# Property Rights in American History

*From the Colonial Era to the Present*

Series Editor

James W. Ely Jr.
*Vanderbilt University*

GARLAND PUBLISHING, INC.
*New York & London*
*1997*

# Contents of the Series

# Property Rights in the Age of Enterprise

Edited with introductions by

James W. Ely Jr.
*Vanderbilt University*

GARLAND PUBLISHING, INC.
*New York & London*
*1997*

**Library of Congress Cataloging-in-Publication Data**

Property rights in the age of enterprise / edited with introductions by
    James W. Ely, Jr.
        p.   cm. — (Property rights in American history ; 2)
        Includes bibliographical references.
        ISBN 0-8153-2684-X (vol. 2 : alk. paper). — ISBN 0-8153-2682-3
    (6 vol. set : alk. paper)
        1. Right of property—United States—History.  2. Industrial laws
    and legislation—United States—History.  3. Trade regulation—
    United States—History.  4. Free enterprise—United States—History.
    I. Ely, James W., 1938–   . II. Series.
    KF562.P76  1997 vol. 2
    330.1'7—dc21                                          97-14432
                                                              CIP

Printed on acid-free, 250-year-life paper
Manufactured in the United States of America

# Contents

# Series Introduction

Protection of private property has been one of the most important and enduring tenets of American constitutionalism. John Locke, the English philosopher who markedly influenced the framers of the Constitution, explained the very purpose of government in terms of property rights. He wrote that the "great and chief end . . . of men's uniting into commonwealths and putting themselves under government, is the preservation of their property."[1] Echoing Locke's viewpoint, as cited in *The Records of the Federal Convention of 1787*, Alexander Hamilton remarked at the constitutional convention of 1787: "One great objt. of Govt. is personal protection and the security of Property."[2] The relationship between property rights and individual liberties was recognized by the leading treatise writers of the nineteenth century. "The absolute rights of individuals," James Kent declared in 1827, "may be resolved into the right of personal security, the right of personal liberty, and the right to acquire and enjoy property."[3]

This longstanding support for private property stems from several philosophical traditions. Since the seventeenth century private property has been intimately linked in constitutional thought with the enjoyment of political liberty. Respect for the rights of property owners was consistent with a major theme of American constitutionalism—the restraint of governmental power over individuals. Property, it has been argued, provides the secure economic base on which to safeguard individual autonomy from governmental coercion and to give effect to liberty. Along the same lines, an economic system resting on private property diffuses power and resources through society at large, and thereby prevents undue concentration of authority. As the prominent journalist Walter Lippman insisted in the early twentieth century, ". . . the only dependable foundation of personal liberty is the personal economic security of private property. . . . Private property was the original source of freedom. It is still its main bulwark."[4] Put simply, private property was commonly viewed both as a means of preserving liberty and as an embodiment of liberty.

Utilitarian considerations also underscored the importance of property in the constitutional order. Many observers linked a strong national economy with private ownership. Security of property and regard for contractual arrangements encouraged the development of investment capital, a vital feature of a modern commercial society. As Morton Keller has aptly observed, "an old concern for private rights and individual freedom coexisted with the desire to foster the development of a national economy."[5]

Constitutional protection of economic rights, therefore, undergirded the free market and helped to secure economic growth.

The framers of the Constitution and the Bill of Rights built upon both liberal and utilitarian arguments, fashioning a constitutional scheme that was designed in large measure to safeguard the rights of property owners. Indeed, the framers did not differentiate between property rights and other personal liberties. From the beginning of the nation, both state and federal courts carefully scrutinized regulatory laws to ensure that they did not infringe upon constitutionally protected economic rights. In so doing, they invoked specific constitutional provisions, such as the contract, due process, and takings clause's in state and federal constitutions. Prior to the New Deal and the "constitutional revolution of 1937", the judiciary generally championed market systems and served as ardent protectors of property rights. Despite this judicial solicitude for economic interests, the Supreme Court never adopted a strict laissez-faire philosophy and in fact sustained most regulatory measures. Yet judicial insistence on upholding property rights marked the boundaries of legitimate governmental authority and thus limited the power of government to intercede in economic relationships.[6]

With the coming of the New Deal and the emergence of the regulatory state, however, the Supreme Court abandoned its traditional commitment to protecting private property from governmental interference. The New Deal sought to strengthen the hand of government over economic affairs and to redistribute wealth through social programs. Henceforth, the justices deferred to legislative judgments about economic and social policy, largely disregarding the impact on the property rights and contractual freedom of individuals. Although some state courts remained committed to economic liberty, constitutional protection of property at the federal level eroded dramatically.

For decades after 1937, property rights were of scant concern to jurists and scholars. Regulation of business activity and land usage multiplied significantly, steadily diminishing the dominion of owners. As Carol M. Rose noted, "land use regulators became accustomed to believing that they were entitled to regulate anything that they pleased . . . ."[7] By the 1970s, landowners increasingly challenged regulatory regimes as a violation of their property rights. At the same time, there was a resurgence of interest in classical economic theory. The result was to undermine the New Deal confidence in regulatory solutions. Responding to these developments and the growing complaint about over-intrusive public controls on private property, judges and legislators began to reassess the importance of property in the constitutional order.

The climate of opinion gradually became more sympathetic to the claims of individual owners. In a series of decisions, the Supreme Court revitalized the takings clause of the Fifth Amendment. Other branches of government also played a role. For instance, in 1991, President George Bush commemorated the bicentennial of the Bill of Rights and urged Americans to renew their commitment to the framers' legacy of limited government. Stressing the key function of private property, he declared:

> The takings clause in the Fifth Amendment is based on a liberating political insight: A person's property serves as a bulwark of individual liberty and that government must pay a fair price whenever it takes private property for public use. By protecting a worker's earnings and savings, a family's home, or a small

businessman's stake from unfair confiscation or ruinous overregulation, this principle seeks to protect the whole of society from gluttonous government.[8]

Although more rhetoric than substance, such expressions of sentiment renew the historic link between property and liberty and help to shape a legal culture in which property rights are again taken seriously.

The vital role of private property rights in a free society has also received dramatic affirmation by recent events in Eastern Europe. Since the collapse of the Soviet Union, many Eastern European nations have sought to create a free market economic system based on stable property rights and freedom of contract. These newly independent countries have taken steps to restore private ownership and to privatize segments of industry. Although this process is far from complete, the new Eastern European constitutions expressly affirm the right of individuals to own and use property. This trend represents implicit recognition of the interdependence of economic rights and political liberty.

For much of our history, the institution of private property was of critical importance in marking the constitutional boundaries of government. There is a vast literature that studies the constitutional protection of property rights from the colonial era to the present. Many of the most important articles dealing with property in American history are brought together in these volumes. The articles provide insight into how courts, legislators, and administrative bodies have addressed the complex issues arising from the safeguards of property found in the Constitution. In these works scholars explore a number of questions relevant to a broader understanding of property rights in American society.

## Notes

[1] John Locke, *The Second Treatise of Government*, ed. J.W. Gough (Oxford: Blackwell, 1946), p. 62.

[2] Max Farrand, ed., *The Records of the Federal Convention of 1787*, rev. ed. (New Haven: Yale University Press, 1937), vol. 1, p. 534.

[3] James Kent, *Commentaries on American Law* (New York: O. Halsted, 1827–1828), vol. 2, p. 1.

[4] Walter Lippman, *The Method of Freedom* (New York: Macmillan Company, 1934) p. 101.

[5] Morton Keller, *Affairs of State: Public Life in Nineteenth Century America* (Cambridge: Harvard University Press, 1977), p. 370.

[6] *See* James W. Ely Jr., *The Guardian of Every Other Right: A Constitutional History of Property Rights*, 2nd ed. (New York: Oxford University Press, 1997).

[7] Carol M. Rose, "Property Rights, Regulatory Regimes and the New Takings Jurisprudence — An Evolutionary Approach," 57 *Tennessee Law Review* p. 589 (1990).

[8] George Bush, *Public Papers of the Presidents of the United States: George Bush, 1989–93*, 1991 Book II (Washington, D.C.: GPO, 1991) p. 1615.

# Volume Introduction

Following the Civil War, Americans experienced a period of enormous economic growth. Industrial expansion and technological innovations proceeded swiftly. Railroads forged a national market for goods and helped unify a fragmented nation. Aided by improved transportation, large-scale corporate enterprises extended their operations across state boundaries. Rapid urbanization spawned unprecedented fiscal and governmental problems and Americans increasingly turned their backs on the Jeffersonian notion of an agrarian republic. Legal developments fostered this economic expansion. Indeed, one historian has concluded that "under the benevolent disinterestedness of a Supreme Court that seemed always to have a conservative majority, Big Business managed most of the nation most of the time."[1]

The Civil War also caused a fundamental alteration of the constitutional scheme. Adopted in 1868, the Fourteenth Amendment prohibited the states from abridging "the privileges or immunities of citizens of the United States" or from "depriving any person of life, liberty, or property, without due process of law." This landmark measure opened the door for enlarged federal judicial supervision of state legislation. The constitutional system remained largely decentralized, and states continued to exercise primary regulatory authority over property and economic activity. However, the states now functioned under a national guarantee of individual rights. Over time, the Supreme Court began to view the Fourteenth Amendment as a safeguard of economic liberty against state infringement. This doctrinal development had profound implications for both federal-state relations and the regulation of propertied interests.

Several factors coalesced to prepare the way for heightened judicial protection of property. The first was a renewed drive for regulation in the post-Civil War era.[2] Not all segments of society benefited from the unbridled operation of the free market. The sweeping economic transformation caused social dislocation and concentration of wealth. Corporate power awakened longstanding fears of monopoly. Agricultural distress during the late nineteenth century found expression in the Granger and Populist movements and demands for legislation to assist farmers. As the most visible symbol of the new industrial order, railroads were a special target for those seeking to impose greater public controls on private enterprise. The upshot was an outpouring of state laws designed to harness the new economic forces. In response, railroads and other property owners sought to employ the Fourteenth Amendment as a shield against what they saw as an unreasonable interference with their economic rights.

Another important factor was the appearance of new constitutional doctrines. In his influential work, *A Treatise on the Constitutional Limitations Which Rest Upon the Legislative Power of the States of the Union* (1868), Thomas M. Cooley encouraged a broad reading of the Fourteenth Amendment. Cooley linked the Jacksonian principles of equal rights and opposition to special economic privileges with due process protection of property. He rejected the notion that due process was merely procedural in nature. Further, Cooley sharply questioned the validity of class legislation, laws that singled out one segment of society for advantageous treatment at the expense of others. Laws that appeared to redistribute wealth were particularly suspect as class legislation. Similarly, in *A Treatise on the Limitations of Police Power in the United States* (1886), Christopher G. Tiedeman championed contractual freedom and maintained that governmental intervention in the economy threatened individual rights. He expounded a narrow view of the state police power and urged judicial protection of economic rights. "The unwritten law of the county," Tiedeman argued, "is in the main against the exercise of police power, and the restrictions and burdens imposed upon persons and private property by police regulations are jealously watched and scrutinized."[3]

An additional consideration was the appearance of a new and more sophisticated understanding of property ownership. Under the emerging view, property was viewed as encompassing not simply title to a physical object but as a cluster of beneficial characteristics, such as the right to possess, enjoy, transfer, and derive profit from one's ownership. As Justice Stephen J. Field presciently declared in 1877: "All that is beneficial in property arises from its use, and the fruits of that use; and whatever deprives a person of them deprives him of all that is desirable or valuable in the title and possession."[4] By the late nineteenth century, property was increasingly defined in terms of market value and earning power, not merely physical possession.[5] As the concept of property shifted, the range of constitutional protection expanded.

Responding to these developments, the Supreme Court gingerly accepted the premise that the due process clause imposed substantive as well as procedural restraints on government. Since the concept of private property was a core value deeply embedded in the legal culture, it was hardly a surprise that the judiciary stressed the economic rights content of substantive due process. Further, the Fourteenth Amendment was designed in part to secure the economic rights of the former slaves. Congress viewed the right to make contacts and acquire property as crucial to the freedmen's participation in the market economy.[6] It seems likely, therefore, that Congress envisioned the Fourteenth Amendment as incorporating substantial economic rights.[7]

During the 1880s, state courts took the lead in fashioning the contours of substantive due process. Under this doctrine, courts asserted the authority to scrutinize both the purpose behind state statutes as well as the means used to accomplish the stated ends. In essence, courts began to review state economic regulations against a reasonableness standard, and invalidated measures seen as unduly restrictive of property rights or promoting the interests of only one class of persons. Judges drew upon common-law doctrines of property and contract law to articulate a baseline from which the reasonableness of economic regulations could be determined. The constitutional problem was to determine whether a given regulation was within the state's police power or represented a deprivation of property without due process. The effect of substantive due process was to establish a potentially broad federal judicial supervision of state economic laws.

Americans of the nineteenth century placed a high value on contractual freedom as a vehicle for private decision-making. James Willard Hurst aptly noted "the overwhelming predominance of the law of contract in all of its ramifications in the legal growth of the first seventy-five years of the nineteenth century."[8] It was thus an easy step for courts to conclude that the right to enter contracts was a vital component of substantive due process and deserved special protection by the judiciary. Accordingly, liberty was defined to encompass the right to pursue lawful callings and to make necessary contracts.

The Supreme Court initially employed substantive due process in the field of railroad rate regulations. In a series of cases during the 1890s, the justices held that the reasonableness of rates imposed on railroads by the states was subject to judicial inquiry under the due process clause. These now largely overlooked victories by the railroads were pivotal in achieving broadened constitutional protection of property interests.[9] The first substantive right recognized under due process was that of regulated industries to receive a reasonable return on investment.

It is important to keep application of the doctrine of substantive due process in perspective. Contrary to the exaggerated accounts of earlier historians, the federal and state courts sustained most of the economic regulations that they considered and never insisted upon a thorough laissez-faire approach to business.[10] Certainly the Supreme Court made no persistent effort to shield business enterprise from legislative moves to impose public controls. Moreover, the use of substantive due process to guard economic rights was congruent with the dominant values of contemporary society. Historian Stephen A. Siegel has cogently pointed out that "in nineteenth-century America, property was considered among the most important civil liberties."[11] In other words, it is a faulty premise to suppose that the Supreme Court was imposing its views upon an unwilling populace.[12]

By the late nineteenth century, the regulatory impulse and judicial response sparked a robust debate in the legal literature over the definition and enforcement of economic rights. Prominent jurists and commentators addressed the place of property and contractual rights in the constitutional system and urged the judiciary to vindicate the economic liberties of individuals against governmental activity. The essays in this volume by Thomas M. Cooley, John F. Dillon, and A.G. Sedgwick reveal the thinking of these leading commentators. Also included are articles by significant judicial figures, David J. Brewer, Henry B. Brown, and William H. Taft, all of whom served on the Supreme Court.[13] Other essays by modern historians probe the evolution, rationale, and use of substantive due process to safeguard property rights. Taken together, they cast light on the effort of the legal culture to adopt the libertarian values inherent in individual property ownership to the circumstances of interstate markets and novel industrial conditions.

Despite its prominence in the jurisprudence of the age, the due process clause of the Fourteenth Amendment was not the only constitutional provision employed to uphold individual property rights. The essays in this volume are closely linked to issues treated in volume four, *The Contract Clause in American History*. In addition, the Supreme Court started to flesh out the protection afforded owners under the takings clause of the Fifth Amendment.[14] Readers will find that the themes developed in volume five, *Contemporary Property Rights Issues*, complement the issues addressed in this volume.

## Notes

[1] Howard Mumford Jones, *The Age of Energy: Varieties of American Experience* (New York: Viking Press, 1971), p. 7.

[2] Kermit L. Hall, *The Magic Mirror: Law in American History* (New York: Oxford University Press, 1989), pp. 195–210.

[3] Christopher G. Tiedeman, *A Treatise on the Limitations of Police Power in the United States* (St. Louis: F.H. Thomas Law Book Co., 1886), p. 10.

[4] *Munn v. Illinois*, 94 U.S. 113, 141 (1877) (Field, J., dissenting).

[5] Morton J. Horwitz, *The Transformation of American Law, 1870–1960: The Crisis of Legal Orthodoxy* (New York: Oxford University Press, 1992) pp. 145–48.

[6] Earl M. Maltz, *Civil Rights, the Constitution, and Congress, 1863–1869* (Lawrence: University Press of Kansas, 1990) pp. 61–78.

[7] Herbert Hovenkamp, *Enterprise and American Law, 1836–1937* (Cambridge: Harvard University Press, 1991) pp. 93–96.

[8] James Willard Hurst, *Law and the Conditions of Freedom in the Nineteenth-Century United States* (Madison: University of Wisconsin Press, 1956), p. 10.

[9] *See* Richard C. Cortner, *The Iron Horse and the Constitution: The Railroads and the Transformation of the Fourteenth Amendment* (Westport, Conn.: Greenwood Press, 1993).

[10] Mary Cornelia Porter, "That Commerce Shall Be Free: A New Look at the Old Laissez-Faire Court," 1976 *Supreme Court Review* pp. 135, 140–43.

[11] Stephen A. Siegel, "*Lochner* Era Jurisprudence and the American Constitutional Tradition," 70 *North Carolina Law Review* (1991), pp. 1, 33 n.154.

[12] Bruce Ackerman, "Liberating Abstraction," 59 *University of Chicago Law Review* (1992), pp. 317, 339–41.

[13] Joseph Gordon Hylton, "David Josiah Brewer: A Conservative Justice Reconsidered," 1994 *Journal of Supreme Court History* pp. 45–64.

[14] James W. Ely Jr., "The Fuller Court and Takings Jurisprudence," 1996 *Journal of Supreme Court History* vol. 2, pp. 120–35.

## Further Reading

James W. Ely Jr., *The Chief Justiceship of Melville W. Fuller, 1888–1910* (Columbia: University of South Carolina Press, 1995).

Joseph Gordon Hylton, "David Josiah Brewer: A Conservative Justice Reconsidered," 1994 *Yearbook of the Supreme Court Historical Society* 45–64.

Morton J. Keller, *Affairs of State: Public Life in Late Nineteenth Century America* (Cambridge: Harvard University Press, 1977).

Patrick J. Kelly, "Holmes's Early Constitutional Law Theory and Its Application in Takings Cases on the Massachusetts Supreme Judicial Court," 18 *Southern Illinois University Law Journal* 357–415 (1994).

Paul Kens, *Justice Stephen Field: Shaping Liberty from the Gold Rush to the Gilded Age* (Lawrence: University Press of Kansas, 1997).

Arnold M. Paul, *Conservative Crisis and the Rule of Law: Attitudes of Bar and Bench, 1887–1895* (Ithaca: Cornell University Press, 1960).

Deborah K. Paulus, "Reflections on Takings: The Watuppa Ponds Cases," 17 *Western New England Law Review* 29–75 (1995).

John P. Roche, "Entrepreneurial Liberty and the Fourteenth Amendment," 4 *Labor History* 3–31 (1963).

Benjamin R. Twiss, *Lawyers and the Constitution: How Laissez-Faire Came to the Supreme Court* (Princeton: Princeton University Press, 1942).

# Laissez-Faire and Liberty: A Re-Evaluation of the Meaning and Origins Of Laissez-Faire Constitutionalism

**Michael Les Benedict**

## I. Legal Scholarship and Laissez-Faire Constitutionalism

Until recently, historians of American constitutionalism agreed that, except for the infamous Dred Scott decision,[1] the most unfortunate decisions of the Supreme Court were those that incorporated the notion of laissez-faire into the Constitution in the late nineteenth century. These decisions permitted the Court to frustrate efforts to secure a more just economic order in the United States until the 1930s. The intellectual foundations of laissez-faire constitutionalism have been so alien to most legal scholars since the 1930s (and equally unintelligible to many even earlier) that they have found it difficult to believe these decisions were the result of efforts to enforce 'neutral' principles of constitutional law, to utilize the terms of Herbert Wechsler's famous analysis.[2] They could not conceive of the Court's rhetoric about liberty and due process as anything but cant, a subterfuge designed to camouflage other purposes.

The orthodox view became that, beneath the rhetoric, 'the major value of the Court . . . was the protection of the business community against government'.[3] During the era of laissez-faire constitutionalism, the 'Supreme Court . . . in fact was an arm of the capital-owning class', legal scholars and historians charged.[4] 'Capitalist enterprise in America generated . . . forces in government and in the underlying classes hostile to capitalist expansion; . . . it became the function of the Court to check those forces and to lay down the lines of economic orthodoxy'.[5] Thus when John P.

**Michael Les Benedict** is professor of history at The Ohio State University.

1. *Dred Scott v. Sandford*, 60 U.S. (19 How.) 393 (1857).

2. Herbert Wechsler, 'Toward Neutral Principles of Constitutional Law', 73 *Harvard Law Review* 1-35 (1959).

3. Robert McCloskey, *The American Supreme Court* (Chicago, 1960) 105.

4. Arthur S. Miller, 'Toward a Definition of "the" Constitution', 8 *University of Dayton Law Review* 633, 647 (1983).

5. Max Lerner, 'The Supreme Court and American Capitalism', 42 *Yale Law Journal* 669-701, 672 (1933). See Arthur S. Miller and Ronald F. Howell, 'The Myth of Neutrality in Constitutional Adjudication', 27 *University of Chicago Law Review*

Frank summarized the instances in which the Supreme Court had invalidated national acts and laws up to 1954, he found that the overwhelming majority 'had no direct bearing on basic liberties'. Rather they involved, among other things, 'economic matters'.[6]

It was to protect the privileges of the wealthy and of corporations, legal scholars concluded, that American judges engrafted upon the Constitution the economic principle of laissez-faire, the admonition that government ought not to interfere with the natural laws that govern economic relations. They did this primarily by reinterpreting the phrase 'due process of law' found in the fifth and fourteenth Amendments to give judges the power to rule laws unconstitutional when their substance, not merely the mode of enforcing them, infringed property rights. This, constitutional scholars insisted, was a perversion of the original meaning of the due process clauses. Although the standard studies of the origins of 'substantive' due process of law found ante-bellum antecedents in the doctrine of 'vested rights', they concluded that the concept of 'substantive' due process had made slight, if any, headway. The Supreme Court had rejected the idea firmly in key cases after the Civil War[7] and adopted it only in the 1880s and 1890s when those opposed to business interests threatened to gain control of the other branches of the national government.[8]

Although challenged, this view is still widely accepted.[9] It plays a key role in the ongoing debate over the proper mode of judicial review. Legal

661-95, 672; Arthur S. Miller, *The Supreme Court and American Capitalism* (New York, 1968) 58, 60-61; John P. Roche, 'Entrepreneurial Liberty and the Commerce Power: Expansion, Contraction and Casuistry in the Age of Enterprise', 30 *University of Chicago Law Review* 680-703 (1963); William F. Swindler, *Court and Constitution in the Twentieth Century: The Old Legality, 1889-1932* (Indianapolis and New York, 1968) 18-38.

6. John P. Frank, 'Review and Basic Liberties', in Edmond Cahn, ed., *Supreme Court and Supreme Law* (New York, 1954) 109, 110.

7. The Slaughterhouse Cases, 83 U.S. (16 Wall.) 36 (1873); Munn v. Illinois, 94 U.S. 113 (1877).

8. Walton H. Hamilton, 'The Path of Due Process of Law', *International Journal of Ethics* xlviii (1938) 269-96; Alfred H. Kelly and Winfred A. Harbison, *The American Constitution: Its Origins and Development*, 5th ed. (New York, 1976) 468-91; Loren Beth, *The Development of the American Constitution, 1877-1917* (New York, 1971); Charles Grove Haines, 'Judicial Review of Legislation in the United States and the Doctrine of Vested Rights', 3 *Texas Law Review* 1-43 (1924); Edward S. Corwin, 'The Doctrine of Due Process before the Civil War', 24 *Harvard Law Review* 366-85, 460-79 (1911); Arnold Paul, *Conservative Crisis and the Rule of Law: Attitudes of Bar and Bench, 1887-1895* (Ithaca, N.Y., 1960) 1-18.

9. Until recently the traditional interpretation has not been much questioned. The standard American constitutional history textbook accepted it. Kelly and Harbison, *The American Constitution*, supra note 8 at 468-91. Likewise leading constitutional law casebooks, such as Wallace Mendelson, *The Constitution and the Supreme Court*, 2d ed. (New York, 1965) 239-40; Alpheus T. Mason and William M. Beaney, *American Constitutional Law: Introductory Essays and Selected Cases*, 6th ed. (Englewood Cliffs, N.J., 1978) 356-59; John E. Nowak et al., *Handbook on Constitutional Law* (St. Paul, Minn., 1978) 394-97. And standard histories of the Supreme Court, for example

scholars have cited the incorporation of the doctrine of laissez-faire into the Constitution as one of the worst examples of judicial abuse of power. When Justice Rehnquist denounced the judicial-activist notion of 'a living Constitution' in 1976, he cited the apogee of laissez-faire constitutionalism, *Lochner v. New York*,[10] and *Dred Scott* together in his *argumentum ad horrendum*.[11] Nothing can so damn a decision as to compare it to *Lochner* and its ilk. As John Hart Ely has written, these laissez-faire cases 'are now universally acknowledged to have been constitutionally improper'.[12]

---

McCloskey, *American Supreme Court*, supra note 3 at 115-35; Fred Rodell, *Nine Men: A Political History of the Supreme Court of the United States from 1790-1955* (New York, 1955) 145-51; Bernard Schwartz, *A Basic History of the Supreme Court* (New York, 1968) 50-53; Swindler, *Court and Constitution*, supra note 5 at 28-29. Also the standard treatment of the rise and fall of laissez-faire notions of American government, Sidney Fine, *Laissez-Faire and the General-Welfare State* (Ann Arbor, Mich., 1956) 126-64, and some of the most influential recent work in general American legal history (as distinct from constitutional history), for example Morton J. Horwitz, 'The Rise of Legal Formalism', *American Journal of Legal History* 19 (1975) 251-64.

Even Mary Cornelia Porter's recent, seminal re-evaluation of laissez-faire constitutionalism fails to note any connection between the Supreme Court's decisions and liberty. Porter, 'That Commerce Shall Be Free: A New Look at the Old Laissez-Faire Court', 1979 *Supreme Court Review* 135-59.

10. 198 U.S. 45 (1905).

11. William H. Rehnquist, 'Observation—The Notion of a Living Constitution', 54 *Texas Law Review* 693-706, at 700-704 (1976).

12. John Hart Ely, *Democracy and Distrust: A Theory of Judicial Review* (Cambridge, Mass., 1980) 14. For other examples of the use of laissez-faire constitutionalism to condemn active judicial promotion of 'fundamental values', see the classic Wechsler, 'Toward Neutral Principles of Constitutional Law', supra note 2 at 24-26 (1959) and such arguments as Robert H. Bork, 'Neutral Principles and Some First Amendment Problems', 47 *Indiana Law Journal* 1-35, 11 (1971); Raoul Berger, *Government by Judiciary: The Transformation of the Fourteenth Amendment* (Cambridge, Mass., 1977) 265-69; Berger, 'Michael Perry's Functional Justification for Judicial Review', 8 *University of Dayton Law Review* 465-532, 475-76 (1983); Joseph D. Grano, 'Judicial Review and a Written Constitution in a Democratic Society', 28 *Wayne Law Review* 1-75, 21-24 (1981); 'Symposium--Constitutional Adjudication and Democratic Theory', 56 *New York University Law Review* 259-582, 533 (1981); Earl M. Maltz, 'Murder in the Cathedral--The Supreme Court as Moral Prophet', 8 *University of Dayton Law Review* 623-31, 625-26 (1983).

Even those who defend active judicial protection of 'fundamental values' not specifically identified in the constitutional text quaver before 'the terror of Lochner'. Thomas Gerety, 'Doing Without Privacy', 42 *Ohio State Law Journal* 143-65, 159-60 (1981). See Paul Brest, 'The Fundamental Rights Controversy: The Essential Contradictions of Normative Constitutional Scholarship', 90 *Yale Law Journal* 1063-1109, 1086 (1981): '*Lochner* remains an embarrassment for proponents of fundamental rights adjudication and a cause for skepticism about the practice'. A few scholars, such as Perry, are now reluctantly conceding that the laissez-faire decisions are part of the heritage of judicial activism. Michael Perry, *The Constitution, the Courts, and Human Rights* (New Haven, Conn., 1982) 115-117; Thomas C. Grey, 'Do We Have an Unwritten Constitution?' 27 *Stanford Law Review* 703-18, 706-10 (1975); Burton Caine, 'Judicial Review--Democracy Versus Constitutionality', 56 *Temple Law Quarterly* 297-350 (1983). They are forced to argue that such evidence of judicial

However, this traditional interpretation reflects the depth of the chasm separating the world view of the twentieth century from that of the nineteenth more than it reflects the real origins and meaning of laissez-faire constitutionalism. Law does not develop in isolation from the perceptions and ideas of the general community. Changing understandings of how society operates, changing standards of fundamental right and wrong help to shape legal doctrine. When those general perceptions and standards change, whole areas of the law based on them may become unintelligible to those who imbibe the new.

The world view of most Americans—and the mainstream of the American intellectual community—gradually underwent such a change between the 1880s and the 1930s. Common to most western societies, this shift constituted 'one of the greatest intellectual and moral upheavals in western history', according to a legal scholar who has described its impact on American law.[13] It left the era of laissez-faire constitutionalism a 'dark age', in the sense described by the great philosopher of history, R.G. Collingwood: '[S]ometimes whole generations of historians . . . find in certain periods of history nothing intelligible, and call them dark ages; . . . such phrases tell us nothing about those ages themselves, though they tell us . . . the persons who use them . . . are unable to re-think the thoughts that were fundamental to their life'.[14]

As the intellectual commitments forged in the Progressive and New Deal eras have faded, and as older notions we now call 'conservative' have revived, it has become possible once more to make sense of laissez-faire constitutionalism. As a consequence, the traditional interpretation has slowly been eroding. Scholars have pointed out that government regulation was widespread throughout the nineteenth century. Courts entertained challenges to relatively few of these regulations and overturned even fewer; they

---

'fallability' should be weighed against the greater benefits of 'noninterpretivist' review. Perry, ibid. at 115-17, 125; Laurence H. Tribe, 'Seven Pluralist Fallacies: In Defense of the Adversary Process—A Reply to Justice Rehnquist', 33 *University of Miami Law Review* 43-57, 55-56 (1978).

For the discomfort with Lochner defenders of judicial activism manifest by trying to distinguish the new judicial activism from the old, see J. Skelly Wright, 'The Role of the Supreme Court in a Democratic Society—Judicial Activism or Restraint?' 54 *Cornell Law Review* 1-28, 3-4 (1968); Paul A. Freund, 'The Supreme Court and Fundamental Freedoms', in Leonard Levy, ed., *Judicial Review and the Supreme Court* (New York, 1967) 124-40; Harry H. Wellington, 'Common Law Rules and Constitutional Double Standards: Some Notes on Adjudication', 83 *Yale Law Journal* 221-311, 270-311 (1973). As one critic has observed, '[T]he maintainability of a . . . line between *Roe v. Wade* [410 U.S. 113 (1973)] and *Lochner* . . . seems critical to thoughtful acceptance of the role they are espousing for the Court'. Samuel Estreicher, 'Platonic Guardians of Democracy: John Hart Ely's Role for the Supreme Court in the Constitution's Open Texture', 56 *New York University Law Review* 547-82, 550, n.12 (1981).

13. Calvin Woodard, 'Reality and Social Reform: The Transition from Laissez-Faire to the Welfare State', 72 *Yale Law Journal* 286-328, 288 (1962).

14. R.G. Collingwood, *The Idea of History* (Oxford, England, 1946) 218-19.

can hardly be denominated rigidly laissez-faire in outlook, these analysts have suggested.[15] A series of reassessments sympathetic to such pillars of laissez-faire constitutionalism as Thomas McIntyre Cooley, Stephen J. Field, and even David J. Brewer, have appeared. In the case of each jurisprudent, scholars have found that their ideas transcended mere devotion to business interests. Rather, their concern after all was the relation of individual liberty to government, and they were willing to take positions counter to those of powerful economic interests when their principles called upon them to do so. The most recent edition of the leading American constitutional history textbook reflects some of this revisionism, recognizing the Jacksonian origins of some of the doctrines that made up laissez-faire constitutionalism and stating merely that they were '*used* for a generation to organize and protect the new system of industrial and finance capitalism' (italics mine), rather than charging that the justices intended them for that purpose.[16]

But despite nascent revisionism, there is as yet no full description of the ethical, libertarian foundation of laissez-faire constitutionalism. It is the purpose of this essay to provide that description and to show how traditional

15. Robert A. Lively, 'The American System: A Review Article', *Business History Review*, xxix (1955) 81-96; Lawrence M. Friedman, *A History of American Law* (New York, 1973) 384-402, 311-18 (I think the point will be seen most clearly if the passages are read in the reverse of Friedman's order); Loren P. Beth, *The Development of the American Constitution, 1877-1917* (New York, 1971), 41-42; John E. Semonche, *Charting the Future: The Supreme Court Responds to a Changing Society, 1890-1920* (Westport, Conn., 1978) 15-164 passim; Morton Keller, 'Business History and Legal History', *Business History Review* lii (1979) 297-301 (1979); Porter, 'That Commerce Shall Be Free', supra note 9; James Willard Hurst's seminal *Law and the Conditions of Freedom in the Nineteenth-Century United States* (Madison, Wis., 1956) is from beginning to end an implicit repudiation of the notion that Americans adhered to laissez-faire doctrines in the 1800s, although he does not attend directly to the contradiction between his conclusions and traditional accounts of late nineteenth-century judicial decisions.

16. Alfred H. Kelly, Winfred A. Harbison, and Herman Belz, *The American Constitution: Its Origins & Development*, 6th ed. (New York, 1983) 398; Alan Jones, 'Thomas M. Cooley and the Michigan Supreme Court: 1865-1885', *American Journal of Legal History* 10 (1966) 97-121; Jones, 'Thomas M. Cooley and "Laissez-Faire Constitutionalism": A Reconsideration', *Journal of American History* liii (1967) 751-71; Peter F. Walker, 'Thomas Cooley: Abolition, Law, and "The Day of Better Things"', in Peter F. Walker, *Moral Choices: Memory, Desire, and Imagination in Nineteenth-Century American Abolition* (Baton Rouge, La., 1978) 330-50; Charles W. McCurdy, 'Justice Field and the Jurisprudence of Government-Business Relations: Some Parameters of Laissez-Faire Constitutionalism, 1863-1897', *Journal of American History* lxi (1975) 970-1005; Robert Goedecke, 'Justice Field and Inherent Rights', *Review of Politics* xxvii (1965) 198-207; Semonche, *Charting the Future*, supra note 15, at 102-104; William B. Scott, *In Pursuit of Happiness: American Conceptions of Property from the Seventeenth to the Twentieth Century* (Bloomington, Ind. and London, 1977) 137-46; Robert E. Garner, 'Justice Brewer and Substantive Due Process: A Conservative Court Revisited', 18 *Vanderbilt Law Review* 615-41 (1965). See also David Gold's *John Appleton and Responsible Individualism* (tentative title) (forthcoming).

American constitutional and legal beliefs suggested constitutional sanctions for laissez-faire.

In doing so, I do not mean to suggest that economic interests played no role in establishing laissez-faire constitutionalism. People rarely will pursue a grievance unless they have some stake in rectifying it. The parties who believed that economic regulations violated their rights had something to gain from pursuing the matter; so have defendants who have challenged criminal procedures and so have black Americans who have pressed for racial equality. On the other hand we all acquiesce every day to rules that run against our self-interest; we concede their legitimacy and we feel no grievance. The thing to be understood is, why did those who challenged various economic regulations in the later nineteenth century feel that grievance, and why did judges, lawyers, the overwhelming majority of intellectuals, and millions of ordinary Americans agree with them? Once we understand that, we will be able to accept laissez-faire constitutionalism for what it was—not an embarrassment but part of a long heritage of protection for liberty, as it has been understood by Americans at different times in our history.

To arrive at that understanding one must recognize that there were two related but distinct justifications for the laissez-faire principle in the later nineteenth century. The first was based directly upon classical economists' conception of the 'laws' of economics. It suggested that almost any government effort to overcome or channel those laws was doomed to failure. The second was based on a concept of human liberty implicit in the principles of classical economics. It militated only against certain kinds of government interferences in the economy, not against all interference. That concept was that the power of government could not legitimately be exercised to benefit one person or group at the expense of others. It was this conviction—not the notion that all government economic activity violated 'immutable' economic laws—that lay at the heart of laissez-faire constitutionalism. It was a principle in which Americans had long believed, that drew upon a libertarian heritage broader than classical economics, and that judges had enforced against legislative transgressions long before capitalists used it to defend what they believed to be their rights. Laissez-faire constitutionalism received wide support in late nineteenth-century America not because it was based on widely adhered-to economic principles, and certainly not because it protected entrenched economic privilege, but rather because it was congruent with a well-established and accepted principle of American liberty.

## II. Classical Economics and Laissez-Faire

At the foundation of classical economics lay the conviction that it was man's nature to seek to gratify his desires with the least possible pain and effort. From this basic fact 'scientific' analysis could adduce a whole series of laws that governed men's economic relationships. (By 'scientific'

nineteenth-century economists meant the careful classification and definition of terms; they did not mean the process of hypothesis-formation and
testing that we would today say defines the scientific method.) Since they
were based on unalterable human nature, the laws discovered by this process
were natural laws, as much so as those that governed the physical elements
of the universe. Furthermore, insofar as God had created human nature (and
in America many leading economists were also clergymen), those laws
could be said to reflect divine will.[17]

Among the laws classical economists posited was that the value of any
good or service was determined by the intensity of the demand for it
compared to its scarcity. Another was that men would always seek to
produce goods or provide services that brought the greatest return for the
least expense and effort. These they would trade for goods they could
provide for themselves only at greater expense and with more effort. Their
trading partners, of course, were doing the same thing and thus both sides
benefited by getting the most goods possible with least possible expense and
effort. Therefore the most complete freedom of exchange promised the
greatest prosperity for all.[18]

Labor was a form of service. As any service, its value was determined in
a bargain based on supply and demand. The supply of labor depended, of
course, on the number of workers available but also upon their character.
The individual members of an educated working class that valued its leisure
time would refuse to sell their labor too cheaply, thus raising wages in
general. Moreover, educated, responsible, sober workers would be in
greater demand than shiftless, ignorant ones. On the other hand, most
laissez-faire economists believed there was a limit to the possible demand
for workers, as expressed in wages. Workers could not be paid more than
the amount of accumulated capital in the country less other costs of
production. This amount was what laissez-faire economists called a 'wage
fund'. A few classical economists also believed the notion developed by
Malthus that the needs and numbers of human beings inevitably outstripped
production, and that therefore the prices of most goods would always be out
of the reach of most men and women. But by no means did all American
classical economists share such pessimism; on the contrary, many were
joyfully optimistic that the ability of men and women, to control population

17. For the best general discussions of post-Civil War American laissez-faire economic
theory, see Joseph Dorfman, *The Economic Mind in American Civilization: Volume
Three, 1865-1918* (New York, 1959) and Fine, *Laissez-Faire and the General-Welfare
State*, supra note 9 at 3-95.

18. Francis Wayland, *The Elements of Political Economy*, recast by Aaron L. Chapin (New
York, 1878) 3-7, 11-14, 163-74; Wayland, *Elements of Political Economy* (Boston,
1856) 15-22, 25; Arthur L. Perry, *Elements of Political Economy* (New York, 1876)
56-117; Simon Newcomb, *Principles of Political Economy* (New York, 1886) 3-7,
57-65, 199-226, 248-56; Amasa Walker, *The Science of Wealth: A Manual of Political
Economy Embracing the Laws of Trade, Currency and Finance* (Boston, 1874) 8-17,
77-102. Julian M. Sturtevant, *Economics, or The Science of Wealth: A Treatise on
Political Economy* (New York, 1877) 53-56.

growth and their desire to produce goods in order to acquire other goods promised ever-increasing production and prosperity.[19]

Once men progressed beyond the stage of mere barter, classical economists believed, the value of goods, services, and labor was expressed according to a standard of value, that is, money. In the opinions of some of them, God had ordained that precious metals, especially gold, serve that purpose. In the opinion of others, precious metals, and especially gold, had simply proved to be the best possible measure of value over the centuries, because of the universal desire for it, its easy transportability, and the general stability of its supply.[20]

All classical economists agreed that these natural laws provided the most efficient mechanism possible for the promotion of prosperity and the maintenance of economic stability. When particular goods became too scarce and the demand for them drove prices up, men would rush to increase production in order to take advantage of the high prices, thus increasing supply and bringing prices down. Likewise, when a particular good became too plentiful in relation to demand and therefore prices dropped, men would shift their productive capacities to other goods, thus lowering supplies and raising prices. No producer could keep the prices of goods artificially high, because consumers would turn to his competitors, who would take advantage of the opportunity to sell more goods at fair prices. Goods would always be available to each person at the lowest possible cost because he would purchase them with money earned from that activity which offered him the highest return for the least effort. If there were a real demand for a good or service, men would provide it, and at a cost commensurate with the demand. If men were unwilling to pay a price that made the production of a service worthwhile, then they could not have been so anxious for it after all, and productive energies would be better spent on something else.

However, the forces of supply and demand could maintain this ideal balance only if men were free to enter and leave the market in response to the push and pull of higher returns in the production of one good or another, or the provision of one service or another. Thus classical economists demanded a system of 'unfettered competition'. Government had the responsibility of assuring that no one used force or fraud to restrain such

---

19. Francis Bowen, *American Political Economy* (New York, 1870) 173-204, 125-50; Perry, *Elements of Political Economy*, supra note 18 at 138-58; Wayland, *Elements of Political Economy*, supra note 18 at 291-314 (1878); Wayland, *Elements of Political Economy*, supra note 18, at 166-90 (1856); Walker, *Science of Wealth*, supra note 18 at 254-63; Francis Walker, *The Wages Question: A Treatise on Wages and the Wages Class* (London, 1884), 101-108, 128-73. For the classical economists on Malthus, see also Archer Jones, 'Social Darwinism and Classical Economics: An Untested Hypothesis', *North Dakota Quarterly* xlvi (1978) 19-31, 22-23.

20. Wayland, *Elements of Political Economy*, supra note 18 at 282-95 (1878); Perry, *Elements of Political Economy*, supra note 18 at 249-311; Bowen, *American Political Economy*, supra note 19 at 237-72; Walker, *Science of Wealth*, supra note 18 at 126-31; Irwin Unger, *The Greenback Era: A Social and Political History of American Finance, 1865-1879* (Princeton, N.J., 1964) 126-31.

competition, whether labor unions or business conspirators cooperating to rig prices or markets. But human laws could not improve on the system itself; they could only interfere with it, thus the adage 'laissez-faire', the 'let-alone principle'.

At its extreme the doctrine of laissez-faire ran almost to anarchism. Herbert Spencer, the Social Darwinist philosopher who was better known here than in his native England (though hardly as influential as some historians have believed), urged the elimination of public education, sanitation laws, and the public postal system, among other government institutions.[21] But no American devotee of laissez-faire went this far. Instead they demanded that government cease its interference with freedom of trade through protective tariffs; stop its subsidization of industrial and transportation development through tax policies, tariffs, postal subsidies, and land grants; permit nothing but gold to be legal tender; resist the temptation to cure economic abuses with regulation; and desist from efforts to improve wages and many shortcomings in working conditions through legislation.[22]

Merely cataloging these positions on the issues of the late nineteenth century indicates that most Americans found unpersuasive the argument that government could not improve upon the 'natural' laws of economy. Over laissez-faire objections the national government maintained protective tariffs throughout the last half of the nineteenth century;[23] until the mid-1870s it subsidized railroad development;[24] throughout the era it provided postal subsidies to steamship and other transportation companies.[25] In the 1860s

21. Fine, *Laissez-Faire and the General-Welfare State*, supra note 9 at 32-46, has a full discussion of Spencer's views. Fine may have been accurate in calling him 'the most influential opponent of the state in America' (p. 32), but that does not tell us just how influential opponents of the state really were. The answer is, not very. Spencer was read widely in America, as are many intellectuals who carry commonly held ideas to logical but absurd conclusions. As R. Jackson Wilson has pointed out, American social scientists—although laissez-faire in outlook—read Spencer mainly to dispute him. Wilson, *In Quest of Community: Social Philosophy in the United States, 1860-1920* (New York, 1968) 155. See also Thomas L. Haskell, *The Emergence of Professional Social Science: The American Social Science Association and the Nineteenth-Century Crisis of Authority* (Urbana, Ill., 1977) and Jones, 'Social Darwinism and Classical Economics', supra note 19.

22. For the position of laissez-faire activists on these issues, see John G. Sproat, *'The Best Men': Liberal Reformers in the Gilded Age* (New York, 1968); Fine, *Laissez-Faire and the General-Welfare State*, supra note 9 at 47-91 passim: Dorfman, *The Economic Mind*, supra note 17 at 49-82 passim.

23. F.W. Taussig, *The Tariff History of the United States*, 8th rev. ed. (New York, 1931) 155-283.

24. John Bell Sanborn, *Congressional Grants of Land in Aid of Railways* (Madison, Wis., 1899); Lloyd J. Mercer, *Railroads and Land Grant Policy: A Study in Government Intervention* (New York, 1982) 32-67 and passim.

25. Marshall Henry Cushing, *The Story of Our Post Office: The Greatest Government Department in All its Phases* (Boston, 1893) 34-35, 137-51; D.D.T. Leech, *The Post Office Department of the United States of America: Its History, Organization, and Working* (Washington, D.C., 1879) 24-25, 30-34, 69.

and 1870s the national government augmented the nation's supply of currency with 'legal tenders' that were not backed by specie. It regulated the money supply by speeding and slowing and sometimes reversing the rate that these notes were withdrawn from circulation.[26] In 1878 the national government began coining limited amounts of silver.[27] In 1887 it created the first great regulatory agency, the Interstate Commerce Commission, to regulate railroads and their customers;[28] in 1890 it passed the Sherman Anti-Trust Act.[29] As early as the 1870s Congress passed a law limiting the working day to eight hours for government employees and after a good deal of debate decreed that there would be no proportional reduction in pay, even if that led to wages higher than those that would have been dictated by the laws of supply and demand.[30] All this was enough to persuade the authors of the leading textbook in American constitutional history to dub the late nineteenth century 'The First Era of National Economic Regulation'.[31]

On the state level government was more active, and in more active violation of laissez-faire economic tenets. Local authorities in many areas continued to promote transportation development with tax abatements, debt guarantees, and public subscriptions to stock issues. At the same time, many states passed stiff new regulations to govern the conduct of their transportation enterprises.[32] In yearly addresses on the state of American law, the presidents of the American Bar Association reported law after law promoting and subsidizing economic development, regulating business practices, employment conditions, and labor relations.[33] As one scholar, reviewing the literature on the relation between government and private enterprise in the nineteenth century has concluded, 'From Missouri to Maine, from the beginning to the end of the nineteenth century, governments were deeply involved in lending, borrowing, building, and regulating'.[34]

---

26. Margaret G. Myers, *A Financial History of the United States* (New York & London, 1970) 148-222; Unger, *Greenback Era*, supra note 20.

27. Bland-Allison Silver Purchase Act, 20 Stat. 25 (1878).

28. Interstate Commerce Act, 24 Stat. 379 (1887).

29. 26 Stat. 290 (1890).

30. Eight-Hour Day Law, 51 Stat. 77 (1868); Eight-Hour Day Proclamation, 17 Stat. 955 (1872).

31. Kelly and Harbison, *The American Constitution*, supra note 8, at 513. The most recent edition, prepared by Herman Belz, has eliminated the words but not the perception. Kelly, Harbison, and Belz, *The American Constitution*, supra note 16 at 380-89.

32. Carter Goodrich, *Government Promotion of American Canals and Railroads, 1800-1890* (New York, 1960), 230-62; George H. Miller, *Railroads and the Granger Laws* (Madison, Wis., 1971).

33. See the presidents' annual addresses in volumes 2-12 of the *Reports of the American Bar Association* (1878-1899).

34. Lively, 'The American System', supra note 15 at 86. See also Gerald D. Nash, *State Government and Economic Development: A History of Administrative Policies in California, 1849-1933* (Berkeley, Cal., 1964) 139-224.

Those who urged the government to adhere to the 'let-alone principle' certainly did not perceive their ideas to be in the saddle. They perceived themselves to be reformers, not defenders of the status quo. They continually deplored the American tendency to over-legislation. Early in the 1870s a contributor to the *North American Review* lamented: 'The average man-
. . . is singularly subject to all kinds of political deception; he loves above all things, to be doctored; and, if a political organization desire, it will take no great cunning or skill to compound some soothing syrup . . . to meet the present demand; an additional "lie upon the statute-book" is a matter of no great consequence'.[35] Fifteen years later, in what is generally thought of as the heart of the laissez-faire era, the dean of American laissez-faire propagandists, William Graham Sumner, complained that exponents of the laissez-faire principle still were received 'with . . . irritation and impatience'.[36]

If the principle of laissez-faire was less than compelling to the public at large in the years that the Supreme Court developed the doctrine of substantive due process, neither was it widely held among the businessmen whom it was supposed to protect. Of course it was businessmen who pressed Congress for the protective tariff and who sought public support for economic development. But businessmen, especially merchants, were also active promoters of state regulation of railroads and later of federal regulation.[37] Businessmen were hardly united behind the laissez-fairist's beloved gold standard, many of them urging inflation as a tool to promote economic prosperity.[38] Of course they were willing to marshal laissez-faire economic arguments against legislation that they perceived to be contrary to their interests, and they shared a vague notion that economic problems were

35. 'The Butler Canvass', *North American Review* civ (1872) 155-56.

36. William Graham Sumner, 'State Interference', in Albert G. Keller and Maurice R. Davie, eds., *Essays of William Graham Sumner* (New Haven, Conn., 1934) ii, 149 (originally published in 1887) (hereinafter Sumner, *Essays*). For laissez-faire reformers' general gloom over the direction of politics and legislation see Sproat, *'The Best Men'*, supra note 22 at 273-81 and passim.

37. Miller, *Railroads and the Granger Laws*, supra note 32 at 19-23, 96, 107, 115, 125-31, 154-55, 164-68; C. Peter Magrath, 'The Case of the Unscrupulous Warehouseman', in John A. Garraty, ed., *Quarrels That Have Shaped the Constitution* (New York, 1966), 109; Lee Benson, *Merchants, Farmers, and Railroads: Railroad Regulation and New York Politics, 1850-1887* (Cambridge, Mass., 1955); Gabriel Kolko, *Railroads and Regulation, 1877-1916* (Princeton, N.J., 1965) 20-44; Ari and Olive Hoogenboom, *A History of the ICC: From Panacea to Pallative* (New York, 1976) 8-17.

38. Unger, *Greenback Era*, supra note 20 at 44-67, 220-25, 324-27, 403; Unger, 'Business Men and Specie Resumption', *Political Science Quarterly* lxxiv (1959) 46-70; Jack P. Sharkey, *Money, Class, and Party: An Economic Study of Civil War and Reconstruction* (Baltimore, 1967) 141-71; Allen Weinstein, *Prelude to Populism: Origins of the Silver Issue* (New Haven, Conn., 1970) 47-52, 55, 125-29, 263-300 passim; Dorfman, *The Economic Mind*, supra note 17 at 116-17.

not amenable to government-imposed solutions.[39] But they conceded that government activity was useful in too many cases to be called laissez-fairist. As a leading business historian has concluded, businessmen developed 'an unformulated pragmatic social philosophy that accorded with their economic interests but not with any existing system of thought'.[40]

The justices of the Supreme Court were no more dogmatic than businessmen when it came to evaluating laws that attempted to 'interfere' with the 'natural' laws of economics. For example, they conceded government power to regulate practices, rates, and prices in a broad category of economic enterprise: those businesses 'affected with a public interest'.[41] They regularly sustained government regulations of property, business practices, contracts, and working conditions when they were designed to promote the safety, morals, or health of the community.[42] They sustained national power to determine what constituted legal tender.[43]

Of course the limits the justices put upon these powers were crucial. The 'public interest' in a business that government had subjected to economic regulation had to be demonstrable; the regulations had to be 'reasonable' and not 'confiscatory'.[44] Regulations of businesses not affected with a public interest had to be designed to protect health, morals, or safety, not to secure economic benefits to any particular group.[45]

But it is in these limitations that the libertarian rather than economic basis of the Court's position becomes apparent. The *economic* argument for laissez-faire was based on the conviction that all government regulation of economic relations were inefficient, if not unenforceable. But the limitations that the justices put upon the power of government to regulate economic enterprises were quite irrelevant to this objection, which would have imposed barriers to almost any regulation, if the justices had accepted it.

Neither the justices in their opinions, nor counsel in their briefs and arguments, objected to economic regulations because of their interference

---

39. See Edward C. Kirkland, *Dream and Thought in the American Business Community, 1860-1900* (Chicago, 1964) 1-28.

40. Thomas C. Cochran, *Railroad Leaders, 1845-1890: The Business Mind in Action* (Cambridge, Mass., 1953), 181.

41. *Munn v. Ill.*, 94 U.S. 113 (1877).

42. *Holden v. Hardy*, 169 U.S. 366 (1898); *St. Louis, Iron Mountain & St. Paul Ry. Co. v. Paul*, 173 U.S. 404 (1899); *Minnesota Iron Co. v. Kline*, 199 U.S. 593 (1905); *Muller v. Oregon*, 208 U.S. 412 (1908); *McLean v. Ark.*, 211 U.S. 539 (1909).

43. *Juillard v. Greenman*, 110 U.S. 421 (1884).

44. *Stone v. Farmers' Loan and Trust Co.*, 116 U.S. 307, 329-30 (1886); *Chicago, Milwaukee, and St. Paul Ry. Co. v. Minn.*, 134 U.S. 418 (1890).

45. See, for example, *Lochner v. N.Y.*, 198 U.S. 45 (1905), which overturned a state regulation of bakery workers' hours on the grounds that it could not be justified as a protection of health or safety. The majority of the justices sustained similar regulation of other industries in *Holden v. Hardy*, 169 U.S. 366 (1898) and *Muller v. Oregon*, 208 U.S. 412 (1908) when such a justification could be made out.

with immutable economic laws. Rather, they insisted that certain kinds of legislation violated rights. Those rights were closely enough related to principles of classical economics to impart apparent justification to Justice Holmes's famous complaint that decisions protecting them were 'decided upon an economic theory which a large part of the country does not entertain'.[46] But it was a concept of rights implicit in classical economics and not a total inhibition on government action that the court was enforcing. This is apparent in Holmes's indictment itself. It was Herbert Spencer's *Social Statics*, not Adam Smith's *Wealth of Nations*, that Holmes complained was being written into the Constitution, and Spencer's opus was not an economic study at all. It was rather an effort to define 'a strictly scientific morality' as deduced from a fundamental moral, not economic, principle, what Spencer called the 'law of equal freedom', the principle that 'every man has freedom to do all that he wills, provided he infringes not on the equal freedom of any other man'.[47]

## III. 'Class Legislation'

Classical economics implied both a broad definition of property rights and a definition of liberty that made government regulation an object of suspicion. As already noted, according to classical economists no object or service had any intrinsic value; value was always determined by the bargain between buyer and seller, which in turn was dependent on supply and demand. Therefore any government attempt to interfere with that bargaining process affected property in the only way that had any meaning: by changing its value. To differentiate diminution of the value of property from deprivation of property itself made no logical sense. Moreover, it was natural for classical economists to look upon the value set upon goods or services by the laws of supply and demand as their *real* value. Insofar as government action either raised or lowered prices by interfering with the operation of a free marketplace, it was taking the property of one party to the bargain and giving it to another. This was 'class', or 'special' legislation—using the power of government for the benefit of a particular group at the expense of the rest of society. It made government the means of theft, the direct antithesis of the legitimate purpose of government, which all knew was to offer protection against such wrongs. It was this conviction, a fundamental idea about right and wrong, not a doctrinaire belief in the inefficiency of government economic intervention, that lay at the heart of American laissez-faire constitutionalism.

Despite their commitment to a value-free, 'scientific' approach to economics, many of the laissez-faire economists explicitly challenged the

46. *Lochner v. N.Y.*, 198 U.S. 45, 75 (1905).

47. Herbert Spencer, *Social Statics; or, The Conditions of Human Happiness Specified, and the First of Them Developed* (New York, 1890) 13, 121.

justice of such legislation. But this was not the primary thrust of their 'scientific' works, and it is unlikely that economic texts were very widely read, even by the American elite or by that portion of it that practiced law. Rather, the laissez-faire doctrine of liberty was drummed into the conscience of American intellectual (and legal) leaders in the course of public debate on specific issues. Laissez-faire propagandists—such as professor and former special revenue commissioner of the Treasury Department David A. Wells, Boston textile manufacturer Edward Atkinson, Yale sociologist William Graham Sumner, journalists Edwin L. Godkin and Horace White, and professional economists Lyman Atwater, Arthur L. Perry, and Simon Newcomb (who was also a respected astronomer)—wrote hundreds of articles and tracts and delivered just as many lectures and political addresses denouncing specific instances of 'special' and 'class' legislation and the tendency towards such injustice in general.

In the opinion of the laissez-faire propagandists, the great danger to liberty had always emanated from the temptation to misuse the powers of government for the benefit of those who controlled it. In darker ages it had been princes and aristocrats who had possessed such power. But in modern, democratic times, the danger seemed to lie in the opposite direction. As Sumner worried, 'Now that the governmental machine is brought within everyone's reach the seduction of power is just as masterful over a democratic faction as ever it was over king or barons'.[48]

To the laissez-fairist this willingness to enact 'class legislation'—to use government power to improve the condition of one group in society at the expense of other, or to alter through state action the relative bargaining positions of laborers and employers or consumers and producers—defined socialism and communism. No matter how limited the interference, the principle was the same. 'There are no socialistic schemes . . . which do not upon analysis, turn out to mak[e] those who have share with those who have not', Sumner explained. 'If . . . the question is raised, what ought the State to do . . . for a class or an interest, it really is the question . . . . What ought Some-of-us to do for Others-of-us'.[49] Or as the great, and by no means reactionary, economist, Francis A. Walker, put it: 'I should apply the term "socialistic" to all efforts, under popular impulse, to enlarge the functions of government, to the diminution of individual initiative and enterprise, for a supposed public good'.[50]

As advocates of laissez-faire looked about them, they grew ever gloomier about the prospects for liberty in the United States. '[T]he activity of the

---

48. Sumner, 'State Interference', supra note 36 at 146. See also Francis Parkman, 'The Failure of Universal Suffrage', *North American Review* cxxvi (1878) 1-20; Sproat, *'The Best Men'*, supra note 22 at 205-42.

49. Sumner, 'The Challenge of Facts', in Sumner, *Essays*, supra note 36 at ii, 117; William Graham Sumner, *What Social Classes Owe Each Other* (New Haven, Conn., 1925); 11-12 (originally published in 1883).

50. Francis A. Walker, 'Socialism', in Francis A. Walker, *Discussions in Economics and Statistics* (New York, 1899) ii, 250 (originally published in 1887).

State, under the new democratic system, shows itself every year more at the mercy of clamorous factions', Sumner mourned, 'and legislators find themselves constantly under greater pressure to act . . . in such a way as to quell clamor'. The omens were particularly grim in the teeming and growing cities. 'Here the dangerous classes are most numerous and strong, and the effects of flinging the suffrage to the mob are most disastrous', the historian Francis Parkman wrote. In cities democracy 'hands over great municipal corporations, the property of those who hold stock in them, to the keeping of greedy and irresponsible crowds controlled by adventurers as reckless as themselves, whose object is nothing but plunder'.[51]

Parkman's comments were especially trenchant, but his concern was widely shared. For example, future President James A. Garfield confided to a friend, 'It has long been my opinion that universal suffrage is a failure as applied to municipal corporations . . . . The root of the difficulty is this: one naturalized foreigner can by his vote neutralize the vote of A.T. Stewart [the millionaire New York merchant]. Thus two men without a dollar can dispose of the pecuniary interests of a man worth many millions'.[52] 'Our money is spent and our taxes are laid by insignificant ephemeral creatures', laissez-fairists grieved. Because of the influence of Tammany-style corruptionists upon the ignorant and propertyless mass of urban voters, 'the educated and wealthy [man] . . . felt himself as much disfranchised as if he had been excluded from the polls by law'.[53] Under such circumstances the taxes levied upon urban property holders took on the character of confiscation, 'organized communism and destruction of property under the guise of taxation', Simon Stern called it.[54]

Given such convictions and fears, it was natural that the laissez-fairists should have supported efforts to weaken the power of the political 'machines' through reform of the civil service and that they should have sympathized when southern Conservatives used similar arguments to justify the elimination of Negro influence from southern politics.[55]

Even more obvious examples of class legislation, of 'socialism' and 'communism', were efforts to improve the conditions of labor, either by direct government regulation of the terms of labor contracts or by removing

---

51. Sumner, 'State Interference', supra note 36 at 146; Parkman, 'The Failure of Universal Suffrage', supra note 48 at 20.

52. Garfield to Burke A. Hinsdale, Jan. 21, 1875, in Mary L. Hinsdale, ed., *Garfield-Hinsdale Letters: Correspondence Between James Abram Garfield and Burke Aaron Hinsdale* (Ann Arbor, Mich., 1949) 314.

53. Richard H. Dana to George P. Marsh, Apr. 23, 1871, Dana Family Papers, Massachusetts Historical Society, Boston, Mass.; J. Francis Fisher, quoted in Simon Sterne, *On Representative Government and Personal Reputation* (Philadelphia, 1871) 74. See Alexander B. Callow, *The Tweed Ring* (New York, 1966) 261-68.

54. Simon Sterne, *Suffrage in the Cities* (New York, 1878) 26.

55. On both issues, see Sproat, *'The Best Men'*, supra note 22 at 29-44, 244-71, and the laissez-faire organs—the *Nation*, *Harper's Weekly*, and the *North American Review* generally.

legal obstacles to the right of unions to strike for higher wages or better
working conditions. In the former case, for example restricting the work day
to eight hours or banning payment of wages in company scrip, the state
plainly was interfering on the behalf of one of the parties to a bargain,
insofar as unfettered bargaining based on the supply of and demand for labor
would have led to a different outcome. Moreover it was not only, perhaps
not primarily, the employer who was being deprived of his rights through
the state's intervention. The real loser, according to the laissez-faire theorists, was the worker who would have been willing to work longer hours or
accept company scrip in exchange for the job in question. The 'lazier'
worker had used the power of government to protect himself from the
competition of the more diligent.

Modifying conspiracy laws so as to permit effective strikes raised the
same objection. A worker or group of workers might have the right to refuse
to work for a certain wage or under objectionable conditions, but they could
not deprive other workers of the right to accept the terms they had rejected.
Nor could they seek to limit access to crafts by requiring apprenticeship
before entry. To do either was as much to engage in a combination in
restraint of trade as was a conspiracy among producers to raise prices by
preventing goods from reaching the market. Government tolerance of such
behavior would sanction the grossest kind of private wrong, depriving men
of protection for the fundamental right to exchange labor for sustenance.
Finally, since most laissez-fairists believed that only a fixed amount of
capital was available to employ labor—a wage fund—any artificial rise in
the remuneration of one worker had to come at the expense of others.[56]

To seek these goals through political pressure was to promote the most
obvious sort of class legislation. To labor reformers' complaints that
workers were merely seeking to defend themselves against the political
power of monopolistic corporations, laissez-faire analysts responded, 'If
capital has gained an advantage by special legislation, this is to be counter-
balanced, not by special legislation to favor the other side . . . but by
earnest united protests against all special legislation'. By doing otherwise
workers 'play into the very hands of monopoly, by following its example . . . . The era of social justice will not be ushered in by those who
have nothing better to urge than the old strife of classes for supremacy'.[57]

56. Perry, *Elements of Political Economy*, supra note 18 at 158-67; Bowen, *American Political Economy*, supra note 19 at 110-16; Walker, *Wages Question*, supra note 19 at 385-408 passim; Francis Walker, 'Legal Interference with the Hours of Labor', *Lippincott's Monthly Magazine* ii (1868) 527-33, esp. 530; W.A. Croffut, 'What Rights Have Laborers?' *Forum* i (1886) 294-96; Sumner, *What Social Classes Owe Each Other*, supra note 49 at 129-30; Samuel Johnson, *Labor Parties and Labor Reform* (Boston, 1871); D. McGregor Means, 'Labor Unions Under Democratic Government', *Journal of Social Science* xxi (1886) 73-74; *The* (New York) *Nation*, May 11, 1866, 594 (1866). See Sproat, *'The Best Men'*, supra note 22 at 228-29.

57. A.L. Chapin, 'The Relations of Labor and Capital', *Transactions of the Wisconsin Academy of Sciences, Arts, and Letters* i (1870-1872) 60; Johnson, *Labor Parties*, supra note 56 at 4-5; Means, 'Labor Unions', supra note 56; Wayland, *Elements of Political Economy* (1878), supra note 18 at 110-11.

Another piece of plainly class legislation was the 'discriminating' income tax, one that exempted incomes below a certain level. Such an act 'has no claim to be considered a tax, but is simply confiscation', the laissez-faire tax expert, David A. Wells, expostulated. '[I]f the State may take five per cent from the man with $5,000 income, and ten per cent from the man with more than $5,000, why stop at these limits? . . . Why not take all that such individuals receive in excess of the average income of the masses? . . . The individual proposing such a tax [is], then, in theoretical intent, a communist of the most radical type . . .'.[58] It could be defended, said a congressional opponent, 'only . . . on the same ground that the highwayman defends his acts'.[59] It was '[c]lass legislation on a tremendous scale'.[60]

Laissez-faire libertarians hardly looked more kindly upon what they believed to be farmer efforts to set aside the normal bargaining process that set railroad rates. No matter what the farmers' grievances, '[w]hen the Grangers had once proclaimed that their object was to "fix rates", or, in other words, to declare by law what proportion of the market value of services they themselves should pay. . . . it was perfectly clear that the Granger movement was rank communism', Godkin thundered.[61]

But more crucial than any of these issues were the two that dominated political discourse throughout the late nineteenth century, regulation of the currency and reduction of the protective tariff. It may seem strange today that expounders of laissez-faire liberty identified protectionism with socialism, but one must remember that most of its advocates justified the protective tariff on the grounds that it protected American workers from competition with products made by cheap foreign labor.[62] To Sumner the issue was simple: the protective tariff raised the price everyone had to pay in order to protect those engaged in a particular industry; it was a 'question

---

58. David A. Wells, 'Rational Principles of Taxation', *Journal of Social Science*, vi (1875), 120-33, at 123. See also Wells, 'The Communism of a Discriminating Income-Tax', *North American Review* cxxx (1880) 236-46; Elmer Ellis, 'Public Opinion and the Income Tax, 1860-1900', *Mississippi Valley Historical Review* xxvii (1940) 225-42.

59. Senator Justin S. Morrill in the *Congressional Globe*, 39th Cong., 1st Sess., 2783 (1866).

60. *New York Tribune*, quoted in *Public Opinion*, July 25, 1891, 372-73.

61. *The Nation* (New York), January 27, 1876, 58; Wells, quoted ibid., October 29, 1874, 282-84; Charles Francis Adams, Jr. 'The Granger Movement', *North American Review*, xx (1875) 394-424, esp. 406-12. See also W.A. Russ, 'Godkin Looks at Western Agrarianism: A Case Study', *Agricultural History* xix (1945) 233-42; Sproat, *'The Best Men'*, supra note 22 at 223-24.

62. Horace Greeley, *The Tariff Question: Protection and Free Trade Considered* (New York, 1856); William D. Kelley, *Speeches, Letters, and Addresses on Industrial and Financial Questions* (Philadelphia, 1872) 9-84, 322-91; James G. Blaine, *'olitical Discussions, Legislative, Diplomatic, and Popular* (Norwich, Conn., 1887) 426-28, 443; Peter Cooper, *Letters on the Necessity of a Wise Discriminating Tariff to Protect American Labor* . . . (1866); Timothy Otis Howe, *The Tariff: Farmers, Iron Workers, and Laborers—The Trinity of the Nation's Strength* (Milwaukee, 1881) (speech originally delivered in 1866).

17

whether the government shall make A give a part of his product to B, to support B in an unproductive industry'.[63] The counter-argument that society was obligated to guarantee a worker's 'right' to labor for a high wage did not persuade the free traders. 'The argument is pretty much that of the communists to this day', they responded. 'Would a tariff bill be tolerated for a moment, if its object was declared in the title as "An act to maintain high wages for a small portion of the people . . . by means of a heavy tax on the remainder" . . . ?' they asked. Do protectionists 'believe in communism'? Are they 'prepared to say it is within the proper function of government to attempt to fix the rate of wages and to provide specific work for all'?[64]

Laissez-fairists recognized that the primary beneficiaries of the protective tariff were industrialists rather than workers. But that did not vitiate the equivalence between protectionism and socialism. No matter who received its benefits, the protective tariff was 'an adoption by the National legislature of the *principle of special legislation*'. 'Protection differs from communism only in this', Atkinson insisted, 'that it attempts to enforce inequitable distribution of our annual product . . . , while communism, or socialism, invokes the force of law under the mistaken idea that a more equitable division may be had . . .'.[65]

The currency question involved the same issues. It was bad enough that the government had turned to the expedient of issuing 'greenbacks', legal tender not redeemable in gold, in order to finance the Civil War. Insofar as a debtor paid a creditor in that depreciated currency instead of the gold-backed currency the creditor had expected when he agreed to the contract, the creditor had been forced to loan the government his gold, without any interest. He was left with notes that the government promised to repay in gold at some unspecified date. 'It was a direct violation of the law of ownership', one economist complained. 'The government took the property of the owner without consent either granted or even asked.' When the Treasury Department released another tide of greenbacks in the wake of the Panic of 1873, Atkinson made the same objection. It was 'a precedent for a Secretary of the Treasury to collect a forced loan . . . at any time'.[66]

---

63. Sumner in his preface to Abraham L. Earle, *Our Revenue System and the Civil Service: Shall They Be Reformed?* (New York, 1878) vii.

64. Francis Lieber, *Notes on Fallacies of American Protectionists* (New York, 1870) 11-15, 17; Edward Atkinson, *Revenue Reform: An Essay* (Boston, 1871) 29.

65. Earle, *Our Revenue System*, supra note 63, at 11; Atkinson, *Revenue Reform*, supra note 64 at 18; See also *The* (New York) *Nation*, January 21, 1869, 44; April 28, 1870, 263; December 12, 1872, 374; Perry, *Elements of Political Economy*, supra note 18 at 380; David A. Wells, 'The Meaning of Revenue Reform', *North American Review* cxiii (1871) 104-53, esp. 148; Wells, 'Rational Principles of Taxation', supra note 58 at 122; William Graham Sumner, *Protectionism: The Ism Which Teaches that Waste Makes Wealth* (New York, 1885); Fine, *Laissez-Faire and the General-Welfare State*, supra note 9 at 64-67.

66. Sturtevant, *Economics*, supra note 18 at 83; Atkinson to Henry L. Dawes, February 2, 1874, Dawes Mss., Manuscripts Division, Library of Congress, Washington, D.C.

Even worse was pressure to issue greenbacks, or later to coin silver, for the direct purpose of stimulating the economy by making debts easier to pay. This was class legislation pure and simple, taking from the creditor and giving to the debtor. 'Men ought to be made to pay what they agreed and expected to have to pay', Godkin wrote in the *Nation*. 'Their escape from this obligation, through the laxity of the laws, is a great misfortune; but their escape through the connivance . . . of government is a still greater misfortune.' Artificial inflation of the currency amounted to a 'sanction given by the law to the wholesale cheating by fraudulent debtors'. It was 'a license . . . to defraud . . . creditors'.[67] Laissez-faire opponents of inflation consistently inveighed against the morality, perhaps even more than against the policy, of the proposal. In a typical expression of disgust, Charles Francis Adams, Jr., wrote a friend, 'We are now educating ourselves into a nation of swindlers; who, whenever their debts press upon them, ease themselves off by invalidating all existing contracts.'[68] For laissez-fairists, only gold was 'honest money'.[69]

Modern scholars of American legal and intellectual history have not been kind to late nineteenth century laissez-faire spokesmen. Their laissez-faire principles may have been part of a liberal heritage, but the laissez-fairists had forgotten its essence, Sidney Fine concluded. 'Those . . . who continued to advocate the laissez-faire brand of liberalism tended to establish economic freedom as an end in itself rather than a means to an end.'[70] Louis Hartz, the great historian of American liberalism, charged that the 'wealthier, conservative strand' of American liberalism had turned the tenets of the more egalitarian, libertarian strand against its advocates, Whigs masquerading as Democrats, he described them.[71]

But the purpose of the laissez-faire propagandists was not to protect the property of the rich from the ravages of the poor. Their purpose was to preserve liberty. They were convinced of one truth beyond doubt: liberty could not survive in a polity where control of government enabled those in power to secure their interests at the expense of those without. It made control of government too important. It invited strife. It invited corruption. Adams, himself Massachusetts's first Commissioner of Railroads, expressed their common conviction when he warned of the dangers inherent in government regulation of the railways: 'He who owns the thing knows that

67. *The* (New York) *Nation*, February 17, 1870, 100.

68. Adams to Carl Schurz, December 3, 1875, Schurz Mss., Manuscript Division, Library of Congress.

69. See Sproat, *'The Best Men'*, supra note 22 at 169-203; Unger, *Greenback F-a*, supra note 23 at 120-44.

70. Fine, *Laissez-Faire and the General-Welfare State*, supra note 9 at 31.

71. Louis Hartz, *The Liberal Tradition in America: An Interpretation of American Political Thought Since the Revolution* (New York, 1955) 21n, 203-27. See also Robert Green McCloskey, *American Conservatism in the Age of Enterprise* (Cambridge, Mass., 1951) 1-21; Clinton Rossiter, *Conservatism in America*, 2d ed. (New York, 1955) 128-32, 153-54.

19

he must also own the legislature which regulates the thing. . . . The man who owns will possess himself of the man who regulates.'[72] As usual, Sumner expressed it best: '[T]he advocate of interference takes it for granted that he and his associates will have the administration of their legislative device in their own hands. . . . They never appear to remember that the device, when once set up, will itself be the prize of a struggle; that it will serve one set of purposes as well as another, so that after all the only serious question is: who will get it?' To press for legislation to benefit the majority at the expense of those who accumulated capital was suicidal to democracy, Sumner insisted. Unable to resist the will of the majority in a democratic system, capitalists inevitably would try to protect their interests by subverting it. 'Modern plutocrats buy their way through elections and legislatures, in the confidence of being able to get powers which will recoup them for all the outlay and yield and ample surplus besides.' Plutocracy, the 'political form in which the real controlling force is wealth', 'the most sordid and debasing form of political energy known to us', not an ideal, egalitarian society, was the inevitable consequent to class legislation. This was what was 'new and threatening' and 'the issue which menaces modern society'.[73]

Throughout his life Sumner feared that the great threat to liberty emanated from below, from the subversion of democratic liberty that would follow the demand for class legislation on behalf of the have-nots. But most laissez-fairists perceived the danger as running the other way. It was the unfair advantages sought by the rich and powerful that taught workers and farmers to turn to government to promote their interests. Commenting on the railroads, even the rigidly laissez-faire economist Julian Sturtevant observed, 'Surely while these great companies set so stupendous an example of combination to resist competition, no one should be surprised that their employees combine for higher wages, and that everywhere strikes are of frequent occurrence. Such examples in high places are very likely to be followed.'[74] When Massachusetts bankers persuaded their state legislature to stay debt collections during a liquidity crisis in 1878, Henry Adams called it 'infamous'—'as flagrant a breach of faith as was ever sanctioned by a legislature'. It overshadows the western granger legislation', he exploded.[75] Sumner inveighed against efforts to subsidize the restoration of the American shipbuilding and shipping industry.[76] It was the demand of the rich and powerful for special legislation that inspired similar demands by others. Since 'the mass of the people . . . perceive that some are made richer by means of one statute, they infer that others may gain either high wages or

72. Quoted in Dorfman, *The Economic Mind*, supra note 17 at 23-24.

73. Sumner, 'Democracy and Plutocracy', in Sumner, *Essays* ii, 213-19; Sumner, 'Definitions of Democracy and Plutocracy', ibid. at 220-25.

74. Sturtevant, *Economics*, supra note 18 at 242.

75. Adams, 'Oppressive Taxation and Its Remedy', *Atlantic Monthly* xlii (1878) 765.

76. William Grahamn Sumner, 'Shall Americans Own Ships?' *North American Review* cxxxii (1881) 559.

leisure, or some other desirable end, by the enactment of another statute', Edward Atkinson explained.[77]

Nowhere was this more apparent than in capitalists' pressure to maintain protective tariffs. Of all the special legislation sought and acquired by business interests, the protective tariff was the most colossal fraud. Repudiating the fiction that the tariff was designed to protect the wages of American workers, its laissez-faire opponents characterized it as 'the aggrandizement of capital by law', an abuse of the taxing power by special legislation'.[78] Laissez-faire reformers warned capitalists that protectionism was the parent of socialism. 'It is a significant fact that the agitation of the labor question in this country comes most urgently from persons employed in those branches of occupation which are most affected by a protective tariff.' Atkinson observed. 'It cannot but be obvious to . . . workers that many of their employers have thus gained wealth by force of law.'[79] 'Both grow in the same soil,' another free trade advocate insisted. '[T]he common conditions for the existence of both . . . are to be found in the doctrine of State aid and governmental interference'.[80] Exasperated by the failure of such logic to shake capitalists' commitment to the protective system, Sumner fumed, 'The English land-owners [who fought repeal of the Corn Laws] were no whit worse than American manufacturers'.[81]

To what we might call laissez-faire libertarians, all these instances of special legislation, whether to promote the interests of businessmen, or farmers, or laborers, were of a piece. 'Whether they are paper-money schemes, tariff-schemes, subsidy schemes, internal improvement schemes, or usury laws, they all have this in common with the most vulgar of the communist projects', Sumner wrote, 'and the errors of this sort in the past which have been committed in the interest of the capitalist class now furnish precedents, illustration and encouragement for the new category of demands.'[82]

The laissez-faire concept of liberty became the common currency among the elite in the United States. It formed the basis upon which discussions of

77. Edward Atkinson, 'The Inefficiency of Economic Legislation', *Journal of Social Science* iv (1871) 123; Earle, *Our Revenue System*, supra note 63 at 12-13.

78. Ibid. 11; Sumner, *Protectionism*, supra note 65 passim and esp. 111; Lieber, *Fallacies of Protectionists*, supra note 64 at 6; Perry, *Elements of Political Economy*, supra note 18 at 379-81; Parke Godwin, 'Our Political Degeneracy', *Putnam's Monthly* v (new series) (1870) 602-603; David A. Wells, *The Creed of Free Trade* (Boston, 1875) 17; Lawrence Laughlin, 'Protection and Socialism', *International Review* vii (1879) 427; Atkinson, *Revenue Reform*, supra note 64 at 18.

79. Atkinson, 'The Inefficiency of Economic Legislation', supra note 77 at 129.

80. Laughlin, 'Protection and Socialism', supra note 78 at 427; Earle, *Our Revenue System*, supra note 63 at 22.

81. Sumner preface to ibid. at x.

82. Sumner, 'The Challenge of Facts', supra note 49 at 117. See also Simon Newcomb, 'The Let-Alone Principle', *North American Review* cx (1870) 1-33.

liberty proceeded.[83] Inevitably it made a tremendous impact upon lawyers and judges, and their arguments and decisions are redolent of its concepts. But the widespread acceptance of laissez-faire notions of liberty must be attributed, at least in part, to the fact that its major thrust, hostility to 'special' and 'class' legislation, was already ingrained in American law and political theory.

## IV. 'Special Legislation'

The American heritage of hostility to 'special legislation' can be traced at least as far back as the seventeenth century, when the common law courts began to challenge royal grants of special privileges to favorites. At the turn of the seventeenth century such grants were still conceived to be within the royal prerogative, an inheritance from the days when the governance of England was the king's feudal right, when the royal treasury was his own property, government officers members of his personal household, his courts part of a proprietary right to administer justice over his own *desmesne*, when, in sum, the activities we identify with the state were instead part of the king's *estate*.[84] In those days the king could sell or give away the exclusive right to hold a market, for example, in the same way he could dispose of a wardship (the right to the profits of an estate while its heir was in his minority). He could bestow a monopoly in the privilege of selling salt as easily as he could bestow an escheated manor. He could, and did, decree that only the merchants of certain towns, the 'merchants of the staple', could import goods from abroad; he could grant a charter to a 'gild', granting exceptions from ordinary tolls and taxes or giving its members a monopoly in a certain craft and permitting them to enforce that monopoly in their own courts.[85] By the seventeenth century the English monarchs

---

83. Fine, *Laissez-Faire and the General-Welfare State*, supra note 9 at 29-31, 32-164 passim; Rossiter, *Conservatism*, supra note 71 at 146-51; Ralph Gabriel, *The Course of Democratic Thought*, 2d ed. (New York, 1956) 162-63.

84. As J.E.A. Jolliffe described in his classic *Constitutional History of Medieval England from the English Settlement to 1485* (New York, 1961; originally published 1927) 183: '[T]he crown of England was honorial and its lands and rights were the demesne of the king'. For the personal origins of royal government in England, see ibid. at 139-201; Austin Lane Poole, *From Domesday Book to Magna Carta, 1087-1216* (Oxford, England, 1951) 8-10. A reading of W. Cunningham, *The Growth of English Commerce and Industry During the Early and Middle Ages*, 4th ed. (Cambridge, England, 1905) 148-237 indicates how closely taxation, supervision, and economic promotion were related to the king's feudal rights. See also Frank Barlow, *The Feudal Kingdom of England, 1042-1216* (London, 1955) 107-13 and passim.

85. See E. Lipson, *An Introduction to the Economic History of England* (London, 1920) 238-60, 1270-1390; Edward P. Cheyney, *An Introduction to the Industrial and Social History of England* (London, 1901) 59-71, 154-58; J. LeRossignol, *Monopolies Past and Present* (New York, 1901) 41-64; Cunningham, *Growth of English Commerce*, supra note 84, at 206-11, 341-43, 445-47; George Unwin, *The Gilds and Companies of*

justified, as exercises of the royal prerogative, a growing number of monopolies in domestic and foreign trade, a policy designed both to augment royal revenues (such privileges were *bought*) and to regulate commerce.[86]

Naturally, many Englishmen who opposed the royal practice of granting such special privileges did so on the grounds that they deprived other men of the specific right to practice their trades. By the early 1600s Englishmen considered men's labor one of their property rights, and in an era when the common law was conceived to be the protector of the subject's property, it was inevitable that men would argue that it protected this right too. Even a royalist member of the Commons conceded by 1610 that 'the Kinge cannot take away the meanes of any Man's living nor grant that one man shall have the sole trade of an occupation to the overthrow of others'.[87]

Perhaps more important was the development of the idea of 'commonwealth'—the notion that government regulations must promote the good of all, not of a special few nor of the king alone. For those who opposed royal grants of special privileges as a violation of the principle of commonwealth, the gravamen of the wrong was not in harm to specific individuals, but rather, in the words of economist John R. Commons, that the 'franchises, patents, privileges granted by the sovereign . . . served only to extract private wealth from the commonwealth without increasing the commonwealth'.[88] Or, as Sir Edward Coke put it at the time, 'if the stealinge of a sheepe be felonie, much more were the robbinge of a whole state' by granting a monopoly of trade in wool.[89]

Objections to the grants of such monopolies were raised in the Parliaments of 1566 and 1598 and their elimination became one of the key demands of the parliamentary opponents of the Stuarts in the early 1600s. In 1624 James I was forced to accede to the Statute of Monopolies, declaring

---

*London*, 4th ed. (London, 1963); Cecil T. Carr. ed., *Select Charters of Trading Companies, A.D. 1530-1707* (London, 1913) xiv-xvii, lv-lxii; on fairs and markets: Franklin D. Jones, 'Historical Development of the Law of Business Competition', 35 *Yale Law Journal* 905-38 (1926); Lipson, *Economic History of England*, supra at 201-12; Cheyney, *Industrial and Social History of England*, supra note at 75-79.

86. Unwin, *Gilds and Companies of London*, supra note 85, at 293-328; W. Cunningham, *The Growth of English Industry and Commerce in Modern Times: The Mercantile System* (Cambridge, England, 1903) 214-49 passim, 285-94; Godfrey Davies, *The Early Stuarts, 1603-1660*, 2d ed. (Oxford, England, 1959) 331-35; *Select Charters*, supra note 85 at lxii-lxxxi.

87. Margaret Judson, *The Crisis of the Constitution: An Essay in Constitutional and Political Thought in England, 1603-1645* (New York, 1964; originally published in 1949) 37.

88. John R. Commons, *Legal Foundations of Capitalism* (Madison, Wis., 1968; originally published 1924) 183-84.

89. Quoted in Judson, *Crisis of the Constitution*, supra note 87 at 291. On the idea of 'commonwealth', see ibid. at 274-300; Whitney R.D. Jones, *The Tudor Commonwealth, 1529-1559* (London, 1970) passim and esp. 13-23.

23

such grants void, with several major exemptions. While the parliamentarians accepted the idea that 'companies' of craftsmen should regulate their trades and that only members of the companies should practice them, they worked to open control of the companies to all with the appropriate skills, so as to eliminate their monopolistic features. Likewise, they eliminated for a time many of the special privileges earlier granted to the great foreign trading companies.[90]

At the same time, opponents of monopolies turned to the common-law courts. In a series of decisions at the turn of the seventeenth century the king's justices subverted the charters by which he had granted such special privileges.[91] Gild monopolies, insisted Sir Edward Coke, the palladin of the common law, 'are against the liberty and freedom of the subject and are a means of extortion and drawing money from them'.[92] When the king agreed to the Statute of Monopolies in 1624, the principle, though not yet the practice, was firmly embedded in the common law, justifying the prideful claim made twenty years before that 'This land shall never feare the mischief and misgovernment, which other countries . . . have felt. Oppression shall not be the badge of authorities. . . . The people shall every one sit under his Owne olive tree, . . . his face not grinded with extorted sutes, nor his marrow sukt with most odious and unjust Monopolies.'[93]

This notion of 'commonwealth' remained a principal commitment of the English radical Whigs, whose ideas proved so influential in America. They regarded themselves as the 'Commonwealthmen', who continued to believe that the governance of England must be for the benefit of all Englishmen.

90. Judson, *Crisis of the Constitution*, supra note 87 at 278, 290-92; Davies, *The Early Stuarts*, supra note 86 at 24-25; Elizabeth Read Foster, 'The Procedure of the House of Commons Against Patents and Monopolies', in William Appleman Aiken, ed., *Conflict in Stuart England: Essays in Honor of Wallace Notestein* (New York, 1960) 57; Unwin, *Gilds and Companies of London*, supra note 85 at 293-343; Cunningham, *Growth of English Commerce*, supra note 86 at 218; *Select Charters*, supra note 85, at lxii-lxxxi. Stephen D. White, *Sir Edward Coke and 'The Grievances of the Commonwealth', 1621-1628* (Chapel Hill, N.C., 1979) 95-141.

91. *Davenant v. Hurdis*, Trin. 41 Eliz., Moor, 72 Eng. Rep. 576 (K.B. 1599); *Darcy v. Allen*, 11 Coke 84 (K.B. 1602); Case of Monopolies, 11 ibid. 86, 77 Eng. Rep. 1260 (K.B. 1602); Case of the Tailors of Ipswich, 11 Coke 53, 77 Eng. Rep. 1218 (K.B. 1614). For a brief discussion, see Michael Conant, 'The Antimonopoly Tradition Under the Ninth and Fourteenth Amendments: Slaughterhouse Cases Re-Examined', 31 *Emory Law Journal* 785-831, 792-97 (1982).

92. Case of the Tailors of Ipswich, 11 Coke 53, 77 Eng. Rep. 1218 (K.B. 1614). Godfrey Davies, 'Further Light on the Case of Monopolies', 48 *Law Quarterly Review* 394-414 (1932); Commons, *Legal Foundations of Capitalism*, supra note 88 at 225-31.

93. Richard Martin, *A Speech Delivered to the King's Most Excellent Majestie*, quoted in Judson, *Crisis of the Constitution*, supra note 87 at 41. Of course with the emergence of parliamentary supremacy at the end of the seventeenth century, Parliament was able to grant monopolies, and it did so regularly to promote trade. Nonetheless this had to be justified on the grounds that the public received a benefit and therefore the grant increased rather than diminished the commonwealth. Cunningham, *Growth of English Commerce*, supra note 86 at 214-18 passim.

More traditional Whig politicians, according to these radical Whigs, had been corrupted by the blandishment of the English monarchs, who plundered the realm for their own benefit and that of their favorites.[94] The revolutionary generation of Americans inherited this idea of 'commonwealth'. It lay at the root of their passionate fear of 'faction'—the danger that in a republic men would succumb to the temptation to use government to secure their own special interests instead of governing only for the good of the whole population.[95]

In government economic policy, the commonwealth ideal led to active state efforts to promote prosperity. The bounty of the new world was the common inheritance of its (European) inhabitants, Americans believed, to be exploited by every man. American legislatures and courts followed policies designed to encourage the distribution of the nation's wealth to all with the energy and talent to exploit it. In this process it was legitimate to offer special privileges so long as the result was an increase in the commonwealth. People might receive special privileges—charters of incorporation, tax exemptions, or grants of land, for example—in exchange for building a bridge, a canal, or a railroad, or to encourage the establishment of banks or factories. Not only did such activity add to the commonwealth, but Americans' confidence in the unlimited abundance of their land was so great that such grants generally were not perceived to limit the opportunities of the rest of the community. State and national policies were 'distributive' of wealth, in the parlance of recent analysts of public policy, rather than 'redistributive'.[96]

Nonetheless, when Americans were persuaded that those who had received such privileges were conspiring to prevent their further distribution, reaction was swift. The commonwealth idea itself 'dictated that a course of partial legislation, which aided some but not all, was intolerable', as Harry Scheiber has observed of Ohio's economic development.[97] Convinced that

---

94. See generally Caroline Robbins, *The Eighteenth-Century Commonwealthman: Studies in the Transmission, Development and Circumstance of English Liberal Thought from the Restoration of Charles II until the War with the Thirteen Colonies* (New York, 1968; originally published 1959); Lance Banning, *The Jeffersonian Persuasion: Evolution of a Party Ideology* (Ithaca, N.Y. 1978) 21-69.

95. Gordon Wood, *The Creation of the American Republic, 1776-1787* (New York, 1972; originally published in 1969) 53-65; Banning, *Jeffersonian Persuasion*, supra note 94, passim; Oscar Handlin and Mary Flug Handlin, *Commonwealth—A Study of the Role of Government in the American Economy: Massachusetts, 1774-1861*, rev. ed. (Boston, 1969) 28-31.

96. Theodore J. Lowi, 'American Business, Public Policy, Case-Studies, and Political Theory', *World Politics* xvi (1964) 677-715; Richard L. McCormick, 'The Party Period and Public Policy: An Exploratory Hypothesis', *Journal of American History* lxvi (1979) 279-98; Lively, 'The American System', supra note 15; Handlin and Handlin, *Commonwealth*, supra note 95 at 28-31, 51-181; Harry N. Scheiber, *Ohio Canal Era: A Case Study of Government and the Economy, 1820-1861* (Athens, Ohio, 1969) 88-94, 355.

97. Ibid. at 92.

Federalists were pursuing a policy providing legislative benefits for the few, Jeffersonian Republicans made 'equal rights for all, special privileges for none' the central plank of their platform. It was 'a theme that reappeared in Republican rhetoric in endlessly different forms like a Wagnerian leitmotif', one of the leading historians of the first party system has written.[98] Whether combatting the established churches in New England, the monopoly on banking privileges in New York, or the special privileges the government accorded the incorporators of first national bank, the Republicans charged Federalists with promoting 'measures of government less to the interest of the many than of a few'.[99] Jefferson's opposition to 'aristocratic' government rested firmly on opposition to that kind of class legislation. As Vernon L. Parrington perceived years ago, Jefferson was convinced that 'a class will serve class interests. Government by aristocracy is government in the interest of the aristocracy'.[100] But it should be reiterated that Jefferson only opposed granting special privileges that deprived the rest of the community of some right or opportunity. Where they provided clear benefits to the commonwealth and did not work such deprivations, Jefferson was willing to use all the tools at government's disposal to promote prosperity.[101]

The modern Democratic party was founded upon Andrew Jackson's opposition to legislation for the benefit of the privileged few, as he perceived it in the charter of the second national bank. 'Men have not been content with equal protection and equal benefits, but have besought us to make them richer by act of Congress', he glowered. Inevitably, 'we have in the results of our legislation arrayed section against section, interest against

98. Paul Goodman, 'The First American Party System', in William N. Chambers and Walter Dean Burnham, eds., *The American Party System: Stages of Political Development* (New York, 1967) 56-89, 69.

99. James Madison, 'A Candid State of Parties', in Gaillard Hunt, ed., *The Writings of James Madison* (New York, 1900-1910) vi, 176-79. Recent studies of the Jeffersonian Republican party at the state level suggest that it was 'a diverse coalition . . . against entrenched interests . . . who thwarted the desires of newcomers and outsiders, rising merchants and ambitious office seekers, religious dissenters and landless yeomen eager to share access to authority and to broaden social opportunities'. They perceived the Federalists to stand 'for monopoly of local office, charter privileges . . . and the religious, institutional and professional life of the community'. Paul Goodman, *The Democratic-Republicans of Massachusetts: Politics in a Young Republic* (Cambridge, Mass., 1964) xi, 76. Thus their opposition to special privileges secured through legislation was part of a general attack upon 'aristocracy'. See ibid. at 70-127; Richard Buel, Jr., *Securing the Revolution: Ideology in American Politics, 1789-1815* (Ithaca, N.Y., 1972) 77-90. This understanding is implicit, I think, in Lance Banning's notion that the Jeffersonian Republicans were a 'country party' opposing what they saw as a 'court party'. Banning, *Jeffersonian Persuasion*, supra note 95.

100. Vernon L. Parrington, *Main Currents in American Thought* (New York, 1917) i, 347-62.

101. See William D. Grampp, 'A Re-Examination of Jeffersonian Economics', *Southern Economic Journal* xii (1946) 263-82; Stuart Bruchey, *The Roots of American Economic Growth* (New York, 1965) 114-22; William Appleman Williams, *The Contours of American History* (Cleveland, 1961) 181-91; Charles M. Wiltse, *The Jeffersonian Tradition in American Democracy* (New York, 1960; first published in 1935) 145-50.

interest, and man against man'. To his political banner he called those ready to 'take a stand against all new grants of monopolies and exclusive privileges, against any prostitution of our government to the advancement of the few at the expense of the many'.[102] Among the thousands who responded were the young Stephen J. Field and Thomas M. Cooley. Not only did they join the Democratic party, but they were heavily influenced by the views of those in the party who took Jackson's strictures most literally: the New York intellectuals—William Leggett, William Cullen Bryant, Parke Godwin, David Dudley Field—whose views were expressed in the New York *Evening Post*, and who powerfully influenced the thinking of radical Democrats throughout the North.[103]

Jackson, the young Cooley and Field, and the other radical Democrats of the 1830s and 1840s, in the words of Cooley's biographer, 'sought constitutional limitations to legislative power because they feared arbitrary and unequal legislation'.[104] They perceived the threat of such legislation to emanate from the machinations of the rich and powerful. 'Power and wealth are continually stealing from the many to the few', Leggett worried, always seeking 'to monopolize the advantages of the Government, to hedge themselves around with exclusive privileges, and elevate themselves at the expense of the great body of the people'.[105] But they never suggested greater indulgence towards class legislation for the poor. Their watchword was 'Equal Rights'. '[E]xclusive privileges granted to one class of men . . . impair the equal rights of all others', Leggett insisted.[106] Such a stricture operated upon all class legislation. Fifty years later Godwin recalled the fundamental principles his friend Bryant had articulated ever since the 1830s: 'Government', he said, 'is the organ and representative of the whole community, not of a class, or of any fraction of that community . . . [I]ts functions are . . . to protect and maintain rights . . . and not . . . to encourage, nurse, and coddle interests, save in so far as those interests are general, or common to every member of the community'.[107] These ideas were hallowed in the words of the great Jackson himself. 'Equality of talents, of education, or of wealth cannot be produced by human institutions', he was convinced. What he aspired to was a government that

102. James D. Richards, ed., *Messages and Papers of the Presidents of the United States* (Washington, D.C., 1896-1899) ii, 590.

103. Stephen J. Field read law in the office of his brother, David Dudley Field. Carl Bent Swisher, *Stephen J. Field, Craftsman of the Law* (Chicago, 1969; originally published in 1930) 21. For the influence of Leggett and other radical Democrats on Cooley, see Jones, 'Cooley and "Laissez-Faire Constitutionalism"', supra note 16 at 753; Jones, 'The Constitutional Conservatism of Thomas McIntyre Cooley: A Study in the History of Ideas' (Unpublished dissertation, University of Michigan, 1960) 20-26.

104. Jones, 'Cooley and "Laissez-Faire Constitutionalism"', supra note 16 at 755.

105. Theodore Sedgwick, ed., *Political Writings of William Leggett* (New York, 1840), i, 66-67.

106. Ibid. 145.

107. Parke Godwin, *The Life of William Cullen Bryant* (New York, 1883) i, 253-54.

'would confine itself to equal protection, and, as Heaven does it rains, shower its favors alike on the high and the low, the rich and the poor . . . '.[108]

As the 'commonwealth' ideal eroded in the 1830s and after, Democrats, especially the radical 'locofoco' wing of the party[109], challenged legislative grants of special privileges as inherently inequitable. While Whigs generally continued to insist such grants were justified by the benefits they conveyed to the community, Democratic rhetoric became stridently antimonopolistic. They demanded either the special privileges be made available to all upon the same terms (as when they supported general incorporation laws) or that such legislation be eschewed completely (as in Pennsylvania's 'anti-charter' movement). It seemed the 'very salvation of their party depended upon keeping up the cry of "monopoly", "monopoly",' an opponent noted bitterly.[110] Democratic actions may have fallen short of their rhetoric ('Can it be possible that a party which believes banks to be monopolies can go on so rapidly creating them'? the same opponent asked). But it was the rhetoric more than the reality that was important in developing American ideas about 'special legislation'.[111]

It is unlikely, given our modern understanding of mass voting behavior, that voters were attracted to the Jeffersonian Republican or Jacksonian Democratic parties because of those parties' general opposition to the use of government to win special privileges. A Boston Baptist was more likely motivated to vote Republican in the early 1800s because of his hostility to

---

108. *Messages and Papers of the Presidents*, supra note 102 at ii, 590. For Jacksonian hostility to privilege and commitment to equal rights, see Marvin Meyers *The Jacksonian Persuasion: Politics and Belief* (New York, 1960) 185-233; Arthur M. Schlesinger, Jr., *The Age of Jackson* (Boston, 1945) 306-21. However, Schlesinger's argument that Jacksonism was a working-class movement is untenable. Jacksonians opposed class legislation of any sort, not only that which benefitted the wealthy.

109. For the principles and influence of the 'locofoco' wing of the Democratic party, see William Trimble, 'The Social Philosophy of the Loco-Foco Democracy', *American Journal of Sociology* xxvi (1921) 705-15; Richard Hofstadter, 'William Leggett: Spokesman of Jacksonian Democracy', *Political Science Quarterly* lviii (1943) 581-94; Joseph G. Rayback, *A History of American Labor* (New York, 1959) 75-92; Schlesinger, *Age of Jackson*, supra note 108, at 190-209.

110. Joshua F. Cox, quoted in Louis Hartz, *Economic Policy and Democratic Thought: Pennsylvania, 1776-1860* (Cambridge, Mass., 1948) 77.

111. Ibid. For political controversies in which competitors used the rhetoric of 'equal rights' and 'special privileges', see Glyndon G. Van Deusen, 'Some Aspects of Whig Thought and Theory in the Jacksonian Period', *American Historical Review* lxiii (1958) 305-22; Lee Benson, *The Concept of Jacksonian Democracy: New York as a Test Case* (Princeton, N.J., 1961) 86-109; Handlin and Handlin, *Commonwealth*, supra note 95, at 182-228 (the Handlins do not discuss the relationship of the breakdown in commonwealth ideas to parties but recognize the consequent drive against 'special privilege'); James R. Sharp, *The Jacksonian versus the Banks: Politics in the State After the Panic of 1837* (New York, 1970); Peter D. Levine, *Behavior of State Legislative Parties in the Jacksonian Era: New Jersey, 1829-1844* (Rutherford, N.J., 1977) 112-78.

the Congregationalist establishment than because he had arrived at the general principle that government should not grant special privileges to particular individuals or groups. A German immigrant in Illinois was no doubt more impressed with Jacksonian Democrats' opposition to prohibition laws than with their argument that such an effort by one group of people to impose its own values upon another was an odious example of 'special legislation'. But their parties campaigned on the general principle as much, if not more, than on the specific instance, and to the degree that they came to identify with the party, they came to identify with its principles too.[112]

These principles were perceived to be so fundamental that different versions of them were incorporated into the constitutions of nearly every state before the Civil War. In language later copied by several states, Virginia and North Carolina in 1776 expressed the inhibition against grants of special privileges inherent in the idea of 'commonwealth': '[N]o men or set of men are entitled to exclusive or separate emoluments or privileges from the community, but in consideration of public services'.[113] New Hampshirites, modifying slightly an earlier version framed in Pennsylvania, more clearly articulated the 'commonwealth' premises upon which this inhibition lay: 'Government [is] instituted for the common benefits, protection, and security of the whole community, and not for the private interest or emolument of any one man, family, or class of men'.[114] As a consequence of such convictions, from their earliest stage nearly every state banned 'hereditary distinctions' and titles.[115] In other sections of their early constitutions they insisted that 'perpetuities and monopolies are contrary to the genius of a State, and ought not to be allowed'.[116]

112. For studies indicating that early nineteenth-century voters divided along religious and cultural lines, see Robert Kelley, *The Cultural Pattern of American Politics: The First Century* (New York, 1979) 109-40, 160-84; Ronald P. Formisano, *The Birth of Mass Political Parties: Michigan, 1827-61* (Princeton, N.J., 1972); Benson, *Concept of Jacksonian Democracy*, supra note 111; William G. Shade, *Banks or No Banks: The Money Issue in Western Politics, 1832-1865* (Detroit, 1972) passim. That political parties themselves became 'positive references'—sources of attitudes and values—for voters is generally accepted in the political science literature. See Robert E. Lane, *Political Life: Why and How People Get Involved in Politics* (New York, 1965) 299-303; Angus Campbell et al., *The American Voter* (New York, 1960) 128-36.

113. Va. Const. (1776), Bill of Rights, sec. 4; N. C. Const. (1776), Dec. of Rights, sec. 3; Ky. Const. (1792), art. XII; Miss. Const. (1817), art. I, sec. 1; Ala. Const. (1819), art. I, sec. 1; Tex. Const. (1845), art. I, sec. 2.

114. N.H. Const. (1784), art. I, sec. 10. See also Pa. Const. (1776), Dec. of Rights, art. V; Vt. Const. (1777), Dec. of Rights, art. VI.

115. N.C. Const. (1776), Dec. of Rights, sec. 22; S.C. Const. (1776), art. IX, sec. 5; N.H. Const. (1784), art. I, sec. 9; Pa. Const. (1790), art. IX, sec. 24; Ky. Const. (1792), art. XII; Del. Const. (1792), art. I, sec. 19; Tenn. Const. (1796), art. XI, sec. 30; Ohio Const. (1802), art. VII, sec. 24; Ind. Const. (1816), art. I, sec. 22; Miss. Const. (1817), art. I, sec. 26; Conn. Const. (1818), art. I, sec. 20; Ala. Const. (1819), art. I, sec. 26; Me. Const. (1820), art. I, sec. 23; Mo. Const. (1820), art. XIII, sec. 20; Fla. Const. (1838), art. I, sec. 25; Md. Const. (1851), art. I, sec. 40; Kan. Const. (1859), art. I, sec. 19.

116. N.C. Const. (1776), Dec. of Rights, sec. 23; Tenn. Const. (1796), art. XI, sec. 23;

By the 1840s these general principles were incorporated into more concrete constitutional prohibitions. 'The general assembly shall not grant to any citizen or class of citizens privileges and immunities which upon the same terms, shall not equally belong to all citizens', the people of Iowa wrote in their fundamental law of 1846. The people of Indiana utilized similar language in 1851, as did those of Oregon in 1857.[117] Fifteen states wrote general incorporation laws into their constitutions between 1845 and 1872.[118] Five barred all state aid to private enterprise.[119] Eight more barred stock subscriptions, loans, or pledges of credit.[120]

The more flexibly phrased of these constitutional provisions, such as those barring 'exclusive privileges . . . but in consideration of public services' or those not clearly prohibitive ('perpetuities and monopolies . . . ought not to be allowed'), could hardly form the bases for judicial review of legislation until jurists became used to adjudging the reasonableness of legislation in the late nineteenth century. By that time the prohibition against taking property 'without due process of law' had become the rubric under which such judgments were made. But even the more stringent prohibitions were undermined by the clear necessity for some kinds of 'monopolies'. There was no reasonable way to permit free competition in street railway or municipal gas service, for example, and ultimately most courts were compelled to exclude these from the class of monopolies and special privileges barred by their state constitutions.[121]

At the same time, the notion that the community as a whole benefitted when special privileges were granted to some private enterprise, that although private they were dedicated to a 'public use', frustrated legal

Ark. Const. (1836), art. II, sec. 19; Fla. Const. (1838), art. I, sec. 24; Tex. Const. (1845), art. I, sec. 18; Md. Const. (1851), art. I, sec. 39.

117 Iowa Const. (1846), art. I, sec. 6; Ind. Const. (1851), art. XXIII; Ore. Const. (1857), art. I (Bill of Rights), sec. 21.

118. La. Const. (1845), art. CXXXIII; N.Y. Const. (1846), art. VIII, sec. 1, 4; Ill. Const. (1848), art. X, sec. 1, (permitted exceptions at legislative discretion); Mich. Const. (1850), art. XV, sec. 1; Md. Const. (1851), art. III, sec. 47: Ohio Const. (1851), art. XIII (Corporations), sec. 1, 2; Minn. Const. (1857), art. X, sec. 2; Ore. Const (1857), art. XI (Corporations), sec. 2; Nev. Const. (1864), art. VIII, sec. 1; Mo. Const. (1865), art. VIII, sec. 4; Neb. Const. (1866), art. II (Corporations), sec. 1, 2; Ark. Const. (1868), art. I, sec. 48; S.C. Const. (1868), art. XII (Corporations), sec. 1; Tenn. Const. (1870), art. XI, sec. 8; W. Va. Const. (1872), art. XI, sec. 1.

119. Ill. Const. (1848), art. III, sec. 38; Pa. Const. (amended 1857), art. XI, sec. 5-7; Fla. Const. (1868), art. XIII, sec. 8; Ga. Const. (1868), art. III, sec. 6; Va. Const. (1870), art. X, sec. 12-15.

120. N.J. Const. (1844), art. VI, sec. 6(3); La. Const. (1845), art. CXXI; Ky. Const. (1850), art. II, sec. 33; Mich. Const. (1850), art. XIV, sec. 6, 8; Ohio Const. (1851), art. VIII, sec. 4; Minn. Const. (1857), art. IX, sec. 10; Mo. Const. (1865), art. XI, sec. 13; Miss. Const. (1868), art. XII, sec. 5.

121. *Norwich Gas Light Co. v. Norwich City Gas Co.*, 25 Conn. 19 (1856); *California State Telegraph Co. v. Alta Telegraph Co.*, 22 Cal. 398 (1863); *City of Memphis v. Memphis Water Co.*, 5 Heisk. (52 Tenn.) 1495 (1871); *State v. Milwaukee Gaslight Co.*, 29 Wis. 454 (1872); *Grant v. City of Davenport*, 36 Iowa 396 (1873).

arguments that such legislation violated fundamental law.[122] When a few state courts finally decided in the 1860s and 1870s that such a 'public use' could not justify taxation for the benefit of private corporations—specifically taxation to pay for bonds donated to railroad corporations or to buy stock in them,—they could not find legal precedents directly in point.[123]

But on the general proposition that the powers of government could not be used for the benefit of one citizen at the expense of another, or one group of citizens at the expense of the rest, there was massive agreement in the courts. It was one of the fundamental principles underlying the concept of 'vested rights', what the great constitutional historian, Edward S. Corwin, called 'the basic doctrine of American constitutional law'.[124] Citing that doctrine, courts throughout the United States regularly voided legislation that seemed to them arbitrarily to transfer property rights from one citizen to another. That, they insisted, was not a legislative power. Once a right to property had vested in an individual, that right could not be divested except in a judicial proceeding, either as a punishment for crime or because in a civil case someone else proved a superior claim.

Such legislative usurpations were most obvious when legislatures attempted to change the law in the middle of court proceedings in an effect to sustain the claim of one of the parties, or even more blatantly when they tried to reverse decisions already rendered or forced rehearings under new laws. It was such an effort that precipitated the famous Supreme Court case of *Calder v. Bull*: 'There are certain vital principles in our free republican governments, which will determine and overrule an apparent and flagrant abuse of legislative power', Justice Samuel Chase insisted. Among the laws which exceeded legislative power would be 'a law that takes property from A. and gives it to B'.[125] On the same principle, changes in laws by which property rights were determined could apply only to rights that accrued after the new law was passed. Courts uniformly insisted on adjudicating cases according to the law in force at the time rights accrued.[126]

---

122. *Beekman v. Saratoga and Schenectady R.R. Co.*, 3 Paige 45 (N.Y. Ch. 1831); *Raleigh & Gaston R.R. v. Davis*, 2 Dev. & Batt. 451 (N.C. 1837). See Harry N. Scheiber, 'The Road to *Munn*: Eminent Domain and the Concept of Public Purpose in the State Courts', in Donald Fleming and Bernard Bailyn, eds., *Law in American History* (Cambridge, Mass., 1971) 362-73.

123. Iowa ex rel. *Burlington & Mo. R.R. Co. v. County of Wapello*, 13 Iowa 388 (1862); *People v. Twp. Bd. of Salem*, 20 Mich. 452 (1870).

124. Edward S. Corwin, 'The Basic Doctrine of American Constitutional Law', 12 *Michigan Law Review* 247-76 (1914). Besides Corwin's essays, the best discussions of the doctrine of vested rights are Charles Grove Haines, 'Judicial Review of Legislation and the Doctrine of Vested Rights and of Implied Limitations on Legislatures', 2 *Texas Law Review* 257-90 (1924); Wallace Mendelson, 'A Missing Link in the Evolution of Due Process', 10 *Vanderbilt Law Review* 125-37 (1956).

125. 3 U.S. (3 Dall.) 386, at 388 (1798).

126. For example, *Merrill v. Sherburne*, 1 N.H. 199 (1818); *Ogden v. Blackledge*, 6 U.S. (2 Cranch.) 272 (1804); *Dash v. Van Kleeck*, 7 Johns. 477 (N.Y. 1811).

As Corwin has pointed out, such 'retrospective legislation' seemed to early American jurists to be akin to criminal enactments, in that they took property as effectively as would a fine for violation of the criminal law. Yet they did so by the terms of the law itself, with no judicial determination of guilt or innocence and no suggestion that the victim had done anything wrong. Thus these laws seemed akin to illicit *ex post facto* laws and bills of attainder.[127]

But while this perception formed one of the bases for the vested rights doctrine, the conviction that such enactments constituted 'special legislation' provided another, closely related one. For example, in the leading case of *Dash v. Van Kleeck*, Chancellor William Kent affirmed the nullity of 'retrospective legislation' with a learned treatise citing English authorities that stressed its similarity to *ex post facto* laws.[128] But his colleague, Smith Thompson, reached the same conclusion by arguing that such legislative interference with vested rights 'is repugnant to the first principles of justice and the equal and permanent security of rights', because it 'take[s] by law, the property of one individual without his consent, and give[s] it to another'.[129] Bankruptcy and exemption laws designed to apply retrospectively met the same objection: 'They take the property which in honesty and fair dealing belongs to the creditor and, without his consent transfer it to the debtor'.[130] Most state constitutions specifically banned their legislatures from impairing 'the obligation of contracts', as did the Constitution of the United States, and in 1827 the Supreme Court made the same distinction between retrospective and prospective bankruptcy and exemption provisions as did the state courts.[131]

Moreover there were occasions when inhibitions against 'special legislation' plainly were more applicable to legislative enactments than inhibitions based on the illegitimacy of 'retrospective legislation'. The former underlay the uniform agreement among early nineteenth century courts that legislatures could not authorize the taking of private property for private purposes without the consent of the owner (although they disagreed about which purposes were private and which were public). When dissident Philadelphians challenged the city's right to use their tax-money to buy stock in railroad companies, for example, Pennsylvania Chief Justice Jeremiah Black conceded, 'transferring money from the owners of it, into the possession of those who have no title to it, though done under the name and form of a tax, is unconstitutional', even as he sustained this particular tax's legitimacy on the grounds that promotion of railroads was a 'public use' of the funds.[132] In eminent domain cases, too, courts agreed that 'the right of

127. Corwin, 'Basic Doctrine of American Constitutional Law', supra note 124, at 248-55.

128. 7 Johns. 447, 500-512.

129. Ibid. at 493.

130. *Quackenbush v. Danks*, 1 Denio 128 (N.Y. Sup. Ct. 1845).

131. *Ogden v. Saunders*, 25 U.S. (12 Wheat.) 213 (1827).

132. *Sharpless v. Mayor of Philadelphia*, 21 Pa. 147, 169 (1853). In a powerful dissent, one

eminent domain does not . . . imply a right in the sovereign power to take the property of one citizen and transfer it to another, even for a full compensation, where the public interest will be in no way promoted by such transfer'.[133]

Likewise New York Democratic politicians and judges complained that special assessments levied upon adjacent property owners for 'public improvements' violated the principle of 'equal rights'. A small number of property owners were forced to pay for improvements that benefitted the whole community at best, or a small group of speculators at worst. A general tax 'falls upon the . . . property of the constituents, equally', they explained '[T]he security against its abuse is found in the mutual interests and mutual relations of both'. But when special assessments were levied upon a particular group of taxpayers, 'the only security against injustice and oppression is taken away'.[134]

The essence of the complaint against special legislation, legislation that took A and gave to B, was that it forced the transfer without resort to the judicial procedures that alone could justify it. That is, special legislation transferred property from one person to another without due process of law. The growing tendency between the 1830s and the 1850s for judges to nullify such legislation because it violated constitutional provisions prohibiting deprivation of property 'except by due process of law' or according to 'the laws of the land' (which nineteenth century jurisprudents held to be synonymous phrases) were merely a logical consequence of that complaint.[135]

Daniel Webster linked the concepts as early as 1819, in his argument before the Supreme Court in the *Dartmouth College* case. Webster urged the

---

of Black's colleagues denied that a railroad subsidy was a 'public use' of tax money, arguing it was an unconstitutional instance of special legislation, in violation of the constitutional guarantee that one's property could be taken only by the judgment of one's peers or by the law of the land. The dissent, not recorded in the report, may be found in 2 *American Law Register* 85-112 (1853-1854). The citation to the 'law of the land' clause of the Pennsylvania state constitution is ibid. at 105.

133. *Beekman v. Saratoga & Schenectady R.R. Co.*, 3 Paige Ch. 45, 73 (N.Y. Ch. 1831). See the cases cited in Thomas M. Cooley, *A Treatise on the Constitutional Limitations Which Rest Upon the Legislative Power of the States of the American Union*, 3d ed. (Boston, 1874) 622.

134. *People ex rel. Griffin v. Mayor of Brooklin*, 9 Barb. 535, 548 (N.Y. Sup. Ct. 1850). See Stephen Diamond, 'The Death and Transfiguration of Benefit Taxation: Special Assessments in Nineteenth-Century America', 12 *Journal of Legal Studies* 201-40, 214-18 (1983), for a discussion of opposition to special assessments in New York in the 1830s and 1840s.

135. For the incorporation of the doctrine of vested rights into the concept of 'due process of law' before the Civil War, see especially Mendelson, 'Missing Link', supra note 124; Corwin, 'Basic Doctrine of American Constitutional Law', supra note 124 and Corwin, 'The Doctrine of Due Process', supra note 8 at 460 are very useful for the information they contain, but Corwin dismisses far too casually the degree to which ante-bellum lawyers and jurists had come to accept what we would recognize as a 'substantive' notion of due process.

33

court to overturn the New Hampshire law that had transferred control of the college from one board of trustees to another: 'Have the plaintiffs lost their franchises by "due course and due process of law"'? he asked. 'On the contrary, are not these acts "particular acts of the legislature, which have no relation to the community in general, and which are rather sentences than laws;" By the law of the land, is most clearly intended, the general law. . . . The meaning is, that every citizen shall hold his life, liberty, property and immunities, under the protection of the general rules that govern society'.[136]

Thirty-five years later the New York Court of Appeals made the point more succinctly in overturning the Married Women's Property Act as it applied to property husbands had acquired through marriage before its enactment: 'The act does not fall within the meaning of *due process of law*. The provision was designed to protect the citizens against all mere acts of power. . . . [N]o power in the state can legally confer upon one person or class of persons the property of another person or class, without their consent. . .'.[137]

It is ironic that in the Dartmouth College case and in many others, lawyers made the charge of 'special legislation' against laws themselves passed, usually by Jeffersonian Republican or Jacksonian Democratic legislators, to reverse previous grants of special privileges.[138] Nonetheless, antebellum American law was suffused with the principle that special legislation was illegitimate, and that conviction had already been linked to the fundamental maxim that no person could be deprived of property but by due process of law or by the laws of the land.[139]

---

136. *Dartmouth College v. Woodward*, 17 U.S. (4 Wheat.) 518, 557-58.

137. *Westervelt v. Gregg*, 12 N.Y. 202, 212 (1854).

138. This was true of the *Dartmouth College* case, where the newly elected Republican legislature of New Hampshire sought to replace the old, Congregationalist board of trustees with one drawn from the entire religious community. Richard N. Current, 'The Dartmouth College Case', in Garraty, ed., *Quarrels That Have Shaped the Constitution*, supra note 37, at 15-29; Francis W. Stites, *Private Interest and Public Gain: The Dartmouth College Case, 1819* (Amherst, Mass., 1972) 12-38. In the famous *Charles River Bridge* case, 36 U.S. (11 Pet.) 420 (1837), Bostonians had sought to undermine the monopoly over bridge traffic between Harvard and Cambridge held by the Charles River Bridge Company, much of the stock of which was owned by Congregationalist Harvard University. Stanley I. Kutler, *Privilege and Creative Destruction: The Charles River Bridge Case* (Philadelphia, 1971) 18-34. Arthur B. Darling, 'Jacksonian Democracy in Massachusetts, 1824-1848', *American Historical Review* xxix (1924) 271-87. In *University v. Foy*, 5 N.C. 58 (1805), perhaps the first decision to cite a 'law of the land' clause of a state constitution in overturning special legislation, Jeffersonian Republican legislators had repealed a land grant to the Episcopalian-dominated University of North Carolina. James H. Broussard, *The Southern Federalists, 1800-1816* (Baton Rouge, La., 1978) 323-26.

139. By the outbreak of the Civil War the linkage had received judicial articulation in North Carolina, Tennessee, Pennsylvania, New York, and the Supreme Court of the United States. *University v. Foy*, 5 N.C. 58 (1805); *Hoke v. Henderson*, 15 N.C. 1 (1833); *Vanzant v. Waddell*, 10 Tenn. 270 (1829); *Sheppard v. Johnson*, 21 Tenn. 285 (1841):

## V. Symbiosis: Laissez-Faire Constitutionalism

In the 1850s the focus of American legislation slowly began to shift from promotion of economic development towards greater regulation of that development. As a consequence, lawyers launched an ever-increasing number of attacks upon laws that they claimed exceeded legislative power. Some of these challenged regulations involved morals; but more and more involved some degree of redistribution of resources. Lawyers challenged prohibition statutes,[140] early zoning-type regulations,[141] special assessments,[142] disaster relief,[143] public payment of Civil War draftee's commutation fees,[144] tax exemptions and subsidies for businesses,[145] and railroad regulations.[146]

The judicial response is instructive. In those cases where counsel complained merely that legislation was a 'retrospective' violation of 'vested rights', that is, that it made it illegal to hold property that was legal when acquired, judges nearly always sustained the legislative power. Thus only the courts of Indiana and New York ruled prohibition unconstitutional.[147] Other judges sustained it as a health and moral measure well within the police power.[148] Likewise, courts sustained ordinances restricting the operation of dangerous, unsanitary, or entertainment-oriented businesses to certain locations.[149] But in these cases there was no suggestion of 'class legislation', no clear transfer of property or its benefits from one portion of

---

*Sharpless v. Mayor of Philadelphia*, 21 Pa. 147, 167 (1853); *Taylor v. Porter*, 4 Hill 140 (N.Y. Sup. Ct. 1843); *Westervelt v. Gregg*, 12 N.Y. 202 (1854); *Bloomer v. McQuewan*, 55 U.S. (24 How.) 539 (1852); *Dred Scott v. Sandford*, 60 U.S. (19 How.) 393, 450 (1856). It had also been developed in Anonymous, 'The Security of Private Property', 1 *American Law Magazine* 318-47, 335ff. (1843).

140. See the cases, infra notes 147 and 148.

141. See the cases, infra notes 149 and 150.

142. See the cases, infra notes 155-157.

143. *Lowell v. Boston*, 110 Mass. 454 (1873).

144. See the cases, infra note 154.

145. See the cases, infra notes 158-160.

146. *Toledo, Wabash, & Western Ry. Co. v. City of Jacksonville*, 67 Ill. 37 (1873); *Munn v. Illinois*, 69 Ill. 80 (1873); *Loan Association v. Topeka*, 5 F. Cas. 737 (C.C.D. Kans. 1874) (No. 2734); *Chicago, Burlington & Quincy R.R. v. Iowa*, 5 F. Cas. 594 (C.C.D. Iowa 1875) (No. 2666).

147. *Wynehamer v. New York*, 13 N.Y. 378 (1856); *Beebe v. State*, 6 Ind. 501 (1855).

148. *Lincoln v. Smith*, 27 Vt. 328 (1854); *Goddard v. Jacksonville*, 15 Ill. 589 (1854); *State v. Gallagher*, 4 Gibbs 244 (Mich. 1856); *Fisher v. McGuirr*, 1 Gray 1 (Mass. 1854); *State v. Paul*, 5 R.I. 185 (1858).

149. *State v. Noyes*, 10 Foster 279 (N.H. 1855); *Metropolitan Bd. of Health v. Heister*, 37 N.Y. 661 (1868); *Inhabitants of Watertown v. Mayo*, 109 Mass. 315 (1872).

the community to another. Judges were far less sympathetic to legislation where such a transfer could be demonstrated.

The famous *Slaughterhouse Cases*[150] had elements of both. The challenged law was designed to protect public health by establishing a single slaughterhouse for the use of New Orleans' butchers, away from residential areas. But it authorized a single company of seventeen incorporators to build it and its appurtenances. The butchers would be forced to rent facilities from them. The butchers 'claim an interest, a privilege, a property, in their labor, and the faculty of applying their labor in useful occupations; of which they cannot be deprived for the profit or gain of other persons or corporations', their counsel, former Supreme Court Justice John Archibald Campbell, insisted.[151] Their business 'by this Act . . . has been converted into a *Monopoly* for the benefit of *Seventeen selected* persons'.[152] As is well known, the Supreme Court sustained the law by the narrowest possible majority, with the dissenters deeming it unconstitutional both as a violation of the privileges and immunities of citizens of the United States and as a deprivation of liberty and property without due process of law.[153]

In other cases the transfer of property from one group to another was even plainer, and in those cases judges by the 1860s were establishing the clear foundations of laissez-faire constitutionalism and, more slowly, substantive due process of law. For example, several states permitted local communities to levy taxes to pay commutation fees that would enable their young men to escape the draft. But in the opinion of many judges, such a tax was too clearly an imposition on the taxpayers of the community for the benefit of a smaller class. The commutation fee was really a penalty for refusing to serve, a Maine judge explained as he concurred in ruling such laws unconstitutional. 'A tax for such purpose is not only a tax on A. for the benefit of B., but it is also a tax on A. to reimburse B. the amount of the penalty.'[154]

Special assessments for local improvements raised similar problems. Did not the whole community get the benefit at the expense of those assessed?

---

150. 83 U.S. (16 Wall.) 36 (1873).

151. Supplemental Brief for Plaintiffs, *Fagan v. State of Louisiana* [The Slaughterhouse Cases], Philip B. Kurland and Gerhard Casper, eds., *Landmark Briefs and Arguments of the Supreme Court of the United States: Constitutional Law* (Arlington, Va., 1975) vi, 580.

152. Brief for Plaintiffs, ibid. 537.

153. Slaughterhouse Cases, 83 U.S. (16 Wall.) 114-16, 118 (1873) (Bradley, dissenting).

154. *Thompson v. Inhabitants of Pittston*, 59 Me. 545, 556 (1871) (Dickerson concurring). See also *Perkins v. Inhabitants of Milford*, 59 Me. 315 (1871) and *Freeland v. Hastings*, 92 Mass. 570 (1865). The New Jersey courts decided that such laws did serve a public purpose and therefore did not amount to special, or class, legislation. But they clearly were troubled by the case and took pains to articulate the principle that 'the power of taking one man's property and vesting it in another, is in no sense a legislative power; and . . . a law which attempted to do this under the name of a tax would be wholly unauthorized and void'. *State, Wagner et al. v. Collector of Delaware*, 31 N.J.L. 189, 195 (1865).

That concern led the New Jersey courts to impose a strict requirement that local government compensate the difference between an assessment and the actual value of the improvement to those assessed. Finally in 1874 they ruled unconstitutional all frontage assessments for street improvements.[155] The New York courts, on the other hand, regularly sustained special assessments, holding that 'there is nothing in the Constitution of this State, which requires taxation to be general . . . or that it shall be equal. . . .'.[156] But by 1872 the weight of anti-class legislation legal opinion forced a *caveat*. When residents of Brockport challenged a law requiring them alone to pay for a normal school open to all state residents, the Court of Appeals sustained the law, citing earlier recognition of expansive state taxing power. However, the judges added, 'It would be going too far to deny that the provisions of the Constitution, which declare that no person shall be deprived of property without due process of law, and that property shall be taken for public use upon just compensation, would afford no protection to the citizen against impositions made nominally in the form of taxes, but which were in fact forced levies upon individuals or confiscations of private property . . . to pay for benefits conferred upon others who bore no proportion of the burden'.[157]

But it was subsidies for private businesses that were most likely to offend judges' constitutional sensibilities, and they were among the first to be overturned in a large number of jurisdictions. Such subsidies of millers, manufacturers, and railroad companies blurred the line 'between what is for public and governmental, and what is for private purposes, between general legislation for the whole people and special for the individual', Maine's Supreme Court warned.[158] 'If it were proposed to pass an act enabling the inhabitants of the several towns by vote to transfer the farms or the horses or oxen . . . from the rightful owner or owners to some manufacturer whom the majority might select, the monstrousness of such proposed legislation would be transparent. But the mode by which the property would be taken from one or many and given to another or others can make no difference in the principle.' Maine's constitution forbade the deprivation of one's property except by 'judgment of his peers or the law of the land', the court pointed out. 'Property taken by taxation is not taken by the judgment of our peers. A statute in direct violation of the primary principles of justice is not "the law of the land" within the meaning of the constitution.'[159] '[T]hough the money demand of the citizen is called a tax, it is not such', wrote Iowa's Judge John F. Dillon in ruling Iowa's railroad subsidy law unconstitutional. It 'is, in fact, a coercive contribution in favor of private railway corpora-

---

155. *The Tidewater Co. v. Coster*, 18 N.J.Eq. 518 (1866); *State v. Mayor of Hoboken*, 39 N.J.L. 291 (1873); *State, Agens, Pros. v. Newark*, 37 ibid. at 415 (1874).

156. *People ex rel. Crowell v. Lawrence*, 41 N.Y. 137 (1869).

157. *Gordon v. Cornes*, 47 N.Y. 608 (1872).

158. Opinion of the Justices, 58 Me. 590, 591 (1870).

159. Ibid. at 593-95.

tions, and violative, not only of the general spirit of the [Iowa] Constitution . . . , but of that specific provision which declares *that no man shall be deprived of his property without due process of law*'.[160]

In 1863, as lawyers and judges ever more clearly linked the concept of 'class' or 'special legislation' to that of 'due process of law', Thomas McIntyre Cooley, the locofoco Democrat-turned-Republican, published his immensely influential *Treatise on Constitutional Limitations*.[161] That treatise made him 'the principal contributor to the cause of constitutional laissez-faire in the era following the Civil War', scholars have agreed.[162]

Cooley gathered together and organized the disparate cases in which judges had applied different specific constitutional prohibitions in order to protect vested rights from retrospective and class legislation. Despite his own stress upon enforcing such prohibitions with restraint, he provided judges with a catalogue of justifications for restriction of state power. His treatise was by no means designed to protect special interests from government regulation. Far from it. Two years after its appearance, Cooley suggested his real animus when as a justice of the Michigan Supreme Court he used its principles not to sustain but to reject the power of states to subsidize private corporations. '[W]hen the State once enters upon the business of subsidies, the strong and powerful are most likely to control legislation, and . . . the weaker will be taxed to enhance the profits of the stronger', he wrote.[163]

Nonetheless, Cooley's *Treatise on Constitutional Limitations* merits Benjamin R. Twiss's description as 'almost . . . a direct counter' in the world of law 'to the appearance of Karl Marx's *Das Kapital*'.[164] After all, the heart of *Das Kapital*, and of socialism, is the conviction that class welfare is inevitable and that control of the institutions of the state is its object until the final victory of the proletariat and establishment of socialism makes it irrelevant to the social order; the heart of Cooley's *Treatise*, and of laissez-faire constitutionalism, was opposition to class and special legislation. State subsidies were illicit no matter who they were intended to benefit, weak or powerful, Cooley insisted from the Michigan court's bench. '[T]he discrimination . . . is an invasion of that equality of right and

---

160. *Hansen v. Iowa*, 27 Iowa 28 (1869). See also *Allan v. Jay*, 60 Me. 124 (1871); *Lowell v. Boston*, 110 Mass. 454 (1873); *Weeks v. Milwaukee*, 10 Wis. 342 (1860)); *Curtis v. Whipple*, 24 Wis. 350 (1869); *Whiting v. Sheboygan and Fon du Lac R.R. Co.*, 25 Wis. 167 (1870); *People v. Twp. Bd. of Salem*, 20 Mich. 452 (1870).

161. Cooley, *Constitutional Limitations*, supra note 133 (1st edition published in 1868).

162. Clyde E. Jacobs, *Law Writers and the Courts: The Influence of Thomas M. Cooley, Christopher G. Tiedeman, and John F. Dillon Upon American Constitutional Law* (Berkeley and Los Angeles, 1954) 27; Benjamin R. Twiss, *Lawyers and the Constitution: How Laissez-Faire Came to the Supreme Court* (Princeton, N.J., 1942) passim; Fine, *Laissez-Faire and the General-Welfare State*, supra note 9 at 128-29.

163. *People v. Twp. Bd. of Salem*, 20 Mich. at 487.

164. Twiss, *Lawyers and the Constitution*, supra note 162 at 18.

privilege which is a maxim in State government. . . . [I]t is not the business of the State to make discriminations in favor of one class against another'.[165]

Cooley's views are emblematic of the symbiotic relationship between the concept of rights articulated by laissez-faire propagandists in the Gilded Age and the legal and political heritage of hostility towards 'class legislation' which seemed to sanction their views. The attacks that laissez-fairists levied upon 'class legislation' in post-Civil War America resonated with principles already deeply embedded in American legal thought. Inevitably, the two merged. When John F. Dillon, now federal judge and American Bar Association president, described the income tax as 'a forced contribution from the rich to the poor' and 'class legislation of the most pronounced and vicious type' he was not only engaging in a laissez-faire polemic; he was calling for judicial intervention against any proposal so manifestly 'violative of the constitutional rights of the property owner'.[166]

Ultimately, the courts responded to this sort of appeal, made in speech after speech, legal and popular article after article, legal brief after brief. It would require a new essay to discuss how courts, both state and national, slowly came to do so. That is a study that wants doing, and which requires far more than the traditional account of the progression from *Slaughterhouse* and *Munn* to *Lochner*, by way of the Mississippi and Minnesota rate cases,[167] *Smyth v. Ames*,[168] and *Allgeyer v. Louisiana*.[169]

However, it should be clear from the foregoing that when the courts did respond, they did not simply spin the doctrine of 'substantive due process of law' and the other underpinnings of laissez-faire constitutionalism out of thin air, in order to protect the position of the privileged. They responded because they perceived 'class legislation' where a new generation would see laws designed to benefit everyone. An American heritage of liberty dictated revulsion against such enactments, and a concept of 'due process of law' that had been developing for almost a century seemed to provide a sanction against them.

---

165. *People v. Twp. Bd. of Salem*, 20 Mich. at 486.

166. Dillion, 'Property—Its Rights and Duties in our Legal and Social Systems', *Proceedings of the New York State Bar Association* xviii (1895) 33-64, 46.

167. *Stone v. Farmer's Loan & Trust Co.*, 116 U.S. 307 (1886); *Chicago, Milwaukee, and St. Paul Ry. Co. v. Minnesota*, 134 U.S. 418 (1890).

168. 169 U.S. 466 (1898).

169. 165 U.S. 578 (1897). For examples of the traditional, Supreme Court-centered account, see Hamilton, 'Path of Due Process', supra note 8; Kelly, Harbison, and Belz, supra note 16 at 397-418.

**Commencement Number.**

# NEW ENGLANDER

AND

# YALE REVIEW.

No. CCLVI.

AUGUST, 1891.

Article I.—PROTECTION TO PRIVATE PROPERTY
FROM PUBLIC ATTACK.

An Address delivered before the Graduating Classes at the
Sixty-seventh Anniversary of Yale Law School, on June 23,
1891, by Hon. D. J. Brewer, LL.D., Justice of the Supreme
Court of the United States.

*Mr. President and Gentlemen of the Graduating Classes:*

" We hold these truths to be self-evident, that all men are
created equal, that they are endowed by their Creator with
certain unalienable Rights, that among these are Life, Liberty,
and the pursuit of Happiness." This was the natal cry of a
new nation. It is the illuminating and interpreting voice of
the Constitution. I know it is by some thought clever to
speak of the Declaration as a collection of glittering gener-
alities. The inspired apostle said: "And now abideth faith,
hope, charity—these three; but the greatest of these is charity."
This affirmation is only a glittering generality; but subtract
from Christianity all that it implies, and what is left is as
barren as the sands of Sahara. The Declaration passes beyond

VOL. XIX. 7

the domain of logic—it argues nothing. It appeals to the intuitions of every true man, and relying thereon, declares the conditions upon which all human government, to endure, must be founded.

John Adams was a member of the committee which drafted this Declaration, and in 1780, he prepared the Bill of Rights for the new Constitution of the State of Massachusetts. Its first article is in these words: "All men are born free and equal, and have certain natural, essential, and unalienable rights; among which may be reckoned the right of enjoying and defending their lives and liberties; that of acquiring, possessing, and protecting property; in fine, that of seeking and obtaining their safety and happiness." There is no additional truth in this article. Its last clauses simply define what is embraced in the phrase—"the pursuit of happiness." They equally affirm that sacredness of life, of liberty, and of property, are rights—unalienable rights; anteceding human government, and its only sure foundation; given not by man to man, but granted by the Almighty to every one; something which he has by virtue of his manhood, which he may not surrender, and of which he cannot be deprived.

In the Constitution, as originally adopted, there was no reaffirmation of these fundamental truths. Why this omission? The men who had joined in the Declaration of Independence were the framers of the Constitution. In the lapse of years had they grown wiser? Were they repudiating that Declaration, or were they still filled with its spirit? While putting into the cold phraseology of the Constitution the grants and limitations of governmental power, did they forget or repudiate the truths which only eleven years before they had affirmed to be self-evident? I shall not stop to argue before you that the Constitution was no departure from the Declaration. On the contrary, I assert and appeal to history in support of the truth thereof—that the spirit of 1776 was present with and filled the convention of 1787, and that the corner-stone of the foundation upon which the Constitution was built, and upon which it rests to-day, was and is the Declaration of Independence. I read into the one the affirmation of the other, that some truths are self-evident, existing before and superior to constitutions, and, therefore, unnecessary of mention therein. Life, liberty, and the pursuit of happiness are lifted beyond the touch of any statute or organic instrument. From the time in earliest records, when Eve took loving possession of even the forbidden apple, the idea of property and the sacredness of the right of its possession has never departed from the race. Whatever dreams may exist of an ideal human nature, which cares nothing for possession and looks only to labor for the good of others—actual human experience, from the dawn of history to the present hour, declares that the love of acquirement, mingled with the joy of possession, is the real stimulus to human activity. When, among the affirmations of the Declaration of Independence, it is asserted that the pursuit of happiness is one of the unalienable rights, it is meant that the acquisition, possession, and enjoyment of property are matters which human government cannot forbid, and which it cannot destroy; that except in punishment for crime no man's property, nor any value thereof, can be taken from him without just compensation. Instead of saying that all private property is held at the mercy and judgment of the public, it is a higher truth, that all rights of the State in the property of the individual are at the expense of the public. I know that, as punishment for crime, the State may rightfully take the property of the wrongdoer. Fine and confiscation have been always recognized as suitable means of punishment. The object of punishment, as well as its justification, is to protect society and deter from crimes against it. The public must use the best means therefor—death, imprisonment, stripes, or fine and confiscation. Whatever may theoretically be said as to the idea of pecuniary compensation for crime, it must be recognized that there are many offenses against human law, particularly those which are in the nature of *malum prohibitum*, and not *malum in se*, in respect to which physical punishment seems a cruelty, and the only other available recourse is a pecuniary infliction. But this seizure of a criminal's money or property is only by way of punishment, and not because the public has any beneficial claim upon it. It is not an appropriation of private property for public uses or public benefits. It is therefore in no manner inconsistent with that security of property which is among the unalienable rights of man.

I come now to the theme of my remarks, and that is :

## THE PROTECTION OF PRIVATE PROPERTY FROM PUBLIC ATTACKS.

The long struggle in monarchical goverments was to protect the rights of individual against the assaults of the throne. As significant and important, though more peaceful in the struggle, is this government of the people to secure the rights of the individual against the assaults of the majority. The wisdom of government is not in protecting power but weakness; not so much in sustaining the ruler, as in securing the rights of the ruled. The true end of government is protection to the individual; the majority can take care of itself.

Private property is sacrificed at the hands of the police power in at least three ways: first, when the property itself is destroyed ; second, when by regulation of charges its value is diminished ; and third, when its use or some valuable use of it is forbidden. Instances of the first are these : when in the presence of a threatening conflagration a house is blown up to check the progress of the flames : when a house has been occupied by persons afflicted with small-pox or other infectious disease, and so virulent has been the disease, and so many afflicted, that the public health demands the entire destruction of the house and contents by fire to prevent the spread of that disease : when to prevent an overflow in one direction, by which large and valuable property would be destroyed, a break is made in a dyke or embankment, and the water turned elsewhere and upon less valuable property, and crops swept away in order to save buildings and lives. In these and like cases, there is an absolute destruction of the property,—the houses and crops. The individual loses for the public weal. Can there be a doubt that equity and justice demand that the burden of such loss shall not be cast upon the individual, but should be shared by those who have been protected and benefited. It may be, that at common law no action could be maintained against the State or municipality by the individual whose property has been thus destroyed. But the imperfections of the law do not militate against the demands of justice. *Salus populi suprema lex* justifies the destruction. But the equity of compensation is so clear that it has been recognized by statutes in many States, and provisions made for suit against a municipality to distribute upon the public the burden which it is inequitable that the individual should alone bear. And in enforcing such an equity, no regard is or ought to be paid to the character of, or the use to which the building or property is appropriated. It is enough, that property held by an individual under the protection of the law, is destroyed for the public welfare.

Second, under the guise of regulation, where charges for the use are so reduced as to prevent a reasonable profit on the investment. The history of this question is interesting: certain occupations have long been considered of a quasi public nature,—among these, principally, the business of carrying passengers and freight. Of the propriety of this classification, no question can be made. Without enquiring into the various reasons therefor, a common carrier is described as a quasi public servant. Private capital is invested, and the business is carried on by private persons and through private instrumentalities. Yet, it is a public service which they render, and by virtue thereof, public and governmental control is warranted. The great common carriers of the country, the railroad companies, insisted that, by reason of the fact that they were built by private capital and owned by private corporations, they had the same right to fix the prices for transportation that any individual had to fix the price at which he was willing to sell his labor or his property. They challenged the attempts of the State legislatures to regulate their tariffs. After a long and bitter struggle, the Supreme Court of the United States, in the celebrated " Granger " cases, reported in the 94 U. S., sustained the power of the public, and affirmed legislative control. The question in those cases was not as to the extent, but as to the existence of such control. Those decisions, sustaining public control over the tariffs of railroads and other common carriers as a part of the police power of the State, were accompanied by the case of Munn *vs.* Illinois, 94 U. S., 113, putting warehouses in the same category. The scope of this decision, suggesting a far-reaching supervision over private occupations, brought vigorously up the question as to its extent. If the tariff of common carriers and warehouse-men was a matter for public control, could the public so reduce the charges that the receipts of the carrier or the ware-house-man would not only furnish no return to the owners, but also not equal the operating expenses ;—so that the owner having put his property into an investment, permanent in its nature, and from which he could not at will withdraw, might be compelled to see that investment lost, and his property taken from him by an accumulation of debts from operating expenses ?

On this line the struggle was again renewed and carried to the Supreme Court, which in the recent case of Railway Company *vs.* Minnesota, 134 U. S., 418, decided that regulation did not mean destruction ; and that under the guise of legislative control over tariffs it was not possible for State or Nation to destroy the investments of private capital in such enterprises ; that the individual had rights as well as the public, and rights which the public could not take from him. The opinion written in that case by Mr. Justice Blatchford, sustained as it was by the Court, will ever remain a strong and unconquerable fortress in the long struggle between individual rights and public greed. I rejoice to have been permitted to put one stone into that fortress.

The other class of cases, is where, in the exercise of the police power, some special use is stopped, and the value flowing from that use is thus wholly destroyed. In principle, there is no difference between this and the preceding cases. Property is as certainly destroyed when the use of that which is the subject of property is taken away, as if the thing itself was appropriated, for that which gives value to property, is its capacity for use. If it cannot be used, it is worth nothing ; when the use is taken away, the value is gone. If authority were wanting, reference might be had to the decisions of the Supreme Court of the United States, and the language of some of its most eminent judges. In the leading case of Pumpelly *vs.* Green Bay Co., 13 Wall., 166, which was a case where land was overflowed in consequence of the erection of a dam, the Supreme Court thus disposed of this matter.

" It would be a very curious and unsatisfactory result, if, in constru-ing a provision of constitutional law, always understood to have been adopted for protection and security to the rights of the individual as against the government, and which has received the commendation of jurists, statesmen, and commentators as placing the just principles of the common law on that subject beyond the power of ordinary legislation to change or control them, it shall be held that, if the government refrains from the absolute conversion of real property to the uses of the public, it can destroy its value entirely, can inflict irreparable and permanent injury to any extent, can, in effect, subject it to total destruction without making any compensation, because, in the narrowest sense of the word, it is not taken for the public use. Such a construction would pervert the constitutional provision into a restriction upon the rights of the citizen, as those rights stood at the common law, instead of the government, and make it an authority for invasion of private rights under the pretext of the public good, which had no warrant in the laws or practices of our ancestors."

In the case of Munn *vs.* Illinois, 94 U. S., 141, Mr. Justice Field used this language :

" All that is beneficial in property arises from its use, and the fruits of that use ; and whatever deprives a person of them, deprives him of all that is desirable or valuable in the title and possession. If the constitutional guaranty extends no further than to prevent a deprivation of title and possession, and allows a deprivation of use, and the fruits of that use, it does not merit the encomiums it has received."

But surely authority is not needed for a proposition so clear. If one of you own a tract of land usable only for farm purposes, and the fiat of sovereign power forbids its use for such purposes, of what value is the naked title ? No profit or advantage comes to you from the possession of that which you cannot use, and no one will buy that which in like manner he cannot use. So whether the thing be taken or its use stopped, the individual loses, he is deprived of his property ; and if this is done in the exercise of the police power, because the public health, morals, or welfare demand, his property is sacrificed that the public may gain. When a building is destroyed that a fire may not spread, the individual's property is sacrificed for the general good. When the use of his property is forbidden because the public health or morals require such prohibition, the public gains while he loses. Equal considerations of natural justice demand that he who is thus despoiled for the public good, should not alone bear the burden, but that the public which is benefited should share with him the loss. It is unfortunate that this question came into the courts along the line of deep feeling, and in the furtherance of a lofty and noble effort to suppress the enormous evils of intemperance. I reluctantly refer to this, for having had some judicial experience in connection with it, I know how angry was the feeling, how biased the judgment, and how bitter were the denunciations. It is unfortunate, I say, that this question came into the courts along the line of such controversy, for it is a familiar saying, "hard cases make bad precedents," and it is seldom easy, under the pressing burden of a great evil, to examine questions in the calm light of simple justice. We look back to the execution of the witches in Massachusetts by judicial decrees as a sad blot on the records of its courts. No one doubts the integrity of the judges by whom those decrees we entered, or does not feel, by way of apology, that the burden of the awful danger supposed to rest upon the community swayed the judicial mind, and bent its judgment.

When the great State of Kansas, in whose past I glory, and in whose future I believe, proclaimed by the voice of its people through constitutional amendment, that the manufacture and sale of intoxicating liquors as a beverage should cease within its borders, humanity rejoiced, and I am glad to have written the opinion of the Supreme Court of that State, affirming its validity and rightfulness. I regret to be compelled to add, that in the glory of success and the furtherance of a good cause, the State forgot to be just. There were four or five breweries, with machinery and appliances valuable only for one use, worth a few thousand dollars, a mere bagatelle in comparison with the wealth of the State, built up under the sanction of the law, owned by citizens whose convictions were different from those of the majority, and who believed the manufacture and sale of beer to be right and wise. As good citizens it was fitting that they should yield to the judgment of the majority. As honest men, it was fitting for the majority not to destroy without compensation; and to share with the few the burden of that change in public sentiment, evidenced by the constitutional amendment. It will be said hereafter to the glory of the State, that she pioneered the way of temperance; to its shame, that at the same time she forgot to be honest and just, and was willing to be temperate at the expense of the individual. Had this question come to the courts along other lines, who can doubt that a different result would have followed.

Powder is a confessedly dangerous article. The police power, caring for the public safety, may regulate its storage, its use, its manufacture, and regulating, may prohibit. In the State of Delaware are the Dupont Powder Mills, a large manufacturing property. Had the State of Delaware, by its legislation, prohibited the manufacture and sale of powder as it had a right to do, and thus put an end to this great manufacturing industry and destroyed its value, who can doubt that in proceedings along that line of absolute justice which all men feel, the courts would have hastened to declare that such destruction of property, at the expense of the Duponts alone, could not be tolerated; that the State that enforced such destruction should share with them the burden. Would they not have promptly reaffirmed the thought of Chancellor Kent, —that what the State takes it must pay for; and paraphrasing, added,—that what the public destroys, it must also pay for ?

There is not only justice, but wisdom in this rule, that, when a lawful use is by statute made unlawful and forbidden, and its value destroyed, the public shall make compensation to the individual. It restrains from hasty action. It induces a small majority to hesitate in imposing upon an unwilling and large minority its notions of what is demanded by public health, or morals, or welfare. The pocket-book is a potent check on even the reformer. If this rule had been always recognized as in force, would the State of Pennsylvania have enacted that foolish law, forbidding the manufacture and sale of oleomargerine, and thus destroying a legitimate and beneficial industry ? or if it had, would the judicial eye have been so blind as not to see through the thin disguise of a pretended regard for public health, to the real purpose of the act,—the protection of another and no more deserving industry, that of the dairy? When a law which is obnoxious to the beliefs of a large minority is forced upon them by a small majority, and that law infringes upon their habits, and destroys their property, all experience demonstrates the difficulty of enforcing such a law. Witnesses commit perjury, jurors forget the obligations of their oaths, public peace is disturbed, animosities are engendered, and every instance of the defeat of the law is welcomed with applause by the sullen and angry minority.

Private property is subject to governmental attack in three ways: First, through taxation: Second, by eminent domain; and, Third, in the exercise of the police power.

So far as the first is concerned, the idea of taxation is the support of the Government by those who are protected by it, and no one can complain of a tax which responds to that obligation. While there is no return of money or property to the tax-payer, there is no arbitrary taking of property without compensation. It is always understood that the government, the public, returns a full consideration. In fact, taxation, whether general or special, implies an equivalent: if special, increased value to the property by the contiguous improvement; if general, protection to person and property, security of all rights, with the means and machinery for enforcing them and redressing all wrongs. Taxation on any other basis cannot be justified or upheld. Whenever it becomes purely arbitrary, and without an implication of an equivalent in one way or another, so that the public takes the property of the individual giving nothing in return, or when the burden is cast wholly upon one or two, and all others similarly situated are relieved, the act passes beyond the domain of just legislation, and rests with the rescripts of irresponsible and despotic power. It is not to be expected that any law of taxation can anticipate or adjust itself with mathematical accuracy to all the various conditions of property. It must always be adjudged sufficient, if the general scope of these statutes is uniformity and justice. Errors which may and do arise in the enforcement of the general rules of such a statute, are not available to deny its validity or impugn its justice. We stand to-day at the threshold of two thoughts and two demands; one is, that land is the common property of all,—as air and light: that ownership of land is as much against common right and justice, as an appropriation of the free light and air of heaven: that, in view of existing social and economic relations, and to sugar-coat the pill by which title in land shall be destroyed, the burden of taxation should be wholly cast upon land, a burden growing until not only the needs of government be satisfied, but the support and education of all the poor be provided for; and in that way the owners of such property be despoiled thereof not directly, but indirectly and through taxation. The other door, which is as yet but slightly ajar, opens to the proposition which, ignoring all differences of property, says that he who toils and accumulates, and is protected by the State in that toil and accumulation, has all the obligations of protection discharged at his death; and that then all his accumulations should pass to the State,—leaving only to his heirs the same freedom of toil and accumulation, and the like protection which he has enjoyed. I do not care to enter into any discussion of the merits of these measures; but pass with the single observation, that in a democratic government, which means the equality of the individual from his cradle to his grave in all matters of common right, the latter proposition is more just, and more in accord with the principles of human equality. Indeed, I think it is worthy of most serious consideration, whether a partial enforcement of this rule is not demanded in a government of the people;—a government based on person and not on property, whose theory is not of class by accident of birth, but of original equality in the individual, and no other aristocracy than that of personal toil and accumulation.

With regard to the second attack, that through the exercise of the power of eminent domain, the established law is, that where the exigencies of the government demand the appropriation of private property to public use, full compensation in money must be paid. This is generally enforced by constitutional provisions; but. even if there be no such provision, I endorse the thoughtful words of the great commentator of American law, when he says: "A provision for compensation is a necessary attendant on the due and .constitutional exercise of the power of the lawgiver to deprive an individual of his property without his consent; and this principle in American constitutional jurisprudence is founded in natural equity, and is laid down by jurists as an acknowledged principle of universal law."

But the matter to which I wish to call your special attention, and which is the main subject of my talk, is the spoliation and destruction of private property through the agency of that undefined and perhaps indefinable power, the police power of the State. I say undefined and perhaps indefinable, for no man has yet succeeded in giving a definition which, in anticipating future contingencies, has prescribed exact limits to its extent. It is that power by which the State provides for the public health, and the public morals, and promotes the general welfare. It is the refuge of timid judges to escape the obligations of denouncing a wrong, in a case in which some supposed general and public good is the object of legislation. The absence of prescribed limits to this power, gives ample field for refuge to any one who dares not assert his convictions of right and wrong. For who, against legislative will, cares to declare what does or does not contribute to public health or public morals, or tend to promote the general welfare? *Omne ignotum pro magnifico.* I am here to say to you, in no spirit of obnoxious or unpleasant criticism upon the decision of any tribunal or judge, that the demands of absolute and eternal justice forbid that any private property, legally acquired and legally held, should be spoliated or destroyed in the interests of public health, morals, or welfare, without compensation.

But it is said, and said by high authority, that when, by legislative act, a particular use of property is forbidden, its subsequent use is unlawful, and a party thereafter attempting such use, may rightfully be deprived of the value of property as a punishment for his crime. This ringing changes on the words immoral, unlawful, crime, and punishment is the mere beating of Chinese gongs to conceal the real question. No one doubts, that if, after the legislature had prohibited a particular use of property, any individual devotes his property to that use, he is guilty of a criminal act and invites and deserves punishment, even to the destruction of the value of that use which he has attempted to create in defiance of the law. But it is a very different proposition,—that, when a party has created the use in obedience to and with the sanction of the law, a legislature has a right to prohibit such use in the future, and by making it unlawful, destroy without compensation the value which was created under the sanction of the law. In criminal matters, *ex post facto* legislation is always denounced. If one does an act which to-day is within the sanction of the law, no legislature can, to-morrow, by a statute prohibiting such acts, reach backward and make that unlawful which was lawful when done, or punish him as a criminal for that which when done he had a right to do. Neither can it, in civil matters, disturb vested rights. If there be no law against usury, and a person loans money upon a contract to pay ten per cent. interest, no subsequent legislation making five per cent. the extreme lawful rate, and forfeiting all principal and interest in case more is taken can destroy that contract, or release the borrower from his obligation to pay the lender principal and ten per cent. interest. No more can the value of a use created under sanction of the law be taken away from its owner, by a mere arbituary declaration of the legislature that such use must stop. Legislation looks to the future and directs its conduct. It does not look backward, or turn a lawful act into a criminal one ; nor may it, under the guise of the police power, rob an individual of any lawfully acquired property or value.

So, out from these considerations I work this thought . That while the government must be the judge of its own needs, and in the exercise of that judgment may take from every individual his service and his property, and, in the interests of public health, morals, and welfare, may regulate or destroy the individual's use of his property, or the property itself, yet there remains to the individual a sacred and indestructible right of compensation. If, for the public interests and at the public demands, he sacrifices his time, his labor or his property, or any value therein, he has a right to demand and must receive at the hands of the public compensation therefor. The full, absolute, and unqualified recognition and enforcement of this right are essential to the permanence of all governments, especially of those by, of, and for the people. In the picture drawn by the prophet of millenial days, it is affirmed that " They shall sit every man under *his* vine and under *his* fig tree, and none shall make them afraid ; for the mouth of the Lord of hosts hath spoken it." If we would continue this government into millenial times, it must be built upon this foundation. To accomplish this, we must re-cast some of our judicial decisions ; and if that be not possible, we must re-write into our Constitution the affirmations of the Declaration of Independence, in language so clear and peremptory that no judge can doubt or hesitate, and no man, not even a legislator, misunderstand. I emphasize the words clear and peremptory, for many of those who wrought into the Constitution the Fourteenth Amendment believed that they were placing therein a national guarantee against future State invasion of private rights, but judicial decisions have shorn it of strength, and left it nothing but a figure of speech.

Young gentlemen, you stand at the open door of a great profession,—at the morning hour of an era of great social changes. The motto of that profession is "justice." Justice not alone to the public, but equally to the individual. Not alone to the strong and wealthy, but also to the feeble and poor. Not alone to the popular, but to the unpopular side. The men whose names shine illustrious on the rolls of that profession,—Hale, Mansfield, Erskine, Marshall, Chase, and Lincoln, voice their great appeal to you not alone by the magnificence of their ability and the wealth of their learning, but as much by their devotion in times of trial, and in the midst of threatening and popular feeling, to the demands of absolute and unfailing justice. From the halls of Westminster, Lord Mansfield looked out on the swelling mass of an angry mob, and, gazing beyond the present to the heights of the future, boldly declared,—" I wish popularity ; but it is that popularity which follows, not that which is run after. It is that popularity, which sooner or later never fails to do justice to the pursuit of noble ends by noble means." In this coming era, great social changes will take place. A more equal distribution of the wealth of the world, and the elimination of the pauper from our midst will be secured. Many and various will be the means suggested for accomplishing these desired and glorious changes. To the lawyer will come the sifting and final judgment on the righteousness and justice of these various schemes. Into that profession, and into this era, I welcome you,—and welcoming, I bid you remember that not he who bends the docile ear to every temporary shout of the people ; but he only who measures every step,—even in defiance of angry passions, by the unchanging scale of immutable justice, will win the crown of immortality, and wear the unfailing laurels. In all your lives, and in all your acts, bear with you the motto of our profession : *Fiat Justitia.*

ANNUAL ADDRESS

BY

# HENRY B. BROWN,

WASHINGTON, D. C.,

ASSOCIATE JUSTICE OF THE SUPREME COURT OF THE UNITED STATES.

## THE DISTRIBUTION OF PROPERTY.

The history of civilized society is largely a story of strife between those who have and those who have not—between those who are ambitious to acquire more and those who are compelled by adverse circumstances to put up with less than they consider their proper share. In the most primitive stage of society it is the master who owns absolutely the labor of the slave; or the noble who commands the allegiance of the serf, and ties him to the estate upon which he was born. As civilization advances, it is the patrician who lords it over the plebeian and oppresses him by unjust laws; and in later and modern times, it is the man who furnishes the capital and the employee who makes it available, both having, nominally at least, an equal voice in the enactment of laws for their mutual benefit and protection. In all these relations, however, there is a tension, which, so far from diminishing as the position of the laboring man becomes more comfortable, apparently increases from generation to generation.

The right of private property, which marks the first step in the emergence of the civilized man from the condition of the utter savage, has been the cause of so much of envy, hatred, malice and all uncharitableness that the whole system is denounced by a certain school of theorists as not only an error, but a fraud; in short, that property is robbery; that the State is or ought to be the sole proprietor, and the individual only the recipient of its bounty.

(213)

By another school it is insisted that, as nearly everything we consume or enjoy is the product of labor, the laborer is entitled to the product. The logical consequence is that the capitalist has few, if any, rights which the laborer is bound to respect. Exactly what his rights are upon this theory no one has as yet had the hardihood to proclaim.

These conflicts between capital and labor are not of recent date. Indeed, they have occurred from a time whence the oldest historical records run not to the contrary. One of the earliest recorded annals of the race is that of the exodus of the Israelites from Egypt, which seems to have been a national protest against the oppression of capital, and to have possessed the substantial characteristics of a modern strike. How far this revolt was due to the order of Pharaoh that the Israelites should provide their own straw to make bricks, and how far to the hereditary aversion of the Jewish race to manual labor, we shall never know, at least until we hear the Egyptian side of the story. It is true they despoiled the Egyptians— a feature not wholly unknown in modern strikes; but there is no evidence that the Israelites ever claimed a proprietorship in the cities they had built for them, or used any violence to prevent others working for them at the same rate of wages. The boycott had not then been invented. The Egyptians are said to have been reluctant to let the strikers go and to have pursued them across the Red Sea; but the pursuit was fruitless, though attended by somewhat unpleasant consequences to the pursuers.

A later manifestation of the same spirit was shown by the Roman commons who, in the early days of the republic, driven to despair by the oppression of the patrician class, withdrew in a body to the Sacred Hill, whence they dictated their own terms, and obtained the appointment of Tribunes of the people for their protection from the cruelty of the burghers. The latter, who were as reluctant to part with the commons as the Egyptians had been with the Israelites, were quickly brought to concede everything they demanded. The Romans were pre-eminently an industrious people. Trade unions or guilds existed from the time of the kings, and often came into collision with the patricians, who found the plebeians indispensable, but at the same time despised them.

The history of the Middle Ages is replete with accounts of conflicts with feudal lords, who descended from their castles, waylaid the traveller, plundered him of his property, seized his person, and, unless ransomed, sold him as a slave. The merchant dared not risk his person and property in foreign parts. If shipwrecked, it was the universal practice to confiscate his goods as the property of the lord on whose land they were thrown. Indeed, for some hundreds of years the seas were so infested by pirates, commerce was subjected to such exactions, and the crews of shipwrecked vessels were treated with such inhumanity that intercourse between nations practically ceased, commerce was abandoned and the laws regulating it were forgotten and lost. In great industrial centres like the Netherlands the manufacturing guilds were in a state of almost constant warfare with the nobles, who lost no opportunity of robbing them of their earnings. In 1329 a strike of brass workers is said to have taken place in Breslau, Silesia, which continued for a year. In 1385, fifty-six years later, a strike of blacksmiths was started in Dantzic, which ended only when the local authorities issued an edict to the effect that any workman refusing to obey the lawful orders of his employer as to continuing work should be summarily deprived of his ears. England had scarcely begun to be a great manufacturing nation when the battle between capital and labor was opened, and strikes became of frequent occurrence. Parliament at first took the side of the capitalists, and it said by a writer in the *Quarterly Review* that as many as thirty statutes were enacted against trades unions or combinations. " These acts continued in existence as late as the year 1824, when they were all repealed. Legislation was abandoned, because its total failure had been conclusively proved. It was found that combinations were not prevented by repression, but, on the contrary, they multiplied in all directions, though in secrecy, and were an increasing source of crime and outrage of the most detestable character. Vitriol-throwing, arson and assassination were practiced upon such masters and workmen as made themselves obnoxious to the trades unions; the operations of trade and capital were seriously interfered with, and it was felt that not only was it impossible to stop combination, but, by confounding right and wrong, and treating unionists as felons, men were led to regard things really vicious with less aversion than formerly." After the repeal of these statutes, and particularly during the reign of the present sovereign, parliamentary legislation has gravitated toward the laboring man, and combinations of laborers, which were formerly indictable as conspiracies, are now recognized by law. The workmen are left free to enter into legal combinations for the purpose of fixing the rate of wages or regulating the hours of labor, determining the quantity of work to be done, and inducing others to quit and return to their work, provided no violence be used. In England, in 1833, the workingmen demanded that their employers should abandon the practice of erecting buildings on the system of sub-contracts. The masters complied, but the cession only led to other demands from the workingmen, who proceeded to issue a series of regulations to abide by certain rules respecting the equalization of wages, the machinery they were to employ, the number of apprentices they were to take. The masters again complied, but the workingmen proceeded to even more dictatorial measures, such as levying fines upon their employers when they had violated any of their regulations, ordering their masters to appear before them at their meetings, and commanding them to dismiss and take back such and such men and to obey such and such rules. Non-compliance with these tyrannical decrees was in several instances followed by an immediate strike of all the hands in the shop. The employers at length formed themselves into an association for mutual defense, and determined to employ no workman unless he signed a declaration that he did not belong to a trade union. A general strike was the consequence, which lasted six months, and of course resulted in the defeat of the workingmen.

Nor was this country behind the others in that particular. No sooner were manufactures introduced upon a considerable scale than employers and their workmen began to come into collision. Mr. McMasters, in his fascinating " History of the People of the United States," says that as early as 1795 the journeyman tailors of Baltimore struck for higher wages, and in 1805 a series of strikes was inaugurated and some of the strikers were brought to trial charged with conspiracy to raise their wages. The strikers in this instance were shoemakers, and were convicted, and soon afterwards opened a warehouse of their own, and appealed to the public to save them and their families from abject poverty. From this time strikes became common, and it is curious to notice that the methods which have become so familiar to this generation were resorted to then to enforce compliance with their demands. Says Mr. McMasters, speaking of the journeyman tailors, "Not only had they refused to work for the old wages, but they forced men who were willing to work to stop, and had threatened to tar and feather any lawyer who prosecuted them." Speaking also of a strike of shoemakers in 1789, he says, "Every journeyman coming to the city must join the society, or a strike against the shop where he was employed would follow. When he did join the shop he ceased, so far as his trade was concerned, to be a freeman : he could not agree with his employer as to the wages for which he would work ; he could not remain in the shop if the master cordwainer employed an apprentice who was not a member of the society, or employed more than two apprentices who were members of the society. If a member broke any of the rules a demand was made on his employer for his discharge, and if not complied with, a strike was ordered against the shop." All this has a familiar sound to the present generation.

From this brief historical sketch it is apparent, first, that strikes, so far from being peculiar to modern industrial enterprise, as seems to be generally supposed, are as old as civilization itself; second, that they prevail most extensively in the most enlightened and wealthy communities, and so far from being an indication of extreme poverty, are equally as frequent in times of general prosperity ; third, that the wit of man has as yet devised no scheme whereby they may be prevented or even alleviated.

Underlying all these conflicts between the different classes of society, whatever shape they take, is the desire of one class to better itself at the expense of the other ; the desire of the rich to obtain the labor of the poor at the lowest possible terms ; the desire of the poor to obtain the uttermost farthing from the rich. The cause and the result of it all is the unequal distribution of property. There is, however, nothing unnatural or undesirable in this. While in the Magna Charta of July 4th, 1776, we solemnly declared that all men are created equal, we are forced to recognize the fact that this is true only of men in their political capacity ; that as no two persons out of the millions of the human race look exactly alike, no two have exactly the same endowments. One is strong, another weak ; one is wise, another foolish ; one is cautious, another reckless ; one is industrious, another lazy ; one is prudent, another improvident ; one generous, another parsimonious ; and so on through the whole catalogue of personal qualities. Education may do something to equalize men, and to soften the asperities of character, but inherent defects can never be wholly remedied, nor inherent virtues wholly suppressed. In the words of the maxim which so well expresses the popular idea, "Blood will tell." From these differences in our intellectual and physical constitutions the inevitable result is that, in the pursuit of wealth, some are vastly more successful than others, and acquire an amount of riches which makes them an object of envy to those who have been less fortunate.

While enthusiasts may picture to us an ideal state of society where neither riches nor poverty shall exist, wherein all shall be comfortably housed and clad, and what are called the useless luxuries of life are unknown, such a Utopia is utterly inconsistent with human character as at present constituted ; and it is at least doubtful whether upon the whole it would conduce as much to the general happiness and contentment of the community as the inequality which excites the emulation and stimulates the energies, even if it also awakens the envy, of the less prosperous. Rich men are essential even to the well-being of the poor. It is they who build our railroads, open our mines, erect our costly buildings, found our great corporations, and in a thousand ways develop the resources of our country and afford employment to a countless army of workingmen. One has but to consider for a moment the immediate consequences of the abolition of large private fortunes to appreciate the danger which lurks in any radical disturbance of the present social system. Think of the tens of thousands who are engaged in the manufacture of luxuries, in the erection of expensive houses, in the manufacture of carriages, jewelry, plate glass, china and porcelain, silks—from the man who breeds the worms to the man who sells the finished silk over the counter—tapestries and rugs, high class furniture and bric-a-brac, in domestic service and in the creation of works of art, and we can understand the distress that would be produced by the sudden cessation of these industries. When we reflect even upon the number engaged in the manufacture of wines, cigars, tobacco and alcohol in its various forms, we are ready to exclaim with Napoleon: "If our virtues could only be made to pay as well as our vices the maintenance of large armies would be an easy matter."

We are told, however, by a certain school of political philosophers, which, for the want of a better name, we will call the Henry George school, that in the progress of modern social life the gulf between the rich and the poor is constantly growing wider—in other words, that the rich are growing richer, while the poor are becoming poorer. If this were true, it would doubtless afford just cause for alarm; but while it sounds well as an aphorism, unfortunately, or rather fortunately, it is wholly untrue. While, in this country at least, private fortunes are larger than they have ever been before, the condition of the laboring class has improved in an equal ratio. To say nothing of the emancipation of some four millions of slaves—of itself an immense gain to the laboring class involved—there was never a time when the working classes were so well paid, or when their wages could buy for them so many of the comforts of life as now.  Even so firm a friend of the working man as Walter Besant, in his " Fifty Years Ago," frankly admits that, comparing his condition with what it was the year Queen Victoria was crowned, there has been a vast improvement.  Not only are his wages higher, but his hours of labor are shorter.  He is better housed, better clad, better fed, better taught, reads better and cheaper papers, sends his children to better schools, and enjoys more opportunities for recreation and for seeing the world than ever before.  He not only practically dictates his own hours of labor, but in large manufacturing centers he is provided with model lodging houses for his family, with libraries, parks, clubs, and lectures for his entertainment and instruction, with cheap excursion trains for his amusement on Sundays and holidays ; and not only absolutely but relatively to the rich is vastly better off than he was fifty years ago. Indeed, it is not too much to say that the American working man who does not own his own home must charge it to his own idleness and improvidence, or to other circumstances usually within his own control.

It is true, as already stated, that large fortunes are larger and more numerous than ever before ; but the cause of this is not far to seek.  That process of centralization which has been steadily going on since the introduction of railways and telegraphs, and which has been such an important factor in the political world, consolidating small states into great ones, combining the petty principalities of Germany into a powerful empire, unifying the discordant states of Italy into a single kingdom, and cementing together the United States of America into a compact federation, has also exercised a most powerful influence upon social life.  Indeed, it was impossible that a system of communication which reduced the days of the lumbering stage coach to the hours of the palace car, and which enables the New York merchant to correspond with his agent in Constantinople in less time than it took him a hundred years ago to reach a customer in Philadelphia, should not affect the business relations of the entire world. This effect may be epitomized in the single word *combination.* Not only have laws against workingmen been repealed, but capitalists, taking their cue from the workingman, have themselves combined in defiance of the laws to control and regulate production. It is not the laboring men, however, who have suffered from this, but the small manufacturers and dealers who are ground between the upper millstone of the great corporation and the nether millstone of the exacting laborer. This result, I think, is to be regretted, since it is better for the country that there should be a hundred small producers of a single article than one great one. In other words, that the profits accruing from the manufacture of a given product should be distributed among a hundred different people rather than be monopolized by one. There is this to be said, however, as a strong mitigating circumstance in favor of large manufacturing corporations, that their stock, and incidentally thereto their profits, are usually widely distributed among stockholders, so that each stockholder is in effect a small producer, receiving the profits upon his production through the agency of the corporation. The evil effects of these corporations are seen rather in their ability to crush out competition, and thereby control the price of the thing produced.

It is evident that combinations between the producers of certain articles which were out of the question fifty years ago, by reason of the difficulty and tediousness of communication and the different prices obtained throughout different parts of the country, have become perfectly practicable since the introduction of railroads and telegraphs. Producers are thereby enabled to keep up constant and instant correspondence with each other, to feel the pulse of the market, to pool their products and to increase or diminish their output as the exigencies of the trade require.

In this connection, however, it will not escape our notice that certain of the causes which have been effective in the amassing of large fortunes are already ceasing to operate, and as the country becomes more perfectly developed and more thickly inhabited, will cease to be important factors. In the settlement of new countries mines are discovered, which, skillfully and unscrupulously handled, are veritable mines of wealth to their promoters. New inventions are made which return fabulous incomes to the patentees ; new manufactures are to be started; railways to be built; commerce by sea to be promoted, and enterprises to be inaugurated in a hundred different directions which return large profits to those who, to use a slang phrase, "are in the ring." The time is coming, however, when the country will have all the railways required ; when the production of manufactures will exceed the demand, and the wages received so near the price of the article produced as to leave little or no profit to the manufacturer. This tendency has been already seen in the older countries, where the competition of American and other foreign food products has made serious havoc with the farmers and land-owners, and will ultimately result in the breaking up of the great estates which have represented the largest fortunes of European countries.

Let us assume, however, that we may be mistaken in this ; that the process of centralization which has been going on so steadily for the past fifty years may continue. Let us consider the possibility that the man who forty years ago was president of a small railroad of a hundred miles and is to-day the absolute master of a system ten thousand miles in length, stretching half across the continent, may in another fifty years control the entire traffic of half of the United States. Let us admit the possibility that a corporation which to-day controls the entire output of one of the prime necessaries of life may in fifty years from now be but one of a hundred other corporations, each controlling the entire product of a certain other article. Let us consider that there is nothing to prevent the man who, fifty years ago, was worth twenty millions of dollars, and was thought incredibly rich, and who, to-day, is the possessor of three hundred millions, being able in fifty years from now to wield the mighty influence which the possession of three thousand millions would put into his hands. If legislatures and other municipal bodies are not now always proof against the corrupting influence of large fortunes, what would they be if these fortunes were multiplied ten-fold? What would become of our legislatures, our courts, and even the boasted immunities of our Constitution? Laws, be they never so clear, may be evaded, ignored or defied. Even the Constitution itself may be obeyed in the letter and disobeyed in the spirit. Indeed, unless rumor does great injustice, one of its most important provisions guaranteeing to each state a republican form of government does not prevent in one of our largest states something very nearly approaching an autocracy. The tendency of large fortunes is to become larger, and in able and unscrupulous hands there is nothing but the life of the holder that stands between him and an indefinite increase. Fortunately for society, the ability and the disposition to accumulate do not ordinarily pass to the heirs, and the wealth gathered together by the frugality of the father is usually dissipated by the improvidence of the son or grandson.

These gross inequalities in the distribution of property have become a favorite topic of discussion with modern sociologists; and schemes without number are suggested to remedy the evils, real or fancied, which arise from them. None of these devices, however, have sufficiently commended themselves to the good sense of the community to be embodied in legislation; and it is extremely doubtful whether legislation can do anything more than cut off some of the vicious growths which the good nature and apathy of the public have permitted to incumber the legitimate avenues of trade. It is clear that the fundamental law of supply and demand cannot be set aside. It is impossible to deny to the laboring man the right to determine the number of hours he shall work, and the wages he is willing to accept. But no possible legislation can compel the employer to pay more than he is willing to pay, or to carry on his business at a loss. The success of every strike would only result in the transfer of manufactures to other localities where the work would be carried on under more favorable circumstances. This is what has actually happened in more than one instance. The writer in the *Quarterly Review*, to whom reference has already been made, says, speaking of trade unions fifty years ago, that in Ireland, where the laboring men with true Celtic vehemence threw themselves heart and soul into the unions, strikes were so numerous that industries were ruined, flannels, silks and laces almost ceased to be manufactured, and the Irish workman who was willing to work was obliged to emigrate to England and Scotland to find employment. Dublin, formerly the seat of extensive and prosperous manufactures and trades, was driven from the market. The shipwrights and sawyers carried every point with their masters, and in the course of a few years there was not a single master shipwright in Dublin. If vessels frequenting the port required repairs, they were merely cobbled up to insure their safety across the channel to Glasgow or Liverpool. Another manufacturer, anxious to execute some metal work in Dublin in order that Irish industries might have the benefit, found to his dismay that he could not compete with England—not by reason of any local disadvantage, but solely on account of the regulations enforced by his own workmen. In an investigation made by a committee in 1830, it was shown that the combination of weavers was such as to result in the total extinguishment of the blanket trade at Kilkarney. Daniel O'Connell himself admitted that the trade unions had wrought more ruin to Ireland than even absenteeism and Saxon maladministration.

The truth is, that five dollars out of every six we spend is spent in labor of some form. Take, for instance, a house, which is built chiefly of brick, stone, iron, glass and wood. Brick, in the form of clay as it lies in its bed, is absolutely worthless, while iron ore, stone in the quarry, sand and standing timber are of merely nominal value, as compared with the labor put upon them in the condition in which they are used for the purpose of construction. The price of labor thus becomes the price of everything which labor produces. If the manufactured product becomes too dear, people will simply cease to buy, and no possible legislation can compel them to buy if they do not choose to do so. Legislation is as powerless to permanently affect the law of supply and demand as it is to affect the law of gravitation. As a good many men in different spheres of activity are just now finding out, there are no laurels to be won in waging war upon the laws of nature. The State may itself become an employer of labor by the erection of great public works, and within reasonable limits this is doubtless proper. But, after all, it is but a temporary expedient. It is the people themselves who have to pay for it. What is put into one pocket is taken from the other. Peter is robbed to pay Paul.

Let us consider for a moment a few of the schemes proposed for securing a more equal distribution of property. The most radical and at the same time the most futile of these schemes is what is known as *Socialism*, by which we understand the total abolition of private property and the ownership of all property by the State—the individual retaining only the right to the enjoyment of his proportionate share. The entire community thus becomes in effect a great partnership, in which each partner is expected to contribute his proportion of labor, and to receive an equal share in its product. As a practical question, in this country at least, socialism may be disposed of in a few words. As it involves a practical confiscation of private property, it could only be established legally by an amendment to the Constitution of the State, which would require the assent of a majority of the voting population. It would probably also require an amendment to the Constitution of the United States, which could only be adopted by the consent of three-fourths of the States. Either of these contingencies is so remote that it may be safely relegated to the

15

region of impossibilities. It is equally improbable that socialism can ever be imposed by force, since the owners of property or their dependents are not only in the majority numerically, but, by reason of such ownership, wield a moral and physical influence out of all proportion to their numbers. Socialism, therefore, while furnishing an interesting field for discussion, is not likely for another century at least to present itself as a scheme for practical consideration.

But, even if it were possible to establish socialism as the basis of society, its results could not fail to be disastrous. In short, no greater calamity could overtake civilization. Conceding all the evils which are claimed to flow from the present unequal distribution of property : the enormous fortunes of some and the abject poverty of others, the constant friction and sometimes open war between capital and labor, the frequency of strikes, the oppressive monopolies of great corporations, the arrogance of the rich and the envy of the poor, the fact still remains that no people who did not respect the right of private property have ever emerged from barbarism, that the disposition to acquire and the ability to own are the prime distinctions between the civilized man and the savage ; that the desire to better one's condition—in other words, to make money—is the great incentive to labor, in fact, lies at the basis of all social progress. Grant that it breeds a spirit of emulation, a desire to live in a better house than our neighbors, to eat better food, to wear finer clothes and to drive a handsomer equipage—this is not in itself objectionable. It only becomes so when it leads to the oppressive use of the power which great wealth wields. It stimulates a man to labor beyond what he actually needs and prevents one who has acquired a competence from relapsing into idleness.

The radical difficulty with socialism is that it takes away the incentive to labor for anything beyond the actual necessities of life. The man who will work every hour in the day wherein labor is possible and lie awake nights inventing schemes whereby his labor will be made more profitable, and a fortune accumulated for his family, would quickly sink to the general level, if he once became conscious that his utmost exertions would realize him nothing beyond his infinitesimal share as a member of the State. While men with whom the habit of work has become strong do sometimes continue to labor for reputation alone, it is the desire to earn money which lies at the bottom of the greatest efforts of genius. The man who writes books, paints pictures, moulds statues, builds houses, pleads causes, preaches sermons, or heals the sick, does it for the money there is in it; and if, in so doing, he acquires a reputation as an author, painter, sculptor, architect, jurist, or physician, it is only an incident to his success as a money-getter. The motive which prompted Angelo to plan the dome of St. Peter, or paint the frescoes of the Sistine Chapel was essentially the same as that which induces a common laborer to lay brick or dig sewers. The love of power or a great name comes only after a pecuniary competence has been secured, and our every-day experience teaches us that the spark of genius is rarely kindled in the breasts of those who are born rich.

This, however, is but one of the innumerable obstacles to the practical success of the socialistic idea. Imagine the confusion that would ensue from an attempt to assign to each individual his proper sphere of labor, the number of administrative officers it would require to keep the machinery of the State in motion, the anxiety of everyone to obtain one of these offices, or, if that were impossible, to obtain employment congenial to the tastes of each individual,—an easy berth, the universal desire to avoid the coarser forms of labor,—to say nothing of the efforts of the idle, the vicious and the criminal to live upon the State while contributing nothing to its support. Of course, all those who are now engaged in the production and sale of luxuries would be at once thrown out of employment, since the underlying idea of all socialism is to insure to everyone the comforts of life, and until this was accomplished there could be no demand for luxuries. But this is not the worst. There is in every civilized community much coarse and repulsive, though indispensable, work to be done. There are sewers and ditches to be dug, canals to be excavated, stables and vaults to be cleaned, railways to be built, and a dozen other forms of labor, which no one would undertake except under the pressure of a dire necessity.

In view of these difficulties, which seem to us insuperable, society at least has a right to demand of the socialists a practical test of the feasibility of their doctrines ; and the very fact that no disposition seems to be evinced to put them to such test is calculated to engender an uncomfortable suspicion that socialism may be after all only a disguised attempt—an attempt as old as civilization itself—to plunder the rich for the benefit of the poor. Why do not the socialists themselves put in practice what they preach ? I know of nothing to prevent any number of individuals from agreeing to hold their possessions in common, to make equal contributions of their labor, and to receive a proportionate share of the proceeds. If authority be now wanting it could easily be procured for the formation of a large corporation for the purchase of lands, the erection of houses, the cultivation of farms and the establishment of various industries upon communistic principles. If capital were needed it could doubtless be raised by the contributions of those who see the evils of society as at present organized, and would be glad to know whether the Social Democratic State is likely to prove the panacea for such evils. If the believers in socialism are unwilling to make this experiment, how can they expect to make converts of the unbelievers ? The burden is certainly upon them to prove that a social system which has existed from the dawn of civilization and under which nations as well as individuals have grown rich and prosperous, and within the last century especially have grown almost incredibly richer and more prosperous, is a failure; and if socialism is likely to remedy the evils which confessedly do exist, and to increase the general happiness, well-being and contentment of the community, the sooner we know it the better: but nothing short of a practical demonstration of its success upon a large scale will satisfy us. This is the country for novel social experiments, and no time can be more favorable than the present.

Some such experiments have been made upon a small scale at various times during the past century, but the results have not been encouraging. In some cases the communities have fallen a prey to internal dissensions and been dissolved. In others, a few unambitious congenial spirits, animated by strong religious convictions, have maintained the communistic principle for a long time, but the organization has shown little vitality, no power of expansion, no increase of numbers, and no promise for the future. The oldest and best-known of these communities is that of the Shakers, several families of which are found in different parts of the country. They are a highly respectable but simple-minded sect of religious enthusiasts who have been engaged for more than a century in the cultivation of farms and in a few simple manufactures. As they live in a state of celibacy, no provision is made for the propagation of the race, and none for replenishing their own numbers except by adoption in infancy from the outer world. It is a well-known fact that the ambitious and enterprising of both sexes pair off in early youth and run away, and that the residuum is content with a plainness of living and severity of dress that would be intolerable in a community of high intelligence and aspirations. While many of the families have become wealthy, several have been suffered to die out, and it is not unlikely that another century will witness the entire extinction of the order. To speak of them as a success, even under their very exceptional circumstances, is at least doubtful: to regard them as indicating the probable success of socialism upon a large scale is absurd. The same remark may be made of the Oneida Community, which was founded upon the idea of a community of wives as well as property, and of other similar organizations more or less prosperous throughout the country. All of them are of select material: none of them take account of the very classes whose presence in any community is dangerous, and whose presence in a socialistic state would be sure to work disaster and ruin.

Upon the whole, socialism, so far from serving as a remedy for the evils which afflict society, would only aggravate them tenfold; so far from being an advance, it would be a distinctly retrograde movement, a return to the barbarous ideas of our remote ancestors.

There is another coarser form of social regeneration known as *anarchism*, of which little need be said. Anarchism openly avows its intent to destroy all existing social institutions by force, while offering nothing to take their place. Its aim is not to reconstruct society, but simply to destroy it. Threats are its sole argument, dynamite its principal weapon. Its motive is hatred of the higher classes, not love of the lower. So far, no writer of distinction has been found bold enough to advocate its claims; indeed, it does not condescend to argue; it simply strikes. Happily, its disciples are few, and, to the credit of the American character let it be said, almost exclusively aliens. Society has nothing to fear from them except so far as it fears the dangerous animal or the venemous reptile. They are fit subjects for the application of the scriptural maxim that those who take the sword shall perish by the sword. Those who fight with fire must expect to be fought with fire. Society is neither meek nor long-suffering and will rigorously exact an eye for an eye and a tooth for a tooth. Those who openly defy and trample upon the Constitution and laws have no moral right to their immunities and no just cause to complain if society makes war upon them as mercilessly as they war upon society. But too much has been said already of this unrecognizable element of this community.

Another most plausible but thus far most elusive plan for a more equal distribution of property consists in *co-operation*. If an intelligent combination of laboring men, under which they were to manufacture and sell solely for their own profit, were possible, it would be hailed by the entire non-capitalistic portion of the community as a happy solution of the problem.

Man has a natural right to the fruits of his own toil, and his obligation to share them with another usually arises either from his own fault or from circumstances to a certain extent within his control. Two causes have hitherto operated to defeat the success of co-operation in manufacture. (1.) The difficulty of securing a faithful and competent manager. (2.) The necessities and the improvidence of the laboring men themselves. The success of every large manufacturing establishment depends in great measure upon the ability of its leading spirit. Men capable of managing such establishments are rare, and command salaries larger than workingmen are able or willing to pay, and the consequence usually is that they embark in business on their own account and become capitalists themselves, or are seduced from their allegiance by offers of a larger salary.

But the principal cause for the failure of co-operation arises from the necessities or improvidence of the laboring man himself. If every season were equally prosperous, if the workingman were always sure of a return equal to his wages, one of the chief difficulties would be removed; but in all branches of production there are unprofitable seasons—years in which the owner is compelled to do business at a loss and to fall back upon his reserved capital to save his plant. If he has such reserve, he may tide his business over to better times; if not, he goes to the wall. But the faculty of accumulation is, after all, comparatively a rare one. Four out of five, perhaps nine out of ten, of the laboring class do not possess it, but are forced or tempted to spend as they go. Taking no thought of the morrow, they look for every season to be as prosperous as the present, and make no provision for panics or depressions. Such men must have fixed wages or starve. As a compensation for their failure to receive their proportion of possibly large profits, they are guaranteed a weekly stipend payable so long as the business is carried on.

A few philanthopic men have introduced a kind of mixed system—paying their operatives fixed wages and at the same time allowing them a certain share in the profits. This method is said to have been attended with satisfactory results and is certainly deserving of imitation.

This, however, like all other schemes of co-operation, must depend entirely upon the voluntary action of the parties. Legislation is powerless to affect it. It can neither compel the employer to pay his employé a share of his profits nor compel the latter to deny himself the benefit of a fixed stipend. In truth, as the law now stands, any laborer in the employ of our great corporations may become a sharer in their profits by purchasing stock, and the wonder is that more do not avail themselves of the privilege. Indeed, half the stock of our manufacturing companies might and ought to be owned by the operatives, who would thus become co-operatives in the best sense of the word. And yet how trifling is the sum that is so owned! This fact itself is a strong indication that the failure of co-operation is rather the fault of the laborer than the capitalist.

Upon the whole, it may be said that while co-operation may, at some time in the future, furnish a satisfactory solution of the labor problem, it requires for its success such a radical change in the character and habits of the laboring classes that it promises but little for their present amelioration. Many, per-haps a majority, of our most successful capitalists were originally laborers. The qualities which raised them from the rank of laborer to that of capitalist were thrift, industry, energy and sagacity—virtues which the majority of men unhappily do not possess. Legislation can neither supply them nor offer any-thing to take their place. Any radical improvement of the working classes must be wrought by the practice of the same old-fashioned virtues which from year to year and from decade to decade are constantly raising men of the higher and wealthier class from the general level.

Considerable has been said of late of the feasibility of *compulsory arbitration* as a means of insuring to the laboring man a fuller appreciation of his rights. Compulsory arbitra-tion is a misnomer—a contradiction in terms. One might as well speak of an amicable murder or a friendly war. The very idea of arbitration implies a voluntary submission of matters to persons mutually agreed upon to decide them. If force be used either to compel submission or to fix upon the arbitrators, it ceases to be arbitration and takes on the ordinary incidents of a suit. To make such proceedings compulsory, therefore, there must be a judge or judges designated by law, process to compel the attendance of defendant and power to enforce the performance of the decree; in other words, such proceedings would be an exercise of the judicial power, and the decree of such tribunal must be conformable to law. Now, the chief value of arbitration is that the arbitrators are not bound by the ordinary rules of law, but may make any award which they may deem just or reasonable, provided it be not absurd or impossible. It is just at this point that compulsory arbitration would fail. If, for instance, workmen had agreed to labor for their employer a certain time for a certain rate of wages, no tribunal constituted by law could disregard or impair the obligations of this contract, though arbitrators voluntarily chosen might say that the circumstances had so changed as to make its full performance inequitable. It is incredible, too, that any court could be found to compel a manufacturer to carry on his business at a loss, to take from him its control and put it into the hands of his operatives, or to employ certain men and refuse to employ others. It is equally incredible that it should compel the workingman to labor a greater number of hours or for a less amount of wages than he had agreed, or to make his service compulsory, since this would be to re-establish slavery under a different name. In other words, compulsory arbitration logically results either in confiscation to the employer or in slavery to the employee.

Even if it stopped short of this and permitted the employer to discontinue his business, if he could not afford to pay the wages decreed, it would not only work a serious injury to the employees who are thrown out of work, but to others who stand

75

ready to take their places. The truth is that the right to contract and to have contracts respected is one which cannot be
taken away without involving the parties in difficulties ten-fold
more serious, and throwing the whole social system into confusion. Where the question between the parties turns upon
the rate of wages or the number of hours of labor, a voluntary
arbitration frequently affords a satisfactory method of adjustment; but where it involves the control of one's business it is
something which a self-respecting employer will not be likely
to surrender even at the behest of arbitrators.

Perhaps it may be proper in this connection to say a word
upon the proposed nationalization of land or ownership of land
by the State, which a new school of political theorists would seek
to accomplish by the imposition of all taxes upon land in its
unimproved state. This is commonly known as the *Single
Tax* theory. There is certainly something to be said in its
commendation. It would have a strong tendency to encourage
the purchase of land for actual use and the erection of valuable
buildings or other improvements, since they would be exempt
from taxation. It would put a complete stop to the purchase of lands for speculative purposes, which doubtless
operates to retard the growth of our cities and towns
and to the leaving of large amounts of vacant and unimproved
property within our municipal limits. Builders are thus driven
out of town to find lots suitable to their means, where if land
were free or comparatively so, they would prefer a location
upon the nearest unimproved lot. How far it would tend to
improve the relations between capital and labor, to obviate
strikes and to open new avenues for employment and for trade
is an open question. My impression is that its advantages in
these particulars have been greatly overestimated.

Upon the other hand, there are practical difficulties in the
adoption of this method of taxation in an old settled community
which seem almost insuperable. Most of our State constitutions provide for a uniform assessment of all property for the
purposes of taxation, and there is no moral or legal right to

shift the whole burden upon a single class. While the woes of the land speculator do not move us to tears, he is certainly entitled to be protected against confiscation under the name of taxation. The first result of imposing the whole burden upon land would probably be the complete destruction of its value and the abandonment of all unoccupied land to the State. This would necessitate a large increase of taxation upon improved land—a taxation which *must* be gauged by the value of the improvements, or else it would fall with crushing force upon the poor man. Let us suppose, for instance, two vacant adjoining lots of equal value. The taxes upon each are the same. Upon one, A builds a house worth $100,000 ; upon the other B builds a modest home at a cost of $1000. The tax upon A's lot would be a bagatelle to him ; that upon B's would ruin him. Shall it be said that A shall pay no more than B ? If he does pay more, then he necessarily pays upon the improvement and not upon the land, and thus we have returned to the old system. It is safe to say that men of modest fortunes would never be content with such a gross discrimination in favor of the rich. It is difficult to see how the system could be carried out not only without the complete destruction of the value of vacant lands, but also of the value of all those in the hands of the poorer classes.

Thus far I have endeavored to show that legislation is incompetent to effect any radical change in the social status or in the relations of employés and employed, and that even if such change were possible it would be attended by evils which would inevitably throw the whole system into confusion. Does it, therefore, follow that legislation can do nothing to improve those relations, or to palliate the evils of the present situation ? I think not. It may fix the number of hours of a legal day's work, provide that payment be made at certain stated periods, protect the life and health of the workingman against accidents or diseases arising from ill-constructed machinery, badly ventilated rooms, defective appliances or dangerous occupations, and may limit or prohibit altogether the labor of women and children in employments injurious to their health or beyond their strength. It may go deeper. Bearing in mind that the most grievous cause for complaint lies in monopolies and combinations, it may by constitutional amendment, if necessary, forbid the charter of business corporations for any other purposes than those of mining, manufacturing, insurance or transportation, and especially may inhibit those for farming or trading purposes, or trafficking in any manner in the necessaries of life. With the aid of the judicial power, it may put an end to combinations having for their object the control and monopoly of particular articles of manufacture, or may accomplish the same purpose by authorizing such articles to be placed temporarily upon the free list. It may put a stop to the vicious system of building railways and other public works through construction companies organized by the directors of the road in their own interest, to whom all the bonds and all the available stock are turned over, and equipping the same through car trust certificates, also issued to the directors, who thus retain to themselves title to the rolling stock—a most cunningly devised scheme by which the stockholders and creditors are first defrauded for the benefit of the bondholders, and the bondholders are then defrauded for the benefit of the directors. By the election of competent and fearless executive officers, the people may do much to secure the management of corporations for the benefit of the stockholders and the public, and may throttle those corporate Frankensteins, which, created by the legislature, have misused their powers to corrupt the will and paralyze the arm of their creators. Upon the other hand, it is equally their duty to protect the laboring man, whether union or non-union, in his right to work for whom and at such wages as he pleases, and to secure his person against violence. In protecting the public against the tyranny of capital, it is equally incumbent upon the legislature to guard it against the tyranny of labor.

There is another field, upon which it seems to me, legislation may enter, experimentally at least, and, perhaps, with great ultimate benefit to the public, that is, in the direction of the State ownership of monopolies.  Much has been said upon this subject of late, but I am by no means satisfied that the old maxim, that the country which is governed least is governed best, may not, in these days of monopolies and combinations, be subject to revision.  I have never been able to perceive why, if the government may be safely entrusted to carry our letters and papers, it may not with equal propriety carry our telegrams and parcels, as it has done in England and other foreign countries for several years ; or why, if our municipalities may supply us with water, they may not also supply us with gas, electricity, telephones and street cars ?  They are all based upon the same principle of a public ownership of the streets and highways, and a power to grant franchises to third persons, which the municipality, if it chooses, may reserve to itself.  Whether the State should go farther and take to itself the proprietorship of railways and canals, may be left to be determined by the success of minor undertakings in the same direction.  In several foreign countries, the State ownership of railways is no longer an experiment.  For years, many of the principal railways of Germany, France, Austria, Hungary, Sweden and Norway have been owned by the State, and operated for the benefit of the public and the employés.  Some of the municipalities of Great Britain have also taken upon themselves the entire burden of rapid transit, which of late has been such a fruitful source of complaint in some of our American cities. How far the public is the gainer by these undertakings is still, to some extent, an unsettled question.  The system has, however, put almost a complete stop to those terrible conflicts between capital and labor which have resulted in little beside loss to the corporations, inconvenience to the public, and disaster to the employés.  It is scarcely possible to pay too great a price for such a boon.  I see no reason to doubt why, under governmental control, these works should not be carried on with as little friction, as little danger of strikes, and as satisfactorily to the public as the post office establishment is at present.

The main objection to the State ownership of natural monopolies arises from the fear that the patronage thereby vested in the Government would be used for partisan purposes. The objection is undoubtedly entitled to great weight, and, in the present condition of the civil service, is decisive against the adoption of the plans. Even the most unblushing advocate of the spoils system will hesitate to favor an extension of that system to new departments of government. This is a tribute which he pays most reluctantly to the views of the civil service reformer. Indeed, it requires no stretch of patriotism to look with apprehension upon the possible addition of some thousands of telegraphers and express messengers, to say nothing of some hundreds of thousands of railway employees to the disposable forces of the Administration,—to become its active agents upon election day, to hold their places at its will and to be removable at its pleasure, after each quadrennial election. How this relic of a corrupt and half-enlightened age came to be fastened upon the body politic of one of the most civilized nations of the earth at the very opening of a new era in its history, when old things were passing away and all things becoming new, and how it came to survive for more than half a century after it had been discarded by all the other great powers, will be an interesting study for the political philosopher of the twenty-first century. It is impossible to suppose that a system which is fraught with so much of evil, so demoralizing to the young men of the country, a system which tends to breed a race of place-hunters who live half their lives upon the government and the other half upon expectation; a system which discourages efficiency and offers a premium upon timidity, favoritism and sycophancy—a system which divides parties not upon lines of policy but upon the hope of spoils—in short, a system upon which no private corporation could be conducted except to disaster and ruin, will become a permanent feature of our governmental polity. The fifty years it has already obtained are but a span in the life of a nation. That which was possible with twenty millions of people will fall by its own weight when applied to the government of a hundred millions. Indeed, the system is already in its decrepitude. The past fifteen years have witnessed a popular awakening upon the subject to which Congress has, I fear somewhat reluctantly, responded. The outrage which has more than once been perpetrated within the memory of men now living, of a President making a clean sweep of his own office-holders, not because they belonged to the opposite party, but because they could not subscribe to a new policy he had dictated, would no longer be possible. Each successive administration has taken a step in advance of the prior one. The heads of the great departments are known to be almost universally in favor of a reform, but find themselves unable to resist the pressure from below. The politicians, loath to yield an atom of their prerogatives, but seeing the inevitable trend of affairs, content themselves with calling the reformers bad names,—always an encouraging sign. Whenever men in public life can be brought to a thorough appreciation of the fact that patronage is a source of weakness rather than of strength, that the interference of officers to control elections, with the independence of thought existing in this country, alienates more voters than it wins, and that even in the case of individuals, the filling of every office makes three enemies and but one friend—in short, that the supposed benefits of the spoils system are but a delusion and a snare, we may look with confidence for the establishment of the civil service upon a sensible basis, whereby the tenure of offices shall be limited and fixed by law, and honesty and efficiency shall receive their appropriate reward.

With a service such as that which the long experience of private corporations has shown to be most efficient, the government might safely embark upon undertakings now closed to it by a popular jealousy of its interference. How far it should go in this direction could only be ascertained by experiment. That it could safely take to itself many functions now performed by private corporations the experience of other countries amply justifies us in believing.

Legislation may also uo something toward securing a more equal distribution of property by limiting the power of a testator to dispose of his estate by will. The laws of all civilized nations recognise in every man a natural right to the enjoyment of his own property and to the increment thereof, nor do they limit in any way his right of accumulation. Such limitation would obviously be impracticable, even if it were desirable. His right to dispose of it after his death, however, stands upon a different footing. While recognized to some extent as a natural one, it is, after all, purely a creature of statute and subject to the legislative will. Prior to the reign of Henry the Eighth, it did not extend to real estate at all, and was limited as to personal estate wherever the testator left wife or children. "If he had both he could dispose of but one-third of his personal estate by will, the other two-thirds being regarded as the reasonable share of the wife and children respectively; while if he had a wife or child, but not both, he might dispose of one-half, the remainder belonging to either the wife or child." While these restrictions have long since been abolished in England, and never existed in this country, the right of the widow to her dower and to a share of the personal estate is ordinarily secured to her by statute, and the verdicts of juries have usually proved adequate to protect children against an unreasonable disinheritance. By the Code Napoleon, gifts of property whether by acts *inter vivos* or by will must not exceed one-half the estate, if the testator leaves but one child, one-third if he leaves two children, and one-fourth if he leaves three or more. If he have no children, but leaves ancestors both in the paternal and maternal line, he may give away but half his property, or three-fourths if he leaves ancestor in only one line. By the law of Italy, one-half a testator's property must be distributed equally among all his children; the other half he may leave to his oldest son or to whomsoever he pleases. Similar restrictions upon the power of disposal by will are found in the codes of other Continental countries as well as in the State of Louisiana. Most of them are intended to prevent the bestowal of the entire estate upon the oldest son, a precaution quite unnecessary in this country ; but the principal of securing a more equal distribution of the estate is a wise one.

One of the early steps in the settlement of this country was to abolish the law of entails and primogeniture, but the right to leave an enormous fortune by will to a single child or to one of several children is still recognized by law. With its unlimited power to dispose of decedents' estates, I know of no reason why the legislature may not limit the amount which any single individual may take by gift or devise, and thus bring about to a certain extent the breaking up of enormous fortunes upon the death of the owner. Were this amount, for instance, fixed at a million dollars, it would compel a man worth one hundred millions to create a hundred beneficiaries, many of whom would probably be charitable institutions, and that, too, without doing injustice to the natural objects of his bounty. Probably not two hundred estates in the country would be affected by such legislation, but the amount of good which could be accomplished would be almost incalculable. Indeed, it would remove the main objection to the growth of these large fortunes.

It is not intended to suggest that such legislation is either necessary or desirable in the present state of the country; but if these fortunes should multiply in the next half century as they have in the last, drastic remedies may have to be invented. But, as once before stated, there are good reasons for believing that the era of these great fortunes is nearing its culmination, and that, with the more complete development of the country, they will cease to be a threatening danger.

But, whatever of peril there may be in store for us, we may rest assured will be surmounted with the fortitude we have more than once displayed in our life as a nation. As a people we are unusually tolerant of grievances, but when they become unendurable, we have never failed to apply a sharp and decisive remedy. So long as we can be represented in legislative halls by upright and intelligent men who will stand

16

for the most enlightened sentiment of their constituency, we may safely bid defiance to all other dangers.

A recent writer in the *Forum*, who purports to know whereof he speaks, says that lobbyists invariably agree that of all classes of men most easily accessible to corrupt influences the leaders of workingmen's or farmers' political movements are the first; and that, in estimating an elected body, the numbers elected on such tickets are placed on the directly purchasable list without much inquiry. That next to these come the editors of country newspapers and newspapers in small cities. If this be true it is certainly a melancholy commentary upon our methods of representation; for, next to judicial corruption, I know of nothing more perilous than corrupt representatives and a venal press. We are sadly obliged to admit that our democratic system as applied to the government of large cities is very far from being what it ought to be, but in the administration of the National and State Governments it may be said to have fully justified the faith of its founders. The task of the coming century will be to remove the few remaining blots upon our institutions, to cleanse the admirable structure erected by our fathers of all that is debasing or unseemly, and to transmit it to posterity strengthened and adorned with all which the wisdom of ages shall have taught to be essential to a free and stable government.

# LIMITS TO STATE CONTROL OF PRIVATE BUSINESS.

IT was a new departure in government when the people of the American States planted their institutions on fundamental principles which embodied a distrust of their own representatives. Distrust of irresponsible power may indeed be accepted as one of the conditions of liberty; and from the days of King John there had been no want of it among English-speaking people. Representative institutions had grown out of it, and these had taken such root and expanded with such vigor that their branches at length overshadowed all else, and liberty was supposed to be secure in proportion as the representatives of the people were powerful. All this time, however, distrust had the crown for its object, not the legislature; and while it was not doubted that hasty or extravagant action on the part of the legislature was possible, the restraining influence of the two houses on each other, and the undefined checks which the kingly authority might in certain ways impose, were supposed to be ample to protect against serious evils. With the crown under due restraint, the people felt no alarm: it might be said that the sovereignty was still in them, and that the legislature held by delegation a trust only; but it was, nevertheless, a trust conferred in such boundless confidence, that the beneficiaries were content to retain, in respect to it, only such ultimate control as is implied in the right of revolution. The theoretical compact of government between the people on the one hand and their rulers on the other, though supposed to be conditioned on a just exercise of the powers conferred, was really one under which the only means of enforcing

16

the condition must be such as an oppressed people might find in the implements of war. But what need of any condition whatever when those to be protected were the very persons delegating the trust, and who selected the recipients from their own number, limiting the delegation to a brief period, at the end of which time they were at liberty to recall and dismiss in disgrace the agent who proved unfaithful?

The American people, however, even for the brief period of a representative's term, conferred no unlimited authority. From the first, they separated the judicial from the law-making authority, and in creating a legislative department they made it the depository of a special trust, in the execution of which it was to act as a special agent only. In the new fabric of government, legislative omnipotence was no more allowed a place than was executive irresponsibility; and for the period, however brief, of representative authority, the delegated function must be exercised within limits previously defined, and subject to which the delegation had been made. If, therefore, in England, the representative for the time being might be said to hold a general letter of attorney, the American, on the other hand, held a special and limited authority: with the former, the act done would stand as its own justification; the latter, at the peril of having whatever he might do disregarded and annulled, must keep within the letter of his warrant.

It must be conceded, nevertheless, that in the original establishment of American constitutions no special distrust of legislative bodies was manifested. On the contrary, these bodies were from the first the chief depositaries of power, and the restraints imposed resulted as a consequence of a written charter of government and of the division of power under it, instead of having been an object in view in creating the government. Legislative powers were granted by the first American constitutions in very general terms, and the doctrine that the representative was subject to any other than a political responsibility, or that legislative acts might be questioned elsewhere, did not readily take root in American soil. It was the judges, not the legislature, who first became subject to popular mistrust, and those who first refused to obey an unconstitutional law were proceeded against as offenders. Disregard of legislative action seemed to popular apprehension an affront to the people, and was punished accordingly.

But the country was not slow to discover the need of some other check upon representatives than that which was afforded in frequent elections. The Yazoo grant of 1795, in Georgia, brought about by fraud and deception, was so enormous in magnitude and interested so many persons, that it attracted the attention of the whole country, and presented in clear light the possibility that fraud might infect the whole legislative body, and that corrupt inducements might incline the representative to connive at or assist in the robbery of his constituents. From that time to the present, the number of constitutional restrictions imposed for the express purpose of keeping the law-making department in close restraint within prescribed limits and under prescribed forms of action, have been steadily increasing in number, until in some States the presumption that the legislature possesses a general power to make laws in its discretion has almost passed away. The general power has now so many limitations, and must be exercised under such carefully prescribed conditions, that the experienced legislator is excusable if he sometimes stumbles into difficulties, and finds to his surprise that something in his legislation will not bear the test of all the rules that have been prescribed for his observance. To prove this, let the reader examine almost any of the new or recently revised constitutions. An inspection will show the following state of things: *First,* That a number of subjects are removed altogether from legislative cognizance. *Second,* That upon a still larger number of subjects the legislature is forbidden to act, except by general law. *Third,* That when acting upon any subject, certain set forms must be observed, which are imposed for the purpose of forcing upon the legislature a care, caution, and deliberation not otherwise likely to be secured. These forms are thus made a condition to valid legislation, and the necessity of observing them is imperative. The principal of these are, that each act shall embrace but a single object, which shall be expressed in its title ; that the bill shall have several readings on different days, and shall be passed only on a recorded vote by yeas and nays. Peculiar provisions are made in some States which are even more stringent.

It would, however, be a great mistake to suppose that constitutional restraints have really narrowed the field actually
occupied by legislation. On the contrary, excepting a few years
immediately following the Peace of 1783, when the terrible oppression of public and private debt impelled to public disorder,
and led to the legislative abuses usually accompanying the acts
making paper a legal tender in the payment of debts, the early
legislation was in general more careful, more circumspect, and
less open to criticism as encroaching on private rights or sound
principles, than much of that more recent. In late years the
channel of legislation has been narrowed, but the stream has
risen in proportion, and by far the larger part of all the doubtful legislation which the history of the country presents has
taken place since the year 1846, when radical ideas began to be
characteristic of State constitutions, and the theory that officers
of every department should be made as directly as possible
responsible to the people after short terms of service was accepted as a political maxim. The one may not be a consequence of the other, but the times have invited legislative
experiments, and the invitation has been freely accepted.

Evidences of this may be found in abundance. The legislation in aid of private individuals and corporations would first
attract attention, not only because of its magnitude, but because
around it has clustered much that was questionable, and not a
little that proved to be corrupt. The grants made for these
purposes within the last thirty years have been of all sorts and
under all pretences, and compared with some of them the
Yazoo grant sinks into insignificance. They were made by the
nation and by the States; and majorities of local communities
were permitted to assume burdens, not for themselves merely,
but also for the non-assenting minorities, to purchase stock in
business enterprises. On all hands it will be conceded that
this legislation pressed hard upon the implied limits of legislative power; but the reasons favoring it were always plausible,
because the nominal purpose in view was always one in which
the community was more or less concerned. This was particularly the case when the assistance was given to railroad enterprises; and it was often asserted by the projectors that railroads were public highways, and assistance was demanded on

that ground. The evils that have resulted from such legislation, equally with the incidental benefits, are foreign to the present discussion, but the grants themselves and the ground on which they have been made may have some bearing. Questionable legislation can never stand by itself : if it is accepted, whatever is within the principle underlying it must be accepted also, and so must all that necessarily pertains and is incidental to it.

The present purpose is to inquire whether, in the matter of the regulation of property rights and of business, legislation has not of late been occupying doubtful, possibly unconstitutional grounds. The discussion in the main must be limited to fundamental principles, aided by such light as legal and constitutional history may throw upon them, since the express provisions of the constitutions can give little assistance. They always contain the general guaranty of due process of law to life, liberty, and property, but in other particulars they for the most part leave protection to principles which have come from the common law. And what is due process of law can never be settled as an abstract question : it has a new phase with every new case, and judicial history shows that judges differ concerning it at the present day when peculiar cases arise, as radically as they did when ship-money was in question, and when the king's warrant was supposed by some to be sufficient justification for an arrest, though it specified no cause.

The general right of the state to prescribe rules for the regulation of property and business is so plain, that no one disputes it. The right is a necessary one in government : a man could securely have nothing and safely enjoy nothing if the limits of interference by others were not prescribed by law. The laws of property are in themselves regulations, and the rules which give remedies for the invasion of rights are what render civilization and orderly society possible. Bentham, in his Principles of the Civil Code, has expressed this with great force and clearness. "Law," he says, "has accomplished what all the natural feelings were not able to do ; law alone has been able to create a fixed and durable possession which deserves the name of property. The law alone could accustom men to submit to the yoke of foresight, at first painful to be borne, but afterwards agreeable and mild ; it alone could encourage them in labor, superfluous at present, and which they are not to enjoy till the future. Economy has as many enemies as there are spendthrifts, or men who would enjoy without taking the trouble to produce. Labor is too painful for idleness, it is too slow for impatience, cunning and injustice underhandly conspire to appropriate its fruits; insolence and audacity plot to seize them by open force. Hence security, always tottering, always threatened, never at rest, lives in the midst of snares. It requires in the legislator vigilance continually sustained and power always in action to defend it against his constantly reviving crowd of adversaries. The law does not say to a man, 'Work, and I will reward you,' but it says to him, 'Work, and by stopping the hand that would take them from you, I will insure you the fruits of your labor, its natural and sufficient reward, which without me you could not preserve.' If industry creates, it is the law which preserves; if at the first moment we owe every thing to labor, at the second and every succeeding moment we owe every thing to the law."

This is a strong statement, but it is literally true and exact. Every man's rights are necessarily relative, and they are measured by means of the limits which are set to the rights of others. It is vain to say, except in the most general and popular sense, that every man has supreme dominion within the boundaries of his own freehold; for his lands are not only charged with servitudes for the benefit of his neighbor, but his management of his lands is restrained in various ways by rules prescribed for the benefit of others. Whatever he does upon his premises that would be offensive to his neighbor, and that the laws of good neighborhood would not sanction or excuse, may render him liable to prosecution for creating a nuisance. His lawful calling he is entitled to pursue at discretion, but if the calling he has chosen be one whose tendency is to disturb the peace or destroy the comfort of the immediate neighborhood, he might be driven from any thickly settled district as a malefactor if he should attempt to establish it there; and the importance and usefulness of his trade would not protect him. The state leaves the rites of sepulture and the manner of disposing of the bodies of the dead to the affections and the sense of propriety and decency of surviving friends, but not wholly without supervision; for if these were to import into any Christian state the custom of some savage tribes of exposing their dead on scaffolds to foul birds of prey, the law would assuredly visit them with condemnation and punishment. Indeed, every item of individual property, real or personal, every kind of business, every movement of the living person where he may come in contact with others, the conduct of the living and the disposal of the dead, are all brought within the control of regulations established by the state, or by customs which the state adopts, and which thus become its regulations. Men cannot escape from these if they would, and they would fall back into a state of savagery if they could and did.

But while this is asserted in very positive terms, it is affirmed with equal positiveness that there ought to be and are some limits to the right to establish such regulations. An unlimited power in the state to control and regulate private property and private business would make freedom and content as precarious as would an unlimited power in every individual to interfere at will in the concerns of his neighbor. The latter would arm every man against his neighbor; the former would be liable at any time to direct with crushing force the power of the state against any interest which for the time had the popular feeling arrayed against it. To-day the unpopular interest may be the professional or mercantile class, to-morrow it may be corporations, and the day following the laborers upon railroads or in mines. Security can only be found in general principles, and the same general principle that will protect one must protect all. If any general principle can be put aside in order that the state may reach one interest, it may also be put aside when any other interest seeks its protection. Constitutional law can know no favoritism; if principles are not fixed and permanent they are not constitutional, and may be suspended or overridden to suit the passion or caprice of the moment. And as security and content can only repose in settled principles, the question of the relative advantage of republican and autocratic institutions will be very much narrowed if it be conceded that the state may exercise in respect to private property and private business the powers an autocrat assumes. Indeed, it may almost be said to be narrowed to this : Whether many persons, having the powers of sovereignty intrusted to them for exercise, would probably exercise them with more wisdom, discretion, impartiality, and justice than would a single person with similar powers.  Upon such a question the most ardent republican might well hesitate before expressing a definite opinion ; for the advantages of government are not to be found in its forms exclusively : they must be perceived also in its results.

That there are some limits to state interference will probably be denied by no one.  Those who go farthest in the direction of what is sometimes called paternal government by state or nation would claim some exemptions on their own behalf, and would be compelled to concede some to others.  What the limits are and how they are to be found, is the question.  Where they are not prescribed by the constitution of a state, probably it will be said they must be sought in the common law and in the constitutional history of the people.  This is the common and necessary resort when questions arise concerning the proper functions of government.

But if you assume that the government may do whatever it may find precedents for in constitutional history, you assume the existence of a practical legislative omnipotence, restrained only as limitations are expressly imposed.  Taking as a strong illustration the matter of regulating prices, and you may easily prove in this way that the legislative power is ample.  Edward II. regulated prices by proclamation in 1314, and whoever refused to sell ox, sheep, hog, goose, pigeon, or egg at the price he named forfeited it to the king.  Edward III. followed the example by proclamation in 1330, and afterwards by statute.  In the time of Henry IV. the price at which foreign corn was permitted to be sold in the realm was prescribed by law for the benefit of the farmers ; and Henry VIII., on the other hand, for the benefit of those who purchased from the farmers, limited by law the prices of their beef, pork, and mutton, thereby holding them under the like restraint to that which he imposed upon importers of wines.  The rates of wages were perhaps oftener limited by law than the prices of wares, and the method of regulation was specially objectionable, in its being generally left to the local authorities, who would be interested, if at all, in keeping the wages low ; but this method was continued down to the time of the American Revolution. Elizabeth thought public policy demanded of her that she should prescribe the size of lot a man might build his cottage upon; and she did so, following the example of her father, who restricted the number of sheep a farmer might keep, and of her grandfather, who limited the number of acres a single farmer might cultivate. For sumptuary laws there are not only precedents, but reasons even in recent times. Montesquieu thought them important in republics, and John Adams in 1778 had some words of regret because he thought the people would not endure them. They were almost as frequent in English history as laws to prevent extortionate prices. By turns Parliament prescribed the length of a man's shoe and the cut of his coat; it sometimes forbade his indulging in the extravagance of foreign cloths, and sometimes limited the courses at his table. Montesquieu said that in Venice the people were compelled by the laws to moderation. "They are so habituated to parsimony that none but courtesans can make them part with their money. Such is the method made use of for the support of industry; the most contemptible of women may be profuse without danger, whilst those who contribute to their extravagance consume their days in the greatest obscurity." It is not without curious interest in this connection that when the Parliament of James VI. of Scotland undertook to put down extravagance in dress among women, and to limit their expenditures for that purpose to what they could afford, they enacted "that it be lauchfull to na wemen to weir abone their estait *except*" this same shameless class. Doubtless the purpose was to make female extravagance disreputable, by branding it as an advertisement of shame. But James, though he humorously indorsed upon it, "This act is verray gude," had the sense also to add his veto. Notwithstanding this, James, when he came to the throne of England, thought proper to prescribe the quantity of ale which should be sold for a penny, as the Lord Mayor and Council of London had done before him.

Precedents in the line of sumptuary laws, and laws regulating prices, though less abundant, are no more wanting in this country than in England. The former may be passed by, as not specially important here, and with the admission that they

93

were neither numerous, nor, under the circumstances of the country, such as should call for very severe criticism. Nor on the score of prices was any persistent and permanent policy established; what was done was meant rather for special emergencies, than to establish the general course of government. Among one of the earliest of Massachusetts colonial statutes was "An act against oppression," which subjected to fine and imprisonment such evil-disposed persons as should oppress and wrong their neighbors by taking excessive wages for their work or unreasonable prices for their wares. The two towns of Boston and Charlestown appointed porters and prescribed their lawful charges; but this may perhaps be considered as a grant of special privilege, with an accompanying restriction. In 1672, the weight of a penny-loaf was fixed by law in the colony, but in the least obnoxious way possible, for it was by a sliding scale regulated by the price of wheat. This was after the manner of the English assize of bread, and was followed to some extent in other parts of this country. In 1777, under the stress of a doubtful war, a strong effort was made to unite the colonies in an agreement upon prices which could be fixed by law, and the New England colonies came to an agreement which had the approval of Congress, but the others failed to concur. It has generally been supposed that the attempt to fix prices by law in this country came to an end when independence was firmly established and liberty secured. Up to that time some of the towns assumed the authority to regulate prices. It may safely be asserted, however, that all attempts in that direction were unsatisfactory. Hubbard, in his General History, gives this account of the Massachusetts experiment of 1633: "Many new plantations going on at this time made laborers scarce, and the scarcity made workmen demand excessive wages, for the excusing of which it was pleaded that the prices of wares with the merchants were proportionable. For the preventing of oppression in the one and in the other, orders were made in the General Court that the artificers, such as carpenters and masons, should not receive above 2s. per diem, and laborers not above 18d.; and proportionably, merchants should not advance above 4d. in the shilling above what their goods cost in England. But these good orders were not of long continuances, but did expire with the first and golden age of the New World, things being raised since to treble the value well-nigh of what they were." The experiment, it will be seen, was in the nature of a protective tariff, applied as between different classes in the same small community. It seems not to have occurred to the good minister to inquire whether the abandonment may not have been due to the fact that the restriction was found beneficial to neither party, and that the wise men, of whom Massachusetts had her full share in those days, were brought by observation and reflection to the conclusion, that there were laws determining prices which were inherent in the nature and circumstances of civilized society, and that the operation of these was not likely to be improved by legislative interference. Similar considerations probably led to the abandonment of the laws in Maryland, and perhaps some other colonies, which made the planting of a certain area of corn by each taxable inhabitant compulsory.

It is not understood to be now pretended that any general right to fix the price of commodities or to limit the charges for services can exist as a part of any system of free government. It seems to be tacitly understood, that whatever power may once have existed for that purpose has been lost or taken away, and that business in general is protected against the interference of the state in such matters. Possibly there may be single individuals or small organizations of men who hold extreme views on this subject, but these would resist the authority as promptly as any one if the power were to be exercised in the restriction of the wages of labor, or in restraining agreements among laborers having for their object to put up or maintain the standard of prices for their services. It is a fact, however, of common observation, that there are some cases in which the legislature is accustomed to limit the charges for services and for the uses of property, and that the exercise of the power is acquiesced in as being rightful. These cases, then, must be supposed to stand upon some principle which distinguishes them from all others, and what the principle is, and how the cases may be separated in which the government may interfere for the prevention of extortion from those in which it may not, is among the important questions that have recently attracted attention. There must be or should be a clear line of distinction somewhere; one that the legislature and the courts may clearly perceive and apply without danger of serious error.

By some persons this question has been approached from what may be called the negative point of view; that is, the general right of regulation in the discretion of the legislature is assumed, and those who dispute its rightfulness in the instance are called upon to point out wherefore it is not permitted. For the general right, the strong illustration is given of the regulation of profits from loans of money. Money, it is said, is the most valuable and the most greatly desired of all property; the right to acquire and use it for all lawful purposes is undoubted; and yet from time immemorial the legislature has laid down rules limiting the charges for the use of it, and imposing severe penalties for demanding or receiving more; and this has been done without so much as a suggestion from any source that constitutional power for the purpose was wanting. The fact cannot be disputed, though it may not be possible to justify it in principle. The general rule the world over has been that usury was condemned, and only in modern times has the policy of usury laws been questioned. In part this probably comes from the fact that government makes money, establishes its value, and, as this nation knows to its cost, changes its value at will. If the coin bear the image and superscription of Cæsar; if Cæsar may make it of gold to-day, of silver to-morrow, and of paper the day following, changing the value of all possessions with every change in the currency—may not Cæsar exercise the comparatively insignificant power to regulate the charges that may be made for the use of it in loans? But in still greater part, perhaps, the ideas concerning usury have come as a part of the Jewish inheritance—as a part of the law delivered by the mouth of Moses in the wilderness. True, the Jews were prohibited only from taking usury of their brethren, but this rule accepted and applied by any other people must at least preclude the exaction of usury by subject from subject. For age after age the condemnation of usury was received by many as a law of perpetual obligation; and when under the operation of the great law of supply and demand men were induced to disregard this divine law, it seemed almost the performance of an obligation of religion when king and people, as the opportunity seemed to be favorable, repudiated their obligation to the usurers, and robbed them of their gains. To spoil the Jews who spoil the people seemed almost a Christian duty ; they were plundered, stoned, and banished ; and so great was the abhorrence of this nation of usurers, that when in the time of the Great Protector (1655) they humbly prayed to be received into the realm, this ruler, so wise in most matters, doubted and hesitated, and spent the next day with his ministers in prayer and fasting ; and yet nothing better came of it than a very zealous remonstrance from Mr. Prynne, who had no difficulty in proving that permission to the Jews to reside in England would be "the greatest affront offered to the Son of God, the author of our redemption, that any Christian government could be guilty of." The history of England in this regard was not singular. Money-lenders the world over, wherever the laws were such as to permit, had been rapacious and cruel, and the poor of every country had suffered at their hands. When Solon set about preparing a code for Athens, he found that the existing laws permitted men to borrow money on the credit of their bodies, and not of their own merely, but those of their wives, their children, and their unmarried sisters ; and failure to meet their obligations subjected the persons pledged to be sold into slavery. Great numbers had been thus sold, and were to be found scattered over Greece, and even in foreign parts. The evil was so enormous and the oppressions had been so cruel, that Solon deemed it necessary to set all the slaves of usury free, and to annul all existing contracts—a measure of repudiation only justified by the most absolute necessity. The statement of Aristotle has been frequently quoted, that money was naturally barren, and that to attempt to make money breed money was preposterous, and a manifest perversion of the purpose for which money was created, which was as a convenience in trade and commerce. When Cato the Censor denounced loans at interest as a crime, he but expressed a very common sentiment.

The common law implied no promise to make compensation for the use of money loaned, though it did imply a promise in the case of other loans for use. When America severed her connection with Great Britain, usury was a penal offence, and the regulation of the interest of money was thought to be one of the most imperative duties of the government. It was furnishing protection for the weak against the strong, the helpless against the grasping and extortionate. American constitutional history consequently begins with money in thrall; from time immemorial the government had established regulations, not only as a matter of course, but in the supposed performance of a great governmental duty. The emancipation of money from this governmental control has since been in progress; in England, by Statute 16th and 17th Victoria, it is now complete, while America lags behind.

The present argument has no concern with the policy of usury laws ; but this may be safely affirmed, that no conclusion in favor of the constitutional right to limit the profits from kinds of property that were never in thrall can be drawn from the fact that corresponding restrictions are not yet wholly removed from property that was never emancipated. To appreciate the illogical character of such a conclusion, there must be kept in view the manner in which the constitutional principles have come to America. They have not, to use the language of Burke in his Letter to the Old Whigs, "been struck out at an heat by a set of presumptuous men," but they have been evolved slowly, and under great trials and difficulties; some of them attained full and rounded proportions before others came to be more than faintly recognized ; the growth of all has been historical, circumstances first giving to one a prominence and a vigor, and afterwards another. With such a growth, a barbarous anomaly, never yet wholly eradicated, and standing among free principles as a great and striking exception, ought to be neither surprising nor misleading. Had the facts been otherwise, had all constitutional principles been planned and settled upon by a body of men meeting for the purpose, and embodying them in a written instrument as an aggregate and harmonious whole, there would be good reason to demand harmony in their construction, and to assume that what seemed an anomaly could only be a principle misunderstood or misapplied. The historical development of a constitution, however, never was and never can be entirely symmetrical; and it must be admitted that the grand old common law, of which American constitutional principles formed a part, and for which the fathers perilled and some of them gave up their lives, had embodied in it more than one feature of barbarism, and indeed, as many believe, is not yet wholly relieved of serious anomalies. Whoever believes that the principles he accepts as fundamental form, when taken together, a complete and perfect code, and insure to the people all the protection that is needful, may glorify it as such; but the wise statesman, though he may insist that the Constitution is the best ever known, will nevertheless admit that it has not yet reached that state of perfection in which it may be regarded as incapable of improvement. And he would be a bold lawyer who would venture to affirm that any code of laws now in existence is wholly free from incongruities.

It has also been thought that the limits of state authority in restricting the profits of business may be determined by a solution of the question whether the property by means of which the business is carried on is "affected with a public interest," whereby it ceases to be *juris privati*, and is brought, like all public interests, within the special supervision and control of the state. But in the attempt to ascertain what it is that affects private property with a public interest one seems to be feeling his way in the darkness, and at the best is compelled to accept and be satisfied with such uncertain light as the instances of state interference can afford. Certain occupations are named which from time immemorial have been subjected to exceptional legislative regulations, and it is assumed that the property employed in these is affected with a public interest, and that in this fact is found the justification for the control exercised. Starting with these as unquestioned and unquestionable cases, the conclusion is drawn that the same authority must exist in certain other cases which are so far analogous as not to be distinguishable in principle.

The phrase "affected with a public interest" is important in this discussion, and as it comes from the treatise "De Portibus Maris" of Lord Hale, it is needful to know in what sense he employed it. The important passage from that treatise is the following: "A man, for his own private advantage, may, in a port or town, set up a wharf or crane, and may take what rates he and his customers can agree for cranage, wharfage, housellage, pesage; for he doth no more than is lawful for any man to do, viz., makes the most of his own. If the king or subject have a public wharf, unto which all persons that come to that port must come and unlade or lade their goods as for the purpose, because they are the wharfs only licensed by the queen—or because there is no other wharf in that port, as it may fall out where a port is newly erected; in that case there cannot be taken arbitrary and excessive duties for cranage, wharfage, pesage, etc., neither can they be enhanced to an immoderate rate; but the duties must be reasonable and moderate, though settled by the king's license or charter. For now the wharf and crane and other conveniences are affected with a public interest, and they cease to be *juris privati* only; as if a man set out a street in new building on his own land, it is now no longer bare private interest, but is affected by a public interest."

To appreciate the exact force of this language, it is necessary to understand that the erection of a wharf on navigable water in Great Britain was never a matter of right, but always of privilege. In the first place, the ports were creatures of the prerogative; no man at will could run his vessel into a haven and land his goods where he pleased, but the haven must first be made a port, and officers of the customs assigned to it. In the second place, the title to the soil of all tide-waters below high-water mark pertained to the crown, and any wharf erected there without lawful permission was a purpresture, and liable to be removed as such. A wharf must therefore be specially and expressly licensed; and if not licensed expressly, it was only in existence by the tolerance of the crown, and on or adjacent to land belonging to the crown, and without the use of which the property could not be made available. Whether, therefore, the wharf was licensed and thereby given special and exclusive privileges, or had been set up without license, Lord Hale had for his assertion that it was affected with a public interest this justification—that it was erected by express or implied public permission, on or in connection with public property, and for the accommodation of the public by means of a private business. This is all that can be claimed from this passage from Lord

Hale; and it seems quite reasonable for him to declare that one who under such circumstances had a monopoly of the business might justly be compelled to deal with the public on reasonable terms.

It is now important to know what classes of private business are so circumstanced that the like reasons will apply. It would seem that these must be very few indeed. The case of the miller is often given as an illustration, and it is said that the state has always controlled the use of his property to some extent, and limited the tolls he has been permitted to exact for grinding his neighbors' grist. It will not be disputed that this was formerly done : the question of authority to do so now is not so plain. As a rule, mills in England were formerly the property of the lord of the manor, who by prescription had an exclusive right to grind grain for his tenants. But an exclusive right of that sort could only exist in connection with reciprocal rights on the part of tenants to be served at fair prices ; and these could only be protected by positive law. The right of statute regulation may thus be said to result as a necessary consequence of the dependence of the tenant upon the mill for his bread. English ideas on the subject were brought by the colonists to this country, and necessity co-operated with these in shaping public policy in respect to mills. Among the earliest legislative acts in Maryland is one providing that " any bargain which the Lt. General and Council shall make with any undertaker for the setting up of a water mill for the use of this colony, shall be levied upon all the inhabitants of the colony, in such manner as the Lt. General and Council shall appoint, so it exceed not 10,000 lb. tobacco in a year, for two years only." This was in 1633—the same year that the first mill was set up in Massachusetts ; and though it may not be affirmed that government aid was given in the case last mentioned, yet as it is stated that it was erected " by leave of the plantation on Neponset River," it seems probable that it was either set up on the common property, or that special privileges were obtained and corresponding duties imposed. One special privilege of the highest importance was certainly granted to millers in the colonial period ; that, namely, of obtaining water-power by means of an appropriation of the lands of others under the sovereign
17

power of eminent domain. This might well be regarded as an equivalent for the obligation which millers were required to assume, to grind corn for a stipulated toll. A reference to the laws of New Hampshire will show how the two things were often coupled together. Thus the law of 1718 by one section limited the tolls for grinding grain; and by another it gave the miller the right to flow the lands of others by means of his dam, on the payment of damages, if any, that should be assessed by a sheriff's jury. Now, when one appeals to the state to put forth on his behalf its sovereign authority to compel another to abandon to him his freehold, he does so on the express and necessary claim that his business is " affected with a public interest," and that in short he proposes to act as an agency for the public in accomplishing some public purpose or supplying some public necessity. In a number of the States the proprietors of grist-mills are still permitted to appropriate for their purposes the lands of non-assenting parties; but in some it is denied that authority can be constitutionally conferred for this purpose unless for mills which are brought under State regulations, compelling them to grind grain for all who come, impartially, and for an established toll. In general, however, it is believed that when the rates of toll are fixed by law, the intent of the law is not to fix a maximum, and thereby to preclude the parties making their own arrangements, but the rate named is merely one which is to govern when the parties deal with each other without special understanding. But whether this belief is well founded or not, it seems apparent that no very forcible argument for the authority to regulate prices in other business can be deduced from a case so exceptional as that of millers. Regulations of their charges certainly began when their business was affected with a public interest ; and if the regulation has continued after the justification for it has ceased, it is perhaps because there has never been provocation to question its rightfulness.

In an early case in Alabama it was decided that the legislature might confer upon a municipality the authority to fix the price of bread. In what are known as the Warehouse Cases, recently decided by the Supreme Court of Illinois, it was said by the learned judge who delivered the governing opinion that this is still permitted by the laws of Illinois. The long experience of that judge in the administration of the law does not admit of any question being raised as to the fact; though whether the authority is conferred by municipal charters in specific terms, or is supposed to rest in some general grant of power, is not stated. If, however, the statutes of any State do now rightfully confer this authority, either in special terms or by general grant, it would seem we might stop the discussion here, and admit that there is nothing in this direction the legislature may not do. In the Alabama case the Court seem to plant the right on the fact that the calling "affects the public interest, or private property is employed in a manner which directly affects the body of the people." Now, why does the baker's calling specially affect the public interest? If it is for any other reason than because he sells to the public one of the necessaries of life, the reason would probably have been mentioned. But the merchant does the same when he sells clothing, the druggist when he sells medicines, the butcher when he sells his meat; and if it is conceded that religious instruction is essential in a free state, as several of the State constitutions affirm, then the clergyman does the same when he imparts religious instruction and advice; and merchant, druggist, butcher, and clergyman may all have the prices of their wares or their services prescribed by law. A distinction in principle between the cases cannot be pointed out, because it does not exist. The right to fix the weight of bread is clear enough; that is only a reasonable regulation to prevent imposition, and stands on the same ground with the requirement of inspection of fish and other provisions.

Ferrymen and owners of toll-bridges, it is said, also have their charges limited by law. This is true. But these parties have special privileges conferred upon them by law—generally. to some extent at least, exclusive; and they are allowed the sovereign privilege of levying toll. The rights they have are not open to general competition; and, as they are given by law, it would be strange indeed if the law in giving could not limit its gift. The law does limit the gift in various ways: it restricts the tolls, and it compels attendance of ferrymen and gate-keepers at all suitable hours, under penalty; it gives special privileges, and it imposes obligations for the public benefit in return. Reference is here made only to those ferries and bridges which are highways, and in respect to which alone does the law undertake to exercise the authority mentioned; if a man sees fit to carry passengers, either by boat or bridge, over a stream, entirely on his own land, his boat or bridge constitutes no part of a public highway, and there is no authority for saying that in doing so he exercises a calling which in any sense is public. He may carry whomsoever he pleases, refusing to carry others; may carry when he pleases, and at any rates agreed upon, or at a reasonable consideration when no rates are fixed; he may attend when he pleases; and if his business is a public business, so as to be brought under legislative control, so must be the tailor's and the cobbler's. In saying this, however, it is assumed that he does not hold himself out as a common carrier; when he does that, he becomes subject to certain exceptional regulations; but whether these can extend to the regulation of prices, is a question which will be referred to a little further on.

The rule may be said to be general, that whenever a special privilege is conceded to private parties, the enjoyment of which requires an exceptional use by them, or in connection with their business, of the public highways, either by water or by land, and the privilege is conferred for some accommodation they are to supply to the public, the property in their business is affected, to some extent at least, with a public interest. This rule will embrace several of the cases in which legislative regulations and restrictions are customarily made. The case is all the stronger where the privilege conferred is in the nature of a monopoly. That was the fact in the warehouse case of All-nutt *vs.* Inglis, decided by the Court of King's Bench in 1810. The warehousemen whose rights were then in question were permitted to receive wines directly from the importing vessels, before the duties were paid; it was an exclusive and valuable privilege, and was given and received in view of common-law rules, which would obligate them to receive the wines for a reasonable compensation. They undertook to appropriate the privilege, and to repudiate any corresponding obligation; in other words, while taking the benefit of the privilege, they practically asserted the prerogative of compelling the public to submit to any charges they might see fit to impose: a monstrous proposition, in view of the fact that the public had no privilege of dealing with others. The controversy is thus stated by Lord Ellenborough : " The question on this record is whether the London Dock Company have a right to insist upon receiving wines into their warehouses for a hire and reward arbitrary and at their will and pleasure, or whether they were bound to receive them there for a reasonable reward only. There is no doubt that the general principle is favored both in law and justice, that every man may fix what price he pleases upon his own property or the use of it; but if, for a particular purpose, the public have a right to resort to his premises and make use of them, and he have a monopoly in them for that purpose, if he will take the benefit of that monopoly, he must, as an equivalent, perform the duty attached to it on reasonable terms." Such a case seems to require no comment: the conclusion of the court is so reasonable and just, that the only wonder is that the doctrine which Lord Ellenborough put aside as untenable could ever have been advanced.

There may also be rejected, as not requiring special discussion or consideration, the case of every employment, the following of which is not of right, but of favor. The case of an auctioneer may be instanced: he performs a public function, and is only allowed to take it upon himself by license. Wherever the business is a privilege, and the taking out of a license is required, the state may impose conditions upon the privilege. The case of hackney-coachmen and draymen may be classed in the same category: their avocations have always been licensed and restrained; and one of the most usual and perhaps most necessary restraints is that which is imposed in respect to their charges. Moreover, these persons are allowed to establish a business in the public highways; they stand there with their conveyances, occupying the streets to the inconvenience, more or less, of the general public, and in ways that would not be permitted but for the special conveniences they afford. Their privileges give them special opportunities for extortion and for practising frauds upon strangers, and the police supervision is required to be exceptionally active and strict. It is not of right that they shall have the privileges which are conceded to them : they might be required to stand for business on private grounds instead of in the streets, just as the merchant awaits his customers at his store, and the mechanic at his shop. The exceptional use which by law or by custom they are permitted to make of the public streets for the conveniences they afford is quite sufficient to affect their vehicles with a public interest ; and they can reasonably no more contest the conditions than could a huckster who should be allowed on special terms to set up a booth on the public market-ground. Moreover, it may be said of this case as of usury, that the regulations are from time immemorial.

Whether the regulation of the business of carriers of persons and goods may extend to the fixing of prices, is a question which has received no little attention, and been the subject of much earnest controversy for the last three or four years. The right in the state to make exceptional regulations of some sort for the case of common carriers is not disputed ; the common law itself made some, the most important of which was the requirement that persons in this business should receive and carry, for all who offered, with impartiality. The Congressional Civil Rights Act of 1875 has supplemented this by a provision forbidding discriminations in the carriage of persons, based on race, color, or previous condition ; and many of the States have regulations to further secure impartiality in the dealings of these persons with the public. But a regulation to secure impartiality is so different in principle from one limiting prices, that the power to establish the one affords no presumption in favor of the authority to do the other. The first is only in furtherance of, and supplementary to, the common-law requirement of fairness ; but the common law is put aside and reversed when the statute undertakes to prescribe what a man shall charge for his services.

When carriers are corporations, so much depends upon their contract with the state that their cases are very apt to be exceptional. It has been decided by a great weight of authority, that where a railway charter reserves to the state an unlimited right of amendment, this right may be exercised in restricting charges for transportation. In the able opinion of the Chief-

106

Justice of Wisconsin to that effect, it is intimated that, independent of this reserved power of amendment, the same thing might be done under the power of police. The idea underlying such a suggestion may perhaps be formulated as follows: 1. Railways, by general concession, are such public conveniences that the sovereign power of eminent domain is allowed to be exercised in their favor in the appropriation of lands of non-assenting parties. 2. It has been claimed, and generally conceded, that the public have such a general interest in railways, that taxes may be levied and paid over to the projectors to aid them in constructing and equipping their road. 3. The argument will then be made that if the state may bring its sovereign power to their assistance, because of the public benefits they are expected to confer, and if it may and does invest its own money in their property, they must, by accepting such assistance, be held estopped to dispute the claim of the state that their property is affected with a public interest. The subject is one having many sides, and so important that any court called upon to consider it would not venture to express any but the most mature and carefully considered opinion. The discussions hitherto have elicited nothing very conclusive or authoritative on the main question.

The case of innkeepers is sometimes said to be one in which the right of the state to limit charges is indisputable; but if an attempt should be made to exercise it, it would probably be contested with vigor. Like common carriers, innkeepers are subject to special regulations at the common law, and the Civil Rights Act also includes them among the persons who are forbidden to discriminate because of race, color, or previous condition. But these regulations, as in the case of carriers, are in the interest of impartiality, and they are not supposed to be burdensome to the business in any sense. Possibly the notions on this subject may have come from the fact that places of entertainment for travellers have generally been places for the sale of intoxicating drinks, and such places are usually required to be licensed, and the number is purposely or indirectly limited. Sufficient reason for this is found in the fact that the business brings many evils upon society, and is so likely to breed disorders and tumult, that exceptional police supervision is imperative.  It is, at best, only a tolerated business, and is always subjected to special restraint when not altogether prohibited. But the business of entertaining travellers has no necessary connection with this ; and it is not only a commendable and useful, but it is also a necessary business.

It is safe to classify, in the following manner, the cases in which usage will warrant one in saying that private property, invested and managed for the benefit of the owners, is affected with a public interest.

1. Where the business is one the following of which is not matter of right, but is permitted by the state as a privilege or franchise.  Under this head would be ranged the business of setting up lotteries; of giving shows, etc.; of keeping billiard-tables for hire ; and of selling intoxicating drinks, when the sale, by unlicensed parties, is forbidden.  Also, the case of toll-bridges, etc.

2. When the state, on public grounds, renders to the business special assistance by taxation or otherwise.

3. When, for the accommodation of the business, some special use is allowed to be made of public property or of a public easement.

4. Where exclusive privileges are granted in consideration of some special return to be made to the public.

In each of these cases the public interest is manifest.  If there are any not coming under these heads, the interest ought to be equally capable of being pointed out.

Passing now to the nature of the control the state may exercise in the regulation of business within the limits of its authority, the following may be suggested as fundamental rules :

1. The state should restrain and seek to prevent whatever would impede its people in making free disposal of their wares or their services on the best terms a free market may offer.

2. The state should abstain on its own part from interposing impediments to its people reaping the advantages of competition in all lawful employments.

As to these rules, there ought to be and probably will be no disagreement.  Indeed, those who have gone farthest in demanding state intervention to limit the profits of business have justified the demand on the ground that the business they desired to have regulated and restrained was a virtual monopoly, so that the regulation was needed to give competition, not to prevent it. In the Warehouse Cases already referred to, this was said; and it was strongly urged that unless the charges of Chicago warehousemen were limited to a maximum, the public had no protection against the extortions of a monopoly.

The word monopoly has an ominous sound to American ears, and whenever the appellation fairly attaches itself to any thing, it is already condemned in the public mind. Monopolies are heard of with great frequency in English history, and at some periods they have played a very important part in public affairs. It must be conceded, however, that those against which the complaints have been loudest were monopolies the government itself had set up; not monopolies of individual establishment, which the government was called upon to curb or to destroy. An instance may be taken of a monopoly in alum, granted by King Henry VI. The king had received a quantity of that article for £4000, which he sold for £8000, granting in the sale an exclusive privilege to the vendees of dealing in alum within the realm for a term of years. King Henry VII. created a similar monopoly in this same article, by conferring upon a Tuscan merchant the privilege of importing a certain quantity, and prohibiting the importation by any one else until he had sold this off. To grant such a monopoly was a favorite resort of the crown when money was needed for personal uses, and as a consideration of some sort was generally received for it, this was equivalent to levying a tax and farming out the collection of it to parties who had paid in advance. But monopolies were not always granted for money. In 1245, Henry III., to spite the London traders, ordered all shops in London to be closed for fifteen days for the benefit of fairs proclaimed by him at Westminster. Similar orders were repeatedly issued afterwards, but it is some satisfaction to be informed by the chronicles that the monopolists profited little, for the rains of heaven sometimes destroyed goods of greater value than all the profits. Queen Elizabeth dealt largely in monopolies, and Sir Walter Raleigh, over whose sad fate men sometimes mourn, did not scruple to find his profit in them. In the great debate upon them in 1601, Sir Robert Wroth said there were then in being patents of monopoly for "currants, iron, powder, cards, ox shinbones, train oyl, transportation of leather, lists of cloth, ashes, anis seed, vinegar, seacoals, steel, aqua vitæ, brushes, pots, saltpeter, lead, accidences, oyl, calamin stone, oyl of blubber, fumachoes or dried pitchers in the smoak, and divers others." "Upon reciting the patents aforesaid, Mr. Hakewell stood up and asked thus: Is not bread there? *Bread*, quoth one; *bread*, quoth another; this voice seems strange, quoth another; this voice seems strange, quoth a third. No, quoth Mr. Hakewell, but if order be not taken for these, bread will be there before the next Parliament." And the queen was pleased to take order concerning these, and to repeal them, protesting that "never did I put my pen to any grant but that upon pretence and semblance made unto me that it was both good and beneficial to the subjects in general, though a private profit to some of my ancient servants who had deserved well; but the contrary being found by experience, I am exceeding beholding to such subjects as would move the same at first." The evil, however, did not stop here, even for this reign; but it rose to enormous magnitude under the first Stuart, and prior to 1623 nearly all the foreign trade of the kingdom was in the hands of a few people in London, who, under their royal grants, were enabled to fix the prices both of imports and exports. In that year the king was forced by the Commons to give his assent to a law which declared monopolies by royal grant illegal, and the most of those in existence were repealed. Of those which escaped repeal was that to the East India Company, which grew to such proportions afterwards. Charles I. revived monopolies, and in 1640, in debate in Parliament, Sir John Colepeper said of them: "I have but one grievance more to offer unto you; but this one compriseth many; it is a nest of wasps, a swarm of vermine, which have overcrept the land; I mean the monopolers and polers of the people: these, like the frogs of Egypt, have got possession of our dwellings, and we have scarce a room free from them: they sip in our cup, they dip in our dish, they sit by our fire; we find them in the dye-vat, wash-bowl, and powdering tub; they share with the butler in his box, they have marked and sealed us from head to foot. Mr. Speaker, they will not bate us a pin : we may not buy our own cloathes without their brokage. These are the leaches that have sucked the commonwealth so hard, that it has almost become hectical. And, Mr. Speaker, some of these are ashamed of their right names ; they have a vizard to hide the brand made by that good law in the last Parliament of King James; they shelter themselves under the name of a corporation; they make byelaws which serve their turns to squeeze us and fill their purses ; unface these, and they will prove as bad cards as any in the pack." The House not only resolved against monopolies, but it resolved that no monopolist or patentee should be allowed to sit in that House ; and several were turned out under this vote. Charles I. even assumed to himself the prerogative of limiting the growth of the city of London, and levied fees for the privilege of building houses in extension of its limits. His assumptions were of course illegal ; indeed, monopolies by royal grant to the prejudice of trade had been judicially declared void in 1602, and in their most odious forms they disappeared when Charles I. lost his head. Meantime America was only suffered to be colonized under the permission of trading monopolies.

It was certainly not this kind of monopoly that was brought under condemnation in the Warehouse Cases, for no grant of special privilege had been given, nor, under the constitution of Illinois, could any have been given. There is another sort known to the English law which has been more or less obnoxious, namely, the monopoly of provisions, effected usually by combination, with a view unnaturally to raise prices. This was a common-law offence, but with several kindred common-law offences has been abolished in England. It is possible that it may in early times, when the means of transportation were imperfect, have been a serious evil, but it is inconceivable that it can be so now, except where it is accomplished through means which are no part of any regular business. If means are employed which public policy cannot sanction, it is competent and proper for the state to interfere.

A monopoly, where the term is employed with the care and accuracy proper in judicial decisions and legal proceedings, must be understood as some exclusive power to dispose of something of value, either generally, or for some definite time, or within certain limits. The method in which it may be secured has nothing to do with its exclusive character, and it is equally a monopoly whether obtained by sovereign grant or secured by individual management. If the exclusive right to dispose of their services in any given capacity at an important business centre were secured in any way by a few persons, those persons would have a monopoly, whether the right were obtained by sovereign grant, by combination, or by employing violence and terror to drive away all who might be competitors. The sovereign grant of monopolies in trade was declared unlawful in England, on the ground that "the sole trade of any mechanical artifice, or any other monopoly, is not only a damage and prejudice to those who exercise the same trade, but also to all other subjects, for the end of all these monopolies is for the private gain of the patentees." There may doubtless be exclusive privileges that would not be subject to this condemnation, but they must clearly be in cases not coming within the reasons assigned. An author or inventor is given for a certain term an exclusive right in that which his talent or ingenuity has produced; but the right here is in something which he himself has created, and which ought to be his property, as much as the wheat he has grown, or the cattle he has raised or bought. Exclusive franchises are sometimes given where in no other way can some public interest be accomplished; but the reasons ought to be of the most conclusive nature, and the state grant ought to be construed with the utmost strictness. To whatever extent special privileges are conferred upon one, he is favored, and equality of right under the government is disturbed. Nevertheless special privileges are sometimes defensible, and sometimes a grant of them may be supported on grounds of necessity.

If the mere fact that a business has or may become a monopoly can give to the legislature an authority to interfere and restrain it, it must be because a monopoly is in itself so manifestly and necessarily opposed to public policy as to be wholly inadmissible. But when any thing is wholly inadmissible, the legislature itself must be without the power to create it. A thing cannot be wrong when growing up independently, and right when set up under a special statute. Therefore, if by enterprise or management a virtual monopoly is created at any point, it must be subject to no more and no other condemnation than would be a monopoly of precisely the same sort expressly created. But in this country men are precluded from claiming that monopolies of legislative creation are subject to special restraints because of their exclusive features. A short provision inserted in the Federal Constitution to prevent the general repudiation of debts has been found to embrace within its protection the grants of exclusive privileges made by the state. Whatever grant, therefore, is made by the state is protected, if the grant was within the legislative competence. Queen Elizabeth might recall the vicious monopolies she had granted, and Parliament might at any time repeal them or bring them under control, but no future Coke in this country can wage the same exterminating war upon them which was waged by the great Chief-Justice in England. It would not be enough for him to show that the object of his attack was a monopoly; he must go farther and show some additional vice, or the legislative grant would be shielded from his attack behind the ægis of the Federal Constitution. *Primâ facie* all legislative grants are made for conclusive reasons; and with the utmost propriety it is always assumed that all laws, whether public or private, have been adopted from honest motives and on sufficient grounds. Therefore, though the benefits may apparently all be of individual and personal nature, the law implies and the judiciary and the executive must hold that public considerations governed the legislative action. In general, however obnoxious the special privilege may seem to be, objectors will be required to show how and in what language it is forbidden in the State Constitution before they can effectually assail it. A few illustrations will give some idea of the extent of State power in the grant of monopolies. Some of the early railroad charters were exclusive, and gave a complete monopoly within certain prescribed limits; and it is notorious that those in New Jersey have caused the country much annoyance. In two or more of the States there have been grants of the exclusive right to navigate public waters, and these have been sustained where they did not come in conflict with the regulations of commerce established by Congress. The Binghamton Bridge case is worthy of special mention. The Legislature of New York at an early day created

113

an incorporation to construct a toll-bridge across the Chenango River, and in the opinion of the Federal Supreme Court the terms of the grant, though not very clear and explicit, were such as to give an exclusive privilege to maintain a bridge across the river for a length of four miles. The growth of towns along this part of the river in time made other bridges essential, and the legislature created another corporation, which it undertook to authorize to build a second bridge within the same limits. The new grant was held to be a violation of the Constitution of the United States, and therefore void. It was in vain that Mr. Justice Grier expressed the opinion that " the power of one legislature to bind themselves and their posterity, and all future legislatures, from authorizing a bridge absolutely required for public use, might well be denied by the courts of New York;" the Court did not concur in this view, and considered themselves bound by the precedents to the contrary. The New Orleans Slaughter House Case deserves at least a passing mention. In the troublous days immediately following the war, when the passions of the people were so inflamed on questions growing out of the civil conflict as to preclude any careful supervision of legislation by the general public, the Legislature of Louisiana granted to a corporate body the exclusive privilege for twenty-five years of slaughtering cattle in New Orleans and its immediate vicinity, limiting their charges it is true, but making them sufficiently liberal. This grant the courts have felt compelled to sustain. If the legislature could lawfully create this monopoly, why not create a similar monopoly of warehousing? And if they did create one, what should prevent their fixing the rates as high as they have ever been fixed by individual warehousemen? It is notorious that the tolls taken on numerous bridges through the country are such as could not be sustained for a day if the legislative protection were taken away, and the tolls were left to competition. A single other illustration of exclusive grants will suffice. In Alabama and Missouri the grant of a lottery franchise has been held irrevocable. It would seem that all the way between the building of railways and the setting up of lotteries there must be room for monopolies almost as numerous as those in England, the schedule of which was given by Sir Robert Wroth. Whatever exist will generally be found now, as in King James's time, "to shelter themselves under the name of a corporation."

But the following question is worthy of serious consideration by legislators : If the state in respect to any particular occupation may prescribe prices, may it not also, on the same reasons and in the same occupation, set up a monopoly? The question is of vital interest, and its consideration requires an examination of the grounds on which exclusive privileges in the nature of monopolies are supposed to be granted. The following may be suggested :

1. The grant of an exclusive privilege may seem to be necessary to the accomplishment of some important public object which, with the privilege, private parties would undertake to accomplish, when without it they would not. The familiar instance is that of a bridge across a river where a highway for teams, etc., is greatly needed. Such a bridge constructed with the privilege in the proprietors to take toll might perhaps be expected to be unprofitable for a considerable period. The state at the time might be unwilling or unable to construct it, but perfectly willing to clothe individuals with the proper franchise for the purpose. These might be quite ready to accept the franchise if they could be protected against ruinous competition by the privilege being made exclusive, when otherwise they would refuse it. Under such circumstances, making the franchise exclusive may seem to the legislature the only condition upon which the needed public convenience may be obtained, and public considerations may apparently preponderate in favor of conceding it.

2. An exclusive privilege may be granted for a consideration received or to be received by the state, and which by adding to the resources of the state would diminish taxation, and thus compensate for any incidental inconvenience or loss felt or suffered by the people in consequence of the grant.

Thus a railroad company having a charter with exclusive features may accept it on condition of paying a certain proportion of its earnings to the state ; another corporation may pay a certain bonus for its charter ; a third may consent to pay an annual license fee in addition to the regular taxes ; and so on.

Many grants have been made on this principle, and in some cases the profit to the state has been large.

3. An exclusive privilege may be granted as a measure of regulation. Thus, in the case of some particular business it may be thought that it is so susceptible of abuses, so liable to be engaged in for the purposes of fraud or extortion, and furnishes such facilities for the one or the other, that the good of the community requires it to be either prohibited altogether or put in the hands of one or of a few persons, who shall first take out a state license under stringent conditions, and afterwards be subjected to a supervision which could not be extended if the business were open to every one. Taking the case of lotteries for an illustration, it might well be said, if lotteries are to be allowed at all, the opportunities they furnish for fraud are so great and so numerous, that the interest of the community would be better subserved by allowing a few persons only, of good reputation, to set up a lottery once a year, paying a reasonable license fee for the privilege, than to allow any man or combination of men to set up one at discretion. So in the case of slaughtering cattle for the markets of a large city, it might be said that if any considerable number of persons made this a business it might prove difficult if not impossible to prevent many nuisances, and since each person must have a separate place of business, there could be no such economy of labor and expense as might be possible with a concentration of the business in one or in a few establishments. Therefore it might be urged that to give an exclusive privilege to a single company or corporation, with a reasonable limitation of the charges which might be made to the dealers in meats, would on the one hand be a matter of general economy and public utility in that it would tend to reduce the cost of one of the necessaries of life, and on the other would assist in the preservation of the public health.

These, apparently, are the two principal grounds which must be advanced in support of the grant of an exclusive privilege when the purpose is one of regulation merely: to obtain more perfect and effectual police supervision and protection against disorders and nuisances, and to effect a general saving to the people in some matter of general or customary expense. The first ought generally to be subordinate, if the business regulated is a necessary and useful business. The police power of the state is so pervading and ample, and it is so plainly the duty of the state to exercise it in such a manner as to protect every man in following any lawful calling he may select, so long as he violates no public law and no rights of others, that for the state to give monopolies as a substitute for such protection, would be to make its own delinquency an excuse for invidious distinctions.

Can, then, a monopoly be granted where the sole or chief purpose is to effect a saving in the cost to the people of something which is an article of public and general need ? For the moment putting aside the consideration of the cases in which any exclusive privileges would be inadmissible, and conceding the right in some cases, let the grounds which must support them be examined. If a saving of individual expense can be a sufficient ground, it must be because the state has devolved upon it a duty to so shape its legislation as to effect such a saving, and the special privilege is a suitable means to the end. This brings us at once upon the ground which must be occupied by the legislature in limiting prices of wares or the charges for services : the reduction is the principal thing, and the legislature in accomplishing this will judge of the available and suitable means, and selecting these will employ them. In one case a direct act of legislation restricting charges might seem the. most suitable and effectual, as it would certainly aim most directly at the end sought. In another case the more practical mode might seem to be to authorize a monopoly. One city might perhaps grant an exclusive privilege in slaughtering cattle ; another, to accomplish the same end, might fix maximum prices by the carcass or the pound of the cattle slaughtered. Each would justify the regulation on the same ground.

It would seem, therefore, that those who claim a right in the state to control prices in certain cases should concede the power to create monopolies in the same cases, and whoever denies the one may deny the other. And if this be so, the question of the rightfulness of special privileges may perhaps be found so intimately connected with the question of state interference to regulate prices as to be incapable of separation.

18

Of the cases in which the legislature has sometimes granted special and exclusive privileges the following remarks may be made :

1. The right to grant these in certain cases not very dis. tinctly classified by any authority is generally conceded. They are always supposed to be granted on public grounds and jus. tifiable occasions, and as it is proper to grant them, so also it is proper to receive them, and the grantees could not, because of their exclusive nature, be subject to reproach or to invidious regulations.

2. Where the grant is to take up some employment which is not of general right, or to exercise some franchise, the author ity in the state to make it exclusive cannot be disputed. The state grants the right or the franchise to one man or body of men, and refuses to grant it to others; it stops with the one grant, as it may lawfully do. This remark assumes that the state constitution contains no express prohibition of exclusive privileges, as some of them do, and that the legislature is left unhampered in that regard.

3. The authority of the state to grant exclusive privileges in the ordinary occupations of life it must be quite safe to deny. If such an authority existed, there would be such a legislative supremacy over the business of the people as could at any time be employed to the destruction of any particular interest ; and this would be inconsistent with regulated liberty. As has already been stated, exclusive privileges of this sort were judi- cially declared unlawful and void in the time of Elizabeth, and have been so held and understood ever since. The cases in which exclusive privileges may be granted would therefore seem to be those which, on grounds already stated, are affected with a public interest.

Some remarks regarding licenses and license fees seem to be called for in this connection. An idea seems to prevail in some quarters that to require persons following any particular occu pation to take out a license is all that is essential to subject them to special regulations. This idea has no foundation. Taxes, in the form of license fees, may undoubtedly be imposed on all occupations, but a free state has no power to compel the taking out of a license as a condition precedent to the following of the ordinary pursuits of life. No despot ever claimed or exercised such a power, and no people not absolute slaves would tolerate its exercise for a single day. It will be remembered that the statutes enacted in the Southern States in 1865-6, which required freedmen to take out licenses for ordinary occupations, and to pay license fees therefor, were set aside, as establishing regulations which in effect compelled this class to submit to involuntary servitude.

Licenses may doubtless be required to be taken out by those employed in occupations the following of which is not a matter of right, and those which are "affected with a public interest" under the principles hereinbefore stated. But in the case of the ordinary and necessary avocations of the day, a license can cut no figure, and to require one to be taken, unless for the purpose of taxation, would be wholly inadmissible. It may be assumed that this statement requires no proof. To suggest the requirement that the farmer or the mechanic shall take out a license, unless for taxation, is sufficient to put before the mind the absurdity of any pretence of such authority.

Of monopolies not created by the legislature, the following may possibly exist:

1. One secured by threats or violence, or other unlawful means. Temporary control of the labor market is sometimes secured in this way; but this is of course illegal, and may be dealt with by the law. The temporary monopoly of the grain market of a particular town, accomplished as a means in gambling operations, may perhaps be classed under this head, inasmuch as it would be competent to make the means illegal by statute, if they are not so at the common law.

2. The monopoly which circumstances give to one by reason of the exceptional location and special advantages of his business, or by reason of his having lawfully acquired an exclusive ownership in something for which there is a public demand. In this, of course, there is nothing wrongful, nothing illegal. Does, then, the mere fact that one owns the whole supply of any thing, whether it be of a certain kind of property or of a certain kind of services, confer upon the state the authority to

119

interfere and limit the price he may set upon his wares or his services? To illustrate with a strong instance: Suppose in some state a single individual should own the only mine in the country of some metal important for use in the mechanical arts; would it be competent for the state, on the ground that competition with him was impossible, to restrict at discretion the price he should be allowed to charge for it? These questions, it will be perceived, present no problem concerning the authority of the state to appropriate exclusive rights, however acquired, under the eminent domain; they raise only the question of the right to limit the prices which individuals may charge for that which is conceded to be their own. Whoever shall undertake to answer these questions in the affirmative should be expected to show how the power may be harmonized with the general principles of free government.

3. The monopolies effected by combination of all who have the required wares or services for sale is of still a different nature. These exist in every part of the country, and it is generally assumed that the state is powerless to interfere and break them up when they limit their action to fixing prices by peaceable means, and when the business is not one over which the state may exercise exceptional power. Whatever may be thought of the wisdom or usefulness of trades-unions, the state, so long as they undertake only to regulate their own charges, is expected to abstain from interference. Letting others alone, these unions must be let alone by others. The state cannot say that their members shall take less than they will voluntarily consent to take; neither, on the other hand, can it compel others to pay more than they will voluntarily consent to pay. And the principle which must apply to them is general.

4. The case of " virtual " monopolies effected by superior industry, enterprise, skill, and thrift, it would seem, might be passed over in silence. When the person who by such means has secured special advantages has done so without the aid of any peculiar privileges, and with every other person at liberty under the law to compete with him, it is a misuse of terms to call his advantages a monopoly. Moreover, such a person is under the condemnation neither of the law nor of public sen-

timent. The qualities he has displayed in achieving his success are likely to bring him applause rather than censure, and he could not be put under restraint because of them, except upon grounds which would authorize the industrious, the enterprising, and the successful to be held in check whenever it was discovered that they were outstripping their fellows.

It seems plain, then, that there are limits which the state cannot overstep in interfering with private business under the pretence of regulation. The rules by which these limits may be determined are, from the nature of the case, incapable of being precisely indicated so as to preclude mistake or controversy, but the following ought to be unquestioned :

1. Whatever in modern times has generally been looked upon as being outside the sphere of legislation, should be regarded as finally eliminated from state authority. To do this is only to take notice of the steady growth of the free principles which have come from common-law rules and usages, and of their gradual expansion with the general advance in intelligence and independent thought and action among the people. The gradual transition from despotism to freedom has been mainly accomplished by the dropping out one by one of obnoxious and despotic powers, and by the recognition of the changes effected as permanent modifications of the constitutional system. Under this head may be classed the power in the state to create monopolies at will. For nearly three hundred years this power has been generally denied to the state, and to exercise and sustain it now is to discard whatever in freedom of industrial effort and competition has been gained in that period.

2. Wherever an extreme power has been supported by special and exceptional reasons, it should be regarded as gone when the reasons have ceased to exist. Thus, if in the founding of a colony it should be found necessary to employ the power of taxation to assist in the establishment and support of mills, yet as the power is an extreme power and only called into use by the extremity of the case, the power should be considered recalled when the necessity has ceased. And when the power to aid mills by taxation is gone, such exceptional power to regulate as must have sprung from it should be considered recalled also.

3. A questionable power, long disused, should be considered abandoned or recalled. Under this head may be instanced the power to fix the price of labor. Such a power belongs to barbarous and despotic times; it is inconsistent with genuine liberty, and it may be exercised to reduce men to virtual slavery. In the American States it has not been exercised since they passed from the colonial condition, and this of itself ought to be accepted as conclusive against the existence of the power. The American constitutions, in providing that no man shall be deprived of life, liberty, or property without due process of law, should be understood as protecting the liberty of employment with the same jealous care with which they protect against unlawful confinement behind bolts and bars.

It is not the purpose of this article to discuss the rulings of any court or to enter upon the examination of any decision. The discussion is upon general principles, and not upon particular cases. The discussion, however, may justify the cautionary remark, that it is a very dangerous thing to make by a precedent an inroad upon one of the fundamental principles of liberty, because precedents tend to beget a habit of thought and action which leads insensibly in the direction in which they point. Every doubtful precedent should therefore be carefully considered, and never accepted when it will not stand the test of settled rules of right. It has recently been said in a case in which a strong exercise of legislative power was under discussion, that the legislature may constitutionally restrict the charges which may be made for the use of property, because profits are not property, and, therefore, constitutional protection cannot be claimed for them. That is as much as to say, the constitution protects a man in his property, but not in the enjoyment of his property; he may have his farm, but the state may take away his profits by limiting his sales to the cost of production. A constitutional protection of this sort is a mere mockery. "The idea of property," says Mr. Bentham, "consists in an established expectation; in the persuasion of power to derive certain advantages from the object, according to the nature of the case." It is true that possible future profits are not property; they cannot be handled or enjoyed, and they may never be realized ; perhaps if one were wrongfully deprived of the opportunity to earn them, he might, because of their uncertainty, not be able to secure suitable redress; but the capability of property, by means of the labor or expense or both bestowed upon it, to be made available in producing profits, is a potential quality in property, and as sacredly protected by the constitution as the thing itself in which the quality inheres. He who denies this may on the same grounds say that while the right to labor is a constitutional right, yet that the profits of labor before they are realized are under legislative control, and may be kept down to prevent, as the early Massachusetts statute had it, " oppression" by " excessive wages."

THOMAS M. COOLEY.

THE

# AMERICAN LAW REVIEW.

MARCH–APRIL, 1895.

## PROPERTY — ITS RIGHTS AND DUTIES IN OUR LEGAL AND SOCIAL SYSTEMS.[1]

### CONSTITUTIONAL GUARANTIES.

From the first settlement of this country the right of private property, in both lands and chattels, has been recognized. It was expressly recognized in the charters of the colonies. The charters and constitutions of the original States contained in general or specific terms provisions for the security of property, as well as of life and liberty. As new States were formed and admitted into the Union, the constitution of each contained similar guaranties. Contracts between individuals are property, and their inviolability has been also secured by the organic law.

Accordingly, the constitution of each State of the American Union contains in terms or substance these provisions: "No person shall be deprived of life, liberty or *property* without due process of law." "Private property shall not be taken for public use without just compensation;" which means, as we all know, that private property shall not be compulsorily taken at all for private purposes, and that when taken for public use the compensation must be actual or in money. In the organic law of almost every State is the provision, borrowed from the

---

[1] Address delivered before the New York State Bar Association at Albany, January 15, 1895, by Hon. John F. Dillon.

VOL. XXIX.    11

Federal constitution, that the legislature shall not impair the obligation of contracts. These are limitations upon the States.

In the Federal constitution similar limitations exist upon the powers of the general government. For, by the Fifth Amendment, it is ordained that " No person shall be deprived of life, liberty or *property* without due process of law; nor shall private property be taken for public use without just compensation." And in the original constitution it was ordained " That no State shall pass any law impairing the obligation of contracts."

As a result of the experience of eighty years of national life came the great provision, born of the travail of our civil conflict, known as the Fourteenth Amendment. This placed the fundamental rights of life, liberty and property in the several States of the Union under the ultimate protection of the national government, for it ordained: " Section 1. Nor shall any State deprive any person of life, liberty or *property*, without due process of law; nor deny to any person within its jurisdiction the equal protection of the law."

Even in this assemblage of learned and distinguished lawyers, judges and legislators, this reference to the more important constitutional guaranties of private property and private contracts, will stand excused, for they constitute the basis of any consideration of the legal rights and legal duties of the owners of property, and they have also an important bearing upon the other aspect of the subject to which I shall refer, namely, the place of property in our social, as well as our legal system.

### THE ESSENTIAL FOUNDATIONS OF OUR SOCIAL FABRIC.

It was on these foundations that our government was laid. It was believed that these principles were those best adapted to insure civil security and social and individual welfare. These foundation-principles assert and imply the right of every man to enjoy personal liberty, to work out in his own way, without State domination, his individual destiny, and to enjoy, without molestation or impairment, the fruits of his own labor. Until lately the conviction among all our people has been general and unquestioned, that these great primordial rights, including the right of private property, whether gained by one's own toil or acquired by inheritance or will, were protected and made firm and secure by our republican system of government.    Such is the established social order.    But in our own day, the utility as well as the rightfulness of these fundamental principles are drawn in question by combined attacks upon them and upon the social fabric that has been builded upon them.    This assault upon society as now organized is made by bodies of men who call themselves, and are variously called, communists, socialists, anarchists, or by like designations.

Presumably movements of the magnitude which these organizations have attained, have some reason for their existence. They cannot be put down by denunciatory epithets, and are entitled to serious consideration as being at all events an organized protest of large numbers of men against the existing social order. This is a wide subject.    I shall make no attempt to discuss it in all its breadth.    My studies have not been such that I would feel competent to do so.    One common principle, however, underlies and pervades all of these various movements, and that is that the institution of private property is wrong and ought to be abolished or essentially curtailed.    I confine myself to this aspect of the subject.

While I do not deny that there is much in our social, industrial, and economic conditions that ought, if possible, to be improved, yet I maintain that the existing social order is sound at the core, and that the remedies proposed which involve, among other consequences, denial of the right of private prperty, or of its full enjoyment, are radically pernicious, or Utopian.    While I shall insist that private property is rightful, beneficial and necessary to the general welfare, and that all attempts to pillage or destroy it under whatever guise or pretext are as baneful as they are illegal, I shall insist with equal earnestness upon the proposition that such property is under many and important duties toward the State and society, which the owners too generally fail fully to appreciate.

### SOCIALISTIC ATTACKS ON PRIVATE PROPERTY.

At the outset let us see whether the statement that these associations question the right of private property and seek its abolition or essential impairment is justified, and at the same time let us also observe what they propose to do with it or substitute for it. " Communism," says the author of the article on that subject in the last edition of the Encyclopedia Britannica, " is the name that has been given to the schemes of social innovation which have for their starting point the attempted overthrow of the institution of private property."

" Socialism " is of various types, but in its original and pure from as it exists on the continent of Europe and generally elsewhere, the abolition of private property in lands and in the means of production is one of the declared ends in view, and the substitution of an economic system in which production is to be carried on in common under State control or supervision, for the common benefit, on some supposed equitable principle of distribution. This was the scheme of St. Simon, the earliest advocate of pure socialism.

Louis Blanc thus expounds his social theory: —

"The want and misery of man," he says, " must be corrected by a new organization of labor, which, abandoning individualism, *private property*, and private competition, the fundamentals of existing society, shall adopt fraternity as its controlling principle." [1]

Proudhon, the great anarch of French socialism, declared in 1840 his hostility to property and property owners in language whose intense ferocity has made it world-famous. " What is property? " he asked; and he answered, " Property is theft " (*La propriété c'est vol*), and " property owners are thieves."

The moderate branch of Belgian socialists advocate the national ownership of land, and as a means of effecting the change favor four measures, which are so suggestive and bear so strongly upon some views which I shall presently present that I quote them in this connection: —

" 1. Abolition of collateral inheritances.

" 2. Proclamation of the liberty of bequest.

" 3. A tax of twenty-five per centum upon all inheritances.

" 4. Enlightenment of the masses so that they shall soon

[1] Ely, French and German Socialism, p. 117.

demand the collectivity of the soil, or, as the English say, the nationalization of land." [1]

Such also are the demands of the "Belgian Labor Party" formed in 1885. That party "looks to the triumph of the political and social system known as collectivistic socialism. The fundamental principle of this system is common or collective ownership of all of the means of production, especially of capital and land. These to be attained through a series of partial and preparatory reforms: such as compulsory primary instruction; the attribution of corporate rights to workingmen's unions; accident, sickness and old age insurance; State ownership of the coal mines; the labor contract; limitation of the hours of labor; *suppression of collateral inheritance, and a heavier tax upon direct inheritance.*" [2]

Karl Mark, the founder of German social democracy and a man of great intellectual ability, declared that "the foundation of the capitalistic method of production is to be found in that theft which deprived the masses of their rights in the soil, in the earth, the common heritage of all." [3]  And so holds Lassalle. The more moderate Rodbertus limits the rightfulness of private property "to income alone." [4]

The "socialistic working-man's party," representing 25,000 members, declared themselves in 1875 in the Gotha Congress, among other things, in favor of "the transformation of the instruments of labor into the common property of society," and "demanded the establishment of socialistic productive associations with State help under democratic control of the laboring people." Encyclopedia Britannica, article "Socialism."

Mr. Kirkup, the intelligent author of the article on socialism in the Encyclopedia Britannica and of a work entitled, "An Inquiry into Socialism," 1887, and who represents what may be called the moderate type of English socialism, while insisting that there is nothing in the fundamental principles of socialism

---

[1] Ely, French and German Socialism, p. 151.

[2] Prof. M. Vauthier, of the University of Brussels, in an article on the new Belgian Constitution, in Pol. Science Quar., Vol. IX, p. 718, December, 1894.

[3] Ely, French and German Socialism, pp. 181, 202.

[4] Ely, p. 168.

in conflict with what is good in existing social institutions, yet admits that socialism contemplates "a new form of social organization based on a fundamental change in the economic order of society." In his view, socialism is "in economics the principle of co-operation or association," and looks to replacing the present economic order " by an economic system in which industry will be conducted with a collective capital and by associated labor and with a view to an equitable system of distribution." [1]

Even in this modified and moderate form, socialism involves a substantial overthrow of the existing social system and, it would seem, the abolition of private property in land and in the means of production.

So far as these various forms of social organizations represent dissatisfaction with the existing economic conditions and seek by peaceful means to improve those conditions, they are open to no criticism. They have been the means of effecting much good in securing the recognition of the unrestricted right of labor combination; shortening the hours of labor; the prohibition of Sunday labor, and of the employment of young children; securing the sanitary inspection of factories and workshops, and in many other ways promoting the welfare and interests of laborers and employes. But so far as these movements challenge the rightfulness of the fundamental basis of the existing political and social system, and advocate the reconstruction of society on the basis of the destruction or impairment of individual liberty and of private property and the substitution of State ownership of land and of the means of economic production, they are founded on illusory or false and pernicious principles, and merit general condemnation. Much, doubtless, there is in existing social, economic and industrial conditions which demands the most thoughtful consideration with a view to improve the condition of the poor or laboring class. But history and experience confirm the conclusions of reason, that the present social order, founded upon the doctrine of individual liberty, on the right freely to engage in any lawful business for profit, and on

[1] Pol. Science Quar., Vol. 3, p. 363.

the institution of private property, is destined to stand, and that all useful reforms and improvements in our social and economic conditions can be better accomplished by grafting them " on the old plant of private property, than by rooting it up altogether and planting the seedling of communism or socialism in its stead." [1]

### RIGHTFULNESS AND UTILITY OF PRIVATE OWNERSHIP OF LAND AND OTHER PROPERTY.

It is thus seen that the main point of socialistic attack is upon the rightfulness of private ownership of land. The main ground of attack is the specious proposition that land is in its nature common wealth, and ought to remain common to all the people, and that private ownership of property of any kind, if admissible at all, should be limited to property which is the direct and exclusive product of the individual labor that creates or produces it, and such ownership cannot rightfully extend to any value which it derives from the general growth of the community. This precise form of attack in terms limited to land, but in principle not capable of limitation to this species of property, takes for its euphemistic motto a demand for the nationalization of land, and for its ground and reason the assumption that land has been converted into private ownership by force or fraud or other indefensible means. This assumption, especially in our own country, is without the slightest foundation in fact. Our whole history, colonial, State, and national, is convincing proof of the rightfulness as well as of utility of private ownership of land.

After the discovery of America this vast continent was in a state of nature, sparsely occupied by barbarous tribes. Colonies were founded with the greatest difficulty, and involved a warfare with nature and savages. Land and its ownership was the great and only efficient inducement to colonization and settlement. At that time nobody dreamed that the ownership of land thus acquired was open to the slightest impeachment on ethical, political, or any other grounds. The hardships and difficulties

[1] Encycl. Brit. (9th ed.), art. Communism."

of the New England, and, indeed, all of the Atlantic colonists and settlers need not be recounted. They are matters of familiar history.

In considering this subject, let it be remembered that land in a state of nature is of little value. It must be reclaimed. Forests must be felled, wild beasts extirpated, savage tribes kept at bay, mines opened, fields plowed, fenced and cultivated, habitations erected; and to bring wild land into a productive state, and to make it of value, involved years of self-denial, privation and toil by the proprietor and his family. The establishment of our independence gave us vast tracts of unoccupied territory beyond the Alleghanies. The history of the conquest and settlement of this remote and almost unexplored wilderness, involving wars with Indians and struggles with nature, need not be here related. If one wishes to refresh his memory on this subject, let him read the graphic story of the settlement of Kentucky, Ohio and the country beyond, in Mr. Theodore Roosevelt's late work, "The Winning of the West." The pioneer went out with his rifle on his shoulder, and "before the land could be settled it had to be won." So in the region beyond the Mississippi, the Missouri and the Rocky Mountains, acquired from France. For forty years of my life I lived on the Mississippi, in a country just acquired from savages, where I have seen the process of settlement constantly going on. A wagon covered with white canvas, containing the pioneer's family and nearly all his earthly possessions, penetrated into a new and, in the main, timberless region. A cabin of logs, a sod house, or a "dug-out" on the side of a hill forms the first habitation, and years of labor were necessary to transform it into a comfortable home and make the land productive and valuable. Witnessing the hardships and toils of these pioneers and early settlers, I have been constrained a hundred times to say, although land was given by the government or sold for the small sum of $1.25 per acre, that in creating and establishing homes thereon under such circumstances, they earned it many fold.

PUBLIC POLICY OF THE UNITED STATES RESPECTING THE DISPOSTION
OF THE PUBLIC DOMAIN — " THE MAGIC OF PROPERTY."

Let it also be remembered that such ownership of the land
has been acquired under an uniform, settled and unchallenged
policy of the government originated and approved by the people
themselves. The wise policy was early adopted by the general
government of selling the public lands at almost nominal prices,
and afterward the still wiser policy of giving them away under
the homestead act, in order that they might be occupied and
cultivated in limited parcels by a large body of *owners*, and not
by tenants. I deny that this was either an unjust or a mistaken
policy. I maintain, on the contrary, that it was a policy founded
on the profoundest wisdom — the wisdom of having the landed
domain broken up into small holdings, and finding its way into
the hands of owners, who have thus the highest motive to develop
and improve it, and a conscious and permanent interest in the
government from which it was acquired, and by which it is protected. It is the real counterpoise of universal suffrage. It is
to-day our great bulwark against the revolutionary schemes of
socialism. This policy of late years has been questioned by
socialistic doctrinaires, and not long since I observed in one of
their publications a lament that the United States had not
retained the ownership of all the vast regions which now constitute forty prosperous States of the Union, occupied by multiplied
thousands of individual owners, and leased the land instead of
selling it. But I deny that it is better to have a land of tenants,
though the landlord be the government, than a land of owners.

Let me illustrate the wisdom of our policy of facilitating and
encouraging the private ownership of land by two or three
extracts from the celebrated travels of Arthur Young in France
just before the French Revolution, which bring out very strikingly what he so aptly describes as " the magic of property."
Under date of July 29, 1787, he writes:—

" Leaving the rocky country of Sauve, these active husband-
men who turn their rocks into scenes of fertility because, I suppose, their own, would do the same by the wastes if animated by
the same omnipotent principle " of ownership.

July 30. " The very rocks of this region are clothed with verdure. It would be a disgrace to common sense to ask the cause: the enjoyment of property *must* have done it. Give a man the secure possession of a bleak rock, and he will turn it into a garden; give him a nine years' lease of a garden, and he will convert it into a desert."

Again, November 7, 1787. " Walk to Rosendale [in Flanders]. Between the town and that place are a great number of neat little houses on the Dunes, built each with its garden, and one or two fields inclosed of most wretched *dune* sand, naturally as white as snow, but improved by industry. The magic of property turns sand to gold."

And why, let me ask, did the American colonist, pioneer, and settler undergo these hardships and make these sacrifices? What was the mainspring of his action? What his controlling motive and real purpose? The answer is obvious. It was to gratify a want that is instinctive in the nature of man and which is rightful in all its depth and scope, as well as beneficent in its operation and results. That want is a spot of earth that a man can call his own — and which by the magic of his affections he can transform into a place dearer to him than all others — a home — a home for himself and his family, where he and they may live in security, and which dying he may transmit to those who are bound to him by the sacred ties of blood and affection. He has thus a title to the land, whether in town or country, which rests upon an undisputable foundation of justice, as well as of sound public policy. The opportunity thus to acquire it was equally open to all; it was acquired by the consent of all; its acquisition wronged no one and was beneficial to all, and I insist that such an owner has the highest of all titles, namely, that its real and substantial value came from the sweat of his own brow, and is the product of his own labor.

And now we are met by the teachers and advocates of socialistic theories who say that all this is wrong, that such ownership is theft; that land belongs of inalienable right to all the people and that it or its full enjoyment ought to be shared by all; and so, on the same principle, as to all other property of whatsoever nature, at least all property which has a productive value — that is, property which yields a return without manual labor bestowed upon it.

Such theories are in conflict with the existing scheme of organized society, and if carried into execution destructive of it. It is not my purpose, nor have I the time, to enter into any extended argument to justify the principle or the institution of private property. Briefly it may be said that it is supported on three grounds — historically, as belonging to every civilization that has advanced beyond the early period of common ownership; ethically, as being mediately or immediately the acquest of labor; and, thirdly, on the ground of utility or the common good. Private property, rightfully acquired, accompanied and limited with just conceptions of its duties, has its justification and support in the nature of man, and the good of society. Man longs for individual ownership. Property therefore connects itself inseparably with the personality of its owner. His dominion over it arises from his personal rights in and concerning it. Properly and legally regarded, the rights of the owner are personal rights, and not that incomprehensible abstraction called the right of things. Ihering puts this in a striking way : " In making the object my own, I stamped it with the mark of my own person; whoever attacks it attacks me; the blow which strikes it strikes me, for I am present in it. *Property is but the periphery of my person extended to things.*" [1]

Labor is the main element of the right. Occupation is necessary in order to bestow labor upon it, and the right of ownership and dominion springs from it, and is justified by labor, and possession is the essential prerequisite and condition of labor. " Only through a lasting connection with labor," says Ihering, " can property maintain itself fresh and healthy. Only at this source is it seen clearly and transparently to the very bottom to be what it is to man." " Communism thrives only in those quagmires in which the true idea of property is lost. At the source of the stream it is not found." [2]

The institution of private property, moreover, is justified by

[1] The Struggle for Law (Am. ed.), 55; Pol. Sci. Quar., vol. 1, p. 604.
[2] Ihering Struggle for Law (Am. ed.), pp. 49, 50; Pol. Sci. Quar., vol. 1, p. 605.

its utility. It arouses man from his natural inertia and love of ease; it induces self-denial, and is the only motive that is certain to enlist his ambition and activity, and to call forth the highest exercise of his powers. Viewed from a mere social or economic stand-point, the man who subdues the wilderness by his labor converts a waste into a productive land, makes the field bloom and blossom into the harvest, does not injure, but benefits, his fellow-men. The benefits to the individual from the ownership thus acquired, and the labor thus bestowed, overflow the boundaries of private proprietorship and inure to the advantage of the whole community. Such a proprietor is a benefactor, and not a robber. The community owes him as much as he owes the community.

### ATTACKS UPON PRIVATE PROPERTY THROUGH THE EXERCISE OF POWER OF TAXATION.

Socialistic organizations in all their forms, being hostile to private property or its full enjoyment, their attacks upon it assume various shapes. I have no time to notice these at length. The most insidious, specious and therefore, dangerous, are those that are threatened, attempted or made in the professed exercise of the State's power of taxation. Forasmuch as the power to tax is supposed to involve the power to destroy, it is boldly avowed by many socialistic reformers, and it is implied in the schemes of others, that the power of taxation is an available and rightful means to be used for the express purpose of correcting the unequal distribution of wealth, and that this may be done without a violation of the essential or constitutional rights of property. Such taxes, may be, amongst others, in the shape of a progressive income or progressive property tax, or both; or a tax on the transfer or devolution of property, limited in amount only by the legislative will, that is to say, not limited at all, so that if the heir or successor gets any thing, it is by legislative grace, and not of right.

Taxation in any of these forms, reasonable and proportional in its character, imposed as a *bona fide* means of raising revenues to help defray the public charges, may doubtless be levied, and under these limitations, presents merely questions of political

expediency.  But when taxes, so-called, are imposed, not as
mere revenue measures, but for the real purpose of reaching the
accumulated fruits of industry, and are not equal and reasonable,
but designed as a forced contribution from the rich for the benefit
of the poor, and as a means of distributing the rich man's property among the rest of the community — this is class legislation
of the most pronounced and vicious type; is, in word, confiscation and not taxation.   Such schemes of pillage are indefensible
on any sound principle of political policy, violative of the constitutional rights of the property owner, subversive of the existing social polity, and essentially revolutionary.  Let us consider
this for a moment.

The State is a commonweal.   It exists for the general good,
for rich and poor alike.   It knows or ought to know no classes.
Universal suffrage is grounded upon this idea.   All vote because
all have an interest in the State, and especially because the personal rights of individuals as distinguished from their property
rights, are matters of universal concern.   The blessings and
benefits of the State are intended to diffuse themselves over
all.   Political duties should ever go hand in hand with political
rights, and it is a serious and even dangerous mistake to permit
them to become separated.   The duty to support the State rests
upon all; and, therefore, the exemption of any class from this
duty while he enjoys the privileges of citizenship, and especially
the elective franchise, may produce, at all events tends to produce,
grave consequences.  The one thing to be feared in our democratic
republic, and therefore to be guarded against with sleepless vigilance, is class power and class legislation.   Discriminating legislation for the benefit of the rich against the poor, or in favor of
the poor against the rich, is equally wrong and dangerous.
Class legislation of all and every kind is anti-republican and
must be repressed.  If universal suffrage shall be guilty of such
short-sighted folly as to seek in the guise of tax laws to
deprive the owner of his property with a view to distribute it among the community, or shall frame our tax laws,
whether imposing direct or indirect taxation, in such manner as
to exempt any class from bearing a proportional and just share
of the public burdens, and distribute and impose those burdens,

either wholly or disproportionately, upon the rich, the results of such injustice will react upon the whole community. Such a course would excite class antagonism, and would also tend to arrest the accumulation of property or cause its flight to other States and countries; it would in these and other ways injuriously affect the general welfare, and the real interests of the laboring and non-taxpaying class of the community.

THE STATE'S TRUE FUNCTION — PATERNALISM — ILLEGAL COMBINATIONS, POOLS AND TRUSTS.

The essential end of government is the common good of all the people who compose it. The State exists, not for the special benefit of any one or more classes less than the whole, but for the commonweal of all. Its benefits must not be denied to any class, or to any person of any class; all who compose the State, the rich and the poor, the plutocrat and the proletariat, all who share in the associated life, are each and equally entitled to the protection, support and care of the State, whose blessings, like the air, the dew, the rain and the sunlight, should fall upon all without discrimination or preference. The State is founded primarily upon the necessity of the individual that his just rights shall be protected from invasion by others, but the complex organization of social or associated life which we call the State, exists for the higher end of the common benefit by enabling each member to enjoy, not only life and liberty, but to pursue happiness, that is, by aid of the State, whatever its form, to develop and perfect his individual and social life and well-being. The scope or limit of the legitimate function of the State in the attainment of the ends or aims of its existence, cannot be conclusively defined or unalterably marked out in advance. All of the many attempts of this character have failed, and from the nature of the case will ever fail. One class of thinkers, extreme individualists, hold that nothing is more pernicious than over activity on the part of the State, which is paternalism, or tending toward it; and hence they maintain that the State's function should be narrowly confined, being principally limited to protection and security of the acknowledged legal rights of individuals; any extension beyond this being regarded as an unwarranted encroachment upon individual liberty. Others, such as extreme nationalists, favor the largest extension of the State's functions, holding that the State should assume the ownership and control of transportation, of capital, and all of the means of productive industry, becoming the general or universal father or guardian of the people in their social or economic relations. Between these extremes are many shades or degrees of opinion as to the true limits of the State's function. I cannot but regard all such *a priori* speculations as of doubtful utility. If the true end, purpose and justification of the existence of the State is the highest development and happiness of the individual and the common good of all, it must be left to experience to determine, from time to time, on the special exigencies and circumstances of the situation, the character and extent of the State's regulation or positive intervention to promote the common and permanent good of society.

### Remedy for Harmful Trusts and Combinations.

These principles are applicable and should be applied in dealing with the modern form of combination known by the name of " trusts."

Industrial problems are constantly assuming new shapes. Transportation and production are largely carried on by corporate aggregations of capital. This cheapens cost and prices and to this extent inures to the public advantage. Competition, sometimes destructive (being often the death as well as the life of trade), is met by combinations which assume the forms of pools or trusts, so-called. These combinations are professedly intended to maintain and steady reasonable prices and to prevent the evils of ruinous competition. When limited to this end, such combinations are not necessarily injurious, and may be beneficial. But they are capable of being used to destroy, not merely to regulate, competition and to increase, for a time at least, prices beyond those necessary to yield a fair return. In these and other ways the injuries to the public may far outweigh the advantages, in which case the question is, What is the remedy? The socialistic theorist says, let the State intervene and assume the ownership of our transportation systems and of the leading productive industries. This is obviously the substitution of social industrialism for the existing order, and implies the surrender to the State of individual's liberty of action.

But no such drastic or heroic remedy — a remedy immeasurably worse than the disease — is at all needful to secure the public welfare. The dominion of the State over the actions of its corporations is supreme within the limits of their constitutional rights, which are mainly rights of property. The State may, with strong hand, suppress every form of combination, whether corporate or individual, which proves to be hurtful to the general good. The State can bridle its corporate agencies, and keep them at all times under effective and salutary control; it can forbid all persons, whether corporate or natural, from courses of action harmful to the public welfare; and thus it is seen that the visionary scheme of social industrialism looking to the State's assumption of private property and of the means of production, and the consequent creation of a socialistic Grand Mogul and the resulting encroachment on the rights and liberties of the citizen, lacks the support of any legal or actual necessity. The State's plain duty is to see that the just interests of the public are protected and secured so far as the law can do this consistently with the rights of others. The real test of the usefulness or hurtfulness of combinations like pools and trusts is experience. It may be the best policy to regulate them, or it may be the best policy to destroy them. The principle on which the State may intervene is plain. If, and in so far as, such combinations shall be found tending to create monopolies, to destroy legitimate and useful competition, thus interfering with the free industry of the people; to yield undue profits at the expense of the consumer, thereby facilitating the creation of enormous private fortunes and the production of inequality of wealth — if such shall be seen or found to be their effect, the State has the power to correct the evil, and it would be its duty to call that power into vigorous activity.

NEEDED REVISION OF OUR LAWS RELATING TO INHERITANCE AND POWER OF TESTAMENTARY DISPOSITION — AMERICAN AND FRENCH SYSTEMS COMPARED.

I come now to consider a phase of the subject of property in its relations to the State and to our social system, which I regard as of the first importance. It is one which has heretofore received among us, I am persuaded, far less attention than it deserves. I regret that the time at my disposal will not enable me to present it with the requisite fullness. I refer to the laws of this country relating to the descent and distribution of property on the death of the owner, and to those relating to the owner's power of disposition during his life and by last will and testament. They are essentially founded, with some modifications, on the feudal and aristocratic notions on these subjects which we derived from England. I regret that the subject which I proceed to consider failed to receive attention in the recent Constitutional Convention in this State.

From the stand-point of political economy and of provident political polity, the existence of enormous private fortunes is of evil tendency, in that it is injurious in its effect upon the owners, inducing idleness and luxury in them and their children, and injurious in its consequences to the community in accumulating in a few hands so large a portion of the property and wealth, which ought to be more generally distributed — thus tending to divide society into classes and to separate by an impassable chasm the rich and the poor. Moreover, the power of the owner of a colossal fortune is so great as to be capable, in bad hands, of much abuse. A wise and provident policy, therefore, dictates that the statesmen and legislators of the present should, by constitutional and legislative provisions, so far as may be consistent with individual liberty and the just rights of property, so shape our policy as to secure, by its continuous and silent operation, as wide a distribution of property as is practicable, thereby preventing the concentration of vast fortunes in a few hands, especially the division and crystallization of society into classes of which property or wealth is the dividing line, and above all into caste-classes, in which the condition of the poor is permanent, and without prospect of improvement. Such a condition is, of all others, the most efficient cause of socialistic movements. Heretofore in this country land has been so abundant and population so sparse as to obscure the importance of this subject. But our available public land is now almost exhausted, population is already pressing upon the means of subsistence, suffrage is universal, the non-property-owner is becoming relatively a much larger part of the community. These are considerations which make the subject of our laws relating to property, and especially real property, as respects its descent, and the power of the owner to fetter it by trusts or dispose of it by deed or will, as he sees fit, one of practical moment. It is very clear that existing laws do not prevent the concentration of wealth. Mainly upon the data supplied by the last census, Mr. George K. Holmes concludes that 4,047 millionaires in the United States own " about one-fifth of the nation's wealth," and " possess about seven-tenths as much as do 11,593,887 families." After giving the details he thus sums up the result: " Twenty per cent of the wealth of the United States is owned by three-hundredths of one per cent of the families; fifty-one per cent by nine per cent of the families (not including millionaires); seventy-one per cent by nine per cent of the families (including millionaires), and twenty-nine per cent by ninety-one per cent of the families." [1]

The right of the owner of property to transmit the same on his death by descent or will, as well as the corresponding right of the heir or devisee to take the same, pursuant to the provisions of the statute regulating the subject of inheritance and of testamentary disposition, has been universally recognized in our laws. By these laws, if the owner dies intestate, his property goes, subject, in general, to dower, curtesy, the homestead right and a few similar provisions, in equal proportions, to his nearest relatives. But by these laws also the owner is given the absolute power to dispose of his property by will as he pleases. The scope of the power is such that the parent may, at his pleasure, with or without cause, disinherit his children entirely,

---

[1] Pol. Sci. Quar., vol. 8, p. 593, Dec., 1893.

or give his property to them in unequal shares. He may tie it up by deed or will in private trusts to be used and enjoyed as he may direct, for long periods of time after his death, the only restriction being that he shall not infringe the law of perpetuities; and for charitable uses without limitation as to time. This almost unlimited power of the owner of property to control its disposition as his whim or pride or passion may dictate, to the extent of disinheriting his children without cause, and this right of the nearest relative however remote to take the whole estate however great, to the exclusion of the State, are very marked characteristics in our laws concerning the descent and devolution of the property; and they have not escaped searching criticism as being unjust to the children of the owner and contrary to the public policy, since they tend to the concentration of wealth in the heir and particularly in the favored devisee or legatee.

And it is precisely at this point that property, or the right to transmit or receive it on the owner's death, is made the subject of socialistic attack. It is argued that there is no such thing as a natural right of inheritance, or natural right to dispose of property by will, since each of these rights rests, it is said, alone upon statute or positive law. It must be admitted that many writers and some courts have so declared. For example, in sustaining the constitutional validity of a collateral inheritance tax act, the judge who delivered the opinion of the Court of Appeals of Virginia broadly declared: " The right to take property by devise or descent is the creature of the law and secured and protected by its authority. The legislature might, if it saw proper, restrict the succession to a decedent's estate, either by devise or descent, to a particular class of his kindred, say to his lineal descendants and ascendants; it might impose terms and conditions upon which collateral relations may be permitted to take it; or it may, to-morrow, if it please, absolutely repeal the statute of wills and that of descents and distributions and declare that upon the death of a party, his property shall be applied to the payment of his debts, and the residue appropriated to public uses. Possessing this sweeping power over the whole subject, it is difficult to see upon what ground its right to appropriate a modicum of the estate, call it a tax or what you will, as the condition upon which those who take the estate shall be permitted to enjoy it, can be successfully questioned."[1]

So, in a case in Massachusetts, Chief Justice Gray said:, "The power to dispose of property by will is neither a natural nor a constitutional right, but depends wholly on statute, and may be conferred, taken away, or limited and regulated in whole or in part by the legislature," and the court held that it was competent for a homestead statute making provision for the widow to limit to that extent the owner's power of testamentary disposition.[2]

It is obvious, if the language of the writers and judges referred to be taken without restriction, that as against the legislative power of the State the right of the owner of property, though held in fee or absolute ownership, would be little if any thing more than an estate or right for life, since the State by denying the right of the owner to transmit, could appropriate the property to its own use, thereby constituting itself the universal successor, and could make this policy effectual by prohibiting gifts, deeds or donations which contravened it. I may be permitted to doubt, however, if the question shall ever arise for solemn judgment under our American constitutions, whether the legislature, while doubtless having full power to regulate the right of succession, can deny it by enactments which are not intended as regulations of the right, or measures of reasonable and equal taxation to raise revenue for public uses, but which are confiscatory in their nature, and intended to appropriate the property to the public use. The doubt is much strengthened by the observation of the present chief justice of Massachusetts in the very recent case of Minot v. Winthrop,[3] sustaining the validity of the Collateral Inheritance Tax Act of that State. And yet I feel constrained to declare that our laws respecting the subject of the owner's power over his property extending to the disinheriting of his children without cause, and apportioning his property unequally among them, as well as his power to tie it up in private trusts and keep it out of commerce and circulation to

---

[1] Eyre v. Jacob, 14 Grat. (Va.) Rep. 1858.

[2] Brettum v. Fox, 100 Mass. 234.

[3] 38 N. E. Rep. 513.

the extent now allowed, are open to grave objections on the ground that they are, in their practical operation, frequently unjust to the heir, and tend to produce those inequalities of fortune which in a republican government should at all events never be encouraged or favored by legislation.

The tenor of this address makes it scarcely necessary to say that I am opposed to any confiscation or appropriation of property on the owner's death for the use of the State, but what I mean is that the laws should be so changed that in their constant and unbroken operation they should secure the equal rights of the children against the ancestor's present absolute power, should tend more effectually to keep the property in free circulation, and to prevent as far as practicable its concentration in single hands. We ought to distinguish between the parent's dominion over his property as respects his children and as respects strangers to his blood. Strangers have no natural claim to a provision out of the donor's or testator's property, and they take through the power of disposition which the law recognizes as an attribute of ownership. The child has all of the rights which spring from this source, and, in addition, those which spring from the parental relation.

The parent is under a natural obligation to provide for his children. He is responsible for their being. In my view, his moral obligation does not cease with their attaining their majority. On the contrary, it is an obligation of perpetual duration. No parent is ever able fully to discharge it. Those writers who maintain that there is no such thing as a natural right in the child to inherit the parent's property, and no such thing as a natural duty on the part of the parent to provide for the child out of his property, take a position in conflict with the universal sentiments and convictions of mankind.

### The French Law of Forced Heirship and Prohibition of Trust Estates — Its Policy and Practical Operation.

For a government founded upon republican institutions and which aims at their perpetuation, the French law is in its fundamental provisions, policy and practical operation, superior to ours. The estates are simpler, more effectual provisions are made to prevent property being kept out of commerce, and also to prevent its accumulation in the hands of single owners. This policy dates from and was the direct fruit of the Revolution of 1789, and assumed its complete shape by the law of November 14, 1792, which prohibited the disposition of property by deed or will whereby one person is to hold it for the benefit of some other person; in short, speaking generally, it prohibits all of the trust estates of the English chancery system. The policy of preventing the suspension of the power of alienation — that is, of securing the right freely to dispose of property and of preventing the concentration of property in single ownership — is effectuated by provisions in the Code Napoleon which restrict the disposition of property by the owner by donation, or transfers either *inter vivos* or *mortis causa.* The principal of these restrictions are:

(*a*) The institution of forced heirship.

(*b*) The prohibition of substitutions, *fidei commissa*, or what we denominate trust estates.

Both of these provisions are important and work to the same end. The doctrine of forced heirship, in the French law, proceeds upon the principle that the relation between ascendants and descendants, and between a child without children and its parents, originates duties so sacred that the law steps in and compels their performance. This it does by making all descendants the forced heirs of a specified portion of the ancestor's property, and which right the ancestor cannot defeat by deed or will, or in any other manner. As to this reserved or legitimate portion, the *legitime*, as it is called, the descendants have the substantial rights of creditors, and can set aside all dispositions in fraud of their rights. Donations *inter vivos* and *mortis causa* may not exceed one-half of the testator's property, where he has but one child, a third where he has two children, and a fourth where he has three or more; and not exceeding a certain portion where the disposer having no children, leaves a father or mother. Under the name of children are included descendants of whatever degree *per stirpes* and not *per capita.* As to the disposable portion, the testator may, for any lawful purpose, do therewith as he pleases, provided the donees are capable of taking it. The principle, you will observe, effectually compels the equal division of the *legitime* or non-disposable estate on the death of the owner, an effect which it is not within his power to thwart.

The prohibition of substitutions, or trust estates, by the famous law of November 14, 1792, was founded in part upon the policy of preserving the simplicity of titles, and to keep the property in commerce, but largely upon the policy that such trusts were aristocratical in their nature and repugnant to the principles established by the revolution, in that they tended to maintain large holdings of land in great families, and to perpetuate in the eldest son or head of the family the *eclat* of a great name, and were prejudicial in these and many other ways to the public and general good.

All the great commentators on the French Code recognize that the law of November 14, 1792, which abolished substitutions and trust estates in France, was based on political reasons as well as on motives of sound political economy. Thus, Laurent says :[1] " Substitutions were the most solid foundation of the aristocracy, and the nobility was inseparable from the throne. * * * Being closely allied to the aristocratic constitution of the old regime, they had necessarily to fall with the old monarchy. The law of November 14, 1792, prohibited all substitutions; they were incompatible with the democratic regime established in 1789; the nobility being abolished, it was necessary to destroy the power which it drew from its immense possessions; and for this reason the law of 1792 was given a retroactive effect. When Napoleon, unfaithful to the spirit of 1789, re-established the monarchy, he desired, also, in imitation of the old regime, to re-establish substitutions. Hence the *majorats* (landed estates descending with a title) created by the Senate decree of August 14, 1800. The new edition of Civil Code, published under the empire, sanctioned this return to the past. Vain effort! The tide of events cannot be turned backward. In Belgium the *majorats* fell with the empire. In France the restoration also tried to bring back the old regime, with its nobility and its sub-

---

[1] Vol. 14, § 389.

stitutions. The law of May 17, 1826, was as powerless for this purpose as the Imperial Act of 1806. The future belongs to the democracy. Whether one rejoices or deplores this fact, it is a providential fact, against which all the efforts of the men of the past have been broken in shipwreck. All these reactionary laws have been repealed, and the democratic wave rolls on increasing. Room must be made for it in society or it will overflow and destroy everything."

Marcade says : [1] " There is not much legislation which has undergone so many changes as that relative to *fidei commissa* substitutions, and the cause of it is that there is no other subject than this more closely allied to governmental forms, and holding a more intrinsic relation to political systems."

Demolombe says : [2] " Among all the subjects of private law, substitutions are most closely attached to public law, and therefore they must inevitably receive the shock of the revolutions which take place in the form of the government and the political system of the country. Hence the history of substitutions in the last half century is nothing more than the history itself of our changes of constitutions."

These laws having been in operation in France for 100 years, their effect is a matter not of speculation but of demonstration. It is thus stated by Brodrick: " Of some 7,500,000 proprietors, about 5,000,000 are estimated to average six acres each, while only 50,000 average 600 acres. This *morcellement* is the direct and foreseen consequence of the partible succession enforced by the Code Napoleon. With some rare exceptions all of the great properties have been gradually broken up. * * * It is a significant fact that neither under the first empire, nor under the restored dynasty of the Bourbons, nor under the Orleanist monarchy, nor under the new Republic has any serious attempt been made to repeal this law bequeathed to France by the authors of the Revolution. It is a guaranty for the respect of property; it conduces to industry and thrift." [3]

The world knows that the wealth and prosperity of France to-day are simply amazing.

[1] Vol. 3, § 456.
[2] Vol. 18, § 62.

[3] English Land and Landlords, chap. iii.

Aware that the French law on the subject of property had been adopted in Louisiana and had been in effect there for nearly a century, I inquired of a distinguished lawyer of New Orleans, Mr. Charles Howard Farrar, concerning its practical operation in that State. He commends the law in unqualified terms. He says: "Under this system no great estates have grown up in Louisiana."

He adds these forcible observations: "Apply these rules to the great estates in New York and elsewhere, where the common law prevails — estates whose portentous dimensions increase with each generation and hang like a shadow over the welfare and prosperity of the republic — and see what would become of them in two or three generations. They would be dissipated so as to be unnoticeable. This then appears to me to be the remedy for the much complained of accumulation of wealth, in a few hands. No people on earth suffered in this regard more than the French people. They found the remedy through a baptism of blood and a carnival of horrors. Will the American people be wise enough to profit by their experience, and wipe out by peaceful legislation the pernicious doctrines of omnipotent power in the testator and of uses and trusts, which persist, like some voracious saurian, from a feudal and aristocratic into a democratic era, devouring the many to exalt the one; or must the red flag of anarchy storm their strongholds before they learn the wisdom of history."

I now leave this important subject. I commend it to your study, examination and reflection. A lawyer who consents to address the bar of the great State of New York, which has left such a deep impress upon the laws and jurisprudence of this country, ought to feel that he has something to say. If this address has any value, it is to be found in the lessons which it is possible to draw from the considerations which I have so imperfectly presented. I do not say that we can or ought to adopt the French law *en bloc*. I only mean to say that, in my judgment, it is possible to introduce into our laws such amendments and changes as will tend, without interference with the just rights of property to make those laws more simple, to insure more effectually the free circulation of property, to prevent the concentration of vast estates in the hands of single owners. Stupidity and selfishness may shut their eyes and fold their arms until red-handed revolution rouses them like a fire alarm in the night from their indifference. True statesmanship looks at the future as well as the present, and makes its chief concern the shaping of peaceful policies so that progress may be assured and revolution may be avoided.

### THE SOCIAL AS DISTINGUISHED FROM THE LEGAL DUTIES OF PROPERTY.

I have thus far spoken only of the legal rights and the corresponding legal duties of property, namely, duties in the lawyer's sense that their performance is or may be enforced by the power of the State. But an important aspect of my subject remains to be noticed. I refer to what, in lawyers' phrase, are termed the imperfect duties of property owners, meaning hereby that they are imperfect only in the sense that, lying beyond the boundaries of civil law, their performance is not enforced or enforceable by the tribunals of the State. These may, for convenience, be called the social as distinguished from the legal obligations of property owners.

In this domain the example and doctrines of the Heavenly Dreamer of the Gallilean Hills, the Divine Teacher, the Blessed Saviour, have unrestricted scope and are destined, as the world grows up to their fuller conception, to a wider and more beneficent sway. The good of His children, who comprise the whole family of man, was the sum total, the beginning and the end of the divine philosophy which was exemplified in His life and teachings. He went about doing good. The fine expression of Kant, that " Humanity is the true end of all our efforts," is essentially borrowed from Him of whom his great apostle said, " He was touched with the feelings of our infirmities." " We, then, that are strong ought to bear the infirmities of the weak." " Come unto me all ye that labor and are heavy laden and I will give you rest." The first beatitude, the opening words of the Sermon on the Mount, was the saying, at once bold and compassionate, " Blessed are the poor." And afterward came the promises of infinite preciousness : " Whoever shall give to drink unto one of these little ones a cup of cold water only in the name of a disciple, verily I say unto you, he shall in no wise lose his reward." "Inasmuch as ye have done this unto one of these, even the least, ye have done it unto me."

If I were required to sum up in one sentence the lesson which existing conditions ought to teach us, it would be the Christian lesson that we must increase and deepen and quicken the sense of the responsibility of society for the welfare of all its members.

The possessor of a large fortune, no matter how honestly acquired, and however firm and exclusive in legal theory is the right of ownership, and however fully he may discharge his legal duties, is yet a debtor to the community. His right and title to his property are of positive institution. The power of the State has protected and preserved it, and the existence of organized society has conferred upon it its chief value. In short, property has in an important sense a public as well as a private side.

The owner of a great fortune owes to society manifold obligations which are entirely beyond the range of legal cognizance. Such a fortune gives power, and power always involves correlative duties. Over some of these let me cast a rapid glance. I do not stop to mention that a rich man ought to avoid the vulgarity of an ostentatious display and parade of wealth. Riches suddenly acquired are especially obnoxious, and every body tries to avoid the splatter and splash of " newly mounted pride." Bearing himself ever with modesty, it is pre-eminently a rich man's duty to identify himself with the communal life in the midst of which he lives and bring to bear for its good the power and influence which wealth always gives. If he is wise he will even cultivate popularity, not by cheap arts but by considerate, active and daily beneficence. The pulsations of his life will be felt for good throughout the community. It is a duty of perpetual obligation on the part of the strong to take care of the weak, of the rich to take care of the poor; and the rich man who fails to interest himself actively in education, in public improvements, and public and private charities, falls not only below the ideal of good citizenship, but he fails to discharge toward society the obligations which spring from the mere possession of large wealth. In no other way can the envy, and even hostility, of the poor toward the rich be so successfully repressed; and therefore the recognition of these social duties not only satisfies a moral obligation, but it is a course founded on a policy of the profoundest wisdom. A public sentiment is rapidly forming which views as a reproach a very rich man who lives or living dies without connecting himself and his name and memory, by substantial benefactions, with works educational, philanthropic or charitable, for the benefit and welfare of his fellow-men. I say it with emphasis, that wealth has some important lessons yet to learn and put into practice. Our very rich men have learned how to gain wealth. They must now learn the more difficult lesson how to use it. Man lives not by bread alone.

If our statesmen and legislators shall adopt the line of policy which I have endeavored to set forth, and if the possessors of large properties shall co-operate with them in the mode I have indicated, we may turn our gaze toward the future of our beloved country, not with gloomy forebodings, but with serene cheerfulness and with the highest hopes. The institution of private property will remain, and there will be no revolutionary overthrow of the existing state or social fabric by any mode of socialistic or communistic attack. But if we are blind to history and to duty, if we idly drift and do nothing, then, with an overcrowded population pressing with augmenting force upon the means of subsistence, with the hopeless separation of the rich and the poor into distinct, hostile and incommunicable classes without common interests and common sympathies, and with the growth of a *proletariat* armed with the ballot in one hand and a gun in the other, the prediction of LaSalle, the great orator of German iconoclastic socialism, may come to pass — may within the next century come to pass, even in this goodly heritage of ours: " The goddess of revolution, after the lapse of a certain time, will force an entrance into our social structure, amid the convulsions of violence, with wild streaming locks and brazen sandals on her feet."

# THE RAILROAD QUESTION REVISITED

## CHICAGO, MILWAUKEE & ST. PAUL RAILWAY V. MINNESOTA AND CONSTITUTIONAL LIMITS ON STATE REGULATIONS

JAMES W. ELY, JR.

Few issues more vexed Americans during the Gilded Age than the regulation of railroads. America's first big business, the railroads wielded enormous economic power and by the end of the nineteenth century represented 10 percent of national wealth.[1] Farmers and other local shippers often viewed railroads as an exploitative monopoly and blamed them for excessive and discriminatory charges. They repeatedly clamored for regulation of the freight and passenger rates fixed by railroad companies. Agricultural interests in the Great Plains states were particularly active in seeking regulatory legislation. Railroad investors and managers, on the other hand, opposed regulatory laws and

James W. Ely, Jr., is professor of law and history at Vanderbilt University. The author of numerous scholarly papers on legal and constitutional history, he is the author or editor of seven books, most recently The Guardian of Every Other Right: A Constitutional History of Property Rights (1991).

[GPQ 12 (Spring 1992): 121-134]

defended their autonomy to determine rates. They feared that governmental control of rates would benefit shippers and farmers at the expense of the railroads by imposing unreasonably low charges. Moreover, they asserted that regulation of rates would likely impair capital investment and thus stifle railroad growth and economic development.

Sectional division was evident in the legislative response to the growth of railroads. The eastern states created advisory commissions that could make reports and recommend reforms but had no enforcement power or authority to set transportation rates.[2] Skeptical about the efficacy of competition, western farmers demanded more stringent governmental control of railroad operations. Their growing resentment was heightened when western railroads passed under the control of eastern investors. During the 1870s the Granger movement spearheaded the drive for the initial wave of more radical state railroad regulations. Many midwestern and southern state legislatures enacted so-called Granger laws to control the prices charged by railroads and related utilities, such as grain elevators and warehouses. They also established powerful commissions to supervise railroad operations and enforce regulatory laws.[3]

In *Munn v. Illinois* (1877) the Supreme Court adopted a deferential attitude toward legislative authority to regulate economic activity. Sustaining an Illinois law that set the rate for storing grain in Chicago elevators, Chief Justice Morrison R. Waite ruled that "when private property is devoted to a public use, it is subject to public regulation." Whether this public interest doctrine applied to a particular enterprise was considered a matter for legislative judgment. Although recognizing that the owner of property "clothed with a public interest" was entitled to reasonable compensation, Chief Justice Waite further declared that the determination of such compensation was a legislative, not a judicial, task. The only protection for property owners against legislative abuse was resort to the political process. Justice Stephen J. Field vigorously dissented, warning that under the *Munn* rationale "all property and all business in the State are held at the mercy of a majority of its legislature." Asserting that grain storage was a private business, he maintained that the due process clause afforded substantive protection to owners in the use and income of their property.[4] In practice state legislatures rarely applied the *Munn* doctrine to control the charges of any major business other than railroads.

During the 1880s judicial attitudes began to change. The Supreme Court receded from the deferential approach of *Munn* and adopted a more skeptical posture toward state regulation of property and business. In *Stone v. Farmers' Loan & Trust Co.* (1886), for instance, the justices upheld a Mississippi statute that empowered a commission to regulate railroad rates, but they cautioned that such authority was not unlimited. Chief Justice Waite observed that "the State cannot require a railroad corporation to carry persons or property without reward; neither can it do that which in law amounts to a taking of private property for public use without just compensation, or without due process of law."[5] Simultaneously the Supreme Court began to formulate a substantive interpretation of the due process clause to safeguard fundamental property rights.[6] This laid the basis for the doctrine of economic due process. The court took

another step away from *Munn* in *Wabash, St. Louis & Pacific Railway v. Illinois* (1886), holding that state regulation of interstate railroad rates unconstitutionally invaded federal power under the commerce clause.[7]

State courts likewise moved toward increased scrutiny of rate regulations. In *Spring Valley Water Works v. San Francisco* (1890) the Supreme Court of California invalidated a municipal ordinance fixing the rates charged by a privately-owned water company. Cautioning that "[r]egulation, as provided for in the constitution, does not mean confiscation, or a taking without just compensation," the court asserted judicial authority to review the reasonableness of regulated prices.[8]

Historians agree that *Chicago, Milwaukee & St. Paul Railway Company v. Minnesota* (1890) was a milestone in the evolution of economic due process.[9] The decision inaugurated an era of increased judicial scrutiny of railroad and utility rate fixing and enhanced the protection of property rights. Yet this landmark ruling has received relatively little attention from scholars. In view of the renewed interest in economic rights,[10] it seems pertinent to examine the litigation that culminated in *Chicago, Milwaukee*[11] and to assess the decision's place in constitutional history.

BACKGROUND OF THE CONTROVERSY

In the early 1870s Minnesota experimented briefly with railroad rate regulation but abandoned the system in 1875 amid fears that governmental controls discouraged capital investment. A decade later many western and southern states joined in a new wave of stringent railroad rate regulations.[12] Minnesota was no exception. Republicans dominated Minnesota politics throughout the Gilded Age, a fact that underscores the public consensus favoring regulation of railroad activities. In March of 1887 the Minnesota legislature enacted a comprehensive scheme to regulate the intrastate activities of common carriers.[13] Building upon 1885 legislation that established the Railroad and Warehouse Commission, lawmakers provided

Fig. 1. A *Chicago, Milwaukee & St. Paul Railway passenger train leaving the Milwaukee Union Depot about 1890.* Photograph courtesy of the Milwaukee Public Library, Milwaukee Road Collection.

that all charges for railroad services "shall be equal and reasonable."

Carriers were required to file a schedule of rates with the commission, and the commissioners were empowered to review the reasonableness of charges. The commission could order a railroad to change any fare deemed unequal or unreasonable and could impose a recommended rate. If a railroad failed to comply with such a rate directive the commission could seek a writ of mandamus. The statute also prohibited unreasonable preferences to any shipper and outlawed rebates and the practice of charging more for transportation for a short distance than a long distance. Because at that time neither the Interstate Commerce Commission nor most state railroad commissions had the authority to

fix charges, the Minnesota law went beyond the prevailing regulatory models.

Organized under Wisconsin law in 1874, the Chicago, Milwaukee & St. Paul Railway Company was the successor to numerous small railroads. By the late 1880s the company owned nearly 6000 miles of completed track, more than 1400 grain elevators, and numerous terminal facilities. The railroad's main line ran between Minneapolis and St. Paul and Chicago, and other lines extended into Iowa, Wisconsin, Nebraska, and the Dakotas. It was one of four major carriers that served the northern prairie states.[14] Operating in states strongly influenced by Granger agitation, the Chicago, Milwaukee & St. Paul Railway had long battled state fare regulations.

In June of 1887 local boards of trade complained to the Minnesota Railroad Commission that the rates charged by the Chicago, Milwaukee & St. Paul Railway for transporting milk from various points within Minnesota to St. Paul and Minneapolis were unreasonably high. The company countered that the milk rates were in fact low. After a hearing at which both the petitioners and the railroad were represented, the commission concluded that the charges for transporting milk from Owatonna and Faribault were unreasonable. The commission directed that a rate of $2^{1}/_{2}$ cents per gallon in ten-gallon cans be substituted for the existing rate of 3 cents per gallon. When the railroad refused to carry out the recommended reduction in milk rates, the attorney general, acting for the commission, procured a writ of mandamus from the Supreme Court of Minnesota directing the railroad to obey the order or show cause why it should not be followed. The railroad challenged the constitutionality of the rate fixing provision on three grounds: (1) that the legislative authority to set transportation rates could not be delegated to the commission, (2) that under its franchise the railroad was entitled to determine transportation rates, and (3) that the commission's order constituted "a pro tanto taking" of the railroad's property in violation of the due process clause of the Fourteenth Amendment. Counsel further argued that the statute did not provide for a hearing and that the reasonableness of rates was a judicial question.[15]

The Supreme Court of Minnesota unanimously upheld the commission's order in April of 1888. After disposing of jurisdictional issues, the court considered the nature of the commission's rate-setting powers. The court construed the statute to mean that rates recommended by the commission "should be not simply advisory, nor merely *prima facie* equal and reasonable, but final and conclusive as to what are lawful or equal and reasonable charges."[16] Consequently the court refused to review the reasonableness of rates set by the commission.

Turning to the constitutional objections, the court relied heavily on the *Munn* decision and stressed the need for legislative control of railroads. The court described railroads as "practically the public highway system of the country," and declared that "no modern civilized community could long endure that their public highway system should be in the uncontrolled, exclusive use of private owners. The only alternative was either governmental regulation or governmental ownership of the roads."[17] The court charged that railroads, "and even the eminent counsel for the respondent in this case," were reluctant to accept the legitimacy of legislative supervision. Nor were the judges sympathetic to the argument that the power to fix rates might be abused and in effect deprive the railroads of property without due process. Last the court rejected the contention that the act improperly delegated legislative power to the commission. The judges reasoned that the legislature had not conferred upon the commission power to make law but simply granted administrative discretion to carry out the regulatory purpose of the statute.

The Chicago, Milwaukee & St. Paul Railway petitioned for a reargument in part on the grounds that the court did not consider later rulings that limited the *Munn* decision. When this petition was denied the company obtained a writ of error to bring the case before the Supreme Court of the United States. Meanwhile, the order of the commission went into effect.

SUPREME COURT DECISION

The appeal was argued before the Supreme Court on 13 and 14 January 1890. The railroad was represented by its able general counsel, John W. Cary. He was experienced in rate litigation before the Supreme Court, having previously appeared in several companion cases to *Munn*.[18] A proponent of laissez-faire constitutionalism, Cary labored to secure judicial protection for the rights of railroads against state regulation. He espoused the principle that property ownership encompassed the right to set the price for its use. Cary argued that in order to vindicate property rights the reasonableness of rates was a matter for judicial inquiry. In short, Cary was prominent among a group of attorneys who were instrumental in promoting laissez-faire values and advocating a strong role for the courts in limiting state regulatory power.[19]

This laissez-faire philosophy guided Cary's arguments on behalf of the Chicago, Milwaukee & St. Paul Railway. He first contended that the rate-setting provisions violated the corporate charter in which the Minnesota Territory granted the railroad directors power to fix "the rate of tolls." Hence the Minnesota legislation unconstitutionally impaired the obligation of contract by interfering with the company's rights under its charter.[20]

More significantly Cary then endeavored to restrict application of the *Munn* decision. Insisting that the right to receive value for use of one's property was an essential attribute of ownership, he charged that the Minnesota court judgment "violates the natural right which belongs to every one to fix the price of his services and of his property or its use." Cary conceded that *Munn* limited a railroad to charging reasonable rates, but he denied a legislature's "right to arbitrarily and finally fix or determine such charges by positive statutes." He agreed that a legislature, under its police power, could regulate railroad operations to protect the safety of persons. Cary maintained, however, that this power did not give lawmakers the right to fix transportation charges. In an impassioned plea, Cary argued that rate regulation was unprecedented and "destructive of the rights of property and more to be feared than the insane ravings of the advocates of socialism and the commune." He charged that railroads could be compelled to provide services at an unremunerative rate, effectively confiscating their property. Thus Cary sought to reopen the broad question of legislative control of railroad fares. Contending that "[i]nvestments in railroad property are entitled to the same protection and consideration as other investments," he maintained that a reasonable rate must include "a fair return on the value of the investment or plant of the railroad."[21] Cary finished by arguing that the Chicago, Milwaukee & St. Paul Railway was engaged in interstate commerce and was not

FIG. 2. *John W. Cary (1817-1895) was the principal legal advisor of the Chicago, Milwaukee & St. Paul Railway for many years and argued on behalf of the carrier in the famous* Chicago, Milwaukee *case. Photograph courtesy of the Milwaukee Public Library, Milwaukee Road Collection.*

subject to the Minnesota law since passage of the Interstate Commerce Act in 1887.

Attorney General Moses E. Clapp defended the Minnesota rate-fixing act. As might be expected, he emphasized the "unbroken line" of Supreme Court decisions commencing with *Munn* that sustained the power of legislatures to establish rates for common carriers. He recognized that a state could not use regulatory authority to confiscate property but disputed the company's allegations that the milk rate was unreasonable. Clapp concluded by emphasizing first that state legislatures could decide what constituted a reasonable transportation rate and second that "the question of the reasonableness of the rate is a question for legislative determination, and when so determined, ceases to be the subject of judicial inquiry."[22]

On 24 March the Supreme Court in a brief opinion ruled that the rate statute, as construed by the Minnesota Supreme Court, deprived the railroad of property without due process of law.[23] Chief Justice Melville W. Fuller assigned the task of preparing the court's opinion to Justice Samuel Blatchford. One historian has suggested that this assignment was prompted by Fuller's belief that Blatchford, a consensus builder, could fashion an opinion that would hold together a precarious majority for a significant constitutional innovation.[24]

The court first rejected the railroad's contract clause argument. Justice Blatchford held that the general language in the company's charter conferring the power to collect tolls did not constitute a contract freeing the company from any legislative control. This finding simply affirmed the settled doctrine that corporate charters were strictly construed.

The justices, however, found a procedural infirmity in the Minnesota rate law. Although the precise nature of the defect was unclear from the opinion, the court was obviously disturbed about the conclusive nature of the administrative process that determined rates. Justice Blatchford pointed out that the statute did not provide for notice or a hearing before the commission or for judicial review of rates.[25] This was a somewhat curious point because, in fact, the company received both notice and a hearing. Justice Blatchford was seemingly concerned that the commission might find rates to be unreasonable sua sponte without any hearing.

The court then moved beyond this procedural objection and asserted the authority to review the fairness of rates imposed by state law. "The question of the reasonableness of a rate of charge for transportation by a railroad company," Justice Blatchford observed, " . . . is eminently a question for judicial investigation, requiring due process of law for its determination." He added:

If the company is deprived of the power of charging reasonable rates for the use of its property, and such deprivation takes place in the absence of an investigation by judicial machinery, it is deprived of the lawful use of its property, and thus, in substance and effect, of the property itself, without due process of law and in violation of the Constitution of the United States.[26]

Blatchford's opinion was somewhat nebulous with respect to the scope of judicial review and did not expressly direct a judicial investigation of rates. But the ruling has generally been understood as establishing that the reasonableness of rates was subject to independent court review. Thus, the Chicago, Milwaukee decision contradicted a fundamental principle of Munn that rate setting was solely a legislative function. Moreover, it signaled the court's acceptance of the due process clause as a substantive restriction on state legislation authority.

Concurring "with some hesitation," Justice Samuel F. Miller provided a more compelling explanation of the constitutional need for judicial review of rates. He recognized that the states could exercise their authority to regulate transportation charges either by direct legislation or through a commission. But states could not apply either procedure to set a rate "which is so unreasonable as to practically destroy the value of property of persons engaged in the carrying business." It followed that there was "an ultimate remedy" for aggrieved parties in the federal courts, which had a duty to inquire into the reasonableness of rates.[27]

Speaking for the three dissenters, Justice Joseph D. Bradley complained that the decision effectively overruled Munn and made the courts "the final arbiter" in rate regulations. He maintained that the determination of reasonable charges was a legislative question, involving considerations of policy as well as remuneration. In his view, judicial relief was only available for fraudulent or arbitrary deprivation of property. He insisted that in this case there was no infringement of property rights "but merely a regulation as to the enjoyment of property."[28]

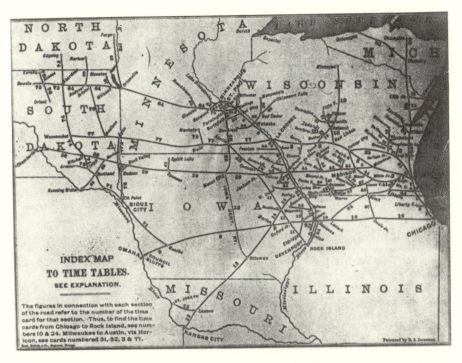

FIG. 3. An 1894 map illustrates the extensive route of the Chicago, Milwaukee & St. Paul Railway through the upper Midwest and eastern Great Plains. Photograph courtesy of the Milwaukee Public Library, Milwaukee Road Collection.

RESPONSE

Whatever the ambiguities of Justice Blatchford's opinion, contemporary observers were quick to perceive a sea change in the Supreme Court's attitude toward rate regulations. "It is everywhere regarded as a most important decision," the *New York Times* reported. Railroad officials were elated. An assistant general manager of the Chicago, Milwaukee & St. Paul Railway commented that "the decision is a ray of hope to railroads oppressed by confiscatory legislation." One railroad agent declared that the carriers "could now feel secure of their property." Another railroad manager added, "I think

the action of the highest court in the country will call a halt on this [granger] class of legislation." The *Winona Daily Republican* quipped: "Whenever you see a railroad man smile now a days you may look to the Supreme court decision for its inspiration."[29]

Reaction in Minnesota was generally hostile. As might be expected, the Populists were particularly bitter. The executive committee of the State Farmers' Alliance unanimously adopted a series of resolutions prepared by Ignatius Donnelly severely censuring the Supreme Court. The resolutions declared that the *Chicago, Milwaukee* decision signified "the subjection of the people and the states to the unlimited control of the railroad corporations of this country." Attacking the concept of judicial review, the resolutions appealed "from this second Dred Scott decision to the people of the nation; and we ask them to consider whether any other race would submit to have their liberties thus wheedled away from them, on technicalities, by a squad of lawyers, sitting as a supreme authority high above Congress, president and people." Last, the executive committee charged that in "our anxiety to protect the rights of property we have created a machinery which threatens to destroy the rights of man."[30]

Newspaper comment, while more restrained, was also largely negative. The *Minneapolis Tribune* maintained that "the Western Legislatures and commissions have in general been sufficiently lenient and reasonable in their demands for reduction of rates." Although agreeing that the railroads should have a right to be heard, the *Tribune* worried that the decision might allow the carriers "through tediously and cunningly delayed litigation to break down" the power of regulation. Similarly, the *Red Wing Argus* observed that the *Chicago, Milwaukee* ruling caused people to wonder "whether the legislators or the courts made the laws of the land." The *Winona Daily Republican* charged that the Supreme Court "takes the purely technical view of the question involved, and . . . looks first of all and chiefly to the interests of the roads."[31]

In contrast, the *St. Paul Dispatch* hailed the *Chicago, Milwaukee* ruling and decried the 1887 act as "the product of an unreasoning warfare upon the railroads." The *Dispatch* called upon the legislature to adopt "the more moderate policy" of the eastern states in supervising railroad operations. Likewise the *St. Paul Pioneer Press* commended the Supreme Court for fixing "an insuperable barrier against the tide of destructive agrarian and confiscatory legislation and judicial decisions which have threatened the unlimited spoliation of all railroad properties."[32]

Leading legal journals tended to look with favor on the *Chicago, Milwaukee* decision. An article in the *Albany Law Journal* defended judicial review of rates "because if otherwise, it would be giving to the Legislature the authority

of deciding the constitutionality of their own acts." One commentator in the *America Law Register* construed the decision as strengthening the rights of property owners against the imposition of rates that resulted in a deprivation of property. He declared that "all lovers of individual liberty, of law and justice can properly rejoice. It is a most momentous decision." Such enthusiasm was not universal. A note in the *American Law Review* sharply criticized the ruling and emphasized the interpretative problems posed by Justice Blatchford's ambiguous opinion. The author was uncertain whether the decision turned on a narrow procedural point or established broad judicial supervision of legislative rate determinations. If it implied the latter, he decried the decision as "an overturning of the fundamental principles upon which all our American governments are founded."[33]

As the debate over *Chicago, Milwaukee* raged, Minnesota officials worked to salvage the regulatory scheme. The railroad commissioners recommended that the law be amended to include judicial review of rates. This approach was adopted by Governor William R. Merriam, a Republican, in his 1891 message to the legislature. Avoiding any criticism of the decision, he pointed out that when the regulatory statute was enacted it was generally understood that the legislature was the final arbiter as to what rates were reasonable. Governor Merriam explained that the Supreme Court

has determined that action upon such matters is not final either in a commission or in the legislature itself. The power of the legislature to make reasonable rates for common carriers is not denied, but whether a given rate so made is reasonable is a judicial question, and must be settled as other matters of law and fact are determined, through the medium of the courts.[34]

Accordingly, he urged a statutory amendment to provide a method of judicial review.

Heeding the governor's request, lawmakers amended the 1887 rate statute. Much of the earlier measure was unchanged, but the amendment stipulated that rates set by the commission should be treated only as prima facie evidence of reasonableness. The amendment also provided for notice and a full administrative hearing before the commission. Finally, the amended statute expressly established the right of a railroad to appeal commission orders to the state district courts, which had jurisdiction to examine "the whole matter in controversy."[35] These changes brought the Minnesota rate law into conformity with the constitutional requirements of *Chicago, Milwaukee*.

ASSESSMENT

Although a major victory for the railroads, the outcome in *Chicago, Milwaukee* did not inaugurate an era of laissez-faire in the transportation industry. The fears of the Populists to the contrary, the Supreme Court continued to recognize the power of state legislatures to regulate railroad and storage rates. The federal judiciary only protected carriers against unreasonable charges, and the railroads had to demonstrate their unreasonableness.[36] Still, the *Chicago, Milwaukee* ruling materially restricted state regulatory authority, and lawsuits seeking to invalidate state-imposed rates multiplied rapidly in the next decade.

Despite the Supreme Court's retreat from the *Munn* doctrine, the decision was not an abrupt departure from existing constitutional norms. Starting in 1886 the court had cautioned in several cases that states could not, consistent with due process, impose confiscatory rates on regulated industries.[37] The justices came to realize that unlimited power of regulation might be used to destroy the value of railroad property. Once the Supreme Court distinguished between rate regulation and confiscation, judicial supervision of rates followed logically. Judicial oversight simply provided a vehicle by which the justices could vindicate property rights against confiscatory legislation. If the states had unlimited power to fix charges, then constitutional protection against confiscation was illusory and regulated industries had only those

rights to use property that lawmakers chose to recognize.

Why did the Supreme Court move away from the *Munn* doctrine of unfettered legislative power to control rates? Scholars have sometimes depicted *Chicago, Milwaukee* as part of a pervasive pro-business bias on the part of the justices.[38] This rationale is problematic. After all, during the Gilded Age the Supreme Court upheld many state-imposed regulations on business activity. A more compelling explanation, offered by Mary Cornelia Porter, is that the court "was less interested in rate regulation per se than in assuring that regulated utilities would continue to attract the investment capital necessary for expanding and improving services to the public."[39] The importance of investment security was clear to contemporary observers. One railroad official revealingly stressed that the *Chicago, Milwaukee* decision "will afford a very great safeguard to railroad investments." He explained that the ruling "comes at a very opportune time, for the reason that the frequent attacks in the West on railroad property by legislators and commissioners were beginning to sap the confidence of investors all over the world in the safety of investments in American railroad properties."[40] This was a crucial point because Europeans invested heavily in many western railroads, including the Chicago, Milwaukee & St. Paul Railway.[41]

Railroads long had feared that legislatively imposed rates would favor local interests and discourage long-term economic growth. An official of the Chicago, Milwaukee & St. Paul Railway explained that

the railways have back of their adjustment of the rates the selfish interest of their own prosperity, which depends upon the prosperity of all the business on their lines, while a political commission if given this power would have nothing at stake but the political success of the influences which placed it in office.[42]

The growing intensity of rate regulation in the

Gilded Age made the court more aware of the deficiencies in the *Munn* doctrine and increasingly sympathetic to the position of the railroads. In short, experience served to undermine judicial confidence in legislative and administrative rate determinations. Gradually the justices saw *Munn* in a new light. While no doubt concerned about unwarranted intrusion on the property rights of the railroads, the court also sought to fashion uniform national standards that guarded investment capital against impairment by inadequate compensation. Further, it became apparent that out-of-state investors had no meaningful opportunity to "resort to the polls" for protection, as suggested in *Munn*. Judicial redress was the only realistic remedy against unduly low rates.

Perhaps the most significant consequence of *Chicago, Milwaukee*, however, was its far-reaching impact on the constitutional protection of property rights generally. By mandating the judicial review of imposed rates, the Supreme Court implicitly recognized that protection of property went beyond title and possession. Ownership encompassed the right to use property for economic value. This step markedly enlarged the range of property interests secured by the Constitution.[43] In addition the decision opened the door for the doctrine of economic due process. Once the Supreme Court accepted the notion that the due process clause mandated reasonableness in the context of rate controls, it was an easy step to apply this substantive restraint to economic regulations generally.[44] Soon the court was assessing regulations against a reasonableness standard and striking down measures it deemed unduly restrictive of property rights.[45]

The *Chicago, Milwaukee* ruling also had implications for the reach of the takings clause of the Fifth Amendment. The court's expressed worry that rate regulations might deprive the railroad of its property without due process portended extension of the takings clause to the states. In fact the dissenters had complained that the majority opinion proceeded on the assumption that the Constitution prohibited the states from taking private property without

compensation. The dissenting justices pointed out that "there is no such clause," and that the states could make their own regulations governing the payment of just compensation.[46] Yet the majority opinion's tendency to assimilate due process protection of property with deprivation of lawful usage foreshadowed a prompt judicial move to enlarge the guarantees available to property owners under the Fifth Amendment. In *Chicago, Burlington and Quincy Railroad Company v. Chicago* (1897) the justices unanimously held that the just compensation requirement constituted an essential element of due process as guaranteed by the Fourteenth Amendment.[47] Hence, the just compensation principle became in effect the first provision of the Bill of Rights to be applied against the states.

The *Chicago, Milwaukee* ruling had a particular impact on the states of the Great Plains. Responding to farmer dissatisfaction with the management of railroads, lawmakers in the prairie jurisdictions enacted a host of laws designed to restrict passenger and freight rates and the charges of grain elevators. Consequently, enlarged judicial review of railroad charges would be felt keenly in the Great Plains. Indeed much of the rate litigation after 1890 originated from the prairie states.[48]

An unresolved question raised by *Chicago, Milwaukee*, of course, was how to distinguish a valid rate regulation from a confiscatory rate. The Supreme Court wrestled with this complex issue in a number of cases during the 1890s. Eventually, in *Smyth v. Ames* (1898), the court unanimously held that a utility was constitutionally entitled to a "fair return" upon the "fair value" of its property.[49] An attempt to protect regulated industries against confiscatory rates, the fair value rule proved difficult to administer. In the ensuing decades federal courts became heavily involved in supervising the rate-making process.[50] At the same time Congress enacted a series of statutes that imposed more stringent federal controls over railroad charges.[51]

CONCLUSION

*Chicago, Milwaukee* was a landmark case in

which the Supreme Court moved toward more vigorous protection of property rights. Historians, influenced by the Progressive school, have often criticized the decision for giving federal courts the power to review the substantive reasonableness of state-imposed rates. Charles Fairman, for example, championed the *Munn* doctrine and Justice Bradley's dissenting opinion in *Chicago, Milwaukee*. "Who can doubt," he asked, "that the Court would have done much better had it never quit the path Justice Bradley first pointed out?"[52]

This analysis, however, is open to dispute. Farmers and shippers who called for railroad rate regulations often pursued an opportunistic course that benefited their economic interests. In a sense, then, the movement for railroad regulation sought a redistribution of wealth from the carriers to consumers. State agencies frequently yielded to parochial pressures in setting rates, thereby threatening the long-term economic health of the railroads. Yet only by generating a profit could the railroads attract capital investment and continue to provide services. It followed that state rate regulations had a direct impact on national transportation policy. Herbert Hovenkamp has pointed out that "the potential for abuse, particularly for free-riding by the states, was substantial, and federal control by either legislation or judicial intervention was clearly necessary." The federal courts, he added, were "the only competent federal arm to control state free-riding and protect the integrity of the national railroad system."[53]

Although criticized for granting the federal courts authority to review the substance of rates, the justices of the Supreme Court followed sound instincts. Judicial review placed some restraint on the marked tendency of legislators and regulators to set railroad rates at unrealistically low levels, often at the behest of special interest groups. Despite the rule of *Smyth v. Ames*, governmental regulation of railroad charges steadily increased in the early decades of the twentieth century. Indeed several scholars have identified heavy-handed rate regulation and cumbersome rate-setting procedures as major factors in the decline of America's railroads.[54] Arguably the

court should have reviewed rates more aggressively to protect the security of capital investment and thus encourage maintenance of an adequate rail service.

Last *Chicago, Milwaukee* has demonstrated impressive staying power. Following the constitutional revolution of 1937 the Supreme Court abandoned economic due process, retreated from meaningful review of rate fixing, and relegated property rights to a secondary position.[55] But the Supreme Court has never overruled *Chicago, Milwaukee* and continues to require judicial review of administrative decisions touching on constitutional rights. Recently the Supreme Court has even shown renewed interest in constitutional restraints on utility rate making. In *Duquesne Light Co. v. Barasch* (1989) Chief Justice William Rehnquist, speaking for the court, reiterated the long-standing rule: "The guiding principle has been that the Constitution protects utilities from being limited to a charge for their property serving the public which is so 'unjust' as to be confiscatory."[56] Rehnquist stressed that a rate must afford adequate compensation. Thus after one hundred years *Chicago, Milwaukee* continues to influence constitutional law and provide at least symbolic protection to property rights.

NOTES

I wish to express my appreciation to Herman Belz, Jon W. Bruce, Barry Friedman, and Nicholas Zeppos for their helpful comments on earlier drafts of this article. I owe special thanks to Paul Woehrmann, Librarian at the Milwaukee Public Library, for locating illustrations from the Milwaukee Road Collection. I also wish to acknowledge the valuable research assistance of Susan E. Raines.

1. Harold U. Faulkner, *Politics, Reform, and Expansion: 1890-1900* (New York: Harper and Row, 1959), p. 75.

2. Kermit L. Hall, *The Magic Mirror: Law in American History* (New York: Oxford University Press, 1989), pp. 197-98; Lawrence M. Friedman, *A History of American Law*, 2nd ed. (New York: Simon and Schuster, 1985), pp. 446-47.

3. Hall, *Magic Mirror* (note 2 above), p. 198; Solon J. Buck, *The Granger Movement* (Cambridge: Harvard University Press, 1913), pp. 123-205. One authority has noted that the "real heart of the anti-

railroad, or 'granger movement' as it is usually known, came in the state regulatory laws of the Middle West." Robert Edgar Riegel, *The Story of the Western Railroads* (New York: Macmillan Company, 1926), p. 143.

4. *Munn v. Illinois*, 94 U.S. 113, 130, 140 (1877).

5. *Stone v. Farmers' Loan & Trust Co.*, 116 U.S. 307, 331 (1886). See also *Dow v. Beidelman*, 125 U.S. 680, 689 (1888) and *Chicago and North Western Railway v. Dey*, 35 F. 866 (Cir. Ct., Iowa, 1888). As early as 1884 Chief Justice Waite observed in a rate challenge: "What may be done if the municipal authorities . . . fix upon a price which is manifestly unreasonable, need not now be considered." *Spring Valley Water Works v. Schottler*, 110 U.S. 347, 354 (1884).

6. James W. Ely, Jr., *The Guardian of Every Other Right: A Constitutional History of Property Rights* (New York: Oxford University Press, 1992), pp. 82-100.

7. *Wabash, St. Louis & Pacific Railway v. Illinois*, 118 U.S. 557 (1886).

8. See Katha G. Hartley, "*Spring Valley Water Works v. San Francisco*: Defining Economic Rights in San Francisco," *Western Legal History* 3 (1990): 287; *Spring Valley Water Works v. San Francisco*, 82 Cal. 286, 307 (1890).

9. John E. Semonche, *Charting the Future: The Supreme Court Responds to A Changing Society, 1890-1920* (Westport, Connecticut: Greenwood Press, 1978), pp. 16-20; David P. Currie, "The Constitution in the Supreme Court: The Protection of Economic Interests, 1889-1910," *University of Chicago Law Review* 52 (1985): 324, 371-75. In a leading law casebook, *Constitutional Law*, 11th ed. (Westbury, New York: Foundation Press, 1985), Gerald Gunther described *Chicago, Milwaukee* as "a significant turning point," but relegated consideration of the case to a footnote, p. 447, n. 8.

10. E.g., Bernard H. Siegan, *Economic Liberties and the Constitution* (Chicago: University of Chicago Press, 1980); Richard A. Epstein, *Takings: Private Property and the Power of Eminent Domain* (Cambridge: Harvard University Press, 1985); Note, "Resurrecting Economic Rights: The Doctrine of Economic Due Process Reconsidered," *Harvard Law Review* 103 (1990): 1363.

11. The different names of the Chicago, Milwaukee & St. Paul Railway over time may give rise to some confusion. The carrier was commonly known as the St. Paul Road in the late nineteenth century. Following a reorganization in 1928 the railroad was popularly called the Milwaukee Road. This article employs the title *Chicago, Milwaukee* to describe the Supreme Court case under investigation.

12. George H. Miller, *Railroads and the Granger Laws* (Madison: Wisconsin University Press, 1971), pp. 117-39; Charles Fairman, "The So-called Granger Cases, Lord Hale, and Justice Bradley," *Stanford Law Review* 5 (1953): 587, 600-606; Buck, *Granger Movement* (note 3 above), pp. 196-97. For agrarian distrust of the railroads in Minnesota see William E. Lass, *Minnesota: A Bicentennial History* (New York: W.W. Norton, 1977), pp. 164-74.

13. An Act to Regulate Common Carriers, and Creating the Railroad and Warehouse Commission of the State of Minnesota, ch. 10, Minnesota Laws of 1887.

14. August Derleth, *The Milwaukee Road: Its First Hundred Years* (New York: Creative Age Press, 1948), p. 137 and Appendix A; John F. Stover, *The Life and Decline of the American Railroad* (New York: Oxford University Press, 1970), pp. 56-57; F. Stewart Mitchell, "The Chicago, Milwaukee & St. Paul Railway and James J. Hill in Dakota Territory, 1879-1885," *North Dakota History* 47 (1980): 11. See also John W. Cary, *The Organization and History of the Chicago, Milwaukee & St. Paul Railway Company* (1893; rpt. New York: Arno Press, 1981).

15. For the factual background and arguments for counsel see *Third Biennial Report of the Railroad and Warehouse Commission as to Amendments and Revisions of the Railroad Laws of Minnesota, 1890, Minnesota Executive Documents for Fiscal Year Ending July 31, 1890*, vol. 3 (1891): 400-442.

16. *State ex rel. Railroad and Warehouse Commission v. Chicago, Milwaukee & St. Paul Railway Company*, 38 Minn. 281, 295, 37 N.W. at 784 (1888).

17. *Id.* at 296-97, 37 N.W. at 785-86.

18. *Peik v. Chicago and North-Western Railway Company*, 94 U.S. 164 (1877); *Chicago, Milwaukee & St. Paul Railroad Company v. Ackley*, 94 U.S. 179 (1877); *Stone v. Wisconsin*, 94 U.S. 181 (1877).

19. Benjamin R. Twiss, *Lawyers and the Constitution: How Laissez Faire Came to the Supreme Court* (Princeton: Princeton University Press, 1942), pp. 70-77, 161-62; John W. Cary, "Limitations of the Legislative Power in Respect to Personal Rights and Private Property," *American Bar Association Report* 15 (1892): 245-86.

20. Brief for Plaintiff in Error, John W. Cary, Counsel, 14-17.

21. *Id.*, at 18, 28, 23, 72.

22. Brief for Defendant in Error, Moses E. Clapp and H. W. Childs, Attorneys, 14.

23. *Chicago, Milwaukee & St. Paul Railway Company v. Minnesota*, 134 U.S. 418, 456-57. A companion case, decided the same day, arose out of a similar factual situation. The Minnesota Commission ordered a small local railroad to reduce its rate for handling and switching cars in Minneapolis. The company protested that the imposed rate was too low and provided an inadequate compensation, thus depriving the company of its property. Reversing the rate decree, the Supreme Court held that the "views

and considerations applicable to" Chicago, Milwaukee "apply with even greater force to the present case." Minneapolis Eastern Railway Company v. Minnesota, 134 U.S. 467, 482 (1890).

24. Semonche, Charting the Future (note 9 above), p. 19.

25. Chicago, Milwaukee & St. Paul Railway Company v. Minnesota, 134 U.S. 418, 457 (1890).

26. Id., at 458.

27. Id., at 459-60. For an analysis of Justice Miller's views, see Charles Fairman, Mr. Justice Miller and the Supreme Court, 1862-1890 (Cambridge: Harvard University Press, 1939), pp. 202-5.

28. Chicago, Milwaukee & St. Paul Railway Company v. Minnesota, 134 U.S. 418, 466 (1890).

29. New York Times, 26 March 1890; quoted in Winona Daily Republican, 1 April 1890; quoted in St. Paul Dispatch, 25 March 1890; Winona Daily Republican, 1 April 1890.

30. Minnesota State Farmers' Alliance, Constitution and By-Laws, Declaration of Principles, Resolutions . . . (1890), 20.

31. Minneapolis Tribune, 26 March, 1890; Red Wing Argus, 3 April 1890; Winona Daily Republican, 26 March 1890.

32. St. Paul Dispatch, 25, 26 March 1890; St. Paul Pioneer Press, 25 March 1890.

33. Henry L. Harrington, "Legislative Interference With the Freedom of Railroad Corporation Contracts," Albany Law Journal 51 (1895): 246, 249; William Draper Lewis, "Can Prices Be Regulated by Law?" American Law Register 41 (1893): 9, 16; Note, American Law Review 24 (1890): 516, 522.

34. Biennial Message of Governor William R. Merriam, 14 January 1891, Minnesota Executive Documents for Fiscal Year Ending July 31, 1890, vol. 1 (1891): 37.

35. An Act to Amend Chapter Ten [1887] Entitled "An Act to Regulate Common Carriers, and Creating the Railroad and Warehouse Commission of the State of Minnesota," ch. 106, Minnesota Laws of 1891.

36. See Alton D. Adams, "Reasonable Rates," in William Z. Ripley, ed., Railway Problems, rev. ed. (Boston: Ginn and Co., 1913), pp. 604-9 (discussing Chicago, Milwaukee and judicial review of the reasonableness of rates). See also Cary, "Limitations on the Legislative Power" (note 19 above), pp. 284-86 for an assessment of the Chicago, Milwaukee decision.

37. See cases cited in note 5 above.

38. Arnold M. Paul, Conservative Crisis and the Rule of Law: Attitudes of the Bar and Bench, 1887-1895 (Ithaca, New York: Cornell University Press, 1960), pp. 39-45. Melvin I. Urofsky has sharply criticized the role of the federal courts in scrutinizing rates and contended that judicial review "gave railroads one more weapon to fight regulation." A March

of Liberty: A Constitutional History of the United States (New York: Alfred A. Knopf, 1988), p. 526.

39. Mary Cornelia Porter, "That Commerce Shall Be Free: A New Look at the Old Laissez-Faire Court," 1976 Supreme Review, pp. 135, 143.

40. Quoted in St. Paul Dispatch, 25 March 1890.

41. Albro Martin, Enterprise Denied: Origins of the Decline of American Railroads, 1897-1917 (New York: Columbia University Press, 1971), pp. 133-34; Dorothy R. Adler, British Investment in American Railways, 1834-1898 (Charlottesville: University Press of Virginia, 1970), pp. 185, 191 n, 199, 210. Riegel, Western Railroads (note 3 above), p. 139.

42. Burton Hanson, Unfair Railway Agitation (Chicago: 1905), p. 51. Another railroad executive urged competition rather than regulation to hold down rates and pointed out that "the great majority of the railways in the United States are the creation of private enterprise and capital, and that the people in their collective capacity have not been taxed in order to construct them." Sidney Dillon, "The West and the Railroads," North American Review 152 (1891): 443, 451.

43. Stephen A. Siegel, "Understanding the Lochner Era: Lessons From the Controversy Over Railroad and Utility Rate Regulations," Virginia Law Review 70 (1984): 187, 210-15.

44. Alfred H. Kelly, Winfred A. Harbison, and Herman Belz, The American Constitution: Its Origins and Development, 7th ed. (New York: W.W. Norton, 1991), pp. 406-8; Urofsky, March of Liberty (note 38 above), p. 500.

45. See Paul Kens, Judicial Power and Reform Politics: The Anatomy of Lochner v. New York (Lawrence: University Press of Kansas, 1990).

46. Chicago, Milwaukee & St. Paul Railway Company v. Minnesota, 134 U.S. 418, 465 (1890).

47. Chicago, Burlington and Quincy Railroad Company v. Chicago, 166 U.S. 226 (1897).

48. E.g., Brass v. North Dakota, 153 U.S. 391 (1894); Smyth v. Ames, 169 U.S. 466 (1898).

49. Smyth v. Ames, 169 U.S. 466 (1898).

50. Siegel, "Understanding the Lochner Era" (note 43 above), pp. 215-59.

51. Stover, Life and Decline (note 14 above), pp. 113-16.

52. Fairman, "So-called Granger Cases" (note 12 above), p. 670.

53. Herbert Hovenkamp, Enterprise and American Law, 1836-1937 (Cambridge: Harvard University Press, 1991), p. 160.

54. Stover, Life and Decline (note 14 above), p. 247; Martin, Enterprise Denied (note 41 above), pp. 354-60. Similarly, Forrest McDonald has maintained that railroads "became the first industry to be destroyed, in the long run, by an excess of regulation." McDonald, A Constitutional History of the United States

(Malabar, Florida: Robert E. Krieger Publishing Co., 1982), p. 184.

55. Ely, Guardian of Every Other Right (note 6 above), pp. 119-34.

56. Duquesne Light Co. v. Barasch, 488 U.S. 299, 307 (1989). See Richard J. Pierce, Jr., "Public Utility Regulatory Takings: Should the Judiciary Attempt to Police the Political Institutions?" Georgetown Law Journal 77 (1989): 2031.

# *Spring Valley Water Works v. San Francisco*: DEFINING ECONOMIC RIGHTS IN SAN FRANCISCO

By Katha G. Hartley

T he place of property and economic liberty in Americans' litany of fundamental rights is the subject of much historical and contemporary controversy.[1] Opinions on the constitutional meaning of "property" often diverge widely as to the nature of the state and the individual within the political community, and may involve radically opposed ideas about the extent to which property's constitutional protections are qualified. Though the Fifth Amendment of the Bill of Rights prohibits the deprivation of life, liberty, and property without due process and bars the taking of property for public use without just compensation, the constitutional text itself offers little guidance in setting precise limits on property rights. In the same way, legislative intervention in economic affairs and the direct regulation of private property has proceeded in American history without stable constitutional guidelines.

Historical analysis of evolving societal and constitutional notions about state power, individual rights, and the ever-elusive "public interest" helps show how constitutional meaning has

Katha G. Hartley is a graduate student in the Jurisprudence and Social Policy Program in the Boalt Hall School of Law, University of California, Berkeley. The author would like to thank Professor Harry Scheiber of the University of California for his helpful comments and suggestions, and Barbara Liebhardt and Jill Frank for reviewing an earlier version of this article.

[1] See, inter alia, Frank Michelman, "Property as a Constitutional Right," *Washington and Lee Law Review* 38 (1981) 1097; Richard Epstein, *Takings: Private Property and the Power of Eminent Domain* (Cambridge, Mass., 1985); Harry N. Scheiber, "Economic Liberty and the Constitution," in *Essays in the History of Liberty: Seaver Institute Lectures at the Huntington Library* (San Marino, 1988); Charles Reich, "The Liberty Impact of the New Property," *William and Mary Law Review* 31 (1990) 295.

been given to property and economic liberty. The late nineteenth century is especially significant in this analysis.

Following a relatively cooperative era between the public and private sectors and a generously distributive political climate generated by rapid economic and institutional growth, legislative activity in the 1870s shifted significantly from promoting economic development toward emphasizing its regulation.[2] The change reflected the increasing social tension arising from the nation's industrial transformation, and created a difficult task for the courts: namely, the demarcation of governmental regulatory action, which was justified in the name of the public interest, but which also set the acceptable limits of governmental intrusion upon private-property rights.[3] The period witnessed a virtual constitutional revolution in government-business relations.[4]

Central to this process was the ratification of the Fourteenth Amendment in 1868. Having adopted verbatim the Fifth Amendment's phrases regarding due-process protections of life, liberty, and property against governmental action, the Fourteenth Amendment became the vehicle by which businesses fought expanding governmental involvement in their commercial affairs. The legal battles over the constitutionality of regulatory legislation that ensued under Fourteenth Amendment claims were as tumultuous as the era. In less than twenty years—from the *Slaughterhouse* cases of 1873 to *Chicago, Milwaukee & St. Paul Railway Co. v. Minnesota* in 1890—the Supreme Court moved from deference toward state regulation, even in the case of obvious legislative corruption, to the substantive due-process

---

[2] Charles W. McCurdy, "Justice Field and the Jurisprudence of Government-Business Relations: Some Parameters of Laissez-Faire Constitutionalism, 1863-1897," in Lawrence M. Friedman and Harry N. Scheiber, eds., *American Law and the Constitutional Order* (Cambridge, Mass., 1978) 246 [hereafter cited as McCurdy, "Justice Field"]; James Willard Hurst, *Law and the Conditions of Freedom in the Nineteenth Century United States* (Madison, 1956) [hereafter cited as Hurst, *Law and the Conditions of Freedom*]; Harry N. Scheiber, "Public Rights and the Rule of Law in American Legal History," *California Law Review* 72 (1984) 217; Harold Hyman and William Wiecek, *Equal Justice Under Law: Constitutional Development* (New York, 1982).

[3] For a discussion of social and political changes in the United States in the late nineteenth century, see Robert Wiebe, *The Search for Order: 1877-1920* (New York, 1967); Hurst, *Law and the Conditions of Freedom*, supra note 2; Stephen Skowronek, *Building a New State: The Expansion of National Administrative Capacities, 1877-1920* (Cambridge, Mass., 1982); on state police power and private property, McCurdy, "Justice Field," supra note 2 at 247; Morton Keller, *Affairs of State: Public Life in Nineteenth-Century America* (Cambridge, Mass., 1977). Police power is defined as "the general power of a government to legislate for the comfort, safety, health, morals, or welfare of the citizenry or the prosperity and good order of the community." Dennis J. Mahoney, "Police Power," in Leonard Levy, ed., *Encyclopedia of the American Constitution*, 4 vols. (New York, 1986) 3:1408.

[4] McCurdy, "Justice Field," supra note 2 at 247.

rulings of the *Lochner* era, which removed that deference in economic matters and which broadly reformulated rights of property and "liberty of contract" as fundamental.

This article focuses on a series of court cases fought between the City of San Francisco and the Spring Valley Water Works, which controlled the city's water supply. Since the cases were heard in the state and federal courts between 1867 and 1890, they illustrate the problems common to courts, legislatures, and corporations at the time. At the state level, they involved judicial attempts to define the reach of the police power, including San Francisco's municipal police power, and the litigants' contractual rights and obligations. At the U.S. Supreme Court level, the dispute fell within a series of Fourteenth Amendment cases that supported legislative discretion in the regulation of business affecting the public interest.[5] However, the last case analyzed here was of a significantly different cast from those preceding it. In 1890 the California Supreme Court abandoned its position of deference regarding legislative regulatory action and ruled substantively on the reasonableness of water rates set by the San Francisco Board of Supervisors. A more comprehensive judicial movement in interpreting the Fourteenth Amendment's due-process clause ensued.

While nationwide developments provide the context of the courts' delineation of San Francisco's regulatory power through the Spring Valley cases, local events and popular sentiment in San Francisco were equally important in this litigation and its ramifications for water policy in California. A radical reform movement was under way in California during the 1870s, characterized by hostility toward concentrated power, and by bitter criticism of corrupt legislative practices. The campaign culminated in the state's adoption of a new constitution in 1879, which gave explicit attention to the "water question."[6] The San Francisco-

---

[5] The "affectation doctrine" was clearly articulated in the *Granger* cases. See Harry N. Scheiber, "*Granger* Cases," in Levy, *Encyclopedia of the American Constitution,* supra note 3 at 2:862, and Harry N. Scheiber, "The Road to *Munn*: Eminent Domain and the Concept of Public Purpose in the State Courts," in Donald Fleming and Bernard Bailyn, eds., *Perspectives in American History* (Cambridge, Mass., 1971) 5:329 [hereafter cited as Scheiber, "Road to *Munn*"]. See also *Beer Co. v. Massachusetts,* 97 U.S. 25 (1878), *Fertilizing Co. v. Hyde Park,* 97 U.S. 659 (1878), *Stone v. Mississippi,* 101 U.S. 814 (1880), *Butchers' Union Co. v. Crescent City Co.,* 111 U.S. 746 (1884), *Stone v. Farmers' Loan and Trust Co.,* 116 U.S. 307 (1886).

[6] The problem of providing an adequate water supply to the state's growing urban areas was distinct from the problems facing irrigators. California's cyclical rainfall patterns created much indebtedness among farmers, who were especially vocal regarding the taxation of mortgages at the state's 1879 constitutional convention. Carl Brent Swisher, *Motivation and Political Technique in the California Constitutional Convention, 1878-1879* (Claremont, 1930) 8 [hereafter cited as Swisher, *Motivation and Political Technique*].

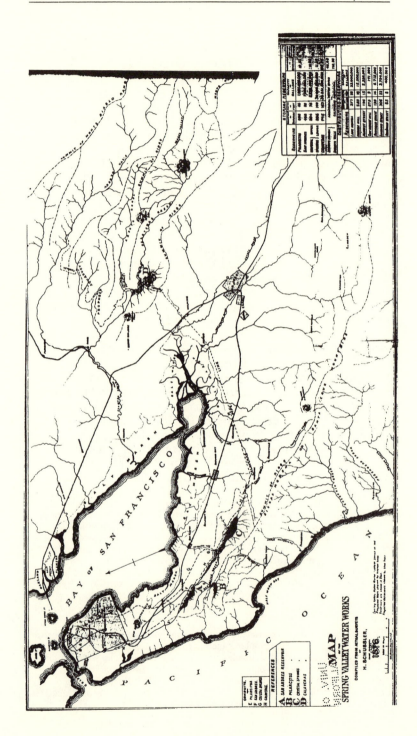

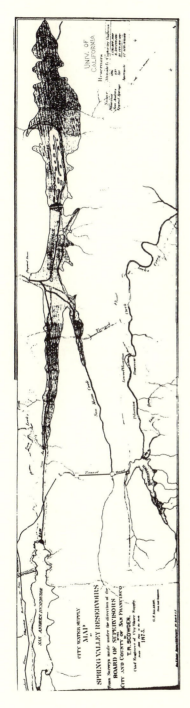

Facing page: map of the Spring Valley Water Works, 1876. (*San Francisco Municipal Reports*, 1876-77)

Left: the Spring Valley Storage Reservoirs, surveyed in 1875 by City Engineer Thomas Scowden. (*San Francisco Municipal Reports*, 1874-75)

Spring Valley litigation and control of the state's water resources emerged as hotly debated issues at the constitutional convention.[7] The compromise solution was Article 14 of the 1879 constitution, which defined water distribution as a "public use," though it was a far from radical conclusion, given the development of public-rights doctrine to that point. The provision grew directly out of the San Francisco-Spring Valley conflict, however, and held important consequences for future water development in the state.

## MUNICIPAL EXPANSION AND EARLY REGULATORY CONTROL

The growth of San Francisco after California's statehood in 1849 was spectacularly rapid, a fact of vital importance to the shaping of the Spring Valley litigation. According to historians William Issel and Robert Cherny, "For thirty years after the discovery of gold, San Francisco stood virtually unchallenged as the economic capital of the Pacific slope."[8] The city quickly came to control trade and financial operations in the West. Between 1860 and 1880, San Francisco's population grew from approximately 57,000 to 234,000.[9] Generally, "The city had more manufacturing establishments, more employees in workshops, greater capitalization, larger value of materials, and higher value of products than all the other twenty-four western cities combined."[10] By the end of the Civil War, San Francisco had securely established its commercial position in the West and in the nation's economy.

---

[7] Spring Valley's president during the late 1870s surmised that the San Francisco-Spring Valley litigation contributed, "perhaps more than any one thing (except ... taxation), towards a radical changing of the constitution of the state." nd, Charles Webb Howard, "The Water Supply of San Francisco. History of the Development of San Francisco's Water Supply, the San Francisco Waterworks and the Spring Valley Water Company," nd, Charles Webb Howard MS, Bancroft Library; Debates and Proceedings of the Constitutional Convention of the State of California, convened at the City of Sacramento, Saturday, September 28, 1878, E.B. Willis and P.K. Stockton, eds., 1880, 3 vols., 1070 [hereafter cited as Debates and Proceedings]; Harry N. Scheiber, "Race, Radicalism and Reform: Historical Perspective on the 1879 California Constitution," Hastings Constitutional Law Quarterly 17 (1989) 66.

[8] William Issel and Robert W. Cherny, San Francisco, 1865-1932: Politics, Power, and Urban Development (Berkeley, 1986) 23 [hereafter cited as Issel and Cherny, San Francisco].

[9] James Hart, A Companion to California (New York, 1978) 338; Swisher, Motivation and Political Technique, supra note 6 at 6. See, inter alia, Earl Pomeroy, The Pacific Slope: A History of California, Oregon, Washington, Idaho, Utah, and Nevada (New York, 1965).

[10] Issel and Cherny, San Francisco, supra note 8 at 23.

To ensure its continued prosperity and growth, the city required
an efficient water-distribution system. When the San Francisco
City Water Works started business in 1857, the city's Board of
Supervisors offered it generous inducements to insure the rapid
construction of its operations. Among these were the terms of its
municipal charter, known as Order No. 46, which stipulated that
rates for the first five years after the introduction of water should
yield a gross revenue of 24 percent per annum upon the actual
cash capital invested, and 20 percent per annum thereafter. The
order was ratified by the state legislature, as required by California's 1849 constitution. Even for that time in the state, the rates
of return were extremely high.[11]

The state relied upon bountiful charter provisions as a means
of promoting investment and thus enhancing economic development.[12] At the same time, Order 46 contained strong regulatory
language that reflected the norm in charters issued in other
states.[13] Section 6 of the order, for example, reserved the city's
right to purchase the entire San Francisco City Water Works
operation after two years, with only thirty days' notice to the
company.[14] Section 4 also provided a pivotal regulatory provision,
reserving for the city the right to the "free use of water . . . for the
purpose of extinguishing fires . . . and for all the public purposes of
said city and county, except for sprinkling of streets."[15]

Shortly after approving the order, the state legislature defined
corporate power more clearly in the 1858 Act for Incorporation of
Water Companies. This offers another illustration of the interac-
tion between distributive and regulatory concerns. The act
granted eminent-domain privileges to any company supplying
water to a city, county, or town in the state. Concomitant with
these privileges were a number of duties: for example, the act
demanded that corporations formed under it should provide the
people they served with "fresh water . . . at reasonable rates,"[16]
and the cities they served with water free of charge "to the extent
of their means, . . . in case of fire or other great necessity."[17] The
act also established that rates should be set by a board of commis-

[11] Act of March 18, 1858, ch. 95, 1858 California Statutes, Sec. 5 at 76 [hereafter
cited as Act of March 18, 1858].

[12] Gerald Nash, *State Government and Economic Development: A History of
Administrative Policies in California, 1849-1933* (Berkeley, 1964) 81.

[13] Scheiber, "Road to *Munn*," supra note 5; James Willard Hurst, *The Legitimacy
of the Business Corporation in the Law of the United States, 1780-1970*
(Charlottesville, 1970).

[14] Act of March 18, 1858, supra note 11, Sec. 6 at 77.

[15] Ibid., Sec. 4 at 76.

[16] Act of April 22, 1858, ch. 262, 1858 California Statutes, Sec. 4 at 219 [hereafter
cited as Act of April 22, 1858].

[17] Ibid.

sioners, with two representatives from the city or town authorities and two from the company, and a fifth chosen by the other
four members.[18] This rate-setting procedure was important, for it
allowed property owners an equal voice with those of elected
authorities in determining the water's selling price.

Popular distrust of concentrated power was directed toward
legislatures as well as private corporations. The fear of legislative-
corporate collusion had shown itself in the state's original 1849
constitution. Article 4, Section 31, prohibited the creation of
corporations other than municipalities under special act, and
reserved for the state the right to alter or repeal all laws, including
those involving incorporation. Despite this restriction, the state
legislature granted a franchise called the Ensign Act, only one day
after its passage of the 1858 General Water Incorporation Act.[19]
Nominally, the franchise authorized entrepreneur George Ensign
to lay water pipes in San Francisco's streets. Sections 3 and 4 of
the act, however, delineated the city's right to tap Ensign's water
pipes and set rates for any water he sold. In other words, the act
opened the door for Ensign's company, the Spring Valley Water
Works, to distribute (or sell) water under terms different from the
state's general water-incorporation act.

The Spring Valley Water Works developed rapidly, rivaling the
San Francisco City Water Works. In 1864, when three employees
of the latter were charged with grand larceny for tapping Spring
Valley's pipes and diverting almost a million gallons of water a
day for several months, the affair was settled out of court and
resulted in Spring Valley's taking over San Francisco City Water
Works' assets and properties.[20]

Spring Valley's original pipe-laying franchise thus evolved into
a monopoly franchise for water distribution in San Francisco. Its
legal status was complicated because technically it operated
under two charters: Order 46, and the Ensign Act. These differed
primarily in the treatment of the public claim to free water use.
Order 46 provided for the city's free use of water for fires and all
public purposes, while the Ensign Act contained more ambiguous
language. Section 3 stated that, in a fire, San Francisco's fire chief
could freely tap the Spring Valley Company's pipes "up to and
until such time" as another company or person introduced water
into the city.[21] If water were brought in by someone else, the act

---

[18] Ibid.

[19] Act of April 23, 1858, ch. 288, 1858 California Statutes 254 [hereafter cited as
Act of April 23, 1858].

[20] James Delgado, "The Humblest Cottage Can in a Short Time Afford . . . Pure
and Sparkling Water: Early Efforts to Solve Gold Rush San Francisco's Water
Shortage," *Pacific Historian* 26 (1982) 37.

[21] Act of April 23, 1858, supra note 19 at 255.

Spring Valley Water Works: outlet of the main tunnel and
commencement of the flume to the city. (Huntington Library)

required that Spring Valley furnish an unspecified quota of its
water for "fire and other municipal purposes."[22]

For two years Spring Valley operated under the San Francisco
City Water Works charter, providing San Francisco with free
municipal water. Naturally, the cost of that obligation increased
as the city's population grew. In 1867 the company attempted to
relieve itself of this responsibility by repudiating the charter and
turning instead to the Ensign Act. Interpreting Section 3 as
requiring free water only in case of fire, Spring Valley notified San
Francisco that unless it made payments and back payments for all
water use, the company would refuse to supply the city with
water for general municipal purposes. In effect, Spring Valley
maintained that its charter contained no regulatory provision
requiring it to provide free municipal water beyond fire extinguishment, and that San Francisco should pay like any other
customer. The city countersued, claiming that the company was
bound to continue its supply of free municipal water.

The ambiguity of Spring Valley's incorporation and the question of the city's entitlement to free water resulted in extensive
litigation in the state courts. Common-law tradition and a long
line of American state court cases supported municipal regulatory
power, especially the legitimacy of corporate obligations such as
free water provision for governmental purposes.[23] However,

[22] Ibid.

[23] Scheiber, "Road to *Munn*," supra note 5.

corporate charters also set the limits of state and municipal police powers within the terms of constitutional law. At issue were three clusters of basic issues in law: private-property rights, reasonable expectations in government-business relations, and obligations of contract. The nature of the particular "property" here was crucial. San Francisco, an expanding city in an arid region, was absolutely dependent upon Spring Valley for its water, a "necessity of life." Besides simply clarifying the terms of Spring Valley's charter, the courts' interpretation of the statutes' language would serve to draw boundary lines between legitimate municipal regulation and the effective confiscation of the company's water.

Four cases argued before the California Supreme Court reveal the difficulties involved. The court moved back and forth between rulings supportive of the city's regulatory authority and rulings protective of Spring Valley's private-property rights in its water. In the first case, in 1870, the court denied San Francisco's demand for an injunction against Spring Valley's proposed shutoff of city water.[24] In the second, in 1873, the court held that the Ensign Act required that Spring Valley provide San Francisco with free water for municipal purposes.[25] The third case was decided a year later, when the court invalidated the Ensign Act altogether under Article 4, Section 31, of the state's 1849 constitution, which prohibited the creation of "special franchises."[26] The court held that Spring Valley should have been organized under the 1858 General Incorporation Act for water companies, the terms of which required that water companies furnish the city or town they served with water "in case of fire or other great necessity, free of charge."[27] The court decided that the phrase "in case of fire or other great necessity" meant that Spring Valley was required only to furnish free water to San Francisco in case of fire, and for no other purpose.[28]

In the fourth case, in 1877, the court offered a new interpretation of the phrase "other great necessity," ruling that it extended beyond fire extinguishment. Justice McKinstry held that Spring Valley's duty included supplying free water to San Francisco for fire and any other activity in which water was "incidental to the discharge" of the supervisors' duties as local legislators.[29] This, he wrote, must be done for "the benefit of the public."[30] Thus, after

[24] San Francisco v. Spring Valley Water Works, 39 Cal. 473 (1870).

[25] San Francisco v. Spring Valley Water Works, 1 Cal. Unrep. 786 (1873).

[26] San Francisco v. Spring Valley Water Works, 48 Cal. 493 (1874).

[27] Act of April 22, 1858, supra note 16, Sec. 3 at 219.

[28] San Francisco v. Spring Valley Water Works, 48 Cal. 515 (1874).

[29] Spring Valley Water Works v. San Francisco, 52 Cal. 121-22 (1877).

[30] Ibid.

seven years of confused litigation with contradictory results, the court finally settled on an interpretation of Spring Valley's charter that forced the company's property-rights claims to yield to the public's interest in water.

## SOCIAL DISCONTENT AND THE 1879 CONSTITUTION

Over the course of the litigation from 1867 to 1877, national political and social conditions had a bearing on the Spring Valley cases and the development of judicial doctrine surrounding state police power. The year 1877 marked the beginning of economic depression throughout the country, and California was hard hit. San Francisco's unemployment rate approached 15 percent.[31] Diverse socioeconomic groups expressed intense and sometimes violent criticism of corporate power and a notoriously corrupt state legislature, demanding fundamental changes in the political process. Elected delegates finally convened for a constitutional convention in 1878.[32]

The San Francisco-Spring Valley litigation had an effect on the constitutional debates and the new document itself. Spring Valley, depicted at the convention as an "evil" monopoly which, through its "old rotten works ... has robbed the city for the last twenty years," was virtually a paradigm for the abusive corporate power many delegates hoped to constrain.[33]

San Francisco's Board of Supervisors also epitomized for many delegates the corrupt political power plaguing the state. The city was still reeling from a major political scandal involving Spring Valley's alleged bribery of several supervisors. In 1875 the company had allegedly offered several thousand dollars' worth of Spring Valley bonds for the votes of particular supervisors, when a decision was before the board regarding Spring Valley's offer to sell its entire operation to the city for $15 million.[34] The purchase price was outrageously inflated. Publicity of the back-room dealings in San Francisco's *Daily Evening Bulletin* and the *Call* roused public sentiment against the purchase. Popular antipathy for the company and distrust of the political process reached new heights, reflected in one editor's view:

---

[31] See Swisher, *Motivation and Political Technique*, supra note 6.

[32] Issel and Cherny, *San Francisco*, supra note 8 at 125.

[33] *Debates and Proceedings*, supra note 7.

[34] "Complaint in Equity, District Court of the Third Judicial District, in and for the City and County of San Francisco, *Theodore Le Roy v. Spring Valley Water Works, et al.*, March 17, 1876"; see generally G.K. Fitch MS; both sources, Bancroft Library.

Published by T. C. BOYD, Wood Engraver. (Iron Building,) corner Washington and Montgomery sts., SAN FRANCISCO.

"The California Water Carrier." Before the San Francisco City Water Works completed the redwood aqueducts to the city in 1858, water was brought by barge from Sausalito and sold from carts. (The Bancroft Library)

The history of the water supply of San Francisco, with the legislation and litigation attendent thereupon, is a record of venality, fraud and corruption, seldom or never equalled in a civilized community, or if attempted, never before allowed to escape its just punishment. If individuals, engaged in private enterprises had adopted such methods, as have been in vogue between city officials and water company employees, some of them would doubtless ere this, have found themselves in the position of convicted criminals, while others would help to swell the population of lunatic asylums, under the order of the tribunals having jurisdiction of the insane.[35]

At the constitutional convention, delegate J.S. Hager from San Francisco insisted that the Spring Valley Company professed to have a claim on all the water in the state; that no water works would be constructed in San Francisco until Spring Valley sold its

[35] "Fraudulent Water Rates," undated news clipping, G.K. Fitch MS, Bancroft Library.

operations, which it would not do for less than twice the price of their actual worth; and that Spring Valley's power was so great that the company always successfully interceded in legislative attempts to curtail its monopoly. He continued: "That which should be open and free to the world has been reduced to private ownership, a thing never heard of in any country in the world except in California, where water, the essential of life, is made the subject of private ownership by individuals and held by them."[36]

Other San Francisco delegates supported Hager's advocacy of public ownership of the state's waters, largely in response to Spring Valley's monopoly.[37] However, this was an extreme position at the time. Whereas state and federal courts' expansion of the public-purpose doctrine clearly justified regulation of municipal water supplies, it did not sanction exclusive public ownership of the resource. Delegates from other parts of California countered the San Francisco representatives' position with views protective of private-property rights in water.

While the 1879 constitution's final provisions concerning water use and regulation were neither radically reformist nor conservatively protective of property, they did specify regulatory procedures and public rights. Article 14 declared that the use of "all water now appropriated, or that may hereafter be appropriated for sale, rental, or distribution," was a public use, and was therefore to be subject to the regulation and control of the state. The article provided that the governing body of the city or town served by a private water company should set the rates in a manner prescribed by state law.

Pursuant to the 1879 constitution's provision nullifying all laws inconsistent with the new state organic law, this last section concerning rate setting had important implications for property claims in relation to municipal police power. Under the 1858 General Act for Incorporation of Water Companies, corporations had been allowed equal representation on rate-setting boards, which provided the property owners with some say in the price of the property. By giving full rate-setting discretion to local governments, the new constitution broadened governmental authority over property affecting the public interest. In other words, this provision brought explicitly to the fore and answered affirmatively the central question posed by Justice Field in his dissent in *Munn v. Illinois* (1876): "whether it is within the competency of a State to fix the compensation which an individual may receive

---

[36] *Debates and Proceedings*, supra note 7.

[37] Ibid. at 1021; see also Mary Catherine Miller, "Riparian Rights and the Control of Water in California, 1879-1928: The Relationship Between an Agricultural Enterprise and Legal Change," *Agricultural History* 59 (1985) 1.

for the use of his own property in his private business, and for his services in connection with it."[38]

Article 11 of the 1879 constitution also contained a response to issues raised in the Spring Valley litigation. Section 19 established that in any city where the municipality did not own or control any public water or electric works, any legally incorporated person or company could use the city streets to provide gas, electricity, or water, on condition that the municipality would regulate the charges. As originally proposed during the constitutional debates, this section stipulated that such companies provide the utility to the city free of charge. In explaining the section's original language, delegate James Reynolds stated, "We understand the reason very well—the power of Spring Valley. . . . It is simply to break the power of overshadowing monopolists."[39] However, over the protests of those from San Francisco, the delegates eventually eliminated the free-service requirement. Several delegates, "disposed to the opinion that there is some other spot on this globe besides San Francisco," successfully argued that such a provision would constrain healthy economic competition in towns with no private-utility monopoly.[40]

## FEDERAL ADJUDICATION AND THE AFFECTATION DOCTRINE

The 1879 constitution's categorization of water distribution as a public use reflected broader judicial developments in the United States concerning state police power vis-a-vis property categorized as private in ownership but public in use. At the federal level, the 1877 *Granger* cases had clearly articulated the affectation doctrine—that governments could regulate private property affected with a public interest.[41] Indeed, California's constitutional delegates framed Article 14 "in accordance with the decisions of the Supreme Court of the United States in the [*Granger*] Cases."[42]

In a series of cases litigated after adoption of the 1879 constitution, Spring Valley made many of the same arguments that had been unsuccessfully put forth by the railroad and elevator operators in the *Granger* cases. The company attacked the 1879 constitution's Article 14, which declared water distribution a public use and provided the terms of its regulation, as violating

---

[38]94 U.S. 138 (1877).

[39]*Debates and Proceedings*, supra note 7 at 1072.

[40]Ibid. at 1073.

[41]Scheiber, "Road to *Munn*," supra note 5. Compare Charles Fairman, "The So-Called Granger Cases, Lord Hale, and Justice Bradley," *Stanford Law Review* 5 (1953) 587.

[42]*Debates and Proceedings*, supra note 7 at 1020.

the U.S. Constitution's contract clause, and the due-process and equal-protection clauses of the Fourteenth Amendment. The state courts, and eventually the federal Ninth Circuit and U.S. Supreme Court, responded, in turn, as had Justice Waite in *Munn v. Illinois,* that

> All property which is affected with a public interest ceases to be *juris privati* only, and becomes subject to regulation for public benefit; and property is affected with a public interest whenever it is devoted to such use as to make it of public consequence and to directly affect the community at large.[43]

Nevertheless, the result of the post-1879, post-*Granger*-cases litigation between Spring Valley and San Francisco was not a foregone conclusion. Writing for the majority in the first of these cases heard before the California Supreme Court in 1881, Justice McKee wholeheartedly embraced the affectation doctrine of *Munn.*[44] However, parts of arguments set forth in a dissent

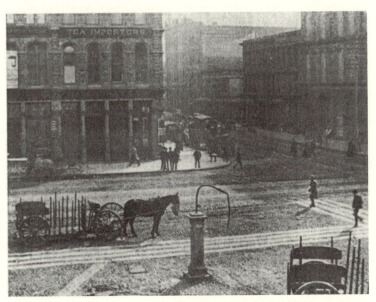

First and Market streets in San Francisco, 1886. A watering-cart hydrant stands in the foreground. (The Bancroft Library)

[43] *Munn v. Illinois,* 94 U.S. 126 (1876), quoted in *Spring Valley Water Works v. San Francisco,* 61 Cal. 8 (1881).

[44] Cal. Const. of 1849, Art. 12, Sec. 31.

written by Justice Ross in that case emerged in arguments of the majority in later cases between the Spring Valley Company and San Francisco. Analogous to Field's dissent in *Munn*, in which Field demanded a clear boundary between public and private spheres for the protection of private-property rights,[45] Ross argued that Spring Valley operated under a contract with San Francisco relating to property rights and to the amount the company should be paid for the property it owned.[46] Spring Valley thus had vested property rights in the water, beyond the reach of any subsequent legislation.[47] Ross made the additional point that if the majority were correct in holding that the new constitution nullified the rate-setting provisions of the charter under which Spring Valley had previously operated, the entire charter should be considered null and void.[48] This would have meant that San Francisco could no longer demand water from the corporation free of charge.[49]

Exactly one year later, in 1882, the supreme court reversed itself and ruled in *Spring Valley v. San Francisco* that all water companies that provided free water for municipal purposes were henceforth relieved of that obligation.[50] Adopting Ross's arguments, Justice Morrison wrote that "if the Constitution took from the Water Company the privilege of having a voice in fixing the rates it might charge for water supplied, it also relieved the company of the duty of supplying the water to the city for any purpose free of charge."[51]

An interesting ideological shift had thus occurred on the court. All but one of the seven justices elected under the 1879 constitution had run on the Workingmen's and Democratic tickets. The Workingmen's Party had been especially zealous in its reform campaign in blasting concentrated wealth and political corruption. While Article 14's provisions on regulation and governmental rate setting corresponded to the general reformist platform of constraining corporations like the Spring Valley Company, the campaign was also aimed at legislative abuses. Spring Valley had once been the focus of public outrage over its high rates, poor service, and legislative influence, but after the constitution's

---

[45] McCurdy, "Justice Field," supra note 1; Charles McCurdy, "Federalism and the Judicial Mind in a Conservative Age: Stephen Field," in Harry N. Scheiber and Malcolm Feeley, eds., *Power Divided: Essays on the Theory and Practice of Federalism* (Berkeley, 1989) 31.

[46] *Spring Valley v. San Francisco*, 61 Cal. 16 (1881).

[47] Ibid. at 17.

[48] Ibid. at 15.

[49] Ibid.

[50] *Spring Valley Water Works v. San Francisco*, 61 Cal. 18 (1882).

[51] Ibid. at 27.

adoption the San Francisco Board of Supervisors was routinely condemned in discussions on the "water question." The complaint expressed in local papers was that San Francisco's longtime insistence on free water for municipal purposes drove consumer rates up and so generated a windfall for large property owners in the city. A flyer circulated in 1880, entitled "An Appeal of the Water-Rate Payers of San Francisco," assessed the situation as follows:

> In no other place in the world is the whole tax of furnishing a city with water imposed solely upon the rate payers, and all other classes and interests allowed to escape. These rate payers pay for all the water used in and about the city, and property contributes not one cent. The wonder is that the people have submitted to this injustice so long. Is there any reason why the rate payer should pay for supplying municipal institutions with so-called free water, or for sprinkling streets and parks, or furnishing the means of putting out fires, that our merchants and capitalists may do business in safety by the purchase of cheap insurance, thereby deriving actual profits from the contributions largely of the poor?[52]

In contrast to McKinstry's holding in 1877 that, "for the benefit of the public," Spring Valley should provide free water for the city, after 1879 the California court pursued much deeper egalitarian objectives while supporting Spring Valley's qualified property rights. Simply put, it appeared right and fair for consumers of all types to pay for water; what was unfair was that private consumers, rather than property owners, should pay for all water used. In his 1882 opinion, Justice Morrison concluded that it was to "distribute the burden more equally that the new Constitution abolished free water."[53]

Though relieved of its burden, Spring Valley nonetheless pursued in federal courts its contention that Article 14 violated the federal contract clause and its Fourteenth Amendment due-process and equal-protection rights. Both the Ninth Circuit Court and the U.S. Supreme Court followed the doctrine of *Munn*, and affirmed McKee's 1881 ruling in California. Chief Justice Waite himself wrote the Supreme Court majority opinion in *Spring Valley Water Works v. Schottler*, decided in 1884. As in *Munn*, he

---

[52] "An Appeal of the Water-Rate Payers of San Francisco; Opinions of the Press and Citizens Upon the System of Water Rates," 1880, Bancroft Library.

[53] *Spring Valley Water Works v. San Francisco*, 61 Cal. 29 (1882).

Entrance to San Francisco Bay, Fort Point at right, Lime Point at left. In the foreground is the water flume that ran from Lobos Creek to the reservoir at Hyde and Francisco streets. (The Bancroft Library)

declared "that it is within the power of the government to regulate the prices at which water shall be sold by one who enjoys a virtual monopoly of the sale, we do not doubt."[54] Field wrote in dissent, as he had in *Munn*, asserting that the majority in this case went beyond "all former adjudications in sanctioning legislation impairing the obligation of contracts made by a State with corporations."[55]

The outcome of the federal cases is not surprising in light of *Munn* and the development of the police-power doctrine as of 1884. However, some of the arguments and opinions presented in these cases foreshadowed a significant change in the way state and federal courts would interpret the due-process clause. The observation made in the Ninth Circuit opinion that "the right [to set water rates] conferred upon the supervisors might, in unscrupulous hands, be abused" is telling.[56] In the Supreme Court, Waite wrote that there "would be time enough" to consider later what constituted reasonable rates set by San Francisco's Board of Supervisors.[57]

---

[54] *Spring Valley Water Works v. Schottler*, 110 U.S. 354 (1884).

[55] Ibid. at 356.

[56] *Spring Valley Water Works v. Bartlett*, Federal Reporter 16 643-44 (1883).

[57] *Spring Valley Water Works v. Schottler*, 110 U.S. 355 (1883).

## TOWARD SUBSTANTIVE DUE PROCESS

A California Supreme Court decision involving San Francisco and the Spring Valley Company, issued while the U.S. Supreme Court case between the two litigants was pending, offers a good example of the judicial deference to legislative regulation of business common in the late 1870s and early 1880s. Against Spring Valley's appeal in 1883 for a writ of prohibition restraining the San Francisco Board of Supervisors from setting water rates, the California Supreme Court issued a brief per curiam response: "In our judgment the matter of fixing water rates is not judicial, and for this reason the writ of prohibition cannot be awarded."[58] In January, 1890, however, the court issued an opinion in *Spring Valley Water Works v. San Francisco* that looked strikingly different from the cases of the same name filed over the years.[59] Waite's cautious statement that enough time existed for the determination of "reasonable" rates thus took on immediate significance. Six years after upholding the San Francisco Board of Supervisors' regulatory authority, the state court was forced to make a substantive analysis of the board's procedures.

In this case Spring Valley claimed that the rates set by the San Francisco Board of Supervisors for use of the company's water were so low that they amounted to confiscation of the company's property without due process, and deprivation of equal protection under the law.[60] Spring Valley appealed to the court for at least a reasonable and just return on its investment. Counsel for San Francisco claimed that the court had no jurisdiction over the matter, since California's 1879 constitution invested the board of supervisors with full discretion to set water rates. The California court thus confronted a question that would plague the legislative-judicial relationship until the mid-1930s: what constituted an appropriate level of judicial scrutiny concerning police-power regulations affecting private property?

The court did not proceed in its review of the rates set by the supervisors unself-consciously. Writing for the court, Justice Works stated:

> The constitution does not, in terms, confer upon the courts of this state any power or jurisdiction to control, supervise, or set aside any action of the board in respect to such rates. . . . [W]hen the board of supervisors have fairly investigated and exercised their discretion in

---

[58] *Spring Valley Water Works v. Bartlett*, 63 Cal. 245 (1883).
[59] *Spring Valley Water Works v. San Francisco*, 82 Cal. 286 (1890).
[60] Ibid. at 301.

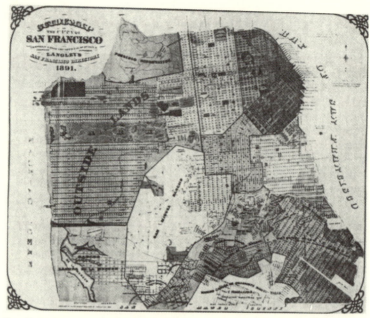

San Francisco city map, 1891. (The Bancroft Library)

fixing the rates, the courts have no right to interfere, on the sole ground that in the judgment of the court the rates thus fixed and determined are not reasonable."[61]

But here the court faced an obvious dilemma:

It seems to us that this complaint presents an entirely different question from this. The whole gist of the complaint is, that the board of supervisors have *not* exercised their judgment or discretion in the matter; that they have arbitrarily, without investigation, and without any exercise of judgment or discretion, fixed these rates without any reference to what they should be, without reference to the expense to the plaintiff necessary to furnish the water, or to what is a fair and reasonable compensation therefor; that the rates are so fixed as to render it impossible to furnish the water without loss, and so low as to amount to a practical confiscation of the plaintiff's property.[62]

[61] Ibid. at 305.
[62] Ibid. at 305-6.

"Picturesque San Francisco, 1896." View from Broadway and Divisadero streets, looking northeast. Angel and Alcatraz islands are in the background. (The Bancroft Library)

Against San Francisco's reliance on _Munn v. Illinois_ and the _Granger_ cases, which clearly established the regulatory powers of the state, the California court countered with Waite's warning in _Spring Valley v. Schottler_: "What may be done if the municipal authorities do not exercise an honest judgment, or if they fix upon a price which is manifestly unreasonable, need not now be considered, for that proposition is not presented by this record."[63] The California court invalidated the rates as set, warning that "regulation, as provided for in the constitution, does not mean confiscation, or a taking without just compensation."[64] The California court issued this decision approximately two months before the U.S. Supreme Court case of _Chicago, Milwaukee & St. Paul Railway Co. v. Minnesota_ (134 U.S. 418), which virtually overruled _Munn_. In that pivotal case, the majority held that the reasonableness of railway regulations was "eminently a question for judicial determination" and required due process of law for its determination.[65]

[63] Ibid. at 312.

[64] Ibid. at 307.

[65] 134 U.S. 458 (1890); Arnold Paul, "Legal Progressivism, the Courts, and the Crisis of the 1890s," in Friedman and Scheiber, _American Law and the Constitutional Order_, supra note 2 at 284.

## CONCLUSION

After the ratification of the Fourteenth Amendment in 1868, the West emerged as crucial to the development of due-process and equal-protection law. The phrase "Ninth Circuit Jurisprudence" denoted staunch defense of the civil rights of Chinese under Fourteenth Amendment protections.[66] The Ninth Circuit's extension of equal-protection and due-process rights in individuals' defense ensued even while the U.S. Supreme Court allowed the transformation of the amendment from a vehicle for protecting newly freed slaves into law invoked chiefly in the protection of private-property rights, often of corporations.

As illustrated by the various phases of the Spring Valley-San Francisco litigation after 1868, the protection of economic rights under the terms of the Fourteenth Amendment—even the basic jurisprudential issue of how "property" should be defined—proceeded with considerable controversy in the social and economic turmoil of the late nineteenth century. Here again the West emerged as important to jurisprudential innovation. Private claims of economic rights and liberty were played out against state power as national constitutional doctrine developed in counterpart with significant changes in state constitutional interpretations. Determination of the limits of private-property claims and the extent to which the public interest necessitated police-power action was essential in regard to water in the West.

[66] See Linda Przybyszewski, "Judge Lorenzo Sawyer and the Chinese: Civil Rights Decisions in the Ninth Circuit," *Western Legal History* 1 (1988) 23; Charles McClain, Jr., "The Chinese Struggle for Civil Rights in Nineteenth Century America: The First Phase, 1850-1870," *California Law Review* 72 (1984) 529.

# The Political Economy
# of Substantive Due Process

## Herbert Hovenkamp*

### I. INTRODUCTION: HISTORICAL EXPLANATION AND SUBSTANTIVE DUE PROCESS

"Substantive Due Process" is the name of a doctrine which the United States Supreme Court and other American courts used from around 1885[1] until the Roosevelt Court-packing crisis of 1937 to determine the constitutionality of regulatory legislation. Under this doctrine, the courts derived a test from the due process clause of the fourteenth amendment of the United States Constitution[2] for evaluating the substantive effect of economic regulations such as wage and hour laws,[3] product quality laws,[4] licensing restrictions,[5] restrictions on entry into business,[6] and price regulation.[7] The language of substantive due process generally spoke not of substantive regulatory stan-

* Professor of Law, University of Iowa College of Law. B.A., Calvin College; M.A., Ph.D., J.D., Univ. of Texas. My thanks to Lawrence Friedman, Robert Gordon, Louis Schwartz, Frank Easterbrook, Ken Kress, Lino Graglia, and Ian Ayres for commenting on an earlier draft.

1. *In re* Jacobs, 98 N.Y. 98 (1885), which struck down a statute forbidding cigar manufacturing in tenement houses, is commonly identified as the first case applying substantive due process analysis.

2. The term "substantive due process" refers also to the Court's fifth amendment jurisprudence in the area of federal regulation. Ever since Adair v. United States, 208 U.S. 161 (1908), and Coppage v. Kansas, 236 U.S. 1 (1915), the Supreme Court has held that substantive due process should be applied to federal legislation under the fifth amendment and state legislation under the fourteenth amendment, using the same legal standard. *See also* Adkins v. Children's Hosp., 261 U.S. 525 (1923) (applying liberty of contract to federal statute under the fifth amendment).

3. *E.g.*, Morehead v. New York *ex rel.* Tipaldo, 298 U.S. 587 (1936) (state minimum wage law); Murphy v. Sardell, 269 U.S. 530 (1925) (per curiam) (state minimum wage law); *Adkins*, 261 U.S. 525 (federal minimum wage law); Lochner v. New York, 198 U.S. 45 (1905) (state maximum hours law).

4. *E.g.*, Weaver v. Palmer Bros., 270 U.S. 402 (1926) (statute regulating quality of materials used to make bedding); Jay Burns Baking Co. v. Bryan, 264 U.S. 504 (1924) (statute requiring standardized weights for bread).

5. *E.g.*, Louis K. Liggett Co. v. Baldridge, 278 U.S. 105 (1928) (state licensing of pharmacists). *See also* notes 49-57 *infra* and accompanying text.

6. *E.g.*, New State Ice Co. v. Liebmann, 285 U.S. 262 (1932) (statute conditioning entry into ice business on demonstration of "necessity" and inadequacy of existing public facilities).

7. *E.g.*, Williams v. Standard Oil Co., 278 U.S. 235 (1929) (statute regulating prices of gasoline); Ribnik v. McBride, 277 U.S. 350, 357 (1928) ("[T]he fixing of prices for food or clothing, of house rental or of wages to be paid, whether minimum or maximum, is beyond the legislative power."); Tyson & Brother-United Theatre Ticket Offices v. Banton, 273 U.S. 418 (1927) (statute regulating prices of admissions to amusements); *see also* Smyth v. Ames,

dards but rather of individual constitutional right. Individuals were said to possess a "liberty of contract" which, like their other constitutional liberties, gave them freedom from governmental interference, meaning, in this case, freedom to make choices affecting individual economic status. As Justice Sutherland put it in *Adkins v. Children's Hospital,* "the right to contract about one's affairs is a part of the liberty of the individual protected by [the due process] clause."[8]

Legal rights are intellectual creations. They reflect the world view of the people who make and defend them. To know a culture's legal rights is to know something about the things its people believe are important. This essay explores one important aspect of pre-Modernist economic policy—the relationship between nineteenth century American political economy and constitutional decisionmaking in the courts. In this period American ideological and scientific values were undergoing an extensive and painful transformation. Post-Darwinian scientists generally thought of themselves as empiricists. They purported to be unimpressed by purely contextual or metaphysical explanations of things. Pragmatism, and later Modernism, inspired an obsession in the social sciences with measurement and verification.[9] By the 1920s, nearly every respectable scientist claimed to believe that no statement about any subject, including humanity and society, was meaningful unless it could be empirically proven or disproven.[10] Today we refer to this transformation of the scientific world view as the "Modernist" revolution.

Two aspects of the Pre-Modernist period in constitutional history, often called the age of "liberty of contract," stand out. First, it was an unprecedented period of judicial activism and creativity. The United States Supreme Court and many state courts reversed a long-standing policy of judicial deference to legislation and began second-guessing the wisdom of lawmakers on a large scale. In the process, courts often created substantive doctrines unsupported by the language or legislative history of any constitutional provision or statute. Second, the doctrine was not only revisionist, but it seemed peculiarly out of step with the dominant political values of the day. The Supreme Court appeared determined to prevent the emergence of the Regulatory and Welfare States, despite substantial support for such change by a variety of interests, including both business and labor, the wealthy and the impoverished.[11]

---

169 U.S. 466 (1898) (striking down "confiscatory" rate regulation and attempting to establish cost-based regulatory standards).

8. 261 U.S. 525, 545 (1923).

9. *See* E. Purcell, The Crisis of Democratic Theory: Scientific Naturalism & the Problem of Value 15-30 (1973).

10. *See id.*

11. For example, labor supported the wage-and-hour laws. *See* J.L. Bates, The United States 1898-1928, at 141-43 (1976); J. Buenker, Urban Liberalism and Progressive Reform 42-79 (1973). Many industrialists supported such things as rate regulation of railroads,

Historians have developed a number of hypotheses to explain this legal theory. The hypotheses are inconsistent with each other, and to one degree or another, all are inconsistent with the hypothesis offered here.

A. *The "Legal Formalism" Hypothesis*

Many critics of substantive due process have observed that those responsible for constitutionalizing the doctrine were out of step with their time.[12] In a world dominated by Darwin, Marx, and the social sciences, how could anyone believe that people had a constitutional right to be free of governmental economic regulation?

One of the most important intellectual events of the 1880s and 1890s was the rise of the modern social sciences—economics, psychology and psychiatry, sociology, and political science.[13] By the turn of the century, social scientists in America were developing a rather high view of themselves: Their self-professed job was to identify social problems and to formulate policies for solving them. Social scientists advocated official implementation of these policies by legislation, executive orders, or judicial rules.[14] They believed the state should adopt these policies because they were scientifically formulated. No one could ever verify the statement of a right, such as "an employer has a right to pay any wage he and his employees agree upon." Progressive Era social scientists like Charles R. Van Hise, Richard T. Ely, Edward A. Ross, and jurisprudent Roscoe Pound believed, however, that statements such as "minimum wage laws provide more efficient use of economic resources" had a scientific, or empirical, meaning that made them more plausible than doctrines like liberty of contract. State legislatures appeared to agree. They passed a wide variety of statutes regulating wages, hours, working conditions, and product quality.[15]

The result was a great tension between the legislative process and the common law. The great economic and industrial expansion of the nineteenth century, the massive growth in the political power of the lower economic classes, and the great increase in state legislation, much of which abrogated the common law, threatened the common law's traditional role as primary economic regulator. One widely accepted explanation of the substantive due process era is that judges

---

at least after the 1890s. *See* G. KOLKO, RAILROADS AND REGULATION 1877-1916, at 87-90 (1965). Likewise, established business firms supported many of the licensing and entry restrictions. *See* Friedman, *Freedom of Contract and Occupational Licensing 1890-1910: A Legal and Social Study*, 53 CALIF. L. REV. 487, 497 (1965).

12. *E.g.*, Pound, *Liberty of Contract*, 18 YALE L.J. 454 (1909).

13. *See generally* E. PURCELL, *supra* note 9; Hovenkamp, *Evolutionary Models in Jurisprudence*, 64 TEX. L. REV. 645 (1985).

14. A leading champion of this position was Roscoe Pound. *See* Hovenkamp, *supra* note 13, at 677-83.

15. *See generally* R. CRUNDEN, MINISTERS OF REFORM (1982); R. HOFSTADTER, THE AGE OF REFORM (1955).

responded to this legislative activity by looking within. They became obsessed with deriving from the common law its own set of values, which required the protection of certain abstractly defined property rights. This critique accuses the judges of the substantive due process courts of being "formalist."[16]

Formalism is law without a policy—except perhaps for the policy that the law must be internally consistent and self-contained, and must not draw its wisdom from outside. Legal Progressives such as Roscoe Pound, who were contemporaries of the substantive due process courts, attacked legal formalism as judicial decisionmaking detached from any policy considerations.[17] Some later historians have also described the period of substantive due process as the age of formalism.[18]

But even formalistic law contains a policy, although it may be the policy of the judges themselves and not the perceived policy of the legislature. For example, when Holmes attacked the majority's decision in *Lochner v. New York*,[19] he did not accuse the Court of creating a legal rule without a policy. He accused it of enacting "Mr. Herbert Spencer's *Social Statics*," and of deciding the case "upon an economic theory which a large part of the country does not entertain."[20] The policy encased in judicial formalism might be that judges should protect the propertied class from the tyranny of the masses, or simply that one economic or social theory is better than another one. Nevertheless, even the most formalistic judge has an idea that his decision will somehow be best for the community. The Supreme Court that decided *Lochner* in 1905 was "formalistic" only because it preferred one economic theory to another, or perhaps because it believed that the prerogative of selecting economic theories belongs to judges rather than legislators.

Another objection to the "formalist" thesis is that it hypothesizes a law that is both static and uncreative.[21] The case law of substantive due process was neither. The law changed very rapidly during the period substantive due process dominated constitutional adjudication.[22] Fur-

---

16. *See* Nelson, *The Impact of the Antislavery Movement upon Styles of Judicial Reasoning in Nineteenth Century America*, 87 HARV. L. REV. 513 (1974); Paine, *Instrumentalism v. Formalism: Dissolving the Dichotomy*, 1978 WIS. L. REV. 997, 1009-12; Scheiber, *Instrumentalism and Property Rights: A Reconsideration of American "Styles of Judicial Reasoning" in the 19th Century*, 1975 WIS. L. REV. 1.

17. *See, e.g.*, Pound, *supra* note 12; Pound, *Mechanical Jurisprudence*, 8 COLUM. L. REV. 605 (1908) [hereinafter *Mechanical Jurisprudence*].

18. *See, e.g.*, H. COMMAGER, THE AMERICAN MIND 359-73 (1950); M. WHITE, SOCIAL THOUGHT IN AMERICA: THE REVOLT AGAINST FORMALISM 59-75 (1957); *see also* W. O'NEILL, THE PROGRESSIVE YEARS: AMERICA COMES OF AGE 93-95 (1975).

19. 198 U.S. 45 (1905).

20. *Id.* at 75 (Holmes, J., dissenting) (citing H. SPENCER, SOCIAL STATICS (London 1851)).

Holmes probably believed there is no such thing as a legal rule without a policy. Twenty-five years earlier he had written that, in spite of what judges say, they in fact base their decisions on what they believe is "expedient for the community concerned." O.W. HOLMES, THE COMMON LAW 35 (1881).

21. *See, e.g.*, *Mechanical Jurisprudence*, *supra* note 17.

22. The law of substantive due process changed substantially during the period 1885-

ther, judges who used substantive due process also produced some of the most creative, noninterpretivist decisions ever written. One example is *In re Debs*, in which the Court cut from new cloth the doctrine that the executive branch has the power to protect interstate commerce from labor disputes, even though Congress had not passed a statute authorizing the executive's action.[23]  Another is *Ex parte Young*, in which Justice Peckham held that the sovereign immunity provision of the eleventh amendment does not apply when a private party seeks to enjoin a state official from enforcing an unconstitutional statute, because the official is "stripped of his official or representative character."[24]  The statute at issue in *Young* was a railroad rate regulation alleged to interfere with the free market. Justice Peckham had no idea what liberal, activist federal courts would do with his decision a half century later![25]

But more important than these novel jurisdictional rulings was the fact that substantive due process was a highly creative substantive legal doctrine at its very core.  It devised a set of economic rules from a constitutional provision in which they were nowhere to be found.  Neither the language nor the legislative history of the fourteenth amendment suggested a congressional concern with minimum wage laws, rate regulation, or business licensing.  Indeed, the legislative history of the fourteenth amendment was all but irrelevant in substantive due process cases.  The judges practiced aggressive, loose construction.

Not even the contemporary proponents of legal formalism articulated a closed system for public law like the one they envisioned for private law.  The paradigm of legal formalism in private law is undoubtedly Christopher Columbus Langdell's 1871 casebook on contracts,[26] which probably did more than any other document to convince two generations of lawyers that legal rules should be derived only from earlier decisions.  But Professor Langdell's work had little analogue in public law.  On the contrary, constitutional scholarship was about to embark on one of its most fertile, interdisciplinary periods.  It would aggressively incorporate another discipline—economics—on a large scale.  The economic theory employed by the courts, whether right or wrong, was an *economic* theory, not the product of legal formalism.

---

1937. In earlier cases such as *In re Jacobs*, 98 N.Y. 98 (1885), and *Lochner*, 198 U.S. 45 (1905), the courts expressed general hostility toward legislation interfering with the market.  Twenty years later in *Adkins*, 261 U.S. 525 (1923), however, the Supreme Court clearly treated statutory regulation of the market price with more hostility than regulation of nonprice terms such as the hours of labor because, presumably, the parties could still bargain around such nonprice regulations by adjusting wages. *See id.* at 554.  During the Chief Justiceship of Edward D. White, 1910-1921, the United States Supreme Court appeared to abandon the doctrine, only to reassert it in the 1920s. *See* Currie, *The Constitution in the Supreme Court: 1910-1921*, 1985 DUKE L.J. 1111, 1129-30.

    23. 158 U.S. 564, 581-82 (1895).
    24. 209 U.S. 123, 160 (1908).
    25. *See* C. WRIGHT, THE LAW OF FEDERAL COURTS 292 (4th ed. 1983) (*Young* provides basis for school desegregation and reapportionment cases).
    26. C. LANGDELL, A SELECTION OF CASES ON THE LAW OF CONTRACTS (1871).

## B.   Economic Hypotheses

Historians often use the word "economic" in a different sense than economists. Many economists, particularly the neoclassicists,[27] believe that economics is a science concerned with the efficient allocation of resources, but not with their distribution.[28] An "economic" question to them is a question about how resources can most efficiently be assigned, regardless of who might be richer and who poorer. Questions about how resources should be divided among conflicting claimants are "political."

When historians, particularly those of the left, use the word "economic," they generally mean "political" in this sense. For example, Charles Beard's famous *Economic Interpretation of the Constitution*[29] does not develop a theory that the Constitution's Framers set out to devise a document that would maximize American wealth or welfare. On the contrary, Beard argues that the Framers represented various interest groups, each of which wished to maximize its own personal wealth. Beard's "economic" interpretation is really a "political," or distributive, interpretation.

Many contemporary legal historians use economic theories to explain the development of the law.[30] However, not all of the persons who have written this history are economic determinists. Economic determinists generally believe that legal rights are nothing more than the consequence of struggles over scarce resources. Karl Marx and William Graham Sumner[31]—two people with extraordinarily different political views—agreed about that. But historians who are not economic determinists believe that people make some decisions that are not dictated by resource scarcity. They do not believe that politics, science, or even religion and the arts developed out of conflicts between economic interests. Although many legal historians have fully justified their broad use of economic explanations for the development of the law, most of them would probably say that some special quality of the

---

27.   The original neoclassicists—Jevons, Marshall, and Pigou—concerned themselves deeply with distributional questions. *See* notes 152-160 *infra* and accompanying text. But modern neoclassicists, such as members of the Chicago School, generally do not share that concern or regard it as not appropriate to economic science.

28.   On the absence of distributive concerns in classical political economy, see P. ATIYAH, THE RISE AND FALL OF FREEDOM OF CONTRACT 335-38 (1979).

29.   C. BEARD, AN ECONOMIC INTERPRETATION OF THE CONSTITUTION OF THE UNITED STATES (1913).

30.   *See, e.g.,* L. FRIEDMAN, A HISTORY OF AMERICAN LAW (2d ed. 1985); M. HORWITZ, THE TRANSFORMATION OF AMERICAN LAW, 1780-1860 (1977); J. HURST, LAW AND ECONOMIC GROWTH: THE LEGAL HISTORY OF THE LUMBER INDUSTRY IN WISCONSIN: 1836-1915 (1964); W. NELSON, AMERICANIZATION OF THE COMMON LAW: THE IMPACT OF LEGAL CHANGE ON MASSACHUSETTS SOCIETY, 1760-1830, at 145-64 (1975); M. TUSHNET, AMERICAN LAW OF SLAVERY (1981); Friedman & Ladinsky, *Social Change and the Law of Industrial Accidents,* 67 COLUM. L. REV. 50 (1967).

31.   *See* W. SUMNER, *Rights,* in 1 ESSAYS OF WILLIAM GRAHAM SUMNER 358 (1934); W. SUMNER, *Some Natural Rights,* in *id.* at 363; *see also* Hovenkamp, *supra* note 13, at 669-70.

law makes economic explanation more appropriate than in some other areas of human expression.

This special quality is the law's own economic consciousness. Law is a cultural activity. It consists only of the things people think about it, and people frequently perceive legal conflicts as economic conflicts. When in a hard case an appellate judge is asked to make a certain rule—perhaps that railroad operators should be liable only for the foreseeable consequences of their negligent acts—the judge understands that she is encouraging or discouraging certain activities by applying economic sanctions. The accumulated weight of a large number of such rules will form a policy about railroads—about how much it should cost to operate them and how the members of society should share this cost. Of course, not every judge has enough vision to consider what role the railroad plays in the American economy and how a particular rule will affect that role.[32] But even the most rule-bound judge asks herself simple economic questions, such as which party ought to be on guard at railroad crossings and who should pay the consequences. Invariably, the judge makes an economic decision.

This essay offers an explanation for the phenomenon of substantive due process that is "economic" in the historian's sense, or political. It argues that American judges had an economic point of view that law treatise writer Theodore Sedgwick offered already in 1836. "What then is the difference between good laws and good public economy?" he asked rhetorically.[33] "None," he answered, "because all good laws tend to the production and just distribution of wealth; all good laws are good economy."[34] The difference between law and political economy, Sedgwick concluded, is that law is positive while political economy is normative. "The former teaches what the law is, which it is the business of the lawyer to learn; the latter teaches what law should be, which is the business of the public economist, or legislator to learn."[35]

But the judges who developed substantive due process behaved more like Sedgwick's ideal legislators, separating those laws which they saw as tending to the production of wealth from those that did not. In the process these judges hid, suppressed, or trivialized underlying conflicts about how wealth should be distributed. Their political economy convinced them that questions about wealth distribution should be treated as nothing more than questions about economic efficiency. Within the classical model of political economy these questions had right answers that legislators had frequently failed to discover.

The importance of this argument is not to show that the judges were right, but that political economy helped them think they were right.

---

32. However, some judges have done so since very early in the nineteenth century. *See generally* M. HORWITZ, *supra* note 30.

33. T. SEDGWICK, PUBLIC AND PRIVATE ECONOMY 31 (1836).

34. *Id.*

35. *Id.*

Substantive due process was another of many failed nineteenth century quests for a "rule of law"—a set of legal rights that could be considered "just" without regard to the way it distributed wealth as between conflicting claimants. In the end, of course, classical political economy was just as temporal and mortal as substantive due process itself. Judicial attitudes toward substantive due process changed when the prevailing economic doctrine changed, in the 1920s and 1930s.

In the late nineteenth century most judges were reluctant to recognize economic conflict explicitly as a justification for changing legal rules. This was not the case with the legislatures. By the turn of the century, a large gap had developed between judicial and legislative perceptions about the role of the law as a wealth distribution device. Many states had enacted legislation that intervened in the market on behalf of labor, regulating child labor, women's maximum hours, and hours or working conditions in certain industries. They had also enacted a host of licensing and regulatory restrictions that benefited established businesses at the expense of prospective entrants, although some of these regulations had health or safety justifications as well. Fierce attacks on classical laissez-faire economic theory by economists such as Charles Francis Adams, Jr.,[36] Richard T. Ely,[37] Edwin Seligman,[38] and John R. Commons[39] provided intellectual support for this legislative reform. But the Supreme Court continued to rely on classical economic theories developed in the late eighteenth and early nineteenth centuries. Why it was so sternly committed to an obsolete economic theory is a perplexing question.

The economic explanation that seems least reasonable, although some scholars,[40] including Holmes,[41] appeared to believe it, is that the Supreme Court Justices who believed in substantive due process were

---

36. *E.g.,* Adams, *The Granger Movement,* 120 N. AM. REV. 394, 399-400 (1875) (questions the laissez-faire conception of competition as the ultimate goal of all markets).

37. *E.g.,* R. ELY, PROPERTY AND CONTRACT IN THEIR RELATIONS TO THE DISTRIBUTION OF WEALTH (1914).

38. *See, e.g.,* Seligman, *Is the Income Tax Constitutional and Just?,* FORUM March 1895, at 56 (criticizing regressive taxation schedules).

39. *See* J. COMMONS, LEGAL FOUNDATIONS OF CAPITALISM (1924).

40. *See, e.g.,* A. PAUL, CONSERVATIVE CRISIS AND THE RULE OF LAW: ATTITUDES OF BAR AND BENCH, 1887-1895, at 232-37 (1960) (the Court responded to conservative pressures and protected the rights of the conservative minority to property); B. TWISS, LAWYERS AND THE CONSTITUTION: HOW LAISSEZ FAIRE CAME TO THE SUPREME COURT 13-17 (1942) (lawyers shaped the arguments and cases before the Court and thus brought about doctrinal support for their clients' property interests).

41. *See* Holmes, *The Path of the Law,* 10 HARV. L. REV. 457 (1897). Justice Holmes wrote: When socialism first began to be talked about, the comfortable classes of the community were a good deal frightened. I suspect that this fear has influenced judicial action both here and in England. . . . I think that something similar has led people who no longer hope to control the legislatures to look to the courts as expounders of the Constitution, and that in some courts new principles have been discovered outside the bodies of those instruments, which may be generalized into acceptance of the economic doctrines which prevailed about fifty years ago . . . .
*Id.* at 467-68.

protecting the interests of the economic classes that had worked to secure their judicial appointments. According to this argument, many of these cases presented a conflict between property holders and unpropertied wage earners. The Supreme Court Justices, most of whom came from the ranks of the propertied minority, consciously or unconsciously voted for "their side" in such cases. This rationale may also explain why the Court upheld comprehensive land use planning, which seemed to interfere with liberty of contract at least as much as did the wage and hour regulations which the Court was striking down under the substantive due process doctrine.[42] The land-use cases were not conflicts between the propertied and the penniless, but conflicts between competing landowners over how land should be used. Wealthy developers who wanted to use their land for industry often challenged zoning ordinances, while affluent businessmen or professionals who wanted to preserve the integrity of their residential or retail neighborhoods often defended them. The Court was willing to allow legislative regulation in these cases, so the argument goes, because the statutes produced no clear benefit to unpropertied wage earners at the expense of the wealthy.

Although it explains some hard cases, this economic interest argument ultimately fails. First, it makes causal assumptions that impeach the integrity of the Justices on the basis of little or no extrinsic evidence. Second, it gives substantive due process a rather odd pedigree. The Court first entertained the doctrine in 1873 in the *Slaughter-House Cases*,[43] in which four Justices were ready to condemn a state statute which they believed gave a monopoly to a group of legislatively favored butchers at the expense of those not so favored.[44] Whatever the statute in the *Slaughter-House Cases* may have been, it was *not* a legislative attempt to transfer money from property owners to the working class.[45] The Supreme Court finally adopted a substantive due process argument in *Allgeyer v. Louisiana*[46] to strike down a statute restricting the sale

---

42. *See, e.g.*, Village of Euclid v. Ambler Realty Co., 272 U.S. 365 (1926).

43. 83 U.S. (16 Wall.) 36 (1873).

44. *Id.* at 83 (Field, J., dissenting).

45. The statute at issue in the *Slaughter-House Cases* was in fact a well-motivated and probably efficient attempt to regulate the slaughtering industry in order to control a major health problem. *See* Hovenkamp, *Technology, Politics, and Regulated Monopoly: An American Historical Perspective*, 62 TEX. L. REV. 1263, 1295-1308 (1984).

46. 165 U.S. 578 (1897). *Allgeyer*'s status as the first substantive due process case in the United States Supreme Court is arguable because the real issue in the case was the scope of a state's power to apply its statutory law to a contract that was made in another state. The Court held that extraterritorial application of a state's insurance regulation exceeded the state's legislative jurisdiction. The Court suggested that there is a "liberty of contract" under which extraterritorial legislation will be scrutinized more severely than legislation applied entirely within the state. *Id.* at 591.

The Supreme Court's subsequent decision in Nutting v. Massachusetts, 183 U.S. 553 (1902), confirms that the Court's primary concern in *Allgeyer* was the extraterritorial application of the state's regulatory power rather than the right to contract itself. In *Nutting*, the Court upheld a statute similar to the one at issue in *Allgeyer*, but which applied only to insur-

of insurance within the state by out-of-state insurance companies. The legislature probably enacted the statute in *Allgeyer* to shield in-state insurance companies from out-of-state competitors.[47] Neither the *Slaughter-House Cases* nor *Allgeyer* can be characterized as the Supreme Court's "choosing sides" with the propertied at the expense of the penniless.

Neither is the hypothesis of vested judicial interest consistent with the later judicial record of substantive due process. Most of the critics of substantive due process were Progressives, or else strong supporters of the ideology of the New Deal. In the process of condemning substantive due process they often drew a distorted picture of the economic impact of substantive due process decisions. For example, they chose to discuss cases that struck down wage-and-hour legislation, thus suggesting that the substantive due process court was "antilabor." In fact, the Court sometimes upheld statutes that interfered quite substantially with the contractual relationship between employers and employees.[48] Further, although some of the better known substantive due process decisions involved conflicts between industry and labor, most cases cannot be so characterized. For example, many statutes creating entry or licensing restrictions for various occupations or professions were overturned.[49]

---

ance contracts formed within the state. The Court recognized a distinguishing principle established in Hooper v. California, 155 U.S. 648 (1895), and followed in *Allgeyer*, by noting that:

> The proposition that, because a citizen might make such a contract for himself beyond the confines of his State, therefore he might authorize an agent to violate in his behalf the laws of his State within her own limits, involves a clear *non sequitur*, and ignores the vital distinction between acts done within and acts done beyond a State's jurisdiction.

*Nutting*, 183 U.S. at 558 (quoting *Hooper*, 155 U.S. at 658-59) (statement also quoted in *Allgeyer*, 165 U.S. at 588). Justice Harlan was the only dissenter in *Nutting*, concluding that the case did not differ in principle from *Allgeyer*. 183 U.S. at 558.

47. *See* W. NELSON, THE ROOTS OF AMERICAN BUREAUCRACY, 1830-1900, at 152-53 (1982). Earlier statutes designed for the same purpose had been struck down by state courts for exceeding the state's power to tax for a "public purpose." *E.g.*, Philadelphia Ass'n for the Relief of Disabled Firemen v. Wood, 39 Pa. 73 (1861) (statute imposing duty on out-of-state insurance companies, but not on in-state companies, and providing that the proceeds should be given to the Philadelphia Association for the Relief of Disabled Firemen, a private corporation, struck down).

An argument can be made, however, that the statute condemned in *Allgeyer* was designed to protect consumers from fraudulent insurance practices. Since the state could not control the practices of out-of-state insurance companies, it simply restricted the sale of their insurance within the state. The statute, which applied to commercial marine insurance, required those offering insurance within the state to maintain an office there with at least one authorized agent. The effect may have been to increase a foreign insurance company's cost of doing business in Louisiana and to permit the state more control over their activities.

48. *See, e.g.*, Chicago, B. & Q. R.R. v. McGuire, 219 U.S. 549 (1911) (approving an Iowa statute which voided limitation of liability for injury clauses in railroad employment contracts).

49. *See, e.g.*, New State Ice Co. v. Liebmann, 285 U.S. 262 (1932); Frost v. Corporate Comm'n, 278 U.S. 515 (1929); Louis K. Liggett Co. v. Baldridge, 278 U.S. 105 (1928); Frost & Frost Trucking Co. v. Railroad Comm'n, 271 U.S. 583 (1926).

State courts also struck down legislative attempts to impose licens-ing[50] in cases involving blacksmiths,[51] undertakers,[52] ticket agents,[53] druggists,[54] and plumbers.[55] Such licensing restrictions almost always protected established businesses from potential new competitors.[56] Many of the courts that struck down such statutes made express find-ings to this effect and condemned the statutes as monopolistic. For example, in 1910 when the New York Court of Appeals struck down a statute setting conditions on the licensing of embalmers and undertak-ers, the court found the "public health" justification offered by the state inadequate. Rather:

> We cannot refrain from the thought that the act in question was conceived and promulgated in the interests of those then engaged in the undertaking business, and that the relation which the business bears to the general health, morals, and welfare of the state had much less influence upon its originators than the prospective monopoly that could be exercised with the aid of its provisions.[57]

Similar sentiments were voiced in decisions employing either sub-stantive due process or its analogue in taxation law, the public purpose doctrine,[58] to strike down legislative subsidies for private business.[59]

---

50.  See generally Friedman, supra note 11.

51.  See Bessette v. People, 193 Ill. 334, 62 N.E. 215 (1901); People v. Beattie, 96 A.D. 383, 89 N.Y.S. 193 (1904); In re Aubrey, 36 Wash. 308, 78 P. 900 (1904).

52.  See Wyeth v. Thomas, 200 Mass. 474, 86 N.E. 925 (1909); People v. Ringe, 197 N.Y. 143, 90 N.E. 451 (1910).

53.  See People ex rel. Tyroler v. Warden, 157 N.Y. 116, 51 N.E. 1006 (1898).

54.  See Noel v. People, 187 Ill. 587, 58 N.E. 616 (1900); see also Commonwealth v. Zacharias, 3 Pa. Super. 264 (1897).

55.  See Schnaier v. Navarre Hotel & Importation Co., 182 N.Y. 83, 74 N.E. 561 (1905); State ex rel. Richey v. Smith, 42 Wash. 237, 84 P. 851 (1906); see also State v. Gardner, 58 Ohio St. 599, 51 N.E. 136 (1898); State ex rel. Winkler v. Benzenberg, 101 Wis. 172, 76 N.W. 345 (1898).

56.  See Cooley, Limits to State Control of Private Business, 1 PRINCETON REV. 233, 263-66 (ser. 4 1878).

57.  People v. Ringe, 197 N.Y. 143, 151, 90 N.E. 451, 454 (1910); see also State v. Walker, 48 Wash. 8, 11-15, 92 P. 775, 776-78 (1907) (Rudkin, J., dissenting). The point is also strongly expressed in Richey:
[E]very legislative session brings forth some new act in the interest of some new trade or occupation. The doctor, the lawyer, the druggist, the dentist, the barber, the horseshoer, and the plumber have already received favorable consideration at the hands of our Legislature, and the end is not yet, for the nurse and the undertaker are knocking at the door.
State ex rel. Richey v. Smith, 42 Wash. 237, 248, 84 P. 851, 854 (1906).

58.  On the development of the public purpose doctrine in taxation as a supplement to substantive due process, see C. JACOBS, LAW WRITERS AND THE COURTS 98-159 (1954); Hovenkamp, The Classical Corporation in American Legal Thought (forthcoming).

59.  United States Supreme Court cases striking down such legislative subsidies include Cole v. La Grange, 113 U.S. 1 (1885), Parkersburg v. Brown, 106 U.S. 487 (1882), and Loan Association v. Topeka, 87 U.S. (20 Wall.) 655 (1874).
Other subsidy cases involving state legislation include Dodge v. Mission Township, 107 F. 827 (8th Cir. 1901) (sugar manufacturer), Sutherland-Innes Co. v. Evart, 86 F. 597 (6th Cir. 1898) (barrel stave manufacturer), United States ex rel. Miles Planting & Mfg. Co. v. Carlisle, 5 App. D.C. 138 (1895) (sugar producer), McConnell v. Hamm, 16 Kan. 228 (1876) (wool man-ufacturer), State ex rel. Griffith v. Osawkee Township, 14 Kan. 418 (1875) (relief to drought-stricken communities), Lowell v. Boston, 111 Mass. 454 (1873) (relief to businesses in area

These decisions simply cannot be characterized as a judicial choice to side with business against labor, immigrants, and the poor. On the contrary, they permitted such groups increased entry into established markets in the face of protectionist legislation designed either to exclude newcomers directly or to give established firms a cost advantage over prospective entrants. Business, like labor, was required to survive the test of the marketplace.

Even Supreme Court decisions striking down legislative price regulations[60] must be characterized as ambiguous. Under the "public interest" view of regulation, these statutes were passed for the benefit of consumers in order to control monopoly pricing by various industries.[61] Today the record suggests just as strongly, however, that the businesses themselves wanted the relief from competition that price regulation can bring, and that they were most often its principal beneficiaries.[62]

---

destroyed by fire), Michigan Sugar Co. v. Auditor Gen., 124 Mich. 674, 83 N.W. 625 (1900) (sugar manufacturer), Clee v. Sanders, 74 Mich. 692, 42 N.W. 154 (1889) (barrel stave manufacturer), Minnesota Sugar Co. v. Iverson, 91 Minn. 30, 97 N.W. 454 (1903) (sugar manufacturer), Weismer v. Douglas, 64 N.Y. 91 (1876) (lumber company), Ferrell v. Doak, 152 Tenn. 88, 275 S.W. 29 (1925) (private box manufacturer), and Ohio Valley Iron Works v. Moundsville, 11 W. Va. 1 (1877) (iron works). *See also* Opinion of the Justices, 58 Me. 584, 592-93 (1870) (advisory opinion that state legislation permitting municipalities to give subsidies to existing manufacturing firms would be unconstitutional) ("Capital naturally gravitates to the best investment. If a particular place or a special kind of manufacture promises large returns, the capitalist will be little likely to hesitate in selecting the place and in determining upon the manufacture."). In Allen v. Inhabitants of Jay, 60 Me. 124 (1872), the Maine Supreme Court subsequently struck down a subsidy statute. *See also* People *ex rel.* Detroit & H.R.R. v. Township Bd., 20 Mich. 452 (1870); Whiting v. Sheboygan & F. R.R., 25 Wis. 167 (1879); Curtis's Adm'r v. Whipple, 24 Wis. 350 (1869); Weeks v. Milwaukee, 10 Wis. 186 (1860).

Railroads were generally an exception to the rules prohibiting public subsidies to private business. *See* C. Jacobs, *supra* note 58, at 114-25. *But see* Hanson v. Vernon, 27 Iowa 28 (1869) (striking down a railroad subsidy). *See generally* J. Dillon, The Law of Municipal Corporations §§ 104-105a (2d ed. 1873) (citing other state law cases and noting that federal law permitted railroad subsidies).

The history of legislative subsidies for new enterprise goes back at least to the beginning of the nineteenth century, and the gross amount of such subsidies was substantial. *See generally* C. Goodrich, Government Promotion of American Canals and Railroads: 1800-1890 (1960); L. Mercer, Railroads and Land Grant Policy: A Study in Government Intervention (1982); J. Sanborn, Congressional Grants of Land in Aid of Railways (1899). For one contemporary scholar's analysis of the cases limiting government's power to aid business, see F. Goodnow, Social Reform and the Constitution 292-328 (1911).

60. *See* note 7 *supra.*

61. *See generally* H. Faulkner, The Decline of Laissez Faire (1951); R. Hofstadter, *supra* note 15. The champion of the public interest theory of regulation was Louis D. Brandeis. *See* T. McCraw, Prophets of Regulation 80-142 (1984).

62. In fact, the left and the right have come to agree that price regulation has often served the regulated firms at the expense of consumers. *See, e.g.,* G. Kolko, Railroads and Regulation (1965); Stigler, *The Theory of Economic Regulation,* 2 Bell J. Econ. & Mgmt. Sci. 3 (1971).

At the risk of some overgeneralization, in the 1870s, when railroads tended to have monopoly routes, they generally opposed rate regulation. By the 1890s, however, when overdevelopment was forcing "ruinous" competition between them, they began to support it. *See* C. Fairman, Reconstruction and Reunion, 1864-1888, pt. 2 (Holmes Devise History of the Supreme Court, vol. VII, 1971); Hovenkamp, *Regulatory Conflict in the Gilded Age: Federalism and the Railroad Problem* 97 Yale L.J. ___ (1988) (forthcoming). *But see* Rabin, *Federal Regulation in*

A more recent economic argument,[63] which gives judges more credit for having a social vision, is built on the observation that laissez-faire legal theory greatly aided American commercial development in the early nineteenth century. According to this theory, business counsel and judges with a vision of American expansion developed an instrumental law that encouraged such development. By the middle of the century, however, the commercial class had succeeded in obtaining legal rules that protected their interests from the threat of competition. When conflicting political interests began to emerge, the legal rules failed to respond. They continued to protect business from external control long after some kinds of regulation and redistribution had become appropriate. The same legal rules that had been novel and instrumental when they were first created became formalistic and outdated, because they no longer agreed with the dominant legislative policy. The old rules were perpetuated largely because the wealthy commercial interests, which commanded the best legal talent, gained enormously from their continuation.

This argument is appealing but it does not answer every question. Most importantly, it does not account for the fact that, when substantive due process first appeared in the state courts, by far the greater number of cases struck down professional licensing statutes or more direct business subsidies, rather than wage and hour regulations.[64] Since the principal beneficiaries of the licensing statutes were established businesses, while the victims were newcomers, substantive due process in this area had an effect precisely the opposite of that which the proponents of this thesis suggest. Likewise, it is difficult to reconcile the effect of the "public purpose" doctrine, used along with substantive due process to strike down business subsidies, with the notion that substantive due process was a great victory for commercial interests.[65]

Furthermore, this argument finds little support in the record of judicial "behavior," in a sense larger than opinion writing. Why were the judges in the 1830s so open to the idea that business needed freedom to expand, but so blind at the end of the century to the equally obvious need for protection of the competing rights of laborers and consumers? Why was it relatively easy for judges like Lemuel Shaw and Roger Brooks Taney to find compelling policy reasons for rejecting estab-

---

*Historical Perspective*, 38 STAN. L. REV. 1189, 1199 (1986) (arguing that even during the 1870s the railroads wanted *some* kind of regulation, although not necessarily of rates). On the 1890s, see G. KOLKO, *supra*. *Cf.* Marvel, *Factory Regulation: A Reinterpretation of Early English Experience*, 20 J.L. & ECON. 379 (1976) (arguing that the 1833 British Factory Act was passed at behest of owners of steam-driven textile plants; the Act placed water-driven plants at a comparative disadvantage and thereby enhanced profits of steam-driven plants). The Factory Acts are discussed at note 118 *infra* and accompanying text.

63. *See* M. HORWITZ, *supra* note 30, at 253-68.
64. *See* Friedman, *supra* note 11; notes 49-59 *supra* and accompanying text.
65. *See* note 59 *supra*.

lished rules in the first half of the nineteenth century, but so hard for judges like Rufus Peckham and George Sutherland to do so later? The intellectual stature of the judges themselves might account for these discrepancies, although, as noted above, the substantive due process era was a period of great judicial creativity.[66] The influence of the organized bar or other political interests in the appointment or decisions of Supreme Court justices might also explain them.[67] However, political conflict alone can not explain the judicial record.

Yet another economic argument is that judges developed substantive due process as a device for combatting special privilege, i.e. instances when a legislature displayed favoritism or unreasonably rewarded one constituency at the expense of another.[68] This argument begins with the observation that one of the earliest concerns expressed in the literature of substantive due process was that "due process" meant fair treatment by the government, whether legislature, executive, or judiciary. It was not fair for the government to "take the property of A. and give it to B.,"[69] or to deprive a large group of butchers of their livelihood in order to give a monopoly to a small, favored number.[70] Under the Commonwealth principle, developed first in England and later in America, the state could intervene in the market in order to make *everyone* better off;[71] it could not intervene in such a way as to benefit some people at the expense of others.

This argument is good as far as it goes, but ultimately it begs the question unless it is accompanied by some sort of conspiracy theory concerning the legislative process. It does not answer *why* it is bad to take the property of *A* and give it to *B*--or, to cast the problem into economic terms, why the courts believed that wealth redistribution forced by the state was a bad thing. Substantive due process would have been a relatively trivial doctrine if it stood only for the proposition that legislatively forced wealth transfers caused by bribery or corruption were void.

One possibility, of course, is that the courts viewed all such legislative transfers as a form of corruption or the product of conspiracy, as in

---

66. *See* notes 23-24 *supra* and accompanying text.

67. *See generally* H. ABRAHAM, JUSTICES AND PRESIDENTS: A POLITICAL HISTORY OF APPOINTMENTS TO THE SUPREME COURT 24-48 (2d ed. 1985); A. MASON & W. BEANEY, THE SUPREME COURT IN A FREE SOCIETY 227-36 (1968).

68. *See* W. NELSON, *supra* note 47; *see also* Les Benedict, *Laissez-Faire and Liberty: A Re-Evaluation of the Meaning and Origins of Laissez-Faire Constitutionalism,* 3 L. & HIST. REV. 293 (1985); McCurdy, *Justice Field and the Jurisprudence of Government-Business Relations: Some Parameters of Laissez-Faire Constitutionalism, 1863-1897,* 61 J. AM. HIST. 970 (1975).

69. Legal Tender Cases, 79 U.S. (12 Wall.) 457, 580 (1871) (Chase, C.J., dissenting).

70. Slaughter-House Cases, 83 U.S. (16 Wall.) 36 (1873).

71. *See* O. HANDLIN & M. HANDLIN, COMMONWEALTH—A STUDY OF THE ROLE OF GOVERNMENT IN THE AMERICAN ECONOMY: MASSACHUSETTS, 1774-1861 (rev. ed. 1969); H. SCHEIBER, OHIO CANAL ERA: A CASE STUDY OF GOVERNMENT AND THE ECONOMY, 1820-1861, at 88-94 (1969); G. WOOD, THE CREATION OF THE AMERICAN REPUBLIC, 1776-1787, at 53-65 (1969).

the *Slaughter-House Cases*.[72]  In *Lochner*, Justice Peckham  voiced his suspicion that many wage-and-hour laws were passed for "other motives" than the ones articulated by the legislative body.[73]  More realistically, however, in the great majority of substantive due process cases there was simply no evidence of corruption, nor even of inappropriate "special privilege," and the courts did not insist on any.  If the special privilege argument is to survive, it must stand for the proposition that the mere legislative transfer of wealth through certain devices, such as price regulation, licensing restrictions, and wage-and-hour laws, is per se an impermissible special privilege. But such a statement is supportable only if there is a theory behind it. Practically every act of government injures one group of people and benefits another, but the great majority are constitutionally valid.

Substantive due process doctrine clearly expressed a concern with special privilege.  Substantive due process judges subscribed to a theory that certain forced wealth transfers were economically irrational and harmful, and that special privilege was one possible explanation for why legislatures would pass such statutes. When courts found explicit evidence of such privilege they were quick to respond.[74]  But the important question for understanding substantive due process is not why the legislatures passed such statutes, but rather why the judiciaries so widely believed these kinds of legislative wealth transfers to be harmful. This question is fundamentally about economic theory, not about imperfections in the legislative process.

This essay argues that judges of the substantive due process era were neither more "formalist" nor more socially biased than judges are today.  Like judges of every era, they drew their wisdom—particularly the wisdom they applied to public law—from outside. To be sure, they operated under a set of rules of form that prevented them from citing this outside wisdom expressly, as judges frequently do today.[75]  They simply accepted and asserted as obvious, doctrine that had become part of the well-established, consensus models of other disciplines. In the case of substantive due process, the judges wrote into the Constitution a unique American perspective on classical economics.

Holmes was right in *Lochner* when he accused the majority of basing its decision on "an economic theory which a large part of the country does not entertain." *Lochner* was supported by the economic theories of the American classical economists, although by 1905 classical economics was rapidly losing ground to institutional economics and welfare ec-

---

72. *But see* note 45 *supra* and accompanying text.
73. Lochner v. New York, 198 U.S. 45, 64 (1905).
74. *See, e.g.*, State v. Santee, 111 Iowa 1, 82 N.W. 445 (1900) (striking down part of a statute generally prohibiting use of certain fuels in lamps but creating exception for the "Welsbach hydrocarbon incandescent lamp"); *see also* People v. Gillson, 109 N.Y. 389, 17 N.E. 343 (1888); Wynehamer v. People, 13 N.Y. 378 (1856).
75. *See* notes 109-110 *infra* and accompanying text.

onomics. More important, classical economics had become largely irrelevant, given the political pressures of the day. The Progressives' rejection of classical economics provided the excuse, not the reason, for the passage of reform legislation.

Nevertheless, Holmes' accusation that the majority relied on an *obsolete* economic theory is not nearly so important or so interesting as his recognition that it relied on an *economic* theory, whether right or wrong, obsolete or current. That economic theory may have been "obsolete" in the sense that it was not the latest theory available. On the other hand, it was very likely the theory that had the largest number of adherents among contemporary American economists.

## II.  THE ECONOMIC FOURTEENTH AMENDMENT

The fourteenth amendment was designed by its framers to give black persons born in the United States the same constitutional protections enjoyed by white persons. Congress passed the Civil Rights Act of 1866 under the powers granted it in the thirteenth amendment, yet the legislation clearly presaged the spirit of the fourteenth. The statute provided that all persons born in the United States are its citizens, and that all citizens, without regard to race, color, or previous condition of servitude should have the same rights "to make and enforce contracts, to sue, be parties, and give evidence, to inherit, purchase, lease, sell, hold, and convey real and personal property, and to full and equal benefit of all laws and proceedings for the security of person and property, as is enjoyed by white citizens."[76] The fourteenth amendment was designed in part to "constitutionalize" the 1866 statute, or at least to resolve doubts about the statute's constitutional status.[77]

Many critics of substantive due process have accused the Supreme Court of "misdirecting" the fourteenth amendment.[78] The gist of their argument is that the amendment was designed to protect the "civil rights" of black freedmen, but it ended up virtually ignoring black Americans, and instead protected employers from pro-labor legislation such as wage-and-hours laws. The pair of Supreme Court decisions identified with this proposition includes *Plessy v. Ferguson* in 1896,[79] which held that "separate but equal" public facilities did not violate the

---

76. Civil Rights Act of 1866, ch. 31, § 1, 14 Stat. 27, 27 (current version at 42 U.S.C. § 1982 (1982)).

77. *See* C. FAIRMAN, *supra* note 62, pt. 1, at 1285-88; Maltz, *Reconstruction Without Revolution: Republican Civil Rights Theory in the Era of the Fourteenth Amendment*, 24 HOUS. L. REV. 221, 277 (1987).

78. *E.g.*, S. FINE, LAISSEZ-FAIRE AND THE GENERAL WELFARE STATE (1956); R. KLUGER, SIMPLE JUSTICE (1976); R. McCLOSKEY, AMERICAN CONSERVATISM IN THE AGE OF ENTERPRISE (1951); R. McCLOSKEY, THE AMERICAN SUPREME COURT 102-05 (1960); W. SWINDLER, COURT AND CONSTITUTION IN THE TWENTIETH CENTURY: THE OLD LEGALITY, 1889-1932 (1969); Soifer, *The Paradox of Paternalism and Laissez-Faire Constitutionalism: United States Supreme Court, 1888-1921*, 5 L. & HIST. REV. 249 (1987).

79. 163 U.S. 537 (1896).

equal protection clause, and *Lochner v. New York*,[80] a decade later, which held that a statute setting the maximum number of hours that bakers could work violated the due process clause.

But such critiques overlook the fact that, in 1868, the concept of "civil rights" of blacks—or, for that matter, of almost anyone—included two elements: (1) the right to equality of treatment in court trials and of access to the agencies of the state;[81] and (2) a set of distinctly *economic* civil rights, namely, the right to make contracts and the right to own property.[82] When the same Congress that drafted the amendment legislated under it, the legislation involved contract and property rights, not the rights of association or privacy or the freedoms of speech or religion. Among the rights not recognized was freedom from racial segregation. Congress did not have segregation in mind when it passed the Civil Rights Act of 1866, when it drafted the fourteenth amendment, or even a decade later when, contemplating the end of Reconstruction, it drafted the Civil Rights Act of 1875, which was subsequently struck down by the Supreme Court.[83] Even Radical Republicans maintained a sharp distinction among "civil" rights, "political" rights, and "social" rights. The fourteenth amendment and the Civil Rights Act of 1866 were designed to protect civil and political rights, but not social rights. And civil rights were fundamentally defined as economic rights.[84]

Thus the fourteenth amendment was economic by design. The freedmen did not need the freedoms of speech or religion or even the fair administration of the criminal process so much as they needed jobs and security. In 1866, Congress selected contracts and property as the civil rights worthy of protection because, within its classical view of the world, the right to make contracts and the right to own property were the keys to economic success. The hard question is not why economic liberties became the central concern of the fourteenth amendment— Congress had that in mind all along—but why the Court used the fourteenth amendment to create substantive rights, rather than merely to ensure that all American citizens of whatever color had the same set of rights, however defined.

The immediate answer is that the due process clause of the fourteenth amendment was not "surplusage," as lawyers sometimes say. If

---

80. 198 U.S. 45 (1905).

81. *See* H. BELZ, EMANCIPATION AND EQUAL RIGHTS: POLITICS AND CONSTITUTIONALISM IN THE CIVIL WAR ERA 109-10 (1978); Hovenkamp, *Social Science and Segregation Before* Brown, 1985 DUKE L.J. 624, 648-51; Maltz, *supra* note 77, at 250. The concept also included the right to vote, which the fifteenth amendment ensured.

82. On the principally *economic* character of civil rights in 1866, see H. BELZ, *supra* note 81, at 109.

83. *See* The Civil Rights Cases, 109 U.S. 3 (1883); Hovenkamp, *supra* note 81, at 648-51.

84. On the historical distinction between civil rights, political rights, and social rights, see H. BELZ, *supra* note 81, at 116; A. BICKEL & B. SCHMIDT, THE JUDICIARY AND RESPONSIBLE GOVERNMENT, 1910-1921, at 753 (Holmes Devise History of the Supreme Court, vol. IX, 1984); Hovenkamp, *supra* note 81, at 642-51.

the purpose of the amendment was merely to give freedmen the same set of rights that white citizens enjoyed, then the equal protection clause would have been sufficient. Congress, however, intended to provide certain absolute rights, protecting freedmen from some kinds of governmental activity. Liberals and conservatives alike agreed about this proposition, and it forms the foundation not only of substantive due process but also of the "incorporation" debate, concerning whether the due process clause of the fourteenth amendment required the states to honor the Bill of Rights.[85]

That these absolute rights should be identified with economic liberties was uncontroversial. The only problem was defining economic liberties. This was the province of political economy. The principal concern of classical political economy was neither price theory, nor industrial organization, nor even trade or tariff policy, but rather identification of the ideal economic regime that would maximize both prosperity and individual liberty.

Francis Wharton, a clergyman-turned-lawyer who became one of America's most prominent treatise authors, wrote his *Commentaries on Law*,[86] on the eve of the rise of substantive due process in the state courts.[87] His interpretation of the fourteenth amendment virtually ignored racial justice themes in favor of economic and business protections. That the legislative history of the fourteenth amendment expressed substantial concern for the rights of black freedmen, and none for the economic rights of others, did not trouble Wharton. He simply observed:

> [T]he provisions contained in these amendments, bearing distinctively on the negro race, are comparatively ephemeral in their character, while the clause before us is likely to be permanent, and to permeate the whole business system of the Union. Almost all the adjudications in respect to the amendment have, heretofore, related to negro rights. But these are now finally settled . . . and the real importance of the amendment, in securing the rights of the people as a body, is now becoming disclosed.[88]

For Wharton, the purpose of the fourteenth amendment was to constitutionalize a particular theory of political economy. Wharton argued that the fourteenth amendment forbids the states from doing by legislation what individuals are able to do better through private business ar-

---

85. *See* Maltz, *supra* note 77, at 267, 273-74; notes 86-97 *infra* and accompanying text.

86. F. WHARTON, COMMENTARIES ON LAW, EMBRACING CHAPTERS ON THE NATURE, THE SOURCE, AND THE HISTORY OF LAW; ON INTERNATIONAL LAW, PUBLIC AND PRIVATE; AND ON CONSTITUTIONAL AND STATUTORY LAW (1884).

87. Although his *Commentaries* were influential, Wharton is not mentioned in the leading secondary works on the origins of substantive due process. *See* C. JACOBS, *supra* note 58; A. PAUL, *supra* note 40; B. TWISS, *supra* note 40.

88. F. WHARTON, *supra* note 86, § 588, at 681 (footnote omitted).

rangements.[89] The "real importance" of the fourteenth amendment was that it gave citizens, particularly when engaged in business, a set of rights against state legislatures similar to those that the Bill of Rights had given the states and their citizens against the federal government. Wharton was among the first "incorporationists," writing at a time when the only civil rights other than those pertaining to government access or court process were economic.[90]

For Wharton, the responsibility for determining when private business can do something better than government can belongs to the courts. Thus judges were invited to adopt a theory about the optimal structure of economic relationships, which is of course what nineteenth century political economy was all about.

In 1884, when Francis Wharton sent out this invitation, British political economy had undergone several revolutions that had substantially undermined the laissez-faire views of the classicists.[91] American political economy had not. Thomas M. Cooley,[92] John Norton Pomeroy,[93] Christopher G. Tiedeman,[94] John Dillon,[95] and Joel Parker[96]—in short, the most prominent constitutional law writers of the post-war period—agreed with Wharton that once the problem of protecting black

---

89.
This clause . . . cures what was previously the great defect of our system. It destroys the power which had been assumed by state legislatures of interfering with private business, and of doing by law that which can be far better done by individual enterprise. And it goes as far as a constitutional limitation can go in establishing the principle, heretofore noticed as one of the first rules of liberal civilization, that government should not exercise functions which can be as well exercised by the people by themselves.
*Id.* § 594, at 711-13.
Looking at the American Revolution itself, and the main body of the Constitution, Wharton concluded that an important purpose of America's liberation was to put a stop to England's interference with "colonial manufactures and trade." *Id.* § 365, at 423. The purpose of the fourteenth amendment was to give the people similar protections against their own state legislatures.
90.
By the first group of amendments, embracing the first eleven, . . . the people of the states, as well as the states themselves are protected from any undue aggressions of the Federal government. But this was not enough. It became evident that the people of the states were in danger at least as much from the aggressions of their own legislatures as from the usurpations of congress. No one can study the statute books of our states without seeing to how vast and pernicious an extent the private rights of individuals have been interfered with by state legislation . . . .
*Id.* § 594, at 700-09.
91. *See* notes 114-168 *infra* and accompanying text.
92. *See* T. Cooley, A Treatise on the Constitutional Limitations Which Rest upon the Legislative Power of the States of the American Union (1868).
93. *See* J. Pomeroy, An Introduction to the Constitutional Law of the United States § 256 (1886); *see also* P. Paludan, A Covenant with Death: The Constitution, Law, and Equality in the Civil War Era 219-48 (1975).
94. *See* C. Tiedeman, A Treatise on State and Federal Control of Persons and Property in the United States (1900); C. Tiedeman, A Treatise on the Limitations of Police Power in the United States (1886).
95. *See* J. Dillon, *supra* note 59.
96. *See, e.g., Constitutional Law*, 94 N. Am. Rev. 435 (1862).

access to the economic system had been solved, the remaining purpose of the amendment was to enable the courts to define individual economic liberties against the states.[97]

III. FINDING POLITICAL ECONOMY IN SUBSTANTIVE DUE PROCESS

The thesis of this article is *not* that American classical political economists "caused" substantive due process by developing a set of economic ideas that were then learned by American judges. The evidence does not support such a proposition. In any event, that is much too simplistic an explanation for how ideas are transmitted.

This paper argues that both American political economists and American judges operated in a uniquely American "market" for ideas.[98] Like all market participants, each American maker of ideas selected from available inputs to produce his own original output. For the American political economist, the inputs included not only British Classicism, but also physical experiences about growth and productivity that were far different for someone living in the nineteenth century United States than for someone living in the British Isles. The inputs of American classical political economy may even have included the decisions of some judges. They certainly included some jurisprudential propositions, such as those asserting the sanctity of property rights. Also included among the inputs into both American political economy and American law was the set of moral and philosophical ideas called Scottish "Common Sense" Realism.[99]

American judges took those ideas that were most available and useful, and they generally perceived the American experience as more useful than the experience in Britain or anywhere else. Political economy was among the most available and most useful of contemporary ideas, for it explained why such things as minimum wage laws or subsidies or state restrictions on entry are bad; and, importantly, why the market worked much better in America than it did in Britain.

Such influence was a two-way street. When the American political economist wrote, he wrote about law as much as about economics—for invariably, in this pre-specialized age he gave his opinions about the sanctity of contracts, strikes, tariffs, national banks, and regulation of interstate commerce. Nearly every one of the great nineteenth century

---

97. *See also* Jones, *Does the United States Constitution Inhibit State Laws Limiting Hours of Private Daily Employment?*, 53 CENT. L.J. 384 (1901); Judson, *Liberty of Contract Under the Police Power*, 25 AM. L. REV. 871 (1891); *Limiting the Right to Contract*, 26 AM. L. REV. 404 (1892); Myrick, *Liberty of Contract*, 61 CENT. L.J. 483 (1905); Pingrey, *Limiting the Right to Contract*, 34 CENT. L.J. 91 (1892); Shattuck, *The True Meaning of the Term "Liberty" in Those Clauses in the Federal and State Constitutions Which Protect "Life, Liberty, and Property,"* 4 HARV. L. REV. 365 (1891). For a later perspective, see Williston, *Freedom of Contract*, 6 CORNELL L.Q. 365 (1921).

98. For a similar argument, applied in a different setting, see G. STIGLER, *Do Economists Matter?*, in THE ECONOMIST AS PREACHER AND OTHER ESSAYS 57 (1982).

99. *See* notes 175-186 *infra* and accompanying text.

American doctrines of constitutional law was also a doctrine of political economy.

It is not particularly difficult to show that American judges were exposed to political economy. In fact, it is hard to imagine how they could have avoided it. British classical political economy was not technical, and it was dominated by large, accessible policy questions.[100] Although American political economists wrote many books, their greatest forum for the exchange of ideas was the general reviews, such as the *North American Review*, the *Yale Review*, or the *Princeton Review*. Judges and lawyers also contributed to the great reviews, which were filled with a wonderfully eclectic mixture of political economy, constitutional law, private law, history, ethics, and even literature.[101] Anyone who was well-read—and that certainly included the elite bar—was exposed to this array of viewpoints. In 1912, when Harvard economist A.N. Holcombe criticized the judicial record in wage-and-hour cases, he placed blame on "the manning of our courts with a set of judges whose economic training was received mainly from the so-called classical school of political economists."[102] Holcombe concluded that "[t]he effect of such judicial interpretation has been to read into the constitution a doctrine that is nowhere expressed therein, namely, the doctrine of freedom of contract."[103]

Substantive due process judges were no more out of date or hostile toward theory and policy than courts in general, including the courts that decided the school desegregation[104] and abortion[105] cases generations later. Elite American judges generally absorb the thinking of elite American intellectuals, although often there is a time lag between intellectual offer and judicial acceptance.[106] Substantive due process fol-

---

100. British and American economic writing did not make widespread use of graphs until the late nineteenth century, nor of complex equations until a generation later. Specialization in the social sciences and economics developed mainly in the twentieth century. The *Quarterly Journal of Economics*, the first specialized academic economics journal in either Britain or America, began publication at Harvard in 1886. The *Journal of Political Economy* commenced publication at the University of Chicago in 1892. The *American Economic Review* began publication under that name in 1911, but it was preceded by the American Economic Association's *Publications*, sometimes called the *Quarterly*, which was first published in 1887, and the *Proceedings* of the American Economic Association, which began in 1887 but was concerned mostly with administrative and organizational matters.

101. For example, the *North American Review*, from 1890 to 1894, published twenty major articles on legal subjects, and eleven major articles on political economy. The *Princeton Review*, which ceased publication in 1888, published eleven major articles on legal subjects, and thirteen on political economy from 1880 to 1884.

102. Holcombe, *The Legal Minimum Wage in the United States*, 2 AM. ECON. REV. 21, 25 (1912).

103. *Id.* at 26.

104. Brown v. Board of Educ., 347 U.S. 483 (1954).

105. Roe v. Wade, 410 U.S. 113 (1973).

106. But sometimes the time lag is not substantial. *See* Hovenkamp, *supra* note 83, at 664-72 (arguing that the Supreme Court's dramatic change of position on the constitutionality of segregation in the late 1940s and 1950s followed very closely after the environmentalist revolution in the social sciences).

lowed quite naturally from the political economy that prevailed at the same time in America's best universities.[107] As a result, understanding substantive due process means understanding the political economy that guided it. This was the political economy taught in American universities in the 1870s and 1880s. Importantly, it was *not* the political economy taught in British universities during that same period. The British were a half century ahead of the Americans, first in economic development and the attendant consequences for the distribution of wealth,[108] second in the resultant theory, and third in legislative incorporation.

One criticism of this historical explanation of the substantive due process era is that the works of the great political economists, British or American, are almost never cited in nineteenth century Supreme Court opinions. The Supreme Court did not begin citing social science data with any regularity until *Brown v. Board of Education*.[109] But this objection is not a formidable one. Even before *Brown*, judges recognized that social sciences could inform adjudication. Rather, *Brown* represents a remarkable change in the etiquette of writing judicial opinions, as the Supreme Court abandoned a longstanding legal tradition of refusing to give explicit credit to intellectual sources from outside lawyers' jurisprudence. Scholasticism, Protestantism, Romanticism, Darwinism, Nationalism, Abolitionism, and many other intellectual

---

107. Lord Keynes' frequently quoted concluding paragraph from *The General Theory* bears repeating:

[T]he ideas of economists and political philosophers, both when they are right and when they are wrong, are more powerful than is commonly understood. Indeed the world is ruled by little else. Practical men, who believe themselves to be quite exempt from any intellectual influences, are usually the slaves of some defunct economist. Madmen in authority, who hear voices in the air, are distilling their frenzy from some academic scribbler of a few years back. I am sure that the power of vested interests is vastly exaggerated compared with the gradual encroachment of ideas.

J. KEYNES, THE GENERAL THEORY OF EMPLOYMENT INTEREST AND MONEY 383 (1936).

108. *See* Lindert, *Unequal English Wealth Since 1670*, 94 J. POL. ECON. 1127, 1152 (1986) (noting that the distribution of wealth in England in 1860 was far more unequal than in the United States). *See generally* Gallman, *Professor Pessen on the "Egalitarian Myth,"* 2 SOC. SCI. HIST. 194 (1978) (American inequality in the distribution of wealth was less pronounced than British inequality in the nineteenth century); Williamson, *Earnings Inequality in Nineteenth-Century Britain*, 40 J. ECON. HIST. 457 (1980) (empirical data shows that British earnings inequality rose sharply from the 1820s to the 1850s followed by a leveling off in the last half of the century).

109. 347 U.S. 483, 494 n.11 (1954). In Muller v. Oregon, 208 U.S. 412, 419 (1908), and Adkins v. Children's Hospital, 261 U.S. 525, 559-60 (1923), the Court referred to the Brandeis Briefs submitted there, but did not cite any of the nonstatutory sources contained in them. In Buchanan v. Warley, 245 U.S. 60 (1917), the Court received a 200-page social science brief on race discrimination, but did not refer to it in its opinion. *See* Hovenkamp, *supra* note 81 at 657-63.

Justice Brandeis first broke the tradition of citing only to earlier case law and a few legal treatises in Adams v. Tanner, 244 U.S. 590 (1917), a substantive due process case decided in the year he joined the Court. Brandeis cited both a social science article and several law review articles in his dissent in *Adams*. *See id.* at 605 n.6 (Brandeis, J., dissenting) (citing Leiserson, *Public Employment Offices*, 29 POL. SCI. Q. 36 (1914)); *id.* at 613-15 nn. 21-25 (Brandeis, J., dissenting) (citing several articles in the *American Labor Legislation Review*).

forces have always shaped the law, even though the seminal works in those areas were never cited by contemporary judges, and only rarely by the writers of legal commentaries and treatises. Political economy was treated no differently. In 1906, Progressive Economist Richard T. Ely complained to Holmes that the Supreme Court had adopted his definition of monopoly almost verbatim, but had attributed it only to "another," and had not mentioned the work in which it was contained.[110]

Consequently, the evidence that the Supreme Court read a particular theory of political economy into the Constitution is necessarily circumstantial. It consists of similarities between the views of the economists and those of the judges, occasional statements in which judges put forward economic theories, and the fact that elite lawyers and political economists wrote for, and read, the same journals and were concerned with the same kinds of policy issues. Justice Holmes relied on this sort of evidence when he accused the Supreme Court of enacting "Mr. Herbert Spencer's *Social Statics.*"[111] Holmes did not cite earlier references to Spencer's work in judicial opinions, for there were none.

Formalism was the *rhetoric* of law in the late nineteenth century, particularly of private law. Lawyers beginning with Langdell or perhaps even earlier wanted the law to be seen as a self-contained system—a science whose "data" consisted entirely of earlier legal decisions—because they were obsessed with placing law on the same epistemological plane as the other sciences.[112] But Langdell's formalism was only a vision. It was never reality, and even formalism at its best (or worst) never did what it said it did. Harvard professor Joseph Beale, who has come to be identified with formalism run amok, often incorporated policy concerns into his legal reasoning, and these policies often drew on the wisdom of other disciplines.[113] Substantive due process was a system of law based on an economic theory.

---

110. *See* Rader & Rader, *The Ely-Holmes Friendship, 1901-1914*, 10 Am. J. Legal Hist. 128, 138 (1966). The decision was National Cotton Oil Co. v. Texas, 197 U.S. 115 (1904). The definition of monopoly came from R. Ely, Monopolies and Trusts 14, 38, 96 (1900). Justice McKenna, who wrote the *National Cotton Oil* opinion, later told Holmes that the definition was probably Ely's. Rader & Rader, *supra*, at 139-40.
111. Lochner v. New York, 198 U.S. 45, 75 (1905) (Holmes, J., dissenting).
112. *See* M. Horwitz, *supra* note 30, at 253-66.
113. *See, e.g.,* J. Beale & B. Wyman, The Law of Railroad Rate Regulation 24-40 (1906) (advocating much more use of economics than historically recognized by courts). Although this treatise is not concerned with the economics of rate regulation, it displays as sophisticated an understanding of the economics of business regulation as many turn-of-the-century economics texts.

## IV. From the British Classical Tradition to American Economic Science

### A. The Breakdown of Classical British Political Economy

Modern political economy was invented by Adam Smith in the 1770s. Before political economy would turn into modern economics, however, it would undergo a utilitarian revolution in the late eighteenth and early nineteenth centuries, and a marginalist revolution in the 1870s and 1880s.[114] Both revolutions substantially undermined support for the laissez-faire theory that dominated Adam Smith's thinking. Political economy in both Britain and the United States experienced the revolutions, but they occurred later in the United States and had very different effects on welfare theory.

Classical political economy had a substantial influence on British legislation in the first half of the nineteenth century.[115] In the second half of the century, consensus among political economists fell apart, however, and their influence diminished.[116] The influence of nineteenth century American political economy on American legislation is considerably less documented than the British experience.[117] One thing seems clear, however. Just as the revolutions in theory occurred much earlier in Britain than in America, so too did the legislative response. Parliament passed the English Factory Acts in the 1830s and 1840s,[118] while widespread legislative regulation of wages and working conditions did not develop in the United States until the 1880s and after. Britain faced a restive labor force beginning in the 1830s; American capitalists faced the same threat beginning in the 1880s and 1890s. Most significantly, Britain reached the limits of its agricultural productivity and faced the prospect of imports and the tilling of inferior land early in the nineteenth century. America contained a great abundance of tillable land throughout the nineteenth century and does so even to the present.

Clearly the difference between classical political economy in Britain

---

114. A third revolution, the ordinalist revolution of the 1930s, was equally important, although not for our purposes here. See Cooter & Rappoport, *Were the Ordinalists Wrong About Welfare Economics?*, 22 J. Econ. Literature 507 (1984).

115. See, e.g., The Classical Economists and Economic Policy (A. Coats ed. 1971); R. Cowherd, Political Economists and the English Poor Laws (1977); R. Kanth, Political Economy and Laissez-Faire (1986).

116. See R. Kanth, *supra* note 115, at 159-60.

117. Most of the existing literature examines the classical Republican tradition. See, e.g., D. McCoy, The Elusive Republic: Political Economy in Jeffersonian America (1980); Foshee, *Jeffersonian Political Economy and the Classical Republican Tradition: Jefferson, Taylor and the Agrarian Republic*, 17 Hist. Pol. Econ. 523 (1985).

118. The most important Factory Acts, which regulated the hours of labor for both adults and children, were passed in 1833, 1844, and 1847. See generally P. Atiyah, *supra* note 28, at 537-42; J. Ward, The Factory Movement: 1830-1855 (1962). On the relationship between the Factory Acts and the classical political economists (Malthus, Senior, John Stuart Mill, and lesser-known figures), see Blaug, *The Classical Economists and the Factory Acts—A Re-examination*, 72 Q.J. Econ. 145 (1972).

and in America was not merely that the Americans lagged behind in theory. But neither do differences in physical environment, labor supply, and rates of industrialization fully explain the difference. Throughout the nineteenth century, American political economy was dominated by a moral, or normative, content that was much less visible in British political economy after 1800. American political economists, much more than the British, clung to the moral ideas of the Scottish "Common Sense" Realists.[119] As a result, utilitarianism—a concept which subordinated natural law and absolute property rights to a pragmatic concept of the good of the many, minimizing the role of moral determinants in the process—had far less influence on nineteenth century American political economy than it did on the British.

Adam Smith was an orthodox Scottish Realist Protestant whose theory of welfare was derived as much from morals as from economics.[120] Smith intertwined the concepts of scarcity, desire, supply, demand, and value into a remarkably sophisticated economic as well as moral theory that included: (1) the Lockean view that each person has a natural right to his own labor—a right that the state cannot take away; and (2) the essentially Lockean notion that value is a function of the labor put into something rather than the demand for it or the marginal utility that it produces—thus, because each person has a natural right to his own labor, he also has a natural right to his own property.[121]

The rule that the market determines the price was considered by Smith to be both normative and positive. Because Smith's theory of economic man was thoroughly intertwined with his theory of moral man, liberty of contract was as much an ethical doctrine as an economic one. For example, Smith adhered to a theory of natural price and believed that part of the natural right of property was a right to this price. He generally rejected the Hobbesian view that a price is "just" merely because it is the product of a voluntary bargain.[122] But Smith also believed that the unrestricted market almost always yielded the natural price. As a result, individual determination of price was an inherent right of property ownership, on both economic and moral grounds.[123]

---

119. On the influence of Scottish Common Sense Realism in American thought, see B. KUKLICK, THE RISE OF AMERICAN PHILOSOPHY: CAMBRIDGE, MASSACHUSETTS, 1860-1930, at 10, 18-21 (1977); H. SCHNEIDER, A HISTORY OF AMERICAN PHILOSOPHY 216-20 (2d ed. 1963); *see also* note 128 *infra.*

120. For the influence of Smith's "Common Sense" moral thinking on American constitutionalism, see generally G. WILLS, INVENTING AMERICA: JEFFERSON'S DECLARATION OF INDEPENDENCE (1978).

121. However, Smith developed a narrow theory of public goods, which was used by later classical political economists to justify more substantial state intervention into economic relationships. See Smith's discussion of the "third duty of government." A. SMITH, THE WEALTH OF NATIONS bk. v, ch. 1, pt. 3 (1776).

122. On the development of distinct Hobbesian "positivistic" and Smithian "normative" theories about price, see P. ATIYAH, *supra* note 28, at 298.

123. *See* Young, *The Impartial Spectator and Natural Jurisprudence: An Interpretation of Adam Smith's Theory of the Natural Price,* 18 HIST. POL. ECON. 365 (1986).

Smith's moral position on economic relations was to have a profound effect on substantive due process evaluation of statutory price controls and minimum wage laws. For example, the position is explicit in the Supreme Court's conclusions that "the right of the owner to fix a price at which his property shall be sold or used is an inherent attribute of the property itself,"[124] and that there is a "moral requirement" of "just equivalence" between the price to be charged for labor and the value the employer places upon it.[125] One could not show liberty of contract to be a bad thing merely by proving it inefficient, for the doctrine was simultaneously grounded in moral and economic considerations.[126] Smith's moral man worked for his wages, and in Smith's moral universe the wages set by the market were almost always normatively correct.[127]

B. *Secularization*

As Smith's followers deviated from his thought, the economic component of laissez-faire theory began to deteriorate. At the same time, the intellectual center of political economy in Britain moved away from orthodox, Presbyterian Scotland, where Smith did his work, toward more liberal, Anglican Oxford and Cambridge, where Scottish orthodox morality was out of fashion by the third or fourth decade of the nineteenth century. By the middle of the nineteenth century the moral content of Smith's position had been undermined in English political economy, particularly by utilitarianism. Not so, however, in America, where Scottish Realism remained the ruling philosophy until after the Civil War.[128] American substantive due process was built on the political economy of an unreconstructed Adam Smith.

1. *Pessimism and monopoly in British classical political economy.*

Two subsequent developments in British political economy undermined Smith's optimistic theory that "the invisible hand" would provide the best society. These developments, the population theory and

---

124. Tyson & Brother-United Theatre Ticket Offices v. Banton, 273 U.S. 418, 429 (1927) (citing Case of the State Freight Tax, 82 U.S. (15 Wall.) 232, 278 (1873)); *see also* Cooley, *supra* note 56, at 271 ("[T]he capability of property, by means of the labor or expense or both bestowed upon it, to be made available in producing profits, is a potential quality in property, and as sacredly protected by the constitution as the thing itself in which the quality inheres."); notes 176-177 *infra* and accompanying text.

125. Adkins v. Children's Hosp., 261 U.S. 525, 558 (1923).

126. In any event, Smith would not have believed such a proof. In his mind there was no disjunction between the economically correct and the morally correct. *See* Young, *supra* note 123.

127. *See* Lewis, *Adam Smith: The Labor Market as the Basis of Natural Rights*, 11 J. ECON. ISSUES 21 (1977).

128. *See generally* T. BOZEMAN, PROTESTANTS IN AN AGE OF SCIENCE: THE BACONIAN IDEAL AND ANTEBELLUM AMERICAN RELIGIOUS THOUGHT (1977); H. HOVENKAMP, SCIENCE AND RELIGION IN AMERICA: 1800-1860 (1978); H. MILLER, THE REVOLUTIONARY COLLEGE: AMERICAN PRESBYTERIAN HIGHER EDUCATION, 1707-1837 (1976); D. SLOAN, THE SCOTTISH ENLIGHTENMENT AND THE AMERICAN COLLEGE IDEAL (1971); G. WILLS, *supra* note 120.

the doctrine of rents, fueled the revolt against laissez-faire theory in British political thought that had developed by the middle of the nineteenth century.

*The population theory.* The first development was the population theory of Thomas Robert Malthus, who became England's first professor of political economy in 1806 at East India College.[129] Malthus' 1798 *Essay on the Principle of Population*[130] drew two conclusions rather ambiguously characterized as empirical:[131] (1) population, when left unchecked, will grow geometrically; and (2) once all good land has been put into production, the food supply can grow, at best, arithmetically. Malthus' observations had profound implications for Britain, which was heavily developed at the time of his writing.

Strictly applied, Malthus' "iron law" of population did not undermine Smith's laissez-faire theory. On the contrary, many later political economists—particularly the Social Darwinists in the United States[132]—believed it strengthened the case for nonintervention. Any interference by the state on behalf of the masses would only increase their numbers in proportion to the food supply and the amount of productive capital. As a result, the amount of starvation would increase. Malthus sometimes personally proclaimed such a severe version of his theory.[133] However, he was strongly influenced by Bentham's utilitarianism, and was quite willing to manipulate Lockean property rights in order to improve the welfare of the poor, provided the price was not too high.[134] Essentially Malthusian arguments carried the Poor Law Reform Bill of 1834 to passage.[135]

Later English political economists quickly softened the severest implications of Malthus' iron law.[136] For example, John Stuart Mill thought a moderate amount of relief to the poor would not unduly in-

---

129. E. PAUL, MORAL REVOLUTION AND ECONOMIC SCIENCE: THE DEMISE OF LAISSEZ-FAIRE IN NINETEENTH-CENTURY BRITISH POLITICAL ECONOMY 80 (1979).

130. T. MALTHUS, AN ESSAY ON THE PRINCIPLE OF POPULATION (E. Wrigley & D. Souden eds. 1986) (1st ed. 1798).

131. In fact, Malthus did not establish either proposition empirically or mathematically. Rather, he simply observed that the growth of population appeared to be outrunning the growth of agricultural productivity, and concluded that the problem would become worse as more marginal land was placed into production. *See* E. PAUL, *supra* note 129, at 83.

132. *See* Hovenkamp, *supra* note 13, at 651-71; note 217 *infra* and accompanying text.

133. *See* Malthus, *A Summary View of the Principles of Population* (1830), in ON POPULATION: THREE ESSAYS 33-40 (G. Himmelfarb ed. 1960).

134. *See* Hollander, *On Malthus's Population Principle and Social Reform*, 18 HIST. POL. ECON. 187, 215-27 (1986) (Malthus personally favored substantial state intervention on behalf of the poor and laboring classes; "iron law" as commonly described is a caricature which can be attributed only to Malthus' intentional exaggerations).

135. The Bill centralized the distribution of relief to the poor, and evened it out according to a schedule. In general, Malthus criticized the poor laws, but it is unclear whether he opposed them in principle, or merely wanted more rationality in their administration. *Compare* R. COWHERD, *supra* note 115, at 27-30 *with* Hollander, *supra* note 134, at 214-27 (Malthus' opposition based on pragmatic concerns).

136. As did Malthus himself in an 1803 revision of his *Essay.* T. MALTHUS, AN ESSAY ON THE PRINCIPLES OF POPULATION at vii (London, 1803).

crease the population, and would greatly relieve suffering. Furthermore, he argued, if the relief were a sufficiently poor alternative to
employment that able-bodied people would be inclined not to take it,
poor relief would have little effect on productivity.[137] Other classical
economists such as Nassau Senior gave lip service to Malthus' work, but
suggested that new technology and improvements in the efficiency of
exchange would tend to offset the productivity problem; as a result,
moderate governmental aid to the poor would not cause starvation.[138]
The strong version of Malthus' iron law appeared prominently in the
late nineteenth century in two places: the writings of Herbert Spencer,
who was much more popular in America than in Britain,[139] and the
writings of American Social Darwinists such as William Graham
Sumner.[140]

*The doctrine of rents.* The political economy of David Ricardo reveals
few vestiges of Scottish Realist orthodoxy, which was waning in Britain.
Ricardo's principal contribution to economic theory at the beginning of
the nineteenth century was the doctrine of land rents, which played a
large role in the mid-century British revolt against laissez-faire
ideology.

We are indebted to Ricardo for establishing that not only monopolists earn monopoly profits.[141] Any time a production input is in short
supply, the price of the final product will rise to monopoly levels,
whether the final product is sold by one vendor or thousands. For Ricardo, the relevant input was agricultural land. He argued that the first
land to be placed into production in any market will also be the most
fertile, for which production costs are the lowest. As demand increases,
more marginal land must be placed into production, and average production costs will rise. To sustain production off the marginal land, the
market price of agricultural products must rise sufficiently to make the
least fertile land in production profitable. As a result, Ricardo observed, the product of the most profitable land can be sold at monopoly
profits, even though the owners of such land constitute only a tiny fraction of all landowners.[142]

From his observations about agricultural land, Ricardo derived a

---

137. *See* E. PAUL, *supra* note 129, at 180-81.
138. *See id.* at 134-35.
139. At least that was Social Darwinist Henry Ward Beecher's view in 1866. *See* R. HOF-
STADTER, SOCIAL DARWINISM IN AMERICAN THOUGHT 31 (rev. ed. 1955). On the refusal of
English political economists to accept the strongest implications of Malthus' iron law, see
Blaug, *The Empirical Content of Ricardian Economics,* 64 J. POL. ECON. 41, 46-48 (1956).
140. *See* R. HOFSTADTER, *supra* note 139, at 143-47, 156-57; Hovenkamp, *supra* note 13,
at 651-71; note 217 *infra.*
141. For modern applications of his work, see Klein, Crawford & Alchian, *Vertical Integration, Appropriable Rents, and the Competitive Contracting Process,* 21 J.L. & ECON. 297 (1978), and
Williamson, *Credible Commitments: Using Hostages to Support Exchange,* 73 AM. ECON. REV. 519
(1983).
142. D. RICARDO, THE PRINCIPLES OF POLITICAL ECONOMY AND TAXATION 38, 70 (1817).
"It is then only because land is of different qualities with respect to its productive powers, and

theory of wages that further undermined Adam Smith's optimism that the "invisible hand" would yield ample provision for every industrious person. Ricardo posited that as increasingly marginal land was placed into production, prices would rise and demand would fall, landlords would earn monopoly returns, and the capitalist entrepreneur would be squeezed between high rental rates and reduced output. Falling demand and rising prices would drive wages to subsistence levels. An important corollary of Ricardo's doctrine of rents was that wages would decline as a percentage of total productivity, thus tending to support Malthus' claim that wages would always be driven to the subsistence level. Ricardo did not personally regard this fact, depressing as it might be, as sufficient to justify substantial state regulation of markets or wages.[143] Later British political economists showed no such reluctance, however, and the doctrine of rents became an important element in the undermining of laissez-faire ideology.[144]

### 2. *Utilitarianism and marginalism.*

Smith believed that an individual's property in his own labor was the sacred, inviolate foundation of all property. As a result, he was opposed, on moral as well as economic grounds, to most legislation that interfered with a person's power to bargain freely.[145] The importance of Smith's moral commitment cannot be underestimated: Even if someone proved that laissez faire is not socially optimal on purely economic grounds, the moral arguments would nevertheless remain.

The development of British utilitarianism under Jeremy Bentham, John Stuart Mill, and their followers undermined this fundamental premise of Smith's political economy. Carried to its logical conclusion, utilitarianism excised natural law from political economy. For example, Smith believed that every commodity had both a "natural price" and a "market price," and that over the long run the latter would approxi-

---

because in the progress of population, land of an inferior quality, or less advantageously situated, is called into cultivation, that rent is ever paid for the use of it." *Id.* at 38.

For example, suppose that the most fertile land in a community produces corn at a cost of $1.00 per bushel. The next qualitative category of land produces corn at a cost of $1.10 per bushel, the next at $1.20 per bushel, and so on. Suppose that demand rises to the point that the demand and supply curves intersect at a price of $1.30 per bushel. In that case the market will "clear"—that is, demand and supply will be in equilibrium—at a market price of $1.30. *All* farmers will obtain that price, for one farmer's corn is indistinguishable from that of the next. As a result, those who till the most fertile land will receive monopoly profits, or "rents," of 30¢ per bushel.

143. *Id.* at 105.

144. The doctrine is particularly apparent in the thought of John Stuart Mill. In fact, Mill preceded Henry George in advocating a tax on landlords to capture their "unearned income"—the monopoly rents that came from their land. Mill was important in the founding of the Land Tenure Reform Association, which had redistribution of land rents as its principal goal. *See* R. KANTH, *supra* note 115, at 105-06; E. PAUL, *supra* note 129, at 161. Even the turn-of-the-century English economist Alfred Marshall accepted the theory and devoted substantial attention to it. A. MARSHALL, PRINCIPLES OF ECONOMICS bk. iv, ch. 3 (1890).

145. *See* notes 123-127 *supra* and accompanying text.

mate the former.[146] Later economists, starting with John Stuart Mill, separated the positive and normative elements of economic theory, and assigned the behavior of the market exclusively to the former. At that point the "natural" price disappeared from economic dialogue.[147]

Likewise, Smith devised a labor theory of value, drawn from the premise that every person has a natural right to the product of his own labor.[148] But Smith's theory of value eventually gave way in the 1870s to the marginal utility theory of value, which assessed not the amount of labor that went into a thing, but rather the amount of incremental satisfaction that it produced.[149]

But the most important effect of utilitarianism was on political economists' perceptions of their discipline. The utilitarian revolution changed laissez-faire theory into an empirical or contingent truth, rather than a moral or necessary one. Once utilitarianism became the accepted predicate for welfare economics, the moral obstacle to state intervention disappeared. Utilitarianism thus was an important predicate for the modernist revolution of the twentieth century.[150]

Nowhere is this influence more obvious than in the development of the theory of public goods and externalities. The concepts of public goods and externalities suggest that some transactions affect people who cannot easily participate in the transaction. In such cases, "market failures"—instances when the market fails to deliver the socially optimal solution—can occur.[151] As a result, the state may have to intervene through legislation to correct the failure.

Utilitarianism also changed political economy by incorporating distributive concerns into economic science. Adam Smith was concerned almost exclusively with maximizing the net social product, regardless of distribution.[152] However, the utilitarians faced the possibility that different distributions of wealth could produce different amounts of total utility. This possibility implied that distribution was an inseparable part of economic science.[153] John Stuart Mill, writing around 1830, defined political economy to include distributional as well as allocative

---

146. See generally Young, supra note 123.

147. E. PAUL, supra note 129, at 155-67, 220.

148. Id. at 23.

149. See P. ATIYAH, supra note 28, at 603.

150. See Coates, Benthamism, Laissez Faire, and Collectivism, 11 J. HIST. IDEAS 357 (1950).

151. For example, a contractor and land owner negotiating to build a high rise building are not likely to consider the increased traffic congestion, loss of light to neighbors, or increased demands on local public services that the building imposes upon others. The people who must bear these costs cannot easily join the negotiation. There are too many of them and their interests are too diverse.

152. Even Nassau Senior, writing sixty years later, attacked the notion that concerns about the "desirable" distribution of wealth were a part of political economy. N. SENIOR, AN OUTLINE OF THE SCIENCE OF POLITICAL ECONOMY 2 (reprint ed. 1938) (1st ed. 1836).

153. A good brief discussion of the influence of utilitarianism on welfare economics can be found in P. ATIYAH, supra note 28, at 324-45.

concerns.[154]  This definition followed from Mill's definition of utility as the aggregate utility of society as a whole, rather than of each individual considered separately.[155]  Since a poor person might obtain more utility from an additional dollar than would a rich person, the state could increase total utility by forcing wealth transfers from the rich to the poor. These ideas quickly entered the mainstream of British economic thought,[156] where they remained until the ordinalists argued in the twentieth century that interpersonal comparisons of utility were impossible.[157]  They entered the mainstream of British *political* thought and never left. When the theory of marginal utility was developed in the 1860s and 1870s, principally under William Jevons, who virtually merged utilitarian ethics and welfare economics,[158] British economists began to propose fairly elaborate schemes to use the state to redistribute wealth in order to enlarge total utility.[159]  That development occurred in England at least a quarter century before it reached America. Furthermore, when marginalism did become part of American economic thinking, principally in the work of John Bates Clark, it was cast into a far more laissez-faire paradigm.[160]

C.  *Summary: Assumptions, Method, and Public Policy*
    *in British Classical Economics*

A traditional view of the political economy of Adam Smith is that his conclusions were either deductive, or based on observations so robust and uncontroversial, such as the inverse relation between supply and demand, that in the nineteenth century they were regarded as universal truths. This view is sometimes assigned to the entire classical tradition in political economy.[161]  But clearly the great classical economists were policymakers who carried political agendas drawn from the economic disputes of their day. Their self- professed "general" solutions to economic problems were in fact pointed at very specific issues, such as the wisdom of the poor laws or the corn laws,[162] just as are the assumptions

---

154. J.S. MILL, *On the Definition of Political Economy; and on the Method of Investigation Proper to It,* in ESSAYS ON SOME UNSETTLED QUESTIONS OF POLITICAL ECONOMY 120 (1844 & photo. reprint 1948).

155. *See* E. PAUL, *supra* note 129, at 152-53.

156. *See* text accompanying notes 307-310 *infra.*

157. *See* Cooter & Rappoport, *supra* note 114.

158. *See* P. ATIYAH, *supra* note 28, at 603.

159. In fact, one could argue that total utility would be maximized when every person had exactly the same amount of wealth, since total utility was maximized when marginal utilities from one person to the next were the same. Jevons, Wicksteed, and Alfred Marshall—the great revisionists of classical political economy—all dealt with the implications of this proposition. *See* E. PAUL, *supra* note 129, at 232-36.

160. *See* notes 311-312 *infra* and accompanying text.

161. *See, e.g.,* J. SCHUMPETER, CAPITALISM, SOCIALISM, AND DEMOCRACY 75 (1942); J. SCHUMPETER, ECONOMIC DOCTRINE AND METHOD 84-85 (1954).

162. *See* R. KANTH, *supra* note 115. The classic statement of this thesis is G. MYRDAL, THE POLITICAL ELEMENT IN THE DEVELOPMENT OF ECONOMIC THEORY (1965). *See also* G. SABINE, A HISTORY OF POLITICAL THEORY 687 (1961).

of economists and other scientists today.[163] Different assumptions led them to different conclusions. For example, Ricardo's doctrine of rents was motivated largely by his opposition to the corn laws, which were designed to encourage domestic production of grain by placing tariffs on imports and bounties on exports. His arguments were supported largely by casual empirical observations made in a relatively static industrial economy.[164] The same thing can be said of Malthus' "iron law" of population[165] or James Mill's defense of England's declining position as an exporter of agricultural goods.[166]

British political economists were also concerned by the problem of class unrest and the growing power of the labor movement. Until late in the nineteenth century, American political economists did not bother to include the risk of substantial labor unrest or even revolution as part of the social cost of a laissez-faire labor policy. In a rapidly expanding economy where wages were perceived as rising and jobs were plentiful, such revolution was unlikely. This was not the case in Britain. In fact, Marx's and Engels' principal theory about the crisis of labor and the need for revolution was drawn from their observations of British poverty during the first half of the nineteenth century.[167]

American political economy differed from British political economy not because of fundamental disagreements over basic principles, but rather because Americans made their observations in a different laboratory. Our perception of differences in principle is distorted by the fact that nineteenth century economists tended to overgeneralize:[168] Ricardo and Malthus in Britain made specific observations but attempted to report universal truths, as did Carey and Vethake in America. The resulting differences left far less room for the interventionist state in America than they did in Britain.

---

163. On the responsiveness of economic theory to political controversy, see generally T. HUTCHISON, ON REVOLUTIONS AND PROGRESS IN ECONOMIC KNOWLEDGE (1978).

164. See Blaug, supra note 139 (arguing that the weight of empirical evidence was against Ricardo— for example, agricultural yields per acre increased throughout the eighteenth century, in spite of the fact that England's agricultural land was fully developed and only more marginal land was being placed into production); see also J. SCHUMPETER, HISTORY OF ECONOMIC ANALYSIS 519-20 (1954).

165. See R. KANTH, supra note 115, at 129-33.

166. See T. HUTCHISON, supra note 163 (noting that early in the nineteenth century England began to import food). By mid-century more than 70% of English grain consumed was imported. The English were thus quite aware of the problem of a growing population and a static land supply. With the help of a little chauvinism, England's import dependency even encouraged the conclusion that more advanced, industrial nations imported food while more backward, agricultural ones exported it. James Mill suggested that no developed country would ever export food, because its population would always rise to the level of complete consumption. JAMES MILL, An Essay of the Impolicy of a Bounty on the Exportation of Grain (1804), in SELECTED ECONOMIC WRITINGS 57 (Winch ed. 1966).

167. See F. ENGELS, THE CONDITION OF THE WORKING CLASS IN ENGLAND (W. Henderson & W. Chaloner trans. 1958).

168. See Coats, The Culture and the Economists: Some Reflections on Anglo- American Differences, 12 HIST. POL. ECON. 588 (1980).

V. The Political Economy of Substantive Due Process: American Economic Thought in the 1800s

Two phenomena distinguished nineteenth century American political economy from that of Britain. One was the persistence of Scottish Realism, which dominated American intellectual life long after the majority factions in Britain had discarded it in favor of more liberal alternatives. The second was the premise of unlimited, rapid economic growth, which Malthus, Ricardo, and their successors had discarded in Britain by the beginning of the nineteenth century, but which survived in America for another one hundred years. Beginning with Malthus in the 1790s, British economists assumed that future economic growth would be slow and painful, particularly in agriculture, that there would be a surplus of labor, and that limitations on the amount of land would permit a small number of people to become wealthy at the expense of the laboring masses. British labor unrest confirmed these fears. By the 1830s, England was already faced with a restive labor force and the threat of organized revolt.[169] Real wages in England were widely perceived as falling during the first half of the nineteenth century, even as they were perceived as rising in America.[170] In reaction to these conditions, British political economists came to believe that a certain amount of wealth redistribution, along the lines of the Poor Laws and perhaps even the Factory Acts, would increase social welfare by reducing the threat of costly revolution.[171] Distribution became a major concern in nineteenth century British political economy.

Americans, on the other hand, saw virtually unlimited potential for economic growth. Room for the entry of new businesses was abundant, provided that the sovereign did not create artificial restrictions on entry, such as monopoly franchises or business licensing. Labor was generally perceived to be in short supply. Early American political economist Willard Phillips noted that labor was sufficiently scarce in the United States that apprentices *received* wages from their masters, while in England they paid wages to their masters.[172] This expansionist view was institutionalized into an "American school" of political economy in the writings of Henry C. Carey,[173] America's greatest antebellum political economist, just at the time that British political economists were beginning to justify radical departures from laissez-faire policy. Carey's view predominated until well into the twentieth century in America.

---

169. *See* E. Hunt, History of Economic Thought 123 (1979).

170. Deane, *Contemporary Estimates of National Income in the First Half of the Nineteenth Century*, 8 Econ. Hist. Rev. 339 (2d ser. 1956).

171. *See* R. Kanth, *supra* note 115, at 147-56.

172. W. Phillips, A Manual of Political Economy, With Particular Reference to the Institutions, Resources and Condition of the United States 117, 134, 149 (Boston 1828 & photo. reprint 1968).

173. *See* L. Haney, History of Economic Thought 315-29 (3d ed. 1936) (discussing Carey and the "American School"); A. Kaplan, Henry Charles Carey: A Study in American Economic Thought (1931); notes 226-233, 277-245 *infra* and accompanying text.

For example, in *Adkins* Justice Sutherland virtually took judicial notice of the fact that wages were increasing.[174]

## A. *The Moral Tradition in American Political Economy*

### 1. *The Scottish Enlightenment and political economy in America.*

Scottish Realism gave way in Britain to utilitarianism. In America, the Scottish Realist tradition persisted. American political economists and jurists subordinated utilitarian solutions to Protestant moral values long after British political economy had abandoned such concerns.[175] One is struck by Justice Sutherland's assertion, again in *Adkins*, that there is a "moral requirement" of "just equivalence" between the value of a worker's labor and the price it should command.[176]

Liberty of contract and other rights recognized under the fourteenth amendment were not merely economic rights. They were moral and religious rights as well. Laissez-faire ideology was an important part of the religious individualism and self-determination that developed in America during the early nineteenth century. The cornerstone of that individualism was the doctrine of separation of church and state—the idea that every person has the right to make certain moral and religious choices without state interference.

Separationism was the cherished doctrine of the dispossessed. Congregational majorities in the Age of Jackson rejected it, while Baptists, Quakers, and even minority Anglicans and Catholics (who had been mixing prelates and politics for centuries) advocated it. Separationism was an ideological product of the Enlightenment, but it achieved polit-

---

174.
We cannot close our eyes to the notorious fact that earnings everywhere, in all occupations, have greatly increased—not alone in States where the minimum wage law obtains but in the country generally. . . . No real test of the economic value of the law can be had during periods of maximum employment, when general causes keep wages up to or above the minimum . . . .
Adkins v. Children's Hosp., 261 U.S. 525, 560 (1923).

175. For more on Scottish Realism and its impact on American Protestant values during the late eighteenth and early nineteenth centuries, see THE ORIGINS AND NATURE OF THE SCOTTISH ENLIGHTENMENT (R. Campbell & A. Skinner eds. 1982), WEALTH AND VIRTUE: THE SHAPING OF POLITICAL ECONOMY IN THE SCOTTISH ENLIGHTENMENT (I. Hont & M. Ignatieff eds. 1983), and note 128 *supra. See also* D. McCoy, *supra* note 117 (study of the relationship between the Scottish Enlightenment and political economy in America before the time of Francis Wayland).

176.
The moral requirement implicit in every contract of employment, viz, that the amount to be paid and the service to be rendered shall bear to each other some relation of just equivalence, is completely ignored [by this statute]. The necessities of the employee are alone considered, and these arise outside of the employment. . . . In principle, there can be no difference between the case of selling labor and the case of selling goods. If one goes to the butcher, the baker or grocer to buy food, he is morally entitled to obtain the worth of his money but he is not entitled to more. If what he gets is worth what he pays he is not justified in demanding more simply because he needs more . . . .
*Adkins*, 261 U.S. at 558-59.

ical dominance in the early 1820s.[177]   The new Jacksonian majority believed that people should be able to worship, think, and manage their affairs with minimal state interference. That view became the principal economic and moral message of the leading democratic political economist of the Jacksonian period, Francis Wayland. Wayland was raised a New York Baptist, but learned Scottish Realism at Congregational Andover Seminary in Massachusetts. He became one of America's leading proponents of the philosophy in the 1830s and 1840s as president of Brown University.

When Scottish Common Sense Realism obtained a foothold in America during the 1760s and 1770s,[178] it imported two ideas about value formation. The first was a unique kind of empiricism that claimed to despise speculation and abstraction. The second was a rationale for individual self-determination that Scottish Realists called the "moral sense." The moral sense enabled a person to know instinctively the difference between right and wrong. "Moral science" was the discipline that used the moral sense to discover the principles of ethical conduct, just as the physical sciences relied on the other five senses to discover the natural principles of the universe. Scottish Realists believed that moral laws are fixed and absolute. They "can never be varied by the institutions of man any more than the physical laws," Wayland wrote in 1835.[179]   However, these laws are discoverable, so that someone well educated in moral science will be able to make the "right" decision when he is confronted with an ethical problem.[180] Most of those ideas came straight out of Scottish Realist Adam Smith's book on moral science, *The Theory of Moral Sentiments*,[181] published seventeen years before the *Wealth of Nations* and all but forgotten by later figures in the British classical tradition of political economy. Like Smith, Wayland felt compelled to write books on both the moral sense and the foundations of political economy. He stated that "[t]he principles of Political Economy are so closely analogous to those of Moral Philosophy, that almost every question in the one, may be argued on grounds belonging to the other."[182]   Wayland's position on the relationship between moral science and political economy was fundamentally Adam Smith's position—but the American Wayland was writing fifty years later.

For Wayland, as for Smith, the individual right to property and the

---

177. The Congregational Churches of Connecticut and Massachusetts were the last churches to be disestablished during a legislative war between Federalists and a Jacksonian alliance of mutually hostile religious groups. *See* 2 W. McLoughlin, New England Dissent, 1630-1833: The Baptists and the Separation of Church and State 1043-1229 (1971).

178. *See* H. Hovenkamp, *supra* note 128, at 3-18.

179. F. Wayland, The Elements of Moral Science 25 (Boston 1835).

180. *Id.*

181. A. Smith, The Theory of Moral Sentiments (London 1759); *see also* G. Wills, *supra* note 120; notes 120-127 *supra* and accompanying text.

182. F. Wayland, The Elements of Political Economy at vi (New York 1837).

profits earned from it was grounded in morals as well as economics. "[W]e are taught, by Moral Philosophy, that by labor exerted upon any substance, in such manner as to give it value, we establish over that value, either in whole or in part, the right of property."[183]

The moral sense provided a broad rationale for individual self-determination in every aspect of human activity. In the eighteenth century, the idea of the moral sense was highly controversial. Scottish Realists asserted its existence in response to the great Scottish heretic David Hume, who had argued that no one could verify the credibility of his own senses. The world "out there," said Hume, is forever unknowable, because each person's knowledge of it is limited to his sense impressions, and he has no way to prove that his impressions are accurate. Likewise, said Hume, "ought" statements can never be verified; thus no one can be sure that a certain action is right or wrong. Hume's view implied either anarchy or ethical positivism, the idea that an action is wrong only if someone in authority says it is wrong.[184]

Against Hume's empirical skepticism the Scottish Realists gave a pragmatic answer that sought to encourage individualism and self-determination. They suggested that no one can think without making certain operative assumptions about the world. We can never prove that our eyes give us reliable information—but our feeling that we really see what we think we see is overwhelming, and any other assumption would make science impossible. Likewise, we can never prove that time is continuous, but if it is not then we can have neither science nor history. Scottish Realism accepted something that earlier modern philosophers had refused to believe: Certain ideas about human understanding seem obvious but they can never be proven. They are like the basic postulates of geometry; we either accept them or we cannot think systematically at all.

Furthermore, observed the Scottish Realists, precisely the same argument demonstrates the existence of the moral sense. Consider two statements: "the grass is green" and "thieves should be punished." Neither can be "verified" in the strong sense of the word. At most we can say we have a powerful feeling that we are looking at something called grass, and that it is green. According to the Scottish Realists, we have exactly the same kind of powerful feeling that theft is wrong. Each of us feels "a distinct *impulse* to do that which we conceive to be right and to leave undone what we conceive to be wrong."[185] This moral sense is deeply implanted in every person—as deeply as our feeling that

---

183. *Id.* at 166. Wayland continued:

If the original capital were our own, we possess that original capital, together with all the additional value. . . . If, by labor upon the capital of another, we have raised its value, we establish a right to a portion of it, to be estimated by the respective values of the labor and capital employed.

*Id.*

184. On Hume and the Scottish Realists, see H. HOVENKAMP, *supra* note 128, at 3-41.
185. F. WAYLAND, *supra* note 179, at 54 (emphasis in original).

our eyes give us reliable information about the external world. This moral sense gives the community a set of shared values from which the state may derive legal rules of conduct. Even as science is impossible unless we trust our senses, guidelines for rational human conduct are impossible if we cannot trust our judgments about right and wrong.

Common-sense Realism offered a rationale for individual moral choice. The moral sense meant that every person has the ability to make moral choices within a set of shared moral rules. Discovering these moral rules and learning to live one's life in response to them were matters of proper education. The purpose of education, said Wayland, is "to render the mind the fittest possible instrument for DISCOVERING, APPLYING and OBEYING the laws under which God has placed the universe."[186]

### 2. The moral tradition, utilitarianism, and the problem of democracy.

Utilitarianism was fundamentally opposed to the Scottish Realist's moral and economic view of the world. It did not become part of the American intellectual mainstream until the rise of Pragmatism and Progressive era social science in the early twentieth century. The reason was plain enough: Utilitarians were willing to subordinate moral concerns to their primary goal of maximizing human satisfaction. Mainstream Americans could not accept that juxtaposition, and many regarded it as "atheistic."[187] The individual seemed to count for so little in utilitarian thinking: His interests could always be bargained away for the good of society. In the United States, utilitarianism was viewed not so much as a fundamental assumption of economic theory, but as a moral view of the world in competition with Protestant orthodoxy.[188] As a result, it was unacceptable to many political economists, such as Wayland, on religious or moral grounds, economic objections notwithstanding.[189]

---

186. Wayland, *Discourse on Education*, in OCCASIONAL DISCOURSES, INCLUDING SEVERAL NEVER BEFORE PUBLISHED 297 (J. Loring ed. 1833).

187. *See, e.g.,* P. KING, UTILITARIAN JURISPRUDENCE IN AMERICA: THE INFLUENCE OF BENTHAM AND AUSTIN ON AMERICAN LEGAL THOUGHT IN THE NINETEENTH CENTURY 139-266 (1986) (concluding that Bentham's theory of legislation had a positive influence on a few Jeffersonian radicals and the codification movement, but that nearly all Americans, liberal and conservative alike, rejected Bentham's ethics); Everett, *Stewart's Moral Philosophy,* 31 N. AM. REV. (1830); Palmer, *Benthamism in England and America,* 35 AM. POL. SCI. REV. 855 (1941) (concluding that Americans—perhaps incorrectly—perceived a dichotomy between natural law theories of justice and utilitarian theories, and almost without exception opted for the former).

Even liberals, such as the American Transcendentalists, disliked Bentham. *See* Kern, *Emerson and Economics,* 13 N. ENG. Q. 678 (1940). Ralph Waldo Emerson called utilitarianism a "stinking philosophy," and apparently associated it with the thought of political economists in general. *See id.* at 692.

188. *See generally* Palmer, *supra* note 187.

189. On the hostility of the American Scottish Realists toward Bentham, see 2 J. DORFMAN, THE ECONOMIC MIND IN AMERICAN CIVILIZATION 1606-1865, at 699, 836 (1946). One source finding substantially more positive Benthamite influence is Everett, *Benthamism in the United States,* in JEREMY BENTHAM AND THE LAW: A SYMPOSIUM 188 (G. Keeton & G.

The response of nineteenth century American political economists to utilitarianism was typical of their response to remote, rather than imminent, heresies. They ignored it. Francis Wayland never discusses Bentham in his *Elements of Political Economy*. Harvard's Scottish Realist political economist Francis Bowen evidently refused to permit his students to read Bentham.[190] The massive, 3-volume *Principles of Political Economy*[191] by Henry Carey never discusses Bentham. Although Carey discusses John Stuart Mill's views on rent[192] and population,[193] he never mentions Mill's utilitarianism.[194] Considering the dominance of Mill's utilitarianism in English political economy, the omission is remarkable.

The laissez-faire judiciary perceived itself as the strongest defender of Smith's and Wayland's moral brand of self-reliance. It often perceived the new interventionist politics of the Progressive Era as the biggest threat to liberty. One of the great liberal myths about Progressive Era social scientists and the legislation they inspired, is that they protected democracy—that the decision in *Lochner* was somehow antidemocratic, while the bakers' hour statute at issue represented democracy at work. To be sure, in the minds of some reformers, the social sciences were designed to give to laborers some of the dignity and freedom that historically only the privileged had enjoyed. However, Progressive Era social sciences were much more paternalistic than democratic. Social scientists became just as elitist as the American judiciary. Economists did not support wage-and-hour laws because the people wanted them but because the economists believed that the laws were good for the people. Almost from the beginning, social scientists were committed to the view that important public decisions should be made by experts.[195]

---

Schwartzenberger eds. 1948). Everett concludes that Bentham's influence can be found in many statements in American legal literature suggesting that a particular legal rule should be adopted because it would serve the "greatest good" to society as a whole. But such statements are as consistent with Jeffersonian or Jacksonian democracy, or for that matter with Whig conservatism, as they are with Bentham.

190. *See* 2 J. DORFMAN, *supra* note 189, at 836.

191. H. CAREY, PRINCIPLES OF POLITICAL ECONOMY (Philadelphia 1837 & photo. reprint 1965).

192. 1 *id.* at 213.

193. 3 *id.* at 68.

194. Some American political economists used the term "utility," but generally to refer only to productive efficiency or usefulness—not in the welfare sense employed by Bentham or John Stuart Mill. *See, e.g.,* H. VETHAKE, THE PRINCIPLES OF POLITICAL ECONOMY, 13-22 (Philadelphia 2d ed. 1844 & photo. reprint 1971).

195. For example, no sooner did psychologists and psychiatrists apply their science to the criminal law than they began to conclude that the jury should serve a greatly reduced function or perhaps be abolished. *See* Hovenkamp, *Insanity and Criminal Responsibility in Progressive America*, 57 N.D.L. REV. 541, 565-66 (1981). Likewise, segregationist statutes, inspired by Gilded Age anthropology and educational psychology, frequently proscribed private activities between consenting adults. *See* Hovenkamp, *supra* note 81. Land-use laws told responsible people how their property had to be developed. *See, e.g.,* Village of Euclid v. Ambler Realty Co., 272 U.S. 365 (1926); Welch v. Swasey, 214 U.S. 91 (1909).

More than one Supreme Court justice attacked wage-and-hour legislation by arguing that the laboring class did not want such laws. Justice Peckham concluded in *Lochner* that "[t]he employé may desire to earn the extra money, which would arise from his working more than the prescribed time, but this statute forbids the employer from permitting the employé to earn it."[196] Mr. Justice Sutherland was presented with a real-life example in *Adkins*, in the case of Mary Lyons. Lyons had been an elevator operator in the Congress Hall Hotel. The contested statute established a minimum wage for all women and children in the District of Columbia that was substantially above the wages received by Lyons. In light of the statute, however, the Congress Hall Hotel decided that her labor would come at too high a price. It converted its elevators to self-service, and Mary Lyons lost her job. She argued that the Congress Hall Hotel had paid her "the best [wages] she was able to obtain for any work she was capable of performing."[197] This argument appealed to Justice Sutherland. Attorney Felix Frankfurter argued to the Court until he was red-faced. He showed the Justices two thousand pages of economic statistics about the cost of living, but the statistics did not convince Justice Sutherland that Mary Lyons was better off without her job than she had been with it.

Legal orthodoxy and the new science often led people to different conclusions about society's goals and values. But these differences in economic or social policy did not alienate American law from the sciences as much as did the new scientific methodology. This new methodology included a willingness to subject long-held beliefs to critical investigation, to change questions of value into questions of fact, and to insist that history, tradition, and dogma are not the best places to look for solutions to hard problems.

The orthodox judiciary looked at the past and found justification for their most cherished beliefs and institutions. They considered tradition and history to be powerful forces in shaping contemporary values. Social scientists, on the other hand, looked at the past and found only traditions and "folkways"—the slowly evolving, often irrational products of social and economic conflict or the often unspoken compromises people make in order to achieve prosperity.

3.  *The exaggerated vogue of Social Darwinism.*

Darwinism unquestionably had a powerful intellectual influence on American scientific thought at the turn of the century.[198] It also had a powerful influence on American jurisprudence.[199] Ever since Richard Hofstadter's path-breaking book on Social Darwinism,[200] it has become

---

196. Lochner v. New York, 198 U.S. 45, 52-53 (1905).
197. Adkins v. Children's Hosp., 261 U.S. 525, 542 (1923).
198. *See* H. COMMAGER, *supra* note 18, at 82-90; R. HOFSTADTER, *supra* note 139.
199. *See* Hovenkamp, *supra* note 13.
200. R. HOFSTADTER, *supra* note 139.

almost commonplace to observe that Social Darwinism guided the United States Supreme Court.

However, Social Darwinism may in fact be the most overrated of Gilded Age ideologies. Justice Holmes' aphorism that "[t]he Fourteenth Amendment does not enact Mr. Herbert Spencer's *Social Statics*"[201] has been interpreted to mean that the United States Supreme Court *had* written Herbert Spencer into the United States Constitution.[202] But more recent scholars have argued that the influence of Social Darwinism was much less than we have been led to believe.[203] There is painfully little evidence that any members of the Supreme Court were Social Darwinists, or for that matter even Darwinian. Even Holmes' credentials are in dispute. Holmes' public and private writings have been scrutinized as carefully as those of any American public figure, but all the evidence that Social Darwinism was an important intellectual influence on his thought comes down to four or five short, personal statements, most from his early career.[204] A much more defensible proposition is that Holmes once or twice used evolutionary metaphors when speaking about law because theories of evolution dominated both scientific dialogue and parlor talk for the entire period of Holmes' professional life. It was no easier for Holmes to avoid evolution than it was for someone growing up in the 1940s or 1950s to avoid relativity.

Herbert Spencer and other Social Darwinists developed explanatory models and rhetorics that could quite easily be appropriated and suitably revised by expansionist, moralistic Protestant Americans. The influence of Darwinism on Holmes, and on the Supreme Court in general, probably amounted to little in comparison to the influence of Orthodox Protestant Realism. The Court's continuous citation in liberty of contract cases to "just equivalence" and "moral requirements" and "natural" or "inherent" rights in property smacked much more of Common Sense Realism than of Social Darwinist naturalism. The degree to which Darwinism and Social Darwinism *failed* to permeate the thinking of the Supreme Court in any obvious way is most amazing.

In both economics and law, "Social Darwinism" was much more an

---

201. *Lochner*, 198 U.S. at 75 (emphasis added).

202. *See, e.g.*, H. COMMAGER, *supra* note 18, at 373 (arguing that Holmes was "wrong").

203. *See, e.g.*, R. BANNISTER, SOCIAL DARWINISM: SCIENCE AND MYTH IN ANGLO-AMERICAN SOCIAL THOUGHT (1979); J. WALL, ANDREW CARNEGIE (1970); Bellomy, *"Social Darwinism" Revisited*, 1 PERSP. AM. HIST. (n.s.) 1 (1984). These scholars argue that evolutionary models guided the sciences and culture much less than we once thought, that most uses of Darwinian or Spencerian metaphors outside the biological sciences were purely rhetorical, and that in reality, Spencer, the leading Social Darwinist, was not cited all that much in American scientific and literary writing. *See generally Spencer, Scientism, and American Constitutional Law*, 33 ANNALS SCI. 457 (1976) (symposium presenting three views of the extent and nature of Spencer's influence on American thought).

204. For an attempt to place Holmes' "Darwinism" into perspective, see Hovenkamp, *supra* note 13, at 656-64. In a letter to Richard T. Ely in 1902, Holmes described Spencer's *Social Statics* as "absurd." Rader & Rader, *supra* note 110, at 132.

epithet than an analytic tool. It added little more than rhetoric to economic theory. In fact, the two scholars who used the rhetoric most, Herbert Spencer in England and William Graham Sumner in America, were either second-rate economists or not economists at all. Social Darwinism ultimately had little to say about the appropriate limits of state regulatory policy, antitrust reform, or poverty relief. Most problematic was Social Darwinism's inability to see anything but the long run. The true Social Darwinist could look at unemployed masses and proclaim their starvation a good thing, callously discounting the possibility of short-run solutions, for which policymakers must continually search.[205] The leading conservative economists in Gilded Age and Progressive America were not Social Darwinists. They were neoclassicists, looking, as most social scientists were, for a scientific method. They were deeply involved in creating a scientific model that would justify competition and define its limits. The Social Darwinists, on the other hand, worshipped competition and believed that it should have no limits.

For most well-educated but nonscientific American Protestants around the turn of the century, Social Darwinism was nothing more than a cosmological argument. This explains how one could be a Social Darwinist without being a Darwinian. Social Darwinism reinforced deeply ingrained Protestant values. Each person bore responsibility for the most fundamental decisions about religious belief, ethical practice, and economic status. The purpose of the state and the church was not to dictate external values, but merely to cultivate and reinforce those values that were confirmed in each person by his own perceptions. Social Darwinism was "background" theory: It enabled people to think that biology tended to confirm the religious ethics that they had already been taught.

The influence of this *moral* theory of laissez faire in the late nineteenth century cannot be overstated. It explains the immense religiosity in Progressive Era reformers, even political economists such as Richard T. Ely and Charles R. Van Hise. Before theologians, economists, or even lawmakers in late nineteenth and early twentieth century America would abandon their commitment to state non-interference and accept extensive social control, the religious and philosophical roots of laissez faire had to be exhumed, examined, and eradicated. The Progressive Era social reformers did just that. However, for their efforts they were castigated and belittled for making economics too easy a mixture of science and religion.

To be sure, the economics of Progressives such as Ely contained a good deal of religious moralizing that proved unacceptable to more

---

205. For example, Social Darwinism had no "theory" of monopoly. Rather, it blithely explained that monopoly resulted from the survival of the fittest and was therefore a good thing, and the best society could hope for was that the monopolist would be benevolent. *See, e.g.*, W. GHENT, OUR BENEVOLENT FEUDALISM (1902).

positivistic economists in the 1930s and after.[206] However, Progressive economists understood something that later generations did not. In 1900, it was not enough to show that laissez faire was not utilitarian or that it did not contain the best economic theory. It was *clearly* not enough to show that laissez faire was not the best application of Darwin's theory to human morality. Any successful critique of liberty of contract had to come to terms with the prevailing belief that laissez faire was *the* Christian economics—even if it produced inequalities of distribution.[207] Moral arguments were absolutely essential to Ely's case. He had the awesome task of showing that laissez faire was not merely bad economics, but bad religion as well.

The subsequent generation of American social scientists generally ignored the religious roots of nineteenth century American economic theory. As a result, they failed to understand the complex philosophy of Gilded Age laissez faire, which was far too orthodox to be truly Darwinian. Later intellectual historians[208] and constitutional or legal historians[209] likewise emphasized the "Spencerian" or "Social Darwinist" nature of substantive due process. They virtually ignored the much older and deeper religious roots. Thus, the laissez-faire Court has been mischaracterized as a bench full of opportunists who adopted a simple-minded popular philosophy and read it into the Constitution, even as many intellectuals were finding it bigoted and naive. Part of the blame for this historical error lies with none other than Justice Holmes, whose most quoted dissent was correct but misleading. He was right when he told the *Lochner* majority that the fourteenth amendment did not "enact Mr. Herbert Spencer's *Social Statics.*" In fact, it enacted Mr. Francis Wayland's *Elements of Political Economy*.

B.  *Political Economy in America: The Perception of Unlimited Growth*

Many American economists believed that the United States was a better laboratory for the study of the principles of political economy than was Britain. As political economist Jacob Cardozo observed in 1826, America was much closer to the state of nature than Britain was.[210] Whether Cardozo and his peers were right or wrong, one thing is clear: American and British political economists made widely differ-

---

206. *See* R. CRUNDEN, *supra* note 15, at 70.
207. The history of that belief, particularly during the decades following the Civil War, is recounted in H. MAY, PROTESTANT CHURCHES AND INDUSTRIAL AMERICA 39-87 (1967).
208. *See* note 198 *supra*.
209. *See, e.g.,* P. MURPHY, THE CONSTITUTION IN CRISIS TIMES, 1918-1969 (1972); *see also* note 40 *supra*.
210.

In this country we feel assured that the laws which regulate Profits, Wages and Rent can be more successfully investigated than in the old world. . . .True theory in investigations of this nature is founded on a comprehensive examination of phenomena as they are presented in a natural state of the social system. It is reasonable to suppose, therefore, that a country whose institutions and laws have done less to derange the natural order of things than where a vicious social organization has re-ent assumptions, which generated profoundly different views of state polity. Occasionally, these assumptions even worked their way into the law. For example, in his small treatise on contracts,[211] Gulian Verplanck observed that Ricardo's observations concerning rents on land might give rise to a perception of unequal bargaining position sufficient to justify the relative willingness of English courts to intervene in private agreements. However, Verplanck opined, American courts never perceived unequal bargaining power, and thus seldom relieved parties from the consequences of their agreements.[212] For the most part, however, legal treatise writers followed an etiquette that forbade them from quoting nonlegal sources, the only common exception being Adam Smith.[213]

### 1. *Malthus in America.*

As noted above, Malthus' "iron law" of population supported a very strong version of laissez faire. Any attempt to interfere with the free market to ease the lot of the working or idle poor would only increase the ratio of poor persons to food supply and productive capital; eventually even more poor people would starve. But most British political economists never took the strictest implications of Malthus' iron law very seriously. The weaker version, adopted rather early in the nineteenth century, tended to undermine the laissez-faire element in British political economy.[214]

Many Americans accepted the stronger implications of Malthus' theory,[215] but they tended to regard it as inapplicable to America's poor.[216] America's capacity to produce food seemed far greater than

---

sulted either from military violence or a selfish policy, will present the fairest field for analysis and speculation into the causes of wealth.
J.N. CARDOZO, NOTES ON POLITICAL ECONOMY at iii-iv (Charleston, S.C. 1826).

211. G. VERPLANCK, AN ESSAY ON THE DOCTRINE OF CONTRACTS: BEING AN INQUIRY HOW CONTRACTS ARE AFFECTED IN LAW AND MORALS, BY CONCEALMENT, ERROR, OR INADEQUATE PRICE 107-31 (New York 1825). *See* Everett, *Verplanck's Essay on Contracts*, 22 N. AM. REV. 253 (1826).

212. Verplanck argued for more intervention on the part of American courts, but on moral rather than economic grounds. G. VERPLANCK, *supra* note 211, at 107-31.

213. *See* notes 109-110 *supra* and accompanying text.

214. *See* notes 134-138 *supra* and accompanying text.

215. Some had what might be characterized as "non-economic" objections to Malthus. For example, Carey argued in his *Principles of Social Science* that Malthus' population argument contradicted the general principle that the more sophisticated the species, the lower the rate at which it reproduces. Because mankind is the highest species, and its entire food supply comes from lower species, the food supply should naturally grow faster than the consuming population. *See* 1 H. CAREY, PRINCIPLES OF SOCIAL SCIENCE 88-93 (Philadelphia 1858 & photo. reprint 1963).

216. However, one of the great attractions of Malthus' theory in America was the moral obligations that attended his theory. Malthus had argued that the lot of the working class would be improved, not by state intervention, but rather by self-restraint. He suggested delaying marriage, which would naturally lead to the births of fewer children. Several American political economists, particularly those most thoroughly engrained in Scottish Realism, used Malthus for precisely this purpose. *E.g.*, H. VETHAKE, *supra* note 194, at 101-02, 110-15. Carey criticized this view, noting that many nations in which various taboos forbade early mar-

any population growth anticipated in the immediate future. Even later in the century, after population growth had outrun most earlier expectations, many prominent political economists in America continued to accept the stronger version of Malthus' principle of population, but did not foresee mass starvation.[217]

John McVikar, a Federalist follower of Hamilton, was the earliest American political economist who wrote extensively on Malthus.[218] He accepted the strongest version of Malthus' principle in theory, but argued that its applicability to countries such as America was several centuries premature, because of their abundance of undeveloped resources. McVikar correctly predicted labor shortages rather than surpluses for many years to come and argued that anticipated production was much larger than anticipated consumption.[219]

Thomas Cooper, a Jeffersonian Democrat, agreed with McVikar about Malthus, if not about much else. Cooper believed that some prudence was important if food shortages were to be avoided in the future, although he thought the problem was far worse in England than in America. His 1826 *Lectures on the Elements of Political Economy*[220] argued that the "iron law" of Malthus clearly established that the English Poor Laws should be repealed. He would even have abolished public education, except at the elementary level.[221]

American critics of Malthus generally made assumptions about economic growth that far exceeded any made by British classical economists.[222] For example, Jacob Cardozo argued that Malthus had

---

riage had experienced common starvation. 3 H. CAREY, *supra* note 191, at 55-57; *see also* Everett, *M'Culloch's Political Economy*, 25 N. AM. REV. 112, 118 (1827).

217. Malthus enjoyed special popularity among America's Social Darwinists, the most prominent of whom was Yale professor of political economy William Graham Sumner. *See* R. HOFSTADTER, *supra* note 139, at 55-56.

218. *See* J. MCVIKAR, OUTLINES OF POLITICAL ECONOMY (New York 1825). An earlier Federalist, Daniel Raymond, had written a 2-volume treatise on political economy that said almost nothing about Malthus. D. RAYMOND, THE ELEMENTS OF POLITICAL ECONOMY (1820).

219. J. MCVIKAR, *supra* note 218, at 120-22. Samuel Newman of Bowdoin College stated the same conclusions more bluntly, but—as is typical for Americans—he made them with reference to the entire world.

The period when the surface of the earth shall be so covered with inhabitants, that population will equal the means of subsistence, is so distant, and all calculations and reasonings relating to this state of things so indefinite and shadowy, that the whole subject is one of no practical importance.

S. NEWMAN, ELEMENTS OF POLITICAL ECONOMY 254 (Andover 1835 & photo. reprint 1973).

220. T. COOPER, LECTURES ON THE ELEMENTS OF POLITICAL ECONOMY (Columbia, S.C. 1826).

221. *See also* G. TUCKER, *On Density of Population*, in ESSAYS ON VARIOUS SUBJECTS OF TASTE, MORALS AND NATIONAL POLICY (1822) (agreeing with views of Cooper). Francis Wayland made similar arguments, although he did not cite Malthus. F. WAYLAND, *supra* note 182, at 125-27.

222. Or alternatively, they suggested that Malthus was so preoccupied with Britain's own agricultural problems that he generalized from Britain to the rest of the world. *See* Denslow, *American Economics*, 139 N. AM. REV. 12 (1884) (suggesting that Malthus' principle of population was wrong, and that Malthus had no doubt derived it by observing the "local phenomenon of emigration from England").

overlooked "the effect of improvements in Agriculture," which tended to undermine his principle of population.[223] Alexander Everett, one of Malthus' most outspoken American critics, argued that when population growth approached the hiring capacity of industry, laborers moved elsewhere, thus spreading economic growth more widely. Everett explained the settlement of the American West in this manner.[224] Clearly, however, these observations were relevant only in a country where plenty of room for such expansion existed, and movement was relatively easy.[225]

Henry Carey was one of the few nineteenth-century Americans to observe that Malthus' theory that population grew geometrically while the food supply grew only arithmetically must be based on empirical observation if on anything at all.[226] Carey's argument displayed a common theme: the contrast of British "speculation" with American "facts," or British "deduction" with the American "Baconian" or inductive method.[227] Carey's "facts" were rather casual as well.[228] But even in densely populated New England, agricultural productivity had appeared to keep up with or even surpass population growth. This view that Malthus had simply gotten his numbers wrong prevailed in the United States for the next half century. Even in the 1880s, a few quick calculations by American Van Buren Denslow in support of Carey revealed that mankind's entire food supply tended to multiply much faster than mankind itself.[229] In all the "bulky volumes written in support" of Malthus, Denslow scoffed, "never has the actual fecundity of a human couple been compared with that of a grain of wheat, a potato, a couple of swine, or a pair of beeves."[230]

The principal difference between Malthus and Carey was context. Malthus looked at London's impoverished masses and saw population constantly pushing against the ability of agriculture and capital to sup-

---

223. J.N. CARDOZO, *supra* note 210, at 44; *see* notes 237-239 *infra* and accompanying text.

224. *See* Everett, *supra* note 216, at 141; *see also* A. EVERETT, NEW IDEAS IN POPULATION (Boston 1823); Everett, *Political Economy*, (Book Review) 28 N. AM. REV. 368 (1829). *See generally* Spengler, *Alexander Hill Everett: Early American Opponent of Malthus*, 9 NEW ENG. Q. 97 (1936).

225. *See also* H. VETHAKE, *supra* note 194, at 109-10, 120-24. Thomas Jefferson himself was once concerned about the implications of Malthus' theory for America. However, the Louisiana Purchase removed his doubts—the supply of land appeared virtually unlimited. *See* D. McCOY, *supra* note 117, at 194-95.

226. *See also* Andrews, *Are There Too Many of Us?*, 155 N. AM. REV. 596, 607 (1892); Denslow, *supra* note 222, at 12-13 (appearing to have taken the observation from Carey).

227. On the distinction, see H. HOVENKAMP, *supra* note 128, at 23-26. *See also* Denslow, *supra* note 222, at 14-16 (crediting Carey with developing an American empirical political economy in contrast to the British deductive method).

228. Carey performed a "simple calculation" showing that even a conservative geometric progression would have the population doubling every generation. Had this happened since the time of Adam and Eve, people would "not now find standing-room upon the earth." 3 H. CAREY, *supra* note 191, at 54; *see also* Andrews, *supra* note 226, at 606 (concluding that Malthus' thesis that population grows geometrically was flawed).

229. Denslow, *supra* note 222, at 12-14.

230. *Id.* at 13.

port it. Carey, on the other hand, believed that the growth of capital permitted the growth of population. He observed that many parts of the world, such as India and South America, experienced horrible starvation in spite of the fact that plenty of idle, fertile land was available for production.[231] The problem was not lack of land but lack of investment. Free movement of capital permitted population to grow, but it permitted agricultural productivity to grow even faster. As a result, the most developed lands tended to have the most abundant food, regardless of their agricultural productivity.[232]

Carey represents unbridled American optimism about the capacity for future growth—against Malthus' relatively dark English pessimism. Both views were inspired by the environments in which these men found themselves. Malthus lived in a country where the amount of investment was seen as relatively high, and the amount of available land as very low. The Malthusian theory, that population growth is a function of the amount of available land, was pessimistic because no new land was being created and, in Britain at least, the best lands were already in production. Carey, on the other hand, lived in a country where land was abundant, but which had experienced chronic underinvestment. The solution to the American problem was therefore simple: encourage investment, and eliminate all artificial constraints on it. The theory of Carey, Wayland, and other Americans, that capital investment permits population growth, was optimistic simply because both undeveloped land and the potential for capital investment were perceived as almost infinite. Such views persisted in America virtually unchanged until the 1880s and 1890s.[233]

### 2. Ricardo in America: rents where land is unlimited.

Ricardo's theory of rents spawned a strenuous reaction to classical laissez-faire political economy in Britain. The theory was that as the proportion of land to population and capital fell, and as increasingly marginal land was placed into production, a higher percentage of the price of commodities would go to monopoly profits for landlords, and wages would decline to subsistence levels. In the United States, Ri-

---

231. 3 H. CAREY, supra note 191, at 54-56.
232. Francis Wayland took essentially the same position:
The prosperity of a nation does not depend simply upon the absolute amount of its capital, but upon the ratio which its capital bears to its population . . . . When the increase of capital is less rapid than the ordinary increase of the human race, there will be, in the lowest class, continual distress . . . .

. . . .

. . . Population always follows capital. It increases, as capital increases; is stationary when capital is stationary; and decreases, when capital decreases. And hence, there seems no need of any other means to prevent the too rapid increase of population, than to secure a correspondent increase of capital, by which that population may be supported.
F. WAYLAND, supra note 182, at 339-40.
233. See, e.g., Andrews, supra note 226; Denslow, supra note 222.

cardo's theory would become the basis of Henry George's "single tax" movement, espoused by some Progressive and socialist politicians at the end of the century.[234] But among Americans, George's application of Ricardo was the exception rather than the rule.

*The doctrine of rents in the American "Classical" tradition.* Ricardo's theory had no significant effect on classical American political economy. Some Americans suggested about Ricardo, as they did about Malthus, that perhaps in some distant future the problem of rents would become significant in the United States. But any American who looked west after 1803 saw a seemingly endless expanse of fertile, untilled land. Its great abundance would keep land prices low for a long time. As a result, rents were not a problem: Land currently brought into production was just as fertile as older land that had been under cultivation for a long time. Classical economists such as Willard Phillips, perhaps American's leading antebellum theorist on economic development,[235] argued that, whatever validity Ricardo's theory might have in Britain, it was of little relevance in the United States, where "a much greater quantity of wheat could be produced . . . without any increase of the expense per bushel in the production."[236]

Other American skeptics of Ricardo looked, not at the vast amount of untilled land, but rather at the relative backwardness of American agricultural technology, and saw increased productivity in the future as substantially undermining Ricardo's doctrine. Jacob Newton Cardozo, in a lengthy attack on Ricardo, argued that rents are much less significant in a world of rapid technological progress, than in one where progress has come to an end.[237] Cardozo was optimistic that increased

---

234. H. George, Progress and Poverty: An Inquiry into the Cause of Industrial Depressions and of Increase of Want with Increase of Wealth—The Remedy (1879). George himself was quite laissez-faire about such things as poor laws. *See* notes 299-305 *infra* and accompanying text.

235. *See* Dorfman, *Economic Thought,* in The Growth of the Seaport Cities: 1790-1825, at 151, 161-65 (D. Gilchrist ed. 1967); Thompson, *Willard Phillips: A Neglected American Economist,* 16 Hist. Pol. Econ. 405 (1984).

236. W. Phillips, *supra* note 172, at 109; *see also* F. Wayland, *supra* note 182, at 382-84.
In newly settled countries, where are found rich and extensive tracts of land, with few to occupy and cultivate them, and where most of the inhabitants are themselves agricultural producers, furnishing supplies of this class for their own wants, though land may be appropriated, no rents will be paid. Soon however, this ceases to be the case; rents will be paid, and as the community continues to make progress in numbers and in wealth, both the amount of land paying rent will become greater, and the rate of rents will advance . . . .
S. Newman, *supra* note 219, at 274.

237. Cardozo argued that land will not produce unjust rents in a competitive market, but that rents might easily exist when a "monopoly of land is established."
[W]hen the soil has been purchased as an instrument of political influence, or as a source of dignity and power, its price will not be subject to the rules which govern its market-value as a commodity, in those countries where it is sought purely for the profit that can be made from it. Something must be paid for the additional value acquired by land in consequence of these circumstances.
J.N. Cardozo, *supra* note 210, at 26-27; *see also* W. Phillips, *supra* note 172, at 122.

productivity would offset any price increases in food brought about by the employment of less productive land.

Ricardo's principal shortcoming, Cardozo argued, was that he neglected to account for government limitations on agricultural production in England, such as the Corn Laws, that reduced incentives[238] and led to inflated prices. Only when the *state* prohibits increased production, argued Cardozo, do rents become possible, and then of course the rents on more fertile land will be greater than those on less fertile land.[239]

Even those who attacked Cardozo in defense of Ricardo found the problem of rents in America to be of a different order of magnitude than it was in Britain. For example, lawyer Jonathan Porter argued that although Ricardo's theory was correct, rents would rise very slowly where plenty of fertile land was available and constantly being placed into production. In fact, they would not rise at all in situations where newly cleared lands were just as fertile as older lands.[240]

However, Henry Carey made the doctrine of rents virtually superfluous in American political economy until the writings of Henry George became popular during the Progressive Era. Carey devoted nearly an entire volume of his *Principles of Political Economy*[241] to questions about how the values of land, capital, and labor are determined. He believed Ricardo's theory outrageously oversimplified a complicated state of affairs. Carey noted that even identifying the "best" agricultural land, at least in a developing country, is extremely difficult. Given equal expenditures of capital and labor, some land will yield more than other land. However, the most productive land may be located far from population centers, may require considerable deforestation, or may lack access to rivers or other forms of transportation. As a result, Carey argued, less fertile land is often placed into production before more fertile land.[242] The choice of which land to place into pro-

---

238. *See generally* D. BARNES, A HISTORY OF THE ENGLISH CORN LAWS FROM 1660-1846 (1930).

239.

> If we suppose on the settlement of a new country that land is of easy acquisition, and that division prevails which is most conducive to the increase of capital and population, in such a case land being obtainable at the price of free competition, its rent can never exceed its productive powers derived from nature. This is on the supposition that capital and population are in due proportion, and that no obstacles exist to a free commercial intercourse with other countries.

J.N. CARDOZO, *supra* note 210, at 26-27. *See also* Cardozo, Book Review, 1 SOUTHERN REV. 192, 205 (1828) (reviewing T. COOPER, *supra* note 220).

240. Porter, *Cardozo's Notes on Political Economy*, (Book Review) 24 N. AM. REV. 169, 176 (1827); *see also* Cardozo, *supra* note 239 (response to Porter).

241. H. CAREY, *supra* note 191. On Carey's critique of Ricardo, see A. KAPLAN, *supra* note 173, at 48-51.

242. *Id.* at 35-40. In short, Carey was arguing that the marginal utility of land was a function of a variety of factors, of which fertility was only one. The other American classical economists generally agreed. *E.g.*, J.N. CARDOZO, *supra* note 210, at 31-32; F. WAYLAND, *supra* note 182, at 386-88.

duction at any given time is made by comparing the gain to be produced from that land with the investment that must be made in it.[243]

Carey also argued that the productivity of land is a function of the capital invested, not only in land but also in labor-saving equipment.[244] As more capital is invested in such equipment, the amount of labor needed to produce a given quantity declines. The relative value of farm land declines as well, for capital investment makes farming possible on a wider variety of land, makes new, more remote land accessible, and increases the amount that can be produced on a given parcel of land.[245]

Did Ricardo and Carey actually disagree? Perhaps, but for the most part they simply made very different factual assumptions. Both probably would have agreed that capital investment is subject eventually to the law of diminishing returns. Carey assumed, however, that the marginal utility of new capital investment was very high.[246] In America, which was relatively undeveloped in the 1830s when Carey was writing, his assumption was quite justified. A new road, canal, or bridge could bring thousands of acres of new land into production.[247] Ricardo assumed a much more developed economy, in which the marginal value of new capital was much lower. As a result, he predicted that future increases in productivity would not be substantial.[248] Similarly, Carey assumed the availability of a great deal of land, which would not be significantly less fertile than land already in production, once it was cleared and made more accessible. Ricardo, on the other hand, as-

---

243. Francis Wayland agreed with Carey, observing that American agricultural efficiency did not increase substantially until the Mississippi Valley was settled and cultivated in the late eighteenth century. F. WAYLAND, *supra* note 182, at 390. Wayland concluded:

> The result has been, that the western farmers have undersold the farmers of the north and east; and now, but little wheat is raised in any part of New England. This result has been increased, by the vast emigration to the west, which has diminished the number of laborers; and at the east, by demand for laborers for manufactures and internal improvements, which has withdrawn men from agriculture, and raised the wages of agricultural labor in the New England States. Hence, by the increased wages of labor, and the reduced price of grain, the profit of agriculture has been reduced, and the price of land has fallen.

*Id.*

244. H. CAREY, *supra* note 191, at 27-35.

245. Even Henry Vethake, perhaps Ricardo's most loyal follower among antebellum American political economists, conceded that technological progress tended to reduce rents insofar as it increased agricultural productivity. *See* H. VETHAKE, *supra* note 194, at 95. Vethake contended, however, that technological advances in nonagricultural sectors would tend to increase rents insofar as they increased the demand, rather than the supply, of agricultural products. Increases in demand would flow from two things: industrial use of agricultural products; and increases in the amount of available income, which would encourage people to purchase more agricultural products. *Id.* at 96.

246. As did Cardozo, who argued that capital as well as land produces "rent," as Ricardo defined it, and that the profitability of agricultural land is in all cases a function of both the fertility of the land and the amount of investment that has been made in it. *See* Cardozo, *supra* note 239, at 199-204.

247. *See also* Carey, *Carey on the Population and Political Condition of Mankind*, 7 N.Y. REV. 306 (1840); Carey, *Carey's Principles of Political Economy*, 3 N.Y. REV. 1 (1838).

248. *See* J. OSER & W. BLANCHFIELD, THE EVOLUTION OF ECONOMIC THOUGHT 348 (3d ed. 1975).

sumed that the best land had been taken and that any new production must take place on significantly inferior land.[249] Under Carey's assumptions, the optimal state policy was to encourage more development without worrying about distribution, which would take care of itself. Ricardo, on the other hand, placed substantially less value on further development, which he believed would exacerbate the problem of maldistribution of wealth and produce only marginal increases in production.

*Rents and the Progressives: the American problem of monopoly.* Except for the work of Henry George, the orthodox Ricardian doctrine of rents was never influential in the United States, not even in the work of the Progressive Era economists, who rejected much of both the classical and neoclassical traditions. More conservative turn-of-the-century economists, such as John Bates Clark, generally agreed with the Progressives that the theory of land rents was inapplicable to the United States.[250] In *Capital and Its Earnings,*[251] Clark attempted to refute the arguments of the socialist economists by showing that the rents that might be derived from land are in no way different than those derived from capital in general. For example, the least efficient ship capable of operating in a competitive shipping market will earn no rent, while the more efficient ones will. But new investment will be made only in the more efficient ships—for capital always goes where the expected rents are the highest. Land is no exception to this rule.[252] Clark conceded the fact that land bears certain "natural monopoly"[253] characteristics because it cannot be infinitely reproduced. But these characteristics are insignificant at best, since most of the elements of value in land, such as proximity to transportation, drainage, irrigation, and clearing, are the product of labor and not inherent in the land itself.[254]

An important difference between the theories of monopoly in American classical political economy and in the Progressive Era is that the latter considered capital investment rather than land to be the chief cause of monopoly. The American classicists followed the British classical economists in viewing land as the only significant producer of monopoly profits. As a result they tended to believe that monopoly and maldistribution of wealth was not a problem in America because of the abundance of good, available land. "Monopoly" would exist only if the state created it by means of monopoly franchises, licensing restrictions,

---

249. To put it more technically, Ricardo believed that the supply curve for agricultural products sloped upwards much more steeply than Carey believed.

250. Joseph Dorfman argues that early in his career, Ely tended to accept the orthodox Ricardian doctrine of land rents, but that he later came to agree with Clark that rents are nothing more than a "species of capital." 3 J. DORFMAN, *supra* note 189, at 257.

251. Clark, *Capital and Its Earnings,* 3 PUBLICATIONS AM. ECON. A. 83 (1888).

252. *Id.* at 122-24.

253. *Id.* at 120.

254. *Id.* at 115-16.

and the like. Up to the time of the Sherman Act in 1890, the word "monopoly" in the United States referred mainly to monopolies created by the sovereign.[255]

When the Progressives began to write, good land was still abundant. Monopoly profits were being earned, not from land, but from railroads, oil, and other forms of industrial development. As a result, America's Progressive Era economists, concerned about the effects of monopoly on wages and productivity, focused their attention not on rents in land, but rather on industrial monopolies and trusts.[256] For American Progressives, technology, rather than land, was the chief producer of rents and the attendant evils of subsistence wages and maldistribution of wealth.

For example, Richard T. Ely, the most prominent Progressive economist, discussed rents at length in his book on property and contract.[257] But he believed that the principal rent-producing engine was not land. Rather, it was large concentrations of capital. Ely identified railroads and telegraph companies as the types of property interests which were causing maldistribution of wealth in the United States. He did not so identify agricultural land.[258] Most Progressives shared Ely's view. In fact, in the literature of both the Granger Movement[259] and the Progressive Era,[260] the farmer was the victim, rather than the cause, of monopoly. Neither farmers nor the owners of agricultural land were ever depicted in American political economy as the rent-stealing monsters that they were in Ricardo's England.

There is one very important difference between the British emphasis on monopoly created by land rents and the emerging American concern with monopoly created by capital investment and trusts. Land cannot be reproduced. British neoclassicists such as Alfred Marshall, a contemporary of the American Progressives, continued to assume that the monopoly profits available from land, which was *inherently* incapable of being increased, were much more problematic than the monopoly profits available from technology, which could be duplicated;[261] they felt the former could only be solved through radical state interference in the market system, such as forcible transfers of monopoly profits. American Progressives generally viewed the "problem of monopoly" created by the trusts as soluble *within* the laissez-faire system. In fact,

255. *See* Hovenkamp, *supra* note 45.
256. *See, e.g.*, R. ELY, *supra* note 110; E. JONES, THE TRUST PROBLEM IN THE UNITED STATES (1924); A. KALES, CONTRACTS AND COMBINATIONS IN RESTRAINT OF TRADE (1918); C. VAN HISE, CONCENTRATION AND CONTROL: A SOLUTION TO THE TRUST PROBLEM IN THE UNITED STATES (1914).
257. R. ELY, *supra* note 37.
258. 1 *id.* at 79-91.
259. *E.g.*, Adams, *supra* note 36.
260. *E.g.*, F. NORRIS, THE OCTOPUS (1901).
261. *See* A. MARSHALL, *supra* note 144, at bk. vii, ch. 10. On the lack of attention to monopoly in neoclassical British economic theory, see P. ATIYAH, *supra* note 28, at 616-17.

the Sherman Antitrust Act of 1890 was dedicated to that proposition. Only the most extreme Progressives proposed the elimination of capitalism as a solution to the trust problem.[262] More moderate Progressives, who were the only ones to achieve substantial political power, sought reform through the antitrust laws. They believed the problem of monopoly created by capital was soluble because it was artificial: Capital itself could be reproduced indefinitely, and only the combinations and conspiracies of investors prevented competition from driving monopoly profits out of the market. American monopoly, when it finally appeared, had a laissez-faire solution.

### 3. Population, rents, and wages: a summary.

Malthus' theory of population and Ricardo's doctrine of rents both predicted the same consequence for the wages of common labor: They would be driven down to the subsistence level or even lower. In Malthus' theory, the relative scarcity of the food supply in light of a large population would tend to drive the price of food up to the point where a worker's wage would barely cover his daily requirements. Ricardo's doctrine of rents predicted three things, all of them bad for the laborer. First, the absolute cost of producing food would increase as more marginal land was placed into production. Second, the price of food would go up faster than the average cost of producing it because all land owners, not merely the marginal ones, would be able to charge the market price for food. Third, real wages would decline as the price of food lowered demand for it and as the supply of laborers increased.

By the 1830s, these theories persuaded most British political economists to depart from laissez-faire ideology and increase support for corrective legislation, such as the Factory Acts.[263] Almost no American political economist before the Progressive Era seventy years later drew the same conclusions. A few conceded that at some future time America may have to face the problem of subsistence wages; most refused to concede even this. Most agreed with Cardozo that Malthus and Ricardo underestimated or ignored economic growth altogether. Once *any* amount of growth is assumed, conclusions about the eventual level of wages become ambiguous. In fact, if economic growth is high enough, wages will rise even as population density becomes quite high. Henry Carey concluded:

> Improvements of cultivation arise out of increased capital, and are the cause why inferior lands pay higher rent than was formerly paid by the most fertile, at the same time that the labourer receives higher wages. Those improvements are constantly going on, and there is no reason to doubt that the worst land in Great Britain will at some future period pay as high a rent as is now paid by the best, leaving to the cultivator

---

262. Some of the more extreme came close, however. *See* C. VAN HISE, *supra* note 256.
263. *See* notes 132-138 *supra* and accompanying text.

higher wages than he now receives.[264]

## C.   *The Policy Implications of American Political Economy*

### 1.   *The wage-fund doctrine in the United States.*

One of the most underrated debates in American intellectual history is the great controversy over the "theory of distribution," or the wage-fund doctrine, that raged in the newly founded academic journals of political economy at the turn of the century. According to the wage-fund doctrine, the aggregate fund available to pay the wages of all laborers in the economy is directly proportional to the aggregate level of capital invested. Total wages in excess of this fixed fund would deplete current capital so that the amount of capital available for the fund in the future would be insufficient to maintain the current level of income.

Most mid-nineteenth century American classical economists subscribed to the wage-fund theory. When the theory came under attack later in the century, an extended debate over the doctrine ensued.

The implications of the debate were awesome: If the classical wage-fund theory were correct, then there was an absolute limit to the total value of wages that could be paid in any given period. According to the theory, actions designed to increase real wages, such as minimum wage or maximum hours statutes or trade unionism, would undermine economic progress and could only harm the laborers they were designed to benefit. "Liberty of contract"—each wage-earner bargaining freely with his employer—was absolutely essential to the welfare, in fact the survival, of both.

The original idea of the wage "fund" is deceptively simple, and explains why the theory was so attractive to the classicists, who were inclined to see order and pattern in all parts of the cosmos. The farmer currently laboring on his plantings must live off that part of last year's crop placed into storage for this purpose. If he consumes it too early he will not live to bring the new crop to harvest. The moral: The amount available for wages at any given time is a function of that which has already been invested. If the workers take more out than has been put in by investors, they will deplete the amount of invested capital, and each year the amount available will grow smaller. But if they take less, the amount invested will grow and the workers will experience increased prosperity. Thus the amount of money available in the economy for the payment of wages at any given time is directly proportional to the amount of capital invested. Also, each worker's share of the fund is inversely proportional to the total working population, because the fund must be divided among them.[265] As William Graham Sumner put it, "[c]hanges in rates of wages can only be produced by changes in the

---

264.  1 H. CAREY, *supra* note 191, at 166; *see also* J.N. CARDOZO, *supra* note 210, at 43-48.
265.  *See generally* Gordon, *The Wage-Fund Controversy: The Second Round*, 5 HIST. POL. ECON. 14 (1973); Phillips, *The Wages Fund in Historical Context*, 1 J. ECON. ISSUES 321 (1967).

amount of capital distributable as wages, or by changes in the number of persons competing for wages."[266] Thus, even though wages in America were relatively high and on the rise, there was a limit beyond which they could not go. Francis Wayland, one of the early American supporters of the doctrine, presented what was to become the standard American perspective:

> The prosperity of a nation does not depend simply upon the *absolute* amount of its capital, but upon the ratio which its capital bears to its population, and the ratio which is maintained between the increase of both. [1] If the increase of capital be so rapid as to allow the simple laborer sufficient wages to support and rear as many children as, under ordinary circumstances, form a human family, there will be no distress in any class. . . . [2] If the increase of capital be more rapid than this, every one will have, beside support and maintenance, many of the conveniences of life; and a large proportion will be continually rising from a lower to a higher grade of employment. [3] When the increase of capital is less rapid than the ordinary increase of the human race, there will be, in the lowest class, continual distress; children will die in great numbers; the average duration of human life will be shortened; and many persons will be sinking from the higher, into the lower grades of employment and comfort.[267]

It is not easy for someone trained in economic theory dominated by late twentieth-century marginalism to picture the wage-fund doctrine, or to appreciate how powerful the idea was during the classical period. The wage-fund idea is distinctively "pre-marginalist" and could only come out of a model in which average, rather than marginal, costs and benefits govern production decisions. Average costs and benefits are those that have already been incurred; marginal costs and benefits are those that are currently anticipated. In short, under the wage-fund doctrine, the amount available for wages is a function of *previously* invested capital, rather than of current productivity. Yale political economist William Graham Sumner, one of the staunchest American supporters of the classical wage-fund doctrine, ridiculed the emerging marginalist theory as suggesting that it "would mean that a man who was tilling the ground in June could eat the crop he expected to have in September, or that a tailor could be wearing the coat which he was making."[268]

For those who believed in the wage-fund doctrine, "artificial" wage

---

266. Sumner, *Protective Taxes and Wages*, 136 N. Am. Rev. 270, 271 (1883).

267. F. Wayland, *supra* note 182, at 339. For a similar description, see H. Carey, Essay on the Rate of Wages 30-32 (Philadelphia 1835 & photo. reprint 1965).

Wayland believed that America fell in category two, while Ireland was in the oppressed category three, largely because the Irish economy was heavily agricultural, but the land was owned by the English, who carried away the rents. *Id.* at 340. Likewise, Newman concluded that wages were the highest in the United States, substantially lower in England, and pitifully low in Ireland. S. Newman, *supra* note 219, at 246.

268. W. Sumner, *Wages*, in Collected Essays in Political and Social Science 36, 50 (1885).

increases above the value of labor—such as those that might result from minimum wage laws or the bargaining power of labor unions—had disastrous implications. First, since more capital would be invested in wages, less would be left for capital improvements. Second, higher wages would increase the price of goods, thus reducing demand below the level set by the invisible hand and ultimately decreasing the demand for labor. Production would decline, and the smaller profit per unit accompanying the higher wages would further reduce investment in capital improvements. This would lead to a vicious cycle: The amount of production would become ever smaller in relation to the population; economic development would grind to a halt or slow dramatically; and the working population would face the prospect of massive unemployment and starvation, until their numbers were reduced substantially or wages were driven back down to a level commensurate with the "fund."[269]

The implications of the wage-fund doctrine cannot be overstated. *Any* kind of forced wealth transfer from capitalists to laborers would upset the equilibrium and spell disaster for the laborer. For those who believed in the wage-fund doctrine, labor unions, minimum wage laws, and graduated income taxes were all bad.[270] More importantly, the true believer could think that they were bad because they were contrary to the laborer's own best interests. The implications of this view are staggering in light of the large number of American political economists who continued to support some version of the wage-fund theory well into the 1890s, long after the British mainstream had abandoned it. In fact, the American debate over the wage-fund theory forced American academic economists to side either with the neoclassical tradition or with the new Progressives. Many chose the former.

The wage-fund doctrine was popular in Britain in the early nineteenth century.[271] John Stuart Mill repudiated it in 1869, late in his life,[272] however, as did 1870s marginalists such as William Jevons[273]

---

269.
That which pays for labor in every country, is a certain portion of actually accumulated capital, which cannot be increased by the proposed action of government, nor by the influence of public opinion, nor by combinations among the workmen themselves. There is also in every country a certain number of laborers, and this number cannot be diminished by the proposed action of government, nor by public opinion, nor by combinations among themselves. There is to be a division now among all these laborers of the portion of capital actually there present.
A. PERRY, ELEMENTS OF POLITICAL ECONOMY 122 (New York 1866). Perry's book succeeded Wayland's text after the Civil War as the most popular American economics textbook. *See* Gordon, *supra* note 265, at 20.

270. *See* Sumner, *supra* note 266.

271. The doctrine was championed by J.R. M'Culloch in the 1820s and by Nassau Senior in the 1830s. *See* J. M'CULLOCH, THE PRINCIPLES OF POLITICAL ECONOMY 292-332 (Edinburgh 1825); N. SENIOR, *supra* note 152, at 2-3, 49; N. SENIOR, THREE LECTURES ON THE RATE OF WAGES 36 (London 1830).

272. Mill, Book Review, in 5 COLLECTED WORKS 680 (J. Robson ed. 1967) (reviewing W.T. THORNTON, ON LABOUR, ITS WRONGFUL CLAIMS AND RIGHTFUL DUES, ITS ACTUAL PRES-

and 1890s neoclassicists such as Alfred Marshall.[274]  The doctrine persisted in the United States until much later.[275]  Prominent mid-century political economists such as Francis Wayland[276] and A.L. Perry accepted it as an article of faith.[277]  It was also accepted in various forms by earlier American political economists such as Jacob Cardozo,[278] Samuel Newman,[279] Willard Phillips,[280] Henry Vethake,[281] and above all, Henry Carey.[282]  Harvard political economist S.M. MacVane adhered to the doctrine in his popular textbook published in 1890.[283]  Prominent neoclassicist Frank Taussig accepted a version of it in the 1890s,[284] as did Social Darwinist and Yale economist William Graham Sumner[285] and the well-known New York lawyer, Henry T. Terry.[286]

A perplexing problem in the history of American political economy is why Americans subscribed to the wage-fund theory so long after most of the British mainstream had rejected it.  The best answer is that, in the United States, where economic growth was rapid and the fund appeared to be growing and making each generation of American laborers better off than their predecessors, the theory was far less brutal than it was in England.[287]  One could accept the wage-fund theory in the United States without accepting starvation as a corollary.  For example, Henry Carey's version of the wage-fund theory was much more optimistic than the classical wage-fund theory.  Carey did believe that the fund that could be set aside for wages was limited at any given time

---

ENT AND POSSIBLE FUTURE (London 1869)); *see also* Ekelund, *A Short-Run Classical Model of Capital and Wages: Mill's Recantation of the Wages Fund,* 28 OXFORD ECON. PAPERS 66 (1976).

273.  *See* W. JEVONS, THE THEORY OF POLITICAL ECONOMY 257-58 (1871); *see also* T. HUTCHISON, *supra* note 163, at 65-66.

274.  *See* Marshall, *The Theory of Business Profits,* 1 Q.J. ECON. 477 (1887) [hereinafter *Business Profits*]; Marshall, *Wages and Profits,* 2 Q.J. ECON. 218 (1888) [hereinafter *Wages and Profits*]; *see also* 1 A. MARSHALL, *supra* note 144, at 567.

275.  The earliest statement of the wage-fund doctrine in America that I have found is in Everett, *supra* note 216.  Two years later, Everett restated the doctrine in Everett, Book Review, 28 N. AM. REV. 368, 384-85 (1829) (reviewing T. MALTHUS, DEFINITIONS IN POLITICAL ECONOMY (London 1827)).  In both of these articles, Everett expresses considerable skepticism about the theory, noting that wages in America were relatively high while, in comparison with England, the amount of invested capital was quite small.  American writers before Everett discussed wages almost entirely as a function of the monopoly price of land.  *E.g.,* 1 D. RAYMOND, *supra* note 218, at 191-203.

276.  *See* note 267 *supra* and accompanying text.

277.  *See* A. PERRY, ELEMENTS OF POLITICAL ECONOMY 122 (New York 1866).

278.  *See* J.N. CARDOZO, *supra* note 210, at 40-41.

279.  *See* S. NEWMAN, *supra* note 219, at 243.

280.  *See* W. PHILLIPS, *supra* note 172, at 117.

281.  *See* H. VETHAKE, *supra* note 194, at 100.

282.  *See* H. CAREY, *supra* note 267; H. CAREY, *supra* note 191, at 15-19.

283.  S. MACVANE, THE WORKING PRINCIPLES OF POLITICAL ECONOMY (1890).

284.  *See* F. TAUSSIG, WAGES AND CAPITAL: AN EXAMINATION OF THE WAGES FUND DOCTRINE 96-107 (1896).

285.  *See* W. SUMNER, *supra* note 268; Sumner, *supra* note 266.

286.  *See* Terry, *Rates of Wages,* 45 NEW ENGLANDER & YALE REV. 798 (1886) [hereinafter *Rates of Wages*]; Terry, *The Services Capital Renders to Labor,* 45 NEW ENGLANDER & YALE REV. 498 (1886) [hereinafter *Services Capital Renders*].

287.  *See* note 267 *supra* and accompanying text.

by the amount of invested capital.[288]   But he also strongly believed that, when one allowed for economic growth, wages would increase more quickly than capital increased.  Assuming rapid economic growth and capital investment and a relative shortage of laborers—actual conditions in nineteenth century America—one could have both the wage-fund doctrine and labor prosperity.

The renewed assertion of the wage-fund theory in the United States at the end of the nineteenth century provoked the largest single debate in America's first economics journal, the *Quarterly Journal of Economics*, during its first two decades of publication.  But the story actually began in 1875, when revisionist economist Francis Walker wrote a seminal article[289] attacking the wage-fund theory.  Walker suggested that the value of wages is determined, not by the amount of previously invested capital, but by workers' current productivity.[290]  A decade later, Walker began developing his own theory of wages, suggesting that optimal wages should equal the workers' productivity and that many workers were in fact paid far less than they produced for their employers.[291]  This perspective inspired Walker to become a supporter of the growing American labor movement.[292]  The theoretical battle between neoclassical and Progressive economists was joined.

The following decade saw an outpouring of scholarship on the "distribution question," or the notion that there was an absolute limit to the workers' share of industrial productivity.[293]  Richard T. Ely and

---

288.  *See* H. CAREY, *supra* note 267; 1 H. CAREY, *supra* note 191, at 15-19.

289.  Walker, *The Wage-Fund Theory*, 120 N. AM. REV. 84 (1875); *see also* F. WALKER, THE WAGES QUESTION 142-44, 405-06 (1876) [hereinafter THE WAGES QUESTION]; Book Review, 124 N. AM. REV. 305 (1877).  Walker, who was president of the Massachusetts Institute of Technology, developed his ideas further in F. WALKER, POLITICAL ECONOMY 364-70 (3d ed. 1888).

290.  Walker asked rhetorically:
Given a certain body of labor employed, what is it that determines the amount which the employer can afford to pay in wages?  Is it the amount of capital at his command, or the value to be realized from that labor?  Surely there can be no hesitation in answering this question.
Walker, *supra* note 289, at 102.

291.  *See* Walker, *The Source of Business Profits*, 1 Q.J. ECON. 265 (1887) (arguing that wages equalled anticipated gross receipts, less the sum of rents, interest, and profits).

292.  *See* J. MUNROE, A LIFE OF FRANCIS AMASA WALKER (1923).

293.  The scholarship on the doctrine can be roughly grouped into a "defender" category and an "attacker" category.  The former includes W. SUMNER, *supra* note 268, Laughlin, *Marshall's Theory of Value and Distribution*, 1 Q.J. ECON. 227 (1887), MacVane, *Business Profits and Wages: A Rejoinder*, 2 Q.J. ECON. 453 (1888), MacVane, *The Theory of Business Profits*, 2 Q.J. ECON. 1 (1887), Patten, *President Walker's Theory of Distribution*, 4 Q.J. ECON. 34 (1889), Sumner, *supra* note 266, Taussig, *The Employer's Place in Distribution*, 10 Q.J. ECON. 67 (1895), *Rates of Wages*, *supra* note 286, and *Services Capital Renders*, *supra* note 286.  The attacker category includes Aldrich, *Some Objections to Profit-Sharing*, 1 Q.J. ECON. 232 (1887), Bonar, *The Value of Labor in Relation to Economic Theory*, 5 Q.J. ECON. 137, 161 (1891), Book Review, *supra* note 289, Clark, *Distribution as Determined by a Law of Rent*, 5 Q.J. ECON. 289 (1891), Giddings, *The Theory of Profit-sharing*, 1 Q.J. ECON. 367, 369-72 (1887), *Business Profits*, *supra* note 274; *Wages and Profits*, *supra* note 274, Walker, *The Doctrine of Rent, and the Residual Claimant Theory of Wages*, 5 Q.J. ECON. 417 (1891), Walker, *A Reply to Mr. MacVane: On the Source of Business Profits*, 2 Q.J. ECON. 263 (1888), Webb, *The Rate of Interest and the Laws of Distribution*, 2 Q.J. ECON. 188 (1888), Wood, *A*

---

other Progressives such as Stuart Wood scoffed at the idea that there was a fixed ratio between capital and wages.[294] When his politics changed, Mill rejected it along with most of the laissez-faire principles of classical economics, as did Francis Walker in America forty years later. America's most prominent neoclassicist of the time, J.B. Clark, eventually rejected the wage-fund theory in favor of a marginal productivity standard.[295] But unlike the Progressives, he continued to oppose labor unions and government employment regulation.[296] No method existed in the nineteenth century to test the wage-fund doctrine empirically.[297] Thus, it was accepted or rejected principally for ideological reasons. Those who accepted it, however, regarded it as "proof" of the disastrous consequences that would attend minimum wage laws, maximum hours laws, or effective union organization.[298]

One fact not widely appreciated is that even liberal American political economists were not generally supportive of wage and hour legislation until after the turn of the century. For example, even in 1898, Henry George believed that the natural law of wages was so absolute that any attempt to regulate them would be disastrous.[299] In *Progress and Poverty*,[300] George's most popular and radical work, he devoted two chapters[301] to disproving the wage-fund doctrine. In its place, however, he substituted his own iron law that the fund for the payment of wages is determined by the "margin of cultivation,"[302] or the difference between the cost of cultivation and the market price of the poorest land currently in production. As a result, wages would tend to be high in new countries where plenty of fertile land is still available.

One man will not work for another for less than his labor will really yield, when he can go upon the next quarter section and take up a farm

---

*Critique of Wages Theories*, 1 ANNALS 426 (1891), and Wood, *A New View of the Theory of Wages*, 3 Q.J. ECON. 462 (1889) [hereinafter *New View*]. For perhaps the coup de grace, see Edgeworth, *The Theory of Distribution*, 18 Q.J. ECON. 159 (1904), and Thompson, *Present Work and Present Wages*, 24 Q.J. ECON. 515 (1910).

294. 1 R. ELY, *supra* note 37, at 2-4; *New View*, *supra* note 293.

295. Clark, *The Possibility of a Scientific Law of Wages*, 4 PUBLICATIONS AM. ECON. A. 39, 49 (1889) ("General wages tend to equal the actual product created by the last labor that is added to the social working force." (emphasis omitted)). For the development of Clark's thinking, see J. CLARK, THE DISTRIBUTION OF WEALTH: A THEORY OF WAGES, INTEREST AND PROFITS (1899), J. CLARK, THE PHILOSOPHY OF WEALTH: ECONOMIC PRINCIPLES NEWLY FORMULATED (1894), Clark, *The Law of Wages and Interest*, 1 ANNALS 43 (1890), and Clark, *Recent Theories of Wages*, 42 NEW ENGLANDER 354 (1883) (appearing to endorse the wage-fund doctrine). *See also* Henry, *John Bates Clark and the Marginal Product: An Historical Inquiry into the Origins of Value-Free Economic Theory*, 15 HIST. POL. ECON. 375 (1983).

296. On Clark's laissez-faire marginalism, see note 312 *infra* and accompanying text.

297. The relevant question—whether wages were paid out of money that would otherwise go to capital or come out of anticipated profits—was arguably an empirical one.

298. *See* R. HOFSTADTER, *supra* note 139, at 145 (noting that the wage-fund doctrine "was not a little favored by the fact that it afforded a complete justification for the existing order of things respecting wages" (quoting THE WAGES QUESTION, *supra* note 289, at 142)).

299. H. GEORGE, THE SCIENCE OF POLITICAL ECONOMY 445 (1898).

300. H. GEORGE, *supra* note 234.

301. *Id.* at 50-79.

302. *Id.* at 206-07, 212-13.

for himself. It is only as land becomes monopolized and these natural opportunities are shut off from labor, that laborers are obliged to compete with each other . . . .[303]

The simplicity of George's argument explains its great success and influence in the late nineteenth century. As long as land was readily available and cheap, wages would have to be at least as high as the return from farming, for any laborer asked to work for less would farm instead.[304] However, under George's version of the wage-fund theory, the total amount of money available for wages could never exceed the amount established by the margin of cultivation: If the gross amount of wages rose, demand for and price of food would rise in proportion and the relative position of the laborer would be no better. Neither would trade unions and minimum wage statutes of less than universal application raise the total level of wages. They would simply transfer wages to the group of workers protected by the union or the statute and away from those not protected.[305]

Progressive economists did not clearly win this battle until after the turn of the century, when nearly every economist of any repute rejected the wage-fund doctrine in favor of some kind of marginal productivity or marginal value theory of wages. But some judges carried the vestiges of the wage-fund debate much later. For example, Justice Sutherland exhumed the theory in *Adkins*, when he observed that a statute that raises wages without raising the amount or the productive efficiency of invested capital addresses only half the problem of labor: "[I]n practice the former half without the latter must lead to ultimate failure, in accordance with the inexorable law that no one can continue indefinitely to take out more than he puts in without ultimately exhausting the supply."[306] This was as orthodox a statement of the wage-fund doctrine as could be found in any nineteenth century manual of political economy.

### 2. *Marginalism and the emergence of welfare economics.*

The marginalist revolution brought about the end of the classical tradition in British political economy, and appeared to undermine most of the classical arguments for laissez faire as a theory of social welfare. Marginalism, with its much more interventionist view of the state, dominated the thought of the leading political economists in Britain after John Stuart Mill: William Jevons in the 1870s, Alfred Marshall in the 1890s and after, and Arthur Pigou in the 1920s and 1930s. Each was more interventionist than his predecessor.[307] In 1920, Pigou, Cam-

---

303. *Id.* at 215.
304. Like other classical and neoclassical economists, George had little appreciation for barriers to entry, which might prevent a laborer from making this move. He assumed that all investment, including labor, flowed smoothly to the highest rate of return.
305. *Id.* at 310-11. For a similar critique, see F. TAUSSIG, *supra* note 284, at 98-99.
306. Adkins v. Children's Hosp., 261 U.S. 525, 557 (1923).
307. *See* T. HUTCHISON, *supra* note 163, at 94-120, 175-99.

bridge Professor of Political Economy, argued that the principal distinction between the wealthy and the working class was that less money had been invested in the productive capacity of the latter.[308] According to the law of diminishing returns, additional investment in development of the poor would produce more social benefits than would equivalent investment in development of the rich.[309] Pigou's thesis carried an important corollary: A dollar *transferred* from the wealthy to the poor would do more good to the poor transferee than it would do harm to the wealthy transferor.[310] The result was an efficiency argument for graduated income taxes, minimum wage laws, regulation of working conditions and hours, product quality, welfare benefits, and the like.

But the marginalist revolution consisted of two quite distinct parts. One part was the public, or "macro," theory that had the implications for welfare described above. The other was a private, or "micro," theory of individual and firm behavior that employed extraordinarily powerful analytic concepts such as marginal cost and marginal revenue. Marginalism as a theory of firm behavior first appeared in American scholarship shortly before the rise of substantive due process, principally in the work of John Bates Clark. Progressive Era economists such as Ely later adopted the welfare theory of marginalism as a *critique* of the doctrine of substantive due process.[311]

Clark, whose contributions to the theory of marginal utility earned worldwide recognition, was just as laissez-faire on matters of state policy as were his classical American predecessors. He believed that the concept of marginal cost could teach business firms how to maximize their profits, and that, in a competitive market, such profit-maximizing behavior tended to maximize social wealth as well, because each person received an amount precisely equal to his marginal value to someone else.[312] Any state-enforced "adjustment," other than one calculated to eliminate monopoly, would interfere with this goal.[313]

The dominant political economy in America on the eve of substantive due process belonged to Clark and the American neoclassicists, not to the much more interventionist British neoclassicists such as Jevons or Marshall, and certainly not to the Progressives, most of whom had

---

308. A. PIGOU, THE ECONOMICS OF WELFARE (4th ed. 1932).

309. Pigou excluded from his argument the "morally, mentally, or physically degenerate" poor, in whom, he opined, public investment was probably pointless. *Id.* at 745. However, he regarded these types as making up only a small percentage of the poor. *Id.* at 746.

310. *Id.* at 746-47.

311. Only shortly thereafter, the British ordinalists, beginning with Lionel Robbins, came to regard the welfare economics component of marginal utility theory as outside economic science because it rested on unverifiable assumptions about interpersonal comparisons of utility. *See* L. ROBBINS, AN ESSAY ON THE NATURE AND SIGNIFICANCE OF ECONOMIC SCIENCE 120-41 (3d ed. 1984) (1st ed. 1932). The result was increased skepticism about forced redistribution.

312. *See* Henry, *supra* note 295; *see also* Jalladeau, *The Methodological Conversion of John Bates Clark*, 7 HIST. POL. ECON. 209 (1975).

313. *See* Henry, *supra* note 295, at 385.

not yet begun to write. Although few of the judges who decided liberty of contract cases were trained as economists, they imbibed the dominant economic thinking of the nineteenth century American tradition, as an occasional reference in their opinions suggests. The judges who developed the doctrine made the unfortunate mistake of attaching themselves to the dominant economic view just as that view was on the verge of falling apart, to be replaced by a more complex, and much more regulatory, economic view of the world.

## VI.  "Affected with the Public Interest": Externalities and the Presumption of Constitutionality

The substantive due process courts upheld more regulatory statutes than they struck down.[314] Both the Supreme Court and state courts exercised a presumption of constitutionality that was usually not defeated. To be sure, the most frequent criticism of the substantive due process Supreme Court charged it with a lack of deference to legislation, a willingness to substitute its own judgment for that of legislators.[315] But the decisions of the *Lochner* era clearly express a form of deference, although perhaps not the kind of deference we would prefer today.

In *Lochner*, Justice Peckham wrote: "This is not a question of substituting the judgment of the court for that of the legislature. If the act be within the power of the State it is valid, although the judgment of the court might be totally opposed to the enactment of such a law."[316] Immediately thereafter, of course, Justice Peckham did substitute the judgment of the Supreme Court for that of the legislature, and found the statute invalid.

But the substantive due process Court was not inconsistent. It analyzed economic legislation with a 2-tier structure not unlike the structure which the Supreme Court uses today in equal protection decisions.[317] In general, it presumed constitutionality. That presumption could be defeated if the legislation at issue appeared to interfere with a right guaranteed by the fourteenth amendment—which encompassed the rights of each seller of property or labor to set his own price, and of each property owner or laborer to receive fair market value in exchange. If a statute was deemed to interfere substantially with one of these marketplace rights, then it would be upheld only if the regulation

---

314. *See* L. Tribe, American Constitutional Law 435 n.2 (1978); Currie, *The Constitution in the Supreme Court:The Protection of Economic Interests, 1889-1910,* 52 U. Chi. L. Rev. 324, 381 & n.341 (1985).
315. *See, e.g.,* P. Murphy, *supra* note 209, at 68-72; L. Tribe, *supra* note 314, at 438-42. Contemporary scholars made the same criticism. *See, e.g.,* Cushman, *The Social and Economic Interpretation of the Fourteenth Amendment,* 20 Mich. L. Rev. 737, 749 (1922); Dodd, *The Growth of Judicial Power,* 24 Pol. Sci. Q. 193, 194 (1909).
316. Lochner v. New York, 198 U.S. 45, 56-57 (1905).
317. *See, e.g.,* L. Tribe, *supra* note 314, at 991-1136.

were justified by a strong public interest. In the words of the Supreme Court, economic regulations would be upheld only if they applied to property "affected with the public interest."[318]

Although identifying property "affected with the public interest" was a judicial rather than legislative prerogative,[319] the judges of the substantive due process era did not have a very clear idea of how to exercise this power. Justice Frankfurter later opined that affectation with the public interest was an "empty formula,"[320] and Holmes once confessed that he regarded it as "little more than a fiction."[321] Even Justice Thomas M. Cooley, who was as instrumental as anyone in developing the law of substantive due process, admitted that the identification of property "affected with a public interest" was a matter of some difficulty.[322] Cooley urged reliance on the teachings of classical political economy. His short list of property so affected included: 1) facilities controlled by the government; 2) monopolies; 3) businesses traditionally permitted only by franchise from the state; 4) businesses that receive special assistance from the state; 5) businesses subject to exclusive privileges granted by the state; and 6) businesses whose regulation is clearly compelled by public safety.[323] In all other types of business, most forms of economic regulation should be deemed improper.

The Supreme Court eventually adopted a position similar to Cooley's, permitting state intervention only where the classical economists themselves would have permitted it.[324] The narrow limits of economic

---

318. Munn v. Illinois, 94 U.S. 113, 127 (1876) (quoting M. HALE, *De Portibus Maris*, in A TREATISE IN THREE PARTS (c. 1670), *reprinted in* 1 A COLLECTION OF TRACTS RELATIVE TO THE LAW OF ENGLAND 45 (F. Hargrave ed. 1787)).

319. *See, e.g.*, Tyson & Brother-United Theatre Ticket Offices v. Banton, 273 U.S. 418, 431 (1927) ("[T]he mere declaration by the legislature that a particular kind of property or business is affected with a public interest is not conclusive . . . . The matter is one which is always open to judicial inquiry." (citing Charles Wolff Packing Co. v. Court of Indus. Relations, 262 U.S. 522, 536 (1923))).

320. F. FRANKFURTER, THE COMMERCE CLAUSE UNDER MARSHALL, TANEY AND WAITE 87 (1937).

321. *Banton*, 273 U.S. at 446 (Holmes, J., dissenting). For other definitional problems, see Scheiber, *supra* note 16.

322.
What circumstances shall affect property with a public interest is not very clear. The mere fact that the public have an interest in the existence of the business, and are accommodated by it, cannot be sufficient, for that would subject the stock of the merchant, and his charges, to public regulation. The public have an interest in every business in which an individual offers his wares, his merchandise, his services, or his accommodations to the public; but his offer does not place him at the mercy of the public in respect to charges and prices.
T. COOLEY, *supra* note 92, at 736.

323. *Id.* at 737-39. Cooley elaborated on his definition in Cooley, *supra* note 56. However, he later expressed some reservations about chartered or franchised firms, particularly if the charter expressly prohibited price regulation. *See* Cooley, *State Regulation of Corporate Profits*, 137 N. AM. REV. 205, 207 (1883).

324. Economic regulation was legitimate only if the regulated firm operated under a charter or franchise issued by the state, was traditionally in a market subject to economic regulation, or had experienced a change in character that compelled public regulation. *See*

regulation under substantive due process analysis are best explained by the narrowness of the concept of externalities in traditional political economy.

By the time of John Stuart Mill, classical political economy had already developed a fairly sophisticated doctrine of "externalities,"[325] which referred to circumstances in which private bargaining could not be trusted to secure the best interests of society because the bargaining agreements affected people who were not a party to the negotiations. For the British classicists, the scope of the doctrine was narrow.[326] Mill, for example, included lighthouses, scientific exploration, and scholarship among the markets in which free competition would not yield the optimal amount or price of service, but nothing resembling the modern theory of private, regulated industry emerged in his thinking.[327]

The doctrine of externalities was most fully developed in British political economy by Pigou at Cambridge University. In 1912, Pigou published *Wealth and Welfare*,[328] which he subsequently enlarged and reissued in 1920 as *The Economics of Welfare*.[329] Pigou observed that certain transactions create a "divergence between social and private net product"[330]—something that later generations of economists would call the problem of "social cost."[331] This divergence occurs when "A, in the course of rendering some service, for which payment is made, to a second person B, incidentally also renders services or disservices to

---

Charles Wolff Packing Co. v. Court of Indus. Relations, 262 U.S. 522, 535 (1923); Tyson & Brother-United Theatre Ticket Offices v. Banton, 273 U.S. 418, 431-32 (1927); *see also* Hamilton, *Affectation with Public Interest*, 39 YALE L.J. 1089 (1930); McAllister, *Lord Hale and Business Affected with a Public Interest*, 43 HARV. L. REV. 759 (1930). Some cases suggest that monopolization of a market would justify legislative intervention. *See, e.g.,* Williams v. Standard Oil Co., 278 U.S. 235, 240 (1929). But the Court was divided on the question of whether de facto monopoly status was sufficient to warrant price regulation. *See* Budd v. New York, 143 U.S. 517 (1892) (6-3 decision); *see also* Hovenkamp, *supra* note 45, at 1309-10.

Cooley's position on unchartered firms that had managed to acquire a monopoly was clear: In the case of " 'virtual' monopolies effected by superior industry, enterprise, skill, and thrift," as opposed to monopolies created by franchise, the state had a duty not to interfere. Cooley, *supra* note 56, at 268. The Supreme Court disagreed with Cooley in Munn v. Illinois, 94 U.S. 113 (1876). *See* Hovenkamp, *supra* note 58.

Some dissenters, such as Justices Stone and Holmes, argued that unequal bargaining power and the resulting unreasonableness in contract terms should also be deemed market failures justifying regulation. *See* Ribnik v. McBride, 277 U.S. 350, 361-62 (1928) (Stone, J., dissenting); *Banton*, 273 U.S. at 448-50 (Stone, J., dissenting); Coppage v. Kansas, 236 U.S. 1, 26-27 (1915) (Holmes, J., dissenting).

325. *See* E. PAUL, *supra* note 129, at 195-96.

326. The one exception among the classicists was Edwin Chadwick, a utilitarian who did most of his writing in the 1830s and 1840s. *See* P. ATIYAH, *supra* note 28, at 332-34.

327. However, Mill did expound a rudimentary theory of natural monopoly based on his observations about gas lighting in London. *See* J.S. MILL, PRINCIPLES OF POLITICAL ECONOMY: WITH SOME OF THEIR APPLICATIONS TO SOCIAL PHILOSOPHY 143 (1848 & photo. reprint 1965).

328. A. PIGOU, WEALTH AND WELFARE (1912).

329. A. PIGOU, THE ECONOMICS OF WELFARE (1920).

330. A. PIGOU, *supra* note 308, at 183.

331. *See, e.g.,* Coase, *The Problem of Social Cost*, 3 J.L. & ECON. 1 (1960); Knight, *Some Fallacies in the Interpretation of Social Cost*, 38 Q.J. ECON. 582 (1924).

other persons . . . of such a sort that payment cannot be exacted from the benefitted parties or compensation enforced on behalf of the injured parties."[332]

The resultant problems cannot be solved "by a modification of the contractual relation between any two contracting parties, because the [problem] arises out of a . . . disservice rendered to persons other than the contracting parties."[333] The obvious solution, Pigou explained, is for the state to intervene through regulatory legislation to protect third-party interests.[334]

Both Cooley and the Supreme Court read into substantive due process doctrine a theory of externalities much like Pigou's. The Court approved regulatory legislation if it was convinced that the regulated exchanges exhibited substantial negative externalities for which the bargaining parties would not account.[335] In order to justify state regulation, its proponents had to show a substantial divergence between "the public interest and private right"—equivalent to Pigou's "divergence between social and private net product." This decisional rule has been overlooked repeatedly by constitutional historians,[336] but it explains the cases in which the *Lochner* era Supreme Court upheld regulatory legislation, including *Muller v. Oregon*[337] and the land-use planning cases.[338] It also explains why the Court generally refused to tolerate inequality of bargaining power as a qualifying public interest. Inequality of bargaining power between capitalists and laborers affected the distribution of wealth between the bargaining parties, but the Court saw no effect on anyone else. Thus, Justice Peckham held that the bakers' hours statute in *Lochner* must fall unless the plaintiffs could show a relationship between the number of hours a baker must work and the "healthful quality" of the bread he produces. The mere fact that long hours of work were bad for the bakers, who were adults capable of protecting themselves, was insufficient to justify the regulation.[339]

---

332. A. PIGOU, *supra* note 308, at 183.
333. *Id.* at 192.
334. *Id.* at 192-96.
335. Justice Stone explained the theory in his dissent in *Banton*:
The constitutional theory that prices normally may not be regulated rests upon the assumption that the public interest and private right are both adequately protected when there is "free" competition among buyers and sellers, and that in such a state of economic society, the interference with so important an incident of the ownership of private property as price fixing is not justified and hence is a taking of property without due process of law.
Tyson & Brother-United Theatre Ticket Offices v. Banton, 273 U.S. 418, 451 (1927) (Stone, J., dissenting).
336. For a recent example of such oversight, see Currie, *supra* note 314, at 378-82.
337. 208 U.S. 412 (1908). *See* notes 340-347 *infra* and accompanying text.
338. *See* notes 348-355 *infra* and accompanying text.
339.
The law must be upheld, if at all, as a law pertaining to the health of the individual engaged in the occupation of a baker. It does not affect any other portion of the

*Muller v. Oregon*, on the other hand, is quite consistent with the Court's public interest affectation theory. Louis Brandeis saved the women's ten-hour statute at issue in *Muller* from almost certain invalidation, given the decision three years earlier in *Lochner*, by submitting his famous "Brandeis Brief" of social science sources to the Supreme Court.[340] Brandeis' great achievement in *Muller* was convincing the Supreme Court that the labor of women was subject to externalities that did not apply to the labor of men.

The Brandeis Brief is an odd assortment of information: domestic and foreign statutes, tracts, writings of clergymen, and reports of regulatory agencies. Much of the information it contained was not "social science" at all, at least not as we understand that term today. Many of the reports Brandeis quoted were purely anecdotal[341] or polemic, and Brandeis was quite careful not to use any term such as "social science" in describing his brief to the Court. Rather, the brief contained a record of "the world's experience upon which the legislation limiting the hours of labor for women is based."[342] The "world's experience" turned out to be that women had less endurance than men, that their reproductive systems were more easily damaged, and that they had less capacity than men to enter into sound business agreements that adequately protected their own interests.[343]

Most importantly, however, Brandeis suggested that women bar-

---

public than those who are engaged in that occupation. Clean and wholesome bread does not depend upon whether the baker works but ten hours per day or only sixty hours a week. . . .

 . . . .

 . . . In our judgment it is not possible in fact to discover the connection between the number of hours a baker may work in the bakery and the healthful quality of the bread made by the workman.
Lochner v. New York, 198 U.S. 45, 57, 62 (1905).
 The notable exception to the Court's stance in unequal bargaining position cases is Holden v. Hardy, 169 U.S. 366 (1898), one of the Supreme Court's earliest substantive due process decisions. In *Holden*, the Court upheld an 8-hour workday law applied to employees in mines, smelters, and refineries, relying in part on inequality of bargaining position as a justification for the regulation. *Id.* at 397. However, in later decisions, the Court read *Holden* as if it had found some third-party interest. In Coppage v. Kansas, 236 U.S. 1 (1915), for example, the Court cited *Holden* for the proposition that regulation of contracts is permissible when necessary "for preserving the public health, safety, morals, or general welfare," but then concluded that such regulation is not permissible if merely designed to level "inequalities of fortune" as between the bargaining parties. *Id.* at 18.

 340. Brief for Defendant in Error, Muller v. Oregon, 208 U.S. 412 (1908) (No. 107) [hereinafter Brandeis Brief], *reprinted in* 16 Landmark Briefs and Arguments of the Supreme Court of the United States: Constitutional Law 63 (P. Kurland & G. Casper eds. 1975).

 341. Much of the brief consisted of statements by workers that they liked factory legislation. Said one worker: "I decidedly prefer to work the hours fixed by the Factory Acts. . . . I have never had any illness since the Factory Act came into operation." *Id.* at 100. Said another: "I have been six years employed in the sewing department. I am very well satisfied with the Factory Acts as they are, and I think all the sewers are of opinion that it is a good law . . . ." *Id.* at 101.

 342. *Id.* at 18.

 343. On sexism in the Brandeis Brief, see Becker, *From* Muller v. Oregon *to Fetal Vulnerability Policies*, 53 U. Chi. L. Rev. 1219, 1221-25 (1986).

gaining with their employers would not protect every interest that society believed needed protection. " 'It is well known that like begets like,' and if the parents are feeble in constitution, the children must also inevitably be feeble."[344] Furthermore, young working women could not be trusted to protect society's interests in the reproduction of healthy offspring.[345]

The sentiments were outrageously Spencerian. Brandeis relied on the fact that a woman's reproductive capacity had always given her a special position at common law, justifying substantial regulation of the health of the unborn. This argument probably saved the women's maximum hours statute. It certainly received all the attention of the Supreme Court. A woman, as distinct from a man, "becomes an object of public interest and care in order to preserve the strength and vigor of the race."[346] As a result, a woman may be "properly placed in a class by herself, and legislation designed for her protection may be sustained, even when like legislation is not necessary for men and could not be sustained."[347]

The doctrine of externalities likewise explains the Supreme Court's seemingly odd defections from liberty of contract in the land-use cases, where it consistently upheld intensive regulation that interfered with the free market for land. For example, four years after he wrote the opinion of the Court in *Lochner*, Justice Peckham authored the majority opinion in *Welch v. Swasey*,[348] which upheld a statute limiting the heights of buildings in Boston. And three years after he wrote the majority opinion in *Adkins*, Justice Sutherland wrote the majority opinion in *Village of Euclid v. Amber Realty Company*,[349] which upheld comprehensive land-use planning—a far more interventionist form of regulation than anything contemplated previously.[350]

---

344. Brandeis Brief, *supra* note 340, at 51 (quoting REPORT OF THE MASSACHUSETTS BUREAU OF LABOR STATISTICS 504 (1871)).

345. "The object of [women's hours legislation] is the protection of the physical well-being of the community by setting a limit to the exploitation of the improvident, unworkman-like, unorganized women who are yet the mothers, actual or prospective, of the coming generation." *Id.* at 50 (quoting Breckinridge, *Legislative Control of Women's Work*, 14 J. POL. ECON. 107, 108-09 (1906)).

346. *Muller*, 208 U.S. at 421.

347. *Id.* at 422.

348. 214 U.S. 91 (1909).

349. 272 U.S. 365 (1926).

350. The presumption of constitutionality may have been stronger in the land-use cases because the Supreme Court was less inclined to suspect the legislatures' motives. For example, in *Lochner*, Justice Peckham suggested that maximum hours statutes were often "in reality passed from other motives" than the ones announced by the legislatures. 198 U.S. at 64. In *Welch*, however, Justice Peckham was willing to presume the existence of externalities sufficient to justify the statute. "These are matters which it must be presumed were known by the legislature, and whether or not such were the facts was a question, among others, for the legislature to determine." 214 U.S. at 108. Likewise, in *Euclid*, Justice Sutherland quoted with approval a state court opinion:

If the municipal council deemed any of the reasons which have been suggested, or any other substantial reason, a sufficient reason for adopting the ordinance in ques-

The Supreme Court's land-use opinions are filled with citations of possible externalities justifying state intrusion. In *Welch*, Justice Peckham cited evidence that the danger of fire was greater with respect to tall buildings than shorter ones, but that the commercial area, where taller buildings were permitted, was both closer to a supply of water and less likely to be filled with women and children who would be endangered.[351] In *Euclid*, as well, Justice Sutherland cited a large number of externalities.[352] All of these examples share one attribute: They are based on the recognition that, because individual parcels are so dependent on the whole, a municipality is composed just as much of "commons" as of individually owned property. A single builder would not consider the costs imposed by the increased risk of fire or the increased traffic caused by his own structure because he would have to bear only a tiny fraction of those costs. As a result, one could expect more than the optimal amount of construction. Indeed, high density in relation to the risk of fire was an important justification for municipal zoning.[353] The political economy antecedents to the Court's land-use cases are explicit in the work of Pigou, who had recognized land use as presenting a problem of externalities prior to the Court's decision in *Euclid*. Externalities arise, for example, "when the owner of a site in a residential quarter of a city builds a factory there and so destroys a great part of the amenities of the neighboring sites."[354] Pigou concluded that the municipal power to control the quantity and type of construction within city limits was virtually "an axiom of government."[355]

Finally, the economic doctrine of externalities explains the Supreme Court's sudden reversal of the long-established doctrine that the takings clause of the fifth amendment applies only to the federal govern-

---

tion, it is not the province of the courts to take issue with the council. We have nothing to do with the question of the wisdom or good policy of municipal ordinances. If they are not satisfying to a majority of the citizens, their recourse is to the ballot—not the courts.
*Euclid,* 272 U.S. at 393 (quoting State *ex rel.* Civello v. New Orleans, 154 La. 271, 283, 97 So. 440, 444 (1923)).

351. 214 U.S. at 107-08.

352. The list included:
promotion of the health and security from injury of children and others by separating dwelling houses from territory devoted to trade and industry; suppression and prevention of disorder; facilitating the extinguishment of fires, and the enforcement of street traffic regulations and other general welfare ordinances; aiding the health and safety of the community by excluding from residential areas the confusion and danger of fire, contagion and disorder which in greater or less degree attach to the location of stores, shops and factories. Another ground is that the construction and repair of streets may be rendered easier and less expensive by confining the greater part of the heavy traffic to the streets where business is carried on.
*Euclid,* 272 U.S. at 391. Justice Sutherland cited other externalities later in his opinion. *See id.* at 394.

353. *See* Behrens, *The Triangle Shirtwaist Company Fire of 1911: A Lesson in Legislative Manipulation,* 62 Tex. L. Rev. 361 (1983).

354. A. Pigou, *supra* note 308, at 183.

355. *Id.* at 192.

ment and not to the states. The Court had reiterated that view in 1896.[356] But in the *Chicago Railroad* case,[357] decided in the next term, Justice Harlan wrote for the majority that "a judgment of a state court . . . whereby private property is taken . . . for public use, without compensation . . . to the owner, is, upon principle and authority, wanting in the due process of law required by the Fourteenth Amendment."[358] Classical economists were, in general, adverse to the concept of government-owned property; the strictest classicists would have limited it to streets, highways, and a small number of other public facilities. But the neoclassicists conceded that the state had a much larger role as property owner, for they recognized many more circumstances in which private markets would not allocate resources efficiently. Just as with substantive due process jurisprudence, the federalization of eminent domain law was the Supreme Court's way of writing its own theory of political economy into the Constitution.

## VII. Conclusion

There is no dichotomy between science and politics. Science *is* a form of politics. One purpose of scientific model-building is to explain observed phenomena and make predictions. But an equally important purpose is to produce consensus. A scientific model achieves success when it convinces those who practice a particular discipline. It may convince by a variety of mechanisms, including many that are political or even rhetorical.[359] Even positivism, the most "scientific" of methods in law, economics, and other sciences, had fundamentally political roots.[360]

The science of political economy in nineteenth century Britain and America was no exception, and neither was the law. The courts of the substantive due process era were guided by prevailing scientific doctrines much as courts are today. They took the law for what it was, a human creation and an intellectual activity, never able to transcend the world view in which it was formed. For example, judges living in an intellectual milieu dominated by genetic determinism in the social sciences are likely to fear racial integration, while those living in an age of environmentalism are not.[361] Likewise, judges trained in the classical tradition of political economy carry that intellectual baggage into their

---

356. *See* Fallbrook Irrigation Dist. v. Bradley, 164 U.S. 112, 158 (1896); *see also* Thorington v. Montgomery, 147 U.S. 490, 492 (1893); Davidson v. New Orleans, 96 U.S. 97 (1877).
357. Chicago, B. & Q.R.R. v. Chicago, 166 U.S. 226 (1897).
358. *Id.* at 241.
359. *See generally* D. McCloskey, The Rhetoric of Economics (1985).
360. *See id.* at 39. Positivism originated in prewar Germany in response to perceived "pseudo-sciences" that were making claims for government support. The mainstream scientific community needed a criterion of acceptability that would transcend the sciences and would distinguish sciences that deserved support from those that did not. The criterion chosen was verifiability—or, as it later developed, falsifiability. *Id.*
361. *See* Hovenkamp, *supra* note 81.

chambers. In the case of substantive due process, they carried American writers' unique perspective on political economy, which for them defined both the content of the property rights protected by the Constitution and the limits of the state's power to regulate those rights. When the dominant American economic ideology changed—not until the first three decades of the twentieth century—the legal ideology followed close behind.

# THE JURISPRUDENCE OF CHRISTOPHER G. TIEDEMAN: A STUDY IN THE FAILURE OF LAISSEZ-FAIRE CONSTITUTIONALISM

*David N. Mayer*[*]

---

[*] Visiting Assistant Professor of Law, IIT Chicago-Kent College of Law; Associate Professor of Law, Capital University (after June 1990). A.B. 1977, J.D. 1980, University of Michigan; M.A. 1982, Ph.D. 1988 (History), University of Virginia.

This Article is based on a paper originally written for a seminar at the University of Virginia and revised for presentation at a colloquium at the Institute for Humane Studies, George Mason University. For their comments, criticisms, and encouragement, I am grateful to Charles W. McCurdy and Calvin Woodard, of the University of Virginia, and to Jeremy Shearmur, Leonard Liggio, and Walter Grinder, of the Institute for Humane Studies. Financial support was provided by the Institute for Humane Studies (the 1987-88 R.C. Hoiles Post-doctoral Fellowship) and by IIT Chicago-Kent College of Law; Craig David Queen, a student at Chicago-Kent, provided research assistance. The views expressed in this Article, of course, are solely those of the author.

## INTRODUCTION

One of the most misunderstood periods in American legal and constitutional history is the so-called "era of laissez-faire constitutionalism" in the late nineteenth century when courts, both state and federal, struck down a score of legislative acts perceived as intrusive upon "substantive" due process rights and, in so doing, incorporated laissez-faire principles into constitutional law.[1] Until recently, scholars have accepted almost as articles of faith the following two assumptions: first, that American judges during this era were motivated by the desire to protect the privileges of the wealthy and of corporations; and second, that the means by which they furthered these interests—for example, engrafting upon the Constitution such laissez-faire principles as "liberty of contract" through the concept of substantive due process of law—represented a perversion of the original meaning of the due

---

1. By "laissez-faire," I refer generally to the notion that government intrusion into individuals' lives should be minimal at best; in other words, that individuals should be "let-alone" as far as possible. Taken to its extreme, the doctrine of laissez-faire implies either anarchism or the reduction of the function of government solely to the protection of individuals from force. Nineteenth-century proponents of this pure laissez-faire doctrine included Herbert Spencer, the English "Social Darwinist" philosopher, and William Graham Sumner, his American counterpart. *See* H. SPENCER, SOCIAL STATICS 13, 121 (1890) (formulating the "law of equal freedom," the principle that "every man has freedom to do all that he wills, provided he infringes not on the equal freedom of any other man"); W. SUMNER, WHAT SOCIAL CLASSES OWE TO EACH OTHER 141 (1982 reprint of 1883 ed.) ("We each owe it to the other to guarantee rights."). Most American proponents of laissez-faire did not go so far as to advocate the wholesale reduction of government to these pure principles, however. Rather, they advocated such reforms as the abolition of the protective tariff; the cessation of government subsidization of industrial and transportation development; the repeal of legal tender laws; and the cessation of the regulation of business practices, employment conditions, and labor relations. *See generally* Benedict, *Laissez-Faire and Liberty: A Re-evaluation of the Meaning and Origins of Laissez-Faire Constitutionalism*, 3 LAW & HIST. REV. 293, 301-303 (1985).

process clauses.[2] Accordingly, legal scholars traditionally have cited the apogee of laissez-faire constitutionalism, *Lochner v. New York*,[3] as one of the worst examples of judicial abuse of power. As one historian recently observed, "Nothing can so damn a decision as to compare it to *Lochner* and its ilk."[4]

The recent work of several scholars, however, has questioned the assumptions underlying this traditional interpretation. In reassessing laissez-faire constitutionalism, these revisionist scholars have attempted to define more closely its ideological underpinnings, tracing connections to such potential sources as a hostility to "special" and "class" legislation deeply ingrained in Anglo-American law and political theory;[5] the dominance of classical economic theory in late nineteenth century

---

2. For examples of this traditional view of laissez-faire constitutionalism, see C. JACOBS, LAW WRITERS AND THE COURTS: THE INFLUENCE OF THOMAS E. COOLEY, CHRISTOPHER G. TIEDEMAN, AND JOHN F. DILLON UPON AMERICAN CONSTITUTIONAL LAW (1954); A. PAUL, CONSERVATIVE CRISIS AND THE RULE OF LAW: ATTITUDES OF BAR AND BENCH, 1887-1895 (1960); B. TWISS, LAWYERS AND THE CONSTITUTION: HOW LAISSEZ FAIRE CAME TO THE SUPREME COURT (1942). Perhaps the earliest exposition of this view is found in Pound, *Liberty of Contract*, 18 YALE L.J. 454 (1909).

3. 198 U.S. 45 (1905). In *Lochner*, the Court held unconstitutional a New York statute prohibiting bakery employees from working more than ten hours a day or sixty hours a week. The majority of the Court considered the statute violative of "the right of contract" between employer and employee, which was "part of the liberty of the individual" protected by the due process clause of the fourteenth amendment. *Id.* at 53. In his famous dissenting opinion, Justice Holmes argued that the majority had decided the case "upon an economic theory which a large part of the country does not entertain" and added that "[t]he Fourteenth Amendment does not enact Mr. Herbert Spencer's Social Statics." *Id.* at 75 (Holmes, J., dissenting).

4. Benedict, *supra* note 1, at 295. Benedict surveys the relevant literature and concludes that this traditional interpretation of laissez-faire constitutionalism and of the *Lochner* case has been pervasive. *See id.* at 294-95 nn.9 & 12 (finding examples of the traditional interpretation in various types of literature, ranging from the leading constitutional history textbooks and constitutional law casebooks to books and articles dealing with the contemporary controversy over judicial activism); *see also* Soifer, *The Paradox of Paternalism and Laissez-Faire Constitutionalism: United States Supreme Court, 1888-1921*, 5 LAW & HIST. REV. 249, 250 (1987) (*Lochner* "is still shorthand in constitutional law for the worst sins of subjective judicial activism.").

5. Benedict, *supra* note 1. Benedict has concluded that the "heart" of laissez-faire constitutionalism "was opposition to class and special legislation." *Id.* at 330. He further argues that laissez-faire constitutionalism received widespread support in late nineteenth-century America "because it was congruent with [this] well-established and accepted principle of American liberty." *Id.* at 298.

America;[6] and the persistence, even after the Civil War, of early nineteenth century "free labor" ideology.[7] Emerging from this nascent revisionism is a far more complex, and less cynical, understanding of laissez-faire constitutionalism—one which attempts more fully to take into account the world view of the nineteenth century.[8]

One reason for the renewed scholarly interest in laissez-faire constitutionalism is that the current debate over judicial protection of civil liberties—and, particularly, of the "right to privacy"[9]—has

---

6. Hovenkamp, *The Political Economy of Substantive Due Process*, 40 STAN. L. REV. 379 (1988). Noting that Justice Holmes was "right" in his dissent in *Lochner, id.* at 393, Hovenkamp argues that "[s]ubstantive due process was a system of law based on an economic theory." *Id.* at 401. Moreover, he argues, judges in the era quite naturally were influenced by the classical economic theories found in the uniquely "American" school of political economy that had become prevalent at American universities by the 1870s and 1880s. *Id.* at 399-400; *see also* Siegel, *Understanding the Lochner Era: Lessons from the Controversy over Railroad and Utility Rate Regulation*, 70 VA. L. REV. 187 (1984) (associating substantive due process with classical "Liberal" economic values and assumptions).

7. McCurdy, *The Roots of "Liberty of Contract" Reconsidered: Major Premises in the Law of Employment, 1867-1937*, 1984 SUP. CT. HIST. SOC'Y Y.B. 20, 26 (associating the "specialness" of the labor contract in American law with the "'free labor' ideology" that was prevalent in the Northern states prior to the Civil War).

8. For discussions of the shift in the "world view" of American intellectuals between the 1880s and 1930s, see S. FINE, LAISSEZ-FAIRE AND THE GENERAL WELFARE STATE (1956); Woodard, *Reality and Social Reform: The Transition from Laissez-Faire to the Welfare State*, 72 YALE L.J. 286 (1962). *See also* Benedict, *supra* note 1, at 296 (quoting Woodard, *supra*, at 288, that the shift from the laissez-faire standard to the welfare state standard was "one of the greatest intellectual and moral upheavals in western history"); Hovenkamp, *supra* note 6, at 437-39 (summarizing the "revolution" that brought about the end of the classical tradition in political economy).

9. Judicial protection of the right of privacy is relatively recent and may be traced to a line of Supreme Court decisions recognizing fundamental rights in such matters as marital and procreative decision-making. *See* Skinner v. Oklahoma, 316 U.S. 535 (1942) (invalidating Oklahoma statute that authorized the sterilization of certain convicted felons); Griswold v. Connecticut, 381 U.S. 479 (1965) (invalidating Connecticut statute that restricted the rights of married persons to use contraceptives); Loving v. Virginia, 388 U.S. 1 (1967) (invalidating Virginia statute that prohibited racially mixed marriages); Eisenstadt v. Baird, 405 U.S. 438 (1972) (extending the right of access to contraceptives to unmarried as well as married adults by invalidating Massachusetts statute that permitted only physicians and pharmacists to dispense them); Roe v. Wade, 410 U.S. 113 (1973) (invalidating Texas law that prohibited all abortions except those performed to save the mother's life). Of these cases, *Griswold* and *Roe v. Wade* are the most important in articulating a constitutionally-protected right

refocused attention on substantive due process protection of nontextual, or unenumerated, constitutional rights.[10] Indeed, a number of scholars have called for the resurrection of substantive due process protection of economic rights as well.[11] Given the close nexus between current controversies over judicial protection of unenumerated rights and scholarly treatment of turn-of-the-century substantive due process, it is surprising that thus far revisionist scholars have neglected one pivotal figure of laissez-faire constitutionalism: Christopher Gustavus Tiedeman (1857-1903).[12] This omission is especially surprising because Tiedeman was the laissez-faire theorist who was most explicit in articulating a rationale for the constitutional protection of unenumerated constitutional rights.[13]

---

to privacy founded either in "penumbras, formed by emanations" from specific guarantees in the Bill of Rights, as the Court said in *Griswold*, 381 U.S. at 484, or in the fourteenth amendment's concept of personal liberty, as the Court suggested in *Roe*, 410 U.S. at 153.

10. The right of privacy was a key concern of the Senate Judiciary Committee during its consideration of the nomination to the Supreme Court of Judge Robert H. Bork in 1987. *See* Power, *The Education of Robert Bork*, 10 U. BRIDGEPORT L. REV. 7, 19-21, 31-32 (1989). Among the questions raised during the Bork nomination hearings were questions about the ninth amendment, which provides that "[t]he enumeration in the Constitution, of certain rights, shall not be construed to deny or disparage others retained by the people." U.S. CONST. amend. IX. The ninth amendment and its potential use for the protection of unwritten constitutional rights have been the subjects of much recent scholarly interest. *See, e.g.*, Barnett, *Reconceiving the Ninth Amendment*, 74 CORNELL L. REV. 1 (1988); Caplan, *The History and Meaning of the Ninth Amendment*, 69 VA. L. REV. 223 (1983); Sherry, *The Founders' Unwritten Constitution*, 54 U. CHI. L. REV. 1127 (1987). For various views on the interpretation of the ninth amendment, see *Symposium on Interpreting the Ninth Amendment*, 64 CHI.-KENT L. REV. 37-268 (1988) (Barnett ed.).

11. *See, e.g.*, R. EPSTEIN, TAKINGS: PRIVATE PROPERTY AND THE POWER OF EMINENT DOMAIN (1985); ECONOMIC LIBERTIES AND THE JUDICIARY (J. Dorn & H. Manne eds. 1987); B. SIEGAN, ECONOMIC LIBERTIES AND THE CONSTITUTION (1980).

12. For a short biographical sketch of Tiedeman, see *infra* notes 29-30 and accompanying text.

13. For a brief but insightful discussion of the significance of Tiedeman's jurisprudence, see Grey, *Introduction*, in C. TIEDEMAN, THE UNWRITTEN CONSTITUTION OF THE UNITED STATES at iii-vii (1974). Grey characterizes Tiedeman's position as one that "by no means was the standard conservative theory of [his] time" and which "bears far more resemblance to the *avant-garde* views expressed by Holmes in *The Common Law* in 1880, and later developed into 'sociological jurisprudence' by Roscoe Pound, and into 'legal realism' by Karl Llewellyn and others " *Id.* at vi.

Tiedeman played a significant role in the unfolding of "laissez-faire constitutionalism" in the late nineteenth and early twentieth centuries. Because he never held a judicial position and had only a limited experience as a practicing lawyer, Tiedeman was not a direct participant in the drama that was occurring in the courtrooms of his time. His role was more indirect and, in a sense, more basic: as a law teacher and a treatise writer, he contributed the ideas which state and federal judges shaped into the evolving doctrines of substantive due process and liberty of contract. Commentators long have regarded Tiedeman's treatise on the limitations of the police power[14] as the preeminent work of laissez-faire constitutionalism;[15] and Tiedeman himself, in the preface to the second edition of his treatise in 1900, with a little modesty noted that the first edition of the book had been quoted by courts with approval in literally "hundreds of cases."[16]

In seeking to explain Tiedeman's influence, commentators have focused invariably upon the purity of his laissez-faire principles.[17] Although Tiedeman shared with business leaders of his age a general aversion to what he called "the radical experimentation of social reformers,"[18] he surely went further than most of his contemporaries

---

14. C. TIEDEMAN, TREATISE ON THE LIMITATIONS OF POLICE POWER IN THE UNITED STATES (1886) [hereinafter C. TIEDEMAN, LIMITATIONS OF POLICE POWER].

15. Clyde E. Jacobs, for example, has called Tiedeman's treatise on the limitations of the police power one of the two most influential treatises of its time, the other being Thomas M. Cooley's *Constitutional Limitations*, which far less clearly sustained and developed laissez-faire constitutional principles. C. JACOBS, *supra* note 2, at 58-59. Jacobs sees the publication of Tiedeman's treatise in 1886 as the climax of a six-stage story of the legal synthesis of liberty of contract: after Tiedeman, he suggests, courts had only but to apply the doctrine which Cooley had suggested, state and federal court decisions had developed, and Tiedeman had synthesized. Benjamin Twiss has been equally generous to Tiedeman, calling the publication of his treatise one of the "outstanding contributions" during the twenty-year period leading up to the "conclusive adoption" of laissez-faire constitutionalism by the United States Supreme Court in *Lochner*. B. TWISS, *supra* note 2, at 110, 122.

16. 1 C. TIEDEMAN, A TREATISE ON STATE AND FEDERAL CONTROL OF PERSONS AND PROPERTY IN THE UNITED STATES at ix (1900) [hereinafter 1 C. TIEDEMAN, STATE AND FEDERAL CONTROL].

17. For example, Clyde Jacobs has argued that much of the force and prestige of Tiedeman's book "undoubtedly derived from its logical consistency and rigor," for while other authorities might be lacking in or hostile to a given proposition of laissez-faire, "the bench and bar might confidently refer to the works of Tiedeman for support." C. JACOBS, *supra* note 2, at 62.

18. 1 C. TIEDEMAN, STATE AND FEDERAL CONTROL, *supra* note 16, at viii (preface to first edition).

in denouncing all forms of governmental intervention in the economic sphere. In this respect, Tiedeman outshone the other leading treatise-writer of the late nineteenth century, Thomas McIntyre Cooley, who was far less consistent in his adherence to laissez-faire.[19] Tiedeman condemned as unconstitutional not only laws regulating the hours and wages of workers,[20] for example, but also usury laws,[21] laws regulating morality through the prohibition of such vices as gambling or the use of narcotic drugs,[22] anti-miscegenation laws,[23] and even the protective tariff.[24]

In his thoroughgoing adherence to free market economics and his advocacy of judicial activism in restraining legislation inconsistent with free market principles, Tiedeman justly may be regarded as the purest

---

19. A former justice of the Michigan Supreme Court and, late in his career, the first chairman of the Interstate Commerce Commission, Cooley was author of the influential *Treatise on the Constitutional Limitations Which Rest upon the Legislative Powers of the States of the American Union*, first published in 1868. Comparing Cooley's treatise to Tiedeman's, one historian has noted that Tiedeman's narrow interpretation of the police power "revealed a much more extreme laissez-faire bias than Cooley's treatise." S. FINE, *supra* note 8, at 154. Alan Jones has shown that the conventional portrait of Cooley as a "laissez-faire constitutionalist" is distorted, and that Cooley is best understood as a Jacksonian Democrat opposed to privilege--hence, his concern over "class" legislation. Jones, *Thomas M. Cooley and "Laissez-Faire Constitutionalism": A Reappraisal*, 53 J. AM. HIST. 751 (1967). Similarly, other commentators have argued that Cooley at most only anticipated the rise of liberty of contract in his formulations of the doctrines of class legislation, implied limits on state legislative powers, and substantive due process. *See* C. JACOBS, *supra* note 2, at 62; Twiss, *supra* note 2, *passim*. The contrast between Tiedeman's and Cooley's positions, with respect to one category of legislation, laws prohibiting usury, is discussed *infra* notes 123-27 and accompanying text.

20. On laws regulating wages, see 1 C. TIEDEMAN, STATE AND FEDERAL CONTROL, *supra* note 16, §§ 99, 100, at 316-30. On laws regulating hours, see *id.* § 102, at 333-38; *infra* notes 152-67 and accompanying text.

21. On usury laws, see 1 C. TIEDEMAN, STATE AND FEDERAL CONTROL, *supra* note 16, § 106, at 351-53; *infra* notes 123-27 and accompanying text.

22. On laws prohibiting vices generally, see 1 C. TIEDEMAN, STATE AND FEDERAL CONTROL, *supra* note 16, § 60, at 179-87; *infra* notes 128-51 and accompanying text.

23. On anti-miscegenation laws, see 2 C. TIEDEMAN, A TREATISE ON STATE AND FEDERAL CONTROL OF PERSONAL PROPERTY IN THE UNITED STATES § 188, at 894-95 (1900) [hereinafter 2 C. TIEDEMAN, STATE AND FEDERAL CONTROL]. Tiedeman also condemned as unconstitutional laws against polygamy, at least insofar as these laws violated the religious freedom of Mormons. *See id.* § 189, at 897.

24. On the protective tariff, see 1 C. TIEDEMAN, STATE AND FEDERAL CONTROL, *supra* note 16, § 93, at 292-94.

exponent of laissez-faire constitutionalism. But to say that Tiedeman was a laissez-faire purist does not sufficiently explain his significance. Belief in the rightness of laissez-faire formed only the backdrop of Tiedeman's constitutional thought. At its heart was his understanding of law in general and of the special role played by the judiciary in the American constitutional system.

Ironically, it was the jurisprudential framework of Tiedeman's constitutionalism, and not its laissez-faire substance, that survived him. In the first decade of the twentieth century, Tiedeman's influence eclipsed as suddenly and as profoundly as it had risen. The narrow view of the police power that had been expounded by Tiedeman, Cooley, and other laissez-faire theorists was supplanted by a broader, more elastic conceptualization of the police power.[25] Laissez-faire constitutionalism also met its demise, as judicial decisions during the so-called Progressive era steadily eroded the concept of liberty of contract, signalling the death-knell of substantive due process protection of economic rights.[26] While these developments occurred in constitutional law, an even more significant shift occurred in American jurisprudence during the early years of the twentieth century, as the legal formalism

---

25. *See* E. FREUND, THE POLICE POWER: PUBLIC POLICY AND CONSTITUTIONAL RIGHTS (1903) (discussed *infra* notes 175-87 and accompanying text).

26. Arguably, the Supreme Court's retreat from liberty of contract was first signaled only a few years after *Lochner*, in Muller v. Oregon, 208 U.S. 412 (1908), when the Court upheld another maximum hours statute applied to female workers because of what it regarded as the "special circumstances" of women. Although the Court clung to liberty of contract for two decades after *Lochner*, *see, e.g.,* Adair v. United States, 208 U.S. 161 (1908); Adkins v. Children's Hospital, 261 U.S. 525 (1923), the demise of substantive due process protection of economic rights clearly came in the 1930s. In Nebbia v. New York, 291 U.S. 502 (1934), the Court upheld, against a due process challenge, the conviction of a store owner who had sold two bottles of milk at a price below that set by a New York milk control board. The rational relationship test fully emerged in West Coast Hotel v. Parrish, 300 U.S. 379 (1937), which overruled *Adkins*. In that case, Chief Justice Hughes, for the majority, said that "[t]he Constitution does not speak of freedom of contract. . . . Liberty under the Constitution is . . . subject to the restraints of due process, and . . . regulation which is reasonable in relation to its subject . . . ." *Id.* at 391. Finally, in the famous fourth footnote in United States v. Carolene Prods. Co., 304 U.S. 144, 152 n.4 (1938), the Court implicitly drew a line between economic liberties and other rights specifically guaranteed by the Constitution, holding that the presumption in favor of constitutionality was broader when legislation implicated only the former. Summarizing the history of the demise of liberty of contract, G. Edward White has observed that the doctrine, "having been 'interpreted' into being, . . . could be interpreted into obscurity." G. WHITE, PATTERNS OF AMERICAN LEGAL THOUGHT 40 (1978).

of the nineteenth century gave ground to legal realism and positivism.[27]    Underlying twentieth-century legal realism was a new,
sociological conception of the law, a conception of the law traceable back
to the same late-nineteenth century German jurists who influenced
Tiedeman's jurisprudence.[28]

This Article examines in depth Christopher Tiedeman's laissez-faire
constitutionalism, explaining it in terms of its jurisprudential roots and
suggesting reasons for its failure in the early decades of the twentieth
century.

Parts One and Two of the Article explore Tiedeman's sociological
conception of law, a conception influenced by the German jurisprudence
of his day and made evident in his 1890 treatise, *The Unwritten
Constitution of the United States*. In Part Two, Tiedeman's treatise is
closely examined, showing how his understanding of constitutionalism
led to his zealous advocacy of an activist judiciary defending both
enumerated and unenumerated constitutional rights.

Part Three of the Article examines the practical application of
Tiedeman's laissez-faire constitutionalism: his limited conception of the
police power of the states (and, by analogy, of the commerce power of
Congress), articulated in his *Treatise on State and Federal Control of
Persons and Property in the United States*, a two-volume second edition,
published in 1900, of his earlier treatise on the limitations of police
power. Certain key sections of Tiedeman's treatise are closely examined
as illustrative of his conceptualization of substantive due process.

Finally, Part Four of the Article concludes this study of Tiedeman's
laissez-faire constitutionalism by analyzing its relation to a basic
problem associated with American judicial review—the problem of
reconciling majority will with the protection of minority rights. The
inability of Tiedeman's jurisprudence to deal adequately with this
problem—and, in particular, with the problem of judicial protection of
unenumerated constitutional rights—is posited as an explanation for the
demise of substantive due process protection of economic rights. In
addition, some questions are raised, and tentative conclusions drawn,
concerning the relationship between jurisprudence and constitutional
law—a matter of vital importance in the modern debate ·over the

---

27. *See generally* White, *From Sociological Jurisprudence to Realism:
Jurisprudence and Social Change in Early Twentieth Century America*, 58 VA.
L. REV. 999 (1972).

28. Thomas Grey has noted the irony in the fact that German sociological
jurisprudence—the source of the "peculiarly modern view of law generally" that
is found in Tiedeman's thought—in later years served to undermine the laissez-
faire constitutionalism that he played so large a part in formulating. Grey,
*supra* note 13, at v-vi. The character and sources of Tiedeman's sociological
jurisprudence are more fully discussed *infra* notes 29-45 and accompanying text.

validity and scope of judicial protection of such unenumerated constitutional rights as the right to privacy.

## I. TIEDEMAN AND NINETEENTH-CENTURY JURISPRUDENCE

Tiedeman was born in Charleston, South Carolina in 1857. He spent his childhood and youth in Charleston, where he also completed his secondary and college education, graduating from the College of Charleston with A.B. and A.M. degrees in 1876. The following spring he went to Germany, where he spent one and a half years attending courses at the Universities of Goettingen and Leipzig. Upon his return to the United States in the autumn of 1878, Tiedeman enrolled at Columbia Law School; he obtained his law degree the following spring. After a short period of practice, first in Charleston, then in St. Louis, in 1881 he accepted an assistant professorship of law at the University of Missouri. He was made a full professor in 1882 and retained that position until 1891. During his tenure at Missouri he wrote a treatise on the law of real property (1884), the treatise on the limitations of the police power (1886), a treatise on the law of commercial paper (1889), and *The Unwritten Constitution of the United States* (1890). He became professor of law at the University of the City of New York in 1891, remaining until June, 1897, when he resigned to devote time to his writing. While at New York he wrote a treatise on the law of sales of personal property (1891) and, after his resignation, a treatise on equity jurisprudence (1893), a treatise on the law of municipal corporations (1894), and by 1900 his *Treatise on State and Federal Control of Persons and Property in the United States*. Tiedeman also edited a casebook on real property (1897) and a textbook on the law of bills and notes (1898). By the time he accepted the deanship of the law school at the University of Buffalo in 1902—a position he held until his death in August, 1903—at least thirty-six law schools were using Tiedeman's texts. Personally well-liked, he was, in the words of a successor at Buffalo, "a most cultured and thorough gentleman in every sense of the word."[29]

---

29. Summers, *Christopher Gustavus Tiedeman*, in 9 DICTIONARY OF AMERICAN BIOGRAPHY 531 (D. Malone ed. 1964). In addition to contributing to legal education through teaching and writing, Tiedeman also severely criticized the case method, which he regarded as far inferior to the European system of formal lectures. *See* Tiedeman, *Methods of Legal Education*, 1 YALE L.J. 150-158 (1891) [hereinafter Tiedeman, *Methods of Legal Education*] for Tiedeman's contribution to a symposium on legal education. Among other things, Tiedeman argued:

> if the duty of the teacher is to explain and discuss the principles and rules of law, he can do so more effectively and can accomplish more

While in Germany at the University of Goettingen, Tiedeman studied under Rudolf von Jhering (1818-1892).[30] Jhering was a leader in the German social-philosophical school of jurisprudence which at the end of the nineteenth century was challenging the precepts of the historical school, which had dominated earlier in the century.

The German historical school · of jurisprudence was founded by Friedrich Carl von Savigny (1779-1861) as a reaction to both natural rights theory and the codification movement of the early nineteenth century. Savigny and his followers—who included Sir Henry Maine (1822-1888), founder of the English branch of the historical school—were opposed to rationalistic speculation. They believed in the slow and organic evolution of law by the energy of the "Volksgeist," or the spirit of the people. Academics rather than statesmen, they were skeptical of the notion that the mere effort of reason could devise a perfect system of law—the notion which had underlay such efforts as the Code of Frederick the Great, the Austrian code of 1811, and the Napoleonic codes. The teaching of the historical school was rooted in the romanticism and political conservativism of the early decades of the nineteenth century; distrusting legislation and adverse to action, the historical school conceived of law as something to be found, not made. Moreover, law was to be found through historical study—and, in particular, through the study of Roman law as it had been adopted and developed in the German common law.[31]

---

in a given time, if he is not obliged to take up his time with catechising the students, and listening to their opinions, which even in the case of college-bred men must be the immature reflections of a tyro. *Id.* at 151.

30. In his essay criticizing the case method, Tiedeman praised the system of teaching—formal lectures expounding on the lecturer's own treatise on the subject of his instruction—that he "learned to admire while sitting under the skillful instruction of the celebrated von Ihering." Tiedeman, *Methods of Legal Education, supra* note 29, at 151. He went on to recommend that American law schools follow the methods of legal instruction pursued at the German universities, to avoid "the great danger of driving out of the schools all scientific study of the fundamentals of the law in the unchecked study from the cases of isolated propositions of the law." *Id.* at 157. The pervasive influence of Jhering on Tiedeman's conception of the law generally is revealed both in this essay and in his *Unwritten Constitution of the United States,* discussed *infra* notes 45-108 and accompanying text.

31. R. POUND, INTERPRETATIONS OF LEGAL HISTORY 14-18 (1923); Schwarz, *John Austin and the German Jurisprudence of His Time,* 1934 POLITICA 178, 184-86. Pound describes the historical school's conception of law as follows:

Law was not declaratory of morals or of the nature of man as a moral entity or reasoning creature. It was declaratory of principles of progress discovered by human experience of intercourse in civilized

Jhering and his contemporaries later in the century condemned both the nationalism and the abstract character of the historical school. Their ideas signaled a trend toward a more flexible, less conservative or static, jurisprudence. This social-philosophical school followed many paths. The approach that Jhering took was the social-utilitarian approach, so called because it insisted upon law as a means to the achievement of social ends.[32]

In his great work, *Zweck im Recht* (originally published in two volumes, respectively, in 1877 and 1883), which translated roughly as "Purpose in Law," or "Law as a Means to an End," Jhering argued that all law exists for the furtherance of social ends, and "the end [*Zweck*] is the creator of the entire law." This is true not only of law, but also of morality, of social custom or usage, of etiquette, and even of fashion. Rules intended to subserve social ends govern the whole social life; and these rules, worked out in social life and enforced by social pressure, constitute the system of social order. The nature of the sanction distinguishes rules of law from other social rules. While purely "psychological" or "internal" coercions enforce rules of morals, social usage or fashion, "external" or "mechanical" coercions enforce rules of law. Behind the law stands, in the last instance, the physical force of the community, and this force is directly exercised, where necessary, upon the person or property of the individual. In early society this physical coercion is unorganized—appearing as lynch-law, clan feud, or self-help of a wronged party. The modern state reserves the application of physical coercion to the state and its governmental organs, and thus national law becomes the command of the state.[33]

This positivist conception of law most clearly distinguished Jhering's jurisprudence from that of Savigny and the historical school. According to Jhering, the historical jurist of the early nineteenth century, like his predecessor, the natural-law jurist of the eighteenth, erring by assuming that legal rules developed from abstract principles, whether discovered in nature or through history. Jhering held that the means of serving human ends are discovered and fashioned consciously into laws. His was a "jurisprudence of realities," in which legal precepts are tested by their results and by their practical application, not solely

---

society; and those principles were not principles of natural law revealed by reason, they were realizings of an idea, unfolding in human experience and in the development of institutions—an idea to be demonstrated metaphysically and verified by history.

R. POUND, *supra*, at 9.

32. R. POUND, OUTLINES OF LECTURES ON JURISPRUDENCE 15-16, 23 (5th ed. 1943).

33. Smith, *Four German Jurists*, 11 POL. SCI. Q. 278, 290-91 (1896) (quoting R. JHERING, ZWECK IM RECHT (2d ed.)).

by logical deduction from principles discovered through historical study of Roman and Germanic law.[34] Jhering argued, "The standard of law is not the absolute one of truth, but the relative one of purpose. Hence it follows that the content of law not only *may* but *must* be infinitely various." Law, in a way, was like medicine:

> As the physician does not prescribe the same medicine to all sick people, but fits his prescription to the condition of the patient, so the law cannot always make the same regulations[;] it must likewise adapt them to the conditions of the people, to their degree of civilization, to the needs of the time.[35]

Thus, he concluded, "A universal law for all nations and times stands on the same line with a universal remedy for all sick people. It is the long sought for philosopher's stone, for which in reality not philosophers but only the fools can afford to search."[36]

In its reaction against Savigny and the historical school, however, Jhering's jurisprudence also reacted against competing systems of jurisprudence in the latter half of the century: on the one hand, the system outlined by the English positivist school, founded by John Austin (1790-1859); and, on the other, the system outlined by German idealists, including both neo-Kantians such as Rudolf Stammler (1856-1938) and neo-Hegelians such as Josef Kohler (1849-1919).[37]

Unlike the positivists, who essentially defined law as whatever the sovereign commands, Jhering defined it as "the sum of the conditions of social life . . . as secured by the power of the State through the means of external compulsion."[38] In other words, to Jhering, it was not the enunciation of commands by state authority, but their enforcement by state power, which makes them legal rules. On the other hand, unlike the idealists, to whom law was simply the expression of will (whether of God or society or the state), Jhering insisted on going behind the will and considering the motive. This, he declared, was always something to be attained, an end (*Zweck*): law was a means to the ends of society, and rights were means to individual ends. Neither laws nor rights were

---

34. Pound, *The Scope and Purpose of Sociological Jurisprudence*, 25 HARV. L. REV. 140, 141-42 (1910); *see also* Smith, *supra* note 33, at 682-85 (summarizing Jhering's leadership of the reaction against the excessive generalization of Savigny's historical school, towards a more practical jurisprudence; concluding that Jhering "was by instinct a realist").

35. R. JHERING, LAW AS A MEANS TO AN END 328 (I. Husik trans. 1913).

36. *Id.*

37. R. POUND, *supra* note 32, at 12, 23.

38. R. JHERING, *supra* note 35, at 380.

intelligible unless one considered the social end (in the case of a rule of law) or the personal end (in the case of a right).[39]

Jhering considered both laws and rights solely from the social point of view; hence, to him, individual ends were means to securing social ends. Private rights existed only because there was a large domain of social life in which egoism, in pursuing its own ends, realized the ends of society. And private rights were subject to limitations at the point where egoism menaced or thwarted a social interest[40]—hence, the limitations which the law imposed upon freedom of contract and upon the employment and disposition of private property.[41]

---

39. Smith, *supra* note 33, at 292-93.

40. Raising the question whether there are any absolute limits of the state and the law over the sphere of individual freedom, Jhering dismissed the arguments of Wilhelm von Humboldt and John Stuart Mill (from Mill's *On Liberty*) and concluded that it was not possible to posit a formula that would define the legitimate scope of the law. "Legislation will, in the future as in the past, measure restrictions of personal liberty not according to an abstract academic formula, but according to practical need." R. JHERING, *supra* note 35, at 409.

41. Smith, *supra* note 33, at 292-93. An interesting example of Jhering's view that a social purpose underlies all law is summarized by Smith. In analyzing the principle behind the prevention of cruelty to animals, Jhering "shows that the purpose of such laws is purely social, they are made for the sake of man, and that to explain them by attributing rights to animals would logically constrain us all to become not only anti-vivisectionists, but vegetarians." *Id.* at 299.

The pervasiveness of Jhering's influence upon Tiedeman is evident in the parallel between this summary of Jhering's theory of law and the discussion of Tiedeman's theory in *The Unwritten Constitution of the United States*. *See infra* notes 46-108 and accompanying text. A more precise example of this parallel between Jhering and Tiedeman can be found in Tiedeman's critique of Henry George's *Progress and Poverty*. Tiedeman, *What is Meant by "Private Property in Land?,"* 19 AM. L. REV. 878 (1885). Associating George's proposal for a single tax on land with Herbert Spencer's proposal in *Social Statics* to replace private ownership of land with tenancy, Tiedeman argued that neither author advocated a genuine change in the law; they merely mischaracterized Anglo-American property law. "[T]here is no 'private property in land,' in the sense in which Mr. Spencer and Mr. George employ the term." *Id.* at 883. Rather, Tiedeman noted, citing his own treatise on the law of real property, an individual's property or interest in land "must always be qualified," for "the State has the right and power to stipulate the conditions and terms upon which the land may be held by individuals," including the power to tax the land or to appropriate it for a public use. *Id.* at 882-83. Similarly, in *Zweck im Recht*, after discussing a variety of limitations that the law placed on private property, Jhering concluded:

All rights of private law, even through primarily having the individual
as their purpose, are influenced and bound by regard for society.
There is not a single right in which the subject can say, this I have

Jhering's philosophy of law thus rejected the notion of an objective foundation of law—based on nature or on history—while at the same time fell far short of declaring that law was merely whatever the sovereign willed the law to be. His jurisprudence, in short, was both social and teleological. It was social in that Jhering taught that law, rather than being something that the individual invoked against society, was something created by society through which the individual found the means of securing his or her interests, so far as society recognized them.[42] His philosophy of law was teleological in that it employed a teleological method, stressing the purpose of the law. It is not enough for the jurist to know that law is a development or even to understand how the law has developed; rather, as perceived by Jhering, the jurist must understand for what purpose and to what end. Legal doctrines and legal institutions have not worked themselves out; human minds fashioned them to meet human ends. "The sense of right has not produced law, but law the sense of right."[43]

As a result, the sociological jurisprudence of Jhering separated law from the will of the sovereign. Both in *Zweck im Recht* and in his earlier work, *Kampf ums Recht* ("The Struggle for Law") (1872), Jhering stressed "[t]he life of the law is a struggle." All law resulted from strife: "Every principle of law which obtains had first to be wrung by force from those who denied it; and every legal right—the legal rights of a whole nation as well as those of individuals—supposes a continual readiness to assert it and defend it."[44] Hence, Jhering emphasized not

---

exclusively for myself, I am lord and master over it, the consequences of the concept of right demand that society shall not limit me.
R. JHERING, *supra* note 35, at 396.

Despite the similarity between Tiedeman's view of property rights and Jhering's overall view of the law, however, Tiedeman nevertheless did draw a line—in his treatises on the limitations on the police power, discussed *infra* notes 109-67 and accompanying text,—beyond which, he argued, the law had no legitimate purpose. As suggested in Part IV of this article, this tension between Tiedeman's sociological jurisprudence and his theory of constitutional limitations may help explain the sudden end of his influence in American constitutional law in the early twentieth century. *See infra* notes 168-225 and accompanying text.

42. Pound, *supra* note 34, at 143.

43. *Id.* at 141 (quoting R. JHERING, ZWECK IM RECHT (2d ed.)).

44. R. JHERING, THE STRUGGLE FOR LAW 1-2 (J. Lalor trans. 2d ed. 1915). Jhering cited the symbol of Justice as a metaphor for this process:

Justice which, in one hand, holds the scales in which she weighs the right, carries in the other the sword with which she executes it. The sword without the scales is brute force, the scales without the sword is the impotence of law. The scales and the sword belong together, and the state of the law is perfect only where the power with which Justice carries the sword is equalled by the skill with which she holds

only the limitations the law placed on the individual but also the individual's obligation—a duty that was both social and personal—to assert one's rights. Law, then, was "an uninterrupted labor, and not of the state power only, but of the entire people."[45]

## II. THE UNWRITTEN CONSTITUTION AND JUDICIAL REVIEW

The influence of Jhering's jurisprudence upon Tiedeman is most clearly evident in Tiedeman's 1890 treatise, *The Unwritten Constitution of the United States*. That work is, as its subtitle states, "a philosophical inquiry into the fundamentals of American constitutional law."[46] Tiedeman ultimately concluded that judicial review of acts of legislation, as against both the written and unwritten constitutions, was not only justified but also necessary to the continued existence of popular government in the United States. He reached that conclusion by applying social-utilitarian concepts of law to the peculiar characteristics of the American constitutional system.

Significantly, Tiedeman began by refuting the legal positivism of John Austin and his followers. "I cannot believe," Tiedeman wrote, "that he [Austin] was unconscious of the natural sequential development of the law, operated upon by all the social forces, out of which civilization is in general evolved."[47] Tiedeman conceded "there is no living law without a sanction or penalty," but emphasized—as did Jhering—"it does not necessarily follow that that penalty must be enforced by an organized government, or that its enforcement by such a government essentially changes the character of the rule."[48] Lynch-law in frontier America provided one example.[49] The life of a rule of law derives not

---

the scales.
*Id.* at 2.
45. *Id.*
46. C. TIEDEMAN, THE UNWRITTEN CONSTITUTION OF THE UNITED STATES (1890) [hereinafter C. TIEDEMAN, UNWRITTEN CONSTITUTION].
47. *Id.* at 2.
48. *Id.* at 3-4.
49. *Id.* at 4-5.
If a man is murdered or a horse stolen in such a community [on the American frontier], and the offender is captured by the vigilance committee, tried by Judge Lynch, and punished in accordance with the custom of the country, he has suffered the penalty of the law, as much as the criminal in an orderly, more civilized community, who is tried and condemned by a regularly organized court, and punished by the ordinary administrative officers of government. The only difference between the two cases is the degree of development in the administration of the law. Lynch-law, in a community not possessed of a properly organized government, is as much law as the enactment

from a government's commands, but from "its habitual and spontaneous observance by the mass of the people."[50] A legal rule, then, is the product of social forces, reflecting "the prevalent sense of right," or *Rechsgefuehl*, as it evolves in the society.[51] Legal rules change over time, as the prevalent sense of right changes, but Tiedeman carefully emphasized that this change is not the quiet, smooth, uneventful development (as in the growth of a language) claimed by "jurists of the Savigny-Puchta [that is, the German historical] school." Rather, he observed—citing Jhering—new principles of law emerged only after vigorous contests between opposing forces.[52]

As Tiedeman moved his analysis from municipal law to constitutional law, the influence of social-utilitarian jurisprudence became even more pronounced. The fundamental principles which form the constitution of a state, he argued, "cannot be created by any governmental or popular edict; they are necessarily found imbedded in the national character and are developed in accordance with the national growth."[53] Hence it followed "constitutions are effective only so far as their principles have their roots imbedded in the national character, and consequently constitute a faithful reflection in the national will."[54] (Jhering's adaptation of the concept of *Volksgeist*, from the historical school, immediately comes to mind.) John Locke's draft of a written constitution for the Carolinas and Napoleon's "paper constitutions" which he imposed upon conquered nations and "unhappy France" were two examples Tiedeman cited of "fruitless attempts to impose constitutions upon people whose principles are not in harmony with the popular political sentiment."[55] It follows that the failure or success of a form of government or constitution in the experience of one people ought not indicate any "inherent and universal demerits or excellences," or assure

---

of an American legislature or the acts of Parliament. *Id.*

50. *Id.* at 6.

51. *Id.* at 7.

52. *Id.* at 11-12. Tiedeman cited and quoted in German from Jhering's work, KAMPF UM RECHT ("The Struggle for Law"). *Id.* at 12 n.1. In a later chapter, on the interpretation and construction of written constitutions, Tiedeman also cited Jhering. *Id.* at 145 n.1. Throughout the book, the influence of Jhering is implicit in Tiedeman's frequent references to law as a reflection of "the prevalent sense of right" in society, or to legal change as the outcome of struggles between opposing forces in society. *See, e.g., id.* at 7, 42-43, 151.

53. *Id.* at 16.

54. *Id.* at 18.

55. *Id.* at 19.

a similar experience if adopted by others.[56] "The English and American constitutions work well, . . . not because of their inherent and abstract excellences . . . but because they are in complete correspondence with the political sentiment of the respective nations, and are themselves the natural products of Anglo-American civilization." Free government in England and the United States is assured not so much by what is found in their written constitutions but rather by "the conservative, law-abiding, and yet liberty-loving character of the Anglo-Saxon."[57]

The excellence of the American constitutions, state and federal, was to Tiedeman a result of the "complete harmony of [their] principles with the political evolution of the nation," rather than "the political acumen" of the conventions that drafted them.[58] The American constitutions "are but natural sequential developments of the British constitution, modified as to detail and as to a few fundamental principles of the new environment."[59] Tiedeman emphasized three of these new principles traceable to the American experience: federalism, popular sovereignty, and judicial review.[60] These principles in turn reflected a profound

---

56. *Id.* at 20. Tiedeman thus questioned the efficacy of a written constitution, modelled after the American and other western constitutions, in Japan—"notwithstanding the wonderful adaptiveness of the Japanese character to political and economic innovations." *Id.* at 18.

57. *Id.* at 19-20.

58. *Id.* at 21.

59. *Id.* Comparing the British and American constitutions, Tiedeman identified two basic similarities: the localization of power ("an unvarying determination to confine the exercise of governmental power to the local authorities in every thing affecting only the local interests") and the separation of powers. *Id.* at 22, 24. He argued that it was not surprising that the framers of the American constitutions—particularly the Federal Constitution of 1787—imitated the British constitution, since they were "thoroughly acquainted with English constitutional law." In addition, he noted, "the universal political sentiment," influenced by Montesquieu, regarded the British constitution as the best the world had ever known. *Id.* at 25-26.

60. *Id.* at 37-40. Federalism, of course, refers to the division of powers between the federal government and the states. Popular sovereignty, in the sense used here, refers to the principle that all government agencies are the creatures of the will of the people and thus subject to limitations imposed on them by popular will—in other words, that government officials are the servants; the people are the masters. A corollary to this "fundamental doctrine of American democracy," as Tiedeman described it, is the doctrine that, inasmuch as the people alone may alter or amend their constitutions, any act of the legislatures or Congress that transcends the provisions of the constitution would be unconstitutional and void. This doctrine Tiedeman identified as "the fundamental doctrine of American constitutional law." *Id.* at 38-39. Finally, the third principle—judicial review, or the power of the courts to declare void

difference between American and English contitutionalism:    the establishment of written constitutions in America, which materially altered constitutional development in the United States.[61]

Despite this emphasis on written constitutions as distinguishing features of American constitutionalism Tiedeman also stressed that the United States Constitution differed in an essential aspect from the constitutions of most of the states.  State constitutions reduced many, if not most, of the details of constitutional law to writing; therefore, they required the calling of constitutional conventions "more or less frequently for the purpose of revision."[62]    The federal Constitution, on the other hand, as understood by Tiedeman

> contains only a declaration of the fundamental and most general principles of constitutional law, while the real, living constitutional law, . . . the flesh and blood of the Constitution, instead of its skeleton, is here, as well as elsewhere, unwritten; not to be found in the instrument promulgated by a constitutional convention, but in the decisions of the courts and acts of the legislature, which are published and enacted in the enforcement of the written Constitution.[63]

This "unwritten constitution of the United States," argued Tiedeman, "within the broad limitations of the written constitution, is just as flexible, and yields just as readily to the mutations of public opinion as the unwritten constitution of Great Britain."[64]

---

legislative acts that contravened constitutions—was a consequence of the second principle, popular sovereignty.

> The courts are obliged to construe and determine the law, whenever a question is raised before them by parties litigant, and, being the servant of the people, they must obey the Constitution rather than the act of the legislature which violates the Constitution. For such an act of the legislature is not law. It being the duty of the courts to declare what is the law, they are obliged to determine when legislative acts are constitutional or unconstitutional.

*Id.* at 39-40. This was essentially the same justification for judicial review enunciated by John Marshall. *See* Marbury v. Madison, 5 U.S. (1 Cranch) 137 (1803).

61. Popular sovereignty, "the fundamental doctrine of American constitutional law," is only feasible where there are written constitutions containing explicit grants and limitations of power, Tiedeman argued.  C. TIEDEMAN, UNWRITTEN CONSTITUTION, *supra* note 46, at 38.

62. *Id.* at 42. Tiedeman noted the general rule that "the fragility and instability of a constitution are in direct proportion to the multiplicity of its written rules." *Id.* at 43.

63. *Id.*

64. *Id.* at 43.

As two examples of provisions of the "unwritten constitution," originating in practice and sustained by popular opinion or custom, Tiedeman cited the process by which a President is elected and the practice of limiting the Presidency to two terms.[65] But by far the most important provisions of the "unwritten constitution"—including many of those that protected the rights of minorities against the will of the majority—were those which originated in the courts, through their exercise of the power of judicial review.

Early in the book, when formulating his general theory about law, Tiedeman discussed *stare decisis* as a principle "absolutely binding, only [insofar] as it also reflects the prevalent sense of right."[66] Thus, although public sentiment required rigid adherence to *stare decisis*, judges have overturned previous rules, even if only under a fiction, where "the variance between the law and the prevalent sense of right was so distressing that the courts have been justified by public sentiment in abrogating an established rule."[67] The modification of the doctrine of vested rights, formulated in the Dartmouth College case and gradually eroded by the courts, furnished one example of a change in constitutional law following a change in public opinion.[68] In a similar way, judges must interpret statutes and constitutional provisions in keeping with "the prevalent sense of right." This implied to Tiedeman a power in the judiciary to limit by construction the undesirable effects of popular legislation. For example, the English Statute of Uses, although enacted to abolish uses and prevent the creation of equitable interests in lands, was given a "distorting, technical construction," which was not only consistent with the sentiment of the English middle class, but also has formed the basis for the modern law of trusts.[69]

The obligation of judges to interpret or construct according to the prevailing sense of right also implied to Tiedeman a power in the judiciary to alter, or even abolish, obsolete statutes or constitutional provisions. Responding to what he called "the fallacy of the doctrine that the government 'derives its just powers from the consent of the governed,'"[70] Tiedeman emphasized that the enactment of laws rested

---

65. *Id.* at 46-53. One other example of the unwritten constitution is the President's exercise of war powers in times of great national emergencies, such as the Civil War (or, as Tiedeman identified it in a chapter heading, "The War of Secession"). *Id.* at 89-90.

66. *Id.* at 13.

67. *Id.*

68. *Id.* at 66.

69. *Id.* at 8. The example illustrates the general rule asserted by Tiedeman, that "the legislature cannot completely enslave the popular will by an enactment not endorsed by the prevalent sense of right." *Id.* at 7.

70. *Id.* at 121.

its authority, not upon the consent of the governed, but upon the ability of the law-makers to compel obedience to their edicts. The "living part of municipal law . . . consists of those rules which the great mass of people habitually and spontaneously obey, and which they compel the rebellious minority to obey, in order to prevent injury to the law-abiding individual or to the commonwealth."[71]     Hence, it followed that the binding authority of law "does not rest upon any edict of the people in the past; it rests upon the present will of those who possess the political power."[72]

From this theory of law and the source of legal obligation, Tiedeman derived his basic theory of judicial interpretation—a theory which emphasized, not the intent of the original lawmakers, but rather the will of the present generation. "[A] true interpretation of the law" turns indeed on the meaning of the lawgiver, but in the United States "the real lawgiver is not the man or body of men which first enacted the law ages ago; it is the people of the present day who possess the political power, and whose commands give life to what otherwise is a dead letter."[73]     The "utterances of dead men" are binding as law only when

---

71. *Id.* at 122.

72. *Id.* An interesting corollary to this line of Tiedeman's thought is that "the right of secession is nothing more than the right of revolution," which is "never legal, until its successful exercise has wrought a transfer of the political power from one aggregation of individuals to another." *Id.* at 127-28. Here, two circumstances of Tiedeman's background—Tiedeman as a native son of South Carolina, and Tiedeman as a student of German sociological jurisprudence—may have had a joint influence on his interpretation of the outcome of the secession crisis of the 1830s (and, perhaps, the Civil War). Tiedeman stated:

> since all law derives its binding authority from the present commands of those who now control and mould public opinion, and not from any original compact or consent of the governed, the supreme power is that aggregation of individuals, which now has the ability to enforce obedience to its commands. The people of the United States exercised supreme power over the State of South Carolina and prohibited its secession from the Union for the same reason and on the same ground as they exercised supreme power over the Mexicans, who became American citizens, in consequence of a cession by Mexico to the United States of the territory in which they lived. It was because in both cases the United States had the ability to assert supreme power over the objecting individuals. The fact that the United States holds these peoples in subjection makes the people of the United States the depositary of sovereign power; and whenever that fact ceases to exist, and the supreme power has in fact been transferred to some other aggregation of individuals, sovereignty will no longer be in the people of the United States.

*Id.* at 125-26.

73. *Id.*

voiced by the living, "[f]or the present possessors of political power, and not their predecessors, are the lawgivers for the present generation."[74] In interpreting—or, more precisely, in construing—the written word of the Constitution, judges should follow that interpretation or construction which "best reflects the prevalent sense of right:"[75]

> While, therefore, as a general rule, the written word remains unchanged and confines the operations of the popular will to a choice of the shades of meaning, of which the written word is capable—until the written word has been repealed or modified by the proper authority,—the practical operation of the law will vary with each change in the prevalent sense of right; and the judge or practitioner of the law, who would interpret the law rightly, . . . need not concern himself so much with the intentions of the framers of the Constitution or statute, as with the modifications of the written word by the influence of the present will of the people.[76]

The judge "who would interpret the law rightly," therefore, must follow "what the possessors of political power now mean by the written word."[77]

Tiedeman did not stop here; judges were not to be mere rubber stamps of popular will. As a chapter in the middle of the book, *The Doctrine of Natural Rights in American Constitutional Law*, reveals, Tiedeman perceived the function of the judiciary as a check upon majority will.[78]   But even here, Tiedeman did not depart from his

---

74. *Id.* at 150.

75. *Id.* Although he used *interpretation* in the broad sense, encompassing what some scholars regard technically as construction rather than interpretation, Tiedeman cited the distinction made by Francis Lieber: that interpretation involved ascertaining the meaning that the framers attached to a particular constitutional provision, while construction involved applying the provision to new circumstances, not known to the framers. *Id.* at 151-52 (citing F. LIEBER, LEGAL AND POLITICAL HERMENEUTICS 168 (Boston 1839)). Drawing upon both Lieber and John Marshall, in his opinion for the Court in the Dartmouth College case, Trustees of Dartmouth College v. Woodward, 17 U.S. (4 Wheat.) 518, 644-45 (1819), Tiedeman concluded that his rule of interpretation was not merely speculative, but was "acted upon and recognized by all the leading American authorities." C. TIEDEMAN, UNWRITTEN CONSTITUTION, *supra* note 46, at 151-52.

76. *Id.* at 150.

77. C. TIEDEMAN, UNWRITTEN CONSTITUTION, *supra* note 46, at 150-51.

78. *Id.*, ch. vi, at 67-82. The text of this chapter originated in an address Tiedeman delivered to the Missouri Bar Association in 1887, *The Doctrine of Natural Rights in Its Bearing upon American Constitutional Law*. Tiedeman, *Missouri Bar Association Annual Address for 1887*, in REPORT OF THE SEVENTH ANNUAL MEETING OF THE MISSOURI BAR ASSOCIATION 97-117 (1887) (summarized and quoted in A. PAUL, *supra* note 2, at 24-27) [hereinafter *Doctrine of*

conception of law as based in the prevalent sense of right, or from the broader jurisprudential base which he shared with Jhering.

Tiedeman began this chapter by observing that legal positivists—those whom Tiedeman described as "jurists of the Bentham-Austin school"—went too far in their reaction against the doctrine of natural rights: they failed to note "popular notions of rights, however wrong they may be from a scientific standpoint, do become incorporated into, and exert an influence upon, the development of the actual law."[79] This is especially true in the United States, where the bills of rights of the state and federal constitutions have formulated and made a part of the organic law of the land "the prevalent doctrine of natural rights."[80] These rights, in their particular content, change over time; for there is "no such thing, even in ethics, as an absolute, inalienable, natural right. The so-called natural rights depend upon, and vary with, the legal and ethical conceptions of the people."[81] But, whatever those rights might

---

*Natural Rights*].

79. C. TIEDEMAN, UNWRITTEN CONSTITUTION, *supra* note 46, at 71-72. Tiedeman attributed the origin of natural rights theory to the influence of the Roman law doctrine of *jus naturale, i.e.*, an ideal law that one might conceive to be in force in the state of nature. *Id.* at 69. This doctrine, argued Tiedeman, was developed to "the extreme limits of absurdity" by its merger with the notion of the "social contract" in post-medieval legal thought. *Id.* at 70. He further argued that the doctrine in this form—absolute natural rights grounded in a pre-social contract state of nature—had "all-powerful influence" on modern jurisprudence, until challenged by jurists of the Bentham-Austin School. In the reaction of these jurists against the doctrine, "the pendulum of modern scientific thought has swung too far in the opposite direction," Tiedeman explained. "Defining law to be the command of a sovereign to a subject, and recognizing the will of the sovereign to be the only standard of right," the positivists excluded altogether from the province of jurisprudence the consideration of "any so-called natural rights." *Id.* at 71.

80. *Id.* at 78. The subtlety of Tiedeman's argument here was missed by Arnold Paul, who contrasted Tiedeman's argument in *Doctrine of Natural Rights, supra* note 78, that there was "no such thing" as an absolute, inalienable natural right, with his argument in C. TIEDEMAN, LIMITATIONS OF POLICE POWER, *supra* note 14, that "[t]he private rights of the individual . . . belong to man in a state of nature." A. PAUL, *supra* note 2, at 25 & n.15. The explanation for the apparent inconsistency is not that the former argument was "delivered to a select group of professional colleagues" while the latter was a "textbook statement intended for use in law schools and courts," as Paul suggests. Rather the explanation lies in the passage from *Unwritten Constitution* previously quoted: that, however wrong Tiedeman regarded the doctrine of natural rights from the "scientific viewpoint," he recognized it as a part of the "prevalent sense of rights" in nineteenth-century America, which judges are obligated to follow. *See supra* text accompanying notes 76-77.

81. C. TIEDEMAN, UNWRITTEN CONSTITUTION, *supra* note 46, at 76.

be at any given time, the American constitutions "make it the duty of the courts to prevent any violation of these rights by the other departments of the government by refusing to enforce laws which contain such violations of constitutional rights."[82]

What doctrine of natural rights was prevalent in 1890, at the time Tiedeman wrote? The obvious answer is the doctrine of rights consistent with the philosophy of laissez-faire, a philosophy which Tiedeman noted had appeared "with the general growth and spread of popular government" and which held as its fundamental maxim "that society, collectively and individually, can attain its highest development by being left free from governmental control, as far as this is possible, provision being made by the government only for the protection of the individual and of society by the punishment of crimes and trespasses."[83] Consistent with this philosophy, the doctrine of natural rights "as presently developed" is, tersely,

> a freedom from all legal restraint that is not needed to prevent injury to others; a right to do any thing that does not involve a trespass or injury to others; or, to employ the language of Herbert Spencer, "Every man has a freedom to do aught that he wills, provided he infringes not the equal freedom of any other man." The prohibitory operation of the law must be confined to the enforcement of the legal maxim, *sic utere tuo ut alienum non laedas.* ["So use your own [property] as not to injure another's"][84]

---

82. *Id.* at 78.

83. *Id.*

84. *Id.* at 76 (quoting H. SPENCER, SOCIAL STATICS 121 (1890)). Tiedeman argued that "[t]his right of freedom from needless restraint has been guaranteed to the British subject by the Magna Carta, the Petition of Right, and the Bill of Rights." *Id.* at 77. The *sic utere* formulation indeed had a long history in Anglo-American law. *See generally* Reznick, *Empiricism and the Principle of Conditions in the Evolution of the Police Power: A Model for Definitional Scrutiny,* 1978 WASH. U.L.Q. 1. State courts in the nineteenth century frequently used the *sic utere* formulation, or something very much like it, in discussing the scope of the police power. *See, e.g.,* Commonwealth v. Alger, 61 Mass. (7 Cush.) 53, 84-85 (1851) (observing that all property may be so regulated "that it shall not be injurious to the equal enjoyment of others having an equal right to the enjoyment of their property"); Thorpe v. Rutland & Burlington R.R., 27 Vt. 140, 153 (1854) (holding that the police power may be validly applied "in regard to those whose business is dangerous and destructive to other persons' property or business"); State v. Paul, 5 R.I. 185, 191 (1858) (observing that property rights are not absolute but are restricted "as they necessarily must be, by the greater right of the community to have them so exercised within it as to be compatible with its well-being").

This philosophy of laissez-faire, wrote Tiedeman, had "until lately, so controlled public opinion in the English-speaking world, that no disposition has been manifested by the depositories of political power to do more than control the criminal classes, provide for the care of the unfortunate poor and insane, and make public improvements."[85] But a change has come over the thought of the country, Tiedeman warned:

> Under the stress of economic relations, the clashing of private interests, the conflicts of labor and capital, the old superstition that government has the power to banish evil from the earth, if it could only be induced to declare the supposed causes illegal, has been revived; and all these so-called natural rights, which the framers of our constitutions declared to be inalienable, and the violation of which they pronounced to be a just cause for rebellion, are in imminent danger of serious infringement.[86]

Popular demands for greater government intervention in economic matters endangered individual rights:

> The State is called on to protect the weak against the shrewdness of the stronger, to determine what wages a workman shall receive for his labor, and how many hours he shall labor. Many trades and occupations are being prohibited, because some are damaged incidentally by their prosecution, and many ordinary pursuits are made government monopolies. The demands of the Socialists and Communists vary in degree and in detail, but the most extreme of them insist upon the assumption by government of the paternal character altogether,

---

85. C. TIEDEMAN, UNWRITTEN CONSTITUTION, *supra* note 46, at 78-79. Tiedeman's view that the philosophy of laissez-faire "dominated" public opinion in America and England in the nineteenth century is largely a myth; various historical studies have shown that the law was used frequently to attain economic ends other than the few identified by Tiedeman here. *See generally* S. FINE, *supra* note 8, at 18-23 (summarizing the extent of federal and state government intervention in the economy of antebellum America); Woodard, *supra* note 8, at 289-90 & n.6 (identifying several studies of nineteenth century England and America which have reached this conclusion). Nevertheless, "laissez-faire" is a useful and appropriate paradigm for nineteenth-century America and England, to distinguish these societies—dominated to a great extent by classical liberal politics and economics—from the "welfare state" paradigm that took hold in England in the latter decades of the nineteenth century and in America in the early decades of the twentieth. *See* A. DICEY, LECTURES ON THE RELATION BETWEEN LAW AND PUBLIC OPINION IN ENGLAND DURING THE NINETEENTH CENTURY 126-302 (1905) (Lectures VI-VIII, tracing the shift from the "Age of Benthamism or Individualism," in the period 1825 to 1870, to the "Age of Collectivism" that followed); Hovenkamp, *supra* note 6, at 402-39 (contrasting nineteenth century American and British political economy).

86. C. TIEDEMAN, UNWRITTEN CONSTITUTION, *supra* note 46, at 79-80.

abolishing all private property in land, and making the State the sole possessor of the working capital of the nation.[87]

Considering "these extraordinary demands of the great army of discontents" and their apparent power, with the growth of universal suffrage, to enforce their views "upon the civilized world," Tiedeman further warned that "the conservative classes stand in constant fear of the advent of an absolutism more tyrannical and more unreasoning than any before experienced by man,—the absolutism of a democratic majority."[88]

Tiedeman immediately followed these warnings with a spirited defense of judicial review—or, more precisely, of judicial protection of unenumerated "natural rights." He wrote, "in these days of great social unrest, we applaud the disposition of the courts . . . to lay their interdict upon all legislative acts which interfere with the individual's natural rights, even though these acts do not violate any specific or special provisions of the Constitution."[89]

---

87. *Id.* at 79.

88. *Id.* at 79-80.

89. *Id.* at 81. Tiedeman cited Judge Cooley, stating that "the right to follow all lawful employment" is an important civil liberty and thus protected by the due process clause. He also quoted the broad definitions of the rights to life, liberty, and property suggested by the New York Court of Appeals in Berthoff v. O'Reilly, 74 N.Y. 509, 515 (1878):

The right to life includes the right of the individual to his body in its completeness and without dismemberment; the right to liberty, the right to exercise his faculties and to follow a lawful avocation for the support of life; the right of property, the right to acquire property and enjoy it in any way consistent with the equal rights of others and the just exactions and demands of the State.

C. TIEDEMAN, UNWRITTEN CONSTITUTION, *supra* note 46, at 82. Despite this "broad and liberal interpretation" of the due process clause, the *Berthoff* court upheld the New York "civil damage" act that made owners of business premises at which intoxicating liquors were sold liable for damages caused by an intoxicated person. (In this case, the plaintiff suffered property damage indirectly caused by the intoxicating liquor sold to the plaintiff's son by the lessee of the defendant, a hotel owner. The plaintiff's horse died from overdriving by the plaintiff's son while he was intoxicated, as a consequence of "repeated potations" at the bar in the defendant's hotel.) Observing that the right of the state to regulate the traffic in intoxicating liquors was long-established and "not open to question," the New York court concluded that the statute, although it restrained the freedom of the owner in the use of his property and thus impaired its value, nevertheless did not constitute "a taking" of the property within the meaning of the Constitution. *Berthoff*, 74 N.Y. at 517, 521.

It is easy to conclude from these passages that what some historians might refer to as Tiedeman's "class bias" influenced his support of
judicial review to check this perceived danger.[90]   But, despite Tiedeman's personal identification with "the conservative classes" and his
abhorrence of socialism, it would be wrong to conclude that Tiedeman's
apparent conservativism led him to contradict his social-utilitarian
jurisprudence.   Two facts are important.   First, Tiedeman saw the
American constitutions as requiring that the courts protect the "so-
called natural rights," that is, those rights which contemporary society
values.   Second, he regarded the political philosophy of laissez-faire not
only as the "prevalent sense of right" in terms of popular opinion but
also as the "end" of American (or, at the very least, nineteenth-century
American) society, in Jhering's sense of the term.

   Like Jhering, Tiedeman adhered to a jurisprudence which, in
contrast to both the positivists and the idealists, separated law from
popular will.   Much of what the "great army of discontents" was calling
for was legislation contrary to Tiedeman's perception of social reality.
The "ills of life," which were the consequences of sin and ignorance and
other "frailties of human nature," were not curable by legislation,
Tiedeman was convinced, because "the stream can never rise higher
than its source, nor can it be expected that legal rules, which are but a
reflection of the moral habits of a people, can effect their moral
elevation," least of all the moral elevation of a people living under
popular government.[91]

---

   90. *See, e.g.*, C. JACOBS, *supra* note 2; B. TWISS, *supra* note 2. Arnold Paul
also regards Tiedeman as a self-conscious "conservative;" but, in speculating
about the reason for the rise of laissez-faire constitutionalism, he criticizes the
"circular explanations" proposed by these and other historians, noting that by
calling it "bias," they may be doing no more than to "name (and thus hide) what
we do not understand." A. PAUL, *supra* note 2, at 236 n.33 (quoting Mendelson,
Book Review 49 AM. POL. SCI. REV. 560 (1955) (reviewing C. JACOBS, LAW
WRITERS AND THE COURTS: THE INFLUENCE OF THOMAS M. COOLEY, CHRISTO-
PHER G. TIEDMAN, AND JOHN F. DILLION UPON AMERICAN CONSTITUTIONAL LAW)
(1954)).

   91. C. TIEDEMAN, UNWRITTEN CONSTITUTION, *supra* note 46, at 6.
Tiedeman's argument here nicely illustrates what Calvin Woodard has described
as "the *laissez-faire* standard" regarding the problem of poverty. This standard
was composed of three tenets: first, that poverty was an inevitable condition of
human life; second, that a person's worldly condition, by and large, reflects that
person's moral character; and third, that private voluntary charity is the proper
source of relief for the legitimate needs of the poor. Woodard, *supra* note 8, at
293. Woodard contrasts this standard with what he describes as the "welfare
state" standard, which rests on virtually opposite assumptions: that "poverty is
an 'economic' phenomenon that can, must, and should be abolished;" that "the
state is the sole social institution capable of dealing with the economic forces

One way to explain Tiedeman's laissez-faire constitutionalism, then, is that his reasoning was tautological: laissez-faire principles, according to his understanding of social reality, framed the only legitimate base for legislation; and, since law was a means to society's end, they also framed that end. Hence, it followed that the only legitimate legal rules were those consistent with laissez-faire principles.

Another way of explaining Tiedeman's constitutionalism, however, avoids such a simplistic explanation by instead focusing more closely upon Tiedeman's concept of judicial review and its applications.

Tiedeman's jurisprudence led him to the conclusion that judges must interpret the law according to the prevalent sense of right. As I have shown, this gave the courts power to modify or disregard unpopular or obsolete legislation. Tiedeman's jurisprudence also gave the courts power to modify or disregard statutes or even constitutional provisions which, however popular or current, were out of step with the will of the people, rightly understood. Here one must distinguish will from whim, or caprice.[92]

Tiedeman's discussion of the Slaughter-House Cases[93] illustrates

---

which give rise to that phenomenon;" and that therefore "the chief responsibility for abolishing poverty rests on the state and the state must, in turn, exert its faculties toward that end." *Id.* at 288.

92. As discussed below, Tiedeman considered the "veto power" of the courts to be "but an obstacle 'in the way of the people's whim, not of their will.'" C. TIEDEMAN, UNWRITTEN CONSTITUTION, *supra*, note 46, at 164 (quoting J. LOWELL, DEMOCRACY, AND OTHER ADDRESSES 24 (1887)).

93. Slaughter-House Cases, 83 U.S. (16 Wall.) 36 (1872). In these cases the Court upheld a Louisiana statute which, among other things, granted a particular company "the sole and exclusive privilege of conducting and carrying on the live-stock landing and slaughter-house business" in New Orleans. In his opinion for the majority of the Court, Justice Miller, impressed with the "one pervading purpose" of the fourteenth amendment—to guarantee to blacks the equal protection of the laws—and apparently determined to keep the amendment limited to that purpose, severely undercut the scope of the privileges and immunities clause. The fourteenth amendment prohibited the states from abridging "the privileges and immunities of citizens of *the United States*," the Court emphasized, not the privileges and immunities of citizens of the several states. *Id.* at 74 The former encompassed a relatively select group of well-defined (but hardly controversial) rights such as the right to come to the seat of national government, the right of free access to seaports, or the right to demand protection while on the high seas or in foreign jurisdictions. *Id.* at 79-80. In his opinion for the Court, Justice Miller also interpreted the equal protection clause quite narrowly, noting, "We doubt very much whether any action of a State not directed by way of discrimination against the negroes as a class, or on account of their race, will ever be held to come within the purview of this provision," which was "so clearly a provision for that race and that emergency, that a strong case would be necessary for its application to any other." *Id.* at 80. Finally,

the point. The fourteenth amendment if applied literally, argued Tiedeman, would have destroyed the federal system of government.[94] That dangerous result was, however, "happily averted by the bold and courageous stand" taken by the Supreme Court.

> Feeling assured that the people in their cooler moments would not have sanctioned the far-reaching effects of their action; that they lost sight of the general effect in their eager pursuit of a special end, the court dared to withstand the popular will as expressed in the letter of the amendment; and, by giving it a narrow and close construction, to cut off its injurious consequences . . . .[95]

---

with respect to the due process clause, Justice Miller's opinion said very little, merely concluding that "under no construction of that provision" could the statute be deemed a deprivation of liberty. *Id.* at 81.

Justice Field in his dissent argued that if the clause were meant to cover only those privileges and immunities that Justice Miller distinguished as those pertaining to citizens "of the United States," the amendment was "a vain and idle enactment." *Id.* at 96. Field would have included among those privileges and immunities the freedom of economic pursuit, "the right to pursue a lawful employment in a lawful manner, without other restraint than such as equally affects all persons." *Id.* at 97. By granting a special and exclusive privilege to one company, the legislature infringed the rights of others to carry on the business, within the same district under similar conditions; therefore, Field concluded, the Court ought to have declared the statute unconstitutional. *Id.* at 110.

94. Presumably, Tiedeman agreed with Justice Miller's conclusion that to interpret the fourteenth amendment so as to empower the national government to guarantee the "privileges and immunities of the citizens of the States as such" would be impermissible, because it would "constitute this court a perpetual censor upon all legislation of the States, on the civil rights of their own citizens, with authority to nullify such as it did not approve as consistent with those rights, as they existed at the time of the adoption of this amendment." *Id.* at 78. Such an interpretation, Justice Miller argued, would destroy federalism.

> [W]hen, as in the case before us, these consequences are so serious, so far-reaching and pervading, so great a departure from the structure and spirit of our institutions; when the effect is to fetter and degrade the State governments by subjecting them to the control of Congress, in the exercise of powers heretofore universally conceded to them of the most ordinary and fundamental character; when in fact it radically changes the whole theory of the relations of the State and Federal governments to each other and of both these governments to the people; the argument has a force that is irresistible, in the absence of language which expresses such a purpose too clearly to admit of doubt.

*Id.*

95. C. TIEDEMAN, UNWRITTEN CONSTITUTION, *supra* note 46, at 102-03.

Tiedeman cited the Court's majority opinion, written by Justice Miller, to support his contention that the Court saw itself as interpreting the fourteenth amendment in accord with the true will of the people:

> But however pervading this sentiment [the desire for a strong national government] and however it may have contributed to the adoption of the amendments we have been considering, we do not see in those amendments any purpose to destroy the main features of the general system. Under the pressure of all the excited feeling growing out of the war, our statesmen have still believed that the existence of the States, with powers for domestic and local government, including the regulation of civil rights—the rights of person and of property—was essential to the complex form of government, though they have thought proper to impose additional limitations on the States, and to confer additional power on that of the nation.[96]

Admitting "so-called strict constructionists" might regard the Court's rewriting of the Constitution as an unwarranted exercise of judicial power, Tiedeman nevertheless defended the majority's decision as one that kept the operation of the fourteenth amendment "within the limits which they felt assured would have been imposed by the people, if their judgment had not been blinded with passion, and which in their cooler moments they would ratify."[97]  The decision of the Court in the *Slaughter-House Cases* was "a successful modification of the rule found in the fourteenth amendment," concluded Tiedeman, because "no attempt was made to overrule it by additional legislation; nor was there any outcry against it, after the people had recovered from their surprise at this bold limitation of their written commands."[98]

Tiedeman concluded his *Unwritten Constitution* by answering the question, of what value is a written constitution? To Tiedeman, having a written constitution as a safeguard to limit the powers of government was less important than the power of judges to use that written constitution to put into effect the limitations. The real value of the written constitution is "to serve as a check upon the popular will in the interest of the minority."[99]  By making the federal judiciary hold office

---

96. *Id.* at 106 (quoting *Slaughter-House Cases*, 83 U.S. (16 Wall.) at 82).

97. *Id.* at 108. Tiedeman nevertheless quoted, with apparent agreement, the opinions of dissenting Justices Field, Swayne, and Bradley, to the effect that the majority's construction of the "privileges and immunities" clause made that part of the fourteenth amendment essentially useless. *Id.* at 100-01 n.2.

98. *Id.* at 108-09.

99. *Id.* at 163. Tiedeman added that a written constitution was "not needed for the protection of the people against the tyranny of the officials," *id.*, after having explained that "the danger of official tyranny has been successfully dissipated in the American constitutional system,—except so far as such tyranny

during good behavior, and by providing in the Constitution for one permanent Supreme Court, "the means have been provided, in ordinary times of peace, of protecting the minority against the absolutism of a democratic majority."[100]   The institution of judicial review, as exercised by the federal judiciary, thus was essentially anti-democratic:

> It enables a small body of distinguished men, whose lifelong career is calculated to produce in them an exalted love of justice and an intelligent appreciation of the conflicting rights of individuals, and the life-tenure of whose offices serves to withdraw them from all fear of popular disapproval; it enables these independent, right-minded men, in accordance with the highest law, to plant themselves upon the provisions of the written Constitution, and deny to popular legislation the binding force of law, whenever such legislation infringes a constitutional provision.[101]

With judicial review, the real value of a written constitution, then, is that it "makes possible and successful, the opposition to the popular will."[102]

It seems difficult to reconcile this conception of judicial review—the power to veto popular legislation vested in a small group of "independent, right-minded men"—with Tiedeman's general conception of law as "the product of social forces, reflecting the prevalent sense of right," as it evolves in the society. But Tiedeman was not self-contradictory—he emphasized that judicial review, "when most successful, does not serve as a complete barrier to the popular will."[103]   This was so, he argued, for two reasons. First, "the judges themselves fall under the influence of the prevalent sense of right, and ordinarily give in their decisions an

---

may be demanded by a popular majority,—by the frequency of the elections and the short terms of service." All classes of government officials are "too anxious to secure popular approval;" "[t]hey have their fingers constantly upon the public pulse, and every expression of popular approval and disapproval is noted." *Id.* at 162.

100. *Id.* at 163.

101. *Id.*

102. *Id.* at 163-64. Indeed, to Tiedeman, the secure tenure of the federal judiciary was virtually the only feature of the American system of government that made the written Constitution worthwhile. Noting that "the direct and constant responsibility of almost all classes of officials to public opinions, through frequent popular elections, goes very far towards nullifying any superior merit which the written constitution possesses over an unwritten constitution," he added that if federal judges were elected for short terms of office, as are many state judges, "the written Constitution would serve very little purpose." *Id.* at 162-63.

103. *Id.* at 164.

accurate expression of it." Second, "the various checks upon this veto power of the courts also serve to make their action only a dilatory proceeding."[104]   Citing James Russell Lowell in calling the power of the Supreme Court "but an obstacle in the way of the people's whim, not their will,"[105] Tiedeman concluded that this constitutional system has successfully established "what exists nowhere else, a popular government without democratic absolutism."[106]

Thus, to Tiedeman, the rules of law as expounded by the courts, even more so than legislative enactments, were the concrete results of the opposition of social forces through which the "prevalent sense of right" evolved. In his essay on legal education, published about a year after *The Unwritten Constitution*, Tiedeman stated even more explicitly the view of the judiciary that emerged from his sociological jurisprudence. "Law is not *made* by the courts, at the most promulgated by them," he emphasized, explaining that law was "not the independent creation of the judicial mind" but rather was "the resultant of the social forces reflecting the popular sense of right."[107]   The judge, therefore, was "but an instrument for the promulgation of this popular sense of right in its particular application to the cause at issue." Like the legislature, the judge does not make "living law" but "only declares that to be the law, which has been forced upon them, whether consciously or unconsciously, by the pressure of the popular sense of right, that popular sense of right being itself but the resultant of the social forces which are at play in every organized society."[108]   Tiedeman's view of

---

104. *Id.* This "extraordinary judicial power" itself was limited by the Constitution's separation of powers and checks and balances, Tiedeman observed. For example, the President and Congress are not bound by the Court's judgment on constitutional questions and are able to alter the size of the Court and its composition. By such means "the popular will may be realized" and the Court's ability to disregard it, thwarted. *Id.* at 160-62.

105. *Id.* at 164 n.1 (quoting J. LOWELL, DEMOCRACY AND OTHER ADDRESSES 24 (1887)).

106. *Id.* at 165.

107. Tiedeman, *Methods of Legal Education, supra* note 29, at 154.

108. *Id.* As noted here, Tiedeman's view that law is not "made," but rather results from the popular sense of right, applied equally to courts and legislatures. Tiedeman regarded as "an unwarrantable fiction" the notion that *either* the judge or the legislator "made" law; as he envisioned it, "all law, so far as it constituted a living rule of conduct, whether it takes the form of statute or of judicial decision, is but an expression of the popular sense of right through the popular agents, the legislator or the judge as the case may be." *Id.* From this conception of the law, Tiedeman proceeded to the heart of his criticism of the case method of legal education. "[T]he whole law or any appreciable part of it, on a particular subject, cannot be learned from the study of a few leading cases, but only from a very large number of cases." In addition to the physical

the judiciary, then, was not a rigid, formalistic conception of the judge as a scientific arbitrator, but rather a conception of the judge as an impartial expounder of the consensus that emerged from conflicting social forces—in a sense, the "conscience" of the popular will. It is this conception of the judiciary that lies behind Tiedeman's analysis of the limitations upon the legislative powers of the states and the federal government.

## III. CONSTITUTIONAL LIMITATIONS AND THE POLICE POWER

### A. *Tiedeman's Conception of the Police Power: The Definitional Limitation*

In the original preface to his treatise on the limitations of the police power, Tiedeman—using the same language that he used in his *Unwritten Constitution*—warned of the danger of "the absolutism of a democratic majority." With candor he indicated his purpose was to "awaken the public mind to a full appreciation of the power of constitutional limitations to protect private rights against the radical experimentations of social reformers." The object of the treatise was "to demonstrate, by a detailed discussion of the limitations upon the police power in the United States, that under the written constitutions, Federal and State, democratic absolutism is impossible in this country." This is true, argued Tiedeman, "as long as the popular reverence for the constitutions, in their restrictions upon governmental activity, is

---

impossibility of reading enough cases to learn the law—literally thousands of cases, Tiedeman argued—was the problem that the beginning law student, the "legal tyro," was not "mentally capable" of extracting the principles of the law from the adjudicated cases. *Id.* at 154. Learning the fundamental principles of the law was, he wrote, "not an elementary work which may be entrusted to beginners;" collecting together and formulating correctly the principles on which the adjudications rest was a task for "[a] few men of extraordinary mental powers"—presumably the editors of casebooks or the authors of treatises, like Tiedeman himself. *Id.* at 154-55. Under the case method, the "higher aim" of law professors—to make students "conspicuously original investigators in the law"—was "lost" on the average law student, Tiedeman argued. *Id.* at 155. He feared that the average student who studied law by the case method alone would become "what is so generally deprecated, a case-lawyer, who thinks the whole business of advocacy consists of persuading the court that the cases he cites . . . are to be followed, not because they enunciate a profound scientific truth, but merely because they have given judgment . . . on a similar set of facts." *Id.*

nourished and sustained by a prompt avoidance by the courts of any violations of their provisions, in word or in spirit."[109]

Tiedeman listed several specific constitutional provisions limiting the exercise of the police power: for example, the article I, section 10, prohibition upon bills of attainder, *ex post facto* laws, and the impairment of the obligations of contracts; and the fourteenth and fifteenth amendments.[110]  Tiedeman also cited Justice Chase's opinion in *Calder v. Bull*, that "certain vital principles in our free republican governments" also limit the legislative power.[111]  Although recognizing

---

109. C. TIEDEMAN, LIMITATIONS OF POLICE POWER, *supra* note 14, at vii-viii; 1 C. TIEDEMAN, STATE AND FEDERAL CONTROL, *supra* note 16, at vii-viii (preface dated Nov. 1, 1886).

110. 1 C. TIEDEMAN, STATE AND FEDERAL CONTROL, *supra* note 16, § 4, at 18-20. Tiedeman's complete list of provisions in the United States Constitution that limited governmental power, state or federal, encompassed provisions in article I, sections 9 and 10; most of the Bill of Rights (the first, second, third, fourth, fifth, and eighth amendments); and the Civil War Amendments (the thirteenth, fourteenth, and fifteenth amendments). Recognizing that some of these limitations—as they were then interpreted—limited only the federal government, Tiedeman nevertheless argued that comparable provisions could be found in the bills of rights of most state constitutions. *Id.* at 20.

111. *Id.* at 9.  Calder v. Bull, 3 U.S. (3 Dall.) 386 (1798), involved a challenge to the constitutionality of a Connecticut statute that set aside a decree of a probate court and granted a new hearing. The plaintiffs in error contended that the law was void as an *ex post facto* law, prohibited by the Constitution. ("No State shall . . . pass any . . . ex post facto Law . . . ." U.S. CONST. art. I, § 10, cl. 1.) The case thus presented to the Supreme Court for the first time the question of judicial review of acts of a state legislature. The Court affirmed the decision of the Supreme Court of Connecticut, which had held that there were no errors; the prohibition of *"ex post facto"* laws was interpreted to apply to criminal laws only, not to civil cases. Following the Court's practice at the time, each justice delivered his own opinion *seriatim.*  In his opinion, Justice Chase nevertheless presented a broad rationale for judicial review of legislative acts, applying not only the provisions of the written Constitution but also unwritten constitutional limitations as well.  The relevant portion of Justice Chase's opinion is worth quoting in full, as Tiedeman did in both editions of his treatise. (*See* C. TIEDEMAN, LIMITATIONS OF POLICE POWER, *supra* note 14, at 5-7; 1 C. TIEDEMAN, STATE AND FEDERAL CONTROL, *supra* note 16, § 2, at 8-10.)

> There are acts which the *Federal*, or *State* Legislature cannot do, *without exceeding their authority*. There are certain *vital* principles in our *free republican governments*, which will determine and overrule an *apparent and flagrant* abuse of *legislative* power; as to authorize *manifest injustice by positive law*; or to take away that security for *personal liberty*, or *private property*, for the protection whereof the government was established. An act of the legislature (for I cannot call it a *law*), contrary to the *great first principles* of the *social compact*, cannot be considered a *rightful exercise* of *legislative*

"courts have no authority to override the legislative judgment on the question of expediency or abstract justice in the enactment of a law," Tiedeman nevertheless observed that "a law which does not conform to the fundamental principles of free government and natural justice and morality, will prove ineffectual and become a dead letter." The reason, as he had suggested in the *Unwritten Constitution,* is that no law can be enforced, particularly in a country governed directly by the popular will, which does not receive "the moral and active support of a large majority of people" or which "violates reason and offends against the prevalent conceptions of right and justice."[112]

By far the most important limitation which Tiedeman would place on the police power was neither tied to explicit constitutional limitations nor based exclusively upon the prevalent sense of right or justice; it was, instead, a limitation which inhered in Tiedeman's very definition of the police power. The police power of the government, "as understood in the constitutional law of the United States, is simply the power of the government to establish provisions for the enforcement of the common as well as civil law maxim, *sic utere tuo ut alienum non laedas.*"[113]

---

authority. The obligation of a law, in governments established on *express compact, and on republican principles,* must be determined by the *nature of the power,* on which it is founded.

A few instances will suffice to explain what I mean. A law that punished a citizen for an *innocent* action, or, in other words, for an act, which, when done, was in violation of no *existing* law; a law that destroys or impairs the *lawful private* contracts of citizens; a law that makes a man *a judge in his own cause;* or a law that takes *property* from A. and gives it to B.: it is against all reason and justice, for a people to intrust a legislature with such powers; and therefore, it cannot be presumed that they have done it. The *genius,* the *nature* and the *spirit* of our state governments, amount to a prohibition of *such acts of legislation;* and the *general principles of law and reason* forbid them. The legislature may enjoin, permit, forbid and punish; they may declare *new* crimes; and establish rules of conduct for *all* its citizens in *future* cases; they may *command* what is right, and *prohibit* what is wrong; but they cannot change *innocence* into *guilt;* or punish *innocence* as a *crime;* or violate the right of an *antecedent lawful private contract;* or the *right of private property.* To maintain that our federal, or state, legislature possesses *such powers,* if they had not been *expressly* restrained; would, in my opinion, be a *political heresy,* altogether inadmissible in our *free republican governments.*
*Calder,* 3 U.S. (3 Dall.) at 388 (emphasis in original).

112. 1 C. TIEDEMAN, STATE AND FEDERAL CONTROL, *supra* note 16, § 2, at 11.

113. *Id.* § 1, at 4-5. Defined this way, exercise of the police power necessarily involved the imposition of restrictions and burdens upon the natural and other private rights of individuals. *Id.* at 4. Accordingly, Tiedeman

Any law which goes beyond that principle, which undertakes to abolish rights, the exercise of which does not involve an infringement of the rights of others, or to limit the exercise of rights beyond what is necessary to provide for the public welfare and the general security, cannot be included in the police power of the government.[114]

Tiedeman cited a mid-nineteenth-century state court decision stating "it must of course be within the range of legislative action to define the mode and manner in which every one may so use his own as not to injure others."[115] But Tiedeman was unwilling to leave such a determination solely to the legislature. He noted there have been "so many unjustifiable limitations imposed upon private rights and personal liberty," particularly sumptuary laws and laws for the correction of personal vice, "laws which have in view the moral and religious elevation of the individual against his will, that the modern world looks with distrust upon any exercise of the police power."[116] Hence, judges are to construe police regulations strictly: "The unwritten law of this country is in the main against the exercise of the police power, and the restrictions and burdens, imposed upon persons and property by police regulations, are jealously watched and scrutinized."[117]

In the first edition of his treatise on the police power, published in 1886, Tiedeman had made an effort to comprehend all branches of the law relevant to the police power.[118] By the time of the second edition of the treatise, case law had so expanded that Tiedeman required two volumes to "corral every important adjudication, which has been made by the State and Federal courts, on the various branches of the subject."[119] The expansion of Chapter IX, *Regulation of Trades and*

---

organized his treatise not in terms of types of regulations, but rather in terms of the types of rights restricted or burdened, with a threefold general classification: personal rights (including personal security, liberty, and private property), relative rights (arising between husband and wife, parent and child, guardian and ward, or master and servant), and statutory rights. *Id.* § 5, at 20-21.

114. *Id.* § 1, at 5. Tiedeman added that such a law is "a governmental usurpation," violating "the principles of abstract justice, as they have been developed under our republican institutions." *Id.*

115. *Id.* (citing the opinion of Chief Justice Redfield in the 1854 Vermont case, Thorpe v. Rutland & Burlington R.R., 27 Vt. 150 (1854), briefly discussed *supra* note 84).

116. *Id.* § 2, at 11-12.

117. *Id.* § 3, at 13. Tiedeman here also cited the holding of the New York Court of Appeals in Berthoff v. O'Reilly, 74 N.Y. 509 (1878), discussed *supra* note 89, that the due process clause is to be interpreted broadly, as the main guaranty of private rights against unjust legislation.

118. C. TIEDEMAN, LIMITATIONS OF POLICE POWER, *supra* note 14.

119. 1 C. TIEDEMAN, STATE AND FEDERAL CONTROL, *supra* note 16, at ix.

*Occupations,* illustrates the change that had occurred in the law during the fourteen-year interval between the publications of the two editions of the work. Tiedeman added a score of new sections: regulations to prevent fraud, the reasonableness of regulations of prices and charges, regulations of wages of workmen, regulations of hours of labor, regulations of the business of insurance, antitrust regulations, prohibition of trade in vice, monopolies and franchises, and so on.[120] Also, in recognition of the expanding jurisdiction of the national government through the interstate commerce clause, Tiedeman not only expanded the last chapter (*The Location of Police Power in the Federal System of Government*) but also changed several chapter headings from "police regulations" to merely "regulations" and the title of the treatise itself from *Limitations of Police Power* to *State and Federal Control of Persons and Property.*[121]

## B. *Tiedeman's Conception of the Police Power in Practice: Three Examples*

Tiedeman's discussions of three particular types of regulations—laws prohibiting the charging of usurious interest, laws prohibiting trade in vice, and laws regulating the hours of labor—illustrate his conception of the police power and how that conception relates to his overall philosophy of law.

With each, Tiedeman drew a basic distinction between legitimate regulations—that is, regulations that affected only trespasses or other matters of legitimate governmental concerns under Tiedeman's formulation—and regulations that went beyond the proper scope of the police power. It is clear from Tiedeman's discussion of these particulars that he sought not merely to summarize the state of the law as it had developed by his time, but rather to show what the law should be, given his general formulation of the police power. Thus, his treatise was not

---

120. *Id.* §§ 85-131, at 233-612.

121. Despite this explicit recognition of the greater role played by the federal government in the control of persons and property, Tiedeman's own constitutional theory limited the power of Congress under the commerce clause by a fairly strict adherence to federalism: because the federal government is one of enumerated powers—i.e. powers granted by the Constitution to the United States government either expressly or "by necessary implication"—the police power generally resides in the states. 2 C. TIEDMAN, STATE AND FEDERAL CONTROL, *supra* note 23, at 1018-1019; *see also* C. TIEDEMAN, UNWRITTEN CONSTITUTION, *supra* note 46, at 142 (United States government, as one of enumerated powers, cannot exercise any power unless it is expressly or impliedly delegated to the United States).

a "conservative" interpretation of the legal precedents; it was in fact a treatise that urged innovation, even radical innovation, in the law.[122]

### 1. Legislation Regulating Interest Rates

Tiedeman prefaced his discussion of usury laws by distinguishing two kinds of regulation of interest: the determination by the legislature of the rate of interest recoverable on contracts for the payment of money in the absence of express stipulation by the parties; and the determination by the legislature of the rate of interest the parties to a contract may agree upon. The first is a valid police regulation, the object of which is to aid the parties in effecting settlements when they have not previously agreed upon any rate of interest. If the parties disagree with the statutory rate, they can agree on any other rate. The second is not a valid regulation. "Free trade in money is as much a right as free trade in merchandise" because "[i]nterest is nothing more than the price asked for the use of money," and price is determined by the law of supply and demand.[123] Tiedeman recognized only one justification for

---

122. For example, with respect to the distinction he drew between laws prohibiting trade in a vice (which he deemed legitimate exercises of the police power) and laws prohibiting indulgence in the vice itself (which he did not deem legitimate police regulations), a distinction discussed *infra* notes 128-51 and accompanying text, Tiedeman observed that this distinction "ha[d] not been endorsed by the courts." In the second edition of his treatise, nevertheless, he did not change the text "because the adverse decisions have not convinced me that the distinction is unsound." 1 C. TIEDEMAN, STATE AND FEDERAL CONTROL, *supra* note 16, § 121, at 510.

123. 1 C. TIEDEMAN, STATE AND FEDERAL CONTROL, *supra* note 16, § 106, at 351. In the section of his treatise that followed, Tiedeman maintained that free trade was "an undoubted constitutional right," and he defined free trade as essentially the right to determine whether, with whom, and on what terms one shall have business dealings. *Id.* at 353. Thus he considered the common law prohibitions against forestalling, regrating, and engrossing to be invalid exercises of the police power. *Id.* § 107, at 355-56. Similarly, speculation—even if one were to "corner the market" in a given commodity—should not be restrained, he argued:

> Because one man has the capital wherewith to buy up all the corn or wheat in our great Western markets, and to cause in consequence a rise in the value of these commodities, does not justify State interference with his liberty of action, any more than would police regulation of the whole capitalist class be permissible.

*Id.* at 354. Tiedeman also argued:

> It is, without doubt, an immoral act, to ask an unconscionably high price for a commodity, taking advantage of the pressing wants of the people; and it may, under a high code of morals, be held to be an extortion, for one to purchase and hold merchandise for the purpose

usury laws: the lending of money was a special privilege, conferred by Parliament, in the days when the common law condemned as usury any taking of money for the use of money. This reason furnished no justification for the present existence of such laws, since in the light of modern opinion the lending of money on interest is "in no sense a privilege."[124] Tiedeman recognized that long acquiescence in the constitutionality of usury laws "render it very unlikely that the courts will pronounce them unconstitutional, however questionable legal writers and authorities may consider them." But Tiedeman argued that such acquiescence ought not preclude an inquiry into constitutionality.[125] Tiedeman's position on usury laws stands in contrast to that of Thomas M. Cooley, who also recognized that this form of governmental regulation of prices as "an exception difficult to defend on principle;" but Cooley maintained that the power to regulate the rate of interest "has been employed from the earliest days, and has been too long acquiesced in to be questioned now."[126] Tiedeman, consistent with his discussion of *stare decisis* in the *Unwritten Constitution*, thought that judges must invalidate rules which became "difficult to defend on principle."[127]

## 2. Legislation Dealing with Vices

In another section of *State and Federal Control of Persons and Property*, Tiedeman made a distinction that was not endorsed by the courts but he nevertheless believed sound. The distinction was between vice and trade in vice.

---

of gaining from its sale more than a fair profit; but it cannot be claimed that there is a trespass upon the rights of others in doing so, or that the rights of others are thereby threatened with injury. One is simply exercising his ordinary rights in demanding whatever price he pleases for his property.

*Id.* at 357. Tiedeman distinguished certain kinds of combinations in restraint of trade—including "cornering" the market by fraud—which he generally regarded as proper objects of prohibition under the common law and modern state and federal antitrust legislation. *See generally id.* §§ 110-13, at 371-416.

124. *Id.* § 106, at 352.

125. *Id.* at 352-53.

126. T. COOLEY, GENERAL PRINCIPLES OF CONSTITUTIONAL LAW 246 (2d ed. 1891).

127. Citing Cooley's observation concerning usury laws, T. COOLEY, *supra* note 126, Tiedeman noted that he "differ[ed] with the learned judge in his opinion that long acquiescence in such laws preclud[ed] an inquiry into their constitutionality." 1 C. TIEDEMAN, STATE AND FEDERAL CONTROL, *supra* note 16, § 106, at 353.

Tiedeman defined vice as "an inordinate, and hence immoral, gratification of one's passions and desires," which primarily damages one's self. So defined, vice was not a trespass upon the rights of others, and therefore was not subject legitimately to police regulation.[128]  On the other hand, no one can claim the right to make a trade in vice; "a business may always be prohibited, whose object is to furnish means for the indulgence of a vicious propensity or desire."  According to Tiedeman, fornication was not a punishable offense, but prohibiting the keeping of houses of prostitution was acceptable; the state could not punish gambling, but the state could prohibit the keeping of gambling-houses or the sale of lottery tickets.[129]

Tiedeman recognized that, because of the interdependence of individuals in society ("*no man liveth unto himself*"), no one could be addicted to vices, even of the most trivial character, without doing damage to the material interests of society, and affecting each individual of the community. But these evils are "indirect and remote and do not involve trespasses upon rights," he maintained.[130]  Indeed, these evils are "so remote that very many other causes co-operate to produce the result," making it "difficult, if not impossible, to ascertain what is the controlling and real cause."[131]  This uncertainty, and the practical

---

128.	C. TIEDEMAN, STATE AND FEDERAL CONTROL, *supra* note 16, § 60, at 180-81. Tiedeman explained:

> The object of the police power is the prevention of crime, the protection of rights against the assault of others. The police power of the government cannot be brought into operation for the purpose of exacting obedience to the rules of morality, and banishing vice and sin from the world. . . . The municipal law has only to do with trespasses. It cannot be called into play in order to save one from the evil consequences of his own vices, for the violation of a right by the action of another must exist or be threatened, in order to justify the interference of law.

*Id.* at 181.

129.	*Id.* § 121, at 509-10. Tiedeman did not explain why trade in vice "may always be prohibited;" he simply asserted that "[a] business that panders to vice may and should be strenuously prohibited, if possible." *Id.* at 508. As discussed *infra* notes 147-51 and accompanying text, Tiedeman's distinction is untenable.

130.	1 C. Tiedeman, State and Federal Control, *supra* note 16, § 60, at 180-81.  Crimes involved direct "trespasses upon rights," not the "secondary or consequential damage to others" that might result from an individual's indulgence in one's vices. *Id.*

131.	*Id.* at 181. Tiedeman gave the example of an alcoholic husband whose intemperance "may result in the suffering of his wife from want, because of his consequent inability to earn the requisite means of support." *Id.* at 181 n.1. The husband's vice may be a cause of the wife's suffering,

> [b]ut she may have been equally responsible for her own suffering on account of her recklessness in marrying him, or she may be extrava-

inability to determine responsibility, has resulted in the rule of proximate causation in tort law—a rule of objective validity that Tiedeman applied in his constitutional analysis.[132] To make acts criminal that did not result in trespass upon others—acts that would not be actionable in tort because the damages they caused were too remote—would be an unconstitutional deprivation of liberty, without due process of law, he argued.[133] Thus, for example, "[i]t cannot be made a legal wrong for one to become intoxicated in the privacy of his

---

> gant and wasteful; or she may by her own conduct have driven him into intemperance, and many other facts may be introduced to render it very doubtful, to which of these moral delinquencies her suffering may be traced as the real moving cause.

*Id.*

132. Tiedeman regarded the rule of proximate causation as one not merely of expediency but rather as one that "has its foundation in fact," a rule that was "deduced from the accumulated experience of ages, . . . a law of nature, immutable and invarying." *Id.* at 184. In extending the tort law principle to the status of a constitutional limitation upon the criminal law, Tiedeman reasoned as follows:

> If this is a necessary limitation upon the recovery of damages where a clearly established legal right is trespassed upon, there surely is greater reason for its application to a case where there is no invasion of a right, . . . When, therefore, the damage to others, imputed as the cause to an act in itself constituting no trespass, is made the foundation of a public regulation or prohibition of that act, it must be clearly shown that the act is the real and the predominant cause of the damage. The intervention of so many co-operating causes in all cases of remote damage makes this a practical impossibility.

*Id.* at 182. Thus, Tiedeman concluded, an act cannot be made unlawful simply because in certain cases a remote damage is suffered by others on account of it.

133. *Id.* at 184. Tiedeman even argued that to prohibit acts that were not trespasses would violate "[t]he inalienable right to 'liberty and the pursuit of happiness.'" *Id.* He left open the question whether acts that were not trespasses nevertheless could be made actionable in tort—for example, the leasing of premises where intoxicating liquors are sold, resulting in injury to third parties because of an intoxicated person's acts, as in Berthoff v. O'Reilly, 74 N.Y. 309 (1878), discussed *supra* note 89. Citing the case, Tiedeman noted that the rule of proximate cause "may be changed, and the damages imputed to the remote cause, without violating any constitutional limitation." 1 C. TIEDEMAN, STATE AND FEDERAL CONTROL, *supra* note 16, at 183 & n.1. If this is true under Tiedeman's analysis, then his distinction between vice and crime appears to have a loophole: it permits legislatures to prohibit certain acts *de facto*, not by making them criminal, but merely by making their remote consequences actionable in tort. To be consistent, Tiedeman should have argued that *Berthoff v. O'Reilly* was improperly decided—that it stretched too far the concept of proximate cause; but this apparently Tiedeman was reluctant to do.

own room," because the person who becomes drunk in private "has committed no wrong, *i.e.*, he has violated no right, and hence he cannot be punished" under Tiedeman's analysis, although he conceded that the courts had not endorsed the distinction he drew between vice and crime, which denied to government the power to punish vice as vice.[134]

One court nearly accepted Tiedeman's position. In *Ah Lim v. Territory of Washington*,[135] decided in 1890, the defendant was appealing his conviction under a statute that prohibited the smoking of opium.[136] The appellant's brief was replete with references to the first edition of Tiedeman's treatise. Citing Tiedeman, appellant's counsel put forth the following propositions:

> The inalienable right to "liberty and pursuit of happiness" is violated when a man is prohibited from doing anything which does not involve a trespass on others. That the vice of smoking opium is grossly immoral is no argument in favor of the validity of this statute. The police power of the state cannot be brought into operation for the purpose of exacting obedience to the rules of morality, and banishing vice and sin from the world. The municipal law has only to do with trespasses. It cannot be called into play in order to save one from the evil consequences of his own vices; for a violation of a right by the action of another must exist or be threatened in order to justify interference by law.[137]

---

134. *Id.* at 182, 184-85. As an example of the courts' failure to observe his distinction, Tiedeman cited the Arkansas Supreme Court's decision upholding that state's statute on profanity, which did not confine the offense to swearing in public. *Id.* at 185 (citing Bodenhauer v. State, 60 Ark. 10 (1894)). He further cited several decisions upholding statutes that made it criminal to visit houses of prostitution or to engage in fornication. Tiedeman regarded these statutes as having gone too far: rather than confining their scope to "the offense of providing the means of indulgence in vice," such as the keeping of "disorderly houses"—which would have been a permissible exercise of the police power, under Tiedeman's analysis—they impermissibly prohibited the indulgence in vice itself. *Id.*

135. 1 Wash. 156 (1890).

136. The statute provided, "Any person or persons who shall smoke or inhale opium . . . shall be deemed guilty of a misdemeanor." *Id.* at 166-67. The provision was an 1883 amendment of a chapter of the 1881 territorial code that dealt with opium and which apparently sought mainly to prohibit the keeping of opium dens. *See id.* at 167 (Scott, J., dissenting).

137. *Id.* at 156-57 (citations omitted). In addition to Tiedeman, appellant's counsel also cited Cooley's *Constitutional Limitations* and Blackstone. Counsel for the Territory argued that these alleged violations of rights involved "[n]o special constitutional limitation or inhibition." *Id.* at 157. Counsel for the Territory further argued, "'The question whether a statute is a valid exercise of the legislative power is to be determined solely by reference to constitutional

These arguments did not persuade a majority of the court, however; by a split vote of 3-2, the court sustained the conviction.

Speaking for the majority, Judge Dunbar observed that "if the state concludes that a given habit it detrimental to either the moral, mental or physical well being of one of its citizens to such an extent that it is liable to become a burthen upon society, it has an undoubted right to restrain the citizen from commission of that act."[138] Such a restraint is not an encroachment upon the rights of the individual, but "simply an adjustment of the relative rights and responsibilities incident to the changing condition of society."[139]

---

restraints . . . ,'" not general principles of "'natural justice and equity.'" *Id.* at 158 (quoting Bertholf v. O'Reilly, 74 N.Y. 509 (1878), discussed *supra* note 89, and citing, *inter alia*, Thorpe v. Rutland & Burlington R.R., 27 Vt. 140 (1851), discussed *supra* note 84).

138. *Ah Lim*, 1 Wash. at 164. Judge Dunbar compared the state's interest in the restraint of narcotic drug use to the state's interest in compulsory education. Education is compelled, not for the benefit of the child, but because "the state has an interest in the intellectual condition of each of its citizens . . . ." *Id.* at 163. Because state tax revenues are spent to build and maintain prisons, insane asylums, hospitals, and poor houses, "surely it ought to have no small interest in, and no small control over, the moral, mental, and physical condition of its citizens." *Id.* at 164.

> If a man willfully cuts off his hand or maims himself in such a way that he is liable to become a public charge, no one will doubt the right of the state to punish him; and if he smokes opium, thereby destroying his intellect and shattering his nerves, it is difficult to see why a limitation of power should be imposed upon the state in such a case.

*Id.*

139. *Id.* at 166. The court denied the existence of "an absolute or unqualified right or liberty guaranteed to any member of society;" rather, it held that scope of an individual's rights "depends largely upon the amount of protection which he receives from the government." *Id.* at 165. Hence, if government does little for individuals—for example, leaving to private charity the amelioration of poverty—one may pursue one's own happiness "without much regard to the rights of government." *Id.* at 166. With the rise of the modern welfare state, however, the situation changes:

> [N]ow all civilized governments make provisions for their unfortunates; and progress in this direction has been wonderful even since noted sages like Blackstone lectured upon the inalienable rights of man. Not only is the protection of individual property becoming more secure, but the vicious are restrained and controlled, and the indigent and unfortunate are maintained at the expense of the government, in comfort and decency, and the natural liberties and rights of the subject must yield up something to each of these burthens which advancing civilization is imposing upon the state.

*Id.*

Judge Scott, in his dissenting opinion, argued that the statute was void, as an impermissible exercise of the police power, in that it was "altogether too sweeping in its terms."[140] The dissenting judge did not cite Tiedeman, but did quote Cooley, "'The right of every man to do what he will with his own, not interfering with the reciprocal rights of others, is accepted among the fundamentals of our law.'"[141] More importantly, Judge Scott apparently adopted Tiedeman's distinction between trade in vice and mere indulgence in vice. To prohibit the keeping of opium dens "was a legitimate exercise of police powers;"[142] to prohibit willfully injuring oneself by smoking or inhaling opium may also be a valid exercise of the police power;[143] but to prohibit all smoking of opium—whether it results in injury to the person or otherwise affects society—was "an unwarranted infringement of individual rights, and therefore unconstitutional."[144]

Tiedeman's suggestion that the proximity or directness of the harm determines trespass might help explain the split in the Washington court: the dissenting judge saw no real or substantial relation of the statute to the public health or morals or safety, while the majority saw such a relation. The difference, in other words, was not so much in the understanding of the law—though admittedly, each side of the court applied different rules of construction reflecting contrasting views of

---

140. *Id.* at 174 (Scott, J., dissenting). Judge Stiles concurred in the dissenting opinion.

141. *Id.* at 176 (quoting T. COOLEY, *supra* note 126, at 385).

142. *Id.* at 167.

143. *Id.* at 170. Judge Scott conceded that "[e]very act of the individual which has a direct tendency to render him unfit to perform the duties he owes to society, is a rightful subject of legislation" and that therefore "[s]ociety has an interest in the promotion and preservation of the bodily, mental and moral health of each individual citizen." *Id.* However, noting the obligation of the courts to exercise the power of judicial review as a check on legislative powers, discussed *infra* note 145, he argued that the police power could not legitimately extend to "every self regarding act of the person which the legislature may choose to prohibit upon the ground that it is injurious to the individual." *Ah Lim*, 1 Wash. at 171.

144. *Ah Lim*, 1 Wash. at 173. The judge added, "Individual desires are too sacred to be ruthlessly violated where only acts are involved which purely appertain to the person, and which do not clearly result in an injury to society, unless, possibly, thus rendered necessary in order to prevent others from like actions which to them are injurious." *Id.*

judicial review[145]—but rather in their understanding of what might be called the social facts of the case.[146]

The disagreement between the majority and the dissenters in *Ah Lim* suggests a basic conceptual difficulty with Tiedeman's distinction between vice and trade in vice. Tiedeman offered no explanation why, under his formulation, trade in vice comes properly within the scope of the police power, while indulgence in the vice itself does not. Setting aside the problem of first determining whether something is indeed a "vice,"[147] one confronts the following question: If personal indulgence in a vice involves (by definition) no trespass on the rights of others, why

---

145. The majority stressed that courts generally should defer to legislatures the determination of acts injurious to the public. Whether the moderate use only of opium was not deleterious and consequently cannot be prohibited "is a question of fact which can only be inquired into by the legislature," Judge Dunbar wrote. *Id.* at 164. In contrast, the dissenting judge emphasized the duty of the courts to act as a check upon the legislative power. Judge Scott argued that the majority position permitted the legislature to decide that "every act of smoking or inhaling opium to be injurious to the person so doing, no matter how long or how short the duration, or how great or how small the quantity, or under what conditions or circumstances the same might have been used." *Id.* at 172. For the courts to refrain from reviewing so broad a determination would in effect make the legislature "the sole and absolute judge of the effect upon the individual, of the act forbidden" and hence "the sole judge of the constitutionality of its own acts of this character." *Id.*

146. The majority stressed that smoking opium was "a recognized evil in this country . . . an insidious and dangerous vice, a loathsome, disgusting and degrading habit that is becoming dangerously common with the youth of the country, . . ." and that it therefore had become regarded as "a proper subject of legislation in every western state." *Id.* at 164-65. The dissenting judge, in contrast, explicitly noted that however "repulsive and degrading" the habit of smoking opium had become generally, "There is a distinction to be recognized between the use and abuse of any article or substance." *Id.* at 174-75. Judge Scott stressed that the offense charged in this case "relate[d] purely to the private action or conduct of the individual" and that the statute in question made criminal "a single inhalation of opium, even by a person in the seclusion of his own house, away from the sight and without the knowledge of any other person." *Id.* at 167.

147. Tiedeman provided no definition of "vice," but perhaps there was less room for disagreement in the late nineteenth century than there is today. The differing responses of the *Ah Lim* majority and the dissenting judge to the smoking of opium—the former stressing opium abuse almost in crisis terms but the latter distinguishing use from abuse, as discussed *supra* note 146—indicate that even the smoking of opium had a somewhat uncertain status as a "vice" at the time. Indeed, state and federal legislation criminalizing the use of opiates had a rather recent origin; laws first appeared in the western states where Chinese immigrants had introduced the practice. *See* W. ELDRIDGE, NARCOTICS AND THE LAW 3-4 (1962).

should society prohibit trade in the vice—i.e., business relationships that merely facilitate acts that do not harm others? Put in more concrete terms, does it make sense to insist—as Tiedeman did—that the state may not use the police power to forbid sex between unmarried adults but may prohibit the keeping of a house of prostitution, or that the state may not forbid gambling but may close down gambling parlors?

Tiedeman's rationale for the distinction, like the rationale for the distinctions made by Judge Scott in his dissenting opinion in *Ah Lim*, rests upon the assumption that society has a legitimate interest—one that it may protect through use of the coercive power of the state—in preventing certain acts, even though they do not involve any direct trespasses on others. Apparently Tiedeman regarded the commercialization of virtually any vice as such an act: hence, trade in vice was always legitimately subject to the police power.[148] Tiedeman also distinguished from his general rule a type of vice which he called "social vice:" acts which by their nature involved injury to society, even when indulged in private. An example was the vice of fornication, which created social injury "of a strikingly strong character, in that it makes probable an increase of the public burden by the birth of illegitimate children, as well as it is the occasion of a wrong to the children so born." Tiedeman conceded that punishment of fornication therefore was "justifiable on these grounds," and that the offense was "properly distinguished from such strictly personal vices, involving no trespass upon the rights of others, such as drunkenness."[149]

This further distinction between "social" vices and "strictly personal" vices is an especially troublesome one—one which calls into question the validity of Tiedeman's overall distinction between crimes and vices. Consider, for example, Tiedeman's characterization of drunkenness as a "strictly personal" vice, in the context of his argument against the constitutionality of legislation prohibiting liquor consumption. Again, consistent with his overall rule delineating the scope of the police power, he regarded as constitutional the prohibition of the sale of liquor, but not the prohibition of consumption. Even laws prohibiting the habit of "treating"—that is, furnishing liquor to others—went too far, "inasmuch as the persons who are directly injured . . . are all willing participants, except in the very extreme cases of beastly intoxication . . . ." Such laws therefore were "open to the constitutional

---

148. "The keeping of disorderly houses and places of gambling is, *of course, prohibited, because it is making a business of pandering to vices*; and, for that reason, comes properly within the jurisdiction of the police power." 1 C. TIEDEMAN, STATE AND FEDERAL CONTROL, *supra* note 16, § 60, at 185 (emphasis added).

149. *Id.* at 185-86.

objection of a deprivation or restraint of liberty, in a case in which no right has been invaded."[150]   But could one not use the same argument with respect to fornication, which Tiedeman conceded could be punished because of the social injury it created?   Introduction of the concept of "social" vice, therefore, weakened Tiedeman's analysis by blurring the distinction between trespasses, which clearly were the law's business, and "vices," which were not.   Although perhaps far-reaching for his time, Tiedeman's formulation fell far short of modern libertarian arguments for the decriminalization of "victimless crimes."[151]

### 3. Legislation Regulating the Hours of Labor

Tiedeman's discussion of limitations on the police power more closely resembles the laissez-faire constitutional position, as it has been traditionally understood, when he analyzed labor regulations.[152]   Here,

---

150.  *Id.* § 61, at 188.  This argument appeared in the section dealing with sumptuary laws, which Tiedeman treated as he did laws dealing with vices: he regarded them as "violations of the inalienable right to 'liberty and the pursuit of happiness'" in that they involved "a deprivation of liberty and property—through a limitation upon the means of enjoyment—without due process of law."  *Id.* at 187.  Tiedeman drew a similar distinction with respect to the "vice" of transvestism.  He considered as "probably constitutional" the prohibition of the appearance in public of men in women's garb, and *vice versa*, because the practice "could serve no useful purpose, and tends to public immorality and the perpetration of frauds."  *Id.* at 189.  He drew the line, however, at the prohibition of cross-dressing in entirety; he argued that the state could not constitutionally prohibit the wearing of particular articles of clothing usually worn by the opposite sex.  *Id.*

151.  A more detailed analysis of Tiedeman's distinction between crime and vice, compared with modern libertarian formulations, is of course a topic beyond the scope of this Article.  For a modern libertarian view generally, see Hospers, *Libertarianism and Legal Paternalism,* in LIBERTARIAN READER 135 (T. Machan ed. 1982) (arguing that the state has no right to prohibit actions that do not harm others, and defining "harm" narrowly, in terms of the use of physical force or fraud).  For modern arguments for the decriminalization of "victimless crimes," see generally G. GEIS, NOT THE LAW'S BUSINESS: AN EXAMINATION OF HOMOSEXUALITY, ABORTION, PROSTITUTION, NARCOTICS, AND GAMBLING IN THE UNITED STATES (1979).

152.  One scholar has observed that "liberty of contract," although the juristic equivalent of economic liberty generally, was associated almost exclusively with judicial decisions concerning labor laws. A. PAUL, *supra* note 2, at 67 n.15.  Perhaps this was so because, in the eyes of laissez-faire constitutionalists, it was labor legislation generally that posed the most important challenge to laissez-faire principles.  Tiedeman noted that "[i]n no phase of human relations is there a more widespread manifestation of legislative determination to interfere with and to restrict the constitutional liberty of

too, however, his analysis involved not merely a "conservative" interpretation of legal precedents but rather a reformulation of the law consistent with his laissez-faire principles.

Tiedeman regarded liberty of contract as a right the law should guarantee equally to the employer and the employee. Although recognizing that the legal equality between employer and employee was nothing more than "a legal fiction,"[153] he nevertheless limited the legitimate regulation of the labor contract to the preservation of the health and safety of the worker[154] or to the protection against fraud. All other regulation—including regulation of workers' wages and hours—would violate the constitutional guarantee of liberty of contract, which Tiedeman argued was "intended to operate equally and impartially upon both employer and employee."[155]

---

contract, than in the contract for labor between employer and employee." 1 C. TIEDEMAN, STATE AND FEDERAL CONTROL, *supra* note 16, § 98, at 315.

153. "[T]here can be no substantial equality between the man, who has not wherewith to provide himself with food and shelter for the current day, and one, whether you call him capitalist or employer, who is able to put the former into a position to earn his food and shelter. The employer occupies a vantage ground which enables him, in a majority of cases, to practically dictate the terms of employment." *Id.*

154. Tiedeman regarded as legitimate, or constitutional, regulations that were "reasonable safeguards" of the health and safety of workers, provided the regulations were not in opposition to "the old common law theory of the non-liability of the employer for injuries sustained by the employee, either through accident or the carelessness or negligence of the fellow-servant." *Id.* § 103, at 339; *see also* 2 C. TIEDEMAN, STATE AND FEDERAL CONTROL, *supra* note 23, at 736-49 (discussing the constitutionality of regulations of "unwholesome and objectionable trades," and of the regulations of mines). Therefore, Tiedeman argued that the legislature could enact a law that prohibited, for example, the manufacture of cigars in tenement houses, for such activity was "considered by some to so taint the atmosphere as to endanger the health of the occupants of the house." Although he cited with approval the New York case declaring such a statute unconstitutional, *In re* Jacobs, 98 N.Y. 98 (1885), he did so on the grounds that the court correctly held that the regulation did not tend to promote the public health but, rather, was a "taking" of property without due process of law. The court "would have trespassed upon the powers of the legislature" if it had undertaken to pass on the necessity of the regulation, argued Tiedeman; "[i]t falls within the legislative discretion in every case to decide upon the necessity for the exercise of its police power." 2 C. TIEDEMAN, STATE AND FEDERAL CONTROL, *supra* note 23, at 738.

155. 1 C. TIEDEMAN, STATE AND FEDERAL CONTROL, *supra* note 16, § 98, at 316. Tiedeman had a generally positive attitude toward labor unions, regarding them as legitimate means of reducing the disparity in bargaining strength between employer and employee—and therefore of protecting the worker's liberty of contract. For example, he noted with approval the rejection of the

Discussing different types of laws regulating the hours of labor, Tiedeman again drew a distinction, paralleling the one he made concerning laws regulating rates of interest. Statutes which simply defined what constituted a day's work, in the absence of an agreement otherwise, did not interfere with liberty of contract any more than statutes which merely prescribed the legal rate of interest.[156] But statutes which determined the hours of labor, either directly by prohibiting labor above a proscribed maximum or indirectly by making obligatory extra compensation for overtime, violated the constitutional liberty of contract of persons who were *sui juris*, and hence were not legitimate exercises of the police power.[157]

---

common law rule that regarded labor organizations as criminal conspiracies in restraint of trade; in rejecting this rule, he argued, American courts "have merely secured to the workman the same liberty of contract, which the capitalist has enjoyed at the common law, and which . . . [is] the constitutional right of every man." *Id.* § 114, at 419. Similarly, he rejected the argument that the statutory exemption of labor organizations from the restrictions of the antitrust laws was unconstitutional because it granted special protection to laborers that were denied to capitalists. Rather, he argued, such legislation was "an undoubted, and, from the practical standpoint, probably unassailable determination of the State to diminish the natural inequalities of capital and labor, by prohibiting combinations of capital and permitting combinations of labor." *Id.* at 423. Although the "thorough-going individualist" might justifiably "condemn any restrictions upon voluntary combinations of either capital or labor," Tiedeman noted, "it does not seem unreasonable" for the law to favor combinations of labor. "The individual laborer is completely at the mercy of the employer, if he cannot combine with his fellows to maintain a standard of wages and to control the terms of the labor contract in other matters." *Id.* at 424.

Tiedeman's position may be contrasted with that of his English counterpart, Albert Venn Dicey, who regarded late-nineteenth century English legislation that facilitated collective bargaining as too favorable to labor combinations. Dicey argued that in England the pendulum had swung too far in the opposite direction, in reaction against late-eighteenth century laws that had forbidden labor combinations altogether. He considered the legislation of the transitional period—the early-nineteenth century legislation that tolerated labor combinations, making them not unlawful *per se* but subjecting them to the same legal restrictions as other combinations in restraint of trade—as the best approximation to a policy of "free trade in labor," which treated the employer and employee equally. *See* A. DICEY, *supra* note 85, at 270-71. Unlike Tiedeman, then, Dicey apparently did not regard employer and employee as naturally unequal in their bargaining positions.

156. 1 C. TIEDEMAN, STATE AND FEDERAL CONTROL, *supra* note 16, § 102, at 333-34.

157. *Id.* An exception, of course, was legislation determining the hours of government employees, where the state itself is a party to the employment contract.

Although Tiedeman recognized the legitimacy of child-labor legislation,[158] his understanding of the class of persons who were *sui juris* was quite broad, encompassing virtually all adults. Tiedeman made no exception for women, for as he saw it "the constitutional guaranty of the liberty of contract applies to women, married or single, as well as to men."[159] Neither did he exempt "unwholesome employments" from his rule: the danger to the health of the worker was not a constitutional justification for interference with individual liberty of contract.[160] The State could legitimately regulate the hours of employment only where such regulations affected either public employees or employees of public contractors.[161]

In discussing liberty of contract, Tiedeman acknowledged that the courts did not uniformly follow his analysis, particularly in applying "the constitutional guaranty of the liberty of contract" equally to women, married or single, as well as to men.[162] One court that did accept

---

158. The exception of children from the general rule regarding liberty of contract posed no conceptual difficulty for Tiedeman. "Minors are the wards of the nation, and even the control of them by parents is subject to the unlimited supervisory control of the State." *Id.* at 335. Accordingly, "there has never been, and never can be any question" as to the constitutionality of regulations controlling and limiting the powers of minors to contract for labor. *Id.*

159. *Id.* at 336.

160. Tiedeman presented an *argumentum ad absurdum*:

But if the danger to the health of the workman is a constitutional justification for such an interference with individual liberty of contract, in the case of particularly unwholesome employments; the same reason could be appealed to, only in a less degree, to justify the regulations of the hours of labor in all employments. For there is no other cause, equally common and general, of impaired health, broken-down constitutions and shortened lives, than excessive, and hence exhausting labor; it matters not whether the occupation is wholesome or unwholesome. The same collision between fact and theory, as to the legal equality of all men, again blocks the way to a rational regulation of the unequal relations of employer and employee.

*Id.* at 337-38.

161. Where the regulations applied to government employees, "the constitutionality of the regulation cannot be questioned" because the government, as a party to the contract, had the right to insist on a provision regarding hours of employment. Similarly, the government, as a party to an agreement with a contractor, had the right to limit the hours worked by employees on public works projects. *Id.* at 338.

162. He noted that "[w]hile women, married and single, have always been under restrictions as to the kinds of employment in which they might engage, and are still generally denied any voice in the government of the country, single women have always had an unrestricted liberty of contract." *Id.* at 335-36. Married women, however, generally were denied this freedom "on the ground of

Tiedeman's analysis was the Illinois Supreme Court—not surprisingly, since a modern commentator has regarded that court as "the pathfinder" in making use of the doctrine of liberty of contract.[163]

In *Ritchie v. People*,[164] decided in 1895, the Illinois Supreme Court held unconstitutional a statute providing "no female shall be employed in any factory or workshop more than eight hours in any one day or forty-eight hours in any one week."[165] The court cited Tiedeman's *Limitations of Police Power*:

> In so far as the employment of a certain class in a particular occupation may threaten or inflict damage upon the public or third persons, there can be no doubt as to the constitutionality of any statute which prohibits their prosecution of that trade. But it is questionable, except in the case of minors, whether the prohibition can rest upon the claim that the employment will prove hurtful to them.[166]

---

public policy, in order to unify the material interests as well as the personal relations of husband and wife." This discrimination against married women, however, was gradually being eliminated; given this development, Tiedeman argued, "there seems to be no escape from the conclusion" that the constitutional guarantee applied to all women, as it did to all men. *Id.* at 336. As an example of a court that did not recognize this, Tiedeman cited a decision by the Massachusetts Supreme Court, upholding a law regulating the hours of labor for women "on the ground that women are still more or less under the tutelage of the State, and need the same protection of the State against the oppression of the employer, as do minors." *Id.* (citing Commonwealth v. Hamilton Mfg. Co., 120 Mass. 383 (1876)).

163. A. PAUL, *supra* note 2, at 51 (citing two cases decided in 1892: Frorer v. People, 141 Ill. 171, 186-87 (1892), which struck down a statute prohibiting mining or manufacturing companies from keeping "truck stores," holding that it was "class legislation" which hindered "that freedom in contracting which is allowed to all others;" and Ramsey v. People, 142 Ill. 380 (1892), which struck down Illinois' coal "screening" act on similar grounds).

164. 155 Ill. 98, 40 N.E. 454 (1895).

165. *Id.* at 102, 40 N.E. at 455.

166. *Id.* at 115, 40 N.E. at 459 (quoting C. TIEDEMAN, LIMITATIONS OF POLICE POWER, *supra* note 14, at 199). In the section quoted from the first edition of his treatise on the police power, Tiedeman went on to suggest that pregnant women might fall within the exception: "It may be, and probably is, permissible for the State to prohibit pregnant women from engaging in certain employments, which would likely to prove injurious to the unborn child." With respect to women generally, however, he had emphasized:

> there can be no more justification for the prohibition of the prosecution of certain callings by women, because the employment will prove hurtful to themselves, than it would be for the State to prohibit men from working in the manufacture of white lead, because they are apt to contract lead poisoning, or to prohibit occupation in certain parts

In the second edition of his treatise on police power, Tiedeman returned the favor, citing with approval the court's rationale for its holding that the statute violated the state constitution's due process clause, in that freedom of contract was both a liberty and a property right. "Labor is property, and the laborer has the same right to sell his labor, and to contract with reference thereto, as has any other property owner," the court observed. "In this country the legislature has no power to prevent persons who are *sui juris* from making their own contracts, nor can it interfere with the freedom of contract between the workman and the employer."[167]

## IV. SUBSTANTIVE DUE PROCESS, THEN AND NOW: LESSONS FROM TIEDEMAN'S JURISPRUDENCE

### A. *From Laissez-Faire to the Welfare State: The Police Power Revolution*

Fifteen years after *Ritchie v. People*, the Illinois Supreme Court upheld, as a legitimate exercise of the police power, a statute providing for a ten-hour day for women working in factories and laundries.[168] Justice Hand, in delivering the opinion of the court in this case, *Ritchie & Co. v. Wayman*, acknowledged "[t]he right of the individual to contract with reference to labor" was an "inviolable" property right protected by the Illinois constitution; but he added "certain sovereign powers," among them the police power, inhered in the State, and "the

---

of iron smelting works, because the lives of the men so engaged are materially shortened.
    C. TIEDEMAN, LIMITATIONS OF POLICE POWER, *supra* note 14, at 199-200.
    167. *Ritchie*, 155 Ill. at 104, 40 N.E. at 455, *quoted in* 1 C. TIEDEMAN, STATE AND FEDERAL CONTROL, *supra* note 16, § 102, at 336 n.2.
    168. Ritchie & Co. v. Wayman, 244 Ill. 509, 91 N.E. 695 (1910). The statute at issue was enacted in 1909 and provided, in relevant part, "That no female shall be employed in any mechanical establishment or factory or laundry in this State, more than ten hours during any one day." Violation of this provision was a misdemeanor punishable by a fine of between $25 and $100. *Id.* at 516, 91 N.E. at 696. To test the constitutionality of the statute, suit was filed by W.C. Ritchie & Company and two of its female employees against Wayman, state's attorney for Cook County, and the chief factory inspector for the State of Illinois. W.C. Ritchie & Company was engaged in the manufacture of paper boxes. The bill averred that the company employed 750 women and that during the rush season it was necessary for its female employees to work more than ten hours per day in order for the company to fill its orders. The bill also averred that the factory was situated in a well-lighted, heated and ventilated building and that the working conditions were "sanitary and healthful." *Id.* at 515-16, 91 N.E. at 695-96.

property rights of the citizen are always held and enjoyed subject to the reasonable exercise of the police power by the State." He defined the police power as "that power of the State which relates to the conservation of the health, morals and general welfare of the public."[169]  So defined, the police power was "a very broad power," and "may be applied to the regulation of every property right so far as it may be reasonably necessary for the State to exercise such power to guard the health, morals and general welfare of the public."[170]

In identifying a rational basis for the 1909 ten-hour law, Justice Hand resorted to arguments that are blatantly paternalistic and sexist by today's standards. Like the United States Supreme Court in *Muller v. Oregon*[171] just two years before, the Illinois Supreme Court emphasized that the statute applied only to female employees, the protection of whose health was a legitimate state interest.[172]

Justice Hand also attempted to distinguish the 1909 ten-hour law from the 1893 eight-hour law, suggesting that the court in *Ritchie* would

---

169. *Id.* at 519, 91 N.E. at 697.

170. *Id.* at 520, 91 N.E. at 697.

171. 208 U.S. 412 (1908)

172. Justice Hand's discussion of what the court regarded as the state's interest in the health of women was extraordinarily frank:

> It is known to all men . . . that woman's physical structure and the performance of maternal functions place her at a great disadvantage in the battle of life; that while a man can work for more than ten hours a day without injury to himself, a woman, especially when the burdens of motherhood are upon her, cannot; that while a man can work standing upon his feet for more than ten hours a day, day after day, without injury to himself, a woman cannot, and that to require a woman to stand upon her feet for more than ten hours in any one day and perform severe manual labor while thus standing, day after day, has the effect to impair her health, and that as weakly and sick women cannot be the mothers of vigorous children, it is of the greatest importance to the public that the State take such measures as may be necessary to protect its women from the consequences induced by long, continuous manual labor in those occupations which tend to break them down physically. It would therefore seem obvious that [the statute in question] would tend to preserve the health of women and insure the production of vigorous offspring by them and would directly conduce to the health, morals and general welfare of the public . . . .

*Ritchie & Co.*, 244 Ill. at 520-21, 91 N.E. at 697. The similar decision of the United States Supreme Court in Muller v. Oregon, 208 U.S. 412 (1908), which Justice Hand cited, *Ritchie & Co.*, 244 Ill. at 521, 91 N.E. at 697-98, is briefly discussed *supra* note 26.

have upheld the statute had it fixed a ten-hour day.[173] That distinction makes sense only if the court applied a conception of the police
power fundamentally different from that posited by Tiedeman and
adopted by the court fifteen years earlier. Indeed, Justice Hand's
comments about the "reasonableness" of the ten-hour statute suggest
that the court had adopted the view of the police power advanced by
Louis Brandeis, who was counsel for the state's attorney, Wayman.
Brandeis argued that courts must uphold as legitimate the exercise of
the police power where the act in question had "some reasonable
relation to the subjects of such power"—i.e., "the preservation of the
public health, morals, safety or welfare."[174]

The police power concept implicit in *Ritchie & Co. v. Wayman* was
the concept developed by Ernst Freund in his work on the police power,
published a few years after the second edition of Tiedeman's treatise

---

173. *Ritchie & Co.*, 244 Ill. at 528, 91 N.E. at 700. The court discerned in
*Ritchie v. People*:

> a veiled suggestion which indicates that it was the opinion of the court
> that the limitation of the right to work longer than eight hours was
> an unreasonable limitation upon the right to contract, while the right
> to contract for a longer day, at least under some circumstances, might
> be a valid limitation upon the right of contract.

*Id.* In so distinguishing the earlier case, Justice Hand's opinion focused
inordinately upon language in *Ritchie v. People* that left room for reasonable
regulations necessary for the public health, safety, or welfare, *see* Ritchie v.
People, 155 Ill. 98, 114-15, 40 N.E. 454, 459 (1895), overlooking the clear
language in that decision that said that the liberty of contract rights of women
should be fully the equivalent of those of men. Indeed, Justice Hand even
quoted out of context the passage from Tiedeman's *Limitations on Police Power*,
cited in *Ritchie v. People*, that maintained it would be constitutional for the state
to prohibit certain types of work "'[i]n so far as the employment of a certain class
in a particular occupation may threaten or inflict damage upon the public or
third persons.'" *Ritchie & Co.*, 244 Ill. at 529, 91 N.E. at 700 (quoting C.
TIEDEMAN, LIMITATIONS ON POLICE POWER, *supra* note 14, at 115). As discussed
*supra* note 166, Tiedeman was referring specifically to pregnant women, and he
went on to affirm that to limit the freedom of contract of women generally was
no more permissible than to limit that of men whose occupations might be
hazardous to their health. More importantly, Justice Hand ignored altogether
the arguments in the second edition of Tiedeman's treatise on the police power,
discussed *supra* notes 159-66 and accompanying text, which urged courts, in
their consideration of laws regulating the hours of labor, to treat women no
differently than men, and which had cited *Ritchie v. People* as an example of
such an even-handed judicial protection of liberty of contract.

174. *Ritchie & Co.*, 244 Ill. at 512, 91 N.E. at 700 (summarizing Brandeis'
argument as counsel for appellants).

and a year after Tiedeman's death.[175] Freund's book signaled the impending death of the *sic utere tuo* conceptualization of the police power and of the doctrine of liberty of contract. Freund's book also signified the influential role played by sociological jurisprudence early in the twentieth century, as legal formalism gave way to legal realism, and as the laissez-faire standard gave way to that of the welfare state in political economy.

Freund defined the police power as "the power of promoting the public welfare by restraining and regulating the use of liberty and property."[176] Hence, unlike Tiedeman who saw the exercise of the police power as legitimate only where it enhanced or protected individual liberty, Freund saw every exercise of the police power, by definition, as an infringement of individual liberty. For Freund, the police power must be "elastic," or "capable of development"; it was not "a fixed quantity," but "the expression of social, economic and political conditions."[177] The standard of legitimacy was the nexus between a statute and the public welfare, broadly conceived as "the improvement of social and economic conditions affecting the community at large and collectively, with a view to bringing about 'the greatest good of the greatest number.'"[178] Freund viewed the *sic utere* maxim as merely one segment of the police power, those "self-evident limitations upon liberty and property in the interest of peace, safety, health, order and morals . . . punishable at common law as nuisances."[179] But, added Freund, "no community confines its care of the public welfare to the enforcement of the principles of the common law:"

> The state places its corporate and proprietary resources at the disposal of the public by the establishment of improvements and services of different kinds; *and it exercises its compulsory powers for the prevention and anticipation of wrong by narrowing common law rights through conventional restraints and positive regulations which are not confined to the prohibition of wrongful acts. It is this latter kind of state control which constitutes the essence of the police power. The maxim of this power is that every individual must submit to such restraints in the exercise of his liberty or of his rights of property as may be required to remove or reduce the danger of the abuse of these*

---

175. E. FREUND, THE POLICE POWER: PUBLIC POLICY AND CONSTITUTIONAL RIGHTS (1904).

176. *Id.* at iii.

177. *Id.* at 3.

178. *Id.* at 5.

179. *Id.* at 6.

*rights on the part of those who are unskilful, careless, or unscrupulous.*[180]

Thus, unlike Tiedeman, who confined the legitimate scope of the police power to the enforcement of the *sic utere* principle, Freund stressed "the essence of the police power" was not confined to the prohibition of wrongful acts.

One can see the difference between Freund's broad conception of the police power and Tiedeman's narrow conception by examining what Freund wrote about each of the three types of legislation discussed in Part III of this Article.

First, with respect to usury legislation, Freund too found "inadequate theoretical justification" for such laws since the loaning of money was "neither a business affected with the public interest, nor one particularly concerning safety or morals." He nevertheless viewed regulation of the rate of interest as but "a species" of the regulation of charges, which was a legitimate exercise of the police power so long as the regulation was not discriminatory. He added that "the singling out of that particular class of charges may at least be justified on the ground of historical tradition."[181]

Second, although Freund observed that "the conduct of the individual in the privacy of his home, not involving or affecting his legal relations to other persons, is generally exempt from the operation of the police power," he based his generalization wholly upon the "firmly established principle of legislative policy" that public regulations must not interfere with "purely private acts."[182] His formulation of the general rule thus differed from Tiedeman's in two important respects. First, while Tiedeman based his principle of limitation on a relatively sure definitional footing ("The municipal law has only to do with trespasses"), Freund based his generalization on the far more slippery

---

180. *Id.* (emphasis in original). In a footnote, Freund cited the opinion of Chief Baron Fleming in *Bate's Case* (1606), that the King had absolute power to do that which is *salus populi*, or applied to the general benefit of the people. *Id.* at 6 n.7. While Freund thus saw the police power as concerned with policy (the promotion of the public welfare) and executive in its function, Tiedeman saw it as concerned with justice (the maintenance of private rights) and thus judicial in function.

181. *Id.* at 290. Like Tiedeman, Freund felt that "antiquated and exploded theories should not be allowed to control constitutional principles;" but, like Thomas M. Cooley and unlike Tiedeman, *see supra* text accompanying note 126, he was willing to allow legislation to stand, given long-standing precedent in its favor, even though it was difficult to defend on principle.

182. C. FREUND, *supra* note 175. at 483.

ground of "legislative policy."[183] Second, and perhaps more importantly, while to Tiedeman the critical distinction concerned the direct effect
of a given act (harm to others versus harm to oneself), to Freund the
critical distinction concerned where the act was performed, or more
precisely, whether the act had public consequences. "Purely private
acts" might be beyond the reach of the police power, as Freund
formulated it, but few acts fell within this category. Gambling, sexual
immorality, use of intoxicants—all these private vices may become
matters of public concern, and hence subject to police regulations,
because they are "offensive to the public" and are "apt, in their more
remote and indirect consequences, to produce physical disorder and
crime, and thus to endanger the public safety."[184]

Finally, and most obviously, Freund's formulation of the police
power left little room for the doctrine of liberty of contract. Freund
regarded legislation for the protection of laborers—including legislation
limiting the number of hours in a work day or week—as legislation
"enacted in the interest of health and safety," as well as "to promote
decency and comfort" ("where women and young persons are concerned"), and therefore legislation that rested upon "a clear and
indisputed title of public power."[185] Not unsurprisingly, Freund had
little regard for the decision of the Illinois Supreme Court in *Ritchie v.
People*.[186] "It is not by the assertion of vague principles of liberty, or

---

183. Indeed, given that there was "no direct judicial authority for declaring
private acts exempt from the police power," Freund acknowledged that "it seems
impossible to speak of a constitutional right of private consumption" of liquor or
other intoxicating drugs. He ascribed legislative tolerance of purely private acts
wholly to "policy." He also suggested other practical safeguards:

> Like any other exercise of the police power, control of private conduct
> would have to justify itself on grounds of the public welfare. Aside
> from this, the practical difficulties of enforcement, coupled with the
> constitutional prohibition of unreasonable searches, will in general be
> an adequate protection against an abuse of legislative power in this
> domain.

*Id.* at 486.

184. *Id.* at 172. For examples of permissible regulations of morality, see *id.*
at 173-91 (gambling and speculating), 192-219 (intoxicating liquors, including
the prohibition thereof), 220-23 (lewdness and obscenity), 225 (notorious
cohabitation), 226-33 (prostitution), 485 (use of opium, citing, *inter alia*, Ah Lim
v. Territory of Washington, 1 Wash. 156 (1890)).

185. *Id.* at 295-96.

186. *Id.* at 298. Freund wrote, "The opinion in Ritchie v. People can hardly
command unqualified assent either in the light of reason or authority." *Id.* In
criticizing *Ritchie*, Freund relied upon the Massachusetts Supreme Court's
decision upholding a law limiting women's labor in factories to sixty hours per
week, Commonwealth v. Hamilton Mfg. Co., 120 Mass. 383 (1876), discussed

by the unqualified denunciation of class legislation that the limits of the
police power can be determined," he concluded.[187]

This statement by Freund, inserted in an almost offhand fashion at
the close of his criticism of the Illinois Supreme Court's decision in
*Ritchie*, was a nutshell summary of the vast changes that American
value systems—in law, politics, and political economy—were undergoing
during the early years of the twentieth century. Laissez-faire constitutionalism, with its hostility to "class legislation" and its affirmation
of "liberty of contract," began its demise. Substantive due process
protection of economic liberties received criticism, at first by academics
and later by the courts, until eventually the Supreme Court in the
1930s abandoned it.[188]

Roughly contemporaneous with the gradual demise of laissez-faire
doctrines in constitutional law were three other major, interrelated
developments that occurred during the period between the 1880s and
the 1920s. One was the rise of the modern social sciences: economics,
psychology and psychiatry, sociology, and political science. By the turn
of the century, social scientists—self-professed experts in these new
professional fields—advocated the solution of social problems through
a variety of so-called "Progressive" reforms; and legislatures responded
with, among other things, laws regulating wages, hours, and working
conditions.[189] The adoption of Progressive legislation in turn signaled
the second major development of the period, the emergence of the so-
called "welfare state," or "regulatory state," standard in public policy.[190] Some argue a third major development was the inevitable
response to the tension that had emerged between legislation and the
common law: the shift from "formalism" to "realism" in the law.[191]

---

*supra* note 162.

187. C. FREUND, *supra* note 175, at 298.

188. The Supreme Court's gradual, thirty-year retreat from laissez-faire
constitutionalism—from Muller v. Oregon, 208 U.S. 412 (1908), to United States
v. Carolene Prods. Co., 304 U.S. 144 (1938)—is summarized *supra* note 26.

189. *See generally* R. HOFSTADTER, THE AGE OF REFORM (1955); R. WIEBE,
THE SEARCH FOR ORDER, 1877-1920 (1967).

190. *See generally* S. FINE, *supra* note 8; Hovenkamp, *supra* note 6;
Woodard, *supra* note 8.

191. Hovenkamp, *supra* note 6, at 381-82. As summarized by Hovenkamp,
the rise of legal realism first involved the formulation of the "legal formalism"
hypothesis. In other words, legal scholars of the time and historians subsequently explained the dissonance between substantive due process and
Progressivism by accusing the judges of the substantive due process courts of
being "formalist"—that is, of using too rigidly, or too mechanically, a method of
legal reasoning that deduced first principles from the existing body of rules and
precedents and then applied them to the facts of the case at hand. Christopher
Columbus Langdell's 1871 casebook on contracts was "undoubtedly" the

The rise of legal realism was made possible by the acceptance of sociological theories of jurisprudence by a new generation of legal scholars, including Roscoe Pound, Louis D. Brandeis, Benjamin N. Cardozo, Karl Llewellyn, and Jerome Frank.[192]   These scholars received some inspiration from Oliver Wendell Holmes' famous study of the common law, which he placed in an evolutionary Darwinian framework, arguing that practical expedients were more central to the development of the law than were logical propositions.[193]   Holmes' emphasis on sociological concepts—the perceived needs of human society and the prevalent notions that emerged from the resolution of human conflicts—in turn suggested the pervasive influence of German jurists such as Rudolf von Jhering upon their American contemporaries. Indeed, Roscoe Pound, one of the early leaders of the realist movement, was a student of German jurisprudence.[194]   His early writings severely criticized the "mechanical" jurisprudence of the late-nineteenth century and insisted on the relevance of the ideas of the German sociological jurists. "The sociological movement in jurisprudence is a movement for pragmatism as a philosophy of law," he explained; it sought "the adjustment of principles and doctrines to the human conditions they are to govern rather than to assumed first principles."[195]   Rather than

---

paradigm of legal formalism in private law, Hovenkamp argues; but he argues that it had no analogue in public law. Rather than being static and uncreative, as the "formalism" thesis suggests, the case law of substantive due process was "highly creative," he notes, suggesting that it was the prevalence of classical economic theories and not the dominance of legal formalism that best explains laissez-faire constitutionalism. *Id.* at 382-83.

For a classic criticism of legal formalism by one of the foremost early-twentieth century legal realists, see Pound, *Mechanical Jurisprudence*, 8 COLUM. L. REV. 605 (1908).

192. *See generally* E. PURCELL, THE CRISIS OF DEMOCRATIC THEORY 74-94 (1973). The phrase "legal realism" probably originated with Karl Llewellyn, who in 1930 coined the similar phrase "Realistic Jurisprudence" to describe his suggested approach. *Id.* at 81. The continuing pervasiveness of legal realism is graphically illustrated by the fact that, at many law schools today, Llewellyn's book introducing the study of law, *The Bramble Bush*, remains a staple of first-year student orientation reading.

193. *Id.* at 75-76 (quoting O. HOLMES, THE COMMON LAW 1 (1881) ("The felt necessities of the time, the prevalent moral and political theories, intuitions of public policy, avowed or unconscious, even the prejudices which judges share with their fellow men, have had a good deal more to do than the syllogism in determining the rules by which men should be governed.")).

194. *See, e.g.*, R. POUND, INTERPRETATIONS OF LEGAL HISTORY (1923); R. POUND, OUTLINES OF LECTURES ON JURISPRUDENCE (5th ed. 1943); Pound, *The Scope and Purpose of Sociological Jurisprudence*, 25 HARV. L. REV. 140 (1910).

195. Pound, *Mechanical Jurisprudence*, *supra* note 191, at 609-10.

examine the internal logic of legal rules, he maintained, it was "much more important to study their social operation and the effects which they produce."[196]

Ernst Freund, too, was influenced by German sociological jurisprudence. Although he did not study under Jhering at Goettingen, he began his study of law in Germany, where he undoubtedly studied the sociological theories of jurisprudence posited by Jhering and his contemporaries.[197]

Given the intellectual climate of the legal community in the early twentieth century it is not surprising that Tiedeman's treatise on the police power—a treatise that stressed adherence to the *sic utere tuo* principle as the touchstone for the validity of police regulations—suddenly was no longer a useful guide for the lawyer or law student. Swayed by the "sociological method" employed by Brandeis and other "realist" lawyers in their briefs,[198] courts like the Illinois Supreme Court in *Ritchie & Co. v. Wayman* or the United States Supreme Court in *Muller v. Oregon* found easy justification for upholding labor regulations as reasonably related to the "health, morals, and general welfare of the public" and hence as legitimate exercises of the police power.

## B.  *Judicial Protection of Unenumerated Constitutional Rights: Some Jurisprudential Concerns*

It is ironic that the German sociological jurisprudence that influenced Tiedeman, and which provided the rationale for his advocacy of judicial activism in *The Unwritten Constitution*, also helped bring

---

196. Pound, *The Scope and Purpose of Sociological Jurisprudence, supra* note 194, at 514.

197. Freund was born in New York in 1864. He was educated in Germany and in the mid-1880s studied law at the universities in Berlin and Heidelberg. He continued his legal studies at Columbia University, from which he also received a Ph.D. in political science in 1897. He taught at Columbia in 1892-93, then in 1894 moved to the University of Chicago, where he became a full professor (in jurisprudence and public law) in 1902. THE BOOK OF CHICAGOANS 247 (A. Marquis ed. 1917).

198. As noted above, Brandeis was counsel for the Illinois state's attorney in *Ritchie & Co.* Two years earlier, in Muller v. Oregon, 208 U.S. 412 (1908), his famous "Brandeis brief"—consisting of two pages of legal arguments and well over a hundred of sociological statistics and analysis—helped persuade the United States Supreme Court of the validity of the Oregon maximum hours law that applied to female workers. By the early 1920s Brandeis, then a widely respected judge on the New York bench, was himself a forceful advocate of the "sociological method" as a principal tool of judicial practice. *See* B. CARDOZO, THE NATURE OF THE JUDICIAL PROCESS 51-141 (1921) (lectures II & III).

about the demise of laissez-faire constitutionalism.. The fact that the same philosophy of law which directly influenced Tiedeman also, directly or indirectly, influenced Louis Brandeis or Ernst Freund or Roscoe Pound should nevertheless not be surprising. The conception of law as a means toward social ends, as Roscoe Pound noted, requires courts to keep in touch with life. This does not mean that they must follow the currents of popular opinion, or public "whim." But it does mean that courts must be sufficiently in tune with society to ascertain its "prevalent sense of right." And, as Tiedeman himself recognized and even urged, it obliges courts to "follow, and give effect to, the present intentions and meaning of the people" when construing the law.[199]

The demise of laissez-faire constitutionalism, concurrent with the rise of the welfare state and legal realism, for some time made judicial activism disreputable.    Indeed, critics of judicial activism—and proponents of the opposite theory of "judicial self-restraint"—forcefully made their voices heard at the time when laissez-faire constitutionalism was at its very height,[200] although their collective voice did not definitively gain the dominant ground until the late 1930s, about the same time that the Supreme Court signaled the final demise of substantive due process protection of economic liberties.[201]    Although laissez-faire constitutionalism as a movement is still dead,[202] judicial activism—given new life by the revival of substantive due process by the Warren and Burger Courts—still lives, although it is arguably more controversial today than it has been at any time since the turn of the century.

---

199.  C. TIEDEMAN, UNWRITTEN CONSTITUTION, *supra* note 46, at 154.

200.  *See, e.g.*, Thayer, *The Origins and Scope of the American Doctrine of Constitutional Law*, 7 HARV. L. REV. 129 (1893) (urging a highly restrictive theory of judicial review).  A modern commentator has argued that Thayer's essay later became a major resource and inspiration for critics of judicial intervention:  "The old judicial review had gone wrong; therefore, all judicial review was suspect." This notion, prompted by the negative traditional view of laissez-faire constitutionalism, lent support to the tradition opposed to judicial activism, the "Holmes-Hand-Frankfurter tradition of 'judicial self-restraint.'" A. PAUL, *supra* note 2, at xvi.

201.  *See* United States v. Carolene Prods. Co., 304 U.S. 144 (1938), discussed briefly *supra* note 26.

202.  This does not imply, however, that substantive due process protection of property and other economic rights is dead. Far from having met its demise, economic substantive due process now enjoys a renaissance of sorts, as a number of distinguished legal scholars have urged its revival. *See, e.g.*, R. EPSTEIN, TAKINGS: PRIVATE PROPERTY AND THE POWER OF EMINENT DOMAIN (1985); B. SIEGAN, ECONOMIC LIBERTIES AND THE CONSTITUTION (1980).  *See generally* ECONOMIC LIBERTIES AND THE CONSTITUTION (J. Dorn & H. Manne eds. 1987).

The distinction that Tiedeman drew in his *Unwritten Constitution* between the true "will" of the people, which the courts are bound to follow, and the people's "whim," which the courts on principle are free to ignore, is a distinction of continuing relevance to the modern controversy over judicial activism. It is a distinction that goes to the heart of what is perhaps the fundamental theoretical problem in American constitutionalism: the reconciliation of judicial review with popular sovereignty. Put another way, the problem may be described as that of reconciling the will of the majority with the protection of the rights of the minority—a fundamental problem that is at least as old as the Constitution itself.[203] What follows certainly does not purport to resolve this problem, nor does it even purport to show any clear lessons, relevant to this basic problem, that can be derived from Tiedeman's jurisprudence and the demise of laissez-faire constitutionalism. I do intend, however, to raise some questions and to make some tentative conclusions that suggest the potential lessons learned from this study of Tiedeman's thought and its place in the revisionist interpretation of turn-of-the-century constitutional law.

First, it is interesting to note how similar Tiedeman's arguments on behalf of an activist judiciary protecting property and economic liberty are to arguments raised in the past thirty or so years on behalf of an activist Supreme Court protecting civil liberties. Ronald Dworkin, for example, in defending the activism of the Warren Court, has described the function of the Court in terms of the judiciary's obligation to consistently enforce the principles upon which their institutions rely. Dworkin argues that in making unpopular decisions, the judge is not enforcing his own convictions against the community's, but rather is resolving conflicts or inconsistencies in the community morality.[204]

Striking examples of this notion of the Court's obligation can be found in the writings of both the Court's most "liberal" Justices and the Court's newest "conservative" member. One memorable example is the opinion of Justice Thurgood Marshall in the 1972 death penalty cases. Notwithstanding opinion polls revealing the public about evenly divided on the question, Marshall argued that if the average citizen possessed

---

203. This was the problem that was of most concern to James Madison at the time of the drafting and ratification of the Constitution, and it was the subject of his famous tenth essay in the *Federalist Papers*. *See* Ketcham, *The Dilemma of Bills of Rights in Democratic Government*, in THE LEGACY OF GEORGE MASON 38 (J. Pacheco ed. 1983); THE FEDERALIST NO. 10 (J. Madison).

204. R. DWORKIN, TAKING RIGHTS SERIOUSLY 126 (1978) ("Individuals have a right to the consistent enforcement of the principles upon which their institutions rely. It is this institutional right, as defined by the community's constitutional morality, that Hercules [Dworkin's model for the activist judge] must defend against any inconsistent opinion however popular.").

"knowledge of all the facts presently available," he would find capital punishment "shocking to his conscience and sense of justice."[205] More recently, Justice William Brennan has gone further, arguing that the death penalty is inherently inconsistent with the eighth amendment's "fundamental premise . . . that even the most base criminal remains a human being possessed of some potential, at least, for common human dignity." Noting that this is an interpretation to which neither a majority of his fellow Justices nor a majority of Americans subscribe, Justice Brennan nevertheless insisted "when a Justice perceives an interpretation of the text to have departed so far from its essential meaning, that Justice is bound, by a larger constitutional duty to the community, to expose the departure and point toward a different path."[206]

A very recent example of the Court's functioning of the "conscience" of the nation is its decision that the First Amendment forbids a conviction under the Texas criminal statute prohibiting desecration of the American flag.[207] In his concurring opinion, the Court's newest "conservative" member, Justice Anthony Kennedy, noted that the case illustrated "better than most that the judicial power is often difficult in its exercise." The members of the Court, he observed, must sometimes make decisions that are not only popular but also personally "painful," because "they are right, right in the sense that the law and the Constitution, as we see them, compel the result."[208]

If the notion that courts must, in upholding the true "will" of the people as embodied in the Constitution, sometimes disregard popular sentiment, however overwhelming, poses difficulties in the interpretation of specific constitutional prohibitions such as the eighth or the first amendment, surely that notion poses even greater jurisprudential difficulties with respect to the judicial protection of unenumerated constitutional rights, such as the right to privacy.[209] Thomas Grey has framed the basic question this way:

---

205. Furman v. Georgia, 408 U.S. 238, 369 (1972) (Marshall, J., concurring).

206. Brennan, *Construing the Constitution*, 19 U.C. DAVIS L. REV. 2, 13-14 (1985). Justice Brennan added that "[b]ecause we are the last word on the meaning of the Constitution, our views must be subject to revision over time, or the Constitution falls captive . . . to the anachronistic views of long-gone generations." *Id.* at 13. Compare Brennan's argument with Tiedeman's argument in *Unwritten Constitution*, that the judge "who would interpret the law rightly" is not bound by "the utterances of dead men." *See supra* text accompanying notes 74-76.

207. Texas v. Johnson, 109 S. Ct. 2533 (1989).

208. *Id.* at 2548 (Kennedy, J., concurring).

209. The history of Supreme Court protection of the right to privacy is briefly summarized *supra* note 9.

> In reviewing laws for constitutionality, should our judges confine
> themselves to determining whether those laws conflict with norms
> derived from the written Constitution? Or may they also enforce
> principles of liberty and justice when the normative content of those
> principles is not to be found within the four corners of our founding
> document?[210]

That question, Professor Grey adds, is "perhaps the most fundamental
question we can ask about our fundamental law," excluding the question
of the legitimacy of judicial review itself.[211]

What makes the question so troublesome today is precisely the
reason why it was so troublesome in Tiedeman's day: the absence of a
objectively-based, or universally-recognized, body of fundamental law.
Eighteenth-century jurisprudence had natural law and natural rights,
but as noted in Part One, above, that body of fundamental law had been
rejected by mid-nineteenth century jurists. It was in the void created
by the rejection of natural rights doctrine that, successively, the
historical and the sociological schools of jurisprudence arose. And, as
shown in Part Two, above, it was in this philosophical milieu—a post-
Enlightenment world, devoid of firm ideological footing—that Tiedeman
strove in his *Unwritten Constitution* to provide a jurisprudential
justification for the protection of traditional (which, Tiedeman assumed,
were laissez-faire) values against the onslaught of popular demands for
the "welfare state." Tiedeman's solution was to posit a doctrine of

---

210. Grey, *Do We Have an Unwritten Constitution?*, 27 STAN. L. REV. 703
(1975).

211. *Id.* Grey argues persuasively that the "pure interpretive model" is
inconsistent with much of our substantive constitutional doctrine, pointing out
that a strict adherence to the written text would jeopardize the entire body of
doctrine developed under the fifth and fourteenth amendments—including
application of the equal protection clause of the fourteenth amendment to the
federal government under the fifth amendment due process clause, as well as
application of the Bill of Rights to the states under the fourteenth amendment.
*Id.* at 710-12. It would also jeopardize modern interpretations of specific provisions of the Bill of Rights, which are often far removed from the original,
historically intended meaning. *Id.* at 713. Grey then distinguishes three types
of noninterpretive judicial review, each progressively narrower: first, the
creation (or discovery) of independent constitutional rights "with almost no
textual guidance," such as the right to privacy or liberty of contract; second, the
general application of norms that the written text explicitly applies in a
narrower way, such as the fifth and fourteenth amendment interpretations
discussed above; and third, the extension or broadening of written provisions of
the Constitution beyond the framers' normative content, as in the School
Segregation Cases or the extension of the fourth amendment to cover eavesdrop-
ping. *Id.* at 713 n.46. Here I am concerned primarily with the first, broadest
type of noninterpretive review identified by Professor Grey.

"natural rights," based not on nature but rather on the "prevalent sense of right" of the American people.

History has proven that Tiedeman's use of sociological principles of jurisprudence was an ineffectual basis for laissez-faire constitutional doctrines such as liberty of contract. One reason, scholars have suggested, was that the laissez-faire standard no longer comported with reality.[212] Whether or not this is true, the apparently widespread and long-lived popular support for "Progressive" legislation in the twentieth century has cast serious doubt on any claim that laissez-faire principles were in accord with the "prevalent sense" of right. The "extraordinary demands of the great army of discontents" that Tiedeman in 1890 associated with popular "whim," or caprice, in the twentieth century—certainly by the time of the "New Deal" legislation of the 1930s—did not dissipate and hence seemed more like the true "will" of the people. In a twentieth-century legal culture dominated by sociological theories of jurisprudence and legal realism, judges had no intellectual armor that would enable activist courts to withstand the will of the majority; the laissez-faire constitutional principles espoused by Tiedeman simply had become irrelevant, under his own jurisprudential framework.

If such was the fate of substantive due process protection of economic rights in the twentieth century, what will be the fate of constitutional protection of other unenumerated, and equally controversial, rights in the future? In other words, is the "right to privacy" doomed to fail, as "liberty of contract" did?[213] One need not speculate

---

212. *See* Woodard, *supra* note 8, at 305-11 (explaining the demise of the laissez-faire standard in terms of "a clash with reality," the reality of an industrial society).

213. Late-nineteenth century "liberty of contract" and late-twentieth century "right to privacy" have much in common. They are both nontextual, or unenumerated, constitutional rights, that are, in effect, creatures of the first type of noninterpretive judicial review distinguished by Professor Grey: i.e., independent constitutional rights "created (or found)" by the courts "with almost no textual guidance." Grey, *supra* note 210, at 713 n.46 Both, too, are ultimately based—in jurisprudential terms—on a perceived substantial support from the majority of the American people. Historically, the popular support for liberty of contract proved to be elusive; popular support for the right to privacy may be equally uncertain, outside the rather narrow sphere suggested by the Supreme Court majority in *Bowers v. Hardwick*, discussed *infra* text accompanying notes 214-19. Finally, both liberty of contract and the right to privacy seem to rest upon basic assumptions about the individual's role in society, assumptions that are likely to become less certain under the pressures of economic change. Arguably, the effect of industrialization in the late nineteenth century was to change people's attitudes about the proper role of government, from a negative model (restraining persons from causing harm to others) to a more positive model (creating and protecting opportunities for the individual and

about the future fate of the right to privacy by trying to predict the Supreme Court's treatment of *Roe v. Wade* in the upcoming term. Rather, one may look to the Court's decision in a case decided in the recent past, *Bowers v. Hardwick*,[214] in which the Court upheld the Georgia statute that made sodomy a criminal offense. In a 5-4 decision, the majority of the Court held that the right of privacy did not extend to protect homosexuals. Declaring the unwillingness of the Court to recognize "a fundamental right to engage in homosexual sodomy," Justice White, in his opinion for the majority, construed the right to privacy quite narrowly, arguing that the Court's previous decisions extended privacy protection only to decisions involving traditional family relationships, marriage, and procreation.[215]  In contrast, Justice Blackmun, in his opinion for the dissenters, interpreted the right to privacy far more broadly, arguing that the case was not merely about sodomy, but rather concerned the fundamental "right to be let alone."[216]  The Court's protection of certain rights associated with the family was based, not on the contribution of those rights to the general public welfare, but "because they form so central a part of an individual's life."[217]  If the right to privacy means anything, Justice Blackmun argued, it must extend to an individual's freedom to choose the form and nature of his or her intimate relationships with others.[218]

The disagreement between the majority and the dissenters in *Bowers v. Hardwick*—a disagreement about the very purpose and scope of the right to privacy—illustrates the precarious jurisprudential status of unenumerated "fundamental" rights today. The disagreement in *Bowers v. Hardwick* was a disagreement not only about the law, but

---

enhancing the individual's ability to "cope" with change). One may legitimately wonder whether rapid advances in computer, communications, and other technologies might also bring about changes, in the twenty-first century, in popular attitudes about privacy and the extent to which it should be valued in society.

214. 478 U.S. 186 (1986). The Georgia statute in question prohibited any oral or anal sexual act, and it applied to married as well as unmarried persons. The Court limited its consideration to the respondent's challenge to the statute as applied to consensual homosexual sodomy; it declined to consider the constitutionality of the statute as applied to other acts of sodomy. *Id.* at 188 n.2.

215. *Id.* at 190-91.

216. *Id.* at 199 (Blackmun, J., dissenting).

217. *Id.* at 204 (Blackmun, J., dissenting).

218. *Id.* at 205, 208 (Blackmun, J., dissenting).

about values—"the values most deeply rooted in our Nation's history."[219]   Judicial   protection   of   unenumerated   constitutional rights—whether grounded in substantive dimensions of the due process guarantees of the fifth and fourteenth amendments, or in the nontextual, fundamental rights protected in the ninth amendment[220], or the   "emanations"   from   specific   guarantees   of   the   Bill   of Rights—inevitably involves the courts' identification and assessment of fundamental values.   Even Justice Holmes, in his famous dissent in *Lochner*, did not ignore this fact.   Indeed, his declaration that "[t]he Fourteenth Amendment does not enact Mr. Herbert Spencer's Social Statics" is so often quoted out of context, that scholars frequently overlook the fact that Holmes did not condemn judicial review on substantive due process grounds *per se*; he condemned only judicial review in protection of liberty of contract because it was based "upon an economic theory which a large part of the country does not entertain."[221]   With respect to judicial review generally, Holmes wrote,

> I think that the word liberty in the Fourteenth Amendment is perverted when it is held to prevent the natural outcome of a dominant opinion, *unless it can be said that a rational and fair man necessarily would admit that the statute proposed would infringe fundamental principles as they have been understood by the traditions of our people and our law.*[222]

Thus, even a legal realist like Holmes recognized that certain "fundamental principles" might trump the will of the majority, in the courts' exercise of their power of judicial review.

The identity of those fundamental rights, and the legitimacy of judicial protection of them, remain troublesome points.   Thomas Grey has suggested that the legitimacy of judicial protection of unenumerated constitutional rights is particularly troublesome in an era dominated by

---

219.  *Id.* at 214 (Blackmun, J., dissenting). The disagreement about morality and moral philosophy implicit in *Bowers v. Hardwick* is discussed in S. MACEDO, THE NEW RIGHT V. THE CONSTITUTION 68-79 (1987) (criticizing the "moral skepticism" of the majority).

220.  On the significance of the ninth amendment for the protection of nontextual, or unenumerated rights, see the sources cited *supra* note 10.

221.  *Lochner v. New York*, 198 U.S. 45, 75 (1905) (Holmes, J., dissenting).

222.  *Id.* at 76 (emphasis added). Pointing to this passage, Grey argues that "[i]t is an often overlooked point that Mr. Justice Holmes in his classic *Lochner* dissent did not use the case as an occasion to reject noninterpretive adjudication generally, or even substantive due process as such; quite the contrary." Grey, *supra* note 210, at 711 n.35.

realism in jurisprudence and skepticism in ethics and epistemology.[223] Perhaps in response to such concerns, some scholars recently have urged theories of a "principled judicial activism;"[224] this development may be yet another indication of a broader movement, the decline of positivism and legal realism and the reemergence of normative legal philosophy.[225] Whether or not such a trend indeed is taking place, this study of Christopher Tiedeman's jurisprudence indicates that basic questions of constitutional law cannot be divorced from basic questions about jurisprudence. Prevailing attitudes about the origin and purpose of law generally must be taken into account by the courts in their exercise of judicial review; and indeed, these attitudes—whether explicit or implicit—do determine the contours of adjudication. This is particularly true in eras of profound social change: eras such as Christopher Tiedeman's and our own.

## CONCLUSION

Recent revisionist scholarship has sought to make laissez-faire constitutionalism more understandable by explaining it on its own terms; i.e., by explaining it in terms of the "world view" of the late nineteenth century. This Article has attempted to further our understanding of laissez-faire constitutionalism by examining in some detail the writings of one of its leading exponents, Christopher G. Tiedeman.

Tiedeman is important in two respects. First, the relative purity of his laissez-faire principles distinguished him from contemporaries such as Thomas M. Cooley. Both in his treatises on the police power and in his spirited defense of judicial activism in *The Unwritten*

---

223. Professor Grey concluded his article with the following troubling questions:

> Conceding the natural-rights origins of our Constitution, does not the erosion and abandonment of the 18th-century ethics and epistemology on which the natural-rights theory was founded require the abandonment of the mode of judicial review flowing from that theory? Is a 'fundamental law' judicially enforced in a climate of historical and cultural relativism the legitimate offspring of a fundamental law which its exponents felt expressed rationally demonstrable, universal, and immutable human rights?

Grey, *supra* note 210, at 718.

224. *See, e.g.*, Barnett, *Judicial Conservatism v. A Principled Judicial Activism*, 10 HARV. J.L. & PUB. POL'Y 273 (1987); S. MACEDO, *supra* note 219. *See generally* Dorn & Manne, *preface* to ECONOMIC LIBERTIES AND THE CONSTITUTION (J. Dorn & H. Manne eds. 1987), at xix-xx.

225. *See* Barnett, *Contract Scholarship and the Reemergence of Legal Philosophy* (Book Review), 97 HARV. L. REV. 1223, 1225-36 (1984) (reviewing Farnsworth, Contracts (1982)).

*Constitution,* Tiedeman expounded the most comprehensive and intellectually rigorous theory of laissez-faire constitutionalism. Second, although that theory had a short-lived influence in the law—citations to Tiedeman's treatises peaked at about the turn of the century, and virtually disappeared at about the time of Tiedeman's death a few years later—the sociological theories of jurisprudence on which it was based were quite "modern" for his time; they survived and flourished in the twentieth century.

Paradoxically, Tiedeman's obscurity in the twentieth century underscores the significance of his ideas today. The demise of Tiedeman's laissez-faire constitutionalism resulted not from the failure of a moral or economic theory, but from the failure of constitutionalism itself—that is, from the failure of certain categories of rights to be given lasting constitutional protection by the courts, through judicial review, in the face of sustained majoritarian demands. To the extent that the rise of legal realism was not merely coincidentally related to the demise of substantive due process protection of economic rights, scholars who are concerned about the constitutional protection of other unenumerated rights—such as the right of privacy—should not ignore the importance of jurisprudence in matters of constitutional law.

# Justice Field and the Jurisprudence of Government-Business Relations: Some Parameters of Laissez-Faire Constitutionalism, 1863-1897

CHARLES W. McCURDY

---

Tʜᴇ institutional and economic growth of American society through the mid-nineteenth century entailed close cooperation between the public and private sectors. Antebellum state and local politicians viewed government's resources as a means to attain the developmental goals of a society dedicated to material growth; public officials were more than willing "to seek the public good through private negotiations."[1] State legislatures chartered hundreds of corporations and lavished them with land grants, lottery franchises, eminent domain privileges, and tax exemptions.[2] Local governments, too, engaged in the scramble for regional development and readily opened their treasuries to railroad corporations and other businesses.[3] By the 1870s, however, various socioeconomic groups began to perceive that their interests were no longer congruent with those of the corporations that government had created and subsidized. In that decade, shippers waged successful struggles to impose stiff regulatory laws on grain

This essay received the Organization of American Historians' Pelzer Award for 1973. Charles W. McCurdy is a graduate student at the University of California, San Diego.

[1] Robert A. Lively, "The American System: A Review Article," *Business History Review*, XXIX (March 1955), 93. See also Harry N. Scheiber, "Government and the Economy: Studies of the 'Commonwealth' Policy in Nineteenth-Century America," *Journal of Interdisciplinary History*, III (Summer 1972), 135-51.

[2] James Willard Hurst, *The Legitimacy of the Business Corporation* (Charlottesville, 1970), 13-30; Paul Gates, *History of Public Land Law Development* (Washington, 1968), 341-86; John Samuel Ezell, *Fortune's Merry Wheel: The Lottery in America* (Cambridge, 1960); Harry N. Scheiber, "Property Law, Expropriation, and Resource Allocation by Government: the United States, 1789-1910," *Journal of Economic History*, XXXIII (March 1973), 232-51; John Cadman, *The Corporation in New Jersey: Business and Politics, 1789-1875* (Cambridge, 1949), 56-61.

[3] Carter Goodrich, "Local Government Planning of Internal Improvements," *Political Science Quarterly*, LXVI (Sept. 1951), 411-45.

warehousemen and railroad companies; local governments became "convinced that they had not gotten their money's worth" and repudiated their indebtedness; finally, state legislatures resolutely moved to divest corporations of the valuable special grants that preceeding policy-makers had bargained away.[4] The simultaneous emergence of regulation, repudiation, and revulsion against corporate privileges threatened a multitude of vested interests on an unprecedented scale. Thus, as Justice Stephen J. Field put it in 1890, post-Civil War constitutional controversies "exceed[ed], in the magnitude of the property interests involved, and in the importance of the public questions presented, all cases brought within the same [short] period before any court of Christendom."[5]

The supreme court, armed with an enlarged jurisdiction and three new constitutional amendments as a result of the Civil War, had both the power and the opportunity to forge new doctrine and fix new boundaries between the public and private sectors.[6] In the ensuing thirty year intra-court debate on how to use those powers, and for what purposes, Field was a pivotal figure. He sought to persuade his colleagues to use all the court's powers, "broadly and liberally interpreted," to "close the door . . . on the introduction of improper elements to control" the legislative process and to "draw the line between regulation and confiscation."[7] He was remarkably successful. The post-Civil War court reconsidered the scope of the states' police and eminent domain powers, restricted the range of policy tools government might employ to subsidize private businesses, and imposed new limitations on government's power to regulate prices. The outcome was a constitutional revolution that set the legal basis of government-business relations upon an entirely new footing.

Field's historical reputation largely stems from his role as "pioneer and prophet" of a substantive interpretation of the Fourteenth Amendment.[8]

[4] Harry H. Pierce, *Railroads of New York: A Study of Government Aid, 1826-1875* (Cambridge, 1953), 84; Frederick Merk, "Eastern Antecedents of the Grangers," *Agricultural History*, 23 (Jan. 1949), 1-8; Lee Benson, *Merchants, Farmers, & Railroads* (Cambridge, 1955); Harold D. Woodman, "Chicago Businessmen and the 'Granger' Laws," *Agricultural History*, XXXVI (Jan. 1962), 16-24; Dale E. Treleven, "Railroads, Elevators, and Grain Dealers: The Genesis of Antimonopolism in Milwaukee," *Wisconsin Magazine of History*, 52 (Spring 1969), 205-22; George H. Miller, *The Railroads and the Granger Laws* (Madison, 1971); Charles Fairman, *The Oliver Wendell Holmes Devise History of the Supreme Court*. Vol. VI: *Reconstruction and Reunion, 1864-88* (New York, 1971), 934-1010.
[5] Stephen J. Field, "The Centenary of the Supreme Court of the United States," *American Law Review*, XXIV (May 1890), 365.
[6] Stanley I. Kutler, *Judicial Power and Reconstruction Politics* (Chicago, 1968), 143-60.
[7] *Ex Parte Wall*, 107 U.S. 265 (1883) at 302; *Tool Co.* v. *Norris*, 2 Wall. 45 (1865) at 55-56; *Mugler* v. *Kansas*, 123 U.S. 623 (1887) at 678.
[8] Edward S. Corwin, "The Supreme Court and the Fourteenth Amendment," *Michigan Law Review*, VII (June 1909), 653.

Since the court often invoked the due process clause to "stave off adverse regulation," historians have relentlessly marched to the conclusion that Field was a mere handmaiden for "business needs" who believed that "protection of economic privilege was government's one excuse for being."[9] By focusing on regulatory issues alone, however, scholars get a distorted view of Field's government-business jurisprudence. Regulatory agitation emerged at the very time that state and local governments were also repudiating internal-improvement bonds and divesting corporations of tax exemptions, lottery rights, and other special grants. All the ensuing controversies involved judicial consideration of the legitimacy of governmental interventions in economic life, and all resulted in significant doctrinal innovations—not only under the newly adopted Fourteenth Amendment but also under the contract clause and the inchoate "public purpose" maxim. Moreover, the convergence of litigation on these several questions was especially important in that at common law regulatory and promotional legislation were part of a single doctrinal continuum. Private businesses that had been granted special privileges by state and local governments did not hold their property by "common right" and were therefore subject to regulation.[10] As a result, litigation resulting from regulatory statutes involved a reconsideration of governmental interventions on the promotional side, and vice versa. Thus, "if one regarded each case as though it came up spontaneously and in isolation, one would fail to grasp the great underlying problems" that the justices perceived.[11]

What follows, in this essay, is a reconsideration of the parameters and underlying rationale of Field's jurisprudence on both sides of the promotional-regulatory continuum. The first part focuses on his signal contributions to American property law and reappraises the court's crucial Fourteenth Amendment opinions on government's police and eminent domain

[9] Arthur Selwyn Miller, *The Supreme Court and American Capitalism* (New York, 1968), 50; Robert McCloskey, *American Conservatism in the Age of Enterprise* (Cambridge, 1951), 85, 74. See also Wallace Mendelson, "Mr. Justice Field and Laissez-Faire," *Virginia Law Review*, 36 (Feb. 1950), 45-58; Howard Jay Graham, *Everyman's Constitution: Historical Essays on the Fourteenth Amendment, the "Conspiracy Theory," and American Constitutionalism* (Madison, 1968), 98-151; Carl Brent Swisher, *Stephen J. Field: Craftsman of the Law* (Washington, 1930), 240-45.

[10] Charles K. Burdick, "The Origin of the Peculiar Duties of Public Service Corporations," *Columbia Law Review*, XI (June 1911), 514-31; *ibid.*, XI (Nov. 1911), 616-38; *ibid.*, XI (Dec. 1911), 743-64; Edwin Merrick Dodd, *American Business Corporations until 1860* (Cambridge, Mass., 1954), 158-63; Leonard W. Levy, *The Law of the Commonwealth and Chief Justice Shaw* (Cambridge, Mass., 1957), 258; Harry N. Scheiber, "The Road to *Munn*: Eminent Domain and the Concept of Public Purpose in the State Courts," Donald Fleming and Bernard Bailyn, eds., *Law in American History* (Boston, 1971), 342-402.

[11] Charles Fairman, "What Makes a Great Justice? Mr. Justice Bradley and the Supreme Court, 1870-1892," *Boston University Law Review*, XXX (Jan. 1950), 67.

powers. New light is cast upon Field's concerns in the *Slaughterhouse Cases*—concerns that subsequently spilled over into corporation law generally, and controlled his position in cash subsidy and regulatory controversies. The second part offers a new view of Field's convictions vis-à-vis "economic privilege." Here, postbellum developments in contract clause law are mapped out to delineate Field's role in the formulation of the important but neglected "public trust" doctrine, which ultimately relegated *Fletcher* v. *Peck* to the "status of a judicial relic."[12] In the third part, a line of doctrinal continuity is traced linking Field's landmark dissents in the *Granger Cases* to earlier court rulings on eminent domain, municipal bond, and exclusive privilege questions. Along this route, one discovers that Field's jurisprudence was neither "cut from the same bolt of cloth" as William G. Sumner's Social Darwinism, nor a product "of the Gilded Age with its Great Barbecue for the Robber Barons and for the rest—'let the public be damned. . . .' "[13] Instead, one finds that Field shaped his government-business jurisprudence to provide "final" solutions to the many-faceted, "great underlying problem" of the 1870s: government's legitimate role in American economic life. The final product was an extraordinarily consistent body of immutable rules designed to separate the public and private sectors into fixed and inviolable spheres.

The fundamental theorem of Field's government-business jurisprudence was derived from the Jacksonian, radical antislavery precept that under "the declaration of 1776" each individual had a natural right "to pursue the ordinary avocations of life without other restraint than such as effects all others and to enjoy with them the fruits of his labor."[14] The Fourteenth Amendment, he periodically asserted, was "undoubtedly intended" to protect both the title to a person's property and his liberty to dictate its use and "enjoy" its income.[15] This was a novel proposition in American constitu-

---

[12] C. Peter Magrath, *Yazoo, Law and Politics in the New Republic: The Case of Fletcher v. Peck* (Providence, 1966), 109.

[13] Mendelson, "Mr. Justice Field and Laissez-Faire," 55; McCloskey, *American Conservatism*, 103.

[14] *Slaughter House Cases*, 16 Wall. 36 (1873) at 101, 90; Howard Mumford Jones, *The Pursuit of Happiness* (Ithaca, 1953), 12; Richard Hofstadter, "William Leggett, Spokesman of Jacksonian Democracy," *Political Science Quarterly*, LVIII (Dec. 1943), 581-94; Louis Hartz, *Economic Policy and Democratic Thought: Pennsylvania, 1776-1860* (Cambridge, 1948), 70-72; William E. Nelson, "The Impact of the Antislavery Movement upon Styles of Judicial Reasoning in Nineteenth Century America," *Harvard Law Review*, 87 (Jan. 1974), 513-66. See also David Dudley Field's laudatory 1841 review of William Leggett, *Political Writings*, in A. P. Sprague, ed., *Speeches, Arguments, and Miscellaneous Papers of David Dudley Field* (2 vols., New York, 1884), II, 209-36.

[15] *Barbier* v. *Connolly*, 113 U.S. 27 (1884) at 31.

tional law, if not in social theory, and it exerted a profound impact on government's role in economic life through the third decade of the twentieth century.[16]

Field conceded that state governments had certain inherent powers that necessarily subjected property rights to a degree of public interference. The states could regulate the use of property in order to protect the safety, health, and morals of the community—in short, to exercise the police power. Government might also take a portion of a person's property by way of taxation for the support of governmental operations or local improvements. Finally, the states could provide public improvements—gas and water works, highways, railroads, and the like—and might employ the power of eminent domain on behalf of those ends. Thus property might be taken for public use upon payment of just compensation. All of these powers, however, might be abused by government, and therefore Field subjected each of them to important and essentially coextensive constitutional limitations.

Nineteenth-century eminent domain law was primarily a state matter and the Supreme Court of the United States played "only an occasional, and mainly validating, role in support of the state judiciaries' initiatives."[17] The court did, however, often reiterate that private property could only be expropriated "in execution of works in which the public is interested."[18] Railroads and other public utility concerns might take property at administered prices because "the public at large" could use the facilities by right, "not as a favor," and government might protect the public's interest in those businesses by enacting appropriate legislation, including "public regulations as to tolls."[19] Purely private firms had to make land purchases in the marketplace, for "the right of eminent domain nowhere justifies taking private property for a private use."[20] Thus Field indicated that takings under the eminent domain power were "proper matter[s] for judicial cognizance."[21]

The court's dicta pertaining to the "public use" limitations on the eminent domain power were merely reassertions of doctrine that was well-established in the states.[22] In *Pumpelly* v. *Green Bay and Mississippi Canal*

[16] Edward S. Corwin, "The Basic Doctrine of American Constitutional Law," *Michigan Law Review*, XII (Feb. 1914), 275; Charles Grove Haines, *The Revival of Natural Law Concepts* (Cambridge, 1930), 154-65.

[17] Scheiber, "The Road to *Munn*," 360.

[18] *Boom Co.* v. *Patterson*, 98 U.S. 403 (1878) at 406.

[19] *West River Bridge Co.* v. *Dix*, 6 How. 507 (1848) at 546.

[20] *Olcott* v. *The Supervisors*, 16 Wall. 678 (1873) at 694.

[21] *Boom Co.* v. *Patterson*, 98 U.S. 403 (1878) at 406.

[22] See Philip Nichols, Jr., "The Meaning of Public Use in the Law of Eminent Domain," *Boston University Law Review*, 20 (Nov. 1940), 615-24.

*Co.*, however, the court reappraised and modified a long line of state court decisions on the just compensation provision.[23] Before the Civil War, "the nagging scarcity of fluid capital" that had initially led to governmental promotion of private corporations also encouraged the state courts to develop legal doctrine that reduced the costs of doing business.[24] Indirect legal subsidies were an especially prominent feature of eminent domain law. The several state courts so narrowed the definition of a "taking" that railroad and canal companies had to pay compensation only to persons who had been forced to give up title to their property. As a result, landowners whose crops and buildings were flooded or otherwise damaged in the course of transport construction had no legal remedy.[25] The word "take," Pennsylvania's Chief Justice John Bannister Gibson explained in a widely followed opinion, "means taking the property altogether; not a *consequential* injury which is not a taking at all."[26]

In *Pumpelly*, the court dealt a decisive blow to the antebellum state judiciaries' "general disposition not to cramp these [growth-inducing] enterprises by a too sweeping or extreme compensation."[27] In that case, a canal company had raised the height of its dam on a Wisconsin lake, which had the unintended effect of flooding the farm of an adjoining landowner. Speaking for a unanimous court, Justice Samuel F. Miller held that:

It would be a very curious and unsatisfactory result, if in construing a provision of constitutional law, always understood to have been adopted for protection and security to the rights of the individual as against the government [just compensation clauses] . . . it shall be held that if the government refrains from the absolute conversion of real property to the use of the public it can destroy its value entirely, can inflict irreparable and permanent injury to any extent, can, in effect, subject it to total destruction without making any compensation, because, in the narrowest sense of the word, it is not *taken* for the public use. Such a construction would . . .

[23] *Pumpelly* v. *Green Bay Co.*, 13 Wall. 166 (1872).

[24] James Willard Hurst, *Law and Economic Growth: The Legal History of the Lumber Industry in Wisconsin, 1836-1915* (Cambridge, 1964), 182. See, generally, James Willard Hurst, *Law and the Conditions of Freedom in the Nineteenth-Century United States* (Madison, 1956), 20-30; Morton J. Horwitz, "The Transformation in the Conception of Property in American Law, 1780-1860," *University of Chicago Law Review*, 40 (Winter 1973), 248-90; Lawrence M. Friedman, *A History of American Law* (New York, 1973), 202-27, 261-64.

[25] Joseph M. Cormack, "Legal Concepts in Cases of Eminent Domain," *Yale Law Journal*, XLI (Dec. 1931), 221-61; Scheiber, "The Road to *Munn*," 362-73.

[26] *Monongahela Navigation Co.* v. *Coons*, 6 Watts & Serg. 101 (Penn. 1843) at 114. See also Stanley Kutler, "John Bannister Gibson: Judicial Restraint and the 'Positive State,'" *Journal of Public Law*, 14 (Spring 1965), 181-97.

[27] Theodore Sedgwick, *A Treatise on the Rules which Govern the Interpretation and Application of Statutory and Constitutional Law* (New York, 1857), 525. For the impact of *Pumpelly*, see Cormack, "Legal Concepts in Cases of Eminent Domain," 233-61.

make it authority for invasion of private right under the pretext of the public good, which had no warrant in the laws or practices of our ancestors.[28]

Indeed, in Field's view, the property right entailed the right to use and enjoyment as well as formal title, and therefore the plaintiff's right to compensation was unquestionable. But Field was prepared to go further and, in slightly modified form, extend the narrow "public use" and broad "taking" doctrines of eminent domain law to the police power as well.

The celebrated *Slaughterhouse Cases* came up from Louisiana at a time when northern "adventurers" and old-line southern Whigs had "become convinced that the same industry and commerce which had transformed the North would revolutionize the South."[29] During the late 1860s, virtually all the southern states embarked on massive programs of public aid to railroads and, simultaneously, major marketing centers made desperate attempts to recapture commercial hegemony in "natural" hinterland zones.[30] The New Orleans slaughterhouse monopoly was part of that city's "organic plan" to secure control of the Texas cattle trade.[31] In order to take full advantage of its locational superiority, city boosters advocated both railroad expansion and the construction of efficient slaughtering facilities that could withstand the competitive pressures imposed by packers in St. Louis and Chicago. New Orleans commercial interests ultimately succeeded in procuring the exclusive grant, as the Louisiana Supreme Court later observed, by "corrupting and improperly influencing members of the state legislature."[32] But the statute conferring the monopoly also threw hundreds of meatcutters out of work. The unemployed butchers claimed that the state legislature had divested them of valuable constitutional rights, while counsel for Louisiana defended the measure as a police regulation designed to protect the public health. In 1873, the ensuing litigation evoked the court's first construction of the Fourteenth Amendment.

Field's associates probably concurred with his assertion that the alleged public health rationale of the enactment was a "shallow . . . pretence" for an "odious monopoly."[33] Nevertheless, a narrow majority upheld the statute on the ground that the Fourteenth Amendment had not been de-

[28] *Pumpelly* v. *Green Bay Co.*, 13 Wall. 166 (1872) at 177-78.
[29] Jack B. Scroggs, "Carpetbagger Constitutional Reform in the South Atlantic States, 1867-1868," *Journal of Southern History*, XXVIII (Nov. 1961), 493.
[30] Carter Goodrich, "Public Aid to Railroads in the Reconstruction South," *Political Science Quarterly*, LXXI (Sept. 1956), 407-42.
[31] Mitchell Franklin, "The Foundation and Meaning of the Slaughterhouse Cases," *Tulane Law Review*, XVIII (Oct. 1943), 14.
[32] *Durbridge* v. *The Slaughter-House Co.*, 27 La. Ann. 676 (1875).
[33] *Slaughter-House Cases*, 16 Wall. 36 (1873) at 87, 89. But see also Charles Fairman, *Mr. Justice Miller and the Supreme Court, 1862-1890* (Cambridge, Mass., 1939), 180.

signed to make the court "a perpetual censor upon all the legislation of the states."[34] Field dissented. He conceded that slaughterhouses had long been considered *prima facie* nuisances, and he insisted that state legislatures might altogether prohibit butchers from plying their noxious trade in densely populated cities.[35] But in his view, the state's duty to protect the people from unhealthful businesses could not "possibly justify" legislation framed "for the benefit of a single corporation."[36] Field was particularly concerned with the implications of Thomas Durant's brief for the State of Louisiana, in which it was argued that a state legislature might make any business "the exclusive privilege of a few . . '. if the sovereign power judges that the interests of society will be better promoted."[37] Field flatly stated that Durant's position had no support in the common law. The only business firms which might be granted exclusive privileges, he asserted, were those that held "franchises of a public character appertaining to government."[38] The classic examples were hackmen, wharfingers, bridge proprietors, and ferry operators. Those businessmen could not engage in their calling by common right because they required special easements in the public streets or public rivers and, as *quid pro quo* for the government's grant of privilege, public officials might prescribe "the conditions under which it [the franchise] is enjoyed."[39] Railroad and other public utility corporations had assumed similar liabilities to the public by dint of exercising eminent domain powers.[40] The meat-cutting business, however, was a purely private, "ordinary trade." As a result, Field contended, it had to be open to all persons "without other restraint than such as effects all others."[41] Thus, in his view, the Louisiana statute "present[ed] the naked case, unaccompanied by any public consideration, where a right to pursue a lawful and necessary calling, previously enjoyed by every citizen . . . is taken away . . ." in contravention of the Fourteenth Amendment.[42]

[34] *Slaughter-House Cases*, 16 Wall. 36 (1873) at 78.

[35] *Ibid.*, at 88.

[36] *Ibid.*

[37] "Thomas Durant, Brief of Counsel in Error," *Paul Estaban and Others* v. *The State of Louisiana*, 8-9.

[38] *Slaughter-House Cases*, 16 Wall. 36 (1873) at 88. Field was not innovating here. In the leading case of *Boston & Lowell R.R. Co.* v. *Salem & Lowell R.R. Co.*, 2 Gray 1 (Mass. 1854), Chief Justice Shaw had emphasized the necessity for public consideration—governmental control of rates and services—before exclusive franchises might be granted. See Levy, *Law of the Commonwealth and Chief Justice Shaw*, 124-26.

[39] *Slaughter-House Cases*, 16 Wall. 36 (1873) at 88. See also Field's dissent in *Munn* v. *Illinois*, 94 U.S. 113 (1877) at 148-49.

[40] See the sources cited at notes 10, 18-20.

[41] *Slaughter-House Cases*, 16 Wall. 36 (1873) at 90. Justice John Harlan, speaking for the court, made the same distinction between "ordinary trades" and public utilities. See *New Orleans Gas Co.* v. *Louisiana Light Co.*, 115 U.S. 650 (1885) at 658.

[42] *Slaughter-House Cases*, 16 Wall. 36 (1873) at 88.

Field's vigorous defense of the butcher's right to pursue his calling un-fettered by state-sanctioned monopolies, if not by "legitimate" police reg-ulations, cannot be considered idiosyncratic. Field's colleagues, although not prepared to "proclaim the faith that was in him both in season and out . . . shared [it] none the less."[43] Indeed, the North had just finished fighting a war that, in Abraham Lincoln's words, was a "people's contest . . . for maintaining in the world that *form and substance* of government whose leading object is to elevate the condition of man; to lift artificial weights from all shoulders; to clear the paths of laudable pursuit for all; to afford all men an unfettered start and a fair chance in the race of life."[44] Thus Field was not being presumptuous when he claimed that the in-dividual's right to pursue one of the "ordinary trades" was "in many respects . . . a distinguishing feature of our republican institutions."[45] In his view, the Fourteenth Amendment would become a "vain and idle enactment, which accomplished nothing" if the court continued to permit the state legislatures to "farm out the ordinary avocations of life."[46] And while Field stubbornly maintained his position, he kept his colleagues aware that, on the whole, they shared the same values and convictions. The strategy of dissent and persistence, aided by changes in the court's composi-tion, ultimately succeeded. In 1886 the major components of Field's *Slaughterhouse Cases* dissent received the approbation of the court.[47]

Even as Field persuaded his associates to adopt a substantive interpreta-tion of the Fourteenth Amendment, he became alarmed at the bar's "ap-parent misconception" of his views.[48] In the zeal of dissent Field had indeed maintained several implausible positions, had cited such dubious authorities as Adam Smith's *Wealth of Nations*, and had given the impression that he was an advocate of unrestrained individualism. But after 1874, Field tried to make it clear that he recognized the states' police power "in its

[43] Corwin, "Supreme Court and the Fourteenth Amendment," 654.
[44] James D. Richardson, ed., *Messages and Papers of the Presidents, 1789-1897* (10 vols., Washington, 1897), VI, 30. See also Eric Foner, *Free Soil, Free Labor, Free Men: The Ideology of the Republican Party Before the Civil War* (New York, 1970), 11-39.
[45] *Dent* v. *West Virginia*, 129 U.S. 114 (1889) at 121.
[46] *Slaughter-House Cases*, 16 Wall. 36 (1873) at 96; *Bartemeyer* v. *Iowa*, 18 Wall. 129 (1873) at 139.
[47] *Yick Wo* v. *Hopkins, Sheriff*, 118 U.S. 356 (1886); Graham, *Everyman's Constitution*, 552-84. On the role of counsel in bringing Field's Fourteenth Amendment construction to fruition, see Walton H. Hamilton, "The Path of Due Process of Law," Conyers Read, ed., *The Constitution Reconsidered* (New York, 1938), 167-90; Benjamin R. Twiss, *Lawyers and the Constitution: How Laissez Faire Came to the Supreme Court* (Princeton, 1942), 42-62.
[48] *Bartemeyer* v. *Iowa*, 18 Wall. 129 (1873) at 141; *Missouri Pacific Ry. Co.* v. *Humes*, 115 U.S. 512 (1885) at 520.

fullest extent," and he was in fact prepared to accord state governments considerable policy discretion.[49] He upheld statutes that prohibited certain businesses altogether as detrimental to the public welfare, recognized government's right to prescribe standards of fitness for lawyers and doctors, and sustained legislation that required railroad corporations to erect cattle guards and eliminate grade crossings at their own expense.[50] Moreover, Field acknowledged the several states' authority to improve the condition of "the poor and dependent" classes of society, including "the laborers in our factories and workshops"; hence he readily affirmed laws that prescribed maximum working hours or compelled employers in hazardous businesses to compensate workers who were injured on the job.[51] The court would invalidate police regulations, he asserted in *Soon Hing* v. *Crowley*, only "when persons engaged in the same business are subjected to different restrictions."[52] So-called "special legislation" was not unconstitutional merely "because like restrictions are not imposed upon other businesses of a different kind."[53] Field, then, provided government with ample room to give "the under fellow a show in this life."[54] Eight years after he retired, however, the court invalidated a maximum hour law for New York bakery workers.[55] But in the process, the majority had to disregard the rule Field had handed down in *Soon Hing*, which "was precedent, in order to draw support from his [*Slaughterhouse Cases*] dicta . . . which was not pre-

---

[49] *Bartemeyer* v. *Iowa*, 18 Wall. 129 (1873) at 138.

[50] *Dent* v. *West Virginia*, 129 U.S. 114 (1889); *Crowley* v. *Christensen*, 137 U.S. 86 (1890); *Minneapolis & St. Paul Ry. Co.* v. *Beckwith*, 129 U.S. 26 (1888); *New York & New England R.R. Co.* v. *Bristol*, 151 U.S. 556 (1894).

[51] *Soon Hing* v. *Crowley*, 113 U.S. 703 (1885) at 710; *Missouri Pacific Ry. Co.* v. *Mackey*, 127 U.S. 205 (1887). Field was so antagonistic to the heavy-handed fellow-servant rule that he was simultaneously making doctrinal innovations in private law, designed to enable injured workers to recover damages from intractable railroad corporations. See *Chicago, Milwaukee & St. Paul Ry. Co.* v. *Ross*, 112 U.S. 377 (1884). See also his vigorous, lone dissent in *Baltimore & Ohio R.R. Co.* v. *Baugh*, 149 U.S. 368 (1893), where Justice David Brewer persuaded the court to abandon Ross and make the fellow-servant doctrine applicable throughout the nation.

[52] *Soon Hing* v. *Crowley*, 113 U.S. 703 (1885) at 710.

[53] *Barbier* v. *Connolly*, 113 U.S. 27 at 31; *Pacific Ry. Co.* v. *Humes*, 115 U.S. 512 (1885) at 523.

[54] Field to Mathew Deady, Oct. 29, 1884, Field Papers (Oregon Historical Society). Field told Judge Deady that he was fed up with "the multifariousness of lying from the inarticulate [Henry Ward] Beecher to Pecksniff [George William] Curtis. The Pharisees of old are the loudest proclaimers of their holier-than-thou virtues. The wealthy and the comfortable wonder as before at the grumblings of the needy and are measuring the eye of the needle, which the camels of old had some difficulty in squeezing through [Mark 10:17], to see what chance there is for their passage. They are not so confident of the 'good time' hereafter as they are of the condition of their bank account now. I am on the other side—and would give the under fellow a show in this life. It is a shame to put him off to the next world."

[55] *Lochner* v. *New York*, 198 U.S. 45 (1905).

cedent."[56] Indeed, if Field's landmark dissents ultimately became the "fountainhead" of the dubious "liberty of contract" doctrine, it was because "another generation" of jurists, with entirely different concerns wrenched Field's principles out of their original context.[57]

Field also held that although health and safety measures invariably "lessen[ed] the value of the property affected," government was not required to compensate property owners who had sustained pecuniary losses.[58] Takings under the eminent domain power were compensable, even if government "refrain[ed] from the absolute conversion of real property to the use of the public," because the individual's property was necessary either for the public work itself or, as in *Pumpelly*, as an easement for "water, earth, sand, or other materials."[59] But the police power stood on a different footing. Police regulations impaired property rights because, as Justice Joseph P. Bradley put it, "the property itself is the cause of the public detriment."[60] In Field's view, this was a vital distinction. Effective takings under the police power were justifiable, he declared in *Barbier* v. *Connolly*, because "special burdens are often necessary for general benefits."[61] As long as the public did not make positive use of private property, the courts would "presume he [who thereby suffered] is compensated by sharing in the advantages arising from such beneficial regulation."[62]

Field did make it clear, however, that government's police regulations had to provide "general benefits." Under "the pretense of prescribing a police regulation," government could not create monopolies in the "ordinary trades"; solve unemployment problems by forbidding Chinese laborers

[56] Corwin, "Supreme Court and the Fourteenth Amendment," 653.
[57] Roscoe Pound, "Liberty of Contract," *Yale Law Journal*, XVIII (May 1909), 470.
[58] *Pacific Ry. Co.* v. *Humes*, 115 U.S. 512 (1885) at 520.
[59] *Pumpelly* v. *Green Bay Co.*, 13 Wall. 166 (1872) at 181. See also *Transportation Co.* v. *Chicago*, 99 U.S. 635 (1878).
[60] *Davidson* v. *New Orleans*, 96 U.S. 97 (1877) at 107. Field's position on takings and the police power is best illustrated in cases involving governmental control of navigable waters. In *Weber* v. *Board of Harbor Commissioners*, 18 Wall. 57 (1873), he refused to award compensation to a wharf-owner whose landing had been summarily destroyed as an impediment to commerce. In *Monongahela Navigation Co.* v. *U.S.*, 148 U.S. 312 (1893), however, he joined a unanimous court that required government to compensate stockholders of a company whose lock and dam were expropriated and incorporated into a larger publicly owned system of river improvements. On the one hand, property was destroyed as detrimental, on the other hand, government took it for the public's positive use. See also Ernst Freund, *The Police Power: Constitutional Rights and Public Policy* (Chicago, 1904), 546; Joseph L. Sax, "Takings and the Police Power," *Yale Law Journal*, 74 (Nov. 1964), 36-76.
[61] *Barbier* v. *Connolly*, 113 U.S. 27 (1884) at 31.
[62] *Baker* v. *Boston*, 12 Pick. 183 (Mass. 1831) at 193. See also Levy, *Law of the Commonwealth and Chief Justice Shaw*, 245-54; *Hagar* v. *Reclamation District*, 111 U.S. 701 (1884).

to work for railroad companies; or provide dairy interests with a protective umbrella by proscribing the manufacture and sale of oleomargarine.[63] Field contended that those laws, "as disclosed on the face of the act, or inferable from their operation," manifestly "discriminated against some [persons] and favored others."[64] Since men had property rights in their occupations, statutes of that variety effectively took the property of one class of persons and vested it in another, private group.[65] In other words, Field imposed limitations on the police power not to protect individuals from enactments designed to "promote . . . the general good," but rather to prevent powerful socioeconomic interests, through the use of corruption or the force of sheer numbers, from utilizing the legislative process as a weapon to improve their own position at the expense of other individuals' "just rights."[66] In his view, this was a proper judicial function. As in eminent domain law, only the courts could determine whether public policy actually "carr[ied] out a public purpose."[67]

Field's crusade to fix a precise boundary between private rights and legitimate governmental interventions also entailed a reconsideration of "public purpose" doctrine in taxation law. By the 1870s, this was a particularly muddled area of American jurisprudence. The legal controversy stemmed from the public's clamor for internal improvements, especially rail connections, which after 1840 had resulted in state laws authorizing local governments to commit themselves to stock purchases and outright gifts to privately owned businesses. In the East and Midwest, antebellum local politicians had been mesmerized by boosterism. Between 1840 and 1880 the nation's aggregate local indebtedness leaped from $25 million to $840 million, much of which flowed into the coffers of private corporations.[68] During the 1860s and 1870s, however, local officials from New York to Iowa recognized that they had overestimated both their power to influence rate structures and their ability to service enormous public debts. Thus a wave of repudiation, and bondholder suits to enforce the contractual

---

[63] *In re Tiburcio Parrott*, 1 Fed. Rep. 481 (C.C.D. California 1880); *Powell* v. *Pennsylvania*, 127 U.S. 678 (1888). For Field's circuit opinions on legislative discrimination against California's Chinese population, see Swisher, *Stephen J. Field*, 205-39; Graham, *Everyman's Constitution*, 142-49.

[64] *Soon Hing* v. *Crowley*, 113 U.S. 703 (1885) at 710; *Barbier* v. *Connolly*, 113 U.S. 27 (1884) at 32.

[65] *Slaughter-House Cases*, 16 Wall. 36 (1873) at 88-89. See also the sources cited at notes 20 and 21.

[66] *Barbier* v. *Connolly*, 113 U.S. 27 at 32.

[67] *Ibid.*

[68] Pierce, *Railroads of New York*, 82-83.

obligations of local governments, coincided with the emergence of regulatory agitation.[69]

The cycle of promotion, repudiation, and regulation frightened investors and profoundly disturbed the conservative community.[70] What must have been most unsettling to Field was the fact that in much of the South and trans-Mississippi West the same process was still in its formative stages. Moreover, as one scholar has observed, "the Western provinces" were even more "creative in devising techniques to abet their own self-exploitation" than their eastern brethren had been.[71] In Kansas, for example, local governments not only granted subsidies to railroad companies but also by 1874 had appropriated over $2 million to aid such "ordinary trades" as hotel and manufacturing establishments.[72] The politics of economic policy were particularly chaotic in Wisconsin. During the 1870s, communities in the southeastern portion of the state had both repudiated their indebtedness and forced a regulatory law through the state legislature. At the same time, representatives from the undeveloped northern counties not only opposed regulation but also succeeded in enacting a statute authorizing local aid to railroads, dry dock companies, manufacturing firms, and steamship companies.[73] For Field, these were ominous developments. He was well aware that private firms that had feasted upon government's largesse were, by the same token, subject to regulation. Thus judicial validation of public sector cash grants to the "ordinary trades" would bring manufacturing, hotel, and dry dock companies into the same vortex of hostile governmental regulation that was simultaneously threatening railroad corporations. Field, however, believed that persons engaged in the "ordinary trades" had a natural right, consistent only with the health and safety of others, to dictate the use and "enjoy" the income of their property unfettered by governmental interference. As a result, he concluded that it was up to the judiciary to establish an inviolable boundary—equally applicable for eminent domain,

[69] See the sources cited at note 4.
[70] For example, see James A. Garfield, "The Future of the Republic: Its Dangers and Hopes," *Legal Gazette*, 5 (Dec. 1873), 408.
[71] Gene M. Gressley, *West by East: The American West in the Gilded Age* (Provo, 1972), 12. See also Leslie E. Decker, "The Great Speculation: An Interpretation of Mid-Continent Pioneering," David M. Ellis, ed., *The Frontier in American Development: Essays in Honor of Paul Wallace Gates* (Ithaca, 1969), 357-80; Allan G. Bogue, "To Shape a Western State: Some Dimensions of the Kansas Search for Capital, 1865-1893," John G. Clark, ed., *The Frontier Challenge: responses to the trans-mississippi west* (Lawrence, 1971), 203-34.
[72] Reporter's note to *Citizens' Sav. Assn.* v. *Topeka*, 5 Fed. Cas. 737 (C.C.D. Kansas 1874).
[73] George Miller, *The Railroads and the Granger Laws*, 140-60; Robert S. Hunt, *Law and Locomotives: The Impact of the Railroad on Wisconsin Law in the Nineteenth Century* (Madison, 1958), 85-87; Lewis Mills, "The Public Purpose Doctrine in Wisconsin, Part 1," *Wisconsin Law Review*, 1957 (Jan. 1957), 52.

exclusive privilege, subsidy, and regulatory purposes—that would distinguish purely private businesses from those which executed works in which the public had an interest.

The state courts, however, only contributed additional uncertainty to the existing, unstable state of affairs. In over twenty jurisdictions, the state judiciaries required defaulting communities to adhere to contractual obligations incurred on behalf of railroad development.[74] Jurists in Michigan and Wisconsin, however, refused to provide remedies for bondholders. Judge Thomas M. Cooley, the influential author of *Constitutional Limitations* (1868), was the leading advocate of the latter position. Speaking for the Michigan court in an 1870 bondholder suit, Cooley held that a railroad was "exclusively private property, owned, controlled, and operated by a private corporation for the benefit of its own members . . ."; as such, it was "not distinguishable from any other" variety of private enterprise and therefore was not a legitimate recipient of public subsidies.[75] The Wisconsin court reached the same conclusion only months afterward.[76] At the very time that midwestern legislatures were enacting statutes to protect the public's interest in rate matters, then, influential jurists were ruling that railroads were "exclusively private" for tax purposes. The state courts' response to the convergence of regulatory and promotional issues, Charles Francis Adams, Jr., lamented in 1870, "furnishes a very curious illustration of the extreme difficulty which . . . now attends any attempt to definitely fix legal principles."[77] Field concurred.

Since diversity of citizenship could usually be established, some 300 municipal bond cases came up during Field's tenure on the court. Two of the more important cases were *Olcott* v. *Supervisors of Fond Du Lac County* (1873) and *Pine Grove Township* v. *Talcott* (1874), which came up from Wisconsin and Michigan, respectively, in the years immediately following state court rulings that public aid to railroads was unconstitutional. In each

[74] Isaac Redfield, *A Practical Treatise on the Law of Railways*, 4th ed. (2 vols., Boston, 1869), II, 395-405; Ellis L. Waldron, "Sharpless v. Philadelphia: Jeremiah Black and the Parent Case on the Public Purpose of Taxation," *Wisconsin Law Review*, 1953 (Jan. 1953), 48-75.

[75] *People ex. rel. Detroit and Howell R.R. Co.* v. *Salem*, 20 Mich. 452 (1870) at 477. See also Alan Jones, "Thomas M. Cooley and the Michigan Supreme Court, 1865-1885," *American Journal of Legal History*, 10 (April 1966), 97-121; Clyde E. Jacobs, *Law Writers and the Courts: The Influence of Thomas M. Cooley, Christopher G. Tiedeman, and John F. Dillon Upon American Constitutional Law* (Berkeley, 1954), 106-21; Scheiber, "The Road to *Munn*," 389.

[76] *Whiting* v. *Sheboygan & Fond Du Lac R.R. Co.*, 25 Wis. 167 (1870).

[77] "Summary of Events," *American Law Review*, V (Oct. 1870), 148; Mark De Wolfe Howe, *Oliver Wendell Holmes: The Proving Years, 1870-1882* (Cambridge, Mass., 1963), 55-57.

case, the court refused to affirm the state's "public purpose" doctrine. The court would follow state decisions on "local questions peculiar to themselves," Justice Samuel Nelson asserted in *Pine Grove Township*, but "here, commercial securities are involved" and therefore the issues "belong to the domain of general jurisprudence."[78] The court held that the public's interest in railroad expansion was undeniable: "Where they go they animate the sources of prosperity, and minister to the growth of the cities and towns within the sphere of their influence."[79] Moreover, Justice William Strong contended in *Olcott*, railroads were "public highways" even when constructed and owned by private persons. Their "uses are so far public that the right of eminent domain . . . may be exerted to facilitate . . . construction" and that had "been the doctrine of all the courts ever since such conveniences for passage and transportation had any existence."[80] The conclusion was inexorable, Strong declared, that public funds might be given as subsidies and "tolls and rates for transportation might [also] be limited" by public officials.[81]

The court's municipal bond decisions exerted a salutary effect on American money markets by restoring confidence in an important class of commercial paper.[82] But the bench divided on the legitimacy of the court's heavy-handed use of "general jurisprudence" principles to protect bondholders. Three factions within the court can be identified. Chief Justice Salmon P. Chase and Justices Miller and David Davis generally dissented on the ground that the court lacked authority to overrule state court decisions when bona fide federal questions had not been raised.[83] Justices Nelson, Nathan Clifford, Noah H. Swayne, Bradley, and Strong (with whom later joined Morrison R. Waite, Ward Hunt, and Harlan), stubbornly resisted every form of railroad subsidy repudiation. Those men were, Miller commented:

if not monomaniacs, as much bigots and fanatics on that subject as is the most unhesitating Mahemodan in regard to his religion. In four cases out of five the

---

[78] *Pine Grove Township* v. *Talcott*, 19 Wall. 666 (1874) at 667. On the development of "general jurisprudence," or a federal common law, see Mitchell Wendell, *Relations Between the Federal and State Courts* (New York, 1949), 113-80; Fairman, *Reconstruction and Reunion*, 935-40.

[79] *Pine Grove Township* v. *Talcott*, 19 Wall. 666 (1874) at 676.

[80] *Olcott* v. *Supervisors of Fond Du Lac County*, 16 Wall. 678 (1873) at 695-96.

[81] *Ibid.*, at 694.

[82] Charles Warren suggested that the railroad subsidy cases "probably had a more important effect upon the commercial development of the country than any other of the Court's extensions of National power." Charles Warren, *The Supreme Court in United States History*, 2nd ed. (2 vols., Boston, 1926), II, 528. See also John F. Dillon, *The Law of Municipal Bonds* (St. Louis, 1876), 7.

[83] Fairman, *Mr. Justice Miller*, 211-18.

case is decided when it is seen by the pleadings that it is a suit to enforce a contract against a city, or town, or a county. If there is a written instrument its validity is a foregone conclusion.[84]

In the majority's view, continued economic growth necessitated vigorous judicial protection of bondholders. "Within the last few years," Nelson wrote in *White* v. *Vermont & Massachusetts R.R. Co.*, "large masses of . . . [municipal bonds] have gone into general circulation and in which capitalists have invested their money." If the court then denied their negotiability, the instrumental value of such securities "as a means of furnishing the funds for the accomplishment of many of the greatest and most useful enterprises of the day would be impaired."[85]

Field's views were unique. Before the convergence of promotional and regulatory issues during the early 1870s, he was not certain that local promotion of railroad expansion was legitimately "within the objects to be accomplished" by municipalities.[86] Moreover, he was deeply troubled by the corruption and opportunism that pervaded the local aid process; when entrepreneurs and local politicians conspired to thrust massive tax burdens on unsuspecting citizens, he consistently voted against the rights of bondholders. Thus he often joined the dissenters.[87] *Olcott* and *Pine Grove Township* came up, however, at a decisive moment in the development of Field's jurisprudence of government-business relations and dictated a reevaluation of his position vis-à-vis municipal repudiation of internal improvement bonds. By then the *Slaughterhouse Cases* had been argued, and he was well into the process of formulating his notion of "public use" or "public purpose" with respect to the extent of the states' police and eminent domain powers. Railroad corporations had been granted eminent domain privileges; hence they were clearly not "ordinary trades." As a result, Field joined the majority in both *Olcott* and *Pine Grove Township*. In his view, the need to formulate universal rules determining the legitimate range of public

[84] Quoted in *ibid.*, 232.
[85] *White* v. *Vermont & Massachusetts R.R. Co.*, 20 How. 575 (1858) at 578.
[86] *Rogers* v. *Burlington*, 3 Wall. 654 (1866) at 671.
[87] *Ibid.*: Field, Robert Grier, and Samuel Miller dissented on the ground that the city only had been authorized to borrow money, not to loan it. *Town of Coloma* v. *Eaves*, 92 U.S. 484 (1876): Miller, Field, and David Davis dissented because the voters had authorized stock subscriptions in one road, while city officials conveyed the municipal funds to another. *Town of Venice* v. *Murdock*, 92 U.S. 494 (1876): Miller, Field, and Davis dissented because bonds were issued without voter approval. *County of Moultrie* v. *Rockingham Ten-Cent Savings-Bank*, 92 U.S. 631 (1876): Miller, Davis, and Field dissented on the ground that the bonds had been issued after a state constitutional amendment had prohibited local aid. *Marcy* v. *Township of Oswego*, 92 U.S. 637 (1876): Miller, Field, and Davis dissented because the voters had been duped into authorizing a debt exceeding the assessed valuation of the entire town, despite a statute restricting local aid to one percent of taxable property.

interventions in economic life took precedence over the immediate consequences his position involved, even if it entailed the exploitation of local governments by railroad corporations or irreparable damages to bondholders. For Field, once the character of the use had been fixed, it was immutable and applied to all governmental interventions. At stake in the subsidy controversies, then, was not only government's promotional discretion but also the legitimate scope of the public sector's regulatory powers.

Under Field's "public use" doctrine, it was axiomatic that local governments had no authority to grant cash subsidies to businessmen engaged in the "ordinary trades." The court considered one such instance in the leading 1874 case of *Loan Association* v. *Topeka*.[88] Through a vigorous promotional campaign involving a $100,000 subsidy, the citizens of Topeka had lured the nation's largest manufacturer of wrought iron bridges to their city. Subsequently, the city repudiated its indebtedness; and with only Clifford dissenting, the court ruled that the bondholders' contract with Topeka was not enforceable. Speaking for the majority, Miller held that the general public had not received a consideration—the right to use the facilities on terms set by government—for the city's grant, and the people's tax monies could not "be used for purposes of private interest instead of public use."[89] "To lay with one hand the power of government on the property of the citizen, and with the other to bestow it upon favored individuals to . . . build up private fortunes," he asserted, "is none the less robbery because it is done under the forms of law and is called taxation."[90]

Field was undoubtedly pleased that Miller had invoked concepts and employed language that closely conformed to his *Slaughterhouse Cases* dissent. Nevertheless, he recognized that a gap remained between their respective positions. For Miller, who had written the majority opinion in the *Slaughterhouse Cases* and had filed virulent dissents in the leading railroad subsidy cases, the decisive aspect of *Loan Association* was that it had come up from a federal court on a subject for which pertinent state law had not been formulated. Thus he spurned the due process clause altogether and held that the Topeka "robbery" violated "principles of general constitutional law."[91] More importantly, Miller declared that "it may not be easy

[88] *Loan Association* v. *Topeka*, 20 Wall. 655 (1874).
[89] *Ibid.*, at 664.
[90] *Ibid.*
[91] See Miller's reiteration of his *Loan Association* position in *Davidson* v. *New Orleans*, 96 U.S. 97 (1877) at 105. Not until 1896 was the public purpose maxim incorporated into the due process clause. In the interim, however, the court continued to invalidate local aid to manufacturing enterprises. See *Parkersburg* v. *Brown*, 106 U.S. 487 (1882); *Cole* v. *La Grange*, 113 U.S. 1 (1885); Edward S. Corwin, "Judicial Review in Action," *University of Pennsylvania Law Review and American Law Register*, 74 (May 1926), 669.

to draw the line in all cases so as to decide what is a public use in this sense and what is not."[92] By declining to hand down a firm rule specifying the exact boundaries of the "public use" doctrine, the court retained discretion to include or exclude particular fact situations as new controversies arose. But that was precisely what Field feared. And four years later he stood in lone dissent when the court upheld payment of subsidies to mill owners. The majority, speaking through Hunt, believed that "it would require great nicety of reasoning" to define a public use such that it included "a gristmill run by water, and exclude[d] one operated by steam; or . . . [showed] that the means of transportation were more valuable to the people of Kansas than the means of obtaining bread."[93] Field did not write a dissenting opinion, but he was almost certainly prepared to make the "nice" distinction the majority had dismissed. Owners of grist mills driven by waterwheels held "franchises of a public character" in that they had flooded adjoining land under the several states' mill acts. Steam-powered mills were "ordinary trades" and, in Field's view, could neither be subjected to governmental control nor be recipients of public subsidies. He believed that doctrine separating the public and private sectors had to be immutable if it was to be effective. As a result, Field refused to condone any deviation from his syllogistic version of the "public use" concept, even when he was required to stand alone in order to maintain a consistent position.

Field's exposition of the constitutional limitations on the exercise of the states' inherent powers—police, taxation, and eminent domain—was uncommonly systematic. Indeed, Field would have reduced the legitimate bounds within which the police and taxation powers might be exercised to embody the eminent domain constraint of "public use." By applying the body of rules that logically flowed from the "public use" doctrine, Field assumed he could mechanically maintain a viable separation of public sector and private sector activities. This is the stuff of laissez faire. But Field's principles carried him still further. If individuals had natural rights which required constitutional protection from the vagaries of government, so too did the states have certain social duties which, according to Field, correct constitutional doctrine recognized as inalienable, inherent powers.

Before the Civil War, judicial concern with the reconciliation of private rights and governmental powers largely focused on the protection of rights vested in private corporations by state legislatures. Therefore, Article I, section 10 of the Constitution, which provides that "no state shall pass any

[92] *Loan Association* v. *Topeka*, 20 Wall. 655 (1874) at 664.
[93] *Township of Burlington* v. *Beasely*, 94 U.S. 310 (1877) at 313.

law impairing the obligation of contracts," was by far the signal constitutional limitation on legislative abuse of private rights. Beginning with the
leading case of *Fletcher* v. *Peck*, the Marshall court held that once government had granted land, perpetual tax exemptions, or corporate charters to
private groups, the state could not thereafter take away those privileges.[94]
Most importantly, John Marshall indicated that it was not "within the
province of the judiciary" to take notice of corruption or examine the mis-
chievous effects of legislative grants in determining their validity.[95] "We
have no knowledge of any authority or principle," Justice Joseph Story announced in *Terrett* v. *Taylor*, "which would support the doctrine that a
legislative grant is revocable in its own nature."[96]

The Marshall court's construction of the contract clause became a crucial
"link between capitalism and constitutionalism" during the formative years
of nineteenth-century economic development.[97] Nevertheless, Marshall's
views were subjected to significant modifications in the antebellum era.
First, in *Dartmouth College*, Story suggested in a concurring opinion that
the states might insert special clauses in corporate charters reserving to
themselves the powers of amendment and repeal. Most states quickly
availed themselves of this practice, and by mid-century it was an accepted
feature of American corporation law.[98] Then, two decades later in *Charles
River Bridge* v. *Warren Bridge*, Chief Justice Roger B. Taney held that the
court would thereafter strictly construe corporate charters.[99] In practical
application, this doctrine meant that corporate privileges and immunities
not expressly granted by the legislature were retained by the state.

Taney's approach to the contract clause reflected his concern for the
course of American economic development. He feared that if the court
chose to presume that legislative grants embodied exclusive privileges, it
might discourage investment in new and competing forms of enterprise.[100]
But there were other judicial concerns that made strict construction of corporate charters particularly appropriate at a time when legislatures served

---

[94] *Fletcher* v. *Peck*, 6 Cranch 87 (1810); *New Jersey* v. *Wilson*, 7 Cranch 164 (1812);
*Dartmouth College* v. *Woodward*, 4 Wheat. 518 (1819).
[95] *Fletcher* v. *Peck*, 6 Cranch 87 (1810) at 130.
[96] *Terrett* v. *Taylor*, 9 Cranch 43 (1815) at 50.
[97] Levy, *Law of the Commonwealth and Chief Justice Shaw*, 280. See also Magrath, *Yazoo*,
101-09; Francis N. Stites, *Private Interest and Public Gain: The Dartmouth College Case,
1819* (Amherst, 1972), 99-113.
[98] *Dartmouth College* v. *Woodward*, 4 Wheat. 518 (1819) at 712; Benjamin Fletcher
Wright, *The Contract Clause of the Constitution* (Cambridge, Mass., 1938), 58-61, 84-88.
[99] *Charles River Bridge* v. *Warren Bridge*, 11 Pet. 420 (1837).
[100] *Ibid.*, at 552-53. See also Stanley I. Kutler, *Privilege and Creative Destruction: The
Charles River Bridge Case* (Philadelphia, 1971).

as "annexes to the marketplace."[101] Speaking for the court in *Ohio Life Insurance & Trust Co.* v. *Debolt*, Taney declared:

> For it is a matter of public history, which this Court cannot refuse to notice, that almost every bill for the incorporation . . . is drawn originally by the parties who are personally interested in obtaining the charter; and that they are often passed by the legislature in the last days of its session, when, from the nature of our political institutions, the business is unavoidably transacted in a hurried manner, and it is impossible that every member can deliberately examine every provision in every bill upon which he is called on to act.
>
> On the other hand, those who accept the charter have abundant time to examine and consider its provisions, before they invest their money.[102]

Field agreed. He occasionally referred to the economic rationale of the strict construction rule, but he believed that the doctrine primarily served "to defeat any purpose concealed by the skillful use of terms, to accomplish something not apparent on the face of the act, and thus [it] sanctions only open dealing with legislative bodies."[103] Field, however, was prepared to extend Taney's position further and restrict the application of *Fletcher* v. *Peck*. He believed that "open dealing" alone had failed to arrest the baneful effects of the private quest for special privileges. Adept lobbyists still might persuade policy-makers to waive future powers of amendment and, as Justice John A. Campbell put it, the court's construction of the contract clause made the judiciary "the patron of such legislation, by furnishing motives of incalculable power to the corporation to stimulate it, and security to the successful effort."[104] Field contended that, since the court had, in fact, taken notice of the turbulent resource allocation process, there was no reason why it should not also scrutinize the substance of special legislative grants. In his view, corporations were not created to extort special privileges from the states, nor were governments instituted to dispense their several attributes of sovereignty to the highest bidder. Thus he concluded that the court's proper function was to "close the door . . . on the introduction of improper elements to control" the legislative process and

---

[101] Wallace D. Farnham, " 'The Weakened Spring of Government': A Study in Nineteenth-Century American History," *American Historical Review*, LXVIII (April 1963), 666. See also James Willard Hurst, *Law and Social Process in United States History* (Ann Arbor, 1960), 46; Hunt, *Law and Locomotives*, 33-34.

[102] *Ohio Life Insurance & Trust Co.* v. *Debolt*, 16 How. 416 (1853) at 435-36.

[103] *Slidell* v. *Grandjean*, 111 U.S. 412 (1884) at 438. See also *Wheeling & Belmont Bridge Co.* v. *Wheeling Bridge Co.*, 138 U.S. 287 (1891). Field restated Taney's *Charles River Bridge* concerns.

[104] *Dodge* v. *Woolsey*, 18 How. 331 (1855) at 371. For the persistent criticism of *Fletcher* v. *Peck* by Justices John Campbell and Peter V. Daniel during the Taney era, see Dodd, *American Business Corporations before 1860*, 130-32; John P. Frank, *Justice Daniel Dissenting: A Biography of Peter V. Daniel, 1784-1860* (Cambridge, Mass., 1964), 205-12.

ensure that unwarranted grants, made against implicit public policy, were not enforced.[105]

Field had some support in precedent for his antagonism to sweeping grants of special immunities. In the leading case of *West River Bridge* v. *Dix*, the court held that the property of a corporation, including its very franchise, might be taken for public use under the power of eminent domain, even if that corporation had earlier exercised that power. The sovereign power of eminent domain was inalienable. Into all contracts, Justice Peter V. Daniel asserted for the majority, "there enter conditions which arise not out of the literal terms of the contract itself; they are super-induced by the preëxisting and higher authority of the law of nature, of nations, or of the community to which the parties belong. . . ."[106] Field was prepared to apply this principle to all of the states' essential powers. If the states could not divest themselves forever of their power of eminent domain, he contended, their powers of taxation and police and their ownership and control of the navigable waters within their respective political jurisdictions were to no less a degree inalienable.[107]

Tax immunity controversies swelled the court's docket during the 1870s. Throughout the antebellum period, state legislatures had granted growth-inducing private interests special tax concessions as a stimulus to development. Policy measures of that variety were particularly popular among politicians because no direct allocation of public funds was necessary.[108] Nevertheless, the suspicion persisted, doubtless with some justification, that the source of tax immunity grants lay in "careless or corrupt legislature[s]" rather than enlightened public policy.[109] As a result, when developmental goals had been fulfilled and middle-class groups began to complain about high taxes, public officials invariably waged concerted campaigns against corruption and corporate privilege and attempted to reassert the power earlier legislatures had bargained away.[110] The summary repeal of special tax immunities was particularly threatening to the fifty-five railroad com-

[105] *Tool Co.* v. *Norris*, 2 Wall. 45 (1865) at 55-56.

[106] *West River Bridge Co.* v. *Dix*, 6 How. 507 (1848) at 532.

[107] See Field's equation of these inherent powers in *The Delaware Railroad Tax*, 18 Wall. 206 (1874) at 226.

[108] Lawrence Friedman, *Contract Law in America* (Madison, 1965), 150; Oscar Handlin and Mary Flug Handlin, *Commonwealth: A Study of the Role of Government in the American Economy: Massachusetts, 1774-1861* (Cambridge, Mass., 1969), 109; Cadman, *The Corporation in New Jersey*, 56-61.

[109] *Dodge* v. *Woolsey*, 18 How. 331 (1855) at 370.

[110] For the post-Civil War tax reform movement, see C. K. Yearley, *The Money Machines: The Breakdown and Reform of Governmental and Party Finance in the North, 1860-1920* (Albany, 1970), 37-95.

panies that by 1870 had secured tax exemptions worth some $13 million from at least nineteen states.[111] The result was a flood of litigation in which corporations confidently argued that their position was impregnable: in *New Jersey* v. *Wilson*, the Marshall court had already brought tax immunities within the protective umbrella of the contract clause.[112]

Few of Field's colleagues shared his belief that *Wilson* was not good law. In their view, any ruling by the court that tended to undermine a leading case or impair the sanctity of contracts would give an unnecessary shock to the economic system.[113] Thus in *Home of the Friendless* v. *Rousse*, with only Field, Miller, and Chase dissenting, the court vigorously affirmed Marshall's tax exemption decision. The dissenters, speaking through Miller, filed an uncompromising critique of doctrine that sustained government's right to bargain away its essential powers. The power to tax, Miller declared:

is a power which, in modern political societies, is absolutely necessary to the continued existence of every such society. . . . To hold, then, that any one of the annual legislatures can, by contract, deprive the State forever of the power of taxation, is to hold that they can destroy the government which they are appointed to serve. . . .

The result of such a principle, under the growing tendency to special and partial legislation, would be, to exempt the rich from taxation, and cast all the burdens of the support of government, and the payment of its debts, on those who are too poor or too honest to purchase such immunity.[114]

Indeed, Field believed, as he later indicated in the *Income Tax Case*, that partial and unequal tax laws effectively transferred property from one socio-economic group to another in contravention of the fundamental precept that property could not be taken for private use.[115]

Despite the setback in *Rousse*, Field ultimately succeeded in modifying the relative position of corporations and the public sector in tax immunity controversies. Speaking for the court in two leading cases handed down in

[111] Leslie E. Decker, *Railroads, Lands, and Politics: The Taxation of the Railroad Land Grants, 1864-1897* (Providence, 1964), 11.

[112] *New Jersey* v. *Wilson*, 7 Cranch 164 (1812).

[113] For example, see *Farrington* v. *Tennessee*, 95 U.S. 679 (1878), where the majority refused to disturb Wilson because "contracts mark the progress of communities in civilization and prosperity. They guard, as far as is possible, against the fluctuations of human affairs. They seek to give stability to the present and certainty to the future. . . . They are the springs of business, trade, and commerce. Without them, society could not go on."

[114] *Home of the Friendless* v. *Rousse*, 8 Wall. 430 (1869) at 443. See also *Tomlinson* v. *Jessup*, 15 Wall. 454 (1873) at 458.

[115] *Pollock* v. *Farmers' Loan & Trust Co.*, 157 U.S. 429 (1895) at 586-608. See also Arnold M. Paul, *Conservative Crisis and the Rule of Law: Attitudes of Bar and Bench, 1887-1895* (Ithaca, 1960), 204.

the 1870s, Field held that once business corporations changed hands on sale of execution or consolidated such that the original concerns had forfeited their status as distinct corporations, all franchises and privileges not "essential to the operation of the corporation," including tax immunities, might be revoked by state legislatures.[116] Moreover, the *Rousse* dissenters' unrestrained advocacy of government's inherent power to tax mobilized substantial support both in the legal profession and on the state benches. In virtually every state, jurists refused to uphold the validity of tax immunities.[117] Thus private interests were required either to expend large sums of money on appeal or bargain with state authorities who were often prepared to offer alternative, though less valuable, concessions as *quid pro quo* for giving up perpetual exemptions.[118] State pressures, combined with the court's propensity to invoke all doctrinal weapons short of reversing *Wilson*, effectively destroyed vested rights in special tax concessions. By 1890 the question was of little importance as a practical matter or a legal issue.

Field met less resistance in establishing the inalienability of the police power. The tyranny of established constitutional doctrine was not a factor, as in the tax exemption cases, and "vested rights in liquor, lottery tickets, gambling, and sex never appealed much to nineteenth century judges."[119] The leading cases came up from the South during Reconstruction, when policy-makers had employed the age-old technique of stimulating capital formation by grants of lottery privileges.[120] The giant southern lottery corporations, particularly the infamous Louisiana State Lottery Company, were notoriously corrupt and often "exercised a power greater than that of the State government itself."[121] As "redeemer" governments acquired power, they generally revoked the charters of those concerns, thereby precipitating litigation.

In *Boyd* v. *Alabama*, an agent for a state-chartered mutual aid association had been convicted of selling lottery tickets in violation of the state's anti-lottery law. The 1868 charter of the company, however, not only ex-

[116] *Morgan* v. *Louisiana*, 93 U.S. 217 (1876); *Railroad Co.* v. *Maine*, 96 U S. 499 (1877). See also Ernest W. Huffcut, "Legislative Tax Exemption Contracts," *American Law Review*, XXIV (June 1890), 399-427.

[117] See the long line of state court decisions cited in Thomas M. Cooley, *Constitutional Limitations* (Boston, 1883), 340. See also James F. Colby, "Exemption from Taxation by Legislative Contract," *American Law Review*, XIII (Oct. 1878), 26-39.

[118] Harry N. Scheiber, *Ohio Canal Era: A Case Study of Government and the Economy, 1820-1861* (Athens, Ohio, 1969), 278, 296.

[119] Friedman, *A History of American Law*, 312.

[120] Ezell, *Fortune's Merry Wheel*, 233-70.

[121] C. Vann Woodward, *The Origins of the New South, 1877-1913* (Baton Rouge, 1951), 14.

plicitly granted it the right to carry on a lottery, but the state had also failed to include any provision for amending the twenty-year grant of privilege. Thus Boyd claimed that the statute was void, insofar as it applied to his activities, because it impaired the state's obligation of contract. The court actually resolved the issue by referring to the anti-logrolling provision in the Alabama constitution. The act of incorporation and the grant of lottery privileges were embraced in the same statute, violating the prohibition of laws involving more than one subject. Nevertheless, in his opinion for the court, Field explained:

[he was] not prepared to admit that it is competent for one legislature, by any contract with an individual to restrain the power of a subsequent legislature to legislate for the public welfare, and to that end to suppress [by the exercise of the police power] any and all practices tending to corrupt the public morals.[122]

In *Stone* v. *Mississippi*, the court refused to provide contract clause protection for a lottery corporation on the inalienability doctrine alone.[123] The inalienability of the police power, Field reiterated in 1884, "is a principle of vital importance," because "its habitual observance" by the state "is essential to wise and valid execution of the trust committed to the legislature."[124]

Field's development of the "public trust" doctrine and the simultaneous erosion of *Fletcher* v. *Peck* reached its apogee in the leading 1892 case of *Illinois Central R.R. Co.* v. *Illinois*.[125] In 1869 the State of Illinois conveyed to the railroad corporation, as part of a larger grant, title to the submerged lands along the entire Chicago waterfront. When the state sought to repossess the property, Illinois Central balked and its attorneys attempted to restrain state action by invoking the contract clause. Field, speaking for a narrow majority, held that the contract authorizing the original grant could not be enforced. The state had no right, he declared, to grant away in perpetuity lands covered by the navigable waters of the sovereign. Navigable lakes and rivers were "public highways" which the state held in trust for the use of all shippers and carriers.[126] Thus the state could make grants

---

[122] *Boyd* v. *Alabama*, 94 U.S. 645 (1877) at 650.
[123] *Stone* v. *Mississippi*, 101 U.S. 814 (1880). See also *Beer Co.* v. *Massachusetts*, 97 U.S. 25 (1878); *Fertilizing Co.* v. *Hyde Park*, 97 U.S. 659 (1878).
[124] *Butchers' Union Slaughterhouse Co.* v. *Crescent City Live-Stock Landing Co.*, 111 U.S. 746 (1884) at 754.
[125] *Illinois Central R.R. Co.* v. *Illinois*, 146 U.S. 387 (1892). Joseph Sax, an eminent legal scholar interested in protecting the "public trust" in such matters as wilderness areas and pesticide control, refers to Field's opinion as "the lodestar in American Public Trust Law." Joseph Sax, "The Public Trust Doctrine in Natural Resource Law: Effective Judicial Intervention," *Michigan Law Review*, 68 (Jan. 1970), 487.
[126] This doctrine logically flowed from the court's earlier commerce and admiralty opinions, where the court had recognized navigable bodies of fresh water, like the oceans, to be "public

of them only for purposes of constructing wharves, docks, and other aids to commerce, and then only to the extent that they did "not substantially impair the public interest in the water remaining."[127] The principle permitting limited grants for public benefit, Field concluded:

is a very different doctrine from the one which would sanction the abdication of the general control of the state over the navigable waters of an entire harbor or bay, or of a sea or lake. Such abdication is not consistent with the exercise of that trust which requires the government of the state to preserve such waters for the use of the public. The trust devolving upon the state for the public, and which can only be discharged by the management and control of property in which the public has an interest, cannot be relinquished by a transfer of property.[128]

It was preposterous, Field contended, that "a corporation created for . . . [railroad] purpose[s]" could be "converted into a corporation to manage and practically control the harbor of the City of Chicago, not simply for its own purpose as a railroad corporation, but for its own profit generally."[129] To allow such a grant was to concede that the public and private sectors had common interests. But, as his several references to "management," "purpose," and "profit" indicated, Field believed that public and private institutions had diametrically opposed reasons for existence; legislation that vested public property in private corporations would invariably lead to situations in which the people would be subject to private greed. Thus, in his view, the court had to "meet the very suggestion of evil, and strike down the contract from its inception."[130]

The fact that Field was willing summarily to divest a major American corporation of exceedingly valuable property should be viewed as more than a legal curiosity. In his version of the American system, there was room for neither corruption and special privilege nor a self-denying spirit of largesse on the part of government, and his "radical" opinions on the "public trust" doctrine were an integral part of his larger vision of government-business relations under the Constitution.[131] On the one hand, he enjoined the several state legislatures to refrain from exercising their "trinity of powers"—police, taxation, and eminent domain—so as to arbitrarily transfer property rights from one socioeconomic group to an-

highways." See *The Daniel Ball*, 10 Wall. 557 (1871); Milton Conover, "The Abandonment of the 'Tidewater' Concept in Admiralty Jurisdiction in the United States," *Oregon Law Review*, 38 (Dec. 1958), 34-58.

[127] *Illinois Central R.R. Co.* v. *Illinois*, 146 U.S. 387 (1892) at 452.

[128] *Ibid.*, at 451.

[129] *Ibid.*

[130] *Tool Co.* v. *Norris*, 2 Wall. 45 (1865) at 55.

[131] See the scathing editorial attack on Field's opinion, "The Police Power and the Lake Front Case," *Harvard Law Review*, VI (March 1893), 444-45.

other. And on the other hand, Field reprimanded legislatures that would contract away the right to exercise those very powers and, except in the case of tax immunity grants, succeeded in persuading his associates that the states' inherent powers were "held in trust" for the public and therefore inalienable. What he attempted to take from government with one hand he sought to restore with the other; the doctrine Field handed down in *Illinois Central R.R. Co.* v. *Illinois* demonstrates in disarming proportions the degree to which he was committed to upholding powers which, in his view, fell on the public side of the line. By enlarging judicial cognizance of the consequences of ill-considered public policy and exercising all its powers, "broadly and liberally interpreted," Field believed the court could proscribe virtually every form of special privilege. The result would be a harmonious system in which the public and private sectors pursued appropriate goals within proper spheres of action. But an all-encompassing separation of the public and private sectors was impossible. Certain businesses, though private in ownership, were public in "use." Thus much of Field's judicial energy was expended in formulating rules fixing the areas in which the public might lawfully intervene in the affairs of private businesses and the extent to which any such interference would be a violation of property rights.

The concept of businesses "affected with a public interest," a major constitutional doctrine for over half a century, was born in the 1877 case of *Munn* v. *Illinois*.[132] Deriving its doctrinal reasoning from the seventeenth-century treatises of Lord Hale, the court held, as Justice Bradley explained a year later in the *Sinking-Fund Cases*:

> when an employment or business becomes a matter of such public interest and importance as to create a common charge or burden upon the citizens; in other words, when it becomes a practical monopoly, to which the citizen is compelled to resort, and by means of which a tribute can be exacted from the community, it is subject to regulation by the legislative power.[133]

Grain warehousemen, Chief Justice Waite wrote for the majority, "stand . . . in the very 'gateway of commerce' and take toll from all who pass"; and therefore "exercise a sort of public office" comparable to that enjoyed by wharfingers, ferry operators, hackney-coachmen, and railroad corporations.[134]

[132] *Munn* v. *Illinois*, 94 U.S. 113 (1877).
[133] *Sinking-Fund Cases*, 99 U.S. 700 (1878) at 747. See also Scheiber, "The Road to *Munn*," 355-60; Charles Fairman, "The So-Called Granger Cases, Lord Hale, and Justice Bradley," *Stanford Law Review*, 5 (July 1953), 587-679.
[134] *Munn* v. *Illinois*, 94 U.S. 113 (1877) at 132.

Field dissented. In his view, the affectation doctrine, as employed by the majority, was a contorted misapplication of Hale's precepts. According to Field, when Hale had suggested that property might cease to be *juris privati*, that is when it ceased to be held by private right, he referred to "property the use of which was granted by the government, or in connection with which special privileges were conferred."[135] But the firm of Munn & Scott was a partnership. It held no corporate charter, and it had been granted no special privileges. The firm's property, then, had never ceased to be *juris privati*, and there was no legitimate rationale for regulation.

Field's position in *Munn* did not stem, however, from a careful reading of Lord Hale. Instead, his construction of "practical monopoly" and "affected with a public interest" had been carefully worked out four years earlier in the *Slaughterhouse Cases*. "It is also sought to justify the act in question," Field had asserted in that case,

on the same principle that exclusive grants for ferries, bridges and turnpikes are sanctioned. But it can find no support there. Those grants are of franchises of a public character appertaining to the government. Their use usually requires the exercise of the sovereign right of eminent domain. It is for the government to determine when one of them shall be granted, and the conditions under which it shall be enjoyed. . . . The grant, with exclusive privileges, of a right thus appertaining to the government, is a very different thing from a grant . . . of a right to pursue one of the ordinary trades or callings of life, which is a right appertaining solely to the individual.[136]

In order to fulfill a public purpose, then, special privileges, including exclusive monopolies or cash subsidies, might be conferred on corporations that necessarily employed powers "appertaining to government." Moreover, the governmental character of those businesses subjected them to legislative control of "the conditions upon which" the franchises might "be enjoyed." "The recipient of the privilege," Field explained in *Munn*, "stipulates to comply with the conditions" set by government; and "it is the public privilege conferred with the use of the property which creates the public interest in it."[137] But the public had no interest whatsoever in slaughterhouses and grain elevators. There could be no legal monopoly

[135] *Ibid.*, at 139. If one takes Lord Hale's precepts literally, Field had the best of the argument. "Tho[s]e things that are Juris publici," Hale wrote, "are [s]uch as . . . are common to all the King's Subjects, and are of the[s]e kinds, viz: (1) Common Highways, (2) Common Bridges, (3) Common Rivers, (4) Common Ports." *Analysis of the Law* (Stratford, England, 1713), 63. For a detailed critique of Waite's use of Hale's tracts, see Van Buren Denslow, "Ira Y. Munn and George L. Scott v. The People of Illinois," *American Law Register*, XXV (Sept. 1877), 539-45.
[136] *Slaughter-House Cases*, 16 Wall. 36 (1873) at 88.
[137] *Munn v. Illinois*, 94 U.S. 113 (1877) at 149, 152.

because such firms could not lawfully exercise governmental powers or privileges, and there could be no "practical monopoly," and hence no rationale for regulation, because no special privileges were held and therefore anyone might take up the calling. Munn and Scott had been engaged in the "ordinary trades" only. In that instance, reasonable prices might be determined only by normal market mechanisms.

"The great difficulty in the future," Chief Justice Waite commented shortly after *Munn* was handed down, "will be to establish the boundary between what is private, and that in which the public has an interest. The elevators furnished an extreme case and there was little difficulty in determining on which side of the line they properly belonged."[138] Indeed, the Chicago warehousemen not only "st[oo]d in the very gateway of commerce," but also had collusive lease agreements for the use of railroad rights-of-way; hence they were, in fact, "practical monopol[ists]."[139] But in *Munn*, as in *Illinois Central R.R. Co.* v. *Illinois*, Field was concerned with high policy rather than the outcome of one particular controversy, and the "great difficulty" to which Waite referred molded his dissenting opinion. In his view, there was simply no way for the court to uphold the grain elevator statute without opening the door for any combination of interest groups, through the "magic . . . [of] language," to change an unpopular "private business into a public one" and leave its owner "at the mercy of a majority of the legislature."[140] "There is hardly an enterprise or business engaging the attention and labor of any considerable portion of the community," he remarked, "in which the public has not an interest in the sense in which that term is used by the court. . . ."[141] Yet Field believed that the exigencies of the turbulent 1870s required the judiciary to resolutely perform its "main purpose, namely, that of setting metes and bounds to legislative power."[142] The Granger Laws and public vacillation—first subsidizing private enterprises, then repudiating the bonded indebtedness incurred—had thoroughly disrupted the nation's economy.[143] Moreover,

---

[138] Quoted in C. Peter Magrath, *Morrison R. Waite: The Triumph of Character* (New York, 1963), 187.

[139] See also Morton Rothstein, "The International Market for Agricultural Commodities," David Gilchrist and W. D. Lewis, eds., *Economic Change in the Civil War Era* (Greenville, Del., 1966), 62-72; Woodman, "Chicago Businessmen and the Granger Laws," 16-24.

[140] *Munn* v. *Illinois*, 94 U.S. 113 (1877) at 138, 140.

[141] *Ibid.*, at 141.

[142] Corwin, "Basic Doctrine of American Constitutional Law," 247. Corwin's language is as applicable to the 1870s as to the antebellum era.

[143] In the "Granger" states, where the convergence of regulation and repudiation was most prominent, annual railroad construction declined from 3,086 miles added in 1872 to 550 miles added in 1876. Once the court refused to condone repudiation and the rate laws were

regulatory agitation and the ensuing clash of regional and functional interest groups had increased at the very time that governments in the trans-
Mississippi West and South had increased their promotion—through cash
subsidies and exclusive grants—of otherwise "ordinary trades." In the
*Slaughterhouse Cases, Loan Association* v. *Topeka,* and *Munn,* however,
the court had failed to make a firm distinction between private businesses
and those in which the public had an interest. The court's decisions, Field
indicated, would encourage further ill-advised interventions in economic
life, perpetuate the inordinate instability that had characterized the early
1870s, and necessitate continous debate as to which businessmen engaged
in purely private concerns and which "exercise[d] a sort of public office."
The mechanical "public use" doctrine, however, had been designed to restore stability by resolving for all time the era's pressing policy questions
on both sides of the promotional-regulatory continuum. Through the end
of his long career, Field continued to believe that the majority had committed a grave error and, as Justice Harlan noted, he periodically turned
"his face towards the setting sun, wondering . . . whether the Munn case
or the eternal principles of right and justice, w[ould] ultimately prevail."[144]

The court's decisions in the *Granger Railroad Cases* flowed logically
from the principles articulated in *Munn.*[145] Railroad corporations were
"affected with a public interest" and therefore might be regulated at the
discretion of the legislature. "The controlling fact," Waite wrote for the
majority, "is the power to regulate at all. If that exists, the right to establish the maximum of charge . . . is implied. . . ." And he added, "We know
that it is a power which may be abused; but that is no argument against its
existence. For protection against abuses by legislatures the people must
resort to the polls, not to the courts."[146] Justice Bradley had anticipated and
described the rationale behind this dictum two years earlier in *Baltimore*

one by one repealed (the last in 1878), new construction rebounded to former levels. In
1880, 2,915 miles were added in the former "Granger" states. Although a financial panic and
ensuing depression certainly played a major role in the decline of new construction between
1873 and 1878, contemporaries tended to attribute it to repudiation and regulation alone.
Andrew Allison, "The Rise and Probable Decline of Private Corporations in America,"
*Report of the Seventh Annual Meeting of the American Bar Association* (Philadelphia,
1884), 241-56.
[144] Quoted in Alan F. Westin, "Stephen J. Field and the Headnote to O'Neil v. Vermont:
A Snapshot of the Fuller Court at Work," *Yale Law Journal,* 67 (Jan. 1958), 376. See also
*Budd* v. *New York,* 143 U.S. 517 (1892); *Brass* v. *North Dakota,* ex. rel. Stoeser, 153 U.S.
391 (1894).
[145] *Chicago, Burlington & Quincy R.R.* v. *Iowa,* 94 U.S. 155 (1877); *Peik* v. *Chicago
& North-western Ry. Co.,* 94 U.S. 164 (1877); *Chicago, Milwaukee & St. Paul R.R.* v.
*Ackley,* 94 U.S. 179 (1877); *Winona & St. Peter R.R.* v. *Blake,* 94 U.S. 180 (1877);
*Stone* v. *Wisconsin,* 94 U.S. 181 (1877).
[146] *Munn* v. *Illinois,* 94 U.S. 113 (1877) at 134.

& *Ohio R.R. Co.* v. *Maryland.* The states' power to fix rates charged by transport firms, he asserted, "in its very nature is unrestricted and uncontrolled" because of "the simple fact that they are its own works, or are constructed under its authority."[147] State legislatures, Bradley explained a decade later, had a "duty" to provide transport facilities for the convenience of the public. When a railroad corporation was chartered, government only empowered it to act "as an agent of the State for furnishing public accommodation." Therefore, it was the legislature's

> prerogative to fix the fares and freights which they may charge for their services. When merely a road or a canal is to be constructed, it is for the legislature to fix the tolls to be paid by those who use it; when a company is chartered not only to build a road, but to carry on public transportation upon it, it is for the legislature to fix the charges for such transportation.[148]

According to Bradley, and probably the entire *Granger Railroad Cases* majority, then, a railroad corporation was no different from a state-owned canal or publicly operated toll road; hence the legislature might fix rates of carriage at its discretion.

Once again Field dissented. He conceded that transport firms were devoted to "public use," and he recognized that state legislatures had generally reserved the power to alter rates fixed in corporate charters.[149] As a result, he admitted that the states' power to regulate transport tariffs was incontrovertible. What he could not accept, however, was the court's contention that railroad corporations were mere "agents of the State." In his view, the majority had converted private concerns with public duties into wholly public corporations. That position, Field contended, was neither good policy nor good law. The public's interest in railroads necessitated the mobilization of private investment capital, and the state of railroad credit wholly depended upon certainty of return. But investors could not be attracted and economic growth perpetuated, if their property was entirely at the mercy of hostile legislatures.[150] Thus Field contended that the court's clear duty was to

> define the limits of the power of the State over its corporations . . . so that, on the

---

[147] *Railroad Co.* v. *Maryland,* 21 Wall. 456 (1875) at 471.

[148] *Chicago, Milwaukee & St. Paul Ry.* v. *Minnesota,* 134 U.S. 418 (1890) at 461. See also Bradley's "Outline of My Views," Fairman, "The So-Called Granger Cases," 670.

[149] Balthasar H. Meyer, *Railway Legislation in the United States* (New York, 1903); M. H. Hunter, "The Early Regulation of Public Service Corporations," *American Economic Review,* VII (Sept. 1917), 569-81.

[150] As early as 1859, the fundamental principle of Field's jurisprudence was "security" for private landowners and investors, without which, he declared, "there would be little development, for the incentive to improvement would be wanting." *Biddle Boggs* v. *Merced Mining Co.,* 14 Cal. 279 (1859) at 379.

one hand, the property interest of the stockholder would be protected from practical confiscation, and, on the other hand, the people would be protected from arbitrary and extortionate charges.[151]

Field must have been most upset because only one year earlier, in *Lake Superior & Mississippi R.R. Co.* v. *United States*, Bradley had drawn just such a line in holding that railroad corporations had certain rights in their property which the public could not take without just compensation.[152]

In 1864 Congress granted land on the public domain to the State of Minnesota to be conveyed, in turn, to the Lake Superior & Mississippi Railroad Company as a bounty for the construction of a "first class" line. The statute contained the following provision: "The railroad shall be, and remain a *public highway* free from all toll or other charge [upon] the transportation of any property or troops of the United States." Federal attorneys liberally construed the act to mean that government shipments were to be transported toll-free by the company. The corporation demurred, filed suit in the United States Court of Claims, and after losing there appealed to the Supreme Court of the United States. Speaking through Bradley, a narrow majority sustained the railroad's contention that the government had to pay the company for the cost of its services. The word "public highway," Bradley declared, "cannot, without doing violence to language . . . be extended to embrace the rolling-stock or other personal property of the railroad company."[153]

How Bradley and Waite, who had joined the majority in the land grant case, reconciled government's "unrestricted and uncontrolled" discretion to fix rates with the right of railroad corporations to refuse carriage without compensation is unclear. But for Field, the difference was only one of degree. As a result of the pervasive, rancorous conflict among merchants, farmers, and railroad companies during the preceding decade, Field had imbibed a profound distrust of the legislative process. Thus he was readily convinced that greedy shippers had fixed rates "without reference to the expenses of the carriage, or the obligations incurred in the construction of the roads."[154] In the Wisconsin rate cases, however, the state court had

---

[151] *Stone* v. *Wisconsin*, 94 U.S. 181 (1877) at 184-85. Compare Swisher, *Stephen J. Field*, 372-85. For Robert McCloskey's recent statement that while Field "denied *all* legislative power to fix prices, a decade later he was willing to concede that some such regulation was permissible. . . ." See Robert McCloskey, "Stephen J. Field," Leon Friedman and Fred L. Israel, eds., *The Justices of the United States Supreme Court, 1789-1969: Their Lives and Major Opinions* (4 vols., New York, 1969), II, 1085.

[152] *Lake Superior & Mississippi R.R. Co.* v. *U.S.*, 93 U.S. 442 (1876).

[153] *Ibid.*, at 455.

[154] *Stone* v. *Wisconsin*, 94 U.S. 181 (1877) at 183. Virtually all the contemporary journalists and railroad "experts" asserted that what Field feared had, in fact, occurred. For a

held that even if tariffs fixed by the legislature diminished income below costs, the judiciary could not provide a remedy; and the court, by remanding the companies to the polls, had implicitly sustained the Wisconsin court's assertion that a compensable "taking" necessitated "appropriation by the state itself, for its own use . . . of the whole thing confiscated."[155] That doctrine, however, ignored the crucial transformation of the property right which the court had, in Field's view, brought to fruition in *Pumpelly* v. *Green Bay & Mississippi Canal Co.*[156] If, indeed, rates had been fixed such that carriage was required without remuneration, then the stockholders' track and rolling stock, like the property of landowners in "consequential" eminent domain takings, had been effectively taken for the public's use without compensation. Moreover, Field contended, rate regulation was not analogous to health and safety measures for which compensation need not be paid even if the value of property had been diminished.[157] By regulating railway tariffs, government did not destroy property because it was detrimental. Instead, the public made positive use of the regulated property. In that instance, Field asserted, "if the constitutional guaranty extends no further than to prevent a deprivation of title and possession, and allows a deprivation of use, and the fruits of that use, it does not merit the encomiums it has received."[158]

Field did not reject the court's position in the *Granger Railroad Cases* on eminent domain analogies alone. He believed that his approach to regulatory questions was also deeply rooted in American corporation law and constituted a logical application of contract clause doctrine the court had handed down during the early 1870s. Speaking for a unanimous court in *Tomlinson* v. *Jessup*, Field had conceded that a state legislature might amend corporate charters if a specific reservation retaining that power had been inserted in either the act of incorporation or the constitution of the state. He had added, however, that "rights and interests acquired by the company, not constituting a part of the contract of incorporation, stand upon a different footing."[159]

full analysis of the literature on rate regulation published between 1872 and 1878, see Charles R. Detrick, "The Effects of the Granger Laws," *Journal of Political Economy*, XI (March 1903), 237-56.

[155] *Attorney General* v. *Railroad Companies*, 35 Wis. 425 (1874) at 579.

[156] See the text at note 28. Field quoted Miller's *Pumpelly* dictum in full in *Munn* v. *Illinois*, 94 U.S. 113 (1877) at 144.

[157] *Ibid.*, at 145-48. See the discussion in note 60.

[158] *Ibid.*, at 141.

[159] *Tomlinson* v. *Jessup*, 15 Wall. 454 (1873) at 459. See also William Maxwell Evarts' argument in the Wisconsin rate cases, partially reprinted in Edward Abbott, "The Wisconsin Railroad Acts," *American Law Review*, IX (Oct. 1874), 50-73. Shortly after filing his brief, Evarts mailed a copy to Field, telling him that the "question of the scope of the reservation of a right to repeal, alter, or amend will have to be settled by your Court before long; if this

For Field, then, franchise privileges might be altered or revoked altogether; but the state retained control only over what it granted. Contractual agreements and corporate property made or acquired in the exercise of the charter privileges were collateral to the grant of incorporation and could not be impaired or taken without compensation. Insofar as the property of the corporators—whether in the form of stock, bonds, or commonly held capital goods—had been vested, then, the state might exert no other power than that which it exercised over the property of individuals. "And such must be the case," Field reiterated in the *Sinking-Fund Cases,* "or there would be no safety in dealing with the government where such a [reservation] clause is inserted in its legislation." Otherwise, government "could undo at pleasure every thing done under its authority, and despoil of their property those [investors] who had trusted to its faith."[160]

Field's construction of the contract clause was not unique. In both the state courts and in the supreme court, jurists had long agreed that reservation clauses did not authorize legislative interference with property rights held outside of and collateral to the corporate franchise.[161] The court divided, however, on the application of that doctrine to cases in which government asserted the right to alter maximum rates fixed in the dated charters of railroad and other public service corporations. The *Granger Railroad Cases* majority ruled that the contract clause was inapplicable and held that the only "controlling fact is the right to regulate at all." Field, however, contended that, although the states might regulate the rates charged by businesses that "held franchises of a public character," the policy-makers' discretion was limited by the established principle that "no amendment or alteration of the charter can take away the property rights which have become vested under a legitimate exercise of the powers given."[162] In his view, if a public service corporation was required "to take as compensation" rates which were "less than the expenses" which the company had incurred in building and operating the road, the stock and bondholders would be deprived of property "as effectually as if the legislature had ordered its forcible dispossession."[163] But Field dissented not because the several railroad cor-

opinion of mine has any value it is in that direction." Evarts to Field, May 18, 1874, Field Papers (Bancroft Library, University of California, Berkeley).
[160] *Sinking-Fund Cases,* 99 U.S. 700 (1878) at 758.
[161] See *Miller* v. *State of New York,* 15 Wall. 478 (1873); *Holyoke Co.* v. *Lyman,* 15 Wall. 500 (1873). This doctrine was also assumed to be unquestionable in the several opinions delivered in the *Sinking-Fund Cases.* See *Sinking-Fund Cases,* 99 U.S. 700 (1878) at 721, 742, 748.
[162] *Commonwealth* v. *Essex Co.,* 13 Gray 239 (Mass. 1859) at 253; Levy, *Law of the Commonwealth and Chief Justice Shaw,* 277-81.
[163] *Munn* v. *Illinois,* 94 U.S. 113 (1877) at 143.

porations had conclusively shown that property rights of stockholders had been impaired, but rather to expose fully the disparity between his position and the doctrine handed down by the majority.[164] Subsequently, in *Ruggles* v. *Illinois*, he concurred when the court sustained a maximum rate law "on the ground that no proof was made that the rate prescribed by the legislature was unreasonable."[165] The burden of proof lay with the corporation.[166] The legislature only had to take care that maximum rate laws provided each company with income commensurate with its costs and, since the property right subsumed the right to the fruits of its use, furnished stockholders with a fair return on their investment.

Field never altered this position. He merely waited for the rest of the court to assume his posture. After 1886, however, neither Field nor the court invoked the contract clause as a restraint on rate maxima.[167] But this did not indicate inconsistency or opportunism on his part. Instead, in the *Railroad Commission Cases*, Chief Justice Waite asserted that the states' regulatory power was subject to the "taking" provision of the due process clause.[168] This landmark concession made it no longer necessary to look through the corporate entity to its stockholders and creditors. Thus Field's persistent demolition work on the discretion doctrine of *Munn* bore fruit even as its contract clause rationale became obscured; by 1888, he was able to summarize his position while speaking for a unanimous court. Railroad corporations, he asserted in *Georgia Banking and Railroad Co.* v. *Smith*, were subject to regulation in order to "prevent extortion by unreasonable charges, and favoritism by unjust discrimination" because there had been a "grant to it of special privileges to carry out the object of its incorporation, particularly the authority to exercise the State's right of eminent domain. . . ."[169] But regulation was "subject to the limitation that the carriage

---

[164] Westin, "Stephen J. Field and the Headnote to O'Neil v. Vermont," 363-83.

[165] *Ruggles* v. *Illinois*, 108 U.S. 526 (1883).

[166] In *St. Louis & San Francisco Ry. Co.* v. *Gill*, 156 U.S. 649 (1895), the court unanimously held that when two companies consolidated the new corporation had no defense against a rate that was confiscatory for only one line of the larger system. Instead, the proper test of reasonableness was the rate's effect on the earnings of the consolidated system as a whole. For the difficulties the great-system managers had in producing the requisite proof, see Albro Martin, *Enterprise Denied: Origins of the Decline of American Railroads, 1897-1917* (New York, 1971), 225.

[167] The court did, however, later uphold Field's contention that rates could only be fixed by public officials if the state had reserved the power in the grant of incorporation. See *Spring Valley Water Works* v. *Schottler*, 110 U.S. 347 (1884); *Detroit* v. *Detroit Citizens' Street Ry. Co.*, 184 U.S. 368 (1902); Richard J. Smith, "The Judicial Interpretation of Public Utility Franchises," *Yale Law Journal*, XXXIX (May 1930), 957-79.

[168] *Railroad Commission Cases*, 116 U.S. 307 (1886); Magrath, *Morrison R. Waite*, 198-200.

[169] *Georgia R.R. & Banking Co.* v. *Smith*, 128 U.S. 174 (1888) at 179.

is not required without reward, or upon conditions amounting to the taking
of property for public use without just compensation. . . ."[170] This restriction
was directly applied in the leading case of Chicago, Milwaukee & St. Paul
Ry. Co. v. Minnesota, and in 1898 the court began reviewing state regulatory
legislation to ascertain its probable effect on the distribution of corporate
assets and liabilities.[171] Judicial review of fact in so complex an area as corporate finance added burdensome judicial duties to an already overcrowded
docket. But that was of no consequence to Field. Public and private rights
not only had to be defined, but the rights of each had to be protected from
"arbitrary" encroachment by the other. That, above all else, was what Field
conceived to be the role of law.

In the immediate post-Civil War period, the socioeconomic dislocation
that accompanied three decades of rapid growth eroded the unifying, antebellum conception of "the Commonwealth" and Americans became "obsessed . . . with the necessity for making the distinction between public and
private spheres of action."[172] But the issues arising from the collapse of co-
operation between the public and private sectors affected different groups in
different ways, and men drew the line as their particularistic interests dictated. Thus railroad leaders saw no reason why government should not grant
them tax exemptions, cash subsidies, or even an entire harbor. They claimed
the rate making power, however, as a sovereign right of management "that
cannot be disturbed by any legislative action."[173] Merchants and farmers
were equally opportunistic. In their view, internal improvement bonds might
be repudiated because railroad and manufacturing companies were "exclusively private," but the same firms that were ineligible for subsidies or perpetual immunities might be regulated at the legislature's discretion because
they were "affected with a public interest."[174]

Field's approach to the ensuing constitutional controversies was more than
a narrow philosophy of the bank account. He, too, was obsessed with formulating rules that separated the public and private sectors as far as practicable.
But he refused to provide "a harbor where refuge can be found" for the inconsistent claims of any particularistic interest group.[175] Instead, Field be-

---

[170] Ibid., at 179.
[171] Chicago, Milwaukee & St. Paul Ry. Co. v. Minnesota, 134 U.S. 418 (1890); Smyth v.
Ames, 169 U.S. 466 (1898).
[172] Oscar and Mary Handlin, The Dimensions of Liberty (Cambridge, Mass., 1961), 99.
[173] John W. Cary, "Brief for Appellants in Error," Peik v. Chicago & Northwestern Ry.
Co., 64; Twiss, Lawyers and the Constitution, 70-76; Fairman, "The So-Called Granger
Cases," 634; Miller, Railroads and the Granger Laws, 186.
[174] People ex. rel. Detroit and Howell R.R. Co. v. Salem, 20 Mich. 252 (1870) at 477;
Munn v. Illinois, 99 U.S. 113 (1877).
[175] Missouri Pacific Ry. Co. v. Humes, 115 U.S. 512 (1885) at 521.

lieved that the proper solution to the nation's policy conflicts lay in uncompromising judicial application, or both sides of the promotional-regulatory continuum, of the long-established eminent domain concepts of "public purpose," inalienability, and just compensation for public use of private property. In his view, the body of doctrine that logically flowed from those precepts was so consistent and so conducive to "the peace of society and to its progress and improvement," that he was certain his entire system would ultimately prevail.[176] *Munn* and all other "grave departure[s] from the purposes of the Constitution," he told a New York crowd at the court's centennial celebration, were "bound to die." Any decision that did "not fit harmoniously with other rulings," Field declared, "will collide with them, and thus compel explanations and qualifications until the error is eliminated. . . . [T]ruth alone is immortal, and in the end [it] will assert its rightful supremacy."[177]

But Field's "immortal truths," if viable at all, provided solutions only for the policy issues of the 1870s. The "public use" and inalienability doctrines offered no guidance whatsoever on questions involving labor-management strife or governmental control of such "ordinary trades" as sugar and oil refining. For the judicial conservatives that succeeded him, then, the system of immutable rules that Field had formulated to separate the public and private sectors was irrelevant for the issues that loomed largest in their minds.[178] And by 1920, the court had not only transformed Field's police power dicta into an iron law of "liberty to contract" but also had permitted the states to devolve eminent domain powers to mining companies and had sustained payment of subsidies to housing-construction firms.[179] As a result, when the affectation doctrine of *Munn* was finally overthrown in *Nebbia* v. *New York*, it did indeed no longer "fit harmoniously with other rulings." The concerns of Field's generation had expired, and the court flatly stated that "there is no closed class or category of businesses affected with a public interest."[180] Field's government-business jurisprudence perished, however, not because it had been internally inconsistent or had failed to reflect the ideological commitments of post-Civil War Americans, but rather because his doctrinal system proved to be incongruent with the rapidly changing needs of an ever-expanding capitalist society.

[176] Field, "Centennary of the Supreme Court of the United States," 367.
[177] *Ibid.*, 363.
[178] For a full analysis of the concerns that molded the "new judicialism" of the 1890s, see Faul, *Conservative Crisis and the Rule of Law.*
[179] *Strickley* v. *Highland Boy Gold Mining Co.*, 200 U.S. 527 (1906); *Green* v. *Frazier*, 253 U.S. 233 (1920).
[180] *Nebbia* v. *New York*, 291 U.S. 502 (1934) at 536.

MARY CORNELIA PORTER

THAT COMMERCE SHALL BE FREE:

A NEW LOOK AT THE OLD

LAISSEZ-FAIRE COURT

Shortly before his death, Justice Black warned that the Supreme Court's support of the "new" substantive due process and equal protection would lead, willy-nilly, down the path taken by the discredited laissez-faire Court.[1] Some students of the Court agree.[2] Wallace Mendelson, for instance, fears that the protection of judicially (and thereby subjectively) determined "fundamental rights"

---

Mary Cornelia Porter is Associate Professor of Political Science, Barat College, Lake Forest, Illinois.

[1] The "new" due process and equal protection concepts cover a wide range of cases and propositions. For examples of the proliferating literature on the subject see: Goodpaster, *The Constitution and Fundamental Rights*, 15 ARIZ. L. REV. 479 (1973); Graham, *Poverty and Substantive Due Process*, 12 ARIZ. L. REV. 1 (1970); Gunther, *In Search of Evolving Doctrine on a Changing Court: A Model for a Newer Equal Protection*, 86 HARV. L. REV. 1 (1972); Michelman, *On Protecting the Poor through the Fourteenth Amendment*, 83 HARV. L. REV. 1 (1969); Tribe, *Toward a Model of Roles in the Due Process of Life and Law*, 87 HARV. L. REV. 1 (1973); Tussman and tenBroek, *The Equal Protection of the Laws*, 37 CALIF. L. REV. 341 (1949). For purposes of this article, emphasis is on the rights of those generally considered least able "to take care of themselves," welfare recipients and debtors subject to garnishment and replevin procedures. For discussion of such cases see: Rosenheim, *Shapiro v. Thompson: "The Beggars are Coming to Town,"* 1969 SUPREME COURT REVIEW 303; PIVEN & CLOWARD, REGULATING THE POOR: THE FUNCTIONS OF PUBLIC WELFARE ch. 10 (1971); Countryman, *The Bill of Rights and the Bill Collector: Sniadach v. Family Finance Corp.*, 15 ARIZ. L. REV. 521 (1973).

[2] Lee, *Mr. Herbert Spencer and the Bachelor Stockbroker: Kramer v. Union Free School District No. 15*, 15 ARIZ. L. REV. 457 (1973); Winter, *Poverty, Economic Equality, and the Equal Protection Clause*, 1972 SUPREME COURT REVIEW 41.

of those whose economic, social, and political resources are minimal (welfare recipients, for example, and debtors) amounts, just as did the earlier protection of corporations, to "government by judiciary."[3] Those who have urged the additional responsibilities on the Court appear equally troubled, but for a different reason—believing they must have a rationale which permits approval of the new, and continued disapproval of the old, economic activism.[4]

Whatever the merits of the arguments, and justification for the anxieties, on either side, the fact remains that the Court is behaving in a traditional manner. In the first place, as Philip Kurland observes, it has always acted "as a centripetal force, [modifying] the Constitution in order to sustain the enhancement of national authority and the despoliation of state power."[5] And indeed, the Warren/Burger Court's cautiously extended solicitude for "the poor" is tendered at the expense of state initiative, state fiscal considerations, and state standards of fair play. In the second place the Court, as has been frequently noted, does respond, within the limitations of the judicial process, to the great imperatives of the times. Two articles in the *Yale Law Journal*, written more than thirty years apart, make the point most tellingly. The Supreme Court, given the nature of the American polity, wrote Max Lerner during the depths of the great depression, could not have avoided the economic controversies which it has been asked to mediate. For:[6]

> [C]apitalism pushes ultimately before the Court the clashes of interest that are attendant on the growth of any economic system, with the displacement in each successive phase of elements that had been useful in previous phases, with the antagonisms it generates among those who are bearing its burdens and the rivalry among those who are dividing its spoils. . . . If it be

---

[3] Mendelson, *From Warren to Burger: The Rise and Decline of Substantive Equal Protection*, 66 Am. Pol. Sc. Rev. 1226 (1972). Boudin's *Government by Judiciary* (1932) is a disapproving description of "laissez-faire" jurisprudence.

[4] Gunther and Tribe, note 1 *supra*. "Substantive equal protection . . . suffers from quite the same defects and has itself created some uneasiness even among its proponents. For that reason, we witness the tragicomic phenomenon of both Justices and commentators nervously seeking to distinguish between what they are doing and the rejected and reviled substantive due process of another era." Winter, note 2 *supra*, at 100.

[5] Kurland, Politics, the Constitution, and the Warren Court 58 (1970).

[6] Lerner, *The Supreme Court and American Capitalism*, 42 Yale L.J. 668, 685 (1933).

added to this that modern capitalism is perhaps the least organic system of economic organization the world has seen . . . and that the American social and political structure within which it operates is perhaps more sprawling and heterogeneous than that of any other major capitalist society, some notion may be had of the confusion of interests and purposes out of which it is the task of the Court to bring certainty and uniformity.

Nor, wrote Charles Reich in 1964, should the Court duck the constitutional issues posed by the positive, or what he calls the "public interest" state:[7]

> The most clearly defined problem posed by government largess is the way it can be used to apply pressure against the exercise of constitutional rights. A first principle should be that government must have no power to "buy up" rights guaranteed by the Constitution. . . . The courts in recent times have gone part of the distance toward this principle. . . .
>
> [T]he time has come for us to remember what the framers of the Constitution knew so well—that "a power over a man's subsistence amounts to a power over his will." We cannot safely entrust our livelihoods and our rights to the discretion of authorities, examiners, boards of control. . . . We cannot permit any official or agency to pretend to sole knowledge of the public good. . . . If the individual is to survive in a collective society he must have protection against its ruthless pressures. There must be sanctuaries or enclaves where no majority can reach. . . . [W]e must try to build an economic basis for liberty today. . . . We must create a new property.

Since the Court is not, as Justice Black and Professor Mendelson have said, embarking on an entirely uncharted course, and since the contemporary economic activism should not, within the context of Court history, be particularly surprising, another "exhumation"[8] of the first substantive due process era might be in order. And upon reexamination it can be claimed, I think, that the Court did not single-mindedly shelter "the interests." Such protection as it gave corporations was, in actuality, the Court's (necessarily prescribed) way of acting as a national regulatory agency. And it did the job tolerably well. So, while there may be other, and perfectly good, reasons for

[7] Reich, *The New Property*, 73 YALE L.J. 733, 779–87 (1964).

[8] For an earlier, and most illuminating, "exhumation" see McCloskey, *Economic Due Process and the Supreme Court: An Exhumation and Reburial*, 1962 SUPREME COURT REVIEW 34.

unease about the "new" property decisions, the commonly accepted interpretation of the "old" property-rights Courts' substantive record need not be among them.

What might, on the other hand, give pause is the extraordinary nature of the "laissez-faire" period's brand of judicial activism. For the Court went far beyond simply nay-saying legislatures and "assumed" congressional power. Less striking instances of judicial legislation have been condemned on the grounds that they take a toll, not only in the quality of the Court's work, but in political terms as well. Separation of powers and the viability of the federal system are jeopardized. Support and respect for the Court itself erodes.[9] If one accepts this argument, then it may be asked at what point in a series of activist rulings, be they from the Fuller, White, Taft, Hughes, or Warren Courts, is such a price exacted? And is it, after all, worth the candle? The "old" property-rights majorities, no less concerned with a perception of the public interest than are the proponents of the "new" judicial economic activism, never paused to ask. It is from this perspective, rather than from the "laissez-faire" Court's actual output, that the "new property" advocates—and their detractors—might take their bearings.

## I. The Old Property-Rights Court: A Revisionist View

With few exceptions, most standard histories and accounts of the Court between the 1880s and 1940s assume a pro-business, anti-labor bias on the part of the majority.[10] The account is as follows: Shortly after the regulation of business "affected with a public interest" was sustained in the *Granger Cases*,[11] the Court, persuaded by the American Bar Association and Justices Field and Harlan, hinted that it would henceforth scrutinize state regulatory measures

---

[9] There is a vast literature in praise of judicial self-restraint. See, *e.g.*, Bickel, The Supreme Court and the Idea of Progress (1970); Kurland, note 5 *supra*.

[10] Kelly & Harbison, The American Constitution (1970 ed.); McCloskey, The American Supreme Court (1960); Swindler, Court and Constitution in the 20th Century: The Old Legality 1889-1932 (1969); Swisher, American Constitutional Development (1943); Wright, The Growth of American Constitutional Law (1942). For some specialized accounts see Jacobs, Law Writers and the Courts: The Influence of Thomas M. Cooley, Christopher G. Tiedeman and John F. Dillon upon American Constitutional Law (1954); Paul, Conservative Crisis and the Rule of Law (1960); Twiss, Lawyers and the Constitution: How Laissez-Faire Came to the Supreme Court (1942).

[11] Munn v. Illinois, 94 U.S. 113 (1877).

with greater care. By 1898 Justice Harlan had his day and, speaking for a unanimous Court, promulgated an elaborate (and altogether unworkable) formula for administratively and/or legislatively determined public utility rates.[12] In the meantime, having already forbidden states to regulate the charges of interstate carriers while traveling intrastate,[13] the Court struck down interstate rates established by the Interstate Commerce Commission,[14] decided against the government in its first antitrust prosecution,[15] and overruled one hundred years of precedent in the *Income Tax Case*[16] (most of this, it might be added, over the angry protests of the same Justice Harlan who was so eager to invalidate state regulatory measures).[17] On the labor scene the record was much the same. Eugene Debs remained in prison for his defiance of court orders to halt the Pullman strike;[18] the Danbury Hatters were advised that their labor boycott was in violation of the Sherman Anti-Trust Act;[19] and the *Lochner* decision[20] gratuitously guaranteed New York bakers their "liberty of contract" against legislative restriction of their hours of labor. The first "conservative crisis"[21] ended, so the tale continues, when the Court, impressed by the Brandeis brief, accepted the principle of economic and social regulation[22]—*Coppage v. Kansas*[23] and the *First Child Labor Case*[24] being significant exceptions—only to be suc-

---

[12] Smyth v. Ames, 169 U.S. 466 (1898).

[13] Wabash, St. L. & P. Ry. Co. v. Illinois, 118 U.S. 557 (1886).

[14] Texas & P. R.R. v. I.C.C., 162 U.S. 197 (1896); I.C.C. v. Alabama Midland Ry. Co., 168 U.S. 144 (1897).

[15] United States v E. C. Knight Co., 156 U.S. 1 (1895).

[16] Pollock v. Farmers' Loan & Trust Co., 158 U.S. 601 (1895).

[17] The literature on this great Justice is unaccountably meager. For a listing, and an effort to explain his apparently contradictory position in the economic cases, see Porter, *John Marshall Harlan the Elder and Federal Common Law: A Lesson from History*, 1972 SUPREME COURT REVIEW 103.

[18] *In re* Debs, 158 U.S. 564 (1895).

[19] Loewe v. Lawlor, 208 U.S. 274 (1908).

[20] Lochner v. New York, 198 U.S. 45 (1905).

[21] The term is PAUL's, note 10 *supra*.

[22] Muller v. Oregon, 208 U.S. 412 (1908).

[23] 236 U.S. 1 (1915). The decision invalidated a state statute which prohibited "yellow dog" anti-union contracts.

[24] Hammer v. Dagenhart, 247 U.S. 251 (1918), held that Congress could not prohibit the interstate shipment of goods produced by child labor. Four Justices dissented.

ceeded by another period of reaction. Finally, with the notorious "switch in time," the Court returned in the early 1940s to the principles of the *Granger Cases*.

There have been challenges to this presentation. It has been variously suggested that the picture is one-sided and exaggerated;[25] that the Court was less interested in thwarting reform than it was in preserving "competitive capitalism";[26] that *Lochner*, in fact, accurately reflects organized labor's preference for governmental neutrality in labor-management relations;[27] that the (misdirected) natural rights activism of Justice Field paved the way for the (well-directed) natural rights activism of Justice Douglas;[28] and, finally, that property rights are as worthy of judicial protection as civil rights.[29] This last proposition was recently articulated by the Court, when it invalidated a state wage garnishment law:[30]

> The right to enjoy property without unlawful deprivation, no less than the right to speak or the right to travel, is in truth a 'personal' right. . . . In fact, a fundamental interdependence exists between the personal right to liberty and the personal right in property. Neither could have meaning without the other.

There can be little doubt that a careful study of the wide range of cases decided during the first, and seminal, "laissez-faire" period does give rise to some skepticism about the usual characterization of the Court. So many stringent state economic regulations were sus-

---

[25] BETH, THE DEVELOPMENT OF THE AMERICAN CONSTITUTION, 1877–1917 esp. chs. 5 and 6 (1971); Jones, *Thomas M. Cooley and "Laissez-Faire Constitutionalism": A Reconsideration,* 53 J. AM. HIST. 751 (1967).

[26] Strong, *The Economic Philosophy of Lochner: Emergence, Embrasure and Emasculation,* 15 ARIZ. L. REV. 419 (1973).

[27] Mavrinac, *From Lochner to Brown v. Topeka: The Court and Conflicting Concepts of the Political Process,* 52 AM. POL. SCI. REV. 641 (1958).

[28] Karst, *Invidious Discrimination: Justice Douglas and the Return of the "Natural-Law-Due-Process Formula,"* 16 U.C.L.A. L. REV. 716 (1969).

[29] Learned Hand wondered why nobody "took the time to explain" why "property itself was not a 'personal right.'" McCloskey, note 8 *supra,* at 44, n.50. And Felix Frankfurter wrote: "Yesterday the active area . . . was concerned with 'property.' Today it is 'civil liberties.' Tomorrow it may again be 'property.' Who can say that in a society with a mixed economy, like ours, these two areas are sharply separated, and that certain freedoms in relation to property may not again be deemed, as they were in the past, aspects of individual freedom?" FRANKFURTER, OF LAW AND MEN 19 (Elman ed., 1956).

[30] Lynch v. Household Finance Corp., 405 U.S. 538, 552 (1972).

tained, many involving great expense to business,[31] that it is difficult to claim that the court simply recorded a free enterprise predilection of the majority. The Court beat a hasty, even unseemly, retreat from its negative posture in the early ICC and Sherman Act cases and in the *Income Tax Case* when Presidents Roosevelt and Taft began vigorously to prosecute the trusts, and when Congress gave additional powers to the ICC and moved toward adoption of the Sixteenth Amendment.[32]

There were other, equally prudent, modifications of earlier judicial positions. Consider *Allgeyer v. Louisiana*,[33] the decision which elevated "liberty of contract" to the status of constitutional doctrine. The ruling invalidated a statute which regulated the sale of marine and fire insurance policies. Five years later, with hardly a nod to "liberty of contract," the Court sustained a similar statute.[34] Other judicial shifts and turns will be discussed later. A "liberal" or a "conservative" ruling often rested on the Court's view of its constitutional or statutory powers. For instance, rulings based on the Eleventh Amendment refused[35] as well as granted[36] injunctions

---

[31] Commenting on regulatory legislation sustained by the Court, a contemporary observer noted that "their cumulative effect [was] to impose vast expense upon the [railroad] companies . . . ; [requiring] that [they] supply even at a loss enough trains and adequate service." Swayze, *Judicial Construction of the Fourteenth Amendment*, 26 HARV. L. REV. 1, 17 (1912). For decisions sustaining rate regulation, see Chicago & Grand Trunk Ry. Co. v. Wellman, 143 U.S. 339 (1892); Budd v. New York, 143 U.S. 517 (1892); Brass v. Stoeser, 153 U.S. 391 (1894). For decisions sustaining requirements that the railroads, at their own expense, provide for public health, safety, and convenience, see Atchison, T. & S. Fe R. Co. v. Matthews, 174 U.S. 96 (1899); Mississippi Railroad Comm. v. Illinois Cent. R. Co., 203 U.S. 335 (1906); St. Louis Southwestern Ry. Co. v. Arkansas, 217 U.S. 136 (1910); Chicago, R.I. & P. Ry. Co. v. Arkansas, 219 U.S. 453 (1911). For a comprehensive listing of cases, see CORWIN, ED., THE CONSTITUTION OF THE UNITED STATES 1121–27 (1964).

[32] The Court reversed ICC rulings in: Texas & P. Ry. Co. v. I.C.C., 162 U.S. 197 (1896); I.C.C. v. Alabama Midland R.R., 168 U.S. 144 (1897); ruled against the government in antitrust cases: United States v. E. C. Knight Co., 156 U.S. 1 (1895); Anderson v. United States, 171 U.S. 604 (1898); and struck down the income tax provision of the Wilson Act in Pollock v. Farmers' Loan and Trust Co., 158 U.S. 601 (1895). And see Swift & Co. v. United States, 196 U.S. 375 (1905). Illinois Central R. Co. v. I.C.C., 206 U.S. 441 (1907); I.C.C. v. Chicago, R.I. & P. Ry. Co., 218 U.S. 88 (1910). *Pollock* was severely modified in Knowlton v. Moore, 178 U.S. 41 (1900); Flint v. Stone Tracy Co., 220 U.S. 107 (1911).

[33] 165 U.S. 578 (1897).

[34] Nutting v. Massachusetts, 183 U.S. 553 (1902).

[35] Fitts v. McGhee, 172 U.S. 516 (1899).

[36] Southern Pacific Co. v. Denton, 146 U.S. 202 (1892).

requested by corporations seeking to prevent state officials from enforcing rate regulation laws. Sometimes the Court sustained[37] and other times invalidated[38] state laws which banned corporations from doing business within a state unless they agreed not to avail themselves of a federal statute providing for the removal of suits from hostile state courts to friendly federal courts.[39] Justices Field, Brewer, and Peckham, considered to be the villains of the piece, sometimes rendered surprisingly liberal opinions and dissents in business regulation, antitrust, and labor cases.[40] Justices such as Harlan, Brown, and Holmes moved back and forth between the liberal and conservative ends of the judicial spectrum.[41] Except for *Lochner*, which was a five-to-four decision, and *Adair v. United States*,[42] the Court sustained all challenged labor legislation.[43] And

---

[37] Security Mutual Life Insurance Co. v. Prewitt, 202 U.S. 246 (1906).

[38] Southern Pacific Co. v. Denton, 146 U.S. 202 (1892).

[39] Removal Act of 1875, 18 Stat. 470. For the importance and ramifications of the Act, see FRANKFURTER & LANDIS, THE BUSINESS OF THE SUPREME COURT ch. 2 (1927).

[40] Justice Field: Missouri Pac. Ry. Co. v. Humes, 115 U.S. 512 (1885); Charlotte, C. & A. R. Co. v. Gibbes, 142 U.S. 386 (1892); Central R. Co. v. Keegan, 160 U.S. 259 (1895); Northern Pacific R.R. v. Hambly, 154 U.S. 349 (1894). Justice Brewer: Chicago & Grand Trunk Ry. Co. v. Wellman, 143 U.S. 339 (1892); Chicago, M. & St. P. Ry. Co. v. Tompkins, 176 U.S. 167 (1900); Adams Express Co. v. Ohio, 165 U.S. 194 (1897); Pullman's Palace Car Co. v. Pennsylvania, 141 U.S. 18 (1891); Atchison, T. & S. F. R. Co. v. Matthews, 174 U.S. 96 (1899). He dissented, with Field and Harlan, against the Court's refusal to compel a railroad company to put in stations at specified places, suggesting that the road's refusal to put in a station at Yakima, then the area's most populous center, was due to the road's interest in building up other commercial areas in its own interest. He also hinted that bribery might be involved. Northern Pacific R. Co. v. Dustin, 142 U.S. 492 (1892). Justice Peckham: United States v. Trans-Missouri Freight Assoc. 166 U.S. 290 (1897); Skaneateles Water Works Co. v. Skaneateles, 184 U.S. 354 (1902); Capital City Lt. & F. Co. v. Tallahassee, 186 U.S. 401 (1902); McCullough v. Virginia, 172 U.S. 102 (1898); Ludwig v. Western Union Tel. Co., 216 U.S. 146 (1910); Pullman Company v. Kansas, 216 U.S. 56 (1910).

[41] See Justice Brown's eloquent and angry dissent in Pollock v. Farmers' Loan & Trust Co., 158 U.S. 601, 686 (1895). Justice Holmes concurred in *Ex parte* Young, 209 U.S. 123 (1908), in which the Court, without the case being properly before it, invalidated a state rate schedule. He dissented in an important antitrust case won by the government. Northern Securities Co. v. United States, 193 U.S. 197, 364 (1904).

[42] 208 U.S. 161 (1908).

[43] Legislation limiting hours of labor: Holden v. Hardy, 169 U.S. 366 (1898); Atkin v. Kansas, 191 U.S. 207 (1903); Muller v. Oregon, 208 U.S. 412 (1908); legislation requiring employers to meet specified obligations toward their employees: St. Louis, Iron Mountain & St. P. Ry. Co. v. Paul, 173 U.S. 404 (1899); Knoxville Iron Co. v. Harbison, 183 U.S. 13 (1901); Dayton Iron & Coal v. Barton, 183 U.S. 23

it was during this period, when judges were supposedly averse to governmental interference in the market place, that the Court sustained a congressional prohibition against interstate sales of lottery tickets—thus sanctioning the first exercise of the national police power.[44]

The Court, as a matter of fact, upheld a large number of state regulatory measures.[45] The exceptions were those which controlled public utility rates, and these decisions can be "rationalized" on the ground that the Court was less interested in rate regulation per se than in assuring that regulated utilities would continue to attract the investment capital necessary for expanding and improving services to the public. Charles Warren put it this way:[46]

> As soon as the capitalists found that certain States would not allow them to earn interest on railroad investments, they refused to invest more money in those States. No new roads were constructed; the equipment that wore out was not replaced. While the rates at which wheat was carried to market remained low, a great deal of wheat did not get carried to market at all, owing to lack of the physical means of transportation. The Legislatures could prevent high charges, but they could not prevent deficient service.

Out-of-state financial owners and backers of the roads, who considered their investment jeopardized by rate regulation, could hardly follow the *Granger* suggestion that they "resort to the polls."[47] The alternative was to take their money elsewhere, or to persist in seeking the judicial redress denied by the *Granger* ruling. Eventually, of

---

(1901); legislation abolishing the common-law "fellow-servant" rule: Wilmington Star Mining Co. v. Fulton, 205 U.S. 60 (1907); Chicago, B. & Q. R. Co. v. McGuire, 219 U.S. 549 (1911); legislation providing for a day of rest (Sunday): Hennington v. Georgia, 163 U.S. 299 (1896); Petit v. Minnesota, 177 U.S. 164 (1900); National Safety Appliance Acts sustained in: St. Louis, Iron Mountain & Southern Ry. v. Taylor, 210 U.S. 281 (1908); Chicago, B. & Q. Ry. Co. v. United States, 220 U.S. 559 (1911); the Hours of Service Act sustained in B. & O. R. Co. v. I.C.C., 221 U.S. 612 (1911). While the Court invalidated the Federal Employers Liability Act, in the First Employers' Liability Cases, 207 U.S. 463 (1908), it sustained a similar, more precisely drawn statute in the Second Employers' Liability Cases, 223 U.S. 1 (1912).

[44] The Lottery Case, 188 U.S. 321 (1903).

[45] See note 31 *supra*. See also Minneapolis & St. L. R. Co. v. Minnesota, 193 U.S. 53 (1904); Nashville, C. & St. L. Ry. v. Alabama, 128 U.S. 96 (1888); Minneapolis & St. L. Ry. Co. v. Beckwith, 129 U.S. 26 (1889).

[46] 3 WARREN, THE SUPREME COURT IN UNITED STATES HISTORY 311 (1922).

[47] Munn v. Illinois, 94 U.S. 113, 134 (1877).

course, the Court, having previously agreed that the Due Process Clause of the Fourteenth Amendment protects corporations,[48] did provide a national forum for what were national grievances and national issues.

Stated differently, substantive due process, as it pertained to state regulation of intrastate public utility rates, served as a surrogate for the (then) inapplicable Commerce Clause.[49] The Court, by protecting the public securities market against the actions of parochial, however reform-minded, legislatures, broadened the scope of its traditional responsibility for maintaining a national free trade area. Another way of looking at it would be that just as the Court determines in Commerce Clause cases if challenged state legislation controls subject matter requiring a uniform national rule, so substantive due process provides the means for establishing a uniform national rule for rate regulation—a rule which would have the effect of stabilizing the expectations of those investing in state-regulated utilities.[50]

One may, with justification, protest such juggling of constitutional provisions. My response, not defense, is that the Court, cabined and cribbed as it is, has on other occasions reached for unlikely constitutional tools to do whatever it thought the public interest required. Chief Justice Marshall's Contract Clause[51] and the Warren/Burger Court's "right to privacy"[52] decisions provide examples. One may also contend that even though the Court did remove state impediments to interstate commerce, its rulings departed from generally accepted jurisprudential norms. For in Com-

---

[48] Santa Clara Co. v. Southern Pacific R. Co., 118 U.S. 394 (1886).

[49] There was never any question as to the constitutionality of state regulation of intrastate railroad charges. In Wabash, St. L. & P. Ry. Co. v. Illinois, 118 U.S. 557 (1886), the Court held that only Congress could regulate interstate rates. The following year Congress enacted the Interstate Commerce Act, 24 Stat. 379 (1887).

[50] "A . . . great mission of the Court is to maintain a common market of continental extent against state barriers . . . ." FREUND, ON LAW AND JUSTICE 57 (1968). In Cooley v. Board of Wardens, 12 How. 299, 319 (1851), the Court sustained a local regulation, which had the effect of interfering with interstate commerce, on the ground that the subject matter was local, not requiring a uniform national rule. For a comprehensive statement of the "Cooley doctrine," see Southern Pacific Co. v. Arizona, 325 U.S. 761, 766–70 (1945).

[51] Fletcher v. Peck, 6 Cr. 87 (1810); Dartmouth College v. Woodward, 4 Wheat. 518 (1819).

[52] Griswold v. Connecticut, 381 U.S. 479 (1965); Eisenstadt v. Baird, 405 U.S. 438 (1972); Roe v. Wade, 410 U.S. 113 (1973); Doe v. Bolton, 410 U.S. 179 (1973).

merce Clause cases the Court usually, and simply, invalidates the offending state legislation, leaving the rest up to Congress, which may or may not act. This was not so in the rate regulation cases, for here the Court not only cleared the channels of interstate commerce, but went the next step and fashioned the uniform national rule. Be this as it may, and without judgment as to what the Court should, or should not, have done, it is from this unique Commerce Clause perspective that substantive due process should be understood.

## II. The Court and the Securities Market: Repudiation, Receiverships, and Rates

The Court's interest in public utility investments, developed to a sophisticated level in the rate regulation cases, actually began three decades earlier. The most dramatic example was provided by the municipal[53] and state debt repudiation cases which crowded the docket for over twenty years and which involved the Court in a long series of acrimonious struggles with state courts. The earliest cases in this category resulted from the railroad boom of the 1840s and 1850s when midwestern states authorized communities to vote the requisite taxes and issue bonds in aid of railroad construction. The enterprises were as often as not marked by foolishness on the part of the citizenry and fraud on the part of the railroad builders and speculators, and sometimes local officials as well. Many of the roads went into bankruptcy and were never completed. Some companies never started to build or never finished the spur vital to the town which had pledged its credit. The result was a heavy debt which was to have been paid out of the prosperity accruing from the benefits of the road. In the meantime the bonds had been sold to out-of-state and foreign purchasers. When it became evident that expectations had exceeded realities, local governments tried to get out from under their self-imposed tax burdens. While state courts were sympathetic, the Supreme Court turned a "face of flint"[54] toward the embattled farmers, insisting that obligations be met

---

[53] For a definitive discussion of cases, see FAIRMAN, 6 HISTORY OF THE SUPREME COURT OF THE UNITED STATES chs. 17 and 18 (1971). Also, FAIRMAN, MR. JUSTICE MILLER AND THE SUPREME COURT ch. 9 (1939). For further constitutional and legal implications of the cases, see WENDELL, RELATIONS BETWEEN THE FEDERAL AND STATE COURTS 143–50 (1949). For the role played by Justice Harlan, see Porter *supra* note 17.

[54] DILLON, LAW OF MUNICIPAL CORPORATIONS 7 (1876).

despite empty treasuries and the willingness of local officials to go to
jail rather than obey court orders to collect taxes. Public outcry was
reflected in several unsuccessful congressional proposals to withdraw the cases from federal court jurisdiction.[55] At the same time,
however, Congress vastly increased the federal judicial powers,[56]
which may suggest a willingness to let the courts handle some of the
problems attendant upon the (often unsavory) methods of financ-
ing the nation's railroad system.

The state debt cases, arousing equally strong popular reactions,
presented the Court with the claims of aggrieved holders of bonds
issued (often under equally questionable circumstances) by Reconstruction governments and repudiated by subsequent legislatures.
Thanks to the ingenuity of legislatures and courts of the impoverished South, the Court had little choice but to hold that the Eleventh
Amendment prohibited compelling state officers to pay interest due
on the bonds.[57] Ultimately, however, the Court, engaging in a bit of
legerdemain of its own, held that the states must make good on bonds
worth "many millions of dollars," and which, the Court noted significantly, had "passed into the markets of the world."[58] Clearly, the
cases, despite the constitutional and legal arguments upon which they
were pegged—the Contract Clause, the Eleventh Amendment, the
diversity jurisdiction—raised, in the mind of the Court, questions of
national and foreign commerce.

The railroad receivership cases, fraught in the view of Justice
Miller with "many evils,"[59] made the Court appear even more

---

[55] See Westin, *The Supreme Court, the Populist Movement and the Campaign of
1896*, 15 J. OF POL. 3, 7–9 (1953).

[56] Removal Act of 1875, *supra* note 39.

[57] The leading case is Louisiana v. Jumel, 107 U.S. 711 (1883). For background
and discussion, see WARREN, note 46 *supra*, at 385–93; WOODWARD, THE ORIGINS OF
THE NEW SOUTH 86–100 (1951). The bulk of the litigation came from Louisiana and
Virginia. These states did not directly repudiate their debts (which the Contract
Clause would prohibit), but either "scaled down" the amount of the debt, or made
collection procedures so expensive and time-consuming that it was virtually impossible for bondholders to receive returns on their investments. Antoni v. Greenhow,
107 U.S. 769 (1883); *In re* Ayers, 123 U.S. 443 (1887).

[58] McCullough v. Virginia, 172 U.S. 102, 108 (1898). In the Virginia Coupon
Cases, 114 U.S. 270 (1885), the Court was finally able to compel a state to make
good on its obligations. Following this, Virginia enacted the "coupon crusher" laws.
In *McCullough*, the Court, by exercising its independent judgment of common law,
held, the highest state court to the contrary, that the statute incurring the debt
was valid. Virginia officials were then ordered to pay interest due on the bonds.

[59] Barton v. Barbour, 104 U.S. 126, 137 (1881). The whole matter of railroad re-

solicitous toward capital. What often happened was that a railroad company declared bankruptcy and went into federal court to get itself a sympathetic receiver who would run the road on a business-as-usual basis. Next, the directors and stockholders, posing as "friendly" creditors, sued to settle their "claims" against the company. Genuine creditors, supplymen, and laborers, who tried to collect something on their bills, went away empty-handed. The Supreme Court, in the majority of these cases, condoned lower federal court practices.[60]

The public utility franchise cases, which were first heard in the 1880s, aroused the least controversy—possibly because the Court, as will be discussed later, practically reversed itself. The litigation began when municipalities began building their own water, gas, and electric plants,[61] thus effectively putting privately owned and managed companies, which held "exclusive" state grants, out of business—and effectively depriving investors of their dividends. In early cases the Court, approving injunctions to halt construction of municipal plants, indicated concern that states keep their "plighted faith" with those who had made "large investments."[62]

The rate regulation cases, involving questions of property valuation, were more complex. The valuation problem first surfaced in the *Railroad Commission Cases.*[63] Chief Justice Waite, while warning in dicta that charges so low as to be "confiscatory" would be in viola-

---

ceiverships was described as an "open scandal," filled with "injustice" and "abuse." Chamberlain, *New-Fashioned Receiverships*, 10 HARV. L. REV. 139, 148–49 (1896). For an illuminating discussion of the problems, see also Warren, *Federal and State Court Interference*, 43 HARV. L. REV. 345 (1930); FAIRMAN, MR. JUSTICE MILLER, note 53, *supra*, at ch. 10.

[60] Barton v. Barbour, note 59 *supra*; Hammock v. Loan & Trust Co., 105 U.S. 77 (1881); Quincy, M. & P. R. Co. v. Humphreys, 145 U.S. 82 (1892); Sage v. Memphis & Little Rock R. Co., 125 U.S. 361 (1888).

[61] "The parallel with the early days of railroads is striking. Electric utility promoters were commonly regarded as community benefactors who should be given incentives to invest in a risky and experimental industry. As a result, franchises of great prospective value were freely disposed of with little attempt to safeguard future community interests. . . . The way was open to abuse, and consumer complaints began to mount. It was charged that the utilities imposed excessive rates, overcapitalized their properties, and obtained exorbitant profits." FAINSOD, GORDON, & PALAMOUNTAIN, GOVERNMENT AND THE AMERICAN ECONOMY 70 (3d ed. 1959).

[62] New Orleans Gas Co. v. Louisiana Light Co., 115 U.S. 650, 673 (1885). See also St. Tammany Water Works v. New Orleans Water Works, 120 U.S. 64 (1887).

[63] Ruggles v. Illinois, 108 U.S. 526 (1883); Stone v. Farmers' Loan & Trust Co., 116 U.S. 307 (1886).

tion of the Fourteenth Amendment's Due Process guarantees, sustained the rates. But it is the Field-Harlan dissenting and concurring minority positions that are of import. They indicated that builders and backers of the roads would have thought twice about entering into such vast and expensive undertakings had they known that profits and returns would depend upon rates determined by railroad commissions whose members might be motivated more by political expediency than by expert knowledge of the intricacies of railroad management and finance. Shortly thereafter the Court did edge toward the Field-Harlan view, holding that with no way of estimating the "original" cost of a road, it would have to settle on a commission's judgment as to reasonable charges.[64]

The 1890s saw a change of emphasis. In the *First Minnesota Rate Case*[65] the Court ruled, according to most readings of the decision, that the ultimate determination as to the "reasonableness" of publicly established rates lay with the judiciary. A careful reading of Justice Blatchford's opinion,[66] however, elicits a more modest conclusion. He pointed out that since the statute which created the commission did not require notice and hearing before setting rates, it was up to the courts to supply the missing "machinery provided by the wisdom of successive ages for the investigation judicially of the truth of a matter in a controversy."[67] An administrative procedure, in other words, that did not provide for notice and hearing was arbitrary and thereby contrary to due process of law. On this ground, Justice Miller, no friend to the railroads, concurred separately.[68]

The Court's seriousness about proper administrative procedures

---

[64] Harlan and Field concurred separately in *Ruggles*, 108 U.S. at 535, 541; and dissented separately in *Stone*, 116 U.S. at 337, 342. In Dow v. Beidelman, 125 U.S. 680 (1888), the Court sustained a rate schedule which resulted in a payment of less than 2 percent of the road's bonded debt.

[65] Chicago, M. & St. P. Ry. Co. v. Minnesota, 134 U.S. 418 (1890).

[66] "The opinion of the Court was delivered by Mr. Justice Blatchford; but the line of argument bears the craftsmanship of Mr. Justice Brewer." Hamilton, *Due Process of Law*, in REED, ED., THE CONSTITUTION RECONSIDERED 182 (1938).

[67] 134 U.S. at 457.

[68] For Justice Miller's view of the federal system and his jaundiced view of the practices of railroad corporations, see FAIRMAN, MR. JUSTICE MILLER, note 53 *supra*, at chs. 8–10. "[I]t is necessary that the railroad corporations interested in the fare to be considered should have notice and have a right to be heard on the question . . . . For the refusal of the Supreme Court of Minnesota to receive evidence on this subject, I think the case ought to be reversed on the ground that this is a denial of due process of law." 134 U.S. at 461.

was evidenced by initial refusals to review legislatively determined rates,[69] and by the Court's willingness to sustain rates when public utilities were given an opportunity to present their case. In such circumstances judicial review was not necessary:[70]

> What this court said about the Minnesota statute can have no application . . . unless it be made to appear that the constitution and laws of California invest the municipal authorities of that State with power to fix water rates arbitrarily, without investigation, and without permitting the corporations . . . affected thereby to make any showing as to rates to be exacted or to be heard at any time or in any way upon the subject.

On the other hand, the Court, in dicta, also said that courts, not legislatures, make final determinations as to common-law standards of reasonable rates.[71] This yes and no attitude of judicial review of rates established directly by legislatures was untenable, and the Court moved toward a resolution in the *Texas Rate Case*.[72] Here the legislature, with an eye on the *Minnesota Rate Case* and the various judicial hints about "reasonable" rates, authorized a railroad commission to give notice, hold hearings, then fix rates which would be considered reasonable unless held otherwise by a court. These precautions were of no avail. The Court, adopting the Field-Harlan *Railroad Commission Cases* position, held that the rates, because of the commission's failure to take into account the costs of construction and returns to investors, were indeed unreasonable. And since the Court had shifted focus from process to substance, from the manner in which rates were fixed to the rates themselves, the way was clear to examine legislatively determined rates. This occurred just before the turn of the century in *Smyth v. Ames*.[73]

The litigation challenged Nebraska's Newberry Bill, passed after

---

[69] Budd v. New York, 143 U.S. 517 (1892); Brass v. Stoeser, 153 U.S. 391 (1894). In these cases the Court also noted that there was insufficient evidence to support the contention that the challenged rates were confiscatory.

[70] San Diego Land & Town Co. v. National City, 174 U.S. 739, 749 (1899). In San Diego Land & Town Co. v. Jasper, 189 U.S. 439, 441, 442 (1903), the Court reiterated this interpretation of the *First Minnesota Rate Case*.

[71] In the Railroad Commission Cases, Chief Justice Waite did not preclude judicial review of confiscatory rates. Stone v. Farmers' Loan & Trust Co., 116 U.S. 307, 331 (1886). In the Minnesota Rate Case, 134 U.S. 418 (1890), Justice Blatchford did not specifically order court review of commissioner-established rates.

[72] Reagan v. Farmers' Loan & Trust Co., 154 U.S. 362 (1894).

[73] 169 U.S. 466 (1898).

Populist gains in the 1892 election. It provided for the reduction of freight rates by almost 80 percent, but, mindful of previous Court rulings, the legislature conferred upon the state supreme court the duty of raising rates if the roads could prove existing rates to be unjust.[74] But, again, the state circumspection was futile. A unanimous Court found the rates unconstitutional on the grounds that they did not allow owners a "fair return" on the company's present value.[75] And in order to ascertain that value public rate-making bodies would henceforth be expected to take at least the following into account:[76]

> the original cost of construction, the amount expended in permanent improvements, the amount and market value of its bonds and stock, the present as compared with the original cost of construction, the probable earning capacity of the property under particular rates prescribed by statute, and the sum required to meet operating expenses.

The "*Smyth* rule," as it became known, raised more problems than it settled. Courts, commissions, legislatures, and the legal profession struggled for years with what Justice Frankfurter referred to as its "hodge-podge" components[77] until, in the early 1940s, a chastened Roosevelt Court got out of the public utility valuation business altogether.[78] These highlights overlook, as so many commentators have, the many cases which strongly suggest the Court's interest in public utility investments went beyond a concern for investors, and extended to the larger questions of the background and purposes of such investments. The Court not only assumed a duty to assure the continued flow of capital investment, but assumed a concomitant duty to protect only such investments as were made in utilities which were honestly financed, well-managed, and responsive to the public interest. Well enough aware of such phenomena as "watered stock," wild-cat finance schemes, and unscrupulous speculators, what the Court attended to was a reasonable securities market for business affected with a public interest.

---

[74] For background, see HICKS, THE POPULIST REVOLT ch. 5 (1931).

[75] 169 U.S. at 547.                    [76] *Id.* at 546–47.

[77] F.P.C. v. Hope Natural Gas Co., 320 U.S. 591, 627 (1944). See Goddard, *The Evolution and Devolution of Public Utility Law*, 32 MICH. L. REV. 577 (1934).

[78] Power Commission v. Natural Gas Pipeline Co., 315 U.S. 575 (1942); *Hope Natural Gas*, note 77 *supra*.

III. Public Utility Investment Pro Bono Publico

After chiding the railroad lawyers for making the interests of their clients "the sole test" for determining the validity of the rates, Justice Harlan reminded the triumphant *Smyth* litigants that a:[79]

> railroad is a . . . corporation deriving its existence and powers from the State. [It] was created for public purposes. It performs a function of the State. Its authority to exercise the right of eminent domain and to charge tolls was given primarily for the benefit of the public. It is under governmental control.

That these words were not intended merely to placate the losers is attested by the Court's abrupt about-face in the municipal ownership cases. The Court, once it realized that municipal ownership was an idea whose time had come,[80] was, in the vast majority of these cases, positively eager to stress the "public purpose" and denigrate the private loss aspects of franchise revocation. Builders and backers of privately owned plants were told that they should have known that local governments do not, by implication, bargain away their inalienable powers of police.[81] In one instance when a city, despite specific assurances to the contrary, went ahead and built its own water plant, the Court advised stockholders of the private company that they would simply have to bear the resulting "hardship" as best they could:[82]

> It is said that the company could not possibly have believed that the city would establish waterworks to be operated in competition with its system, for such competition would be ruinous. . . . On the other hand, the city may . . . say that, having once thought of having its own waterworks, the failure to insert in that agreement a provision precluding it, in all circumstances and during a long period, from having its own separate system, shows that it was not its purpose to so restrict the exercise of its powers, but to remain absolutely free to act as changed circumstances or the public exigencies might demand.

---

[79] 169 U.S. at 544.

[80] For a discussion of the late nineteenth-century movement for municipal ownership of public utilities, see Fine, Laissez Faire and the General Welfare State ch. 10 (1969). For some cases, see note 40 *supra*.

[81] Lehigh Water Co. v. Easton, 121 U.S. 388 (1887); Stein v. Bienville Water Supply Co., 141 U.S. 67 (1891).

[82] Knoxville Water Co. v. Knoxville, 200 U.S. 22, 34–35 (1906).

"As the public demands." The idea appears and reappears as importunate suitors were turned out of Court, and, in language bordering on the suspicious to the scornful, warned not to trifle with *Smyth*, or its progenitor, *The Texas Rate Case*. There Justice Brewer had taken the pains, as had Justice Harlan in *Smyth*, to explain that there were circumstances which would indeed warrant, if not cry out for, tariffs such as those established by the state commission. Consumers, for instance, should not be asked to foot the bill for wasteful and incompetent management, for "enormous salaries," for building costs incurred "at a time when material and labor were at the highest price," or for railways "unwisely" constructed in localities where there was not "sufficient business to sustain a road."[83] However, upon examination of the facts of the instant case (and it should be pointed out that when companies did not present adequate evidence of earnings, the Court either sustained the challenged rates or dismissed the suit),[84] it appeared that the company had not only cut expenses to the bone, but had, over a ten-year period, voluntarily reduced tonnage rates. The road, which was in receivership, had not met operating expenses for three years. Investors, who had "never received a dollar's worth of dividends," had, "in order to make good the deficiency in interest . . . put their hands in their pockets and advanced over a million of dollars." Under such discouraging circumstances, worsened by the commission's rate schedule, "would," the Court asked, "any investment ever be made of private capital in railroad enterprises?"[85]

Few companies received such high marks for public spiritedness (or sympathy for a tale of woe). What a utility, for instance, was "pleased to call 'operating expenses'" might not include "exorbitant" salaries[86] or "injudicious expenditures."[87] What another might claim was "original cost" was, in a word, "inflated."[88] If investors expected "any dividends" it behooved them to look toward "prudent and honest management."[89] Otherwise they might be slated for a

---

[83] 154 U.S. at 412.

[84] Dow v. Beidelman, 125 U.S. 680 (1888); Chicago & Grand Trunk Ry. Co. v. Wellman, 143 U.S. 339 (1892).

[85] 154 U.S. at 411–12.

[86] Chicago & Grand Trunk Ry. Co. v. Wellman, 143 U.S. 339, 346 (1892).

[87] San Diego Land and Town Co. v. Jasper, 189 U.S. 439, 442 (1903).

[88] *Ibid.*                    [89] 143 U.S. at 346.

"misfortune . . . which the Constitution does not require to be remedied by imposing unjust burdens upon the public."[90] Valuation, that troublesome concept, might not be based on costs incurred at a time of high prices, but on the "property at the time [it was] being used for the public."[91] A company which had foolishly "embarked upon a great speculation which has not turned out as expected" would have to settle on "more modest" valuations.[92] Excessive, fictitious, and other questionable forms of capitalization could not be absorbed by rates high enough to realize the profits necessary to pay dividends. "Bond and . . . stock issued under such conditions afford neither measure nor guide to the value of stock."[93]

What of returns on investments made in such soundly financed and managed companies which passed judicial scrutiny? Well:[94]

> stockholders [were] not the only persons whose rights or interests [were] to be considered. . . . The public [could not] properly be subjected to unreasonable rates in order simply that stockholders may earn dividends.

In one instance the Court wondered if shareholders in a water company really expected to be "forever entitled to eighteen per cent upon [the original] cost." Dashing such hopes, and sustaining rates based upon the calculations of a commission, the Court noted that "much of the capital was invested between twenty and thirty years ago, and to be able still to realize six per cent upon the money originally invested is more than most people are able to accomplish in any ordinary investment."[95]

The *Smyth* rule that utilities are "entitled to a fair return upon the capital invested" may have been, the Court said, "sound as a general

---

[90] Covington Turnpike Co. v. Sandford, 164 U.S. 578, 597 (1896). Cases decided prior to *Smyth* had considered questions of earnings, rates, returns, and valuation, and were, as was this one, referred to in *Smyth*, 169 U.S. at 544-45.

[91] San Diego Land & Town Co. v. National City, 174 U.S. 739, 757 (1899).

[92] San Diego Land & Town Co. v. Jasper, 189 U.S. 439, 447 (1903).

[93] City of Knoxville v. Knoxville Water Co., 212 U.S. 1, 11 (1909). In this case the Court noted that most of the stock "was issued to contractors for the construction of the plant, and the nominal amount of the stock issued was greatly in excess of the true value of the property furnished by the contractors . . . . It perhaps is unnecessary to say that such contracts were made by the company with persons who, at the time, by stock ownership, controlled its action."

[94] Covington Turnpike Co. v. Sandford, 164 U.S. 578, 596 (1896).

[95] Stanislaus County v. San Joaquin Canal & Irr. Co., 192 U.S. 201, 214, 216 (1904).

proposition," but only should "the conditions of the country . . . permit it." Each case, it was cautioned, would be "determined by its own considerations";[96] and indeed, as has gone entirely unnoticed, the Court, modifying the *Smyth* decree, advised the Nebraska State Board of Transportation that the Court did not lay down "any cast-iron rule covering each and every separate rate."[97] Permission was granted to lower rates selectively, as the situation warranted.

## IV. Laissez-Faire in Perspective

Congressional power over commerce "is as broad as the need that evokes it."[98] What has been under discussion here is the exercise of judicial power to regulate commerce—and under a constitutional pseudonym at that. It is one thing for the Court, substituting its judgment for that of Congress, to invalidate federal legislation. It is one thing for the Court to strike down state laws which it deems to be interferences with interstate commerce. It is quite another thing not only to "free" interstate commerce, but then to go ahead and "usurp" a legislative function. While something akin to this occurred in such civil rights areas as reapportionment and busing to achieve integrated schools,[99] such operations are freakish as far as interstate commerce matters are concerned. And while I maintain that the Court has been unfairly accused of coddling vested interests, there should be no blinking the fact that it did move into a field which the Constitution specifically and unequivocally reserved to Congress. The Court arrogated the commerce power unto itself, going far beyond what is commonly understood as "government by judiciary." For as pertains to an aspect of interstate commerce, the Court did more than exercise a veto power. It ruled.

On the other hand, what the Court did in an unavoidedly haphazard way was not at all unlike what Senator La Follette tried to do in 1906 and what Congress did in 1920 when it ordered the Interstate Commerce Commission to ascertain the aggregate value of regulated roads and to determine what, upon that basis, would be a

---

[96] Minneapolis & St. L. R. Co. v. Minnesota, 186 U.S. 257, 268 (1902).

[97] Smyth v. Ames II, 171 U.S. 361, 365 (1898).

[98] See Carter v. Carter Coal, 298 U.S. 238, 328 (1936) (Cardozo, J., dissenting).

[99] Reynolds v. Sims, 377 U.S. 533 (1964); Swann v. Charlotte-Mecklenburg Board of Education, 402 U.S. 1 (1971).

fair return on investments,[100] and what it did in 1934 and 1935 when it legislated controls over the securities market in general[101] and the market in public utility securities in particular.[102] If one is able, then, to take the Court's extraordinary activism in stride, the first wave of laissez-faire jurisprudence and substantive due process may be viewed as something of a judicial holding action which made a contribution to national economic development. The Court did what it could to establish a national standard for public utilities regulation—a standard which would provide minimal assurances for necessary capital investment[103] as well as guidelines for consumer protection against unwarranted charges. By concerning itself with the relationship between public utility rate regulation and the continued flow of working capital to finance public services, the Court performed what may be described as an indispensable national function.

Scholars and judges who cannot be accused of harboring a laissez-faire bias subscribe, to some extent, and in some manner, to this view. Charles Beard, while severely criticizing the Court's "tenderness" toward "corporate rights," conceded that the power to nurture business growth "vested somewhere in the national government" was "essential to the continuance of industries and commerce on a national scale."[104] Justice Brandeis did not oppose the concept of a uniform valuation standard to be followed by regulatory commissions. On the contrary, his quarrel with *Smyth v. Ames* was that the rule was not very helpful. As a substitute for the "laborious and baffling task of finding the present value of the utility," he proposed the "prudent investment" method of valuation as a means of giving

---

[100] Transportation Act, 41 Stat. 456 (1920).

[101] Securities Exchange Act, 48 Stat. 881 (1934).

[102] Public Utility Act, 49 Stat. 803 (1935).

[103] Commentators have discussed the Court's focus on public utility investment. See, *e.g.*, DICKINSON, ADMINISTRATIVE JUSTICE AND THE SUPREMACY OF LAW 221 (1927): "It became increasingly clear . . . that the security of investments required the announcement of at least some more or less uniform guiding principles." The overriding and dominant valuation question was that the "rate must be high enough to give profit enough to make safe for investors the investment of a billion dollars a year in railroad stocks and bonds–fresh money for railroad extensions and improvements." Cook, *The Legal Legislative and Economic Battle over Railroad Rates*, 35 HARV. L. REV. 30, 33 (1921). My point is that the Court was equally concerned with consumer interests.

[104] BEARD, CONTEMPORARY AMERICAN HISTORY 87 (1914).

the "capital embarked in public utilities the protection guaranteed by the Constitution."[105] Harking back to the spirit of the *First Minnesota Rate Case*, Justices Frankfurter, Clark, Black, Brennan, and Chief Justice Warren have either claimed for the courts the final say in rate determinations or have protested against regulatory commissions behaving in ways that are "arbitrary and unreasonable . . . entirely outside of the traditional concepts of administrative due process."[106] And while the position of the Court now is that "he who would upset the rate order . . . carries the heavy burden of making a convincing showing that it is invalid because it is unjust and unreasonable in its consequences,"[107] the Court has not entirely abdicated responsibility for establishing standards. Investor and consumer interests must be "balanced" and returns on investments, ruled the Court in words reminiscent of the *Railroad Commission Cases* views of Justices Field and Harlan, "should be sufficient to assure confidence in the financial integrity of the enterprise, so as to maintain its credit and to attract capital."[108]

Professor Beard and the more recent members of the Court would undoubtedly be appalled to be associated with substantive due process. But in a real sense they may share a concern of their predecessors—a desire to preserve the very best aspects of capitalism. This meant, toward the end of the nineteenth century, maintaining a wary judicial outlook for excesses and abuses on the part of the captains of industry as well as their regulators. In a period of almost cataclysmic economic change, as Professor Lerner pointed out, great dislocations, and responses to those dislocations, occur. "Clashes of interests" revolve around the question of who is to share in and benefit from new forms of wealth—and how. The mid-nineteenth century American response to the problems associated with the extraordinarily rapid development of industrial capitalism and an interdependent national economy was—incongruously—state regulation. (The effective employment of the Interstate Commerce and Sherman Acts did not begin until the Progressive era.) This localized

---

[105] Southwestern Bell Tel. Co. v. Public Service Commission, 262 U.S. 276, 292 (1923) (concurring).

[106] Frankfurter, dissenting, in F.P.C. v. Hope Natural Gas. Co., 320 U.S. 591, 625 (1944); Clark, Black, Brennan and Chief Justice Warren, dissenting, in Wisconsin v. F.P.C., 373 U.S. 294, 326 (1963).

[107] Hope Natural Gas Co., 320 U.S. at 602.

[108] *Id.* at 603.

reaction to new national demands was, perforce, inadequate; and, since it threatened the investment sources which made economic growth possible, self-defeating as well. The responsibility for averting this negative development, or, put more positively, the responsibility for encouraging continued investment belonged, in Professor Beard's words, "somewhere in the national government." That somewhere turned out, for many years, to be the Court.

## V. Conclusion

The development of the "new" substantive due process and equal protection has raised, for some, the specter of the old laissez-faire Court, and, for others, the problem of reconciling (without the sacrifice of logic and precedent) espousal of judicial protection of "the poor" with antipathy toward judicial protection of corporations. Both opponents and proponents of the "new property" jurisprudence appear to agree that at one time Court decisions not only reflected the economic predilections of the majority, but brought the Court into disrepute. Neither group wishes a repetition, in form if not in kind, of this particular segment of judicial history.

Leaving aside the merits or demerits of the "new property" jurisprudence, the apprehensions of both groups may be off the mark. As some students of the Court again review the period in question, there is evidence that the characterization of the Court as "laissez-faire" is not entirely accurate. And, as I have tried to demonstrate, the Court was interested, primarily, in just one kind of "old property"—investments in public utilities. It is reasonable to assume that the "articulate major premise"[109] of these cases was that public utility investment was the lifeblood of an expanding national economy. The Court, by supervising state supervision of the utilities, established minimal and uniform guarantees for investors. Moreover, and this has been consistently ignored by critics of the laissez-faire Court, the Justices also strongly endorsed state efforts to protect the public. The Court, by balancing the interests of investors and consumers, turned itself into something of a federal regulatory agency. This was an extreme instance of "government by judiciary," for it went far beyond laying down judicial guidelines for state legislatures and administrative agencies, and extended to a lively judicial oversight of a vital element of the national economy.

---

[109] Holmes, dissenting, in Lochner v. New York, 198 U.S. 45, 76 (1905).

On the other hand, a justified condemnation might be tempered by taking the following into account. In the first place, the Court provided, as described by Robert McCloskey, for "the growth of entrepreneurial . . . freedom [which] helped to promote material progress . . . after the Civil War."[110] (Whether the result was, after all, desirable, cannot be assayed here.) In the second place, Congress took its bearings from *Smyth*. The Transportation Act of 1920 instructs the ICC to give "due consideration to all the elements of value recognized by the law of the land for rate-making purposes."[111] And whatever the problems created by *Smyth*, even those who have condemned the decision "as a major barrier to the effectiveness of public utility regulation,"[112] have also, unwittingly, conceded its salutory influence on the Transportation Act which:[113]

> taken as a whole, was a striking departure in railway regulation. Earlier laws had been dominated by a concern with railroad abuses. . . . Abandoning this restrictive approach, while continuing the earlier mandate of "reasonable and just" rates, the legislation explicitly recognized the needs of the carriers for adequate revenue. By protecting the investor, it sought to stabilize railway credit and stimulate a flow of capital into the industry.

Finally, without making extravagant claims for the *First Minnesota Rate Case*, the Court did, in effect, warn against giving what Professor Reich calls unlimited "discretion" to public officials and agencies. The Court asked then, as advocates of the "new property" rights ask now, that "the machinery provided by the wisdom of successive ages for the investigation . . . of the truth of a matter,"[114] *i.e.*, notice and hearing, be made available to those whose property rights are affected or threatened by "authorities, examiners, boards of control."[115] That the property loss might be catastrophic for a welfare recipient deprived of benefits, and minuscule for a railroad corporation whose rates are regulated by the state, is beside the point. What is to the point is that the Court was aware, many years

---

[110] McCloskey, note 8 *supra*, at 48.

[111] § 15 (a) (4), 41 Stat. 489.

[112] FAINSOD, GORDON, & PALAMOUNTAIN, note 61 *supra*, at 79.

[113] *Id*. at 269–70.

[114] Chicago, M. & St. P. Ry. v. Minnesota, 134 U.S. 418, 457 (1890).

[115] Reich, note 7 *supra*.

ago, of the dangers which the "public interest state" could pose to individual liberties. Justice Brewer's protestation (*obiter*, and in dissent in 1894) that the "paternalistic theory of government" was, to him "odious,"[116] has a hauntingly contemporary ring. The pervasive power of the welfare state, disquieting to conservatives, now troubles liberals as well.[117]

In sum, the old "laissez-faire" Court has been misunderstood and thereby disparaged. Its actual "transgressions" (if one takes this view) have, because of failure to comprehend its objectives, been overlooked. And while a reconsideration of this long dead past may seem, in Professor McCloskey's phrase, to be "mere bootless anti-quarianism,"[118] conventional interpretations of the "old" substantive due process are a reference for the "new." For this reason alone, it is instructive to grant the old "laissez-faire" Court its long overdue rehearing.

---

[116] Budd v. New York, 143 U.S. 517, 551 (1892).

[117] "The modern welfare state is a benevolent despot [that] retains the power to direct the behavior of recipients [of its benevolence]. Glasser, *Life under the New Feudalism*, 1 Civ. Lib. Rev. 27 (Winter/Spring 1974).

[118] McCloskey, note 8 *supra*, at 35.

# CONSTITUTIONAL PROTECTION OF PROPERTY RIGHTS.

AMONG the many interesting questions involved in the litigation which has been going on for some years, with regard to the New York elevated railroads, the right of the owners of property on the streets through which they pass, to recover compensation for the injury done them by the construction of the roads, is one of the most practically important. In most cases of the construction of railroads, the right to compensation in some degree is unquestioned, because land is actually taken from the owner, and the title transferred to the corporations; and the compensation paid the latter is merely the payment of its value. But, in the case of the elevated railroads, a different and more delicate question has arisen. In some streets of the city no land has been taken at all, but the value of property has been materially reduced, owing to the fact that the structure over which the trains pass blocks up the street, darkening it and rendering it inconvenient for use, while the trains moving backward and forward close to the windows of the houses annoy their occupants with a constant noise and the smoke and cinders of the engines. In these cases, the actual market value of the property is greatly diminished; yet the elevated railroads have thus far successfully resisted all attempts to obtain compensation; and it is probably safe to say that the general belief among those most competent to form an opinion — that is, the opinion of the bar — is that the courts will never compel them to make compensation. That there ought to be redress for such an injury no one disputes. The State cannot commit an act of more high-handed injustice than that of authorizing a corporation to do wide-spread damage of this sort without making compensation for it. The obstacles in the way of obtaining such compensation grow out of certain peculiarities of legal construction, which curiously illustrate the confusion and consequent injustice that often attend the development of our jurisprudence.

The constitution of the State of New York contains the provision common to all our State constitutions, that "when private property shall be taken for any public use by the State, the owner shall be compensated."*

Now, singular as it may seem, it has been decided by court after court that, to constitute a " taking " of property within the meaning of this clause, there must be some direct, actual, physical interference with land or chattels.

The Supreme Court of Pennsylvania, in construing a similar provision thirty years ago, said: " The constitutional provision for the case of private property taken for public use, extends not to the case of property injured or destroyed."† This may be said to have been the prevailing view of the American courts down to a very recent period, and it is plain that, under this interpretation, the claim of the owners of property diminished in value by the elevated railroads would have no standing whatever.

Within the past few years, however, a new view of the subject has made its appearance, which has received the sanction of a court of high authority, and under which property-owners would be materially better off. In the case of Eaton vs. the Boston, Concord and Montreal Railroad,‡ the facts presented to the court were as follows : The corporation, claiming to act under legislative authority, removed a natural barrier situated north of the plaintiff's land, which had, down to the period of the construction of the road, completely protected his meadow-land from the effects of floods and freshets in a neighboring river. In consequence of this, the waters of the river sometimes flowed over his meadows, carrying stones, sand, and gravel upon them. Here there was nothing but injury, and no appropriation of land whatever. Nevertheless, the court held that this was a taking of the plaintiff's property, within the meaning of the constitutional provision, and that the legislature could not authorize any such injury without making provision for compensation. In reaching this conclusion, the court first states the commonly accepted interpretation as follows :

---

* Const. N. Y., Art. 1, Sec. 7.                    ‡ 51 N. H., 504.
† O'Connor vs. Pittsburg, 18 Penn. St., 187.

"The constitutional prohibition (which exists in most, or all, of the States) has received in some quarters a construction which renders it of comparatively little worth, being interpreted much as if it read, 'No person shall be divested of the formal title to property without compensation, but he may without compensation be deprived of all that makes the title valuable.' To constitute a 'taking of the property' it seems to have sometimes been held necessary that there should be 'an exclusive appropriation,' a total assumption of possession,' 'a complete ouster,' an absolute or total conversion of the entire property, 'a taking the property altogether.' These views seem to be founded on a misconception of the term 'property,' as used in the various State constitutions."

In a strict legal sense, they continue, land is not " property "; but the subject of property. The term property, although in common parlance frequently applied to a tract of land or a chattel, in its legal signification means only the rights of the owner in relation to it. Property is, in other words, the right to possess, use, enjoy, dispose of, rent, sell, give away, devise the thing owned; and anything which interferes with the beneficial enjoyment of all these rights substantially diminishes them, and consequently involves a "taking," *pro tanto*, of the property. The right of using indefinitely is an essential quality or attribute of absolute property, without which absolute property can have no legal existence. This right of using necessarily includes the right and power of excluding others from using the land. If the right of indefinite use is an essential element of absolute property or complete ownership, whatever physical interference annuls this right takes "property," although the owner may still have left him valuable rights of a more limited and circumscribed nature. He has not the same property that he formerly had. Then he had an unlimited right, now he has only a limited right. His absolute ownership has been reduced to a qualified ownership. Restricting A's unlimited right of using one hundred acres of land to a limited right of using the same land, may work a far greater injury to A than to take from him the title in fee simple to an acre, leaving him the unrestricted right of using the remaining ninety-nine acres. Nobody doubts that the latter transaction would constitute a " taking of property." Why not the former?

The case of Pumpelly *vs.* Green Bay Company,* decided by the Supreme Court of the United States, closely resembles the New Hampshire case. In that case it was held that the backing of

* 13 Wall, 166.

water so as to overflow the land of an individual, or any other superinduced addition of water, earth, sand, or other material or artificial structure placed on land, if done under statutes authorizing it for the public benefit, was a taking of property within the meaning of the constitutional prohibition. The court said as to this:

> "It would be a very curious and unsatisfactory result, if, in construing a provision of constitutional law, always understood to have been adopted for protection and security to the rights of the individual as against the Government, and which has received the commendation of jurists, statesmen and commentators as placing the just principles of the common law on that subject beyond the powers of ordinary legislation to change or control them, it shall be held that if the Government refrains from the absolute conversion of real property to the uses of the public, it can destroy its value entirely, can inflict irreparable and permanent injury to any extent; can, in effect, subject it to total destruction without making any compensation, because, in the narrowest sense of that word, it is not taken for the public use. Such a construction would pervert the constitutional provision into a restriction upon the rights of the citizen, as these rights stood at the common law instead of the Government, and make it an authority for invasion of private right under the pretext of the public good, which had no warrant in the law or practices of our ancestors."

This decision seems to treat the submerging of lands as equivalent to the " taking " of them. But, obviously, it is not the lands which are "taken" in such a case, in any true sense. The title to the lands is still the property of the owner; it is the beneficial use of them which is gone, so that as a matter of fact the difference between this and the New Hampshire case is only one of degree. The Supreme Court, in saying that the land is " taken" by overflowing, merely means precisely what the New Hampshire court means when it says that the " property" is taken by an occasional deposit of stones, sand, and gravel through an overflow or freshet. And the New Hampshire court itself says, after using the language we have quoted as to the meaning of the word " property" in the constitutional prohibition :

> " If, on the other hand, the land itself be regarded as 'property,' the practical result is the same. The purpose of this constitutional prohibition cannot be ignored in its interpretation. The framers of the constitution intended to protect rights which are worth protecting; not mere empty titles, or barren insignia of ownership, which are of no substantial value. If the land, 'in its corporeal substance and entity' is 'property,' still, all that makes this property of any value is the aggregation of rights or qualities which the law assumes as incidents to the ownership of it. The constitutional pro-

hibition must have been intended to protect all the essential elements of ownership which make 'property' valuable. Among these elements is fundamentally the right of user, including, of course, the corresponding right of excluding others from the use . . . . a physical interference with the land, which substantially abridges this right, takes the owner's 'property' to just so great an extent as he is thereby deprived of this right. To deprive one of the use of his land is depriving him of his land, for, as Lord Coke said: 'What is the land but the profits thereof?' . . . . The private injury is thereby as completely effected as if the land itself was physically taken away."

As a matter of fact, the land itself is never taken. The land, the corporeal substance, always remains. The possession may be taken, or the entire title, or both, or something less; and in any one of these cases the only "taking" that is possible is a diminution of the right of user. It may indeed be contended that a diminution of the right of user which is effected without any change of possession or title, as in the New Hampshire case, is not a "taking" away of any property rights, but merely a destruction of property rights without any appropriation. But it is just such destruction of property rights which the constitutional prohibition is intended to reach. Otherwise, any railroad which wished to avoid the necessity of compensation might accomplish its object by not attempting to acquire the title to, or "condemn" any land, but by merely constructing its road; and in answer to any claim for damages might contend that it had "taken" nothing.

From a comparison of the early Pennsylvania case which we have cited, and which may stand as representing a whole class of contemporaneous decisions, with the two last decisions (by the side of which many others of a similar tendency might be put), it is obvious that the meaning of the constitutional clause prohibiting the taking of property without compensation has suffered a change, and that the courts are now beginning to show a disposition to treat any injury or destruction of property as a "taking." The meaning of the word "property" seems to be undergoing a modification, and the word to be used in a different sense from that which was formerly current.

There is nothing more difficult than to effect any change in a legal conception once firmly imbedded in a system of jurisprudence, particularly such a one as ours, in which general principles are developed out of adjudicated cases; while each case is, in theory, supposed to be founded upon and governed by another precisely similar; in which, in fact, there is, in theory, supposed to be no change at all. It is not surprising, therefore, that we should find the conception of "property" prevailing till a very recent period in the United States, to be still the same which the word suggested to lawyers of the last century, which Blackstone elaborated in his "Commentaries," and which historically may be traced to the archaic customs which answered the purpose of law in the forests of Germany. It is easy to see that in all early systems of law there is likely to be a confusion between the terms used to express the thing owned and those used to define the ownership of it. The word "property" we find used in Blackstone to express these two entirely distinct ideas: first, the thing owned; and secondly, the entire aggregate of rights and obligations with relation to it imposed by the law upon the owner. "Real property" means land, "personal property" means chattels; but we speak at the same time of property *in* land and property *in* a chattel. These last expressions come from the Roman law, as the word "property" itself is simply the Latin equivalent for ownership. The reason that English lawyers of the last century distorted this legal term from its natural use, and treated it as a convenient synonym for something radically different, is undoubtedly that they had not themselves reached any distinct conception of the nature of property in land. The feudal system was coherent, logical, and intelligible. No feudal lawyer could ever have confounded the land itself with the tenure by which it was held or the quality of the estate. The fee was as distinct a conception in his mind as any *universitas* of rights and duties in the mind of a classical jurist. But the feudal system was, in Blackstone's time, already in a state of decay, and half-understood legal ideas derived from Roman jurisprudence offered a tempting bait to any systematic writer on law. To a man of Blackstone's passion for symmetry and mere style, this was too tempting to be resisted, and the consequence was the production of a work in which we have neither the mathematical accuracy and metaphysical precision of feudal law, nor the civilized classification of the Roman, but often a jumble of the two, in which confusion is made worse confounded by the assumption that it is the perfection of system and order.

That the confusion with reference to everything relating to property, which we find in Blackstone, was wide-spread among the lawyers of his time, there is abundant evidence. It was a period in which it was often uncertain whether cases would be decided upon archaic principles, handed down from the time when Europe was still overrun with savages, or upon the polished and philosophical doctrines of right, elaborated by the classical lawyers of the Empire. A curious and instructive instance of the first is to be found in the opinion of Mr. Justice Yates, in the great copyright case of Millar *vs.* Taylor, in which he traces a close resemblance between the ownership of literary ideas, and that of wild animals, likens the publication of a book to the escape from the control of its captor of a fox or tiger, and hence reaches the conclusion that there can be no copyright at common law. On the other hand, we have the decisions of Lord Mansfield, a judge more familiar, through his familiarity with the principles of equity, with Roman than with English law, deciding case after case without much more regard for common law principles than if they had no existence. It was a time of great legal confusion, and nothing is more natural than that this confusion should by no means have altogether yet disappeared.

The confusion as to the use of the term " property " produced less practical inconveniences at the time than might be supposed, at least so far as land was concerned, because any litigated question which arose with regard to it had to be translated into the terms and conceptions of feudal law, which were still used with all their nicety in decisions and statutes. All actual litigation still concerned, not anything so vague and indiscriminate as "property" in land, but fees, estates tail, reversions, remainders vested and contingent, freeholds, tenancies for life, at will, by sufferance, easements in gross or appurtenant, and the thousand other varieties of title and estate, which the systematic feudal lawyers had been careful to classify and define. It was not until the word "property" came to be used in the written constitutions of the United States that the seeds of any practical trouble were sown.

Singular as it may appear, no such question as that presented by the construction of the elevated railroads has ever caused the English courts the slightest difficulty. There being no written constitutional provision on the subject, there has never been any necessity for defining the word " take," or the word " property," and Parliament and the courts have always given the owner whose property has been injuriously affected by the construction of public works of any kind, full redress, without regard to anything except the fact of injury. The Land Clauses Consolidation Act, passed in 1845, provided that the owner should have compensation for land, or any interest in land, taken or "injuriously affected." A single English case, which resembles in many respects that of the elevated railroads, and decided forty years ago, will show the difference between the American and English law on the subject. In Turner *vs.* The Sheffield and Rotherham Railroad Company,* the plaintiffs were the owners of a starch factory, near which the defendants built a railway station and embankment, by means of which the light and air were shut off, and the premises rendered "dark, close, uncomfortable and unwholesome, and less fit and commodious for the purpose of manufacturing starch therein," and the other purposes for which they had been used. Added to this, "large quantities of earth, soil, dust and dirt" were "carried, drifted, blown, scattered and spread," so that the fixtures, implements, and effects of the starch factory were rendered "dirty, foul and clogged up," by means of which the premises "were greatly deteriorated in value." The court held that the plaintiffs could recover.

That private rights of this sort should be more effectually protected in England without any written constitutional guarantee, than in this country where the subject is carefully provided for in the bill of rights, is a remarkable thing in itself, and is made the more so if, as we believe to be the case, the explanation of the matter is that the American judges of the last generation were driven into a narrow construction of the prohibition by the confusion existing as to the term "property" among the English lawyers whom they attempted to follow. The original source of confusion has been admirably explained by Austin, who, in his lectures on jurisprudence, points out the various meanings of the very ambiguous word "Property." His analysis serves to illustrate at one or two points what we have been saying. First comes the use of the word in its correct or strict sense, the same in which it is used by the Supreme Court of New Hampshire, if not by the Supreme Court of the United States—the right of unlimited user. Then comes what he calls the "loose and vulgar acceptation," to denote "not the right of property or dominion, but the subject of such a right, as where a horse or piece of land is called my property." But Austin, who was probably unaware when he wrote this, that on this side of the water

* 10 M. & W., 425.

our constitutional prohibitions against any interference with private property were already beginning to involve us in a controversy of serious dimensions over the meaning of that word, adds: "I think in English law, unless used vaguely and popularly, the term property is not applied to rights in immovables (land). We talk of property in a movable thing. By absolute property in a movable thing, we mean what the Roman lawyers called *dominium* or *proprietas,* they having no distinction between real and personal property. But in strict law language the term is not applied to a right or interest in immovables. An estate in fee simple, an estate tail, an estate for life, and so on, but never a property strictly speaking. An estate in fee simple corresponds as nearly as may be to absolute property in a personal chattel." In other words, as we have hinted above, the feudal system of tenures admitted no such vague conception as " property."

If the views here suggested are sound, the process of interpretation through which the constitutional provision as to taking "property" is passing, is one under which what Austin calls the true or strict sense of the word is being substituted for the " vulgar acceptation" in which the subject of property is confounded with the property itself.

That the second of these two views must in the end prevail and render the first obsolete, no one who has paid much attention to the development of the law on the subject in this country can for a moment doubt. At the risk of repetition, we shall make one more quotation from Austin, because it shows more clearly still than anything that we have already taken from him, that the view of the subject adopted by the New Hampshire Supreme Court is Austin's, as Austin's was that of the Roman law. He says:

"The right of property or dominion is resolvable into two elements: First, the power of using indefinitely the subject of the right. . . . . Secondly, a power of excluding others (a power which is also indefinite) from using the same subject. For a power of indefinite user would be utterly nugatory, unless it were coupled with a corresponding power of excluding others generally from any participation in the use. The power of user and the power of exclusion are equally rights to forbearances on the part of other persons generally By virtue of the right or power of indefinitely using the subject, other persons generally are bound to forbear from disturbing the owner in acts of user. By virtue of the right or power of excluding other persons generally, other persons generally are bound to forbear from using or meddling with the subject. The rights of user and exclusion are so blended, that an offense against the one is commonly an offense against the other. I can hardly prevent you from plowing your field, or from raising a building upon it, without committing, at the same time, a trespass. And an attempt on my part to use the subject (as an attempt, for example, to fish in your pond), is an interference with your right of user as well as with your right of exclusion. But an offense against one of these rights is not of necessity an offense against the other. If, for example, I walk across your field, in order to shorten my way to a given point, I may not in the least injure you in respect to your right of user, although I violate your right of exclusion. Violations of the right of exclusion (when perfectly harmless in themselves) are treated as injuries or offenses by reason of their probable effect on the rights of user and exclusion." *

The decision of the questions involved in the elevated railroad litigation will form an interesting episode in the history of the interpretation of the word "property" in the clauses of our State constitutions. As we have already said, no land in these cases has been taken. The owners have the same "property" (in its vulgar acceptation) that they had before; but, owing to the construction of the elevated railroads, their right of user, if not of exclusion, is gone. To take a case in which there is no dispute about the facts: the building of the branch of the elevated road through Fifty-third street in New York fills the street, to within a few feet of the upper windows of the houses, with a structure which darkens the whole neighborhood, while over it the passage of the cars and engines produces noise, smoke, and dust, which render the houses unfit for the uses to which they were intended to be put. Their rental and market value is diminished, and the whole character of the street is injured. Now, this case approaches very closely to the case in the Supreme Court of New Hampshire and to that in the Supreme Court of the United States. In the former case, as we have seen, no land was "taken"; in fact, land can never be said to be taken unless we mean by that that the title is absolutely transferred from one person to another, and it has never been maintained that railroads could escape paying damages altogether if they stopped short of "condemning" and acquiring title to land. The plaintiff merely complained that his land was diminished in its beneficial use or value to him by a deposit upon it of sand, stone, and gravel. In the Supreme Court of the United States his complaint was that his land had been flooded. In the case of the elevated railroads, the owners complain that their "property," i. e.. their

* Austin on Jurisprudence, 837.

right of indefinite user, is taken. Substitute smoke, dust, noise, and darkness for sand, gravel, stones and water, and the cases are seen to resemble each other closely. Even if the "taking" be held to require, as has been said in many cases, a physical interference with the land, it would seem to make no difference whether this physical interference were effected through the deposit of some material substance upon the land, or by such agencies as those called into play in the streets of a crowded city.

Whether the elevated railroad cases will be decided in accordance with what may be regarded as the modern meaning of the word "property," or in accordance with the older view that confused the taking of the land with the interference with the enjoyment of it, it is, of course, entirely impossible to tell; it is a curious fact that, in the recent reargument of the question of the property owners' right to damages, little attention should have been paid to the historical side of the use of the terms over which the controversy has so long been going on.

A practical objection has been often made to carrying the right of compensation to the extent recognized by the Supreme Court of New Hampshire—that it is so liberal as to be impracticable. No railroad can be built, it is said, without affecting in a great variety of ways the use to which property is put, and these general changes cannot be taken into account and compensated for, because it cannot be told in advance what they are going to be. In one place, the construction of a railroad, for instance, may bring about an alteration of a most serious character in a whole neighborhood, may make the fashionable quarter of a town unfashionable, destroy the picturesqueness of a view, or frighten fish away from a feeding-ground. The consequences may be slight, or they may be very serious. As was said a generation ago by a learned judge:

"The opening of a new thoroughfare may often result in advancing the interest of one man, or a class of men, and even one town, at the expense of another. The construction of the Erie Canal destroyed the business of hundreds of tavern-keepers and common carriers between Albany and Buffalo, and greatly depreciated the value of their property; and yet they got no compensation. And new villages sprang up on the line of the canal, at the expense of old ones on the former line of travel and transportation. Railroads destroy the business of stage proprietors, and yet no one has ever yet thought a railroad charter unconstitutional, because it gave no damages to stage-owners. The Hudson River Railroad will soon drive many fine steam-boats from the river; but no one will think the charter void because it does not provide for the payment of damages to the boat-owners. A fort, jail, workshop, fever hospital, or lunatic asylum, erected by the Government, may have the effect of reducing the value of a dwelling-house in the immediate neighborhood; and yet no provision for compensating the owner of the house has ever been made in such a case." *

Again, it is said that the changes produced by a railroad are often beneficial; that this is, in fact, one of the most common results of the construction of railroads; in fact, one of the principal objects for which they are built. If damages in any case are to be considered, why should not benefits be taken into account, and why could not the owner, if his land is improved in value, be made to pay the railroad for it, just as the railroad pays if it is diminished in value. There are in this argument two fallacies which are easily exposed. In the first place, with regard to benefits, the matter is wholly separate from the question of damages. If the public ever come to think that railroads should be allowed to tax the members of the community whose lands they pass through, for the benefit conferred by them, it is, no doubt, perfectly competent for the legislature to pass a law for such a purpose. It would be open to all the objections which may be urged against the betterment statutes which permit assessments of benefits accruing through the opening of ordinary highways and streets, and to more beside, because the benefits conferred by railroads are vastly more wide-spread and difficult to determine accurately than those conferred by roads and streets, which generally affect land within a very narrow compass and in a very definite way. But, granting that such statutes might be passed, there is no evidence that anybody thinks they ought to be passed, and no likelihood that they ever will be passed; and until there is, any discussion of the difficulty of applying them seems to be merely time wasted. As to the other objection, that there are all sorts of injuries to property, for which no one ever dreams of asking compensation, the answer obviously is that this is merely the question which arises in every lawsuit: whether the wrong is such that, on the general principles governing the administration of justice, compensation ought or ought not to be given. In every case in which the question of the right to compensation for injury is considered, there is always a preliminary question: whether the act complained of is not too remotely connected with the injury

* Radcliff's Executors vs. Mayor, etc., of Brooklyn, 4 Comst. (N. Y.), 195, 206.

to be considered at all, or whether, if the cause is immediate, the damages are not so difficult to calculate as to make it out of the question to give any redress. The reason why a tavern-keeper could not be allowed to recover damages for the injury to his business by the construction of the Erie Canal, is because he could not prove them by means of the common rules of evidence. He might be able to show that his business had fallen off since the construction of the Erie Canal, but how much of it would be due to that cause, and how much to some other, no court of justice could possibly ascertain. If it could, the illustration would fail, because the tavern-keeper would on the general principles of justice be entitled to redress. The reason is precisely the same in the case of the business of a stage or of a steam-boat route destroyed by a railroad, or of a new village springing up at the expense of an old one. A fort, jail, workshop, or fever hospital may be erected without compensation, for precisely the same reasons. No property-owner could possibly prove in a court of justice the difference in value produced by the proximity of such a building. The meaning of the word "property" in the constitutions of the States has been confused already quite enough without this added perplexity. The subject of consequential damages for taking land is too technical for the purposes of the present discussion; but we merely wish to point out that it is wholly separate from the question of the meaning of the word "property." If the New Hampshire view of this is adopted, it will merely be settled that taking property is diminishing the value of ownership. But it will be just as necessary as it was before for the injured owner to prove the extent of the damage, and that it is actually caused by the "taking," and that it is not too remote.

A. G. SEDGWICK.

# Michigan Law Journal.

| Vol. III. | AUGUST, 1894. | No. 8. |
|---|---|---|

## THE RIGHT OF PRIVATE PROPERTY.*

### WILLIAM H. TAFT.

As far back as we can go in the history of the common law of England, the right of property of the freeman was theoretically inviolate. Of course the serf or slave, owned by another, enjoyed no such right. But freedom, and the security of private property were linked together as the ancient liberties of the free English subject. The Norman kings were not as regardful of these liberties as they should have been, and the barons of the realm forced from King John in 1215 the written promise to preserve that which we all of us know as the Magna Charta. The important words of John's promise were: "No freeman shall be taken or imprisoned, or be disseised of his freehold or liberties, or free customs or be outlawed or exiled, or any otherwise damaged, nor will we pass upon him, nor send upon him but by lawful judgment of his peers or by the law of the land."

It is needless to say that this guarantee under John's sign manual was often broken by him and his successors, but just in proportion as England became more civililed, the ancient charter and pledge of rights became more sacred.

When our ancestors settled in this country their purpose was to establish here a government and society in which the liberty of the individual and the right of property should be strictly pro-

---

* An address delivered before the graduating class and alumni of the law department of the University of Michigan at the last Commencement. Judge Taft prefaced his address with the following remarks:

*Gentlemen of the Graduating Class:* Since your Dean and Faculty honored me with an invitation to speak to you on this occasion, I have not found it easy to select an appropriate subject of present interest. Last year, the class which preceded you, had the good fortune to hear an able and instructive address on the uses of the science of jurisprudence from one who, though still a young man, is a leading lawyer of the country and is now doing honor to your and his Alma Mater as the Solicitor General of the United States. A careful study of what Mr. Maxwell said in this place a year ago, and

tected. The constitutions of the states which were adopted after the Declaration of Independence and before the federal constitutional convention, contained guaranties, the language of which was borrowed from the foregoing clause of Magna Charta. The Massachusetts constitution of 1780, was especially full in this respect.

When the war of the revolution closed, the territory which lay northwest of the Ohio river and east of the Mississippi, was claimed, under royal grants, by Virginia, New York, Connecticut and Massachusetts. After much controversy these states ceded it all to the old Confederation, making it subject to the government of the Continental Congress, and that body, after several years of intermittent effort, finally passed the ordinance of 1787 establishing over it a territorial government. Its passage was secured largely through the persistent efforts of the Ohio Company, an unincorporated association of revolutionary officers of Massachusetts, organized for the purpose of buying and settling a million and a half acres of land in the new territory. The ordinance is in many respects as remarkable a charter of constitutional liberty as that under which we now live. All the guaranties contained in the Massachusetts constitution of 1780 were embodied in the ordinance, and it also contained a clause forever forbidding slavery in the territory. It was this which so endeared the ordinance to the opponents of slavery in the heated discussion of that institution in the forty years before the war. But the part of the ordinance with which we have most to do, in this discussion, is as follows:

Section 14. It is hereby ordained and declared by the authority aforesaid, that the following articles shall be considered as article of compact, between the original states and the people and states in said territory and forever remain unalterable unless by common consent, to-wit: * * * *

the adoption of his suggestions to your methods of professional work, will make you better lawyers. I cannot hope to confer such a benefit upon you, but I have thought it might not be without public benefit, if I could say something to you, as future members of the legal profession, to awaken or increase your interest in the social conflict now at hand, in which is at stake the security of private property. I am the more encouraged to do so when I observe that among your professors and instructors is that great judge, jurist and law writer, Mr. Justice Cooley (who honors us all by presiding here to-day), than whom no one has done more in this generation on the bench and in his treatises to maintain inviolable the rights I am about to discuss.

## ARTICLE II.

\* \* \* \* \* No man shall be deprived of his liberty or property, but by the judgment of his peers or the law of the land, and should the public exigencies make it necessary, for the common preservation to take any person's property or to demand his particular services, full compensation shall be made for the same. *And in the just preservation of rights and property, it is understood and declared, that no law ought ever to be made or have force in said territory, that shall, in any manner whatever, interfere with or affect private contracts or engagements, bona fide, and without fraud previously formed.*

The authority and origin of the clause with reference to contracts is in dispute. Nathan Dane of Massachusetts many years afterwards, claimed that it was original with him, while Richard Henry Lee of Virginia maintained that he was its author, stating that he intended it as a regulation of the abuse of paper money. Whoever drafted the clause it is probable that it was prompted by Dr. Manasseh Cutler, the agent of the Ohio Company, who was deeply interested for his principal in establishing in the new territory, all the possible guaranties of property and contract rights, because upon such security depended the value and success of his company's proposed purchase. The clause forbidding the impairment of the obligation of contracts by legislative authority was the first restriction of the kind ever contained in a charter of constitutional rights. It suggested the adoption of a similar restriction in the constitution of the United States a few months later, and in some form or other is now found in the constitutions of nearly all the states.

In 1791, a bill of rights was added to the federal constitution and by its fifth article congress and the general government were forbidden to deprive any person of life, liberty or property without due process of law. Following Sir Edward Coke's statement in his Institutes, the supreme court of the United States has held that the words "due process of law" are the equivalent ot the words of Magna Charta "except by the lawful judgment of his peers or by the law of the land." In 1866, after the late civil war, and for the purpose of establishing the security of life and property, so much in peril in the states which had been devastated by war and which were being subjected to radical changes in their social conditions, the fourteenth amendment to the federal constitution was adopted, providing among other things. that no state shall pass laws depriving any person of life, liberty or property without due process of law. Similar restrictions upon the power of state legislatures may be found in all the state constitutions.

There is not time and it is not necessary for me to review the judicial treatment and construction of these guaranties. Suffice it to say that the supreme court of the United States, the ultimate tribunal for the enforcement of them, has lacked neither in a high appreciation of their sacred character, nor in courage to declare void the intermittent attempts of state legislatures and of congress to override them.

I have thus reviewed the guaranties of private property contained in our fundamental law, familiar to us all, for the purpose of showing what a conservative government we live under and how strongly buttressed by written law is our American society against the attacks of anarchy, socialism and communism. While we inherited from our English ancestors the deep seated conviction that security of property and contract and liberty of the individual are indissolubly linked, as the main props of higher and progressive civilization, we have by our complicated form of government, with its many checks and balances, been able to give substantial guaranties of those rights, much further removed from the gusty and unthinking passions of temporary majorities, than has our mother country. The difficulties attending an amendment of the national constitution are so great as to make it practically impossible unless there is an overwhelming and long maintained feeling among the people in its favor. And this, in a less degree, is also true of amendments to state constitutions. Such limitations upon the power of the legislature were unknown when American political history began. The guaranties of English liberty and rights were against the aggressions of the monarch, not those of the legislature. The English parliament had always been omnipotent, and might by arbitrary act deprive the king of his throne, the subject of his property or the creditor of his debt. As Mr. Justice Mathews said in *Hurtado v. California*,[1] "The actual and practical security for English liberty rights of contract infringed by act of parliament. The Irish against legislative tyranny was the power of a free public opinion represented by the Commons."

The history of England even down to modern times affords many instances where property has been confiscated and vested

---

[1] 110 U. S., 531.

land laws of the last fifteen years, if subject to the restrictions of the federal constitution, would certainly have been held to be in direct conflict with all the guaranties of property and contract given in that instrument. The trend of recent English politics indicates that the power of public opinion is not now being strongly exerted in behalf of vested rights. The steps toward state socialism by both the great political parties are quite rapid.

The assaults of socialism upon the existing order in continental countries of Europe are more formidable even than in England, and of necessity therefore property rights are there more seriously threatened. The power of the socialist party in politics is in those countries fast increasing, and we need not be surprised if we shortly see in some one of them the experiment of socialism actually attempted, with the disastrous results and not altogether useless lessons which are sure to follow.

In this country until recent years not only have we had broad constitutional guaranties of property and contract rights, but there has been present in the breasts of our whole people a firm conviction of their sacred character. The fundamental compacts of state and nation have been merely declaratory of that which has been recognized as right and necessary by every individual, no matter how humble, and the immense advantage to our country growing out of the inviolability of property and contract rights has until recently been fully appreciated by all American citizens.

But while there has been no change in our constitutional guaranties, it cannot be denied that there has lately come a change of sentiment in certain of our people, by whom the right of private property is not now as highly regarded as formerly. Constitutional restrictions are generally not self executing but appropriate legislation must be passed for the purpose. Statute laws do not execute themselves, but, to be effective, must be administered by the firm hand of executive power. Events are happening each day which make a thoughtful man fear that if the tendency, indicated by them, is to grow in popular weight and intensity, our boasted constitutional guaranties of property rights will not be worth the parchment upon which they were originally written.

Impatience with the existing social order and contempt for the security of private property have found strongest expression among those who do manual labor for a living. By some of the more radical the wisdom of private property has been already challenged, while others manifest a resentment toward the system

409

without formulating a purpose to destroy it. Then there are others, not confined to the ranks of labor, who would not admit an intention to undermine the constitutional guaranties we have just been considering and yet publicly express so strong a hatred for aggregated capital, and show so marked a disposition to obstruct in every way its lawful accretions, that much comfort and strength is given to the avowed enemies of private property. Now the institution of private property is a good thing or it is not. We who believe in it must be able to give reasons for the faith that is in us. A full discussion of the subject would be too much extended for an address like this, but it may not be out of place briefly to refer to the origin of private property, and its incalculable advantage to our race, and to point out why the laborer of all members of modern society is most interested in maintaining its absolute security.

As soon as man raised himself above the level of the beasts, and began to live in a social state with his fellows, he recognized as a principle of natural justice that one should enjoy what his labor produced. As man's industry and self-restraint grew he produced by his labor not only enough for his immediate necessities but also a surplus which he saved to be used in aid of future labor. By this means the amount which each man's labor would produce was thereafter increased. As social justice requires that the laborer should enjoy his product, so it came to be equally well recognized that he whose savings from his own labor increased the product of another's labor was entitled to enjoy a share in the joint result, and in the fixing of their respective shares was the first agreement between labor and capital. What a man has the full right to enjoy he has the right to give to another to enjoy, and so it happened that when a man was about to die he assumed and was accorded the right to give, to those whom he·wished to enjoy it, that which was his. As the natural parental instinct dictated provision for those whom he had brought into the world, it first became custom and then law that if he made no express disposition of what he had the right to enjoy, it should become the property of those for whose existence he was responsible. In this way the capital saved in one generation was received by succeeding generations, and its accumulation for producing purposes was made much more probable. The certainty that a man could enjoy as his own that which he produced, furnished the strongest motive for industry beyond what was merely necessary to obtain the bare necessities of life. The knowledge that what he saved would enable him to increase and share the result of another's labor was the chief inducement to economy and self control, and this was greatly strengthened as a motive when he came to know that what he saved during his life could be enjoyed after his death by those to whom he was bound by natural affection. In other words, the institution of private property is what has led to the accumulation of capital in the world. Capital represents and measures the difference between the present condition of society and that which prevailed when men lived by what their hands would produce without implements or other means of increasing the result of their labor, that is, between the utter barbarism of prehistoric ages and modern civilization. Without it the whole world would still be groping in the darkness of the tribe or commune stage of civilization with alternating periods of starvation and plenty, and no happiness but of gorging unrestrained appetite. Capital increases the amount of production and reduces the cost in labor units of each unit of production. The cheaper the cost of production the less ·each one had to work to earn the absolute necessities of life and the more time he had to earn its comforts. As the material comforts increase the more possible becomes happiness and the greater the opportunity for the cultivation of the higher instincts of the human mind and soul.

Capital was first accumulated in implements, in arms and personal belongings, the value of which depended wholly on the labor necessary in their manufacture. The rewards of the chase were divided, the flesh being distributed to the tribe and the skin going to the hunter as his own. When the land began to be cultivated the crop belonged to the husbandman but the land was still common. Gradually, however, as more land was needed for the support of all, those in possession of the land asserted a right to permanently occupy it, and maintained it by force or were succeeded in permanent occupation by the stronger. After cycles of progress the ownership of land came to be recognized, and in course of time it was exchanged for what was purely the product of labor on the land. While, therefore, it may be conceded with reference to the land of England and the continent of Europe that private property in land in its rough uncultivated and unimproved state depended originally on mere force and conquest, nevertheless, in the possession of the present owners of it, its value is the accumulated result of the labor of previous generations. The improvements and the increased value due to cultivation are manifestly nothing but the result of labor. This is still more clearly the case in our country, where land was originally given to those who would settle it, and where it only had value after the labor of clearing and cultivating it had been performed. All capital then is nothing but the accumulated savings from labor available for use in making labor more productive, and thus reducing the cost in labor units of producing everything conducive to human happiness. It would seem, therefore, to be plainly for the benefit of every one to increase the amount of capital in use in the world. This can only be done by maintaining the motive for its increase, which we have found to be in the institution of private property.

Labor needs capital to secure the best production, while capital needs labor in producing anything. The share of each laborer in the joint product is necessarily determined by the amount of capital in use as compared with the number of laborers. The more capital in use the higher is the reward of each laborer, while the less the capital in use, the number of laborers remaining the same, the lower the reward of each laborer. To state it in another way, the more capital in use the more work there is to do, and the more work there is to do the more laborers are needed. The greater the need for laborers the better their pay per man. Manifestly then it is to the interest of the laborer that capital should increase faster than the number of those who work. Everything which tends to legitimately increase the accumulation of wealth and its use for production will give each laborer a larger share of the joint result of capital and his labor. It will be observed that the laborer derives little or no benefit at all from wealth which is not used for production. Nothing is so likely to make wealth idle as insecurity of capital and property. It follows as a necessary conclusion that to destroy the guaranties of property is a direct blow at the interests of the working man.

The cry of the critic of our present civilization is that the poor are getting poorer and the rich richer, from which premise it is said to follow that the wealth of the rich is unjustly wrested from the poor. The proposition that the poor are getting poorer is unfounded and with that the conclusion falls. It is not true that the laborer of this country, skilled or unskilled in times of ordinary prosperity, receives less than formerly. On the contrary statistics show that the purchasing power of his wages is decidedly greater than in former ·years. Doubtless there is much misery in the world but there always has been. There is a greater spirit of charity and benevolence to-day than ever before, and society is therefore more conscious of the misery of its unfortunates. But before it can be established that the present system of civilization resting on free labor, free right of contract and security of private property is a failure, it must at least be shown that the average condition of those who depend on manual labor for their existence is growing worse instead of better. This cannot be proved at all, and certainly is not shown by an array of statistics to prove that the rich men are growing richer.

The rapid accumulation of wealth among the comparatively few in the last twenty years in this country has frightened many people beside the laborer, but a careful consideration of the facts fails to disclose any good reason why it should, if the wealth is to be employed only for the lawful accretions of itself. In the last three decades we have witnessed an enormous decrease in the cost of producing nearly all the necessities and many of the comforts of life. This has been brought about in two ways, one by the invention of labor-saving machinery and processes, and the other by the combination and economic organization of capital. The inventors on the one hand, and the men of judgment, courage and executive ability who have conceived and executed the great enterprises on the other, have reaped princely profits, which the world may well accord them for the general good they have done. The profits which they received were the price the world paid for the gain in the purchasing power of labor. But for the pledge of society that the profits might be securely enjoyed the enterprises never would have been undertaken, and the machines never would have been invented. The wealth thus accumulated is not wrested from labor but it is only a part of that which has been added to the general stock by the ingenuity, industry, judgment and ability of those who enjoy it. The other part has been enjoyed by every member of society whose labor has ·been given greater purchasing power. Moreover it is a mistake to suppose, because enormous profits have enured to the leaders of industrial enterprises, that their accumulation of it as private property will not benefit others. On the contrary, if the owner of such wealth would increase it, he must use it with labor, and so increase the dividend of labor and wages per man. If with the growth in the laboring population the condition of man is to improve, new plans

413

for the use of capital to better advantage must be devised which shall at the same time increase capital more rapidly than the population and reduce the cost of living. The aggregation and organization of capital in corporations is therefore for the general good. It is said that this has now gone on in some industrial enterprises called trusts to such an extent as to entirely destroy competition by absorbing all the small producing agencies. That this is one of the objects of the founders of such associations is doubtless true. Whether the intent and its accomplishment are unlawful by statute I do not stop to discuss. Certain it is that even a few years' experience with such unwieldy enterprises shows that those only are successful whose manngers are gradually reducing the prices of the commodities they manufacture, and this they cannot do and live save by reducing the cost of production. The competition of smaller establishments is only effectively avoided by continuously doing that which smaller establishments cannot do, that is, by producing and selling cheaper goods. The possibility that rival enterprises will spring up furnishes the same motive for reducing prices that actual competition would. The ultimate result of such aggregations of wealth is for the benefit of the man who buys what is produced, that is, of every member of society.

What has been said should not be misunderstood. The men who have by economic organization of capital at the same time increased the amount of the country's capital increased the demand and price for labor and reduced the cost of necessities, are not philanthropists in the sense that they have done this from any motive of unselfish and disinterested love for human kind. Their sole motive has been one of gain, and with the destruction of private property that motive would disppear and so would the progress of society. The very advantage to be derived from the security of private property in our civilization is that it turns the natural selfishness and desire for gain into the strongest motive for doing that without which the upward development of mankind would cease and retrogression would begin.

We are told in sounding rhetoric that some one by the present system of private property and contract is worth $50,000,000. Well, what of it? If he is using it in such a way that thousands of workmen are employed at good wages, and the cost of living necessities is being gradually reduced, what good ground of complaint has any one to make, that for the mere sake of seeing his fortune grow, he is willing to give hard mental labor and untiring industry to the economic advancement of society? The men of wealth do not oppress anybody by extending, in every legitimate way, the scope of their great industrial enterprises and thereby increasing their wealth. The working man rarely has cause to complain, and his strikes are very few when production is profitably carried on. It is when the capitalist has not used good judgment in his investment when there are no profits to divide, that the real pinch between capital and labor comes, and then follows the usual result, after a weary conflict against the inevitable, that the investment is abandoned and the laborer is discharged.

But if it is so clearly for the benefit of the workingman that capital should be combined and organized to increase wealth and reduce the price of production, why is it that he and others are so hostile to aggregated capital? There are several reasons for this, one of which at least is founded on a real evil in part traceable to the increase of wealth. Unscrupulous managers of great corporate enterprises, with large amounts of money at command, have not hesitated to use it in corrupting legislative and other depositories of political power for the purpose of securing unjust advantages over the community at large. Unfortunately, men of good reputation who would not stoop so low in their private business, are, when interested in great corporations prone to wink at the dishonesty of such expenditures, and to regard them as necessary under the circumstances, stilling their consciences by carefully avoiding embarrassing inquiry into details. The monopolies secured by legislation are much more dangerous to the public weal than any which may be for a short time maintained by the mere combination and organization of capital. The latter carry in themselves the germ which must shortly either render them beneficial to the community or cause their destruction, while the former supported by positive law are much more difficult for the natural operation of the principle of supply and demand is overcome. It is unfortunate for the public that there have been action and reaction in the matter of political corruption by corporations, which has only increased the sum of it all. While much money has doubtless been spent to secure undue advantages for corporate enterprises, it is also true that sums quite as large have been spent to prevent legislative or executive action unjustly obstructive to legitimate corporate purposes and instigated solely for blackmail. It is the corrupting influence of large corporations which has caused a righteous resentment among the people against the abuses of corporate wealth, and often without any discriminating recognition of the immense amount of real good they have done for the community. Is it a good reason for destroying capital and the corporate agencies for legitimately increasing it, and the resulting addition to the sum of human happiness, that in the flush of rapidly acquired wealth men have been able to corrupt legislatures and other branches of the government? This would be a waste of benefits acquired equal to that described by Charles Lamb in his story of the Chinese method of preparing roast pig. Manifestly the remedy for the evil or corruption is to put men in political control not susceptible to corrupt influences, rather than to take away from everybody that, which, while it is a means of corruption, is also the means of securing every material good. The difficulties of eradicating corruption from politics are immense, but with our confidence still firm in a government of people we should be the last to admit that they are not to be overcome.

A second reason for the hostility of the laborer to the security of corporate wealth is in the want of clear-sighted leadership in many of those unions organized by workingmen for the purpose of securing their common production and benefit.

It is often stated that such organizations are a threat to modern society and civilization, but it seems to me that this is as far from the truth as the opinion that the aggregation and organization of capital are necessarily bad. We live in an age of marked progress in which organization of labor and organization of capital are necessary steps. They both of them make strongly for the public good but they also bring with them the evils that experience and time will cure. They are permanent and necessary features of our civilization and must be recognized and treated as such.

I have said that the increase of capital is for the benefit of the laborer, because it increases the demand for his labor and therefore his wages. As the fruits of production are to be divided between labor and capital, their common interest to increase the fruits is manifest. But in the division of their joint product their interests are plainly opposed. Clearly in such a conflict of interest the laborers united are stronger than when acting singly. Ultimately the division of the fruits is inexorably determined by the law of supply and demand, but during the gradual adjustment, according to that law, the capitalists will gain the advantage unless labor acts as a body. On a rising market, early advantage in the increase of the demand for labor may be taken by the laborers if they act together, and a prompt raising of wages secured, when otherwise it would be grudgingly and slowly granted; while, by the same united action, they may retard their too eager employer in reducing wages on a falling market. Such organizations, when they are intelligently and conservatively conducted, do much I have no doubt to aid their members in the hard struggle for existence, and have materially increased the share of the workingman in the joint product of capital and labor. Take the Brotherhood of Locomotive Engineers in this country. It exercises a wholesome effect upon all the members by enforcing temperance, fidelity and strict attention in the discharge of their important duties, They have a prudently managed life insurance system. They take united action on the subject of wages. They call in experienced chief officers to assist them in a controversy. The result has been that their strikes have been few and their financial and moral condition excellent. There are many others like it and they conclusively demonstrate that the more conservative and reasonable such organizatians are in their dealings with employers, the more useful they are to their members.

But unfortunately for capital and labor, many unions as now conducted are very different from that just described. In them, the turbulent are either in the majority or by mere violence of demonstration overawe the conservative element. The leaders are selected, not because of of their clear judgment and intelligence, but because they are glib of tongue and intemperate of expression. The influx of foreign workmen bringing with them the socialistic ideas which prevail among the laboring classes of Europe, has planted in many unions the seeds of sedition and discontent with the existing order. Hence it is, that whenever a controversy arises between labor and capital resulting in a strike, lawlessness too often follows any attempt of the employer lawfully to continue his business. If this lawlessness is not repressed promptly and firmly, as often it is not, the sympathies of members of the union are awakened in behalf of lawless methods, their former law-abiding disposition is blunted and they manifest an alarming indifference to the necessity for peace and order.

Then many labor organizations appear in politics and their influence is thrown, regardless of party lines, for the candidate who loudly proclaims himself the friend of labor and proves it by denouncing the greed of capital, the slavery of the workingman and his purpose to change all this by legislation. While their members are not in a majority, the united action of such labor organizations, together with the inert partisanship which gives to each of the great parties a certain vote whatever the issue, enables them to exercise an influence in elections far beyond their mere numbers. As there is still much human nature in man, the impulse of most persons in public life is to say and do nothing which will displease them. Thus it is that the workingman is rarely told the exact truth about his relations to capital and is too often encouraged by public men to believe that he suffers from society wrongs which should not be borne. Is it much cause for wonder, that he is skeptical about the wisdom of private property, when he is told in the halls of our national legislature that he should have the right to compel another to employ him at his own price, and that, in a bloody battle waged for him, for this purpose, against private property and its defenders, he is entitled to sympathy? Is his illogical hostility to aggregate capital very strange when in the same place he frequently hears men attacked with virulence and a torrent of epithet, simply because by industry, thrift, executive ability and sound business judgment, they have succeeded in accumulating wealth? Shall we wonder that the labor unions regard themselves as privileged when it is deemed proper by a house of congress to investigate the action of an able and conscientious federal judge in making an order claimed to prejudice the interests of organized labor, on the ground that the order was illegal, and unwarranted? Whether the order was proper or within the jurisdiction of the court were questions of law upon which lawyers and judges might differ, and which would be probably settled by a court of appeals. There was not the slightest evidence that the learned judge's conclusion was influenced by other than a wish to do exact justice. He simply gave to the performance of a disagreeable duty his best judgment. May not labor unions reasonably conclude that such a disregard of the independence of a co-ordinate branch of the federal government is justified only because, in the cause of labor against capital, constitutional restrictions are not to be observed?

When we turn to the state governments, we find even more encouragement to the workingman to think that property has few rights which, in his organized union he is bound to respect. In several states the open sympathy of peace officers with law-breaking strikers has been most demoralizing to the cause of order. The failure to visit the many breaches of the law with adequate penalties accustoms the less conservative labor unions to the use of lawless methods to accomplish their purposes, and the actual security of private property is seriously shaken.

I do not by any means intend to say that hostility to private property will continue to be the tendency of labor organizations for I am sure that, as their members become educated by hard economic experience to the truth that they have a deep interest in sustaining the security of property rights, their action will become more intelligent and more conservative. The trouble has been that many of their members are at present blinded by the new sense of social and political power which combination and organization have given them, and they fail to perceive the limitations of that power, which are fixed, not only by the inexorable law of economics, but also by the mighty force of Ameaican public opinion, which, after a long suffering patience, sometimes manifests itself with terrible emphasis.

The power which labor organization have, if directed in proper channels, could exert an influence for good which can hardly be overstated and all lovers of our county will say God speed the day. But it will not be by bringing about legislative or executive action or nonaction, which shall weaken the power of society to protect property and capital. Of the many good things labor organizatians could do in politics, let me mention but one. The use of wealth which injures labor is for the corruption of legislatures, national, state and municipal. This is most expeditiously and safely accomplished through the political boss. He lives by virtue of the spoils system and the machine. A concerted movement to abolish the use of public office to perpetuate political power would do much to deprive unscrupulous rich men of the means of manipulating legislatures, councils and city governments. It would bring about the payment of the same wages by the public as a private employer, and would relieve enterprises in whose success the workingman has every interest, of the heavy weight of taxation which so much interferes with their prosperity. It would give him cheap gas, cheap water, and cheap intramural transportation.

As it is, however, anything which injures corporate interests is thought in some mysterious way to work good for the laborer. The same spirit pervades many of the rural communities of this country, and so it is popular openly to favor legislation hostile to corporate interests. The regulation of corporations, particularly railroad corporations, has been so severe and unjust in many instances that insolvency has followed and thereafter has come a poor or indifferent service to the public, because the purchaser will not expend further capital within a jurisdiction so inimical to enterprise. Many state legislatures are now engaged in devising plans of taxation which shall affect only corporate property and remove the necessity of increasing the rate of general taxation in order to pay the increased expenditures of government. Thus they are discouraging the large investment of capital within their jurisdiction and directly injuring those of their constituents who earn their daily bread by the sweat of their brows. When the populist party came into control of the state government of Kansas with its threatenings against capital and corporations, all capital in movable form fled the state as if from a pestilence and it became apparent how little civilization could improve without capital.

The populist party has grown enormously among the farming communitins of the south and far west because of the discontent produced by the present industrial depression. There were in times of prosperity on the one hand an extension of areas of agriculture beyond the limit of profitable cultivation, and on the other the planting of new territory enormously fertile, which made living competition with it by older farms impossible. The hardships and consequent discontent have led to the approval by the populists of those quack remedies for hard times that are so fascinating to the human imagination and so pernicious in their effects. They are based principally on the proposition that the government is all powerful to give every one a living because it has an inexhaustible supply of wealth to draw from, that it can create wealth by stamping as money what was before worthless, and that it is its duty to distribute it when so created, among the people. They forget that the state is nothing but an aggregation of many men, and that it cannot use a cent which it does not take from the men who compose it. They seek to avoid the simple truth that there is nothing good to be enjoyed for which labor has not been expended. From one fallacy they have drifted to others, until the difference between what is advocated in populist platforms and socialism is hard to state. Suffice it to say that many of the planks are directed against accumulated capital and the rights of private property.

In the large cities where foreign labor is congested, we find bodies of avowed socialists. The socialist objects to the ownership by an individual of any means of production, that is, of capital. That, he contends, should be wholly vested in the state, while the results of production should be distributed among all members of society for consumption only, in proportion to their labor, the comparative value of the labor of each to be fixed by a governing committee. It is hardly necessary to point out the immense loss in production which such a plan would entail in depriving the community of the benefit it now derives from the motive for accumulation given by the security of private ownership, or the entirely impracticable plan of governing committees to determine the comparative rewards of different kinds of labor, or the waste and corruption necessarily incident to state managed enterprises.

In addition to those already named who are engaged in a movement against the security of private property, there are others who look on with complacency at the popular resentment at large corporate interests, but would be much alarmed at any disposition to infringe upon the property rights of individuals of moderate means. They would be willing to see a man's power of accumulation limited by law to a substantial size. What shall the sum be? Shall it be a million or a hundred thousand or fifty thousand or less? In either case such a limitation would be a fatal blow at the institution of private property and its beneficent effect. The right of property and the inviolability of contracts carry with them, by necessary implication, the right to use property as capital for the lawful accretion of the same, and if the right to limit lawful accretions be once conceded and inequalities of wealth are to be remedied by legislation, there is no logical stopping place between that and practical socialism.

It seems to me that enough has been stated to show that, while we have the strongest guaranties of the rights of property in our fundamental laws, there is a growing tendency to weaken the firm maintenance of those guaranties, so far at least as they relate to corporate capital; that everything which weakens this security of corporate capital cannot but affect that of individual private property; and that if the present movement against corporate capital is not met and fought, it will become a danger to our whole social fabric. I do not think the present state of social unrest is any ground for a pessimistic view of modern civilization. We are passing through an era of tremendous economic changes and the apparently alarming phenomena in the social horizon are only the necessary results of an adjustment to new conditions. But this view does not, in the slightest degree, diminish the necessity for reducing the friction of the adjustment, so that it may not be retarded, or for preventing a temporary impairment or destruction of the chief agent in the material progress of the human race, the security of private property and free contract.

How then can we stay the movement I have described against property rights? It is by telling and enforcing the truth that every laborer, and every man of moderate means has as much interest to preserve the inviolability of corporate property as he has that of his own. It is by defending modern civilization and the existing order against the assaults of raving fanatics, emotional and misdirected philanthropists, and blatant demagogues. It is by purifying politics from corruption. It is by calling to strict account our public men for utterances or conduct likely to encouage resentment against the guaranties of law, order and property and by insisting that equal and exact justice shall be done as well to a corporation as to an individual in legislative and executive action. The friends and believers in our modern civilization with its security for private property, as the best mode of a gradual elevation of the race, must make their views and voices heard above the resounding din of anarchy, socialism, populism and the general demagogy which is so wide spread to-day.

In the days of old, the charter guarantees were given it was supposed, for the benefit of the poor and lowly against the oppressions of the rich and poweful. To-day it is the rich who seek the protection of the courts for the enforcement of those guaranties. The judges of federal and other courts are sworn to administer justice fairly between the rich and poor. When the oath was formulated it was doubtless feared that the temptation would be to favor the rich. To-day, if a judge would yield to the easy course, he would lean against the wealthy and favor the many. While this seems to be a change, it is not really so. The sovereign to-day is the people, or the majority of the people. The poor are the majority. The appeal of the rich to the constitution and courts for protection is still an appeal by the weak against the unjust aggressions of the strong. Mr. Justice Miller, speaking for the supreme court in *Loan Association v. Topeka*,[2] a case where the majority of the voters of a city were seeking to impose upon its property holders against their consent, a tax to build a private factory for the use and ownership of a private individual, uses this language in reference to the right of the property owner to object to the taxing of his property for the personal advance ment of another. "It must be conceded that there are such rights in every free government beyond the control of the state. A government whigh recognized no such rights, which held the lives, liberty and property of its citizens, subject at all times to the absolute disposition and unlimited control of even the most democratic depository of power is, after all, a despotism. It is true it is a despotism of the many, of the majority, if you choose to call it so, but it is none the less a despotism."

The immediate burden of this conflict for the security of private property will, I suppose, fall upon the courts until by discussion and longer experience, light shall come to its opponents. The bench must rest for its strength upon the bar. As Judge Dillon said in his address as president of the American Bar Association: "The prominent present duty of the American bar and judiciary is to maintain the ascendency of our constitutions and to see that their guarranties are made effectual in favor of all persons, all rights and all interests which they were devised and designed to protect."

And for this reason I have addressed you. As you enter upon your professional life you will be required to swear that you will support and defend the constitution of the United States and of the state of Michigan. Many of you will become foremost in the communities where you live as leaders of public sentiment. Many of you, I hope, will take part in politics. You will go to the legislature and to congress. As public teachers, as public men, as politicians, you will not cease to be lawyers, or lose your allegiance to the fundamental compacts you have sworn to uphold and defend. It has seemed to me fitting, at such a time, to remind you that in those compacts there is secured as sacred the right of private property, and that unless you do everything that in you lies to maintain that security and guaranty, you will be false to the oath you take. You are about to enter a profession which a great French chancellor said was "as old as the magistrate, as noble as virtue, as necessary as justice." In ancient times the members of that profession were the bulwark of freedom and of the vested rights of property. I do not doubt that they will continue to be so in the future. The freedom of the citizen is secure. It is the right of private property that now needs supporters and protectors.

---

[2] 20 Wall., 655.

# Acknowledgments

Benedict, Michael Les. "Laissez-Faire and Liberty: A Re-Evaluation of the Meaning and Origins of Laissez-Faire Constitutionalism." *Law and History Review* 3 (1985): 293–331. Reprinted with the permission of the University of Illinois Press.

Brewer, David J. "Protection to Private Property from Public Attack." *New Englander and Yale Review* 55 (1891): 97–110.

Brown, Henry B. "The Distribution of Property." American Bar Association, Report of the 16th Annual Meeting (1893): 213–42.

Cooley, Thomas M. "Limits to State Control of Private Business." *Princeton Review* 54 (1878): 233–71.

Dillon, John F. "Property—Its Rights and Duties in Our Legal and Social Systems." *American Law Review* 29 (1895): 161–88.

Ely, James W., Jr. "The Railroad Question Revisited: *Chicago, Milwaukee and St. Paul Railway* v. *Minnesota* and Constitutional Limits on State Regulations." *Great Plains Quarterly* 12 (1992): 121–34. Reprinted with the permission of the Center for Great Plains Study.

Hartley, Katha G. "*Spring Valley Water Works* v. *San Francisco*: Defining Economic Rights in San Francisco." *Western Legal History* 3 (1990): 287–308. Reprinted with the permission of the Ninth Judicial Circuit Historical Society.

Hovenkamp, Herbert. "The Political Economy of Substantive Due Process." *Stanford Law Review* 40 (1988): 379–447. Reprinted with the permission of the Board of Trustees of the Leland Stanford Junior University. Copyright (1988).

Mayer, David N. "The Jurisprudence of Christopher G. Tiedeman: A Study in the Failure of Laissez-Faire Constitutionalism." *Missouri Law Review* 55 (1990): 93–161. Reprinted with the permission of the University of Missouri–Columbia. Copyright 1990 by the Curators of the University of Missouri.

McCurdy, Charles W. "Justice Field and the Jurisprudence of Government-Business Relations: Some Parameters of Laissez-Faire Constitutionalism, 1863–1897." *Journal of American History* 61 (1975): 970–1005. Reprinted with the permission of the *Journal of American History*.

Porter, Mary Cornelia. "That Commerce Shall Be Free: A New Look at the Old Laissez-Faire Court." *Supreme Court Review* (1976): 135–59. Reprinted with the permission of the University of Chicago Press, publisher. Copyright 1976 University of Chicago.

Sedgwick, A.G. "Constitutional Protection of Property Rights." *North American Review* 135 (1882): 253–65.

Taft, William H. "The Right of Private Property." *Michigan Law Journal* 3 (1894): 215–33.